The Tent of the Meeting

Illustrating God's Plan of Salvation

Peter Russell-Yarde

Printed in the United States of America
Library of Congress Control Number: 2025923880
ISBN: Softcover   978-1-969213-24-3
           e-Book   978-1-969213-25-0
Republished by: TwinVerse Prime
Publication Date: 10/20/2025

To order copies of this book, contact:
TwinVerse Prime
Phone: (725) 257-6538
clients@twinverseprime.com
www.twinverseprime.com/

CONTENTS

Being a personal consideration
of the purpose and importance
of this structure which God designed
and Moses constructed

DEDICATION

To our wonderful and almighty God
The Lord God of Israel
Who alone saves to the uttermost.

May God alone receive all the praise due to His Holy Name

Biblical Comment:
The Origin of Life : God's Relationship with Man in Genesis
God Rescues His People : Birth of Nation According to Exodus
The Wilderness Training School : Powerful Lessons in Numbers
Seeing Into the Future : Understanding the Revelation of John
The Path of Wisdom : A Study of Proverbs Chapters 1 to 4
Proverbs 5 to 12
Hosea
Joshua
Deuteronomy - Moses Last Discourses
Epistle to the Ephesians
Epistle to the Colossians
Epistle to the Romans
Epistle to the Hebrews
Epistle to the Galatians
Letters to the Thessalonians
The Return From Exile - Ezra, Nehemiah, Haggai and Zechariah

Matters of Faith:
Are There Demons? & Other Matters of Faith
Letters to the Seven Churches in Revelation
Lost Souls : The danger of losing sight of God
Covenant & Testament : God's rules for God's people to obey
Belief and Faith : Understanding the Essentials
Ordinary People : Extra-ordinary faith
So You Think You Know About Faith : Learning to Trust God
A Fresh Look at Easter
You Will Receive Power
Assuredly God IS!
Truth & Doubt
Christ IS King : A Guide for Doubters
Law & Grace (Lessons from the Kings of Judah & Israel)
The Return from Exile

Autobiographical:
A Tale of Three Men (Provides background information about how these books came to be written and distributed)

What our faith is all about
The Tent of the Meeting : Illustrating God's Plan of Salvation

ACKNOWLEDGMENTS

To Rabbi Aaron, who asked me to write this book
and Derek, two Israelites who have
become remarkable servants of their Messiah and a major
influence on my life in His service.

Ramon of TwinVerse Prime designed the book cover

INTRODUCTION

Jesus said to the Pharisee, a lawyer by profession, "You shall love the Lord your God with all your heart, with all your soul, and with all your mind.' This is the first and great commandment. (Matt. 22:37, 38)

God is not flesh and blood as we are, but spiritual and therefore cannot be seen by the human eye. When God created man, He designed into every individual an inner space that only He can fill, it is when that space is empty that many questions come into people's mind such as: Who is God? Why can't we see God? How can we find Him and get know Him? What is salvation and why do we need it? Clearly the only book that provides us with answers is the Bible.

The purpose of this book is to methodically answer those questions and explain the way God introduced His plan of salvation to mankind and how He developed that plan through the course of human history to its fulfilment in the birth, life and sacrificial death of the Messiah. The more I prayerfully studied the design of the Tent of the Meeting, also known as the Tabernacle of Moses, the more I realised that in its design God clearly illustrated the fundamental principles of what His salvation was all about.

Two words of advice for the reader: prayerfully ask God to give you spiritual understanding as you read the text, and have an open Bible alongside you for the references. Otherwise allow the text to speak for itself.

My thanks to Margaret Harvey, the proof reader of the first edition, whose personal, abiding faith in the Lord Jesus and her love and respect for the Lord's word shone through all her comments. But, as she reminded me from time to time, this is my work and I must one day give account of what I have written to the God of Israel, which I am very happy to do.

This second edition has been greatly changed and has not been proofread so please excused any grammatical and other mistakes, focusing on the message of the book.

I pray that you, the reader, will enjoy a similar or even greater life-enhancing and life-changing spiritual experience I have had whilst writing this book.

May God richly bless you as you read and study this book along with God's eternal Word.

Peter

1 THE BEGINNING

"For if by one man's disobedience many were made sinners,
So also by one man's obedience many will be made righteous"
(Ro. 5:19)

Relationships in the Beginning

When God created man, He created him in His own image and likeness. Man was to be God's unique creation; an earthly creature, made from the dust of the ground, who was to be God's representative on the earth. He was to be clothed with authority from God and to own the ability to rule as visible head and monarch of the world; a world which was unique in the universe in that it, alone, supported animal and human life. Because of that uniqueness it became the centre of the universe where God and man could meet in total harmony.

By virtue of being God's chosen representative on earth, man was separate from all others. Although made in God's image and likeness, the first man had no past, only a future; yet he stood erect with the features of a man who had intellect; that is the ability to reason, to think for himself. But there was one particular aspect of his being that made him stand out from the rest of the creation and that was his moral standing or original righteousness.

It is important that we do not make the same mistake the early church made in believing that the creation followed a neat plan of development according to their understanding of a developed creation. The Bible text does not give a line-by-line narrative of how the earth or any living thing was created.

All we know is that *God said ...* and as a result another aspect of the development of the earth and all that is on it came into being, BUT we do not know how it was done or how long it took.

If the scientists of succeeding generations are able to discover that knowledge, then that is to our advantage, so long as what they tell us is based on fact and is not the result of speculation or assumptions; particularly if they are the result of their standing as a believer or unbeliever. (See Appendix B.)

What we are told specifically regarding the creation of man is that when man became a living air breathing human being, created in the image and likeness of God, *God breathed into his nostrils the breath of life*. This created within man a spirit that allowed him to speak with God, something accorded to no other living thing.

Man + Breath of God — Body · Soul · Spirit

Animals — Body · Soul

Also, the first man was a living person; he had experienced some life before a rib was taken from him to produce the first woman. These are specific facts that have been written down according to God's knowledge of the events for He alone was present when the earth was created.

Like all creatures, man had a soul, which was the real person within the body. But what was to separate man from the rest of creation, by elevating man out of the animal kingdom, was that God breathed into the nostrils of the first man the breath of spiritual life. In the account of the creation, no other living being experienced this personal and intimate contact with God.

What did this action mean for the man God had created from the dust of the ground? In this way God gave man not life as an air breathing individual, but spiritual life that allowed him to enjoy an intimate relationship with Him because through that relationship God is able to provide us with spiritual food that keeps the spirit alive (Matt. 4:4). It is interesting that God is able to give life, not just spiritual life but also physical life and take it away, for it is essentially His life that He is giving.

When the waters covered the earth at the time of Noah, we are told that all those in whose nostrils was the breath of the spirit of life died. (Gen. 7:22) Their life was taken away by the waters of judgement, suffocating them.

Our Lord visited the spirits (souls) imprisoned (I Pet. 3:18 – 20) as a result of that 'judgement of God', which emphasises that the true life of man is not in the body, which is made from the dust of the ground, but in the God-breathed spirit that gives life to the body and soul of man and has the potential to bless us with eternal life. The blood within the body keeps the body alive and is essential to life (Gen. 9:4), but the true God-given, God-focused life is in the spirit of a person which is sustained by the Spirit of God.

The son of the widow with whom Elijah lodged was sick, and his sickness caused him to stop breathing. Elijah, in the privacy of his room, called on God not to restore the child's breathing, but to restore his soul which is the gift of personality and life from God (I Kgs 17:21) to each and every individual. The Hebrew word nephesh is, for the most part, translated as soul and the word soul comes from the Latin solus meaning alone or sole, meaning that it is unique to every individual.

Right from the beginning God wanted man to be eternally His and initially established man on the earth not only for it to be a testing ground, a test which God knew beforehand that man would fail, but to train man in His ways, which as the creator He had every right to do.

Because the emphasis of scripture is the Spirit of God dealing with the spirit of man (God is Spirit and they that worship Him must worship Him in spirit and in truth - Jn. 4:24) it is important that we understand the difference between spirit and soul and the breath of life that God breathed into the nostrils of Adam.

When God gave man life, He did two things. He gave man a body in which he lived with the ability to breath on its own, which is our earthly life, and to become a unique individual (the soul). What elevates man above the animal kingdom, the members of which do not exists after their physical death, is He breathed into the nostrils of the first man an individual spirit that was able to communicate with the Spirit of God and cause man to become eternal.

As the spirit in man cannot communicate with the human body, for one is formed from the earth and the other is a gift from God, the soul acts as the intermediary. When the body dies the soul and the spirit live on in a spiritual environment.

All living beings have a soul, as the above illustrations show, but only man has a God breathed spirit which is the reason why animals die and disappear, but man through that breathed spirit from the eternal God lives on after his physical death.

Life on the earth was to be a temporary measure[1]; it was to be a place of testing for although God wanted man to abide with Him forever in His place of rest, He would only accept into that place of rest those who lived lives that were in tune with Him and His instructions for life; after all He was the creator and knew the best and only practical way for man to live a life that was in tune with His design.

With His foreknowledge God knew that man would fail the test that he had set, and that the failure in that test would introduce sin[2] into the world, and that sin would separate them from Him. So not only did He plan into His creation a means of salvation, but also a place where those who did not live according to His instructions for how to live their lives according to His will and purpose, which is a place where God is forever absent, a subject that will be dealt with in detail throughout this book.

---

[1] This is why Jesus said, *It is the Spirit who gives life* (that is eternal life); *the flesh profits nothing* (because it is temporary, for life on this earth only). *The words I speak to you are spirit, and they are life.* Being consumed with this earthly life will only lead us away from God and into the arms of Satan, to be rewarded with an eternity in hell.

[2] Sin is being disobedient to the instructions laid down by God for how man should live his life on the earth.

The Beginning

It is important that we understand this matter of how we live our lives according to God's instructions for our relationship with God depends on it.

The things of earth and the things of heaven are completely separate for the things of earth are temporary[3], particularly since sin entered into the world, but the things of heaven are eternal and pure. Although Satan had access to God, as we will see in the book of Job, his position in the heavens changed once he had become rebellious towards God, and his ultimate future was to be consigned to hell, which we will learn is the place where God is not.

This then is the make-up of man which allows the body, made from the dust of the ground, the soul and the spirit, which are to live within the physical body that we see, the 'physical house' in which we live on earth, until it is released from the physical body when the body dies. It also explains why the virgin birth was so vital to the Son of God being able to visit the earth in human form as we will discover later:

Body	Soul	Spirit
Flesh	The real individual	Spirit that communes with God

In calling for the soul, or life of the child to return to him, Elijah was also calling back the spirit of the child for the two elements, the soul and spirit are both necessary for the body to live and become that recognisable person.

Thus God gave us:

❖ a **body** of flesh, made from the dust of the ground and therefore firmly based in the earth and entirely physical, in which we are able to live and breathe on the earth and that others see and recognise,

❖ a **soul,** the real person within the body, the created individual personality with its individual characteristics, that lives within the body whilst on earth,

❖ a **spirit** which was given to man and man alone when God breathed into Adam's nostrils the breath of life, through which God gave man his life-giving spirit, enabling man to not only communicate with God, hence Adam being able to speak with

---

[3] From the beginning God put a time limit on the life of the earth. Because of God's design, towards the end of the life of the earth it would gradually heat up for God gave man the ability to find and use the resources He designed into the structure of the earth that would cause that heating up to take place.

God in the garden, but be the way in which an individual enjoys and eternity with Him in heaven.

That spirit is recreated in every new born baby, and it is that spirit which elevated man out of the animal kingdom, for no other creature has been given such a spirit within them, or is able to communicate directly with God. It is also that spirit, which with the soul, lives on for eternity after physical death. Sadly sin kills the spirit's ability to communicate with God causing the soul and spirit of a man to suffer in that pace where God is forever absent except for those who have committed their lives to God during their physical life.

What is important about Elijah calling back the soul of the young son is that by doing so God returned the soul and the living spirit that had left the body causing it to die. In returning the soul, life returned to the human body of the child. It was when the spirit returned to his body that the child's soul was activated by the power of God, and the body started to breathe again so that Elijah was able to return the living child to its mother.

Surely this demonstrates beyond all doubt that it is the soul with the spirit that is the life within us; the real 'us' as a person that connect us to the living God and provides us with eternal life whether we go to heaven or hell. It is also reasonable to accept that because of the lack of knowledge of the spiritual aspect of God, many of the leading religious Jews of old were unable to fully understand this concept. Indeed, the Pharisees and the leading religious clergy had no idea of the spiritual aspect of God and therefore could not understand the fact that the spiritual Son of a spiritual God had the ability to come down to the earth and inhabited a human body to become a living human being in order to pass on information that the Father wanted us to know.

With the understanding of the virgin birth that is available to us now (See Appendix A), and the ability of the Spirit that was the Son of God to actively live in the body provided for Him by Mary, we are more able to understand the technicalities of this matter that were hidden from those who have gone before us, just as the truth of the coming of the Messiah was more evident to those nearer the time of His arrival on this planet than, for example, to Abraham.

We are all the more overwhelmed by the knowledge that, not only are we made in the image of God, but that the gift of who we are and able to do, and the life we have within us, is contained within the God breathed spirit of life within us. Where that breathed spirit in an individual has been devoid of spiritual food (Matt. 4:4) it has become inactive, although it will still cause the person to live through the eternal life provided by the spirit but in a place where God never goes.

The Beginning

This body, being made from the dust of the ground, will not survive after our physical death for it will decay and return to the earth from whence it came, but the soul and the spirit that is the real 'us in communion with God' will live on, and will need to be clothed in a new incorruptible body (1 Cor. 15:44) in which we meet with our creator God, if we are numbered amongst the true believers[4]. It is essential that instead of being imprisoned by only accepting past knowledge, we must seek for fresh inspiration from God

It cannot be stressed enough that we owe our very lives to God; who we are, our character and our individual personality. God made us in His likeness and image but He did not make us exactly the same as Him or the same as each other. We are all different.

Yesterday I noticed two people walking together deep in conversation. This brought to my mind the following thoughts:

- ❖ Two people do not walk together unless they agree because they have a similar interest, whatever that interest may be, possibly the basic need of friendship or company.

- ❖ The two men on the way to Emmaus had a mutual interest in the tragic death of the man they believed to be the Messiah, the Saviour of Israel. They were joined on their walk by someone else with the same interest, for the Messiah needed to tell them personally that He had risen from the dead, exactly as the prophets had foretold and as recorded in scripture. It was, therefore, through their personal witness and experience of meeting and talking with Him 'in the flesh' that they would be able to tell others and encourage them to believe that He was alive.

- ❖ Adam walked in the garden with God at first because they agreed; they enjoyed each other's company and had things of mutual interest to discuss. They walked together by mutual agreement.

To be able to walk with God, we must also be in tune with Him who put the stars in their place; there can be no agreeing to disagree for the purpose of walking together. In our relationship with God, for it to be effective and long lasting, there has to be complete mutual agreement.

It is important at this stage to also identify, particularly within those whose spiritual awareness has not been totally anaesthetised by Satan, that

---

[4] True believers are those who totally believe in God as the eternal creator Spirit and His Son who came to the earth and gave Himself up as our sacrifice for sin and have not only accepted that sacrifice but have totally committed themselves to God through Christ and receive into themselves the dwelling of the Holy Spirit as in the day of Pentecost when the disciples receive the baptism of the Holy Spirit. They accept the inerrancy of the word of God through which God speaks to them through the ability of the Spirit of God to open up its meaning to them.

there is an inherent desire within us to see God's face.

Such is the relationship we have with Him that we want to see Him face to face. His intention is that this will happen. Moses wanted to see Him in that way but was treated to a veiled and carefully managed sight of God; for the purity of His being is such, and Moses' sinfulness and filthiness was such that Moses could not have survived the experience: indeed, God has warned us that *No man can see Me, that is My face which is my supreme glory, and live. (Ex. 33:20).*

This then is the remarkable situation at the beginning regarding the personal relationship between man and his creator. They could meet with each other and see each other face-to-face; such was the right-ness (sinlessness) of man and the compatibility of man with God. Indeed, we read in Genesis 3 that the Lord God walked in the garden with man, for when Adam hid from Him the Lord called out to Him, *Where are you? I am looking for you so that we can meet together and talk with each other.*

Theirs was an easy relaxed relationship; a mutual enjoyment of each other's company. That was the way God had intended it to be; the whole purpose of the creation. In creating the world, the complete structure and content and integration of the temporary natural world, God had man in mind, thus creating a purpose for his initial existence. Adam had the task of keeping the Garden of God in trim, using his authority over the creation to keep order and not to allow any one created item to dominate another.

Such was God's pleasure in man, who He had made in His own image, that pinnacle and final act of His creation, that when He viewed everything that He had made He pronounced it very good and allowed man to stamp his authority over it by naming everything.

But notice that man was created as an adult human being from the start, for God made him in His own image and likeness; conversing with man from the very beginning. Surely this in itself makes the creation of man so remarkable in that man had the power of speech and the knowledge and understanding of the language of God that enabled him to freely converse with God, to speak to the woman when she was created and for both of them to converse with Satan when he made his appearance in the garden to tempt them into sin. Adam, therefore, did not experience birth and childhood, as we have experienced them, for he was the first of all human creation.

There is still much that we do not understand with regard to the early years of the earth. How do we explain the dinosaurs and their disappearance from the earth? When was man created in relation to the animals of all types? All we do know, and can be sure about, is that God created all things in His own way and in His own time (2 Pet. 3:8) and that has to be sufficient for us. Including the fact that the whole of the creation is temporary, and all the creatures short lived, with only man being eternal.

The Beginning

The purpose of this study is to try to understand man in relationship with God starting with the purity of relations at the beginning, how this relationship was soured and how God sought to provide a way back to a new relationship with Himself that was available to all men.

It was not God's intention for man to be confined to the earth with a certain lifespan, for in the garden He planted a tree, the tree of Life. Had Adam chosen to eat of its fruit he would have been able to enter into an even more intimate relationship with his creator than he had at the beginning. It would have been possible for Adam to experience eternal life with God if he had eaten of the tree of Life, although in a different place than the earth.

Along with the soul of man, the spirit of man does not die at the point of physical death; it goes on to face judgement before God. As we shall see as we study the development of God's plan of salvation, there are just two destinations for the soul, heaven and hell, with heaven being where God is and hell where God is not. Only those who positively respond to God's way of salvation through repentance and trust in Him, and willingly allow themselves to be transformed into His likeness through the work of God's Holy Spirit, becoming true believers through faith in His word.

These alone will enter into the place of His rest which is the heaven in which He has lived since completing the creation of all that is seen and unseen. But this will become clearer as we discover the gradual revelation of the plan of salvation and how it affects us today.

Such was God's concern for man, that when He saw him in the garden, He had created especially for him, God realised that all the other inhabitants of the earth had a female companion but that man was on his own. Surely this emphasises how important man was to Him, for He did not see man as merely a creation, but an eternal being with whom He wanted to become involved. It was only when the creation had been completed and God viewed His creation from above that He realised that man was on his own and could become lonely.

To solve the problem God carried out the first surgical operation in the history of the world. Giving man a general anesthetic, *God caused Adam to enter a deep sleep (Gen. 2:21)*, He removed a rib from his body, closed the wound and then proceeded to create woman from the man's rib, to ensure their compatibility and bonding so that to Adam she became *bone of my bones and flesh of my flesh (Gen. 2:23)*

Therefore, it is said that woman was made from man but man is born of woman so that neither can claim greater importance before God. As we shall see, though, man has been given authority over woman (it is he who named all the animals, thereby stamping his authority over creation), it is an authority that should be exercised in love just as God has shown His love towards man (See Eph. 5:22 – 33).

Man's relationship with God and the relationship between man and woman must be viewed in the context of how God created us for it is He who set up the relationship we were to have with Him and also that between man and woman. The moment of the fall of man can be viewed as being the first moment when Adam did not take seriously the authority over Eve he had been given by God.

Abram made the same mistake of not taking authority in the situation created by his wife and going with Hagar at Sarai's request, even though God had promised him a son through Sarai. He gave away his authority to his wife when he resorted to human practice to overcome the problem of the lack of a son because of Sarai's bareness; yet that barrenness was no problem to God, as we know from the birth of Isaac.

Abram's error caused problems with Ishmael, who was rejected at the age of eleven, a rejection that is being experienced today in the Middle East. Sin is just as much a failing to accept our God ordained position within this life as is our direct disobedience, or lack of obedience, to God Himself. This leads us easily into our consideration of just what sin is all about.

Relationships Contaminated

God trusted man and gave him authority over all the living things of the earth (Gen. 1:26). At some time, however, in the spiritual sphere of God's creation a rebellion occurred. An archangel referred to as Lucifer, called *Son of the Morning*, who was probably the most senior and greatest angel God created, decided he wanted be take God's place and be God. He is described as being the *seal of perfection, full of wisdom and perfect in beauty* (Eze. 28:12). Such was his radiance that he was said to have been covered in precious stones and gold, his musical prowess was with timbrels and pipes; this had been prepared in him on the day he was created.

He was appointed the guardian angel for the world as it was at the beginning. He is said to have been perfect in all his ways, with unrestricted access to God Himself, and he wielded great power over God's angelic host (Eze. 28:12 – 19). Such was his power and authority that when the archangel Michael disputed with this same angel (the Devil) over the body of Moses, Michael did not have the authority to accuse him directly but called on a higher authority saying, *The Lord rebuke you!*

Although the passage in Ezekiel 28 concerns the King of Tyre, the reference to Eden, the Garden of God, gives the true identity of the person involved for it to refer to this angel, Lucifer, who appeared to Eve as an angel of light to convince her that to eat of the forbidden tree was good and not really against God's instruction to Adam.

But how did this remarkable cherub, so blessed by God, end up by being brought so low? The text tells us that his heart was lifted up because of his beauty. It is worth recording here that in the context of scripture the heart is considered to be the centre of a person's will and intellect.

Not satisfied with the gifts of looks and music and the position of power he held in God's kingdom, (which he received from God when he was created and did not have to earn it for himself), he wanted more and turned his wisdom to corrupting ways for the sake of his splendour.

It must be emphasised that all that he had was not his by right; it had been given to him when he was created. It is essential for each one of us not to allow ourselves to be puffed up before God, particularly if we have an outstanding skill or talent for you have received it as a gift from God for (Zech. 9:2b – 4) the good of all men.

Let us consider this passage carefully, for it tells us a great deal; not only about the prince of this world but also about his influence on men, in this case a king ruling in Tyre (which still exists today). He was probably called Ethbaal and had been a priest before taking the throne from its former occupier.

Ethbaal, who gave his daughter in marriage to Ahab, started the worship of Baal in Israel. He considered himself a demi-god and even wiser, in his own opinion, than Daniel, whose fame had spread north to Tyre. His wealth through trade was very great and his influence over the surrounding nations extensive. This attempt to destroy God's plan of salvation through distracting Israel away from the truth through the worship of false gods was a typical sign of his continued influence and work in the world (See Appendix C).

We cannot allow ourselves to be deviated from the central theme of scripture which is all about God's relationship with this world that He has created and the people that inhabit it; and conversely man's relationship with God and the spiritual world that He created along with the world of the flesh.

We must recognise the fact that He created all things and that His power over all of His creation is undiminished through time as men's power decays for through His unlimited power He sustains all things; this means that we must take God seriously. Hear what Isaiah has to say on this matter:

"Have you not known from all that you see around you
and the events that have occurred?
Have you not heard God speaking through His prophets
and all that He has created?
Has it not been told you from the beginning in the Torah
When the earth was formed and came into being?
Have you not understood from the foundations of the earth
how night follows day
And the seasons do not falter?

It is God who sits so high above the circle of the earth
that the people appear small and insignificant like grasshoppers.
Be assured it is God who stretches out the heavens like a curtain
Using them as tent for Himself.
He has absolute power over all men that rule with power over others
Able to bring their schemes to naught.

It is He alone who distributes power to the weak
And those seemingly insignificant in the eyes of men.
Those who try to live in their own strength shall grow weary,
But those that seek the Lord with all their heart,
Desiring to know Him and serve Him
shall continually renew their inner spiritual strength:
Indeed, supplied with His power they shall mount up on wings like eagles
They shall run and not be weary
They shall walk and not faint.
(See Is. 40:21 – 31 Consider Ps. 34)

It is essential when considering all these things that we maintain in the back of our minds the realisation that the God who made all things is still the same supreme God to whom we must direct our obedience. The thoughts and devices of unbelieving men will undoubtedly come to naught; for they are here one minute and departed the next and their influence and the effect of their lives on the world disappear over time and eventually have little or no effect on future generations.

The greatest danger for anyone is to believe that they are greater than they are, for from the dust our human bodies were made and to the dust our bodies will return. It is only the God gifted soul and spirit within us that will live on, at which time our influence on the earth will have ended and we will be completely at the mercy of God. It is His decision alone that will allow us access to heaven, where He lives, or send us to hell, the place where He is not, according to His rules and not our interpretation of those rules.

In speaking through the prophet Ezekiel, who had been appointed to speak to God's people Israel (Eze. 2), and referring to the Prince of Tyre God says:

your heart is lifted up,
And you say, 'I am a god,
I sit in the seat of gods,
In the midst of the seas.'
Yet you are a man, and not a god.
(Ez. 28:2)

So what are the facts surrounding this king that will help us understand something of what God is saying to us?

The king had his headquarters on an island off the coast which was considered to be sacred to the god Hercules; to the extent that the colonies, the peoples in the surrounding area, considered Tyre to be the mother city of their religion and also of their particular political existence.

Such a situation encouraged the king to gain an inflated opinion of his position, coming to the belief that he was a god, even believing that he was God. Daniel's fame had spread to that area and the king thought he was even wiser in his own opinion of himself than Daniel, yet Daniel knew that his wisdom came not from himself but from the Lord God of Israel, the God he had, in obedience to the Torah, committed himself to loving with all his heart, mind and strength.

The king was very clever and had great wisdom in trade so that his riches increased. But he allowed those riches, the beauty of his possessions and his powerful position (not only in his own kingdom but amongst his neighbours) to lift his heart, so that he thought he had attained the high level of a god.

God is saying in this scripture that He would show this ruler with an inflated ego that he was as frail as everyone else and would die at the hands of the aliens God would send against him. The very seas that he thought protected him would be the scene of his demise. For God asks him through the prophet Ezekiel,

> *Will you say before him who slays you, 'I am a god'? You shall die the death of the uncircumcised (unsaved heathen) (Ez. 28:9, 10)*

There is an intrinsic danger in scripture in taking literally what is expressed figuratively, and figuratively what is meant to be taken literally. Such is the information contained in the lamentation for the king of Tyre. But there is a matter of equal importance which is the fact that two creations co-exist and operate side by side.

The cherubim (above the mercy seat) and seraphim (Is.6:2) were representatives of a different creation and were continually in the presence of God. In this lamentation there is a bringing together of these two creations for what happened to Lucifer is reflected in the manner of the inflated, self-opinionated pride that led to the fall of this king (Eze. 28:11 – 19).

> *"You were the seal (the completion) of perfection*
> *Full of wisdom and perfect in beauty.*
> *(v12)*

Such was his rank within the spiritual realm that no one could bring a charge against him except by calling on a higher authority such as in the case when he was there to make accusations against Joshua the high priest; the angel had no recourse but to call on the Lord to rebuke Satan (Zech. 3:1, 2).

Indeed, Satan had complete access to Eden, the garden of God, and the holy mountain of God. He was most magnificently attired that was provided on the day that he was created; for it must be realised that Satan is a created being who was anointed to be before the Lord to be the worship leader of the heavenly host. This guardian cherub with overshadowing wings was blameless in all his ways until iniquity was found in him. Such was his beauty and the glory of his person and the power of his position that he wanted to trade on all that he was and had in order to achieve the highest goal which was none other than the throne of God Himself.

> *You have said in your heart:*
> *I will ascend into heaven,*
> *I will exalt my throne above the stars of God;*
> *...........*
> *I will be like the Most High.'*
> *(Is. 14:12 - 15)*

Remember that man was the pinnacle of God's physical creation, and His delight. For Satan to achieve his ends of becoming like the Most High, what more did he have to do but to take authority over the world which would allow him to rule the centre of the universe, creating for himself considerable power and influence outside heaven. In order to do that Lucifer needed to gain authority over man to whom God had given authority over every living thing on the earth.

With a proud heart and an inflated ego, he corrupted the wisdom that Adam had received from God because of what he saw in himself. In so doing Satan had defiled the sanctuaries in which he had authority and would be brought low. His desire for power, played out by taking power for himself over man, did not turn out as he had imagined, for although God had given authority to the man, He, as creator, had never given His ultimate authority over His creation as a whole. Man was required to be obedient to his creator and could only do that which was within the bounds God had set.

Satan too was a created being, even a cherub of the highest order, but he was still under the authority of God (Job 1).

How are you fallen from heaven

15

The Beginning

O Lucifer, Son of the Morning!
How are you cut down
you who weaken the nations!

... you shall be brought down to Sheol
(the place of the dead)
To the lowest depths of the Pit
(Is. 14:12b, 15; see Lk. 10:18)

Like the reference in Ezekiel, Isaiah prophesied against a ruler, in this case the King of Babylon. However, the underlying message is for Satan (also known as the Devil) who is still working quietly in the background through those who have rejected God, and who want to gain power in this life.

Unfortunately, such people forget that all men will die and have to face an eternity in the spiritual world, finding out when it is too late that what they will face and experience which will not be to their pleasure but to their grief. Satan raises men up in order to bring them low, whereas God brings men low, to the point of repentance, before raising them up to great and unspeakable joy.

This is perhaps the most important and essential lesson that anyone interested in coming into a true and real and dynamic relationship with God must understand and have fixed in their hearts. God wants men and women to seek Him face to face. Satan, on the other hand, does not want them to know who he (Satan) is but hides himself; except when he appears as an angel of light, believing it will have a greater effect on his victim. He prefers to put suggestions in the mind of an individual and direct their attention away from the things of God to the things of the world that he has perverted.

Gradually we are being prepared for the entrance into this world of the man of sin (2 Thes. 2:1 – 12) and the other incarnations referred to in the book of Revelation which will lead us to the climax, when God will demonstrate His glorious power. So, why do we need to know all this?

God in His wisdom gave man a free will. He wanted man to desire a relationship with Him of his own free will, not enter into it through force. Yes, our relationship to God must be a marriage-type of relationship, but a willing marriage, not a shotgun, and that is as true today as it was then because God's love must be at the centre of that relationship.

The Bible is very clear about the choice we have to make if we are prepared to study the instructions it contains. Unfortunately, the majority of mankind does not understand the critical importance of scripture to our eternal future so the decision they have made, without realising it, is to reject the creator God.

Man was created with the potential to live forever, but only if he was prepared to accept that marriage relationship with God. As a test God planted two trees in the centre of the Garden; the tree that leads to (spiritual) life and the tree that leads to (spiritual) death.

Most people forget the most important tree in the centre of the garden, the Tree of Life, the fruit of which was freely available to man and would have given him eternal life from the moment he had eaten of it. In which case the other tree would have ceased to have any importance and would have inevitably disappeared. As God planted it, He could just as easily uproot it.

When God created man, He created him in love and wanted man to freely love Him in return. Although God placed within man a need for a relationship with Himself as the creator, so that man could love Him in complete freedom, He also allowed man to have a free will which also gave him choice.

By the eternal God breathing into the nostrils of the first man the breath of life (not the first woman as she gained her life from the man), He also gave man an eternal spirit within him. Freewill required the individual to make choices. But what choice was there for the first man and woman in that garden of God? By planting two trees in the middle of the Garden of Eden and putting a restriction order on one of them, God was giving man the choice of eternal life with Him or rebellion and therefore eternal separation from Him.

From the first man, every individual human being is required to make a choice of being for or against God. It is a choice that has to be made, whether consciously or not, it does not matter but it is an inescapable choice that has to be made. The fruit of one of the two trees had to be eaten at some stage of Adam's life, and the choice of which one decided whether he desired to follow God or reject God. As it was, Satan persuaded Adam and Eve to eat of the tree of rebellion which introduced the DNA of sin into man. Every individual since Adam has had to make the same decision, although not by eating of the fruit of one of the trees, which disappeared from his view when man was ejected from the garden.

The question we must all ask ourselves is, "Am I for or against God?" Those who decide not to make a decision are in fact deciding to reject God, because theirs is a decision to ignore Him, which is tantamount to rejecting Him. For those who decide to love God in return for His love, their future prosperity is assured, if not in this world, then certainly in the world to come where they will be called into His presence forever.

The problem for man was the focus Lucifer had on obtaining power over the earth. We know from experience that we are surrounded by evil men who will do anything to get what they want.

Personally, we have been conned out of large sums of money because of evil men working the Time Share scheme; which in its original concept was a very good idea until it was taken over by unscrupulous business men who decided it was their way to a 'better and more comfortable life in this world'.

It is helpful when considering the conversation Satan entered into with Eve to remember certain essential facts.

The authority for the woman was the man, Adam. Feminists will complain about such a statement but according to scripture this is correct. It is the way God the creator designed us; creating the man first and then woman from the bone of the man. Any decision about eating from either tree rested with the man not the woman. This is amply confirmed by God because it was Adam who was accused of sinning against Him, with the woman attracting the lesser charge of being deceived.

Satan automatically went to the woman knowing that God's instruction about the two trees had not been given to her directly from God, for she had received the man's interpretation of it. Satan therefore considered her an easy target for his deception.

Satan did not draw attention to himself; indeed, it is true to say that the last thing that Satan wants a person to do is to recognise him. The very fact that we think of him as a snake is a deception. The Hebrew word for Serpent is nachash meaning to hiss, mutter, whisper as do enchanters. The fact that Satan is not actually named as such in the first testament, it is clearly he who is described figuratively in Genesis 3, for his methods were serpent-like.

This is a technique used alongside factual reporting to bring factual information more forcibly to the reader's attention. This is enforced when linking it with the reference to *that old Serpent called the Devil and Satan* in the last book in the Bible (Rev. 12:9). What is important for believers to realise is that, although his purpose is to deceive, he is able to appear as an angel of light and be very plausible, which is why Eve was cognizant of him and acted on his suggestion (2 Cor. 11:3-4, 14).

Because of his persuasive nature Satan has convinced many prominent men and women to believe him and not God the creator of all things. Hence the prominence of the Big Bang theory, with no suggestion of there being an intelligent mind behind the creation of all that we see around us. It is only when we set our minds to search for God to find out the truth that we will receive truth.

Notice too that the place of this encounter was right by the forbidden tree, although the Tree of Life would also have been very close. All Satan had to do was to focus the woman's attention on the fruit of the forbidden tree and then begin his mesmerising conversation as an angel of light who Eve thought she could trust (1 Cor. 11:14). It is also probable that the man was nearby for they would have wanted to keep within sight of each other in the garden.

By understanding the deceptive methods of Satan, we are better prepared to withstand the wiles of the evil one (1 Cor. 11:1 – 15).

So, what happened there in that garden at the beginning of the human history of the earth?

The Matter of Genesis Chapter 3

We must be very careful when considering the events which led man to sin against God because within the text figurative and literal language vie for position in a mixture than can be confusing if we are not careful. This means that if we want to understand scripture, we need to seek the guidance of the Holy Spirit; only then will we be guided by God, who inspired those who contributed to that word, to understand the deeper truths hidden within it.

It is also essential that we take the occasion of the fall of man as a complete whole; to dissect the text word by word would lead to confusion and error.

The tempter is being referred to as a serpent but he is also described as being wiser that any beast (any living being) of the field which the Lord God had made which means that the 'serpent' referred to here had intelligence far above that of any member of the animal kingdom.

Therefore, it is reasonable to assume, particularly given what we have just discussed in detail, that the serpent (snake) is no more a snake than King Herod was a crafty fox (Lk. 13:32) or Nero a [mighty or ferocious] lion (2 Tim. 4:17), who put many believers to death using various traumatic methods including allowing them to face hungry lions in the arena, or Judah a lion's whelp (Gen. 49:9) who would ultimately be mightier than all his brothers for it was the tribe of Judah that would give birth to the Messiah. The fundamental purpose of Satan's activity in the garden was all about his desire to control the earth in order to try and become like God.

Balaam's ass was given the ability to speak to the prophet by the angel of God because of God's creative skills. No one else has the level of creative skill to get a creature of any sort to speak and this is the only occasion in scripture where such a thing happened.

It is important, therefore that we are careful not to allow ourselves to be confused by the language used concerning this critical time in the history of man. Could a snake of itself, with no organs of speech whatsoever, articulate words and speak with sufficient intelligence and persuasiveness to get the woman to do what she understood to be fundamentally wrong? Indeed, why would a single snake seek to converse with a human being anyway? What would be its motive, and did it have the intelligence or the cunning to be able to do so? What snake, as a reptile, could possibly have complete understanding of the word God spoke to Adam and of itself decide that it wanted to deceive the woman? A positively bizarre suggestion that is believed by many people today

Therefore, to give Eve credibility, it is more likely that Satan, as the fallen angel Lucifer, the most senior angel in God's spiritual creation, appearing as an angel of light and with considerable persuasive skill due to his great God-given wisdom, sought to persuade her of the advantages of eating of the fruit of the forbidden tree. Why? Because it was he alone who believed he had the most to gain from man rebelling against God.

As we have already seen, the Hebrew word for serpent, nãchãsh, means to hiss, mutter, whisper; as do enchanters, with the secondary senses of to divine, enchant. Therefore, the most likely scenario is that Satan acted 'as a snake' in his efforts to persuade Eve to eat of the forbidden tree, and this understanding is reflected in Paul's concern for those in Corinth:

> *"But I fear lest somehow, as the serpent deceived Eve by His craftiness,*
> *So, your minds may be corrupted from the simplicity which is in Christ.*
> *For Satan himself transforms himself into an angel of light.*
> *Therefore, it is no great thing if his ministers also*
> *Transform themselves into ministers of righteousness"*
> *(2 Cor. 11:3, 13,14)*

Therefore, it was Satan, the arc angel responsible for the earth, who was greater than all the living creatures amongst which the first man and woman were living at that time. Thus, this exalted, glorious and wise cherub, supreme in the angelic kingdom that God had made, presents himself to Eve at a moment when she was near the forbidden tree.

Satan started his conversation with the woman by asking her the question,

Are you sure that you are not allowed to eat any of the fruit in the garden?

It is essential that we consider the elements within this question to gain the greatest benefit from it for it will help us when the evil one tries to divert us from the truth.

What God said to man whilst he was on his own regarding the two trees He had planted in the midst of the garden (Gen. 2:16, 17) was:

Of every tree in the garden you may eat freely ...

Notice that in this part of the instruction God does not name the tree of Life, including it along with all the other trees in the garden. One would have expected Adam to have gone round and sampled the fruit from each of the trees, but this obviously did not happen for the world would have been a completely different place if he had.

The thought has come to me and will not go away that this world was always intended by God to be a testing ground and that the new creation (the New Jerusalem as revealed in the book of Revelation) was planned to replace this earth and heaven at some point even if Adam had eaten of the tree of Life. The reason for this thought is that the world is of a certain physical size and if the first couple had done as instructed to *be fruitful and multiply* there would surely have come a time when there would have been a state of over population. I must stress that these must be considered as my thoughts for I cannot be sure God put them into my mind. It is worth considering, particularly at this time when there is so much talk of over-population and the increasing birth-rate.

But one aspect of what God said does stand out, and that is, by not identifying the tree of Life *Of every tree in the garden you may eat freely* ... God is showing us that He has never put pressure on man to seek eternal life; it is a free-will choice. God does not want to force people to love Him. His love is free to all and it is up to each and every individual to return that love if they so desire.

For God to be a totally impartial judge it is essential that He does not force, or predestine, anyone to do something He desires them to do. After all is not God the offended party because of man's sin that has caused a chasm to open up between them? Therefore, God does not cause, or force us to love Him, rather He wants us of our own free will to return to Him and love Him by way of the salvation He has provided.

We are totally free to make our own informed choices according to the information we receive throughout our lives. However, God does have the ability to know the deep thoughts of our hearts, which are the thoughts and beliefs we keep buried deep within ourselves.

This is why God knew Jacob had a heart for Him but Esau did not, and it is this ability that allows God to intervene in our lives to direct us to Him through gentle guidance, but the choice of whether or not to believe in Him is always our responsibility.

More than that God, who exists outside of time, has foreknowledge which is why He chose Jeremiah and commissioned him as a prophet before he was even born, for He said, ... *before I formed you in the womb, I knew you* ... *(Jer. 1)*. Therefore, God knew the sort of person Jeremiah would be not just when he was a child but the sort of person he would be when he reached the mature age of 30 when priests started to become active in the services of the temple.

No one is predestined to be a believer. However, those who do believe are predestined to behave in a certain way because of God's influence in their lives. To put it another way, those who do accept God as their Lord and Master, by surrendering their lives to Him, will adopt a predestined pattern of behaviour because of God's involvement in their lives, even as Joseph did throughout his eventful life.

For Joseph, in spite of all the reverses he experienced because of the acts of men (particularly his brothers) who did things seemingly for selfish ends, ... *you meant it for harm* ... realised through the Spirit of God that ... *God meant it [allowed it to happen] for good* ... (Gen. 50:20; see also Ro. 8:28). It is for this reason that he never blamed God for his problems. (See Appendix F) Remember, it is clearly written in scripture that God had told Abraham what would happen in the future, knowing that Joseph would be there to obey Him.

God has predestined us, those like Jeremiah who He foreknew, to be ... *conformed to the image of His Son* ... our Lord (Ro. 8:29). If we accept God as our Lord and Saviour, a strictly personal choice, then we will conform to a pattern He has set down, for we will then come under the influence of His Holy Spirit who brings us into conformity.

Those He foreknew He chose to be holy and without blame before Him (Eph. 1:5) because they would have first realised their sin, repented of that sin and been cleansed, even to the purifying of their consciences, by the blood of the Passover Lamb of God (Heb. 9:14).

Predestination is therefore all about the type of transformed life those, who choose, of their own accord, to come under the authority and saving grace of God, would live. This is why it is essential for those who enjoy studying the word of God to treat the whole Bible, from beginning to end, as a complete whole. Those who only study one testament but not both, for whatever reason, will be confused and follow wrong teaching to their detriment.

It remains a fact that the one tree in the middle of the garden that God did identify was the tree of the Knowledge of Good and Evil:

> *... But of the tree of the Knowledge of Good and Evil you shall not eat*
> *(Gen. 2:17)*

God's instruction was very clear. Adam was not to eat of any part of the tree of the Knowledge of Good and Evil, not its fruit, its leaves, its bark or its wood, thus restricting Adam's freedom of choice, but only in regard to one tree out of all the variety of trees that were there for his needs.

Having clearly identified this tree from among all the other trees in the garden, God then gives the reason why.

> *... for in the day you eat of it you will surely die,*

God was effectively asking Adam, 'Are you willing to put your trust in Me; and Me alone? Mentally making the choice of trust and submission rather than rebellion and separation?'

It was not that the tree was poisonous or would cause Adam to have an upset stomach. The purpose of this test was moral and spiritual. Adam would surely die if he ate of any part of that tree. It was a complete death sentence: *... you will surely (or most certainly) die*. But it would be death from the intimate spiritual relationship he had with God his creator, starved of the spiritual food which is *every word that proceeds from the mouth of God*. To put it another way (a question we all need to ask ourselves), "Do you want to be earth bound in life and thought and after death exist in that place where God, who is the source of love, is forever absent, or spiritually connected and inspired (like Joseph) and assured of entering into the New Jerusalem where God's overwhelming love permeates the atmosphere?"

Although this aspect of the test would not necessarily have been understood by Adam, the simple truth of it was for him to obey God or defy Him. From our point of view in the twenty-first century there is much that we know about the life of the world, which should be to our advantage.

With the dramatic changes in weather patterns and ever-expanding population, and with wars and rumours of wars, man has come to the conclusion that the world cannot survive unless something is done to reduce harmful chemicals being released into the atmosphere, stop increasing the size of the population and stop the harm being done to the population and nature through destructive wars. But wars are the result of sin in the world which causes man to come under the influence of Satan who is the author of chaos and conflict amongst people and peoples.

The Bible has been telling us since the second testament was published that the world has only a specific life span. Because of the inevitability of death, both the world and the Bible are telling us that not only will we die, but there will ultimately be an end to this world as we know it, for it will disappear as quickly as it appeared. That prospect for many is scary. Therefore, we need to ask ourselves the question: 'What is beyond this life?'

Remember that the woman, Eve, had not then been created. We have no way of knowing the time scale between the moment God warned Adam about the one tree that He identified, and Eve being created.

Having analysed what God actually said, now let us look into what Satan said to Eve, knowing that all she had to go on was what Adam actually said to her, the details of which of course we will never know.

So God said to Adam:

Of every tree in the garden you may eat freely ... (Gen. 2:16)

However, Satan's question to Eve was:

Has God really said, "You shall not eat of every tree in the garden? (Gen. 3:1)

Notice that Satan suggested he was quoting what God said, but in such a way that a totally different interpretation of what God has said was put forward. Not only would such a restriction mean that a whole range of foodstuff would be denied them, he very craftily twisted the word that God had given Adam, enabling it to be twisted even more as the conversation went on.

When tempting the Lord Jesus, immediately after His forty days and nights in the wilderness without food and water, Satan tried twice to use God's recorded word to get our Lord to do something contrary to God's will. He failed and therefore tried to directly secure Jesus' allegiance to himself by offering all that the Lord could see physically. An empty gift for it was very limited and temporary.

It is essential to understand that in taking over the authority of the earth divinely given to man, Satan had only what was earth-bound to offer. Therefore, in the temptation of the Messiah, Satan's focus was earthbound as follows:

In the first temptation Satan calls into question the legitimacy of the Messiah by saying, *If you are the Son of God...* Yet shortly before, the words from the Father had proclaimed Him as His beloved Son, in whom He was well pleased. Casting doubt is Satan's primary means of attack. Is this not the question on the lips of all those who refute the person of the Messiah as being the Yeshua[5] of Nazareth?

Satan then asked the Lord to command stones to be made into bread, so that He could satisfy the physical hunger He must have experienced after 40 days and nights without food or water. The Lord immediately changed the focus to heaven, and embraced the whole man, saying that man shall not be dependent on physical bread alone to survive but on the spiritual food that only God can provide (Matt. 4:3, 4). However important physical food is to the body, for the whole man, spiritual food from God is also an essential element of life. The two types of food have been provided since the first man trod the earth, for he had the vegetation and fruit of the trees to eat to satisfy his physical body, but his contact and communion with God engaged his spiritual self which was also an essential element of his life; as we know by the tragic events of Adam's life after he was forced out of the garden.

With this in mind it is important to remember that Adam was brought to life as a eternal living soul not through physical food but through God breathing into his nostrils the breath (the spirit) of life. This is clearly brought to prominence when our Lord said,

---

[5] Hebrew for Jesus

> *It is the Spirit who gives (spiritual) life;*
> *the flesh (physical life) profits nothing[6].*
> *The words I speak to you are spirit and life.*
> *(Jn. 6:63)*

The instructions we receive from hearing the words of God direct us to things eternal. Do not forget that food is only of use in this life; once we die food is of no use to the spirit within us that lives on. Therefore, it is essential that we hear, and take to heart, the words of God that instruct us how to live eternally with Him our creator.

In the second temptation Satan again tries to pervert the word of God by taking the Lord in the spirit to the pinnacle of the temple, suggesting He throw Himself off to demonstrate that angels would come and catch Him so that the word would be fulfilled,

> *He shall give His angels charge over you*

and

> *In their hands they shall bear you up,*
> *Lest you dash your foot against a stone*
> *(Matt. 4:5, 6 from Ps. 91:11, 12)*

Obviously, this is not right because Satan is asking the Lord to do something that is entirely irresponsible, just to see if God saves Him as spoken of in the Psalms. So what does it really say? The key is in what Satan did not include in the first reference:

> *For He shall give His angels charge over you,*
> *To keep you in all your ways*
> *(Ps. 91:11)*

Were the ways of our Lord best served by doing something completely irresponsible, to test the promises of His Father with whom He had been intimate for eternity? What would it prove anything that could be of benefit to the salvation of mankind which was, after all, His true mission on earth? Indeed, in another part it says,

> *You shall not tempt the Lord your God*
> *As you tempted Him in Massah*
> *(Deut. 6:16 cf Ex. 17:2)*

Therefore, by twisting, or not quoting exactly, what scripture (the Word

---

[6] Because it is temporary

of God) says, Satan is able to fool people into believing him; which is exactly what he was doing with Eve without Adam contradicting him.

Our Lord used that verse, *You shall not tempt the Lord your God ...* to tell Satan that His task on earth was to serve the Father faithfully (see Jn. 17:20 – 23). This was yet another attempt by Satan to maintain his strangle hold on the earth, on man in particular, and destroy the Messiah's mission to save mankind.

In the last temptation Satan showed his true objective by taking our Lord in the spirit to the top of an exceedingly high mountain to show Him all the kingdoms of the world. Satan said to the Lord that He could have all the kingdoms of the world if only He would fall down and worship him.

But why would the Word made flesh, who existed before the creation and took part in the creation of all that was made that was made (Jn. 1:1 – 3), including the angel Lucifer himself who became Satan the deceiver, want to bow down and worship a created being who controlled so little for he could only do what God permitted him to do? To Pilate our Lord spoke of a kingdom that is not of this world (Jn. 18:33 – 37) for He came into the world to bear witness to the truth; God is truth.

Also, how could God shake the heavens and the earth unless His kingdom was unshakeable? If it was not unshakeable, He would shake His own kingdom also, but it is unshakeable! The reference in Hebrews 12:26 clearly indicates that God will shake what He has made so that what cannot be shaken can remain; further proof that God is supreme in all things.

Thus, in answering these three temptations of Satan, our Lord three times used the recorded word of God saying, *It is written ...,* further proof, if it was needed, that the Messiah, the Word of God, had come to earth in the form of Jesus from Nazareth, born in Bethlehem according to scripture to fulfill all that had been written in the Hebrew scriptures.

To return to Satan's conversation with Eve, her reply betrays her lack of knowledge:

> *Of course we can eat of any tree, but we are not to eat from the tree in the centre of the garden or touch it (an embellishment) or we will die". (See Gen. 3:3)*

Now Satan reveals his true character. Having distorted what God had said to Adam when speaking to Eve, and sensing from her response that Eve did not know exactly what God had said, he now voices an alternative explanation:

"*It's a lie",* hissed the serpent (Satan), "*You will not die, for God knows that the instant you eat it you will become like Him* (they were made in His image so they were already at that point *like Him), for your eyes will be opened and you will be able to distinguish good and evil* (but that ability to distinguish good and evil would not be, as we now know, from the view of goodness and mercy, but, because they would be in defiance of God, from the view of rebelliousness and evil which has resulted in violence and wickedness in the world of human relations which Satan introduced and has stimulated that violence and wickedness within humanity over the years of human history).

Now that Satan has got her attention focused on the fruit of the forbidden tree, and with the prospect of the fruit making her wise she instinctively reaches out and takes the fruit and eats it and then gives that same fruit to her husband to eat, which he does.

God's command was for them not to eat of the fruit of that tree. Adam should have stood firm and refused to eat of the fruit in defiance of Satan and then sought God's advice regarding his wife's misdemeanour; but he didn't, preferring to go along with what she had done, thereby bringing upon himself the judgement of God and not only upon himself but all those born of him.

It is a fact that Satan raises the hopes of people who then find those hopes dashed. Jesus knew full well that Satan did not have anything to offer Him except entrapment under his authority and rule. As a created being Satan has no creative ability of himself, so he is reduced to using the powers over the creation that God had invested in him when he was created, along with the deception and lies, hate and cruelty which he has acquired as an independent angelic being.

These rebellious attributes that he acquired he has used to raise false hopes within people because he does not have God's loving heart and concern for them. He raises men up in order to bring them low for he has no ability to enhance people's lives, only to make them worse because he is taking people away from the blessedness God offers. Such is the tragedy of sin, which is a falling short of the high standards of God.

As soon as they had eaten of the fruit, they realised they were naked and hid from their creator God when He arrived in the garden to walk and talk with them. Yet God is the all-seeing God from whom nothing is hidden, particularly our sin (Ps. 69:5). He will have instantly recognised the sign of disobedience under the rule of Satan by noticing how Adam replied when He called him, asking where he was.

> *I heard Your voice in the garden and I was afraid because I was naked; and I hid myself.*

Previously, even though he was naked, Adam had no fear of God and was unaware that he was naked; therefore, the deception of Satan brought about these changes in Adam's understanding of his condition. Notice he spoke regarding himself alone – *"I heard your voice in the garden and I was afraid"*, but Eve would have been with him hiding herself from God and covering herself because of the presence of Adam.

He realised that he was naked, a fact that had not been of any concern to him before. When he was righteous his nakedness did not matter, but now that he had introduced sin into his life, he was looking at himself through different eyes, through eyes of unrighteousness.

The peace within his heart that allowed him to live without clothes and meet with God had now gone. Fear entered in, the fear of being found out because of sin, his conscience was affected because he had done something entirely against God's instructions. It was this fear, through rebelliousness, that has caused the separation between God and man ever since. Sin is the result of the curse of eating the fruit of the tree of testing, which is rebellion against the word of God.

Our need to be obedient to God's word is as true today as it was then. The charge we have regarding the word of God is written at the end of the Book of Revelation (Rev. 22:18, 19). If we add to the words then we will experience the plagues it contains, and if we take away words then we will have our name removed from the Lamb's Book of Life.

There are a number of groups who are perverting the word of God and they should reconsider their ways. In a television interview a previously homosexual man told how he became a Christian, born again through the action of the Spirit of God and realised that his way of life was contrary to scripture and decided to live as God created us to live. He is now married with children and has a totally different outlook on life. The homosexual church, also known as the Gay Christian Church, is a lie and follows Satan's enticement of Eve which is total rebellion against God and His creational design for man. Other churches have their own Bible which is suspicious to say the least.

When God challenged him regarding his confession of nakedness (Gen. 3:11) Adam did not admit freely to eating the fruit of the forbidden tree but, like Satan, focused God's attention on someone else, *The woman / whom You gave to be with me / she gave me of the tree / and I ate.* There was nothing righteous about that reply, it had only accusations, 'It is not my fault but hers / Yours / the fruit of the tree'.

'It is not my fault I ate of the tree. You gave me the woman and she gave me the fruit to eat. Therefore, I am innocent of any charge'! This in any language is the, 'get out of trouble' clause. And the woman was no better for she blamed the serpent for deceiving her.

The ease with which they associated with God previously was now at an end, for God cannot look upon sin, it is abhorrent to Him. Which is why when His Son hung on the accursed tree the Father looked away, and why the Messiah cried out, *Why have You forsaken Me?*

The worst thing that could happen in this event was for them to eat the fruit of the tree of life. So, having slaughtered one or two animals for their skins with which to clothe the couple, God unceremoniously ushered them out of the garden to live a life of hardship and toil, forbidden to re-enter the garden where they had easy access to God. To ensure man's compliance, God placed trusted angels to guard the entrances to the garden.

The controversy of the next few verses are manmade! If you are a Jew who believes that the Messiah has yet to come, the last thing you want to hear is of Messianic prophecies in the book which is central to your faith. On the other hand, if you are a Gentile believer in the life and work of the Messiah, Jesus Christ, then it is reasonable for you to seek out all prophetic references to the promise of His coming and life.

Let us go very carefully through the next few verses to try to understand what was said to whom and for what reason within the context of the prevailing events. I say this having been directed to articles that are clearly a Jewish attempt to disprove the so-called 'Christian Deception'. This is a very negative and dangerous method of studying scripture and is to be avoided at all costs for it will only attract the judgement of God.

Condemnation

It is of particular interest that God speaks to the perpetrator first:

So the Lord God said to the Serpent ..
(Gen. 3:14)

This name-calling has stuck. The fallen angel Lucifer, the accuser of the saints, has, since that time, been hiding behind the appellation 'serpent', rather than the implication of being of a serpent type. We are therefore looking at the snake, not the one who acted like a snake.

But we have been made well aware that it is Satan who is being accused, because God would not look to condemn one of the creatures He had created and who not only did not have any organs of speech, but did not have the brain power to display the wisdom that we were told exceeded that of all the beasts of the field.

Do those who suggest that it was a snake that beguiled Eve really accept that Almighty God would condemn a snake, which relies on pure instinct to live, for something that it was obviously totally incapable of doing? I think not! The fact that God condemned Satan to an attitude of groveling, ... *on your belly you shall go* ... which is further emphasised by, ... *you shall eat the dust of the ground all the days of your life* ..., reveals in figurative language that by his actions Satan is humbled and would, in time, be completely defeated in his attempt to usurp the throne of God. (See Zech. 3:2; Jude 9).

God, being the pure and holy God that He is, is totally incapable of creating anything that is other than pure and holy and good as is clearly

29

The Beginning

indicated in Genesis chapter 1 for we read that God saw that each stage of His creation was good.

Originally Satan was the light-bearer of Divine glory, and such was his princely status before God that to him was entrusted a large part of the universe to rule in God's name (Lk. 4:5-7). How or when rebellious thoughts entered into this angelic being's mind, we have no knowledge except that his chosen act of defiance was established before man was created. It was this event of Lucifer falling away from the perfection of God that lies at the root of all the misery in the universe. But it was the contamination of the mind of man which brought to a head the anger of God and the final sentencing of Lucifer turned Satan.

Let us consider the words of condemnation in the light of what we already know:

> *How are you fallen from heaven*
> *O Lucifer, Son of the Morning!*
> *How are you cut down*
> *you who weaken the nations!*
>
> *... you shall be brought down to Sheol*
> *(the place of the dead)*
> *To the lowest depths of the Pit.*
> *(Is. 14:12b, 15; see Lk. 10:18)*

As the most senior angel Lucifer was above all the cattle in the field, indeed he was a spiritual being and of a different order; yet here the Lord God who created him is saying that he was to be brought low, below the status of cattle and beasts in the fields. This was a very great fall for such a glorious being.

The second stage of his fall from grace is the promise *On your belly you will go* ... But this is meaningless if we consider that Satan would move around on his belly; surely the meaning that would do justice to God's anger at what this being with an inflated opinion of himself had done, is for Satan to be prostrate, in an attitude of pure humiliation[7]. Prostration before God and before kings and rulers has been the physical sign of an inner submission to authority that is far more eloquent than any literal words can describe. Where it says in the Psalms ... *For our souls are bowed to the dust; our belly cleaveth (clings) to the earth, (Ps. 44:25 KJV)* in our minds we are seeing a prostration of prolonged duration that emphasises a submission that is truly very deep and altogether exceptionally respectful in a way that far exceeds

---

[7] All true believers have power over Satan in the name of Jesus Christ, which means he is subservient to believers.

any literal combination of words.

Such a humiliating state is compounded by the promise, *And you shall eat dust all the days of your life,* for he would experience constant disappointments and failures, mortifications and reverses (see Appendix C). Let the question be put again, "Is this really about a snake?" The theatre of action is far above that of a mere creature of the field.

And so we come to a particularly controversial verse.

Again we must remind ourselves who the judge is and in this case to whom the condemnation is being directed.

> *I will put enmity between you and the woman, between your seed and her seed …*

It is important to point out that God can never promote anything that is evil, for God is pure and holy and righteous and no sin can be found in Him. Therefore, for this enmity between Satan and the offspring of the woman to come to pass all God needed to do was to withdraw His calming influence.

The one thing that Satan could not abide was the peace of the Garden. He so hated the relationship between God and man that he sought to shatter it through his deception. Any attempt by God to bring about the salvation of men will be met with opposition from Satan, those angels who followed him out of the service of God and those who have decided to work for him.

The spiritual battle was activated from this moment; a battle that has spilled over into the affairs of this world from time to time but is particularly relevant in the Middle East as the time of the end approaches.

But what about the seed of the woman and that of the serpent, a subject that excites the response of so many people who have an obsession regarding whether or not this is a Messianic prophecy.

It is true that the seed of the woman is the whole of mankind, for all of us stem originally from that first couple. However, we are talking long term here, for due to the foreknowledge of God, the plan of the salvation of men was set before the foundations of the world were laid (Eph. 1:4), before the tragedy in the garden was acted out and before man had chosen to eat of either tree and was still free of sin.

The reference, … *just as He chose us in Him, before the foundation of the world, that we should be holy and without blame before Him in love … (Eph. 1:4)* means that even before the foundation of the world God chose (knew) those who would believe in Him, of their own accord, to be holy. Because of the freedom of choice that God allows each and every one of us, He did not choose any individual to be holy, only those who would respond to His offer of salvation and submit themselves to Him in faith.

The Beginning

There is a matter of God choosing individuals such as Jacob rather than Esau at strategic moments in history, but that was because He already knew (foreknew) what the state of the heart of each individual would be, therefore before they were even born God knew that Jacob would have a heart for Him but the focus of Esau's heart would be on the things of the world.

The seed of Satan are the dragon (Rev. 12) and two beasts the one out of the sea and the one out of the earth (Rev. 13).

God is far more powerful and able than Satan and all his followers, both spiritual and physical. After all it was God who made all things, even them. The choosing of Abram and Moses and King David was all part of His plan. It seems reasonable at this moment of judgement for the end game to be declared.

But just for a moment let us look at another 'Christian deception'.

Now to Abraham and his seed were the promises made.
He said not to seeds, as of many; but as of one,
And to thy seed, which is Christ."
(Gal. 3:16)

The argument goes that the word 'seed' is a compound noun and can mean either one or more than one, depending on the context of the passage in which it is found. According to scripture it is the seed of the man that is passed on, not the seed of the woman. So what is Paul trying to say that complies with the rule that you do not try to make the text say something you want it to say?

Abraham had two sons, one by a slave woman and one by his wife, who was free. One was the son of God's promise and one was the son of man's desire. That is; Abram's wife Sarai persuaded Abram to go with her maid, Hagar, because she herself was without issue and was getting old. But God had promised Abraham offspring, which was made clear after Ishmael's birth, when God said that Sarah would have a son. Therefore, there is promise in selection.

God's promise was first to Abraham and then to Isaac (even though Ishmael was born first), and then to Jacob (even though Esau was born first). If we continue this identification of those selected to be forebears of the Messiah, we come to the logical conclusion that they are all God's choices, that is; all the men and women He chose to be in the ancestral line of Messiah, whose arrival was not only prophesied by Daniel and other prophets but was according to scripture.

Therefore, Paul was correct in saying that Abraham's seed, according to God's promise, was directed through many generations to the one seed of the woman who would have the greatest impact on our relationship with

Satan. That is the Christ, the ultimate Passover Lamb who destroyed the finality of the grave for those who seek Him for in aligning themselves with the Messiah they are assured of eternal life with God. It is the Messiah who said that we were not to fear those who kill the body, but rather to fear Him who is able to destroy both soul and body in hell (Matt. 10:28). This then is Satan's power, which has been restricted to attacking us physically but he has no power to destroy us spiritually (Job 2:6) for eternity. That power is God's alone.

So, what about the woman's seed? Yes, it is in the plural for the simple reason that the woman was the mother of all those in whom the breath of God is found. But the central theme of scripture is not about Israel and the Jews, which is a totally selfish way of looking at scripture.

Rather it is about God's plan of salvation, from choosing Israel to be the means of producing the first fruits (Christ) through an ancestral line, to providing an understanding of the principles of both the way in which we relate to God and the process of salvation; from animal sacrifices to the ultimate sacrifice of God in the Messiah.

The Hebrew Mashiach (Messiah), the promised One had to be fully human. It was man who had sinned and been separated from God. As a stopgap, the animal sacrifices served the need for God to put in place the means of allowing those with a heart for Him to receive forgiveness without offending the purity and holiness of God. But such sacrifices did not have the deep conscience cleansing power necessary for eternal salvation.

Also, the animal sacrifices needed to be repeated time and again for the blood of an animal was unable to ... *make him who performed the service perfect in regard to conscience* ... *(Heb. 9:9)*. The reason why the Messiah, our Lord Jesus Christ, emphasised His humanity by using the name 'Son of Man' is because central to His ministry was the essential nature of His sinlessness, even in His human form, so that he could die for the sins of the whole of mankind, not just the nation of Israel (Jn. 11:49, 50).

His death would not only provide God with the fact that the sentence He had passed on man in the beginning had been carried out, for a perfect man had indeed died as a man and the representative sacrifice for man's sin, but His sacrifice would also provide those willing to accept the way of salvation with a once for all cleansing of their sin before God, along with a cleansed conscience (Heb. 9:13 – 15).

For the Christ to be our sacrifice He had to be pure (Son of God), but also, He had to be man (Son of Man); in that way He provided the perfect Passover Lamb sacrifice, obviating the need for further animal sacrifices.

Finally, we come to the end game, the final battle, when not just the spiritual battle but the spiritual war is won, for in the following two lines we have encapsulated the final state of this rebellious and divisive cherub.

> *... He shall bruise your head,*
> *And you shall bruise His heel.*
> *(Gen. 3:15c)*

Satan would be permitted to bring suffering and persecution on God's chosen people particularly when they were at their most rebellious. For when God withdraws His protection, the enemy steps in as he did on countless occasions through the warlike propensities of the nations around Israel. He would ultimately be allowed to bring affliction to the Messiah; affliction that would result in the physical death of the Messiah, but always according to God's plan and timing.

There would still come the time when the chosen core of God's people would see the fatal blow that the Messiah would inflict on Satan at the end, his head. What is so significant in the book of Revelation is the unfolding of the end times, when Satan is finally sent to the lake of fire, which will be the fulfilment of this passage in Genesis chapter 3. For at that time the two ends of the Bible will be brought together; united.

It is unlikely that Satan realised the full significance of this verse, for throughout the history of Israel he has had a significant part to play as Appendix C makes clear. But his end will be final and eternal.

It is important that we do not leave the condemnation of the man and the woman out. It is interesting that, having dealt with the judgement of Satan, the Lord God then goes on to judge the woman who was sentence as being deceived (v16). Not only would women find the conception, carrying and bearing of children painful to remind them of the danger of Eve's deception, but God set the relationship between the woman and the man in stone.

> *Your desire shall be for your husband,*
> *And he shall rule over you.*
> *(Gen. 3:16)*

This is the key to true family life and is clearly evident when women are observed with men. There is within them the need for the man to take charge. They are the home makers and men the ones who are the protectors and the labourers for food. Any deviation from this God established relationship leads to problems.

The full force of God's anger is directed to the man, who should have taken charge of the woman, his helpmeet, in the first instance before Satan had a chance to do any damage by telling her exactly what God had said to him about the forbidden tree. Now he would find cultivating the ground in order to produce food a tiresome occupation. Suddenly the man became mortal, confined to this earth without the free spiritual contact with God he was previously afforded, liable now to the full measure of all the miseries and difficulties of life on his own in a world he had allowed Satan to rule over.

Satan's suggestion to Eve that by eating the fruit of the tree of the Knowledge of Good and Evil she and Adam would be like God knowing good and evil, was a myth, a means to an end to enable him to gain authority over them. Now they faced an uncertain future fending for themselves. They were to find out just how dire life can get when trust is shattered by deception and disobedience. Their final end was to be a reuniting of their bodies through decay with the dust of the earth from which they were made.

Finally, we have the first animal sacrifice. In this case it is the Lord who has the animals slaughtered; bringing to an abrupt end spiritual and physical peace that brought easy cohabitation amongst the living beings in the garden. They died because of man's sin. Their life blood was poured out so that their skins could be used to clothe the man and the woman who had, through disobedience to the command of God, found themselves condemned by God and cast out of the garden; separated from the One who had lovingly created them and blessed them.

In an instant they had been let loose in the great wild world to be dominated by the evil work of Satan and his demonic servants, angelic and human. The death of animals for the sake of man's wrong doing was not pertinent when, as vegetarians, they were in such an intimate and spiritual relationship with God.

But now, no longer welcomed in the spiritually conducive atmosphere of the garden, the sacrificial death of certain animals, coupled with a true and loving heart towards God of the one offering the sacrifice, was the only way man was able to keep in touch with Him. The immediate intimacy man had previously known was lost. The new relationship had to be built on the foundation of belief, commitment and trust.

It is reasonable to presume that by means of the sacrifice of those animals for clothing, God demonstrated to man his need to offer sacrifices for sin, which Abel so faithfully followed. This violent end to animals for the benefit of man, which would be repeated until the coming of the perfect sacrifice for sin, shattered the peaceful coexistence within the garden of God.

As the pure righteousness of God and the unrighteousness of man could not coexist because they are direct opposites, man was driven from the garden in which he had been created and where he had developed as an individual. The vital fact was that man, in his mortal and unrighteous state, must not be allowed to gain eternal life by eating the fruit of the tree of life.

The judgement of God, which man had brought upon himself, meant that he must be excluded from the presence of God. He would therefore have to individually reapply for a personal relationship with God, a rebirth of his spirit that would lead to eternal life, through repentance and faith in the renewing ability of God through His plan of salvation which we are about to discover together.

Thus, the man and the woman were driven out of the garden of God wherein stood the tree of Life, so that it could be preserved for another time when it would fulfil the task for which it was created; providing spiritually restored man with eternal life in the spiritual kingdom of our God (Rev. 21 & 22 esp. 22:2).

2 LIFE APART FROM GOD

"Humble yourselves
Under the mighty hand of God,
That He may exalt you in due time,
Casting all your cares upon Him,
For He cares for you"
(1 Pet. 5:6, 7)

'For the Lord gives wisdom;
From His mouth come
Knowledge and understanding.
(Prov. 2:6)

Mortal Man

If God made us then our future is with Him, if Satan made us then our future is with him.

This perhaps encapsulates the problem the first man and his wife faced in their dramatically transformed situation. It is a problem we still face today. Who do you believe - God or Satan? Whose kingdom do you want to be a citizen of, God's eternal kingdom that has no territory on earth but fills the earth because of God's ownership of it, the eternal future of which is heaven bound and glorious joyous in the very presence of almighty God who is the source of love and joy, or Satan's kingdom which is initially confined to the earth but has its eternal future in hell where God is not?

Having allowed their physical desire to overrule their spiritual understanding, and having listened to the voice that was not of God, the life of man suddenly became burdensome. What God had told them was true and what the tempter had told them, through self-interest, was not.

Where was their 'god status' now, faced as they were with scratching a living from the earth and pain filled procreation? If anything sealed the fact that 'God is true and everyone else a liar' then this was it.

Looking back towards the garden of God from which they had been evicted, there must have been enormous sadness and a major feeling of trepidation within the man and the woman. Finding themselves outside its embrace was a lesson indeed of their failure to be obedient to the God who had created them and on whom their devotion should have been focused.

They would have seen the cherubim guarding the garden's entrance, which was to the east of the garden in the direction of the rising sun, and clearly marking the frontier of God's eternal spiritual kingdom with the earth. The holy emblem of the flaming sword demonstrated the conservation of the purity and righteousness of His presence, and, in their memories, they would have relived the pleasure and security they had known there.

The purpose of the unidirectional flaming sword was to inform those who could see it that any attempt to enter the garden would be met with certain death, for this was the perfect God guarding His kingdom on earth to prevent anything that was not righteous entering into it. To us that garden is invisible.

With the appearance of the Cherubim[8], God was demonstrating the severing of the spiritual from the physical creation with immediate effect. Man would no longer be able to see the spiritual other than in exceptional circumstances, although the influence of the spiritual creation would continue to work within the world's environment, its unseen activity evidenced in the demeanour, attitude and way of life of those spiritually enlivened by the Holy Spirit. This was a totally new environment for man, and one with which he was now forced to become familiar.

So, having achieved his end in taking control of what is 'of the earth', what was Satan's plan now? Surely it was to keep hold of it. Therefore, the battle for supremacy on earth began; a battle that is still raging today for anything to do with God is anathema to Satan who is referred to as the 'Prince of the Power of the Air'.

Even the Lord Messiah did not challenge him when he said that he was able to give Him all the kingdoms of the world (Matt. 4:8, 9), but the Lord was able to say that the 'Lord your God' should be worshipped for He was, and always will be, greater than Satan.

Away from regular personal and physical contact with God within the safe environment of the secure garden, where everything was peace and love, the man and the woman had to face each day not knowing what would happen to them. A new and uncertain future was their lot.

From the start man was mortal with a spiritual centre. The purpose of the Tree of Life was to make mortal man into an eternal being (the possessor of eternal life), hence God's need to remove the now sinful man from the garden so that access to the tree of life was denied him. Unrighteousness can have no place within the eternal kingdom of God. Now man's mortality would be demonstrated for all to see, for the inevitability of death would cast a shadow over every living soul.

---

[8] Angels are the messengers of God (Heb. 1:14) and can also be people such as Elijah who was a prophet of God and an angel because he was a messenger of God but not of the spiritual hierarchy. Cherubim are the doers, action angels if you like, such as here where they are guarding the garden entrance.

What created the greatest pleasure within the garden was man's God-ward attitude, his enjoyment of being in God's presence. This is what I wrote in my work on the book of Genesis regarding Jacob's son Joseph:

> There is clear evidence in Joseph's life that he had an empathy with God. His brothers, however, were, like Esau, seemingly oblivious to the importance of staying close to God. Joseph therefore shone like a light in a darkening place. Jacob must have sensed a kindred spirit and as a result was seen to love him more than his brothers. The scene that was now opening up took on an unnerving similarity to that of Cain and Abel.
>
> Cain became jealous of his younger brother when Abel's sacrifice was accepted and his was rejected. Now the brothers, seeing Joseph being loved of his father in preference to themselves, followed Cain's example by allowing jealousy to become established in their hearts. (Extract from The Origin of Life)

Let us look at the developing situation.

The multiplication of Man and Social Disorder

Adam and Eve had sexual intercourse resulting in the birth of Cain followed later by Abel. So Cain was the elder brother.

Consider their occupations: Cain was the tiller of the ground (in today's parlance a farmer or market gardener) whereas Abel was a shepherd of sheep.

By breathing into the nostrils of the first man God placed a generic need within all of us for spiritual contact with Himself. We are informed by scripture that God is a spirit and the only way we may worship Him, that is give Him the honour and adoration due to Him who made us, is in spirit (through the spirit that is in us) and in truth (acknowledging and abiding by the instructions we have received from the mouth of God in both the first and second testaments).

As we are made aware God worked six days (stages) to create the world and its surrounding heavens and on the seventh day He rested. In blessing man and calling on him to be fruitful and multiply, which is the first of God's guiding principles of life for man to build a home and rear a family, God also instructed him to subdue the earth, which means to take authority over it and have governance over it.

This would suggest that Adam and Eve would work in the garden, for from the start work was part of man's daily therapy. His task was to tend the garden, and on the seventh day they would rest and spend time with

God. Why do I say this? Because God was insistent from the beginning that the routine adopted by the nation of Israel was for the people to work for six days and then on the seventh to rest; six being the number of man and seven being God's number for on that day he rested, therefore in this context the seventh day is holy to God.

When it is said in Gen. 4:3 that, *In the process of time Cain brought some of the fruits of the soil as an offering* ... it is probable that the routine cycle of working six days and resting on the seventh became so much part of their lives whilst in the garden that the parents of the two boys carried on that same routine even after they were evicted from the garden, for scripture gives us no idea of how long the couple lived at peace in the garden. Outside the garden, the daily work for both the man and the woman was far more arduous and the need for one day of rest each week became very necessary. Therefore, the Sabbath day of rest became synonymous with a time of worship before God.

However, the main change that they experienced was that they were now sinners, separated from God. There is overwhelming evidence of God's love for mankind over the years of human history and of the instructions God has given man on how he can reach out to Him. Realising that the man and woman were now undoubtedly subdued and traumatised by their dramatic change of circumstances, particularly in their relationship with God, it is unlikely that God threw the rebellious pair out of the garden without instruction on how they could maintain some form of relationship with Him in their new situation. That instruction would include the embryonic process of offering animal sacrifices, which became more prominent with introduction of the Passover Sacrifice, and formalised at the inauguration of the Tent of the Meeting.

There are two things about man that are vitally significant and these are that man was made in the image of God and that into man's nostrils God breathed the breath of life. Therefore, as with a woman who gives birth to a child and the child is part of her; in the same way man is part of God for God gave him birth.

God loved man when He created him and God still loves man, for God would have no one perish for the lack of instruction on how to receive forgiveness of sins. He even sent reluctant Jonah to Nineveh to save that great city through instruction (Jonah 4:11). Through Moses God instituted the regular services and sacrifices by which men might receive forgiveness for their sins, albeit covered over for that time until the ultimate sacrifice when their sins will have been completely blotted out.

Without understanding the process (this instruction would come later), man was provided with the means of approaching Him through the shed blood of a lamb, providing him with forgiveness as in the case of Abel.

Central to our relationship with God is blood. To Noah God said that blood is the life of the flesh (Gen. 9:4). In Leviticus we read that not only is the life of the flesh in the blood, but that God has given that blood, initially to Israel, when daubed on the altar of sacrifice, to make atonement for their souls (Lev. 17:11).

Cain brought an offering to the Lord on the Sabbath day. His brother Abel followed.

As a tiller of the ground Cain brought a sacrifice of thanksgiving (thanking God for the fruit of the ground), not of worship to God which is altogether different. To worship God, we must first recognise our need of Him and our indebtedness, not only for the gift of life but also for His grace and mercy. Cain signally did not recognise his sinful state before God or give God glory, for in offering the fruits of the ground he might have acknowledged that God gave the increase, but the act of sowing, tending the crop and then harvesting the crop was the work of Cain's own hands. In seeking to offer to God such a sacrifice, Cain was trying to earn favour with God not submit to Him.

Abel seems to be a completely different character, for he did not want to give of what he had achieved but to offer a life for his continued existence, and to maintain his spiritual relationship with God. By offering of the firstling of the flock he was giving to God the very best of what God had created.

The fat was the choicest of the choice offerings he could present to God. It can also be termed a sin offering which will be identified when we get to the priestly offerings on the altar in front of the tabernacle. This is after all what God demonstrated to Abel's parents when animals were killed to provide them with clothing which they previously did not need because the sun and warmth was provided by God Himself.

But let us consider the events more closely, for we are told that the Lord had respect for Abel's sacrifice but not for that of Cain. Is there some other information that we need to consider to fully understand this and subsequent events?

The words 'had respect to' in Hebrew signify the fact that God looked at the sacrifices with keen interest accepting the sacrifice that was offered (not only according to His instructions but also with a right attitude of heart) by igniting it with fire from heaven, just as with the sacrifice Elijah offered on the top of Mount Carmel before King Ahab and the people (1 Kgs 18:38; also see Lev. 9:24).

A covenant in Biblical terms is a binding agreement between two parties. 'B'rit', the Hebrew word for covenant, actually means "to cut the covenant" and this was done by cutting a sacrifice in two (Gen. 15:9, 10), along with the resulting shedding of blood. Abram went into a deep sleep during which God told him what would happen to his descendants but that they would eventually arrive back in the land through which he was wandering as a stranger. For the covenant to be made legal the parties had to walk between the halves of the sacrifices but as this was a covenant God, being the righteous and holy One, was making with Abram, the sinner made righteous by his sacrifices and obedience to the will of God, therefore it was only God who walked between them in the form of a smoking oven, symbolic of the affliction of Israel (Deut. 4:20; 1 Kngs. 8:51) and a burning torch (1 Kin. 11:36, 15:4). When a covenant was entered into a solemn promise was made of love and protection. It is interesting that God told Abram that his descendants, the Israelites, would leave Egypt with great possessions; this was to enable them to provide much of the materials and treasure for building the Tabernacle.

To the Israelites circumcision was a sign of the everlasting covenant God made with Abraham (Gen. 17:1 – 14) in perpetuity and evident in the living flesh of every male. But Moses went further by instructing the Israelites to circumcise the foreskin of their hearts and be stiff necked no longer (Deut. 10:16). But what did he mean by that statement?

> *"What does the Lord your God require of you,*
> *But to fear the Lord your God,*
> *To walk in all His ways and to love Him,*
> *To serve the Lord your God with all your heart*
> *And with all your soul,*
> *And to keep the commandments of the Lord*
> *And His statutes*
> *Which I command you today*
> *for your good?*
> *(Deut. 10:12, 13)*

Circumcision was an outward sign of the covenant relationship with which God blessed Abram[9], and became the sign of a person's membership of the nation of Israel (Gen. 17:1 – 14). But in the verses above the Israelites were being called upon to do more than just carry an outward sign of that covenant relationship that signified membership of God's chosen people. They were to love and serve the Lord their God with all their heart; they were required to enter into a personal all-encompassing relationship with Him, even to the extent of being in the state of marriage with God, where commitment and service were part of the day-to-day routine of life.

It was not to be a superficial relationship. They had to put the covenant relationship into practice and commit themselves, as Abram had done

---

[9] It was as Abram, that he answered the call of God, but when he was 99 years of age God changed his name from Abram to Abraham (father of nations). Abraham is also the spiritual father of all believers and an example to us. The use of the names Abram and Abraham in this book accords with the time of his life that is pertinent to the text.

(Gen. 12:1) in being totally obedient to God's call, to the God who had done so much for them by choosing them and bringing them out of slavery into a new and free relationship with Himself (Deut. 10:17 – 22). The symbol of the flesh had to be transferred to the heart, deemed the centre of their being, and each and every individual had to embrace the Lord their God as their husband (Is. 54:5; Hos. 2:16 – 20). The relationship had to be intimate and of the deepest and purest kind.

So what do we see here? Abel's sacrifice of a lamb was suddenly consumed by fire but that of Cain's just stayed there untouched. It was not just the choice of sacrifice but the state of the heart before God of the one offering the sacrifice.

God's judgements are sure and not arbitrary. Indeed, the Psalmist says that the judgements of the Lord are true and righteous altogether, which means that there were rules to live by that God had given to Adam and Eve regarding sacrifice, just as He had warned them about the fruit of the tree of 'Good and Evil'. Abel had lovingly observed those rules in presenting his sacrifice to God, but Cain clearly had not.

And we have further evidence concerning God's response to this event, for in speaking to Cain regarding the failure of his offering God says:

> *"If you do well (according to My instructions) will you not be accepted?*
> *But if you continue to be disobedient the act of sin (rebelliousness) lies at*
> *the door. But if you seek out a lamb to sacrifice it will not fear you and*
> *you will be able to offer it for you to be accepted" (Gen. 4:7).*

Why then did Cain maintain his anger? Why did Nadab and Abihu offer strange fire before God when they must have been fully aware of the power and awesomeness of God (Lev. 10)? What is there within the mind of the rebellious sinner that causes them to persist in their rebellion against the will of God? The humiliation experienced by Cain in having his sacrifice publicly rejected hurt his pride and he was unwilling to say sorry to God and change his ways and his attitude because his heart was hardened towards God, not understanding, nor wanting to understand the consequences of his action.

Anger is a reaction that stimulates a person out of tune with God to violence when they are in contact with another person who is in tune with God. It is a clash of good and evil between people caused by the contrast of what state the sinner knows deep within them that they ought to be in rather than the state they were in. It is the demonic in contrast to the pure godly.

Daniel prospered because he had a hearts desire for God that revealed itself as *'an excellent spirit ... in him,'* so much so that the king thought of putting Daniel in charge of the realm under him as king (Dan. 6:3) just as

Joseph was put in charge of Egypt under Pharaoh. This led to all the other governors and satraps being jealous of him.

We read that, as soon as the decree was signed which stopped people petitioning any god or man except for the king for 30 days, Daniel demonstrated the strength of his faith by going to the upper room, with windows that faced Jerusalem, three times that day to pray and give thanks to God.

In this activity he had engaged since early days (Dan. 6:10) and his protagonists knew that. Although what they did not know, but were soon to find out, was the truth and power of God's existence.

Of course, those jealous of his rise to power had conspired to put that decree before the king, knowing what Daniel would do. They were waiting for evidence against Daniel, and reported his actions to the king, who could then do nothing to save Daniel from the lion's den.

Having been forced to condemn Daniel to the lion's den, the king spent a sleepless night, but before the dawn could fully give its light, the king went to the place of execution and found Daniel alive and well because the angel of the Lord had shut the mouths of the lions. Daniel's accusers and their families were not so fortunate, for before they reached the bottom of the pit all their bones were broken.

Jealousy is a tragic condition. Spiritually inspired jealousy is particularly insidious because it acts as a window on the battle Satan is engaged in with God, using men and women as his pawns to do his dirty work.

Those who accused Daniel and thought they could get rid of him with impunity were wrong for they had not accounted for the power of Daniel's God. They met their deaths, they and their families having their bones broken before they reached the ground. But they were not alone, for Haman who had previously accused Mordecai at the time of Queen Esther, was hanged on the gallows he had built on which to hang Mordecai (Est. 7:10, read the whole of Esther to gain an understanding of the situation).

At the time of the Messiah the ancient Jewish court system called the Sanhedrin judged accused lawbreakers, but could not initiate a death sentence. It required a minimum of two witnesses to convict a suspect as laid down by scripture. As there were no attorneys the accusing witness stated the offence in the presence of the accused, and the accused could call witnesses on his own behalf, which is graphically demonstrated by Paul's trial before Felix, Festus and Agrippa (Acts 25:16). The court then questioned the accused, the accusers and the defense witnesses.

The Great Sanhedrin, the supreme religious body of 71 sages that met in the Chamber of Hewn Stones in the temple in Jerusalem, dealt with religious and ritualistic temple matters, criminal matters appertaining to the secular court, proceedings in connection with the discovery of a corpse, trials of adulterous wives, tithes, preparation of Torah Scrolls for the king and the Temple, drawing up the calendar and the solving of difficulties relating to ritual law.

It was before this court that Stephen was brought, being accused of blasphemy (Acts 7). Having outlined his understanding of the history of Israel, to which they listened intently, he then went on to accuse them of being stiff-necked and uncircumcised of heart and ears, resisting the activities of the Holy Spirit as their fathers had done.

Stephen then challenged them regarding the activities of the forefathers who persecuted the prophets, for they disagreed with the message those prophets reputedly gave them from God. Being spiritually blind they were unable to understand the message; it did not touch their spirits as it should have done.

Now the members of this Supreme Court had followed the example of their forefathers by becoming the betrayers and murderers of the Just One who had been promised. They were cut to the heart by such accusations, believing they were supremely holy and pure according to the Law of Moses (Jn. 9 esp. v34, 40, 41). But there are a number of features of their behaviour that would suggest that they were far from the truth in God.

They gnashed their teeth at Stephen, which would indicate a demonic element within them; but when Stephen had a vision of the heavens opening and the Son of Man standing at the right hand of God, the distinct contrast between Stephen's holiness and their lack of understanding of the true things of God became too much for their pride and worldliness to stand. Stopping their ears so that they could hear no more of his holy utterances, and crying out with anger and a sense of personal humiliation and demonic craze, they rushed him out to the place of execution, where they released their pent-up guilt feelings by throwing stones and rocks at him to kill him. They were acting as judge and jury and by default sentencing him to death, which they were not allowed to do for around 30 C.E., the Great Sanhedrin lost its authority to inflict capital punishment.

Was this the correct way for the members of such an august court to behave? Fanaticism is not of God for God is a God of love who seeks to gently lead the sinner to the point of repentance. Compare Stephen's behaviour to theirs. Filled with the Holy Spirit of the living God, as he was, did he not act with propriety throughout this whole episode? *'Father forgive them ...'* was his cry. Their behaviour was truly of Cain and not of Abel.

Religion has ever been the greatest excuse for blood-letting and extreme cruelty. This is Satan at work in individuals and groups.

So what of Cain? It would appear that he was unwilling to listen to the message of God and desired revenge on the one who, quite innocently, obeyed the instructions of God and obtained the reward.

God's question to Cain regarding the whereabouts of his brother was one to which God knew the answer, but He wanted to hear what Cain was prepared to say; just as God knew where Adam and Eve were when He called to them in the garden after they had sinned and were hiding their nakedness, but He wanted them to convict themselves from their own mouths.

The answer Cain gave is no different in its message to the reply given by his father Adam. Cain lied. There were only two of them and the disappearance of one had to be the responsibility of the other. Yet Cain declared that he did not know the whereabouts of his brother, and then asked if he was his brother's keeper.

But God knew the facts, declaring that Abel's blood cried out to Him from the ground. The judgement of God on Cain is severe, pronouncing that the ground and all that it sustained would be barren wherever he lived and that he would be a fugitive all his life. Although his life would be spared because of some identification which prevented others from carrying out rough justice. With no hint of repentance, Cain left the sanctuary of Eden, where his parents now lived, to lead a godless life because of his unwillingness to repent of his sin and seek God's forgiveness; rebellious to the last.

So began a period of unrestricted human self-determination. Cain, through his outward show of devotion but lack of inward piety, demonstrated a nature drawn entirely from the evil one (1 Jn. 3:12), even though he had the breath of God within him.

Whereas Abel brought his first and best because of the spiritual tendency of his heart, Cain brought of the first thing that came to hand because of the predominance of his world-dominated mind over any spiritual understanding or consideration, remembering that they had not known the loving and safe environment of the garden of God. It is possible to be practical and spiritual as Abel clearly demonstrated, but Cain was predominantly practical and saw things from a completely Satanic worldly point of view. This is the danger many members of both synagogue and church face; ritual that replaces the spiritual element of worship with dogma that overwhelms a spiritual consciousness or spiritual seeking that connects the worshippers with the Spirit of God.

In the introduction I said that this is not a Bible study in the true sense of the expression. The purpose of the work thus far has been to illustrate the relationship of God and man before sin entered into the world, how sin made its disastrous appearance and the reaction of men to God after that monumental event. This is supremely important as we consider the historical events leading up to the building of the Tent of the Meeting, otherwise known as the Tabernacle of God.

Man's Descent into Decadence

Whereas love dominated the creative desire of God, Satan, who has no creative skills whatsoever because he was a created being himself, brought to man deception and everything that is anti-God; unfortunately for man, deception and all the other acquired attributes of Satan stimulated the opposite to love, which is both fear and self-aggrandizement such that even the creation is directly affected (Ro. 8:22).

The natural world that lived in harmony within the Garden of God was transformed outside the garden into an environment of deception and fear, particularly in regard to the animal kingdom; this along with the self-seeking of men with the desire to dominate others.

Much has been broadcast, particularly in the twenty first century, of the decline of the natural world and the disappearance of species in all areas of the natural world (as recorded in the book of Revelation) because of the work of sinful man, seeking greedily to surround himself with the 'good things of life' to the detriment of all that is around him; seeking the things of this life rather than blessings in the future with God.

Particularly from man's point of view the environment in which he found himself changed dramatically.

1. Whereas in the garden God was the guide and quietly laid down the governing principles of daily life, putting man in charge of looking after the garden (nature needs to be tamed and managed) and identifying what he could and could not eat; outside the garden, suddenly, there were no fundamental regulations from God, except the instruction to offer sacrifices for sin. But man cut off from the God who created him and provided him with the reason for his existence and purpose in life, now found himself cut adrift with no identified goal or vision, apart from the need to survive each day. Suddenly he had no one to please but himself.

   Certainly, Satan did not have any interest in man except to be the superior being. To Satan man was just a prize; a possession with which he thought to elevate him, drawing him nearer to his true goal of the status of God, whose equal he aimed to be.

   This self-promotional activity of Satan filtered through to man who now found himself under Satan's authority. Unfortunately, Satan's strategy has always been to hide away; to merge with the background so that no one really knows who he is or that he exists, just as he is pleased to be likened to a snake, for in that way no one knows what he is really like.

   Who is the Devil? Has anyone ever seen him? He is mostly in disguise. Just as he appeared to Eve as an angel of light, so he can appear to any one of us in human and many other forms.

The danger for believers is that we are tempted to give credit to Satan when he has had nothing to do with what he is being accused of. But even this adds to his anonymity.

2. The less responsive and more hostile natural environment into which man had suddenly been propelled contained a reduced revelation of nature, conscience and an abbreviated history divorced from the fact of God being its creator.

    From the ease of life under the guidance and protection of God to the almost godless environment into which he had been thrust, man was suddenly faced with providing for himself without the assurance of the protection of God; hence the introduction of fear and uncertainty, for Satan had no plan other than gaining authority over man for his own ends.

    True, man had become like God knowing good from evil but, without the supporting knowledge of God, man was trying to live his life without foresight and in total ignorance. After all, it was God who was responsible for man's existence and it was His intention that man should be closely engaged with Himself for eternity; death being unheard of.

3. With the with drawl of God's supervision, man had to make up his own rules as he went along because Satan was incapable of replacing the true guidance God had previously provided. Satan was only able to cause chaos, which through his rebellion against God, was all he knew.

Cain established the doctrine of self-will for he showed no repentance when his offering was rejected and remained unburnt on the altar. Rather than seeking to understand his state before God and make changes to his lifestyle and approach to the Almighty, Cain's response to God's judgement on his offering was to be angry with his brother, who had understood the need for repentance and the offering of a substitutionary sacrifice of blood being the death of a guiltless sacrifice of the purest kind. Although he acknowledged he was a dependent creature before God, Cain did not believe he was a death-deserving sinner; unfortunately, such people will only find out the folly of their alternative ways after death when it is too late to make a change to their life style (Lk. 16:19 – 31).

According to accepted Jewish teaching, there were to be two appearances of the Messiah. The question is, why did the Jews, at the point where BC became CE, which interestingly happened at the time of the Messiah's appearance however much it is disguised, believe that a warrior king would come first, when God's primary concern was to overcome the penalty of man's sin, introduced by Adam, so that individuals could be saved to the uttermost and enable them to obtain eternal life?

The sin offering was central to the temple worship. Sin was the leaven that had to be cleaned out of Jewish houses at the time of the annual Passover celebration. Forgiveness of sin was essential to man's approach to God. Cleanliness, with all the copious rules for its maintenance, was a central concern for the religious people of that time, yet they did not apply the principle of physical and outward cleanliness to their inner and personal lives (Matt 23:23 – 28).

It will hopefully become clear as we pursue this study of the Tent of the Meeting how central to our relationship with God is the acknowledgement of, and accounting for, our sinful state before God through the full payment of the penalty for sin. This will also give credence to why the first appearance of the Messiah was as the suffering servant leading the way to His second coming as triumphant King.

We have already seen (Appendix C) the reaction of those without that sense of guilt before God towards those who have a spiritual sensitivity. The recorded scriptures are primarily about the history of the line of Israel from the beginning and its relationship with God. Prophets have been particularly high-profile recipients of abuse, from those who, being without God, could not recognise or understand the words as being from God. King or priest made no difference, for each in their own way abused the messengers of God (Matt. 21:33 – 41).

Worthy followers of Cain were Balaam who preferred the riches and acknowledgement of men rather that the service of God (Nu. 22) and Korah who through self-delusion was prepared to challenge and defy Moses, the true servant of God (Nu. 16), and thereby attract supernatural retribution along with his co-conspirators and their families.

The Psalmist admits to being envious of those who seem to succeed even though they are away from God and have no desire to serve Him, until he realises just how important God is to him in his own life (Ps. 73).

'For to be carnally minded (that is of the flesh, worldly)
Is death, because it is enmity against God,
But to be spiritually minded
(that is with the spirit within us alive and
communicating with God as it was in the beginning
with God in the garden)
Is life and peace.
(Ro. 8:6, 7)

Abel pleased God; but, because of his focus on the things of the flesh and the world, Cain found himself unwilling and unable to please God and, without the discipline such a relationship has on a man, Cain left the presence of God to pursue a life detached from Him. This one act of man opened the gates to the confusion of religious thought and observance: from atheism and all those 'isms' that deny the existence of God, to the plethora of cults and pagan religions with which the world is burdened up to the present day.

Confusion of religious focus entered into the world hindering man from finding the true God to worship. Seeking for a spiritual focus for his innermost need, man has floundered around blindly seeking the truth but because of his world focused mind and the confused messages and offers of spiritual fulfilment with which Satan has saturated the environment around him, including within the church, the majority of mankind has been unable to find that truth for which they search so earnestly.

This is an extract from my book Christ IS King : A Guide for Doubters:

> Scotsman James Hudson Taylor was challenged by God to go to China as a missionary doctor in the mid 1800s to heal the sick and preach the gospel and in so doing started the China Inland Mission, which organization was used to send many missionaries out to that vast land which was so full of spiritual darkness. In his autobiography he tells this story:
>
> *"On one occasion I was preaching the glad tidings of salvation through the finished work of Christ, when a middle-aged man stood up and testified before his assembled countrymen to his faith in the power of the Gospel."*
>
> *"I have long sought for the Truth,"* said he earnestly, *"as my fathers did before me; but I have never found it. I have travelled far and near, but without obtaining it. I have found no rest in Confucianism, Buddhism, or Taoism; but I do find rest in what I have heard here tonight. Henceforth I am a believer in Jesus."*
>
> The man was one of the leading officers of a sect of reformed Buddhists in Ningpo (near Shanghai). A short time after his confession of faith in the Saviour, there was a meeting of the sect over which he had previously presided. I accompanied him to that meeting, and there, to his former co-religionists, he testified to the peace he had obtained in believing in the Lord Jesus. Soon after, one of his former companions was converted and baptized. Both now sleep in Jesus. The first man long continued to preach to his countrymen the glad tidings of great joy. A few nights after his conversion he asked how long this gospel had been known in England. He was told that we had known it for hundreds of years."
>
> *"What!"* said he, amazed, *"is it possible that for hundreds of years*

you have had the knowledge of these glad tidings in your possession, and yet you have only now come to preach it to us? My father sought after the Truth for more than twenty years, and died without finding it. Oh, why did you not come sooner?"

In conclusion Hudson Taylor wrote: *"A whole generation has passed away since that mournful inquiry was made; but how many, also, might repeat the same question today? More than two hundred million have been swept into eternity, without an offer of salvation. How long shall this continue, and the Master's words, "To every creature," remain unheeded?"*

It is this growing detachment of mankind in general from God after his eviction from the garden, with individuals who had that spark of spiritual need for Him within them, God initiated His plan of salvation which initially used those individual seekers to re-establish His kingdom within men until, in Jacob, it progressed to being developed into a nation through the furnace of affliction in Egypt.

And Israel is still central to God's plan to provide man with a way back to Himself. However, because of their lack of understanding of the things of God at the time of the first visit to earth by the Son of God when the nation denied the coming of the supreme and final sacrifice, God used those not of the nation of Israel, who had been taught the truth by His disciples, until Israel should see the error of their ways and take back their role as God's representative nation on earth, the main channel He has always tried to use to speak to man. The established church is assisting that process because it is following the example of Israel by becoming de-spiritualised and refocusing on the things of the earth and it too will be transformed into doing what it was designed to do.

Cain the fugitive became the first to build a fixed settlement (Gen. 4:17), a city he called by the name of his son Enoch meaning 'initiation', a fresh start. Does this suggest that Cain was seeking to set aside all that had gone before and to travel towards a life of self-determination, resisting the curse through self-will and with determination to defiantly oppose the Divine word?

It would certainly suggest the founding principles on which all future godless human development has been based. Fleshly energy focused on creating a paradise on earth without the acknowledgement of the sovereignty of God, self-redemption by man for man without the involvement of the Divine persons. Yet true and eternal redemption, that continues after a person had died and in his spirit left this earth, can only be experienced when the human heart is opened as a ready recipient of Divine life-changing activity.

It is interesting that in Genesis 5, under the recorded generations of

Adam, the list does not include either Cain or Abel, ignoring them as though they had never been, although even Abel might have had issue.

It is also important to realise that the line of heritage that ultimately leads to Abram and the birth of the nation of Israel is identified, with many sons and daughters being recorded: it is as though the text following the relevant people in that line is magnified, thus putting into the background all other real people who were born and had their being at the same time as those identified. They are not unknown to God.

Cain and Abel have been included in the generations of the heaven and the earth, making the distinction between the line of godless Cain, righteous Abel and the other sons and daughters born of Adam and Eve. In doing so, the scriptures illustrate the estrangement from God of those who made the decision to enter into a world of religious make-believe.

For Cain is characterised by his defiance at the moment of judgement, even though the Almighty sought to give him a way to recover his relationship with Him by asking him to do as He directed, *"If you do well will you not be accepted?"* and warning him that sin, rebelliousness towards God, lies at the door with a desire for mastery of his soul if he refuses to rule over it. It says in one place, *"... your adversary the Devil walks about like a hungry lion seeking whom he may devour. Resist him ..."* and surely this is what the Almighty was saying to Cain.

Cain probably believed in the permanency of the earth, that he and it would go on forever. But it was created by the one offering the way of eternal life to him, which had nothing to do with earthly living. Therefore, Cain had set off walking along a dead-end road that would lead to personal disaster; a disaster that would involve all those who were persuaded to go along the same road that leads to eternal spiritual death as opposed to an eternal life in the presence of the creator God.

Two ways of life clearly emerge. The way of God and the way of anti-God, the way of the true believer and the way of a pseudo-believer who provides for himself a spiritual element in his life to try to satisfy the spiritual hunger within him, but an unfulfilling spiritual element which does not allow him to submit himself to God who is the only One who can satisfy the inner spirit in man. This is the way of the demonic, the cruel and obsessive imprisonment of the soul to ritual that destroys and de-humanises the sexual and social perfections that God intended man to enjoy.

It is interesting that with the birth of Enosh the son of Seth, who replaced the murdered Abel in the eyes of his mother Eve, we read that men began to call on the name of the Lord but not to glorify it. Enosh means weak, sickly, incurable; and it would seem that it was at this point that those rejecters of God, no doubt encouraged by Satan and those fallen angels who had followed him in rebellion, found other ways of seeking to satisfy their inner spiritual hunger by worshipping things such as the stars, by the name of Jehovah thus profaning that Name. What would Satan like more than to be worshipped by man? Man, in worshipful obedience to the usurper of the position of the Almighty.

As it happens God worked through those willing recipients of Divine grace, using them as witnesses even to this apostate world, to redirect individuals to Himself, such as Enoch. For although men live together in this fallen world, individuals have always been separated according to their understanding and adherence or non-adherence to the God who created them (Dan. 2:43), no matter what their position within the community may be.

Jonathan the grandson of Moses went the way of idolatry (Judg. 18:30), and even Aaron was so weak when faced with a mob crying out for something to worship other than the Lord God who had rescued them from slavery in Egypt that he made for them a golden calf (Ex. 32:4).

But God has not been without a voice in the world for we read in the Word of God concerning Enoch, who walked so closely with the Lord that He took him (Jude 14, 15).

Did not the Psalmist acknowledge God's ability to know us wherever we are and whatever state we are in, even to the understanding of our thoughts (Ps. 139:1 – 4)?

Therefore, it is important to realise that it is the responsibility of each and every individual to make the choice for God; true belief in God, which shall be of the heart, is not inherited from grandparents or parents as one Roman Catholic priest announced at a child's christening service. It is an entirely personal decision. One has only to consider the type of people the twelve sons of Jacob were and how differently they viewed the God of their father, or even the difference between Jacob and Esau, to realise how individuals react to the knowledge of God and how it affects their eternal future.

An Act of Judgement

There are moments in scripture where it says that man had degenerated to a point where God could take no more and steps in to bring judgement on those spiralling out of control down the slippery slope of debauchery. Genesis 6 reveals the first such occasion, *"And the Lord said, "My Spirit shall not strive with man forever, for he is indeed flesh; ..."*. This emphasises the vulnerability of man after the fall to the influence of Satan through the attractions of the world. Whereas before, in the Garden, because of the inbuilt character of God, the propensity of man was to do that which was good, but after the fall man acquired a tendency to do what was bad; which tells us in no uncertain way just how important it is for us to keep close to God.

We read that the sons of God saw how beautiful were the daughters of men so that they took wives for themselves of all whom they chose. But were these angels? Although the phrase 'the sons of God' relates to angels in scripture, in the context of Genesis 6 this does not make sense. Why? It is important that we understand the two creations for which God was responsible. There were two distinct and separate creations, the spiritual and the physical.

Angels were not provided with bodies of flesh. Although they could appear to men as human beings they could equally disappear in an instant, for the physical form was an optical illusion. The bodies were not real; they were not of the flesh, for their life was serving God in His eternal heaven, constantly in the presence of God.

Conversely man was created with a spirit trapped within the flesh. The flesh is of the dust of the ground and the spirit within is eternal and can only be released by the death of the body in which it lives. It is said that Jesus was 'tented' amongst us, which means that just like us the Messiah's spirit lived in the tent, which is the body, which we can see and touch.

It is the eternal future of the spirit within each of us for which the Tree of Life was provided. But man, whilst in the body, cannot exist outside the earth's environment whereas angels move easily between earth and God's dwelling place (Gen. 28:12).

This means that man in the flesh can have no relations with angels who are only spirit. Physically there is no substance in an angel that could possibly be of any use in producing children. It is impossible.

So, what could this expression 'the sons of God' mean? Enoch loved God to the extent that he was translated, which means he did not die in the normal sense but was taken up into heaven before he died a physical death, which God is perfectly capable of doing. We do not know how it was done, such as in the case of Elijah; all we know is that it was.

Now Enoch had many sons and daughters. The expression could well mean that those who were 'of God', the offspring of believing Enoch, were attracted to those who had rejected God, such as the daughters of Cain, because of their beauty and, possibly, their sensuality and brazenness. The problem with that is that the women would bear the children, and then train the children according to their own wayward ways.

The men were supposed to be followers of God. But if they were producing children with the daughters of those who denied God, they were themselves guilty of pursuing deviant ways, so there was no one to set a higher standard of life. Society degenerated to the point where God proclaimed,

"My Spirit shall not strive with man forever..."

and later

'He was sorry that He had made man to the extent that He was grieved in His heart'. (Gen. 6:3, 6)

Fortunately for mankind there was just one man, Noah, whose heart was still God-ward and who maintained a life in keeping with the will and purposes of God. We do not know just how devout his sons were, or their wives. Of Jacob's sons there was only one that we can be sure of whose heart was with God, and that was Joseph; for his life demonstrated for all to see his love and devotion for, and single-mindedness in, the service of God. It is this demonstration of devotion to God that says whether or not a person is a true believer.

We have here demonstrated what man is capable of when separated from God. This is the very reason why God barred the Israelites from marrying pagan women; but this was an instruction that even the priests in Jerusalem at the time of Ezra ignored to their cost. Think of the children abandoned by those erring priests. The priests, who had the task of maintaining the faith of those around them, had rebelled against the oracles of God and married pagan women (Ezra 10:2, 3), who had children by them.

Ezra came from exile and reprimanded them, so they abandoned their wives and children in order that they could be made 'clean' before God. But what damage did this action of abandonment do to the wives and their children and to their extended families? Would they not have joined the ranks of the enemies of Israel? So, whose fault was that but the sinful priests themselves, who lusted after the daughters of men and aligned themselves with the ungodly only to abandon them to save their own skins? There is no honour in that, only dishonour.

What have we learned from what we have studied so far? Is it not the need for each and every believer to be true to the word of God? Eve sinned because she was not fully conversant with what God had said, or its importance. We have the word available to us and the freedom to pray and seek God, therefore it is up to each and every one of us to read the word and be obedient to its instructions.

There is a plethora of written material available to us to teach us the truth, which we need to study with caution until we are sure whether or not it is of God. Are we saved to the uttermost? Have we committed our lives to God in such a way that we have the Holy Spirit of the Living God abiding within us? Are we continually in touch with God for guidance and understanding, for direction and confirmation that we are in the will of God? Or are we, like Eve, ignorant of the word and therefore in danger of eating the fruit of the wrong tree?

Individually we have the responsibility of being in a personal relationship with God. We must not just reach out to Him in an attitude of repentance and faith, but continually and with passion seek after the things of God and be receptive to what He has to say to us, allowing His guiding hand to direct us to the right way that leads to life. It is not easy. But with a submissive heart and a willingness to be totally at His disposal, then He is able to work in our lives. He has in mine.

Do not complain that God does not say anything to you and does not seem to answer your prayers if you are technically living a life that is no different from the multitude of others around you. You must demonstrate to God, just as Noah did, that your heart's desire is to be His child.

We have the witness of the word of God as to what sort of God the Lord the God of Israel is. From what we have read so far, we cannot be ignorant of just what is required of us if we are to be saved. We are no longer to be dependent on animal sacrifices, as we shall find out, but on the blood of the perfect Passover sacrifice of the Messiah of Israel.

To those Jews who reading this are angered or just confused by it, I would recommend just one course of action. The Lord God of Israel is the God of all Truth, therefore seek Him with an open and penitent heart and ask Him to reveal to you the truth of the matter. However, in letting God reveal to you the truth, you must be willing to receive His word whatever it is.

In separating man from God, Satan had brought man low. With no moral code or standards to live by, Satan had allowed man to degenerate to the point where the earth was corrupt and filled with violence (6:11). Without the loving standards and moral codes of God, all flesh had corrupted their way on the earth.

Noah represents the remnant that God has always maintained on the earth. Considering the thousands of inhabitants on the earth by that time, possibly even tens of thousands, just one man was found who was sufficiently God-centred to start a repopulation of the earth. God gave Noah 120 years to build an ark and to provide a witness of the creator God to the population of the earth before God brought judgement on the earth in the form of a flood. Unfortunately, even after all that time there was still only Noah and his immediate family who were worthy of being saved.

It is interesting that we are gradually discovering the route of salvation which God revealed over the passage of time. For example, the slaughter of animals to provide skins to clothe the naked couple, the accepted sacrifice of Abel and the provision of clean animals for Noah to sacrifice once he had been released from the ark at the end of the flood. From these and other events we see a clearer message of how man can come before God with a clean heart. For a more detailed understanding of the flood please see my book The Origin of Life.

Finally released from the safety of the ark, with his family and the animals God wanted to save, Noah offered clean animals as sacrifices to God, seven (God's number) of each type of clean animal as God had instructed him to lead into the ark.

What is so sad is the endemic and insidious nature of inherited sin was ever present within certain men, for it was not long after God gave Noah the covenant sign of the rainbow (Gen. 9:13) that sin again reared its ugly head.

Noah and his family received God's blessing and instructions to populate the earth; they were also told that the animals would be fearful of them and some would be available to them for food.

Blood Central to God's Salvation

Death was the judgement conferred on all men because of that original sin that inevitably resulted in the committing of personal sin by all the offspring of Adam and Eve.

It is essential to our understanding, not only of our relationship to God, but our means of getting right with Him, that we collect these strategic scriptures and put them together to provide ourselves with the full truth regarding salvation.

The warning Adam received from God regarding the fruit of the tree of the Knowledge of Good and Evil was that if he ate of it then he would surely die. As soon as they defied God's command, Adam and his wife were thrust out of the garden and, in a moment, experienced being shut off from face-to-face meetings with the God who created them. The way to the tree of life was guarded by spiritual beings with the purifying power of the fire of God and the ability to kill anyone who would dare try to enter into the presence of God. Moses was told that if he saw God's face he would surely die.

Now with Noah we hear of the truth of the meaning of blood.

"But you shall not eat flesh with its life,
That is its blood still in it.
(Gen. 9:4)

And in Leviticus we have an even more profound explanation of why God held blood as being such an essential part of man:

For the life of the flesh is in the blood, and I have given it to you upon the altar to make atonement for your souls; for it is the blood that makes atonement for your souls (Lev. 17:11)

Blood is sacred, for it is the blood of Abel that cried out from the ground to accuse errant Cain of murder. Such was to be the status of blood that anyone guilty of shedding the blood of man was to have his blood shed - meaning being condemned to physical death – and this also held true for animals killing man.

Just let us take a few more moments considering this matter:

1. We have been made in the image of God; therefore, we are God-centred and in our truly natural state as we were created God focused, or to put it another way, we have been created with a God-focused centre, which is the spirit within us. Hence our intrinsic desire for, and interest in, spiritual things, even if that which is within us has been turned by the fall to be anti-God and anti-spiritual, as with atheists and the like.

2. We are holy unto God because God breathed into the first man His own breath of the Spirit. This action of God not only gave Adam, and every individual born of Adam, independent life, but also created in each of us a spiritual being that is only compatible with God's Holy Spirit. Indeed, we are only truly 'alive' when we are in an active and dynamic 'marriage' type relationship with God through the intermediary work of God's Holy Spirit.

    The Spirit of Life is only effective when we have such a relationship. For consider what Paul (the Jewish Pharisee and onetime aggressive opponent of those who believed) said to the Ephesians, *you He made alive who were previously dead because of sin (inherited and personal)*, and then compare that to what John (the Jewish fisherman and disciple of the Messiah) reported in his Gospel, that the Messiah breathed on them and said, *Receive the Holy Spirit* (Jn. 20:22).

    When the disciples received the Holy Spirit (Acts 2) they were made alive to the extent that they were empowered for the work of witness that the Messiah commissioned them to do (Jn. 20:21). Consider this against the godlessness that Satan has to offer, depriving us of the Spirit of Life. The world has given us nothing. Our parents gave us nothing that God did not give to them first. Therefore, the creator God Himself is our all in all.

    It was God's Holy Spirit who was 'hovering' over the waters in the very beginning of the creation of the earth and is the power in the earth to bring to pass the thoughts of the Father, and the word of the Son. It was that same Holy Spirit who breathed into man's nostrils the breath of life, thus creating within man his spiritual, Holy Spirit compatible, inner being.

    True life exists when man's spirit, in complete obedience and commitment to the first commandment *You shall love the Lord thy*

God with all, becomes united with the Holy Spirit of the Living God; for only then can the Spirit of Life become a reality (Jn. 10:10).

3. It is God who designed us in such a way that the blood that courses through our veins sustains our life. Agreed, if we are deprived of breath then we die, but in basic form it is the blood that uses the oxygen to sustain the body and to be deprived of blood means that we weaken and die. To God therefore our blood is representative of the life He breathed into us and is therefore holy to Him.

4. The penalty for sin is death, for God told man that if he ate of the fruit of the tree of the Knowledge of Good and Evil, he would surely die. It was and still is a certainty! In rebelling against God, Adam forfeited his eternal life, as the disappearance of the Tree of Life, which still survives, so clearly demonstrates.

5. Salvation, which is the message central to the whole of the complete scriptures, is all about the restoration of sinful man to God. But man is condemned to death! Therefore, for salvation to be a reality blood must be shed, and as it is man who sinned it is man's blood that is required.

    But if all men died then salvation is of no practical value because in the animal sacrifices the animals had to be perfect, therefore for the eternal sacrifice the man had to be pure and perfect - sinless. Therefore, God decided that until the time was right for a perfect man to come and die, animal sacrifices would be permitted to atone for the sin of the sinner. Unfortunately, these sacrifices had to be repeated time and again by all men.

We are fortunately in the position where we can see the whole account of the plan of salvation; from the initial introduction given to Adam and Eve on their departure from the garden of God, as illustrated by Abel, through to the account of the sacrifices overseen by the priestly clan of Levi and right up to the fulfilment of the perfect Lamb of God in the Messiah at whose death the earthly Holy of Holies within the temple building became redundant.

This is a complete work of Almighty God from which I have thankfully and gloriously benefitted; a benefit that God has seen fit for me to pass on to others through my skills as an experienced technical writer.

Hear what Isaiah said:

"And He (the Lord the God of Israel)
said, "Go, and tell this people:
'Keep on hearing, but do not understand;
Keep on seeing, but do not perceive.'
Make the heart of this people dull,
And their ears heavy,
And shut their eyes;
lest they see with their eyes'
And hear with their ears,
And understand with their heart,
And return and be healed.""
(Is. 6:9, 10)

God realised that it mattered not that His prophets spoke His words to the people; their eyes were still blinded by the veil (Ex. 34:33) they wanted Moses to put on after he had given them and because of their stubbornness they were unwilling to hear the increasingly spiritual message God wanted to give to them, particularly if it was not what they wanted to hear.

When the prophet Jeremiah told them to surrender to Nebuchadnezzar, the king and the leaders of the people kept ignoring him and putting him in prison because it was not what they wanted to hear, but it was the truth according to the God of truth. Why then should they believe that eternal life, which was the ultimate goal of God's plan of salvation, was finally fulfilled through the death of the anointed One?

It was the stubbornness of the people of Israel that caused the Christian church, which was started by, and was initially led and populated predominantly with very courageous Jewish followers of the Christ, to become predominantly Gentile led and populated. Israel does not, nor ever will belong to the church, nor does the church replace Israel. Rather the church is part of spiritual Israel because it is the fulfilment of all the prophecies received by Israel; its foundation is the long promised perfect Lamb of God, the Messiah (Lk. 20:17, 18).

The church, that is the body of believers, not a building or an organization, is the new spiritual Israel in so far as it takes the fulfilment of God's plan of salvation as the basis of its new spiritual life; this is because the old Jewish religious activities, which focused on the ceremonies of the temple, are now obsolete because the temple, as it was, is no longer part of God's work in the world today. Therefore, the church must be seen as the fulfilment of God's plan of salvation and include as full members all those individuals who have received, in repentance and faith, the message of the Messiah and are prepared to worship Him in spirit and in truth.

The reason the Holy One of Israel spoke to the people in parables and not in plain language (Jn. 3:3 – 8; 10 – 15) according to the purposes of God is:

> 10   *And the disciples came and said to Him, "Why do You speak to them in parables?"*
>
> 11   *He answered and said to them, "Because it has been given to you to know the mysteries of the kingdom of heaven, but to them it has not been given.*
>
> 12   *For whoever has, to him more will be given, and he will have abundance; but whoever does not have, even what he has will be taken away from him.*
>
> 13   *Therefore I speak to them in parables, because seeing they do not see, and hearing they do not hear, nor do they understand.*

This was because they were spiritually dead[10], unable to hear or understand what God was saying to them.

> 14   *And in them the prophecy of Isaiah is fulfilled, which says:*
>   *'Hearing you will hear and shall not understand,*
>   *And seeing you will see and not perceive;*
>
> 15   *For the hearts of this people have grown dull.*
>   *Their ears are hard of hearing,*
>   *And their eyes they have closed,*
>   *Lest they should see with their eyes and hear with their ears,*
>   *Lest they should understand with their hearts and turn,*
>   *So that I should heal them.'*

For all those reading these words I would urge you to humbly, and in an attitude of repentance for your state as a sinner and contaminating sinfulness, and desiring complete and sure faith in God, seek the Lord while He may be found. Call upon Him while He is near (Is. 55:6 – 9; Ps. 51) and be open to His voice. Allow God to fill you with his Holy Spirit and do not approach God in an attitude of knowledge but, as I do, in ignorance; for His ways are not our ways, neither are our ways His ways. Seek knowledge from God for true wisdom comes from Him and Him alone.

Man without God is disaster (consider Proverbs chapters 1, 2 and 3).

Noah, grateful for being saved by God from such a devastating judgement, was keen to say his own thank you to God in the most

---

[10] That is the God breathed spirit within them was totally insensitive to what the Spirit of God wanted to say to them because they had been starved of God's word, neither did they seek after God in a concerted effort to find Him and commune with Him.

appropriate way, which was by offering sin offerings using clean, appropriate animals and birds. How he knew what was clean and unclean we can only understand if we assume God told him.

To offer the sacrifices which were to be presented as holy to God, Noah wanted to raise them off the ground so he became the first man to build an altar. And we read that God accepted these sacrifices not for the death, shed blood and burning of the flesh of the animals, but because of the desire Noah had in his heart to worship and thank God for his salvation in this profound way.

God in His turn promised never again to cause such an all-encompassing flood to come upon the earth and declared that the rainbow would become the sign of that covenant between Him and mankind.

So, the promises made to man at first are reiterated, for God told Noah and his sons to be *fruitful and multiply and fill the earth*. But what is added emphasises the change from the dominance of man over the lesser creation in love within the garden to that of terror, as we know to this day, for most animals and living creatures are terrified of man, and rightfully so because man in his fallen state is a destroyer.

> *"The fear of you and the dread of you*
> *shall be on every beast of the earth,*
> *bird of the air,*
> *indeed, everything that moves on the earth,*
> *And the fish in the sea.*
> *They are given into your hand*
> *for they shall be food for you"*
> *(Gen. 9:2, 3)*

Even Great Men Have Blemishes

Now that Noah was back on the earth, he and his family were effectively alone but he had his experiences as a farmer to fall back on. As I wrote in 'The Origin of Life' it is remarkable how God restored His creation with all the vegetation growing that was there prior to the flood. If the flood, which according to a rough calculation, covered the earth for about a year, all vegetation should have died completely and the seeds in the ground all rotted. But they did not.

So we read that, in time, a vineyard[11] cultivated by Noah produced fruit that he was able to make into an alcoholic beverage. Too much wine has a detrimental effect on a man and Noah, once described as the only man at a

---

[11] Where did the vines come from seeing the earth was under water for so long and had been uncultivated?

time of great wickedness who found grace in the eyes of the Lord, was reduced to incoherence and was unable to control his bodily activity and lay in his tent naked.

There is shame and an easy descent to do evil in God's sight by allowing a liquid to debilitate a man; such is the uncontrolled degradation and profane state into which Noah descended. A man chosen of God because of his unwillingness to descend to the depths of depravity reached by those around him before the flood, and of an outstanding nature, with all those previously around him gone with the flood, now consoles himself with the very fluid which possibly lubricated their fall from God's standard.

The fact that Ham saw his father in that naked and degraded state is not the point; it was an accident. However, it was his actions in making that discovery known, and the way he made it known, that led to his father's condemnation. It was his brothers who covered their father's nakedness discretely. Ham's son Canaan is somehow implicated in this incident for it is he, rather than his father Ham, who is named in Noah's condemnation.

Be that as it may, we can see the incident unfold for Ham. Instead of quietly and secretly covering his father's nakedness and then leaving the area, he went to tell his brothers; possibly, although we are not told in detail, with derisory language of his father's unfortunate state. Ham's older and younger brothers went immediately and very judiciously covered their father, without looking at his nakedness, thus earning his praise.

Probably near to his death Noah prophecies over his sons as Jacob was to do many generations later. Canaan, not Ham is cursed for his actions, which no doubt suggests that those actions came to light after a time. He was to live in a degraded state and be a servant of servants, which meant that his legacy to his descendants would always be, and has proven to be, at the mercy of all others, particularly to the offspring of Shem and Japheth.

Shem, the eldest son, is praised with the prophetic word that Jehovah (the Eternal, Immutable One, who was and is and is to come[12]) would particularly and peculiarly honour the descendants of Shem as the line through which He would speak to mankind and instruct them in the way of salvation until finally and spectacularly visiting the earth in the form of man to bring about the full and certain all-sufficient sacrifice for sin that would allow all men to become sons of God through repentance and faith. The descendants of Japheth would benefit from the promise of God to the descendants of Shem by dwelling in their tents.

Through the pages of this book, we will study God's plan of salvation, how it was revealed and how it unfolded to the point where the ultimate price of the salvation of man was paid in full, and also the incidents that provide us with the proof of its completion. We will also discover that,

---

[12] Which is God in covenant relation with man whom He has created

because it is God's plan, it is He who chose those who would be involved in its development and progress and provide the lineage for the Messiah, despite the fact that many tried by obstinacy and ignorance and pure hardheartedness to disrupt the progress of His plan.

Sadly, there are still far too many who, even today and even though they have been born into the chosen race, try to deceive us, as true though unknowing followers of Satan. They deny that the price of man's sin has been paid to the full and that salvation is within the grasp of all mankind, without first having to become Jews.

But this will all be revealed as we continue to search the scriptures not to promulgate my theories or my interpretation but the truth according to the God of truth. The Lord God almighty who created all things and under whose authority and spiritual control I and others, both Jews and Gentile converts alike, have willingly become submissive servants and worshippers. (See Appendix D)

I repeat the warning included in the Introduction because it is a true and essential reminder to me and all those who read this book of just who we are dealing with. Do not mess with God for although He is a God of Love, he is also a God of Justice, a righteous judge before whom we will one day stand to give account of all that we have done, both good and bad. It is His decision alone as to whether or not we are able to enter into His eternal rest within His unshakable and eternal kingdom.

3 THE WAY OF THE CHOSEN

"The fear of the Lord is the beginning of knowledge,
Fools despise wisdom, instruction and discipline"
(Prov. 1:7; see also Prov. 2:1 – 7; Ps. 14:1)

Confusion of Man (Gen. 11)

Man is incomplete without God as we have seen from what we have discovered up to this point. And it is not just the descendants of Ham who had the propensity to stray from God for, throughout the scriptures we have clear evidence of members of the chosen race diverting from the true God and seeking other gods because the focus of their lives was not on spiritual things, but material things.

We have a considerable advantage over those who lived at the time of the first testament that we are concerned with right now, for we have the whole picture of salvation from beginning to end, just as though we were in space looking down on the earth and seeing the play of history being enacted on the world's stage.

We also have the sum of man's discoveries of the vastness and complexity of what God has created which gives us an incredibly rich insight into the character of God if we are willing to spend time meditating upon it. This means that today we, both Jew and Gentile, are in the position where we can offer no excuse when we stand before the great white throne of the Christ, the Anointed One, and confess that we have not believed in God and His salvation.

Not only that, for those of us who do believe, it is incumbent upon us to confess our faith to others, however, the embarrassment some have concerning the confession of that name, might cause them to be denied access the heavenly kingdom of God. The question is, why should we be embarrassed to confess the name of our beloved saviour?

All those living at the time concerned, had been born of Noah and his wife therefore their language was the same throughout the then known world. Through the discovery of the vast plain of Shinar, in the south of what became known as Mesopotamia, they realised the extent of their civilization and became proud of their extensive family and wanted to preserve it.

In so doing they became introspective, shutting out the God who created them and to whom they owed their lives because of His rescue of

Noah to whom they were all related. How quickly man forgets the goodness of God. But more than that, they were rebelling against the command of God to fill the earth, to explore other delights of God's creation and to populate them.

As it was they saw this vast fertile plain fed by the rivers Euphrates and Tigris that could not only contain their number but provide an easy and comfortable living in a paradise environment. Was it not Abraham's nephew Lot who chose the fertile plain which was the location of the cities of Sodom and Gomorrah, leaving the more rugged land to Abraham? But which of the two remained in the will of God (Gen. 13:10; 19:12 – 17)?

Abraham, as we shall see, was called by God and was determined to follow Him whatever the cost. But these descendants of Noah, seeing the way to an easy life, decided to ignore God's command and make a life for themselves within the confines of this plain.

Being so settled and proud of their civilization they said to themselves, *"Let us make bricks and bake them thoroughly …"*, for they were so determined in their quest that they could not wait for the power of the sun to bake them, rather they used a furnace. However, such bricks are known to only last a relatively short time in world history before crumbling, which indicates considerable ignorance on their part and emphasises the temporary nature of their plans. In contrast consider the eternal promises of God to those who have served Him such as Abraham and David.

Focusing on this world, and seeking after the things of this earth, is short-sighted to the point of blindness, whereas being obedient to the will of God not only attracts the fulfillment of His promises but also eternal life.

Throughout our consideration of the Tabernacle of God that Moses was instructed to build, we will see, and hopefully understand, the secretive, devious and destructive work of Satan. The most important lesson we need to learn is just how aggressive he is in his manipulation of men and nations to pursue his end of diverting, frustrating and, if possible, confounding the plan of God's way of salvation through which man can be saved to the uttermost.

But what was the objective of the descendants of Noah? It was to establish themselves as great on the earth; that is on this isolated, temporary and vulnerable spherical ball that they knew so little about, suspended by the grace of God in the universe. How much more we know than they yet the majority of the population today do not believe in the One who created and sustains all these things, believing instead that we are established on a firm foundation, which is unshakeable. Yet on this planet we have learned to expect the unexpected. Although made in the image of God we are eternal, but not in a physical sense. The eternal side of us is spiritual whether for glory or punishment.

This is the enigma of inherent sin: delusion, believing ourselves to be greater than we are. Yet all around us are the secrets and truths embedded in God's creation of which even in the 21st century many have no concept.

> *"Come,"* they said, *"let us build ourselves a city and a tower the top of which is in the heavens (to be like God); and let us make a name for ourselves, lest we be scattered abroad over the whole earth." (v4).*

But God's plan was that they should be scattered over the whole earth and there was initially no reason that it should not be with the same language!

Sin has made men blind to the truth; they are continually unable to perceive their own corruption because, being in the world, they have become entangled in the thoughts and understanding of the world and therefore limited by it.

Thus is man alienated from God by his own thoughts and conceited belief in his own intrinsic goodness which gives birth to an unwillingness to look outward to the magnificence of all the creation around him. Even gathering more and more facts about the amazing complexity of the natural world about us has not triggered a desire within many to meet with the creator, believing it all happened by chance, thereby missing out on a true understanding and appreciation of the spiritual and physical aspect of it all.

Man may have been essentially good because in the garden with God he was righteous. But rebellion has corrupted man to the extent that although we want to do that which is good, yet we find ourselves doing that which according to the law of God is wrong. It was the law given by God to the Children of Israel through Moses which defined what was good and what was bad thereby providing the standard by which we could compare our 'goodness' (Ro. 7:13 – 25).

Just as God had to step in when the first man sinned, to expel him and his wife from the garden and to prevent him eating the fruit of the tree of Life; so here God had to step in to scatter the people and confuse their language to provide the right environment for the introduction of His rescue plan for mankind, that is of salvation through repentance and faith in Him alone.

Consider these three things that reveal God to us even today:

Nature — *for the heavens declare the glory of God, and the firmament shows His handiwork* (Ps. 19:1; see Job 12:7 – 12). The Big Bang Theory was put forward to try to explain the diversity within the earth. There is no harm in that. Appendix B contains an excellent explanation of how creation and the Big Bang can co-exist and complement each other. The longer men study this world and the 'outer-space' that surrounds it the more questions that are posed and the more men are enticed to seek further answers. And because of the finiteness of men's minds the subject matter being more and more fragmented, demonstrates just how 'small' men are in this vast and seemingly timeless environment.

Conscience — in the dictionary conscience is described as a person's moral sense of right and wrong and is viewed as acting as a guide to one's behaviour. It is a central factor in man's behaviour and to what we are considering in this book. But right and wrong, because we are tainted with sin, cannot be properly distinguished by us, for it is only obtained through learning from the One who is above sin.

The wayward environment in which we live is stimulated, as we are, by the fallen spiritual beings whose only aim is to perpetuate the chaos they have created from the order that existed at the very beginning. One person's right is another person's wrong. So where is original truth to be found? Hear what Moses said:

> *'For I proclaim the name of the Lord:*
> *Ascribe greatness to our God.*
> *He is the Rock, His work is perfect;*
> *For all His ways are justice ,*
> *A God of truth and without injustice;*
> *Righteous and upright is He.*
> *(Deut. 32:3, 4)*

Where can we learn what is right and wrong? Is it not from the God who created us and made us what we are and planted us in that which appeared according to His design? We are made in His image, fashioned according to the person that He is with love and truth being central to all His thinking; we have received a portion of His Holy Spirit because of the breath He breathed into Adam's nostrils at the beginning of human history (which is really His-story for everything on earth points to Him).

It is man who rebelled in the garden and caused the separation between himself and man, removing the spiritual guidance that only God can provide, and replacing it with a purely physical life and worldly understanding that has no eternal value (Jn. 6:63).

Indeed, it has placed man in the position of needing to be reborn of the Spirit (Jn. 3:5; 20:22). Unfortunately, it is sin-contaminated man who has repeated that rebelliousness time and time again to his eternal cost. But God did not make us to be like that; the first man and woman both knew right and wrong without realising it because God's character and attributes were designed into the structure of their inner most being to become part of them.

Worship — The search for something outside ourselves to fill the spiritual emptiness within us has led to the creation of many gods and goddesses throughout the life of mankind, particularly among those who, like Cain, refused to bow down to one supreme being. This hunger for spiritual satisfaction has caused many to create tangible and bizarre images from wood and stone and others of ethereal beings to satisfy that desire to worship someone or thing that is greater than ourselves that God placed within us when we were created. Unfortunately, vast numbers who without thought are like fools declaring there is no God when all that is around them remains otherwise unexplainable.

So where can we learn what is truly right and wrong? How can we obtain a pure conscience?

It is to provide as comprehensive an answer as possible to that question that this book has been written; for having considered the state of the relationship between man and God at the beginning of time, and understood the disastrous process that brought man low and separated him from God, we shall see God's love shining out as He gradually put His previously prepared plan to save men from their sins into action, working out that plan through those individuals who were prepared to seek Him and listen to His instructions and be obedient to Him.

Let us consider certain facts that show us the difference between the true and the deceptive:

Man's History — people's memories in the early stages of man were long and the history of man relatively short but much had been packed into that short period (Gen 1 – 11). The message of God was still there for them to consider and there were those who sought after Him.

Unfortunately, as we have discovered so far, the heathenism introduced through the rebellion and separation of man from God and through the deceptive work of Satan and his evil angelic forces had developed in man an alternative understanding of God and all that surrounded him, even his very existence. It is a perversion of the three-fold original for:

Nature —

or the misinterpretation of the revelation of nature, to which earthly man is prone. If there is no God, let us worship what we see that seems to be greater than, or is different from ourselves. But nature itself and all living things, the earth on which we live and the solar system that surrounds us was also created for it had no hand in its appearance, its design or its development and the complexity of its internal workings.

The focus of man has been on the wonder of what he sees and a desire to understand how it all started without any consideration given to seeking and understanding the meaning of the intricacies of its internal interdependencies or development. The intelligence of those who believe it all happened by chance must be called into question, for their attention seems to be so fixed on the earth, and what is before their eyes, that they are unwilling or unable to consider the spiritual element which would lead them into all truth.

This is the reason Moses reminded the Israelites that they saw no form when the Lord spoke to them at Mount Horeb, warning them not to misinterpret the revelation of God in nature, as those away from God had been persuaded to do. The Israelites were not to worship natural things such as the moon, sun and stars, or to look to the earth to worship anything that crept on the ground, or any animal or any human, or to make images of them in whatever form, perfect or distorted (Deut. 4:15 – 19, cf. Eze. 8). These things are our heritage under God who created them all with the overriding instruction to 'make no graven image!'

Conscience —

any alternative understanding introduced to our created God-centred instinct will cause confusion. The God of peace brings that deep peace of the soul that satisfies for it is only the peace of God that passes all understanding (Is. 26:3; cf. Phil. 4:7). Remove God and try to implant a substitute and peace disappears leaving only conflict of soul.

True History — true history brings with it understanding and the fear of the Lord who created all things (Prov. 1:7) but fools despise wisdom and understanding, believing themselves to be wise (Ro. 1:22). We have the advantage, those of us who have believed the reports of the prophets to whom were given the revelations of God, for having heard and having a heart for God we have believed.

Distorted history hides the truth that is of God, just as Satan hid the true words of God from Eve by deception. The only way heathenism (unbelief in the One true God), however expressed, can survive is by distortion of the truth. But true history remains and the future of the world is in God's hands; deception brings us into conflict with God and as God holds all the power over the earth in His hands, deception will only bring down those who believe it.

Fortunately, the Divine influence on mankind did not end with the separation of man from God, for God holds a powerful attraction to those who seek the truth. Even though Satan is referred to as the Prince of the Power of the Air, he is not the one who is in total control, for we are assured that God is not far from any one of us (Deut. 4:7) so that we are able to find Him, providing we are prepared to search for Him purposefully, with a heart that is open to Him and His ministration through the work of His Holy Spirit (v29).

True, the object of this work is to consider the Tent of the Meeting which is a central feature in God's plan of the salvation of man. What we are seeing at this juncture is man taking his eyes off God and concentrating on the things of the earth. And who is the Prince of the Power of the Air, the earth-bound ruler of the world, but Satan.

Is it not in Satan's interest to be continually refocusing men's minds on the world and the things of the world which he dominates through fallen man and away from contemplating God? It is he who provides men with spiritual ideas and thoughts that do not involve God and which direct the worship of men to himself, and those he took with him when he left God's presence!

'Consider', he says, 'the power of nature and the amazing forces at work in the world. Surely, there are spirits in the sky, on the earth and in the sea; spirits of peace and anger, cyclical forces that provide the seasons, gods of war and many others to be worshipped'. In this way animistic philosophy was born in men's minds and in those who sought after a relationship with demonic spirits which demonstrated their angelic power through men.

Thus did the work of the Devil and his demonic spirits take hold of men. This idea is merely a continuation of the original Biblical revelation of two creations; that of the spiritual world and of the physical world. The rebellion of Adam and his separation from God, who alone is able to provide the spiritual knowledge so essential for man's true understanding of his relationship to the whole of creation, has enabled Satan to distort the truth in the minds of men because of their confinement to the physical creation. To earth-bound man this has brought about the binding of both the spiritual and physical in a marriage of convenience; a humanizing of eternal things.

However, we have not been abandoned by God who has a natural and powerful magnetic attraction to us because of the manner of our creation and formation, having been made alive, and being independent beings with His breath in us. Added to this we are assured that He is not far from each one of us (Deut. 4:7; Acts 17:27).

These then are the principles of truth and deception of which we must be aware as we continue our study of Gods' plan for saving man, revealed to us in this great two-part book that we call the Judeo / Judeo-Christian Bible. For even though some have believed there was a God, as Cain did, they have not been willing to praise Him as God, nor given Him thanks for their existence or for the wonderful world in which they live, but have become vain in their thoughts, allowing their foolish hearts to be darkened (2 Kgs 17:15 – 18; Jer. 2:4 – 8; Ro. 1:20 – 23).

The confusion brought about in man was considerable and it is worth considering here for language is a means of communication using words within a vocabulary which is specific to a people. The grammatical construction of a collection of words to create what we define as sentences and paragraphs that encapsulate the ideas and thoughts of the communicator, the phrasing of the words and construction of sentences to better convey those ideas and thoughts from one person to another and the pronunciation of the individual words and phrases; each identify the race to which we belong that was first formed during the confusion God brought about all those years ago.

Previously, not only was the language uniform throughout the population but so was the mental understanding of it and the means of expressing it. The tone of the voice and intonation along with facial expressions, the use of words and their spelling as well as the type and style of the individual letters used, and the combination of words and positioning within sentences are different according to each nation as we know it today, but then it was the same throughout the world's population.

Now something said in English in Britain could not be said without offence in America. Words in French that are used in English do not necessarily have the same precise meaning. Spanish is completely incomprehensible to one whose only language is English, as are so many others.

The original language used by Adam to name all the animals, and possibly enhanced up to the time of Babel, was shattered into fragments so that each group of people saw only a part of the whole. The whole ethos of each group differed, be it in the area of religion, science, art, philosophy and history, these often contradicting each other because of the individual point of view and cultural perceptions that had resulted from that fragmentation of Noah's enlarged family of descendants. We all see things differently even within close families.

It is interesting and worth considering as we progress in our search for the true developing path of God's plan and Way of Salvation, that at strategic points the coming together of man has been achieved, with possibly the two most significant and influential occurrences being:

1. The Roman Empire allowing free travel between nations.

2. The development of the British Empire allowing a common language to develop for the easy flow of information. Thus, for the first time since Babel there was a common language, but the thought process of each nation and ethnic grouping has still caused confusion. This could only be addressed by the unifying process of the Holy Spirit of the living God in the minds of the leaders and individuals of each nation where God's purposes need to succeed.

However, we view these manmade structures, it will hopefully become clear that in spite of the frailty of man (for there are none perfect), God's hand was an integral part of each one, particularly because Rome was just a city state and Britain just a small island off the continent of Europe. It is not always the large and mighty that God uses, but often the small and insignificant, so that the glory is directed to Him.

Whose Choice?

God not only has the right as the creator of all things to choose those through whom He wishes to work, but He also has the superiority of wisdom, knowledge and understanding, and in regard to the human race the ability to search the hearts of men and make the right choice at the right time.

Such choices were made according to God's own time table, which He set up to both reveal and then bring to completion the way of full and complete salvation for all mankind. Because of this we can legitimately ask the question, "Does Israel have the right to consider the Divine revelation that they have received since Abraham as theirs, to retain for themselves alone?" The answer must be a resounding "No!", for the very reasons identified above! He is the God of all mankind, not just the Israelites.

Israel is undoubtedly the main beneficiary of the Divine revelation that has been received mainly through the devotional service to God of those, like the prophet Moses, and the succeeding generations of the Levitical priesthood and others who have been prepared to commit themselves totally to Him and serve Him whatever the cost. It is through Moses that God gave to mankind in general, and Israel in particular, all the information and spiritual knowledge needed for us to not only seek for Him as individuals but to find Him and enter into a personal relationship with Him.

This is so whether we are born into a true Jewish family or born a Gentile, for it has been through the relationship of successive generations of the nation of Israel that God has given us all the knowledge we require to understand who He is and how we must approach Him and relate to Him.

It is also very clear from the reading of scripture that those who are chosen must realise that what they have received from God is not theirs by right, for not only have they been chosen, but the Divine revelation that they have received is of God and not of themselves. Indeed, as inherent sinners, they are as much in need of the cleansing and healing power of God as anyone else. Therefore, it is not theirs by right, because with the revelation God has given them comes the responsibility to pass on that revelation to those whose hearts God knows will be receptive to it as well as those who need to be told, whether or not they take any notice of it or respond to it such as those living at the time of Noah. Jeremiah and Jonah are clear examples of this.

God was speaking to Israel through Jeremiah with a message regarding not only their attitude and relationship to Him, but their response to Nebuchadnezzar's demand that they surrender to him. Even though the leaders, including the king, refused to listen there will have been others who will have responded. What is clear in this instance is that the warning had to be broadcast.

Jonah, on the other hand, had God's message for Nineveh and it was when Jonah finally acceded to God's instructions to go to Nineveh and deliver it that many non-Israeli souls were saved.

Israel is rightly proud of the fact that, as a nation, it is they who have received the Divine revelation directly from God, as recorded in the Torah and the record of the prophets; but pride can cause the human mind to focus on the wrong things and be dislocated from spiritual thought that is of God. Where, for instance is the sense of responsibility to pass on that revelation, and why have they got to the position where they have refused to accept the completion of that revelation, as recorded by the Jews who realised that their Messiah had come in the person of the Lord Yeshua?

Why did they get themselves into the position where they considered

Gentiles so contemptible that they would not go to their houses and eat with them?

True, fraternising with pagans over the years brought them into conflict with God, but that was because they allowed themselves to learn from the pagans their way of worshipping everything that was not God, instead of seeking to teach the pagan people the truth about the God who had chosen them. Instead of being the student they should have been the teacher as we see in the case of Peter when he was led to the house of Cornelius in the book of Acts, chapter 10.

My search for the God of Israel and my resulting intimate relationship with Him has been brought about because the focus of my search has been on God Himself without any preconceived notion or understanding or training from others. It has been an untainted personal search.

As I understand the situation, Rabbi's under training are given strict instructions not to read the second or New Testament. Why? If God is revealed in it, then what authority do they believe they have to deny others a legitimate search for the truth of God, providing those searching for that truth have a pure desire to know it as I have? It has become my responsibility, with the Divine revelation and understanding I have received from the God of Israel, to pass it on to anyone willing to listen and desiring to look unto Him themselves. I am just one more sign post pointing to the reality and truth God.

There is no compulsion with the Lord; if there were any sense of being compelled to do something for Him we have only to consider the Garden of Eden and the two trees in its midst, and the fact that although God had wanted man to eat only of the tree of Life he didn't force him to do so. All men have the freedom to seek after God as we have seen.

Compulsion belongs to fallen man through the work of Satan alone and his demonic forces through the fanaticism they generate in the minds of those they control. For Satan and his forces, the time is short for their future is in the lake of fire when our Lord returns to take the saved unto Himself at the conclusion of all His plans.

There is no room for fanaticism in God's kingdom; for God chooses men with the potential towards righteousness (Ro. 9:6 – 18), through whom He can demonstrate by example the essence of the out working of His love and salvation (Eph. 2:1 – 10), but He can also pass on the word of truth to them, and it is this truth that has been recorded in the scriptures for our benefit and for those who follow us.

All that we are learning together is what man has recorded in response to the instructions of God they have received through the work of His Holy Spirit (2 Tim. 3:16, 17; 2 Pet. 1:20, 21). This is where His Spirit works with our spirit, which He has 'reactivated', to make it once again not only God-conscious but also God-sensitive causing the spiritual 'ears' and 'eyes' of man to be opened and receptive to His plan of salvation, a plan we need to not just take to heart but to seek to fulfil in our own lives (Ez. 36:26, 27; Eph. 2:1 – 5).

God also chooses to work through those wicked individuals who are so attuned to the world that their God sensitiveness is completely dead, for it is through such people He can display His mighty power. The most prominent of such individuals is the Pharaoh at the time of the Exodus.

God's superior and unassailable authority is completely outside the reach and understanding of men except where man receives within himself from God an understanding of the 'parable' within the event (Matt. 13:1 – 23; 1 Cor. 2:10b – 16). By the time Terah died we can only conclude from the text that Abram had a sufficient understanding of God and such a relationship with Him that when the call came Abram was ready to obey the call. (See Appendix E)

We know that the promises of God are sure, but Abram had to find that out for himself, which, because he was the first one to be called to a dynamic and active based relationship with and in the service of God, was unique at that time. This makes Abram himself far more remarkable than any believer that had gone before or has lived since. He was the first of a new breed of what we can call 'a servant of God' to be established; an example that all those who subsequently aspired to belief and commitment had to follow. Abraham is our example and spiritual father in God, whether we be Jew or Gentile!

It is interesting that Terah had the right idea in wanting to travel to Canaan, but it was not in God's plan for him to do so. Thus they remained at Haran until he died.

What sort of character was this Abram[13] God had chosen? How can we best understand this remarkable man who is our example and the rock from which we are hewn (Is. 51:1, 2)? From the information we have before us we can gain an understanding of him.

He was a:

- business man, for he had obtained much wealth

- leader of men, for he had quite a retinue with the slaves and servants by the time he left Haran. As he was to be the leader of a tribe, which he was assured would become a great nation, he needed to be a leader who led by example.

- man of God, for he had been open to and was able to respond to the initial work of the Holy Spirit by which he was drawn

---

[13] The use of the names Abram and Abraham relates to the time of his life to which the text in which the name appears relates.

into a personal relationship with God.

- teacher for he was able to convince his family and those with him of the reality of the God he had come to love and serve. Consider the attitude of Abraham's senior servant when he went to find a wife for Isaac (Gen. 24:12 – 14). And for Isaac, this was so much part of his understanding and he so trusted in his father that he yielded himself to Abram when it came to Abram honouring God's request for Isaac to be sacrificed saying God will provide a lamb.

- man of principle, for having accepted this God who had met with him he then entered into a binding agreement with Him (God's initial promises of guidance and that he would become a great nation), with honour, and followed God without knowing what was ahead and without question. Throughout his life he never lost sight of the servant position he had before God[14].

- man with frailties just like all men for, as we shall see, there were times when he faced dangerous situations in which he did not trust God to protect him because he assessed the situation as a mere man. He also conceded to his wife's request regarding sleeping with a servant girl when she was concerned that there would be no legitimate heir, even though God had clearly promised him a son by Sarai.

It is worth mentioning at this point that because of the text of Genesis it is possible, with the evidence it contains, to confirm that Abram/Abraham lived at that time with the geographical accuracy being undisputed. This merely emphasises that we must never lose sight of the fact that he was a real man with real choices to make in regard to what he did in life. He knew all the risks of making bad decisions and making a move to another country that proved to be the beginning of disaster.

Abram had to display considerable faith in doing what he did and his previous wealth-creating decisions should not detract from the risky and hard choices he had to make in regard to following this spiritual God he had come to know and love.

In serving this very same God we have to make similar decisions regarding the degree to which we are prepared to put ourselves at His disposal. The decision is real. Trying to understanding this matter is the most difficult for those who have led an uneventful life that is routine and

---

[14] It is important to realise that the covenant Abram had with God when he became Abraham was not an agreement between two equals but a promise of God.

not unlike the life of an unbeliever.

God's recorded promises to Abram, provided he surrendered himself to Him and obeyed Him, are listed as:

- God would guide him to another land

- He would become the father of a great nation

Whatever personal experience Abram had with God before God called him it was sufficient for him to leave his new home in Haran and his family and venture forth into an unknown country to follow an unknown path and serve a relatively unknown and possibly unproven God who was so different from all the other gods that the vast majority of people were worshipping at that time. In this he is our example and the rock from which we are hewn.

Abram Commits His Life to God

The Genesis narrative now provides us with the lineage of the next significant person God chose to continue to develop His plan of salvation. Noah was chosen because, of all the population, only he was sufficiently spiritually sensitive for God to be able to enter into a working relationship with Him. Abram, who was to become Abraham the father of nations, and particularly the father of the Hebrew nation, was born into the promise of Shem and received the covenant that is still in force today with believing Israel. But scripture does not say that he was the only one God could have chosen.

The original revelation of God to man started with the creation of man, followed by his forced exit from the Garden of Eden and the gradual disintegration of his close relationship to God and his descent into unbelief and godlessness. Even the flood and the salvation of Noah and his immediate family did not persuade man to seek after God alone. The inherited sin of Adam had so corrupted the inner man of most men that the propensity of man was no longer to seek for God but to create for himself a belief and an understanding of his situation from what was around him.

With the account of the calling of Abram we witness the birth of a new revelation through chosen men and women through whom the lineage of the Messiah, who was prophesied to be the Saviour of Israel, would be developed.

It is essential at this stage that we realise the Word of God is central to our search for truth and only the proper dissemination of that word before the Almighty God will reveal that which is necessary for our correct understanding of the mind and ways of God. Eternal salvation only comes to those who seek after God with a true and open heart and mind to Him through repentance, prayer and true worship of the heart.

The most important factor for me is that God first sets the scene for His decision making, thus providing us with the information we need to understand why He chose who He chose, and thereby demonstrating His sound judgement in the life-changing decisions He made throughout history.

Notice the progression of Abram's father who decided to move away from the historic family home in the intensely pagan city of Ur of the Chaldees to Haran, which stood at the beginning of the way of Abram's service with God thus preparing the way for Abram and making his decision to serve God that much easier.

We must also be mindful of the situation Abram found himself in at that time. He could have no understanding that his decision to answer the call of God would have such a profound influence on the whole of mankind. Indeed, in his situation at the time of his father's death, all we can surmise is that he had a heart for God and was already in a receptive position to hear God's call. As I wrote in my book "The Origin of Life":

> Surrounded by idols that he realised had no power or ability to do anything but to sit where they were placed, Abram was just such a person who called out to the one true God, ignorant at the time of just who He was. But God saw in him someone He could work with to create a vehicle through which He could reach out to the people of the world with the message of salvation. A nation built from the foundation of one man that would be a focal point, a living, dynamic notice board by which God could not only tell but also demonstrate His salvation to all mankind through all earthly time.

The uniqueness of Abram is his willingness to turn his back on a world that had once again got sidetracked from the focus of Noah's saving faith. A continuation of the strand of gold, that would weave its tortuous way through world history, reappears in the black clouds of a world that had once again forgotten God; seeking instead to produce its own homemade variety of deities. They could worship these with little effort, divorcing them from the creator in obedience to the influence of the Devil and his demonic forces of evil.

Although he was not the first believer (that honour has to go to Abel) nor was he the second (for Enoch and Noah preceded him), Abram's faith was significant in that, whereas the others had believed and remained within the area and within the family setting in which they lived throughout their lives so that they became the central focus for others who were able to believe through them, Abram's faith had a dynamic structure that would allow him to trust in this new-found and persuasively powerful God to launch out into a completely new life away from the influence and confining limitations of family and familiar influences.

We have no way of knowing when or how Abram first met with God nor how long it took him to realise that God wanted him to separate himself from immediate contact with his family and friends and set out on a new nomadic life of trust and service that would fashion a life of uniqueness and blessing for all mankind.

Abram starts his journey to a land that he would never own but which was promised to his descendants, of which he had none at that time. A number of significant events happened that are worth highlighting to reveal a pattern of God's involvement in his life and which can also teach us something about the power of God in the life of a believer and the way in which He both protects and guides us. God communicates with those who desire to hear from Him and who are prepared to listen to Him when He does.

The first major event was when God appeared to Abram to promise to give the land of Canaan, not to him but to his descendants, and Abram built an altar to the Lord there. Abram had first to put the sole of his foot on the ground for his descendants to claim it for themselves.

The next event which is of particular interest is his meeting with the Pharaoh. In those days if a king liked the look of a woman then it was nothing for him to arrange the death of the woman's husband and take her into his harem. Because of this Abram asked his wife Sarai to say that she was his sister, which technically she was (a half-sister), and as predicted Sarai was duly absorbed into Pharaoh's harem and Abram was rewarded with gifts.

What happened is particularly interesting because of the degree of God's intervention and the fact that pagan priests realised that it was Abram's God who caused the plagues in Pharaoh's household. It shows us that God was prepared to protect His plan of salvation, and all those who were to be directly involved with it, from any contamination from the world. His plan was to be kept Holy.

Although old and childless Abram had to believe that God knew the way he was to go and would provide all that he needed. God had promised that he would be the father of nations but without offspring Abram, at that time, had no way of knowing how that would be accomplished; but as it was God's promise, and Abram had taken God at His word when he first set out in accordance with God's instructions from Haran, it was up to Abram to believe that God not only had the will but also the ability to bring that promise to fulfilment.

The problem we humans have is that we cannot see farther than the moment in which we live, being unable to see into the future. We can make a calculated guess as to what we think might happen, but that is all. If God has provided us with promises as to what will happen, then we have no option but to accept those promises and believe that what He has promised will happen.

Sarai was no different to us. She was so concerned about the fact that there was no heir that she persuaded her husband to do what the unbelievers around did in similar circumstances, which was for him to take on another wife, in this case her slave girl Hagar, and produce an heir for her. But such an offspring would not be from Sarai's flesh, and God's promise was that God Himself would provide Abram with an heir, and as Sarai was his wife, that heir would come from her, not a slave girl (Gal. 4:23). Abram in this incident showed that he was human too.

What God was doing, it would seem, was to demonstrate conclusively that what happened in the past was no guarantee that something more amazing cannot happen in the future. For all intents and purposes Sarai was beyond childbearing age. But God was able to allow her, even when both were beyond the normal age of producing children, to have a child which was to be the child of the promise (Gal. 4:22) in response to the covenant God made with Abram and Sarai.

The Abrahamic covenant came as the result of Abram's proven loyalty to and faith in God of which the outward sign was to be circumcision of all the male children born within his household, and to him and his descendants in perpetuity.

It is not my intention to consider Abram/Abraham's life before God as I did in my book "The Origin of Life" but to consider certain aspects of it that will enable us to better understand God's plan of salvation and our necessary response to it.

Melchizedek

The record of Abram's meeting with Melchizedek (Gen. 14:17 – 24) is one of those pieces of information that is very easily glossed over without realising its significance.

The offices of priest and king can only be combined in God. King Uzziah, all the time he was under the tutelage of the priest Zechariah (2 Chron. 26:5), sought God, and God blessed him during that time.

It is reasonable to assume that at some time Zechariah died, and even though it was God who had blessed him as king, Uzziah was not satisfied with just being the King of Israel. He tried also to usurp the priestly function because of pride (2 Chron. 26:16 – 21) and therefore suffered from leprosy for the rest of his life.

It is particularly interesting that the leprosy broke out on his forehead where the Mosaic high priest would have worn the engraved plaque "Holiness to the Lord" (Ex. 28:36 – 38), emphasising the God given right to that office for the person God chose or whom He allowed to occupy that office.

The significance of Melchizedek, which is dealt with in greater detail in a chapter 8 of this book, is therefore that he is called both the king of Salem (Peace) and priest of the Most High God. Elsewhere he is referred to as being:

> *without father or mother, without ancestry, having neither beginning of days or end of life, but resembling the Son of God he continues to be a priest without interruption and without successor* (Heb. 7:3).

It is to this king and priest that Abram gives a tenth of the spoils of a war that he knew God had enabled him to win, and a tenth is only given by a lesser man to a greater one. Therefore Abram, being the founder of the Hebrew race and therefore of Israel, the twelve leaders of the tribes were in his loins at that time, therefore he was acknowledging the greatness and uniqueness of this king and priest above him and all his offspring.

Covenant

A covenant can be unilateral or bilateral and include conditions which are agreed between both parties or, particularly in the case of unilateral covenants, set by the one offering the covenant, the conditions being agreed on acceptance by the other party. This is particularly relevant to the covenants that relate to God's plan of salvation, because the whole process involves God's willingness to provide rebellious man with a way back to Himself.

Covenant, as we will see more clearly as we progress with the subject matter of this book, means 'last will and testament' which only comes into effect on the death of the testator, and is invoked on the death of the one making the covenant.

This was because man rebelled against a fundamental rule God had set in the beginning which was [and still is] that man shall live in accordance with the rules set by Him as man's creator, for only in that way can mutual trust be developed between the two parties enabling God to shower blessings on man that only He, as the creator, can give.

The covenant God made with Abram is the foundation of His relationship not only with Abram, but with the Hebrew race in general and Israel in particular; a relationship that was designed to overflow into the whole human race and bring about a new way of life and relationship between individuals and God. Although this covenant has been built upon by other more specific covenants, its position as a founding covenant remains unchanged.

When God told Abram not to be afraid, for He was his shield and exceedingly great reward, Abram immediately thought about his lack of an heir. Having amassed considerable possessions and a company of people, according to the tradition of the time the manager of his house, a slave called Eliezer of Damascus, would inherit everything if there was no natural heir. God told Abram that Eliezer would not inherit but rather one who would come from Abram's own body.

Abram was accredited with righteousness because of his willingness to believe in God and be totally submitted to Him. But Abram still had a mind of his own and wanted some confirmation that he and his heirs would inherit the land God was offering him. This was the explanation of the confirmation of the covenant in "The Origin of Life".

> The ancient method of making a covenant was to cut an animal in half and for the contracting parties to walk through the portions of the slain animal, thereby they were thought to be united by the bond of a common blood. To assure Abram God used this method to establish a covenant between them and to give him some understanding of future events. Abram, who slayed the animals as God instructed him, was forced to prevent scavenging birds eating them, symbolising the difficulties to be experienced by his heirs when taking possession of the land.

When the sun was setting a deep sleep, similar to that experienced by Adam before his rib was removed to create Eve, came over Abram and a great darkness that stimulated a dread within his spirit, symbolising that the nation that would issue from him would have to pass through bitter times of oppression. The four hundred years relates to four generations before they would be freed from slavery.

In the darkness a smoking furnace and flaming torch, symbolic of the Godhead, passed between the pieces to establish the covenant. So was delivered to Abram a surety that God's promises concerning the future of his tribe and line would be established and prophetic knowledge of what would happen before those offspring would take possession of the Promised Land. (Another Extract from "The Origin of Life")

> This covenant, which was binding on both parties, was God's covenant to Abram who had to agree to accept the conditions of obedience and faith to God that were written into it; for the covenant was a direct result of his believing in the Lord to the exclusion of all others. Thus the irrefutable covenant from God to Abram and his chosen offspring involved the giving of the Promised Land even though Abram would never own it in

his lifetime.

Polygamy is not biblical for the only instruction with regard to marriage is for one man and one woman to become one in body through sexual intercourse; but the custom of a man having more than one wife, as practiced around them, obviously had an influence on them.

Sarai, being concerned that she was beyond the age to bear children, suggested that Abram slept with her maid Hagar to produce an heir. Unfortunately, human nature is fickle and Sarai did not account for Hagar who, when she found herself to be pregnant with a child by Abram, despised Sarai because of her barrenness. Sarai, as the first wife, reacted badly but the situation was of her own making purely for the want of trusting God as her husband had done.

Blaming Abram for her mistake was not the answer. But what is said to her and recorded for us is that, as she acknowledged that children are a gift from God, it was to God to whom she should have directed her plea for a child, as Hannah did very much later (1 Sam. 1:11), which resulted in her giving birth to Samuel.

Hagar, having realised the difficult situation she found herself in, ran away only to be confronted by an angel of the Lord who promised her a son and told her to return to her mistress and submit herself to Sarai (Gen. 16:7 – 15). But Ishmael was of man not of God (Gal. 4:21 – 26).

From Abram to Abraham

Our walk with God is progressive and at times we do not realise just how much God is working in our lives or how much we have changed as the result of His work within us without looking back over our lives using hindsight. However, God does not work in our lives without our agreement. This I have found to be true. And in Abram's case this is certainly true for from the beginning of his walk with God in Haran Abram had established his presence in Canaan and given witness to those who would have taken Sarai for themselves that the God of Abram was far stronger than they or their gods.

It was not until Abram was 99 that God finally confirmed His continuing and special relationship with him by giving him various promises and re-establishing His covenant specifically with him alone and his descendants.

By referring to Himself as the Almighty God, God was establishing the fact that He was everything Abram would ever need. Being addressed by this exalted God, Abram showed his humble obeisance by kneeling and then bowing his head to the ground, demonstrating his acknowledgement of the superiority of God in his mind and heart.

God's covenant with Abram was now to enter a new phase.

1. Their names were to be changed, signalling a completely new state in their relationship with God, from Abram and Sarai to Abraham (Ab - meaning father and raham - meaning multitude) and Sarah (bringing out more forcibly the meaning Princess than the archaic form Sarai). His name change because of the change of circumstances and position before God, was the accepted custom at that time.

2. The outward sign of the covenant was for ALL males within Abraham's household to be circumcised whatever their status, from Abraham and all under his authority to the most lowly servant and anyone else living freely within his household who had either been born or bought into his house.

3. The promise of a son for Sarah. For this promise Abraham must have been overjoyed for he laughed with joy, knowing as he did by then that the ability of God to work miracles should not be questioned.

The covenant sign of circumcision was an outward identification mark of an inward decision to willingly serve God as Abram had done since answering God's call to leave his family and familiar surroundings and follow Him. Abraham's first true son of the flesh was to be demonstrably chosen and whose existence was of God. Whatever Sarah may have thought, God was able to give her a child in her old age and the delay God imposed in allowing her to conceive was specifically to test Abram's faith and to show that nothing is too difficult for Him.

At the age of one hundred Abram received the one gift from God that he had wanted more than anything else; not only the promise of a son which was given with the covenant, but a pregnant wife who produced a son. Abraham was still proud of his son Ishmael who was now 11 and considered him his first born, but to God Isaac was his first born, for Ishmael was born of the flesh but Isaac was born of God, according to God's promise, will and plan.

To all intents and purposes Isaac was a miracle baby and, as prophesied, a boy child. But only God has the power to choose the sex of the naturally produced child He has promised to someone; He also has the power to allow women to produce offspring or to be barren.

The testing of Abraham yet again when God told him to sacrifice the one person dearest to his heart (Gen. 22:2) was the final confirmation of Abraham's total and absolute commitment to God. But more than that, it demonstrated, by the provision of a ram by God at exactly the right moment, His ability to provide a sacrifice that was acceptable to Him.

This incident further emphasises the fact that the Messiah was to be God's unarguable provision of an acceptable sacrifice for mankind. We have in Abraham the start of God's clear plan of salvation. God was, through Abraham's life, showing us by a living example how He was going to absolve man from his sin; not by forgetting it or glossing over it, but in a practical way, using the shedding of blood to cover man's sin completely, providing man is willing, as Abraham was, to leave the world behind and follow Him with the same determined commitment.

Just as at the time of the sacrificing of the first Passover lamb, when the blood of the lamb was daubed around the outside of the door to the dwelling, which sign diverted the angel of death, so in the sacrificing of lambs before that event, the blood was for God to see. Instead of seeing man's sin He sees the blood of the sacrificial animal, providing the sacrifice as offered with a pure heart.

Why did God choose the lamb? Perhaps because of its timid nature and unpredictable ways, and that it is lost without someone to lead and protect it. Isaiah used the image of a lamb with the thoughts of it having so little understanding that it goes meekly to the slaughter and says nothing when it is being sheared (Is. 53:7). Flocks of sheep have no cohesion, so that when a predator strikes the flock scatters, each to its own way without thought or understanding. It is also why the sheep is used to describe the fallen human state for when man was united with God in God's garden all was well, but since his intimate relationship with God was severed, mankind has been lost and confused and without understanding of the fundamental facts of why he is here on the earth or what he needs to do to bring purpose and objectivity to his life.

Therefore, throughout life man wonders around in danger of being led about at the whim of spiritual forces that he does not see or understand or even realise they are affecting him. It is said that Satan prowls around the earth like a lion seeking whom he may devour (1 Pet. 5:8). Those who seek after God have Him to protect them, for we have that wonderful account in Job which tells us that God allows Satan only a limited freedom to do what he wants to us.

For this reason, from the moment the ram was found by Abraham caught by its horns in a bush, the lamb takes centre stage as a symbol of God's willingness to save man from his sin, both inherited and personal, through the shedding of the blood of a sacrificial animal.

Jacob

The interesting thing about Isaac is that he was an essential part of Abraham's walk with, and also testing by, God. He was a demonstration of God's ability to cause a woman to not only bear a child but a child of a determined sex as and when He wanted her to do so.

He was also the subject of Abraham's servant's task to find him a wife from the daughters of Abraham's family in Haran. That God guided the servant to find Rebekah there can be no doubt. And her willingness to be Isaac's wife and travel out of her own familiar territory showed an outstanding character, which was later to be used by God to ensure His choice of a successor to Isaac being chosen.

When Rebekah became pregnant with twins, they fought in her womb with distressing results for her. This battle continued in life with Esau being one for the open spaces and the excitement of the chase and Jacob being more studious. Isaac saw in Esau the person he would have liked to have been because he thought Esau's life more exciting and adventurous than his own more-staid existence[15].

Jacob undoubtedly had a heart for God but, in the normal course of events being the older brother, the future of the tribe would have been in Esau's hands. It was this concern for the God-centred future of the house of Isaac that caused Jacob, possibly in the spur of the moment, to obtain his brother's birthright. This ultimately leads to a series of events that were out of Jacob's control but can be clearly seen as being God inspired.

Esau had no heart for God like his father or grandfather. As the whole purpose of God choosing Abraham was ultimately to found a nation through which He could explain in detail the whole process of His way of salvation, it was essential that each leader of the tribe was focused on Him.

To Esau the immediate was far more important than the future. Feeling hungry after an energetic time in the surrounding area with his close group of friends and servants, Esau needed food not his birthright, and therefore thought nothing of selling it for a mess of pottage. In obtaining Esau's birthright Jacob set in motion the process that led to him receiving Isaac's blessing.

Consider what we know about the moment when Isaac was about to give his blessing to the son who would succeed him as leader of the tribe.

Isaac was old, virtually blind and no longer the man he was. Rebekah was always nearby and overheard Isaac's command to his son Esau. She had held in her heart the prophetic utterances she received from God, when the two babies were fighting in her womb, concerning the elder serving the younger. She had observed through their developing and now mature years which of the two would be more suited to maintain the continued observance of the Godly focus of the tribe for she had willingly adopted the God of her husband Isaac as her God.

Hearing her husband's instructions to Esau to provide him with food, Rebekah immediately realised what she needed to do to ensure that her favourite, who was also God's favoured, son received the blessing in place

---

[15] See my book on Genesis "The Origin of Life" for a full account of Isaac's life

of Esau. The burden of the word of the Lord to Israel through Malachi:

"I have loved you," says the Lord.
"Yet you say, 'In what way have you loved us?'
Was not Esau Jacob's brother?" says the Lord,
Yet Jacob I have loved;
But Esau I have hated (or not loved),
And laid waste his mountains
And his heritage ... "
(Mal. 1:2, 3)

Rather than presenting the perfect animals for sacrifice to the Lord, the priests had resorted to cast offs, *"offering defiled food on God's altar" (v8)*, that is blind, lame and sick animals were an evil approach to the God who had blessed the nation whom He loved with an unconditional love. Love and hate? But these must not be considered from the point of view of human emotions. Let us see why God preferred Jacob.

According to the terms of the covenant the supreme condition for Abraham (his name was changed from Abram to Abraham at a specific time in his life, therefore each name is used in the text according to the time to which it is related) and all succeeding generations of male offspring receiving the sign of circumcision in their flesh was for them to be totally obedient to the Lord God who had chosen Abram and for them to live a life devoted to His service just as Abraham had done from the beginning.

Unfortunately, Esau, although being circumcised on the eighth day according to the covenant, had no time for God which is amply demonstrated in his casual attitude to the value of his birthright as the elder son and his life style in which the service of God had no part. Therefore, he had broken all the covenant conditions making the covenant promises null and void. As far as God was concerned Esau was no longer covered by the covenant He had made with Abraham.

Jacob, on the other hand, for all his faults, had a heart for God and was a man God could work with to develop His Way of Eternal Salvation through a nation which He was involved in creating, which was his goal in calling Abram in the first place. All that we are considering in this book, confining ourselves strictly to the inspired word of God and being completely obedient to the inspiration and leading of His Holy Spirit just as Abraham did, is about God and His plan to save men to the uttermost; nothing else. The Tent of the Meeting, or Tabernacle of Moses, was an essential part of that plan but only at the beginning for it was not the ultimate solution to man's sin that God would provide.

It is an encouragement to us that none of the patriarchs were perfect. They all made mistakes. Yet God was able to achieve His plan through them.

Remember that God's promise to Abraham was that the land he was travelling through would belong to him and his descendants and we know that God instructed Moses and Joshua to annihilate all the peoples inhabiting the land at that time. It was their lack of will to do exactly what God had asked of them which created the basis for much of the conflict in that region today.

There were three factors that necessitated Jacob receiving Isaac's blessing rather than Esau.

1. Esau had rejected God in his heart.

2. He had adopted a life style in which God had no part.

3. He had become contaminated with the pagan people amongst whom they lived by marrying two of the local Canaanite girls. These women were of a people that had totally departed from their creator God and were focused on what He had created. Therefore, their way of life was a downward spiral to ever more evil practices that increasingly separated them from their Creator. And it was these Canaanites who were at a later time to be displaced by the nation of Israel, the sons of Abraham, Isaac and Jacob through whom God would not only demonstrate how man must relate to Him but how He deals with man. Israel was also the nation that would receive the instructions concerning God's Way of salvation.

The deception carried out to ensure Jacob, not Esau, received Isaac's blessing and to ensure that Jacob took over the leadership of the tribe of the Hebrews was clearly of God. This was so that God's eternal plan was not compromised at this early stage, and to fulfil God's prophetic message to Rebekah that the elder would serve the younger.

Consider the elements:

- Isaac had waited before passing on the blessing he had received from his father Abraham and confirmed by God until he was virtually blind and obviously frail.

- Jacob had to be persuaded by his mother to go through with the deception for he was concerned that his father could find him out and the blessing he wanted could turn out to be a cursing. Jacob at this time did not know that he was chosen of God.

- Isaac preferred Esau to Jacob, yet Esau had none of the

characteristics God was looking for in His chosen one.

- A goat was used instead of venison.

- The hide of the goat was used to cover the smoothness of Jacob's skin in the places where Rebekah thought her husband would be bound to feel, and yet it is difficult to understand how the hair of the goat could possibly be the same as the hair on a man. It is noticeable that Isaac only felt a small area, for had he been more concerned he might have gone to the edge of the deceiving hide.

- Isaac heard the voice of Jacob, but the feel and smell of him and taste of the food, all earthly senses, pointed to Esau. Had he been of a mind and perhaps more alert he would have waited because the food had been prepared far too quickly. But he was frail and accepted the situation.

When told that the blessing for the older child had already been given, Esau's tears were those of a spoilt child who had been denied something he believed was his right, not his responsibility. As it was, he received a blessing of sorts which satisfied him to a point. His reaction was hot headed and because of God's protection his threat to kill Jacob came to nothing.

In this way Jacob found himself his father's successor. He could never have imagined the extent and complexity of the task before him nor the trials and tribulation he would face on the way. But it is his experiences of the blessings of God and the increasing sense of security of a life given into His care, as he actively sought for and found the truth about God, that it is an example to us all.

4 A NATION IS BORN [16]

"All we like sheep have gone astray;
We have turned everyone to his own way;
And the Lord has laid on Him
The iniquity of us all."
(Is. 53:6)

The foundations

It is noticeable that God chose shepherds to found the nation that was to carry His name and through whom He revealed Himself and His desire for men's hearts. He also made the lamb central to the Way of Salvation.

Throughout our consideration of the plan of salvation that God was to establish, initially using individuals and then a nation, we must never have far from our minds the reason for this plan, this way back to God, nor should we be unmindful of the severity of the sentence that was knowingly incurred by man in the beginning as recorded for us by Moses in the book of Genesis through the inspiration of the Holy Spirit.

The word sin is used and abused to the extent that mankind tends to ignore it or mitigate the importance of his act of rebellion against God, the creator of all things, in the beginning. The reaction of many is that it was Adam's problem not theirs if, that is, it had actually happened. The proof that it did happen is clearly shown in the attitude of men and women towards the one eternal and almighty God throughout the generations of man's existence.

We have recorded for us what happened to the first created man in the garden God had provided for him, so we have no excuse, nor will we be allowed any excuse at the time of the judgement that will most definitely come.

God told Adam that if he should eat of the fruit of the forbidden tree he would surely die. The fact that he accepted Satan's alternative explanation meant that he was bound to incur God's wrath and receive the promised penalty of death. And this death sentence applies to all mankind, even today, because Adam was the first man and we are his descendants. As Paul said to the Corinthian believers, *"As in Adam all die, so in Christ shall all be*

---

[16] A more detailed understanding of the life of Jacob and Joseph can be found in my work "The Origin of Life".

made alive ..." (1 Cor. 15:22)

We therefore suffer from inherited sin from Adam and have within us a greater propensity to sin as a direct result of that inherited sin and the separation from God that it caused. Although man was created as good, sin has corrupted that goodness within us thus making us basically rebellious sinners. Even those of us who have surrendered out lives to God and accepted Christ's sacrifice on our behalf have to work at dedicating our lives to Him by daily, almost minute by minute seeking Him through repentance and prayer and turning a listening spiritual ear so that we might hear what He has to say to us.

This means that those who do not constantly seek Him and surrender themselves to Him through repentance and faith allow that basic sinful nature to deflect them from hearing Him speak to them and prevent them understanding His way of guiding them through life.

Let us be mindful of the fact that Satan only opposes those who have a heart for God and are active in His service. It is they to whom Satan directs his troublesome activities. Those who proclaim themselves Jew or Christian but just wander through life without that dynamic, intimate, personal spiritual relationship with their creator, are no threat to Satan and could find themselves in the wrong place after death, purely because they have not been saved to the uttermost, that is they have not established their salvation through obedience to the first commandment which is to actively and purposefully love God with their heart, mind and strength.

The whole purpose of the creation was for God to have for Himself living beings to whom He could relate and whose company He could enjoy according to His original design. Everything that appeared through the act of creation God saw as good. And that particularly included the creation of man who was the pinnacle and real purpose of the creation.

The act of rebellion, that was initiated by the most senior angel who was endowed with great beauty and musical ability, became the devastating eruption of tragedy in God's spiritual and physical creation, for through his single-minded determination to usurp the throne of God Satan initiated the corruption of the pure relationship man had with his creator by persuading man to defy God in the very act of eating of the forbidden fruit. (See Appendix C.)

In this way the foundation of God's relationship with man was destroyed and the spiritual food which man received from a daily meeting and fulfilled spiritual relationship with God was cut off from him. Without that relationship man could no longer easily commune with God, his spiritual life was stunted and the focus of his attention became the earth; things of the world. With Satan now established in the earth to become the prince of the power of the air by taking the authority over the earth which God had given to man, man was enslaved to Satan rather than to God.

Yet the future life of the spirit of every man is in God's hands. Through that separation man could no longer live forever in God's presence. Had man eaten of the fruit of the Tree of Life he would have had an eternal future with God, but through his action of rebellion which introduced sin, the penalty of eternal spiritual existence separating man from God became a reality. It is essential that we do not treat this matter lightly or believe that God will not carry out His plan to deal harshly with all those who reject Him in favour of obeying Satan.

God is not soft but perfect in judgement and says what He means and means what He says. The choice He gave to Adam illustrated that. Either the fruit of the tree of life which was free, or the fruit of the tree of the knowledge of good and evil which was not available to them on the penalty of death. And that new existence which would mean them being without God (which state continued after physical death) meant being removed from the love and joy that only God could provide, leaving in its place fear and evil.

Such is hell, for the spiritual emptiness within a person without God in life is bad enough, but to face an eternity in a place where there is nothing to sooth the spirit will only result in the weeping and wailing and a gnashing of teeth that is mentioned in scripture (Matt. 8:12; Lk. 16:24 – 26).

The problem with hell and damnation is that we have no clear picture of what it is really like but the Bible speaks of it being an eternal state (Matt. 18:7 – 9) where there is weeping and wailing and gnashing of teeth. That there is a hell where God is not and where there is much anguish of soul comes from the parable the Messiah told the people as recorded in Luke's gospel chapter 16.

The poor beggar, Lazarus, who sat outside the luxurious home of the rich man, whose name is not given, was in a desperate state of health because he lacked sufficient food to eat and was ignored by the rich man who could have provided for his needs.

In this parable the Messiah tells us that Lazarus finally died and was carried by the angels to meet Abraham. Later the rich man also died and was buried with much ceremony which he could afford. But because of his selfish and uncaring lifestyle, the rich man found himself in hell and in torment. For some reason he had sight of Lazarus being cared for by Abraham and asked that the man for whom he had so little time during his lifetime should do him a service now by providing some cooling water which could only provide him with temporary relief.

Did the rich man find himself in the lake of fire as described later in the book of the Revelation of John? Is the torment he was experiencing eternal or temporary when dying the second death? Some commentators say that God is a God of love and therefore could not be so cruel as to cause the spirits of those people who rejected not only God the Father during their lifetime, but also the sacrificial death of the Saviour to suffer eternal torment.

But surely God's love is amply displayed, for in spite of the gulf that He put between sinful man and Himself because of the abhorrent sin of man, His love, manifests itself in Christ's death, which provided the escape route from the wide road that leads to destruction to the narrow gate that so many people have avoided, ignored or do not want to use. There are two sides to God: that of love and that of justice.

The mercy of God is in the provision of the Passover Lamb which is Christ Jesus, an exceptionally expensive sacrificial cost to pay for the redemption of man. The anger of God is against all those who reject Him

It is essential that in considering the 'love of God' we do not allow ourselves to think that all will be saved whatever they have believed or have done in life, or that the battle between God and Satan is not real and fierce, for there have been many martyrs throughout the centuries when the battle has been at its fiercest (Rev. 6:9; 20:4).

The second death is clearly identified in John's record where he tells us that death and hell were thrown in the lake of fire and it is this action that is identified as the second death and it is into this furnace that the spirit of all those who have rejected God will be cast (Rev. 20:14, 15).

God is not soft but holy and almighty and altogether righteous and just. God dealt with Pharaoh in an appropriate and uncompromising manner when he fought with Him prior to the release of the Children of Israel. Pharaoh drowned not because God wanted him to drown but because he would not accept the will of God regarding the future of the children of Israel. In exactly the same way it is the personal and consistent rebellion of an individual against God (as demonstrated by Satan himself) which sentences them to hell after their physical death.

As we consider the often-turbulent times experienced by those involved with the development of God's eternal plan of salvation, it is essential that we realise and accept God's insistence that anyone desiring to enter into a new and eternal relationship with Him shall become pure in that relationship through the cleansing of the blood of the Messiah. Any deviation from a single-minded focus on God through accepting reasoning from other human sources shall have a detrimental effect on a person's purity of relationship with God (see 1 Cor. 3:11 – 15).

It is no good believing, for instance, that other 'faiths' have an equal knowledge of the way of salvation even though they do not accept the single sacrifice of the Lamb of God, the Messiah of Israel. All 'faiths' do not have an equal, or even a partial say, in God's salvation because their way is not purely of God, rather it is accepted reasoning from men which replaces what God tells us is necessary. This is exactly what Satan wants us to do.

Indeed, it is true to say, that any religion on this earth that provides a holy book or sacred writings that give(s) an alternative explanation of the creation, or our relationship to God, or provides instructions on how we are to live our lives and the way a man might live for eternity that is contrary in both principle and detail to what is recorded in the Judeo/Judeo-Christian Bible is a false religion.

Jacob's journey of discovery

Every individual born of man has a choice of what they want to do in life and the God or gods or no god on whom to focus their attention. For Esau it was the world around him, full of the excitement of the chase. For Jacob it was the spiritual aspect of life that commanded his attention and a curiosity concerning the God of his grandfather and father.

Who was this God and why was He so essential to the life of his forebears? Jacob realised that there was more to life than the immediate and fleeting experiences that appealed to the physical senses; rather there was something deeper within the human psyche that needed satisfying by something or someone outside their physical environment.

There is no doubt that Jacob was led by God throughout his life, because of this sensitivity to spiritual things, to the point where he inherited the patriarchal position of his father instead of his brother Esau. Many people throughout the world, including myself, have been able to look back over their lives and identify a central strand that points to the involvement of a higher authority, which is the Almighty God Himself. Jeremiah was one such; for God told him that He had chosen him whilst he was in his mother's womb.

With the threats against him and the need for him to get a wife from his own true family, rather than the pagan people amongst whom they lived, it was part of God's plan that Jacob should set out on a journey back to the place from which Abraham started, a journey that would prove to be one of discovery regarding the things of God and essential for his future life; a spiritual odyssey no less.

Jacob, therefore, set off on his own to travel to the country of his family, no doubt confused by the sudden turn of events. He had survived the scrutiny of his father and received the blessing his father had wanted to give to Esau rather than the curse he had expected to receive because of the audacity of what he had done at his mother's insistence. The joy of finally receiving his father's blessing had turned to sadness because of the threats from his brother.

On that first night of his travels, he lay down not in comfort but with a stone for a pillow, wondering what was to befall him.

God prefers to deal with people individually, at moments when they are on their own, and particularly when they are in a state where they are receptive. For Jacob this was just such a time. Causing him to dream a dream of a ladder set up between heaven and the earth, God let Jacob realise that spiritual activity was all around him. Although Jacob was led to say, *"Surely God is in this place and I knew it not"*, God the Holy Spirit, being part of the Godhead, was responsible for the imagery of the angelic activity of ascending and descending a ladder Jacob saw in his dream. This gave him a clear pictorial message that God was active on earth through His spiritual messengers.

This was Jacob's first experience of God speaking to him directly which made him aware, probably for the first time in his life, of the reality of the spiritual world of God on earth. Previously all Jacob had to go on was verbal instruction that included Abraham's call and dedication to the God who called him and the experience Isaac had of the aborted human sacrifice and how he was saved by God who Himself provided the lamb for the sacrifice He had asked Abraham to make. This had profoundly affected Jacob and was the motivation behind his efforts to prevent Esau gaining control of the tribe and leading it away from the God of Abraham.

But now as a mature man he was experiencing for himself the immediate involvement of God in his own life. To him the dream was real and the activity he had witnessed happening was symbolic of God being present in that place. Indeed, it excited his spirit which was developing in its sensitivity towards God as He worked out his life. It also showed that there was a connection between earth and heaven that he had not realised before.

The fact that the angels were ascending before descending made him aware of God's continual activity on earth with the need of God's spiritual servants to return to heaven to receive further instruction.

Such was the impact of this experience on his spirit that he made a vow, that if this God would be with him in the future, then he would willingly accept Him as his God and come under His authority just as his father and grandfather had done before him.

This journey to his relatives was starting on the right note with Jacob not only realising the reality of the presence of God, but accepting His authority over him providing God remain with him.

Just like Abraham's servant, Jacob arrived at the watering hole outside Haran hoping to meet with his relatives and in a similar manner to the servant, who met Isaac's future wife as she came to water the sheep. That he was able to meet with a cousin so easily overwhelmed him. The success of his journey excited him so that three times he told Rachel that her father was his mother's brother.

Jacob was to learn many lessons in his uncle's house. Deception, both in regard to the fact that he was tricked into marrying Leah as well as Rachel, which kept him employed for fourteen years rather than just seven, and in the way his then father-in-law managed to find ways to prevent him accumulating wealth for himself which would have enabled him to become independent.

Laban undoubtedly benefitted from Jacob's services, for the way in which the God of Jacob blessed his work; because of this Laban was determined to retain his services for as long as possible by whatever devious method he could employ. It was finally Jacob's wiliness and knowledge of his trade that allowed him to overcome and outwit his cunning uncle. Until, that is, Laban's sons, ignorant of the power of Jacob's God and of their father's deviousness towards him, came to believe that what was happening with regard to Jacob's accumulation of flocks and the demise of their father's flocks was down to Jacob's own deviousness and trickery.

The unfairness of the situation was that through Jacob Laban had suddenly become a very rich man, yet it was Jacob who was being deprived of a fair income and tricked into giving more of his skills and abilities whilst at the same time being accused of malpractice.

This situation must resonate with many people today. Jacob was a clever man, skilled in shepherding and management and most importantly of all blessed by God. Laban on the other hand was a cheat and a bully and his sons lazy being able to enjoy the good life of ease. Yet it was Jacob who was doing all the work to provide them with the riches they had come to enjoy. Such people will go to any lengths to subjugate others to allow them to continue in their unreasonable lifestyle.

It might seem timely that at this point Jacob received a message from God indicating that he must leave Laban. It is not. We must accept that Jacob had entered into an intimate relationship with God from the moment of making his vow and had therefore been focused on Him and, over the years, grown sensitive to His voice. Also, God was fully aware of the growing animosity towards His servant by Laban and his household. Jacob, no doubt concerned for his own and his family's safety sought God for guidance and received it. Certainly Laban's daughters had noticed a change in their father's attitude towards them and were willing to leave him.

We could be cynical and consider Jacob's actions to be those of a man in a difficult situation trying to sort things out to the best of his ability and, if that required some scheming, then so be it. But as we have already seen God loved Jacob and through the work of the Holy Spirit, God had guided and directed him throughout his life to ensure his progress and safety.

Jacob's skills and abilities were God given and he was using them in the service of God for he was an essential element in the progress of God's plan of salvation that was being progressively played out on the earth in the lives of individuals.

We cannot ignore how important Jacob was to God and His goal of providing man with eternal salvation. Therefore, we must not fall into the trap of analysing Jacob's life totally separate to God's complete and saving work of His grace on earth, as that would provide us with a totally false understanding of Jacob's life.

Do not forget that this is not about a normal situation, for Jacob was central to God's developing plan of salvation and any attack on him would be an attack on God Himself. It is essential that we do not read scripture as we would a novel for it is all about God in action through ordinary people's lives and Jacob was an ordinary man albeit having been raised a son in a ruling family and therefore a prince in his own right.

Thus, with an established family of four wives and thirteen children, male and female servants and much livestock, Jacob took to his heels at the most opportune moment. This had been orchestrated by God for Laban and his sons were a significant three days journey away from home, shearing sheep and feasting. Three further days passed before Laban heard of Jacob's departure and by the time he had got his men together, it took him seven hard riding days to make contact with the slow moving caravan of Jacob.

If further proof of God's involvement in Jacob's life were needed, we have it here. God warned Laban not to have Jacob return either by enticement or by force of arms. Jacob was His servant. Thus, with his anger and desire for revenge dissipated, Laban struck a note of injured innocence when he finally caught up with Jacob, yet he had shown no fatherly concern for either of his daughters or their offspring for his attention had been on the wealth-creating abilities of Jacob and just how long he could keep him under his authority.

Just like Esau, his attention was on the things of this world not on those of the next or the spiritual necessity for a relationship with the God who had drawn Abraham away from this ordinary family.

It is important at this point to pause and consider the two main wives of Jacob for there is instruction to be had here.

Leah was not Jacob's favoured wife, Rachel was. Leah was not beautiful, Rachel was. Yet it was Leah whose heart was given to Jacob when they married and it was she who was willing to dedicate her life to him and fully worship his God in her heart, which act of commitment was rewarded by God by the sons she was able to present to Jacob, including the senior son Judah from whose loins the Messiah was promised.

Rachel wanted children but was not willing to give herself to Jacob in the same fulsome manner that her sister was, nor was she willing to accept his God in the same way. Notice that she hid the earth gods of her father, unwilling to give them up to enter into a new life of faith. Yet it was her son, Joseph, who was to become perhaps the most individually famous of all Jacob's sons.

Jacob's transforming experience

Memories of his brother's threat to his life bothered Jacob, even after a long absence. He was fearful about his reception and his brother's reaction to seeing him with such a large retinue, which could be construed as a threat. Even with the experience of God being with him, Jacob reacted in a basic human way to the challenge before him.

Jacob did three things:

1. He divided his retinue and possessions into two camps so that if Esau attacked one camp the other had time to flee.

2. He prayed and put the whole matter before God:

    "O God of my father Abraham … O Lord who said to me, 'Return unto your country'…, I am not worthy of all the mercies, and of all the truth, which you have shown to your servant; for with my staff I passed over this Jordan but now I am become two camps. Deliver me from the hand of my brother … for I fear him lest he come and smite me … And You have said, 'Surely I will do you good and make your seed as the sand of the sea, which cannot be numbered for multitude'.

3. He took as a present some of his possessions for Esau, sending them out before him in several droves with a message that these were a present from Jacob to his brother, and that Jacob was following on behind. Everyone going in front of Jacob was to speak with humility to Esau to defuse any anger and animosity he may still harbour. With space between each drove Jacob would receive ample warning of his brother's intentions, and therefore have time to flee for his life.

The humility and gratitude voiced in Jacob's prayer demonstrated just how much misfortune had developed the nobler impulses of his heart. Twenty years of fixed principles, steadfast purpose, and resolute sacrifice of the present for the future had purified and enabled him. The experiences of God he had had before reaching Laban had been profound, bringing to life all he had learned of Abraham's life of faith and that he had heard from his father, providing him with an immoveable anchor in the deceptive world of his relatives.

It also demonstrated that the apparent self-centredness of this man that so many continually focus on was superficial, disappearing like the mist under the noonday sun. Surely this clearly demonstrates that it is possible for the truly penitent to come nearer to God in a life changing way as opposed to those who have appeared never to have stumbled or fallen into sin. We learn from out mistakes.

A Nation is Born

From his vision of the ladder set up from earth to heaven, through his various experiences whilst serving Laban, initially for his wives and then for his possessions, and his protection from Laban after he had fled from Haran, Jacob's faith must surely have been built up and his sensitivity to spiritual realities become even more highly tuned. Now, fearful for the future and unable to defend himself from so large a force led by the impulsive and physical Esau, Jacob needed the time and space to think things out.

His experience led him to believe that the most profitable thing to do was to seek his God and search his own soul alone in an unpopulated place. All he could envision for the immediate future was to slay or be slain. Neither option was appealing to a very sensitive, peace loving man to whom any confrontation was anathema. All the safeguards he had put in place were designed to defuse a dangerous situation.

Now, alone with his thoughts and seeking the God who had promised to bless him he wrestled with a man until the break of day. Jacob was a fit man and this fitness was amplified within him because of his fear of the future. Even when his thigh was dislocated, Jacob's determination to continue the struggle was undiminished. When the angel (it is more likely to have been the Messiah during one of His several visits to the earth prior to His birth at Bethlehem[17]) conceded and asked Jacob to release him, Jacob would only do so in return for a blessing (Gen. 32:24 – 28).

The change from supplanter to Prince of God, the meaning of the name Israel, signals a new and godlier phase in Jacob's life. All the past struggles and learning experiences had led him to that supreme moment of a physical/spiritual struggle that dramatically changed his experiential belief and faith in God to a steadfast and certain faith.

Notwithstanding his human weaknesses, this faith was to help him overcome fears and uncertainties with the knowledge of a surety that God was with him no matter how bad the situation got in which he found himself. Previously God had to show Jacob that He was present in his trials; in future this would not be necessary.

Almost as a symbol, a reminder of this epic meeting with God, Jacob would henceforth walk with a limp. Just as Abraham's tested faith can be our experience at strategic moments in our lives (a crucial element in this author's life), so Jacob's physical struggle with God is allegorical of every individual's struggles and wrestling with their understanding of, and faith in God when facing up to a forthcoming, or current crisis or major turning point in their lives.

---

[17] God is able to deal gently with us even though He has far greater power than we have, for He is able to control that power according to circumstances. It is also clear that it is God alone who could rename Jacob as Israel, a name God wanted the nation to have that developed from Jacob

This was a pinnacle experience for Jacob, when the physical and spiritual aspects of his life became in a supreme moment irrevocably united, allowing God and man to walk in harmony, achieving a level of spirituality that is an example to all those who want to grow in the eternal God.

What differentiates those who have prevailed from those who have not is undoubtedly the extent to which they have searched for, responded to and sought after the God of Abraham, Isaac and Jacob and, in so doing, have gained an understanding of the promises of God which all three Patriarchs possessed and that provided an inheritance and sure foundation for them, even as they do for those individuals of all subsequent generations, Jew and Gentile alike, who have followed Jacob's example.

The Esau's of this world have their eyes fixed on things they are able to see, feel, smell and hear, oblivious to the greater spiritual wonders of God. Just as Esau himself was denied the great life changing happenings of God that Jacob was able to experience, so are they.

Jacob's new name is a title of victory. Collectively his children had become Israelites, Champions of God and contenders for the Divine, conquering not through their own strength but with the strength and knowledge that comes from God, whilst they remained in a right relationship with Him.

Exactly who the "messenger" was remains a mystery of the Divine, but Jacob's life had been preserved even though he had seen and had physical contact with a divine being.

This was a defining moment in Jacob's life and brought about a land mark event in God's plan of salvation

God Causes Good to Come from Evil

For those steeped in the tradition of the Jews that say Jesus is not the Messiah I would say one thing. The whole purpose of this book is to seek out the true purposes of the Lord God of Israel through total reliance on the Holy Spirit of the Living God for inspiration in studying the Word of God. You will know that to write anything concerning God and His way of salvation that is contrary to His truth is dangerous.

If I were found guilty of misinterpretation, then my future would indeed be very bleak. Yet I have been blessed by what I have written thus far and have that witness that can only come from the God of Israel that I must continue to write. My experience is that I cannot stop writing for as Jeremiah said, *"...His word was in my heart like a burning fire shut up in my bones; I was weary of holding it back, and I could not ..." (see Jer. 20:7 – 9)*. Therefore, I would advise you, even as a Gentile believer, that you read on and only make up your mind as to the truth of what you read at the end. Your future as God's chosen could depend on it.

Jacob's life, once he had made peace with his brother, became that of a nomad like that of his father and grandfather, although not without moments of meeting with God. However, of his twelve sons one stood out from the rest because of an inner desire for the things of God. Jacob loved Joseph more than his other sons because of this and as a result his brothers came to hate this favoured son, because of jealousy.

It is interesting how God chooses men and women to serve Him. But it is those who have a heart[18] for Him or are searching for someone to satisfy their inner longing and for a more complete life that God chooses. They start the search not knowing that it is their spiritual inner selves that need feeding with the pure spiritual food of the Holy Spirit. This is the key to them finding not just peace in their inner being, but a purpose for their lives. Just as Jacob was chosen of God because he had a heart for God, so was Joseph, with both coming under God's protecting arm as can be seen throughout their lives.

The animosity that built up between Joseph and his brothers is a sure sign that they were far from God and had no relationship with Him. They could not have any concept of the importance of the dreams he recounted to them. Because they had received no spiritual awareness of God, they had no belief in Him. In Judah's case, as explained in my work "The Origin of Life", he was quite prepared to live like the pagan families around him; indeed, his son was the result of him going with his widowed daughter-in-law posing as a prostitute (Gen. 38 esp. 24 – 26).

Those under the influence of the evil introduced by Satan, which is pure godlessness, cannot stand being with those who have a portion of the Spirit of God within them, for the God inspired good within a person is an irritant to those without God. It is a fact that just as darkness is the absence of light, so godlessness and anything that is evil is the absence of God who is Love, Light and Righteousness. Therefore, hatred and despicable actions are part of the godless culture Satan introduced and continues to stimulate.

This consuming animosity of the brothers towards Joseph set the scene for his faked killing by his brothers which initiated years of deep sadness within Jacob, who must have thought at one time that Joseph would inherit the blessing from him even though he was almost the youngest.

Jacob himself had inherited the blessing from his father even though he was the younger of the twins. Such was his love for this aspiring spiritual son through a fellowship of understanding and easy spiritual intercourse between them that to Jacob Joseph's death was as though his whole future and purpose in life had been condemned to disaster.

What Jacob did not, could not, realise was that the purposes of God

---

[18] Deut. 4:29; Ps. 27:8 [When David wrote in this Psalm, "My heart said to You …" he was acknowledging the Hebrew understanding of the heart, which is that it is the seat not only of a person's affections but also of the thoughts and will], Amos 5:4.

cannot be seen by men unless God wants them to know what He is doing and reveals this through His Holy Spirit. The pain and suffering Jacob experienced was all part of the work God was engaged in to bring the eleven brothers to Himself as believers in Him. His aim was to establish a God-fearing nation through which He could develop His plan of salvation.

For all those who read the scriptures, part 1 and part 2, it is essential that they look deeply into the text, discarding any preconceived ideas and notions and instructions in dogma from others and put themselves in the hands of Almighty God, asking Him to open their eyes to the truth and then allow the Holy Spirit of the Living God to reveal to them the inner truths that have been deposited there.

I believe the purpose of this book is to show those who are seeking the truth of God not to focus on the tragedies and conflicts but seek out the purposes of God through inspiration. It is so easy to incorrectly interpret God's work and come to a wrong conclusion.

The account of Joseph being sold into slavery is very well known and is a good example of God at work through imperfect men. After all, why should just one of twelve be different when they were brought up in the same family, although of different mothers? It is also significant that this son of Rachel (who was not as prepared as her sister to give up the worship of her family's gods and worship the God of her husband), should be the one most aligned to the belief of his father. What we need to realise is the underlying reason for his eventful life, which is probably less well known.

Joseph was able to demonstrate the depths of his love for God even as one reverse in his life followed another. He could have had no idea of the important part he would play in saving his people from starvation or of being the means of bringing his brothers back to a belief in the God he so diligently served, or that his life would reflect so accurately the life of the promised Messiah who was to come (see Appendix F).

As power goes, only the Pharaoh had greater power than Joseph, therefore he was a man to be feared particularly by those who were not Egyptian and needed some of the stored grain in the time of famine. Joseph used that power to instill fear into his brethren over a period of time so that when he finally revealed himself to them, he was able with the greatest possible impact to demonstrate just how important God had been in his adventures, not just to him but, through him, to them also.

Their guilt in selling him in the first place weighed heavily on their consciences, particularly the major players, Simeon and Judah. But it was in Judah, the head of the tribe into which the Messiah was to be born, that the greatest change was seen.

Through the life of Joseph God was able to demonstrate His ability to achieve great things with a single person who loved Him and was willing to serve Him through apparently good times and bad. But there is far more to

Joseph than the salvation of the tribe of Israel, for he was not to be the one by whom the Messiah of Israel was promised, rather it was through his singular and devout dedication to God that he was able to challenge his brothers to the extent that they were enabled to come close to God.

This is an extract of what I wrote in "The Origin of Life" which is important to our understanding of the work of God Joseph was able to do:

Joseph Tests His Brothers

From Joseph's point of view, he had already witnessed some outward signs of individual grief at their role in his disappearance when they were last before him. But this grief only showed a guilt complex that was more to do with the concern of each brother at their involvement in that embarrassing episode; more of a regret brought on by the thought that they could have been guilty of murder in the first instance, more a niggling doubt about what had actually happened to Joseph than any real sense of sorrow at the cause of their action. There was also the feeling that having kept what they had done secret all these years it still had the potential to re-emerge and cause them more than just a little embarrassment.

Joseph needed to show them through experience that their real sin against him was a hardness of heart, unbelief in the God of Abraham, through whom an understanding of the dreams could have been obtained had they been as close to Him as Joseph and, perhaps most important of all, the hatred they had allowed to dwell and ferment in their hearts that had been the trigger for their actions. The planting of the cup in Benjamin's sack was to provide that testing experience.

This came when Joseph's steward went after them and stopped them just as they cleared the city. Up to that moment they were steadily becoming more relieved to be returning home with both Simeon and Benjamin. When he accused them of returning evil for good by stealing his master's silver divining cup, a very important personal possession and much used in Egypt at the time, there is no doubt they would not have been able to believe what they were hearing. In their state of mind and their fear of the authorities, for them to have done such a thing was totally out of the question, madness. They would have ensured that they kept together; Benjamin would certainly have been guarded. That the servant voiced the accusation in such a way that he seemed to expect them to know about this theft and admit to it was even more outrageous.

The reaction of the brothers, who were unaware of what had

been going on and completely innocent of any wrong doing, will have been one of bewilderment. The servant's suggestion was preposterous. Knowing they were innocent of any possible charge they suggested that the person found with the cup in their sack should die and all the brothers become bondmen, but the servant replied that just the guilty person should become a bondman and the rest of the brothers could go free. Their confidence in their innocence would have been vindicated when each sack was opened and no cup found. However, when the cup was found in Benjamin's sack their shock would have quickly led to despair. Benjamin was the one brother who must not be put at risk, for it would mean the death of their father. Their brother having disappeared through their actions, they could not afford to go to their father and say that the second child of his beloved Rachel was now either dead or the bondman of an Egyptian official.

The Brothers Return for a Third Meeting with Joseph

The brothers needed no persuasion. Packing their sacks, they all returned in haste to Joseph's house to plead their case. A meeting with Joseph, the third, was quickly arranged. Joseph made out that with the cup he was well able to discover the guilty person by divination. Judah conceded that they had little means of proving their innocence since the discovery of the cup in Benjamin's sack condemned them and declared, "God has found out the iniquity of your servants", meaning that God had found them guilty of doing wrong to their father, by the devious means they had used to hide from him their involvement with the disappearance of Joseph.

Although Simeon is considered the one who counselled that Joseph be slain, it is probable that Judah was in agreement until the option of selling him became a possibility when they saw the Ishmaelite caravan. As a natural leader it was his hardness of heart, unbelief and hatred without cause that had encouraged his brothers at that time, and it was this fact that had through the years come to haunt him. Coupled to this was the shame inflicted on themselves by the deception of their father; for by contaminating Joseph's coat with blood and having others take it to their father it gave Jacob the impression that Joseph had been killed.

They could not, in their own selfish-minded state, have conceived the degree of distress such an event would cause their father. This too would have impacted on Judah's memory. To compound the problem of a sense of profound guilt was the growing realisation of the wrong done to their brother Joseph. There is little doubt that over the years in their quiet moments, when they were reminded of their involvement in Joseph's disappearance, a deepening sense of guilt would have plagued them. Judah's admission indicates that the moral regeneration of the brothers was complete. At last the admission came that God had finally got the message through to him concerning his sin and, as a result, his willingness to give up his own life for the sake of his brother Benjamin was revealed.

Joseph's insistence that Benjamin would be his bondman and that the others must return to their father spurred Judah into one final effort to secure his release. It is an eloquent and succinct account of all that had happened to them from the moment of their confession, in response to Joseph's enquiries about any family during their first meeting, of the life of their father and the existence of a youngest brother right up to their present situation (Gen. 44:19 – 33).

Boldly, in front of this awesome and frightening official, Judah desperately recounted the Viceroy's instructions that they would not see his face unless Benjamin was with them and Judah's warning that their father would die if anything happened to the lad. He spoke of Jacob's reluctance to allow the lad to come to Egypt because of the loss of the other son of this wife and that it was only on the Viceroy's insistence that he be brought that their father finally relented. Judah then, in offering himself as a bondman in place of his brother, made their personal situation very clear that should anything happen to Benjamin it would signal his father's death.

> *And your servant my father said unto us: 'You know that my wife bore unto me two sons; and the one went out from me, and I said: Surely, he is torn in pieces; and I have not seen him since; and if you take this one also from me, and harm befall him you will bring down my gray hairs with sorrow to the grave. (Gen. 44:27 – 29)*

Now if the Viceroy's decision was final and they returned without the lad then their father would die through sorrow having lost both sons from his wife.

Judah pointed out that as he had provided surety for the lad, he would bear the blame to his father forever; it was therefore preferable that he should become a bondman in place of Benjamin. Having seen the anguish suffered by his father after the death of Joseph he could not endure seeing the total devastation of his father should he not be able to return with Benjamin. The repetition of the phrase 'with sorrow to the grave' and the fact that their father's soul was bound up with the lad's soul emphasized just how critical the whole matter was.

It was Judah's confession, his repentance and willingness to become a substitute for Benjamin that finally brought Joseph's emotions bubbling to the surface. Unable to contain himself any longer he ordered his staff out of the room and finally broke down in tears. His brothers were bewildered by this sudden turn of events. One-minute Judah was pleading for his brother's life, desperate for the Viceroy to change his mind regarding Benjamin, fearful that his father would die with a broken heart and the next they were alone with this powerful man crying his eyes out and telling them in their own language that he was their long-lost brother Joseph. They were stunned, bewildered and confused.

"*I am Joseph; does my father yet live?*", he needed assurance that his father, who was of a good age when he was taken away from them, should really still be alive and that he should see him once again.

But Joseph's greatest problem was to assure them that he really was their brother. Calling them near to him to give them a better opportunity to check him out, he assured them that it was God's plan that he had come to Egypt to preserve life. The manner of his transportation from home to Egypt had been God's method to affect his ultimate rise to his present position.

Joseph had had time, since his brothers first came to Egypt seeking food, to realise just how God had achieved His purpose in saving his chosen people from starvation and that there had been no other way whereby he could be brought before Pharaoh without there being any feeling of threat.

As a slave Joseph had proved his remarkable abilities first by become the overseer of the estate of the Captain of Pharaoh's Personal Guard and then given the responsibility of running the prison for the Prison Governor. He had been respected in prison. He was always unbowed yet always helpful and supportive of those who ruled over him, practical yet clearly a man of God. Throughout, Joseph had proved himself worthy of trust and a man in whom full confidence could be placed.

The butler was able to give a personal testimony to Pharaoh regarding Joseph's character and standing within the prison and his powers of interpreting dreams. Even Potiphar, who is the one most likely to have been charged with bringing Joseph before the king, will have added his weight to the chief butler's evidence (Gen. 41:14 – 19).

From the moment he had entered Egypt and had been bought from the Ishmaelites by Potiphar to the moment he was brought before the king, Joseph had been in the employ and therefore under the surveillance of senior people in the service of the king. All could vouch for his character and moral stature. When he had given his assessment of what should be done to mitigate the effects of the seven years of drought and Pharaoh wanted to appoint Joseph as Grand Vizier, even as Viceroy, no one raised any objection, indeed the general consensus of the senior palace staff was that it was an excellent appointment. Yet moments before Joseph had been a convict. One wonders what Potiphar's wife made of the whole affair?

However necessary it was that Joseph should be taken to Egypt and sold as a slave for God's plan to become a reality, and however critical to that plan was the action of the brothers, there is no doubt that it was necessary for his brothers to realise that their attitude towards him was wrong and needed to be sorted out. They needed to repent of their sin and seek forgiveness. God's ultimate goal had been to save life and this Joseph was at great pains to point out.

"And now be not grieved, nor be angry with yourselves, that you sold me hither, for God sent me before you to preserve life … and to save you alive for a great deliverance."

"So now it was not you that sent me hither, but God; and he has made me a father (which is an exact transliteration of an Egyptian of state rank, corresponding to 'vizier') to Pharaoh and lord of all his house and ruler of all the land of Egypt."

For believers in the one true God, as Abraham had been, hindsight is the one sure way to confirm that God is with them. From it God's plan and involvement in their lives can be identified to provide assurance for the future.

The son who was dead is not only alive but ruler in the land. There was clear evidence that the God who had blessed him in Potiphar's house and then in prison, was blessing his management of the famine in Egypt. Pharaoh, who was rejoicing in the fact that his country was being saved from starvation and disaster, on hearing that this saviour had been visited by his family in Canaan naturally offered them the best grazing land, the land of Goshen. With his full authority the brothers were to return and bring the whole family into Egypt to be looked after.

But Joseph had to warn them not to fall out along the way.

Jacob Told About Joseph

The brothers, through their traumatic meetings with and experiences of Joseph had had time to come to terms with the fact that this was indeed their long-lost brother whom they thought was dead. Jacob, who had had to rely on what his sons told him, had reached a point where he could no longer believe them. Indeed, so shocked was he with their news that he almost died. The lies they had told him regarding Joseph and their untrustworthiness made it hard to accept they were at last telling him the truth. It was the wagons that Joseph had sent that finally tipped the balance and he was able to believe that his son Joseph, whom he loved so much, was indeed alive.

But it was not the descriptions of the splendour of his appearance and his life and position that enthused Jacob, "It is enough" that Joseph was alive and he would see his son again. That was the true grandness and excitement of the occasion.

Jacob was a man of habit even though he had been a sojourner all his life. From an early age the accounts of how the Almighty God worshipped by his grandfather and father had spoken to them and directed them had been food to his enquiring mind. After his first meeting with this God through the angels ascending and descending the ladder Jacob had himself grown to know that same God, worship Him and ultimately to serve Him. Moving to Beer-sheba, where his father Isaac had built an altar and settled, Jacob offered sacrifices to their God.

During the night God appeared in a dream to Jacob giving him clearance to go down into Egypt where his offspring would be melded into a great nation; his father Isaac had previously been prevented from going down into Egypt. Not only would God go with Jacob into Egypt but He would also bring him back again to the Promised Land, that is, at his death for burial and with his offspring when they went up to take possession of the Promised Land as the nation of Israel. And Joseph would perform the customary duty of putting his hands-on Jacob's eyes at his death.

For the brothers to find out that this despised brother had not died but become as powerful as he had in such a powerful country as Egypt was one thing, but for him to pronounce that his change in circumstances was the direct result of the God of their father Jacob was quite another.

Emotions ran riot when they discovered that this previously feared and powerful governing official, who was respected by Pharaoh and the Egyptian people, was none other than the brother they had caused to be sold into slavery.

Such a discovery resulted in a number of emotionally led changes within the hearts of his brothers:

- Relief that the years of guilt could be set aside because they were forgiven of the crime they thought they had committed so long ago.

- The understanding they received concerning the power of the God of their father Jacob who could achieve such a result from their evil actions.

- The sense of joy that their brother was alive after all and they could commune with him freely.

- The sense of relief that at last they could drop the life of lies and deception that they had had to adopt before their father regarding the fate of his beloved son.

- The forgiveness that they had received after years of carrying their guilty secret within their hearts.

But this could not have happened without the repentance shown by the brothers concerning their vile actions.

The first testament is foundational in our understanding of the salvation that we are discovering God created to attract men (this includes both men and women) back to Himself. Throughout the books contained in the Bible we are discovering, and will continue to discover as we proceed book by book, just how thoroughly God developed His plan of salvation using those who were willing to surrender their lives to Him through repentance and faith in order that they might be of service to Him in whatever capacity He decided.

Patriarch and Prophet, Priest and King, all were chosen by Him because of their willingness to submit to their God just as Abraham had done at the beginning. The requirement for entry into His kingdom and service has not changed.

We need to discover that element of the person and character of the promised Messiah each incident/event is describing, or how we as sinful men need to understand our position before God and how we must prepare and present ourselves before Him to meet with Him.

Jacob in His searching met with God in a way that God knew would bring out the best in him for he saw the vision and was filled with wonder that God, the God he was searching for, should be in that place and worshipped Him there.

Some have a confession of faith that is even more dramatic in that, without the introduction to God that Jacob received, God met with them for their hearts were receptive to His calling them. Men and women from other cultures and religious practices have been touched by the Spirit of the Living God and responded to Him to be saved to the uttermost.

It is all too easy to read this wonderfully expressive and descriptive word of God and come to our own conclusions. It has taken me a life-time of seeking after God and continually seeking His complete authority over me that has allowed God to train me and bring me to sufficient maturity in the Spirit for me to do the work in which I am now engaged. The emphasis must be on Him and not on me, just as the servants of old proclaimed His ascendancy over them in order for His message and His plan to be communicated to men.

Abraham, Isaac, and Jacob (renamed Israel), were all central to the word of God and His work in this world to create and develop His plan of salvation, but it was not just for their personal benefit, it was for the world! The Jews do not own God's plan of salvation! It was given to them to promulgate through repentance, obedience and faith and service to the people of the world. A task an identified few were prepared to take on even at the cost of their own lives.

It can be seen from Appendix F how a Jew who came into knowledge of the complete message of God's salvation was given the inspiration by God to evaluate Joseph's life, and in that way help him in understanding the person of the future Messiah.

But this understanding is available to all Israel if they are prepared, as he was, to seek God's understanding of the Word that He had caused to be written for their benefit. Let us not be unmindful of the fact that it was Moses who wrote the first five books of Holy Scripture by inspiration. They could have been written no other way for he was not alive at the time of the creation or the events leading up to his involvement with Israel.

It was by testing that Joseph demonstrated his deep unshakeable faith and love of God; and it was only by that demonstration of his faith in the God of his parents in the heart of pagan Egypt that allowed the Pharaoh to promote him to such a high position with the agreement of his people.

The life of Joseph clearly shows us the importance of a strong, dynamic personal relationship with God and that that relationship can only come from an individual person's heart being focused on God for his eleven brothers had no such relationship.

It cannot be gained by inheritance. It has nothing to do with our DNA. We are not born with it. But the desire for God must be gained and acted upon by each of us as individuals. It has got nothing to do with others. It is strictly personal for that is the way God made us. Those who tow the party line, who merely accept what they are taught without question, can so easily be made blind and unable to see the truth through poor or inerrant teaching.

It was by testing that the brothers were brought to the point of repentance by Joseph, and gained the knowledge that it was their father's God who had saved them, not only from the act of evil but by using their evil intent and act to bring about eternal good. It was through being faced with the full horror of their sinful act, and suddenly denied their stance of self-denial, that the brothers were brought to the point of confession and repentance.

It was only when they reached that point in their lives when the truth came out that Joseph was able to forgive them, claiming that although they had meant it for harm God had turned it to good. And it is to that point of coming face-to-face with our sin against others, and particularly the full horror of our sin against God, that God wants to bring all errant men and women so that they can confess and repent of their sin and seek His eternal forgiveness.

The Joy and Horror of Egypt

We must not read scripture with a worldly mind, which is why it is essential that we seek after God with all our hearts so that through His Holy Spirit we can receive understanding. This is the only way I have been able to write the library of books that has now been established and distributed around the world.

Just as the brothers were brought to the point of confession through trials, so the whole of God's plan of salvation has been systematically developed through the lives of individuals and nations, particularly God's chosen nation of Israel, in a sinful world through trials and tribulations.

This is understandable because, had the way been easy that plan would not have had a God focus in a sinful world; rather, as we shall see as we continue our investigation of the Tabernacle of Moses, Satan has continuously sought to bring the development of that plan to a hasty and ignominious end.

Therefore, the lives of all those who believe in the one true God are at odds with Satan who became the ruler of the earth by attracting to himself the obedience of man which should have belonged to God, and because he is a spiritual being, he is also the prince of the power of the air with a onetime angelic following that has become demonised because of its anti-God activities.

The entrance of Jacob, now called Israel, into Egypt was a grand affair because of the debt Egypt and the family owed to Jacob's son Joseph who had saved the nations from starvation. From my work "The Origin of Life":

> Right up to the end of his life Rachel's name was never far from Jacob's lips. Not only had he loved her to the extent that the seven years he first worked for her seemed short, but also she had produced a son who had proved faithful to him and had that same desire to reach out to the Almighty God that Jacob had. Indeed, Joseph's life seemed to mirror his own early days, for whereas he had looked heavenward, Esau had looked earthward and preferred the physical attractions rather than the spiritual; now it was Joseph who looked to the spiritual and his other sons to the physical worldly attractions.
>
> Yet it was Leah who was truly faithful to Jacob, abandoning both her family and family gods for her husband and her

husband's God. Her faithfulness was ultimately rewarded because her son Judah became the leader of the eleven brothers, and it was into his line that King David and the Mashiach (Jewish Messiah) were born. Leah also provided Jacob with the greatest number of sons and, through her son Levi, Moses, the greatest of all the pre-Messianic prophets. But her death and place of burial is only briefly recorded *("… where I buried Leah …")* when Jacob explains to Joseph where he is to be buried. Rachel was buried along the way.

It was Judah whom Jacob sent to seek directions from Joseph for the way to Goshen, and they travelled and set up camp there.

Now it was Joseph's turn to seek out his father whom he had not seen for so many years for a meeting filled with emotion. Joseph fell on Jacob's neck and the tears flowed releasing the years of homesickness and yearning for his father from whom he had learned so much about his faith. Joseph honoured his father and loved him. Finally, Jacob was able to declare his willingness to die now that he had seen his long-lost son.

Joseph, aware that the special privilege of his position was in part due to Pharaoh, now took charge of the protocol side of introducing them to the king. All that had happened as Jacob and his entourage entered the country and the emotional meeting of Jacob and Joseph would have been reported in detail to Pharaoh. All the arrangements had to be carefully made so as not to offend the royal family, for shepherds were an abomination to the Egyptians.

The meeting between Pharaoh and the five selected representatives of the family was carefully choreographed with the responses to Pharaoh's questions practised in advance. It is important to observe Joseph's loyalty to his family; that he was able to associate himself with these crude Canaanite shepherds who had tried to do him so much harm and were far removed from the grandeur of the royal palaces in which he now lived. It shows a simple nobility of character to which it is difficult to find an equal in the whole of human existence.

Joseph's one foundational attribute, that allowed him to welcome such brethren with open arms and without animosity, was his sense of divine appointment as the saviour of his people. It was his total trust and faith in the wisdom and faithfulness of the God of Abraham, Isaac and Jacob which had initially triggered the hatred and had then initiated the chain of events that brought about the present situation. Without his father he would not have acquired this faith, therefore he could deny neither his lineage nor his brethren.

Pharaoh's gratitude for Joseph's eminent services to him and his country during the famine was to give to Joseph's people the best of the land. Further to this generous offer was to appoint Joseph's relatives to the position of royal officers, superintendents to the king's herdsmen.

Joseph then introduced his father to Pharaoh. There was an interesting use of words as the two conversed, for the king enquired about Jacob's age, *"How many are the days of your life?"* Jacob in reply referred to his 'days of his sojourning' as being 130 years, making the point that there was a land beyond death, which would be his eternal home, a real life that could not be obtained here. He then referred to the years of his life being few and evil, reflecting on the troubled existence he had endured, and saddened by the fact that his life had been shorter than that of his forebears. Jacob then blessed Pharaoh before leaving his presence.

The family of Jacob now settled in the land, coming under the authority of Pharaoh as citizens and gaining possessions through purchase and were supported by Joseph. As for the Egyptian and Canaanite nations, they gradually paid over first their money, then their cattle and then their land to Pharaoh in exchange for food because the famine was so severe in the land.

Jacob Blesses His Sons

Jacob, having lived seventeen years in Egypt was coming to the end of his life. He was not afraid to die for, as his answer to Pharaoh suggested, he was looking forward to something far greater than he could expect in this life. God had also appeared to him on a number of occasions confirming to him his special status in God's will and plan. However, Jacob was concerned that he should not be buried in Egypt and to that end obtained assurances from Joseph that he would undertake the responsibility for his burial in the family burial ground.

Jacob had lived through tortuous times. Esau, Laban, Dinah and Joseph, names that trigger memories of trials and tribulations; yet it was on the anvil of affliction that the soul of this sensitive man was forged, knowing by experience that he could not travel outside of God's care and concern for him. Such was his faith in God, tried and tested as it was, (often seemingly to the point of destruction) by which he knew of a certainty that God was with him and would never leave him.

Far from being one who never made mistakes, he was able to rise above life's cruel reverses extracting good from each one to end his life blessing those around him. Jacob realised that just as he had had to face the unknown and experience danger, so would his sons.

Then Joseph, being warned of his father's poor condition, brought his two sons to him that he might bless them before he died. His father then recounted the promise God had made to him that the land of promise would be for an everlasting possession for the great nation that his offspring would become. What is more, Joseph's two sons would become as Jacob's sons and counted within the identified tribes of Israel. Indeed, during the history of Israel the name of Ephraim is often used for the northern kingdom after the 2 to 10 split at the time of Rehoboam, (cf. 11 Chron. 25:7; Hos. 5:3; 6:10; 10:6; Is. 7:2; Jer. 7:15).

God is no respecter of persons. Being the first-born has no advantage as has been seen by the preference given to Abel, Abraham, Isaac, Jacob over Esau, Joseph himself, Moses and David. At this important time in his life, Jacob would have been given divine inspiration when dealing with his offspring. Although his eyes were dim his mental ability was sharp. Knowing full well how his son would have positioned his grandsons before him Jacob placed his right hand on Ephraim's head and his left on that of Manasseh, crossing his hands over to do so.

> *"The God before whom my father's Abraham and Isaac walked, the God who has been my shepherd all my life long unto this day, the angel who has redeemed me from all evil, bless the lads; and let my name be named in them and the name of my father's Abraham and Isaac; and let them grow into a multitude in the midst of the earth."*

Although Joseph tried to correct his father by changing his hands over so that the first-born would be recognised, his father protested that he was fully aware of what he was doing.

> *"I know it my son, I know it; he also shall become a people, and he also shall become great; howbeit his younger brother shall be greater than he, and his seed shall become a multitude of nations."*

So Jacob blessed Joseph's sons:

> *"By these shall Israel be blessed, saying: God make you as Ephraim and Manasseh."*

Just as Joseph would not, could not ignore his brethren, so his sons willingly gave up a most exalted social position and an enviable political career in the Egyptian state to align themselves with their kinsmen, the despised shepherd-immigrants. Such was the influence of their father and their own sense of belonging.

With the passing of Jacob and then Joseph, time gradually obscured the truth, and the saving of Egypt from starvation by Joseph the Hebrew gradually dimmed in the minds of the autocratic rulers of the people. The growth in the number of the people of Israel that God was allowing, to establish Israel as a nation in its own right (four generations of growth), and with a different language to that of the Egyptians, gradually suspicion was aroused in the minds of the rulers that this people could become a threat to their nation if an enemy attacked the country. However unreasonable, the thought gained credence with the leaders and the slavery of the Israelites became a reality.

God's prophetic message to Abraham at the time of the covenant making had come to pass (Extract from "The Origin of Life"):

God Makes a Covenant with Abraham

The ancient method of making a covenant was to cut an animal in half and for the contracting parties to walk through the portions of the slain animal, thereby they were thought to be united by the bond of a common blood. To assure Abram, God used this method to establish a covenant between them and to give him some understanding of future events. Abram, who slayed the animals as God instructed him, was forced to prevent scavenging birds eating them, symbolising the difficulties to be experienced by his heirs when taking possession of the land.

When the sun was setting a deep sleep, similar to that experienced by Adam before his rib was removed to create Eve, came over Abram and a great darkness that stimulated a dread within his spirit symbolising that the nation that would issue from him would have to pass through bitter times of oppression. The four hundred years relates to four generations before they would be freed from slavery. In the darkness the smoking furnace and the flaming torch, symbolic of the Godhead, passed between the pieces to establish the covenant. So was delivered to Abram a surety that God's promises concerning the future of his tribe and line would be established and prophetic knowledge of what would happen before those offspring would take possession of the Promised Land.

The seeds of God's activity for His intervention into the affairs of men can take years to germinate and become fully established. Again, it is men of faith who are used to produce a leader through whom God could work. The whole account of Moses' birth and life is a complete picture of God working amongst men. A devout couple of the tribe of Levi became the parents of a beautiful boy at a time when the law required that all male children born of a Hebrew woman had to be killed. Believing this child to be special the woman nurtured him until he reached the age of three months, when it became impossible to hide him because by then he would naturally be more vocal.

In faith the couple built an ark and waterproofed it and laid it in the reeds along the river bank (Ex. 2:3) near where Pharaoh's daughter would wash in the waters. God induced a heart for the child in the princess's heart and at eight years of age, having been taught by his parents the history of Israel and about the God who had chosen them to be His people, he was adopted into the household of Pharaoh to become a prince of Egypt and to be trained in the ways of diplomacy and in their way of life and way of doing business. Indeed, it is thought that he was trained in the Egyptian army as a potential general alongside Pharaoh's natural eldest son.

This is the evidence of God's overruling power that He is able to cause a beautiful boy, who should have been killed at birth, to be born of a devout couple, and for that boy to be later named and raised by the very family with whom God would ultimately do battle to rescue His people from slavery in Egypt.

Even as His chosen people were crying out to Him for deliverance God was already taking action that would take about 80 years to come to fruition. For not only had Moses to be trained in the art of leadership and attain that royal upright stature, but he had also to be trained in leading a nation through the wilderness of Sinai, hence his 40 years as a shepherd during which time he had not only to learn how to survive and understand the wilderness and how to shepherd a flock of sheep (in the future to be the sheep of God's people) but also understand the loneliness of leadership which was the life of a shepherd.

During his first years of instruction within his natural family Moses would have become acquainted with his parent's devout and strong faith in God which would undoubtedly have made a strong impression on him. They would also have wanted to instill in him the essence of their faith in God to prepare him for his time in a pagan family, albeit the Egyptian royal family.

Moses himself, in spite of the pagan teaching he was subjected to by his Egyptian tutors, had retained his sense of the importance of the power of the God of his people (see Ex. 2:11 – 13), for when he met with God at the burning-bush he had no problem recognising who it was that spoke to him. (Ex. 3:6) No man is perfect in God's sight, according to God's scale of righteousness, for all have sinned and fallen short of the glory and perfection of God. But God is able to use fallen and sinful men whose hearts are right with Him to the glory of His name, a name which is above every other name that is named.

5 TRAINING OF A NATION [19]

"Oh, taste and see that the Lord He is good;
Blessed is the man who trusts in Him!
Oh, fear the Lord, you His saints!
There is no want to those who fear Him.
The young lions lack and suffer hunger;
But those who seek the Lord
shall not lack any good thing. "
(Ps. 34:8 - 10)

Sunrise in the wilderness

His training completed it was time for Moses to be called into service.

It is clear throughout the history of man how man on his own, without God, will degenerate into chaos. It has happened time and time again. Egypt, having departed from the state it was in under the rule of Joseph, became a place of slavery not only for the Hebrews but also, through the autocratic rule of the Pharaohs, for the ordinary civilian population themselves.

Paganism had got a hold on society in general and the worship of various gods became the norm, with vast sums being spent on the erection of great temples. Vast building projects were undertaken to ensure each ruler would be acknowledged as a great man by future generations. These have been tourist attractions ever since.

The oppressed people of God, suffering under almost intolerable conditions and with the prospect of an early death through the heavy weight of the toil laid upon them, began to seek after their God for His deliverance.

Moses, challenged by the burning bush and then the voice of the God of his parents emanating from the centre of the bush, will have been overwhelmed by the surreal nature of the event. He had got used to being a shepherd alone in, and surrounded by, the often-cruel beauty of the wilderness. His curiosity about the burning bush led him to a direct confrontation with the God who had organised his life up to that point.

The challenge for God was to persuade Moses to accept the major role

---

[19] For a fuller understanding of Exodus please read my book "God Rescues His People"

in His plan to rescue His people from slavery in Egypt. The challenge for Moses was to believe that this God, who was talking to him, was able and powerful enough to provide him with the wherewithal for him to accomplish that task. It was a daunting prospect and one that would shatter his acquired lonely and intimately private lifestyle that was not without its dangers but which he had come to enjoy, for it suited the intrinsic humility of his character.

Consider what I wrote in my book "God Rescues His People":

Moses' Objections to God's Commission

Moses now puts forward what, to him, were three important obstacles to his acceptance of God's commission:

1. *"Who am I that I should go unto Pharaoh and bring forth the children of Israel out of Egypt?"* Moses had lost the self-confidence and self-esteem that had enabled him to assume the role of an Egyptian Prince. He had taken on a humbleness of character that was to distinguish him from other leaders of history, and it was this that caused him to see himself as being unfit for such a demanding role. But God had trained him for it and God's credibility was on the line. Had Moses failed, God's plan of salvation would also have failed, but God chooses His servants with infinite wisdom knowing their hearts and their characters. In every case it is those who realise their dependency on God for forgiveness and strength who succeed in fulfilling His promises in them.

    > *"Certainly I will be with you and this shall be the token that I have sent you, you will worship Me on this mountain"*

    It is a fact that when God calls someone for a work He never leaves them to it but always provides support, and here God gives Moses a promise of success that, once he had brought the children of Israel out of Egypt, he would serve God in worship on this very mountain.

    It can be confidently stated that people, however well trained by God, cannot accomplish God's commission without His help. That is the way God works. Indeed, it is essential that people commissioned by God be well acquainted with their own failings and inadequacies so that they rely on His strength, His wisdom, His inspiration, His power to see them through. Such an attitude causes the disciple to seek an increasing intimacy with God that develops their spiritual life, so that it is not only what they see with their physical eyes but also what they see with their spiritual eyes and hear with their spiritual ears that enables them to do God's work.

Elisha's servant looked out from the walls of the city of Dothan and saw the army of the King of Syria surrounding the city. In despair he told the prophet the news. Elisha, however, knew that the forces of God outnumbered the King's men. Elisha asked God to open the servant's eyes so that he could see the chariots of fire (2 Kgs. 6:8 – 23). This is no fairy story.

Corrie Ten Boom once described Faith as a 'Fantastic Adventure In Trusting Him'. That is the essence of serving God God's way.

Moses, trust Me!

Only God can give His servants a promise that their work will be successful, only He can know the future with any degree of certainty. The token, the assurance was that Moses and the children of Israel would indeed serve God on the very mountain on which this interview was being held. That is: God's plans for the children of Israel WOULD be accomplished without fail.

How could I have possibly realised, when challenged in 2001, that Derek would ask me in 2002 to write my thoughts on the book of Genesis and that the result of my writing would be broadcast around the world, as it has been; or that I would continue by writing this on the book of Exodus? That is the message God wanted to give me in 2001 when He challenged me with the question, "Do you trust Me?" "Don't try to think about what I want you to do or how you are going to accomplish it, just trust Me for every day." This is exactly the position Moses was in.

2. Thinking from a practical point of view, Moses asks for some identification, a name that he could give to his brethren as proof of whom he was serving. He was naturally aware that someone was bound to ask the question, "What is the name of this God who has sent you to us?"

In reply God gives him a name that describes Him completely. I AM THAT I AM. This name sets the Lord

God of Israel far above all other gods for it describes His self-existent, eternal nature; it declares the unity and spirituality of God, confirming the consistency of the historical record of God in His dealings with men. It does not limit God in any way; indeed, it says that He will be what He will be.

Abraham, Isaac and Jacob all experienced this Almighty, Divine spirituality throughout their lives. Indeed, they grew to depend on it so that at the end of their lives there was no doubt in their minds regarding the awesome nature and spiritual unity of God.

This name was to be the rallying point for Israel for it clearly stated that 'although you have had no evidence of Me during your lives as slaves, be assured that just as I was with your ancestors so I will demonstrate My powerful presence with you and WILL redeem you'. All they had to do was to see the salvation of their God, but the method by which that salvation was achieved must be left to Him. 'I will save you in the way I will save you.'

The use of the name Adonai at this point expresses the loving kindness and faithfulness of God, who has heard their cry of distress and makes known His ways of righteousness to them. The great and living God is about to reveal Himself through Moses; His care for them being made clear to them by His actions.

This act would be, and ever has been a memorial to a God who is known by a very large company of believers as a God who has manifested himself in His providential care of His people throughout the generations. There is never a time when He is not educating, punishing, guiding, encouraging, supporting, correcting, comforting and generally being involved in the lives of those who are prepared to believe in Him, and accept Him as the Lord of their lives.

He is ever awake to hear the cry of the oppressed and to make known His ways of righteousness to the children of men.

Moses was instructed to gather all the elders of Israel and tell them how God was going to take them out of Egypt to the Promised Land, a land flowing with milk and honey. They were to be told that they would not leave Egypt empty handed for the people of Egypt would give them generously all sorts of jewellery and precious things; tokens of friendship and repentance that would eventually be used to adorn and enrich the travelling sanctuary, the 'Tent of the Meeting'; something they could never have envisaged happening. For the people of Egypt this act of giving was a clear indication that the oppression came from the rulers of Egypt, not its citizens.

3. Moses doubted that the elders and the people would accept the message of freedom as being truly from God. Being cautious about some new message, especially one you desperately want to hear is a good thing. We are told to test the message and the messenger that both are of God. A worldly saying is "believe nothing you hear and only half you see". The problem with words is that, however compelling they are, they can be empty and powerless. The Bible teaches that the only way to be certain a prophecy is true is to see if it happens. For Moses the immediate support of the elders was crucial to his mission but he felt that they would find it difficult to believe him.

Before the burning bush Moses was being given proof through words uttered by Almighty God, words that spoke of the future as though it would certainly happen, words that were uttered with the sensation of God's presence and power. For Moses there was no doubting the genuineness of the experience. However, in the cold light of day and with the overriding sense of oppression in Egypt the people of Israel would tend to be far more cynical.

God's promise of surety to Moses that it was truly He who was speaking to him and that the task he was signing up to would succeed was also in the future, for he was promised that after he had led the people out of Egypt he would "... *serve God on this mountain ...*".

It is possible that the people had already suffered with false prophets and speculators. In their hour of desperation they would want some proof, some clear evidence that God was indeed the power behind Moses and his mission to free them from the tyrannical Egyptian rulers; make no mistake that Pharaoh, like many other dictators, could not have kept the whole nation of Israel under slavery without the full support of others.

From the point of view of the elders, they would need to be convinced that Moses was who he said he was before persuading the people to follow him.

As proof God gave Moses three signs that would

convince the elders that He had sent Moses to them:

A rod – Moses was first instructed to throw the rod (probably a shepherd's crook) he was carrying to the ground. As soon as it hit the ground it became a serpent. It is always dangerous to pick a serpent up by its tail because it has the ability to bite the hand that holds it. Moses ran from the snake, demonstrating just how real it was. When God instructed Moses to grab the snake by its tail he would have done so with considerable reluctance. But as soon as he did so it became a rod again.

Whether a rod or a serpent it was under the control of Moses through God's power. Through this sign God was saying to the leaders that ultimately all control belonged to Him.

Pharaoh used the serpent as a symbol of royal and divine power, but here we see evidence of God's mighty power, for He used it to punish Pharaoh and to allow the people he had enslaved to triumph over him and those who supported him.

What is so remarkable about this rod, later called the 'rod of God', is the uses to which it was put. Stretched over the Nile the water turned to blood, pointed at the Red Sea the waters were divided so that the people were able to cross on dry ground, smiting the rock water poured forth, held up high the battle against the Amalekites was won, it flowered to prove that Aaron was the chosen of God. A remarkable shepherd's staff.

Leprosy – a malignant, contagious and incurable disease, the worst form of which caused the skin to become glossy white and ulcerous. Anyone who contracted the disease was immediately sent out from the populated areas to survive as best they could until their death.

What was so miraculous about this sign was that Moses was not only able to contract the disease but cure it at will. Now you see it, now you don't. More compelling proof that God was with him.

"Take of the waters ..." Three is God's sign of perfection. (Those who oppose God consider three as the number of confusion).

God knew those who would be convinced by the first sign, those who would be convinced by the second sign and those who required just one more sign to provide that certainty they needed.

By being similar to the first plague, in this sign the elders would later see continuity in God's efforts to persuade Pharaoh to release His people. With the Nile being 'the source of Egypt's fertility' it was obviously worshipped with a deity, the Queen of the Nile, being the object of their worship. The purpose of the sign was to demonstrate God's ultimate control of the Nile and its fertility, and that any other object of their veneration was a myth and of no account. The God of Israel is the one true God who created all things and ultimately controls all things.

In spite of these three convincing signs and God's promise to be with him and guide him throughout his time as a leader of the people of Israel, Moses persisted in clinging to his 'feel-safe' sense of inadequacy.

For a man who had lost the self-confidence and self-assurance of his youth, the diplomatic and leadership role God had described needed someone of eloquent and convincing speech; a man who could, with a natural confidence, stand first before the elders of his people, then the people of Israel themselves before going to the ruler of Egypt and speak God's word with authority. But Moses did not, indeed could not, know that this was not God's way.

The excuses raised as a smoke-screen to try and divert God from commissioning him for this task were each counteracted until Moses realised that he was not going to succeed in deflecting God from having him accept the honour.

Considering the matter from Moses' point of view; it was a dubious honour, for in his mind he had no direct personal experience of this God, even though it was He who, without him realizing it, had organised his life thus far.

Having had plenty of time to think about his life and the time he was a prince in the household of Pharaoh, Moses could foresee all the problems he would encounter in trying to extricate his people from the dominance of the Egyptian royal family and the hard heartedness of the leaders.

Moses was left with no alternative but to accept the job of leader and was led by God into the most-high profile and productive part of his life. However, we must never lose sight of Moses' view of the situations, many of them highly dangerous and fraught with psychological and spiritual difficulties, in which he would find himself in the future. We must also ask ourselves, would we be prepared to trust God that far ourselves.

Realising that, for him, there was no way out of this commission, Moses went to his father-in-law to seek permission to leave his house and go with his wife and sons and return to his people in Egypt.

Confirming that those who had sought his life after the murder of the Egyptian were now dead, God impressed on Moses the importance of carrying out all His instructions, warning him that Pharaoh would resolutely resist the request for Israel to worship Him in the wilderness.

This whole process, however, was not just about the release of a small insignificant nation from the grip of a tyrant, but a nation that God describes for the first time as His first-born son *("Israel is My son, My first born")*. This establishes the fatherhood of God because if Israel is His first-born then God was to gain other children.

It is also important to realise just how important the nation of Israel was to be to God as His messenger, missionary race. All the promises He gave to that nation were given in perpetuity. Israel is still His first-born, even in the twenty-first century. He still loves them despite all that has gone on over the years since their slavery in Egypt. God remains faithful even if man does not.

True to His word God had Aaron meet Moses and lead him to the family home, a far cry from the sumptuous living that he had previously enjoyed in the royal palaces, but at least the knowledge of his crime was no longer frontpage news.

His first task was to persuade the leaders of the people to accept him as being the man sent by God who would lead the people out of slavery. Knowing that he was one of them (an Israelite), having the knowledge of royal protocol must have been a help in his acceptance by the leaders. But accept him or not, Moses was the man of God whom God had sent to deliver Israel.

The trial by plague that was about to erupt had at its heart a spiritual battle, for Satan had seized control of Egypt and was doing his best to wipe out the people of God by seeking to have all the male children killed and the people enslaved. The girls and women who would have been left would have been assimilated into the Egyptian nation. But the people of His servant Israel, who were chosen by God and were being allowed to grow and to be welded into a nation in Egypt, had stamina and the midwives found themselves party to the work of hiding the new born children from the Egyptian authorities or for the midwives being ignored by the Hebrew women when they gave birth so that the steady increase in the growth of the nation could not be stopped. This is a true sign that Satan has no power against God or His people.

It is in the crucible that pure metals are produced; it is through going out into the bush to hunt for game that young warriors are tested; it is through examinations that students are tested to see if they have understood the subject matter that they have been taught; it is through testing that God sees whether or not a believer is really ready to trust Him with their future. It was through the crucible of a Satan inspired leadership of Egypt that the new nation of Israel would be forged into a cohesive whole.

The initial plagues could be repeated by the magicians of the day who surrounded the king in his court. But then the power of God began to be felt and these wise men began to realise that they were up against a power they had not experienced before and their advice to the Pharaoh was to capitulate in the face of this seemingly all-powerful God. But Satan had far too much to lose and spurred his subject on to the end. All the gods worshipped by the Egyptians, from the sacred Nile to the various insects, were seen to be what they were, completely powerless for they were part of God's creation. (See Appendix C)

During this time the hardship of the labour required from the Hebrews was increased to the point where they were wondering if Moses was really for them or not. But they had entered on a path of progress that provided no alternative way and they were forced to trust that God knew what He was doing.

It has never been God's intention to cause His people to suffer. However, there were times, particularly when His people were in the Promised Land and still being rebellious, that He allowed things to happen to them such as going into exile or being subjected to invaders, to teach them the lesson that they can only live in peace and prosperity when they willingly worshipped Him and served Him faithfully as their Lord and their God.

But woe to the nations He used to punish His people if their treatment of them went far beyond what He had wanted them to do. The situation that arose in Egypt is just such a case for the Pharaoh took over command of them and enslaved them for his own purposes. That is why God, having rescued His people from the nation He had used to punish them, then punished that nation just to show them that they could take no credit for their expansionist activities with regard to the nation of Israel for He was the power to whom they had to account, not their non-gods or self-boasting.

It is important for us to realise that God also uses the times of difficulty that we, as individuals, are bound to experience from time to time to strengthen our faith in Him, because our faith needs to be proved through the trials and tribulations of life (1 Pet. 1). It is also true that our Lord warned us what was clearly evident in scripture, that there is a war going on between the God and the forces of darkness led by Satan. Those of the enemy camp, both spiritual and physical, adopt varying degrees of animosity towards the people of God from dislike to extremes of violence.

When God commissioned Paul as His servant, he was warned that he would have to suffer much from those opposed to the message he would be called upon to preach (Acts 9:16).

First Passover

In my previous work on Exodus[20] I wrote this:

The people were given strict and detailed instructions regarding the first Passover sacrifice with clear knowledge, since it was such a momentous event, that it was to be remembered by an annual celebration year after year in perpetuity. It was also made very clear that this first sacrifice of a lamb was to protect their first-born from the work of the angel of death whom God would send throughout the land and would finally lead to their release from captivity and oppression. Previously God had targeted the plagues at the Egyptian areas of the land thus protecting the Israelites. This time it was their task to protect themselves by acting in obedience to God's instructions.

❖ The time they were in was to be to them the first month of the Israelite religious year.

❖ Annually on the 10th day of this month each family was to obtain a lamb that was to be consumed three days later in the evening with nothing of the animal left over. Small families that could not consume a lamb in one sitting were to join with another family, or other families, and share a lamb; larger families would need more than one lamb.

---

[20] See my book God Rescues His People

❖ The lamb, of the sheep or the goats, was to be of one year old and a male (as for a burnt offering) without blemish, free from any defect (Malachi 1:6-8). The emphasis was that the lamb was symbolically innocent and free from sin.

❖ As the Israeli day was counted from 1800 hours to 1800 hours, the lamb for the Passover sacrifice was to be obtained on the 10th day but sacrificed on the 14th day which was three days later (10/11 [selection]-11/12 [day one]-12/13[day two]-13/14[day three].

❖ The lamb was to be killed by the head of the household at dusk, between three and five, and the blood painted on the lintel and doorposts of the houses in which the people ate the meal. It was called the Pascal or Passover lamb because at the sight of its blood the angel of death would pass over that house leaving the first-born alive. It is this saving of the first-born that led to the instruction that all first-born must be dedicated to God, the first-born children being bought back with an offering before God, just as Isaac was.

❖ The lamb was to be roasted, not boiled, because fire represented purification and sacrifice. It had to be completely consumed (Jn. 6:53 – 58), anything that was left had to be fully consumed by fire with nothing left over for scavenging animals or birds. It was also to be symbolic of Messiah's death, for the Cross represented the consuming fire of sacrifice. Jesus was totally consumed on it because of His death. Not a bone of the Pascal Lamb was to be broken for not a bone in the Messiah's body was broken, whereas the bones of the criminals crucified with Him were (Jn 19:31-37).

By eating the Passover Lamb, the people were taking unto themselves the salvation of God, there being no time to drain the carcass of all its blood. By eating the 'flesh' and 'blood' of the Messiah, His listeners were likewise taking into themselves who He was and the teaching He was giving to them. He was the living Word and Perfect Man who had come directly from God. He, although many did not realise it at the time, was central to their future life with God as the sacrifice for sin on the altar. Accept Him into their lives fully, as with their intake of food and drink, and they were assured of salvation and free to enjoy personal communion with God as a priest.

There are, however, two parts to the problem of sin; our intrinsic sinful nature, which causes us to set our hearts against God, and our personal sinful acts in which we personally rebel against God. From the first we must be delivered, and this is done by the blood of the Messiah not cleansing our hearts but cleansing our conscience from dead works, that is works made dead by the sinful nature within us. With regard to the second, the blood is for our atonement, or at-one-ment with God, and is for God to see. Our spirits cannot become regenerated within us except we open our hearts to God in such a way that He is able to deal with both types of sin.

This Passover sacrifice was a sin offering for the first-born of the Israelite nation and had to be repeated year on year. Christ's sacrifice, on the other hand, is a once only, never to be repeated sacrifice providing the repentant sinner with full cleansing even to their conscience. His sacrifice was, and is, for all those who believe and accept that they are sinners in need of a saviour and who want to be freed from the penalty of death, whether Jew or Gentile. The relationship between the sacrificing of the Passover lamb and the sacrificing of Christ on the cross is that they happened at exactly the same time in God's calendar of feasts the Jews were to follow, fulfilling John the baptiser's claim that Jesus was the Lamb of God; but the blood He shed on the cross was an all-sufficient sacrifice for the cleansing of all the sins of those who would confess their sins and seek God for cleansing. None are turned away. Salvation is available to all.

❖ Bitter herbs were to be eaten representing the bitterness of the Egyptian bondage.

❖ The people had to eat the first Passover meal fully dressed, with shoes on ready to start their journey at a moment's notice.

As Moses and Aaron began to instruct the congregation of the children of Israel, they became God's ambassadors to both Pharaoh and Israel. This change in their role signalled the end of one relationship and the beginning of a new one that would last until Moses' death.

By setting this festival as the first festival to be celebrated at the start of each religious year God was identifying the Passover experience:

❖ as the birth pangs of a new nation; a time when He, by His mighty power, separated them from the world (represented by Egypt) and its oppression in the form of sin (slavery). Israel would utter the cry of freedom on their release but the Egyptians would utter the cry of despair. The Passover was the culmination of years of hardship and grinding oppression. This was God in action; and for those who have come to faith through acceptance of the Son of Man, Jesus Christ, it is just as important to them symbolically as it is to the physical seed of those who finally left Egypt.

❖ with death as the basis of their freedom from the world and the cleansing of personal sin. The blood on the doorpost and lintel was only made available through the death of a lamb without blemish that died in place of the first-born. As they journeyed through the wilderness the people were required to continually sacrifice a lamb for an atonement of their personal sin; that was to restore their at-one-ment with God. This sacrifice for sin was to be repeated year after year until Christ's death on the cross, which represents the moment of our freedom from the oppression of the world. His is the once for all sacrifice that does not need to be repeated; for as we accept Jesus as our Passover sacrifice the Father sees the blood in relation to our sins and the angel of death (that is the second death) passes over us.

❖ with the gateway to the path that leads to the Promised Land. All those who accept Jesus Christ as Lord, whether Jew or Gentile, become members of the redeemed, the remnant of Israel. We no longer look, as those who were released from Egypt did, to the land of Canaan but to the New Jerusalem that God is preparing for us (Rev. 21:9-11; cf. Jn. 14:1 – 6).

❖ as the beginning of a nation that accepted Him as their King and God. All those who left Egypt were to celebrate this festival once a year without fail. But only those men who had been circumcised, and therefore identified as belonging to God, could take part. Slaves and servants were to be circumcised and guests who wanted to join in the celebrations also had to voluntarily be circumcised. This celebration was only for those who were born into the nation of Israel and had been circumcised by believing parents or who wanted to be part of this worshipping nation.

It is important to realise that although the physical mark of circumcision in fulfilment of the covenant was most important, even more important was the attitude of the mind and heart of the individual Israelite. Abraham received the covenant of circumcision because of his trust and faith in God. From an idolater, Abraham became the forerunner of all believers both Jew and Gentile and by turning to God and committing his life to God he became the example we are to follow. Jeremiah called upon his fellow countrymen to cause the physical circumcision to be reflected in the attitude of their hearts by believing and turning over their lives in covenant giving to the Living God (Jer. 4:4, see also Deut. 10:16).

Israel was not just a nation but also a religion, for it had been chosen by and was to believe in Elohim Adonai, the God of Abraham[21], Isaac and Jacob from whom they had descended. No other nation on earth can claim such a heritage; that is, to have been chosen by the creator of all things seen and unseen. To be a discipleship nation to the world is unique. Their whole way of life was to be bound up with the worship and service of God. And of all those not born an Israelite who have come into the faith in this same God, God expects nothing less. We should not live like those in Egypt who are of the world and slaves to it, but unto Him who has called us, just as Abraham did.

This celebration, this Passover festival would further single them out as the Lord's people, as unique, as though He had branded them with His mark on their forehead (Rev. 7:3; 22:4). It would also attract the attention of Satan and his spiritual and human followers. Pharaoh was by no means the first, and is certainly not the last, leader of a nation working to try to bring down and annihilate the nation of Israel and upset the plan of God, even to this very day.

The Passover celebrations that were to continue year after year were used to keep alive the memory of this event and how God had displayed His mighty power over Egypt (representing the world) and saved His people both from slavery of Egypt (the world) and from sin by demonstrating the powerless of men and the forces of darkness (Satan and his demonic forces that use men to do their work of opposing God) represented by Pharaoh and the wizards, sorcerers and the priests of the various gods that the Egyptians worshipped. In like manner the followers of the Jewish Messiah, Jesus Christ, who was recognised as such by more than 12 devout Jews, and the multitude that has come into the knowledge of His sacrifice through the work of God's Holy Spirit remember His death until He returns.

The sacrificing of the Passover Lamb was the most significant event in the history of the people of Israel! For the first time the symbol of a lamb without blemish, without spot, being sacrificed specifically for the saving of individuals was introduced as a required sin offering before God.

Previously it had been the patriarchs who had offered such sacrifices of worship to God; now it was incumbent on all members of the nation of

---

[21] Abraham is the father of all believers whether or not they are his physical descendants.

Israel to individually offer such sacrifices, the Passover lamb being the first occasion.

Uniquely, it was also the occasion for the blood of animals and humans to be elevated in the minds of the people to the position of Divine sacredness, that it is symbolic of God's gift of life to the individual, both human and animal. This is important because it was the shedding of blood before the Almighty God that brought about the forgiveness of sin, therefore it became central to the act of repentance before God by taking on a holy significance; for the people were to treat the blood of the animals and of humans with total respect, or the exalted and holy position of the sacrifice would be denigrated. This is why God's word to Noah is so important:

> *"But you shall not eat flesh with its life within it, that is, its blood."*
> *(Gen. 9:4)*

And in Leviticus is explained why the blood is so important in the worship of God:

> *For the life of the flesh is in the blood, and <u>I have given it to you upon the altar to make atonement for your souls</u>; for it is the blood that makes atonement for the soul.'*
> *Therefore, I said to the children of Israel, 'No one among you shall eat blood, nor shall any stranger who dwells among you eat blood.' (Lev. 17:11, 12)*

Blood is the life of the animal and the penalty of sin is death, therefore the only means of providing man with a means of being cleansed from his sin, and therefore guiltless before God, is for blood to be shed for him. It is this salvation that God would provide that was initially a temporary measure seen by using the blood of the lamb, but ultimately it was to be said, *"It is expedient that one man dies for the nation"* and that sacrifice would be provided by God Himself in the person of the Son of God.

There had to be the death of a perfect man, the representative of all mankind, for the sacrifice to be acceptable to God the Father so that *"all who call on the name of the Lord shall be saved"*. It is not the prerogative of the Jews to decide who should have access to this salvation provided by God Himself; nor are they able to decide the means of that salvation, only God is able to do that for after all He is the injured party and yet He is the one providing man with the way of salvation.

Indeed, as He is purity itself, He was the only one who could rescue the human race He had created from the death sentence He had imposed upon them.

The Training of a Nation

The full procedure for the sacrificing of the Passover Lamb is laid out and explained in my book "God Rescues His People" and had to be strictly obeyed. By daubing the blood from the sacrifice on the outside of the lintel and door posts and the people closing the door and eating the sacrifice within so that nothing was left, they were telling God that they were believers, although events during their travels in the wilderness suggested that the belief of some was somewhat suspect.

The act of sacrifice and eating the sacrifice described what was to happen in the future when the promised Messiah would give totally of Himself, an all-consuming sacrifice, for He died with nothing left of His life. But it also allowed God to bring death to all those families who did not believe in Him and were therefore of the household of Satan, with whom He was doing battle. Rich and poor, slave and free, all suffered if they were not of the people of Israel or those who had come to believe with them and had joined their company.

It was the first born who died, representing the opening of the womb for the first time and representing new life and a new beginning. Therefore, it was the first born of all animals and humans that had to be dedicated to God, because it was He who gave the increase.

Remember Rachel's plea to her husband Jacob for a son? His reply was that he was not God to give her a son. Consider Hannah who prayed in the temple for a son. Samuel was given in answer to that prayer. Then Hannah dedicated him to God for service in the Temple at the time of the high priest Eli (1 Sam. 1) as she had promised she would. And Samuel became the high priest and a great prophet of God. God is responsible for the increase.

By this drastic means in which God demonstrated His power over life itself, the Pharaoh was brought to his knees and finally gave Moses permission to lead the Hebrews out of the land. But why was his permission so important to God? Because in entering into the land Jacob allowed himself and his people to come under Pharaoh's authority and therefore, he would have needed Pharaoh's permission to leave. It was a legal matter which, as it turns out, provided God with the means of putting fear into the heart of the pagan nations in Canaan which would be put to the sword when Israel crossed the border to enter the Promised Land.

Many find the record of the slaughter of so many people in scripture abhorrent and the idea of war and occupying a land through wiping out the population totally alien to their understanding of a loving God. To put their minds at rest we need to go back to the fall of man.

Satan's purpose in persuading man to rebel against God was so that he could gain control over the whole of mankind and take over man's God given authority over the natural earth; in this way man would come under the authority of Satan not God and therefore would, after their physical death, enter a place totally absent of the love of God, and God Himself. Whereas all believers in the one True God, who are rebelling against Satan's authority in the earth and attracting his anger, will be with their loving creator God for eternity, experiencing the joy and peace of His presence.

Satan wants mankind to worship him and him alone. But those who are willing to do this are continuing the rebellion against the God who created them which began with Adam; therefore, they had become enemies of God and moreover have been rejected by Him! In the heavenly places, although not in heaven itself which is God's throne room and 'dwelling place' (don't forget that God is everywhere being of Himself omnipresent), there is a battle going on between the forces of God and those of Satan, a conflict that from time-to-time spills over into the physical creation, becoming evident in this world as Satan seeks to retain and strengthen his power over man and the physical creation. His ultimate aim is to usurp the throne of God, which He cannot succeed in doing because, like us, he is a created being. But that has not stopped him trying.

God wants to purify the earth of the rebellion, but those individuals who support Satan and his demonic forces, the angels who gave Satan their full support when he rebelled against God, are opposing Him, therefore He is removing them.

Let us not forget that the cost of sin and a sinful life is the second death, which is the death of man's spirit in hell, where God is not. All the people who followed pagan ways were on the side of those against God; it is such people as these who were removed prematurely from the earth during one of the many battles that took place, not only when Israel was taking over the Promised Land, but also during their time of living in the land.

They therefore reaped the consequences of their rebellion against the God who created them and to whom they should have owed allegiance. For the nation of Israel only went into the land when the sins of the Canaanite people had reached a degree of ripeness that was an abomination to God and had the potential of exporting that depth of depraved sinfulness to other parts of the then-known world. To God this was unacceptable. He had given them their chance to reach out to Him and they had rejected it.

The whole purpose of the chosen nation and people of Israel was, and still is, to be His representatives on earth. To them have been given all the holy writings of the prophets, also His own words which they received direct from His mouth on Mount Sinai and in this they have surely been very blessed. But in return they, both as a nation and as individuals, have the responsibility to be holy before Him; indeed, all who call on the name of the Lord must be in a right relationship with Him if they are to approach Him in prayer and worship.

The whole purpose of God's plan of salvation that we are discovering has been revealed to man was to prepare men to meet with Him, to get them into a right state of mind and heart through repentance and then through cleansing of blood and the renewed infilling of the Holy Spirit to allow them to communicate with God. Thus, ordinary men and women could approach God and speak with Him, having been made holy through the forgiveness of their sins (See Is. 6:5 – 7; Zech. 3:1 – 5).

The Exodus

The angel of death, or to put it another way the angel of judgement, sent from God took away the lives of the first-born of Egypt, those who were rebellious towards Him, removing from them the breath they had received at the time of creation, as was the breath of members of the animal kingdom, for He is the provider of life.

Pharaoh was distraught at losing his own flesh and blood and in the turmoil of the moment gave the signal for the entire Hebrew population to be released, with the instruction that they should be urgently removed from the country.

The Israelites, already dressed for a quick departure as they had been instructed to do by Moses, left their houses with all the goods they could carry and followed Moses away from the only home they had known into the unknown. However, God knew that Pharaoh would change his mind in the cold light of day and arranged for a confrontation to take place between Himself and the Pharaoh.

Realising that with no forced labour at his disposal, his future prosperity was in jeopardy, Pharaoh collected his forces and went after the fleeing Israelites determined to bring them back. The man was possessed with just one thought, that in spite of all that had happened he should not lose face by seemingly being defeated by a slave nation. But God protected His people by various natural phenomena being activated at the right moment and in such a way that Pharaoh was unable to get near the fleeing people. Yet those same natural phenomena were beneficial to the Hebrews. The pillar of cloud caused by an angel of God, provided light at night and an indication of God's presence during the daylight hours.

Many of the people (possibly Egyptians or other slaves) were merely going along with the crowd, doing what they were told to do. They had little concept of the power of God in relation to themselves even after the grand display of His powers during the plagues, although they were persuaded by the awesomeness and effect of the plagues to join the Hebrews.

When the people, knowing that Pharaoh and his forces were not far behind, suddenly came up against the Red Sea they panicked, loudly complaining to Moses that they had been brought to a dead end, a place where they would be slaughtered just as people of no faith or very little faith would do.

But God had everything in place for His people to be legally released from Egypt. It is at times of crisis that we need to trust God the most. God knew exactly what He was doing for He had brought the Pharaoh to the point of judgement using His people as the bait.

God commanded Moses to order the sea to part thus creating a dry path through the sea. We are not told what natural or supernatural event caused this to happen, although there has been much speculation about how this remarkable phenomenon occurred. With the Pharaoh fast catching up, the people were keen to hurry to cross over on dry land even though the walls of sea towered frighteningly above them on either side.

Directly they had crossed and the Egyptians, with Pharaoh at the head, started to cross the sea bed, which was no longer firm ground for the chariots and horses, God released the sea to flow normally and the Egyptians with their king died; drowned. This tragedy happened because Pharaoh was unable and unwilling to accept the supremacy of the God of Israel. In reality it was just another battle that God fought against his created opponent Satan that was played out in human affairs. But it was God's battle, for Satan wanted at all cost to stop the progress of God's plan of salvation through the nation of Israel.

Going through the sea on dry land was a defining moment for the people. By going through with this one act they were identified as being baptised with the baptism of Moses and from generation to generation the people of Israel were encouraged to recognise that by their forefathers going through this baptism they had also been through it because they were in the loins of their forebears. Their history is essential to all Israelites.

The testing of the people of the new nation is well documented in my previous work on Exodus[22]. Their testing was another way for God to not only cleanse the people from doubters and idol worshippers, but to also demonstrate to them His ability in every situation to provide them with all their needs and to guide them in such a way that they could be assured of His continuing presence and goodness towards them, and that He would allow them to serve Him by being His witnesses on earth.

Take the following incident as an example of their need to trust God:

The Israelites then moved on to Rephadim via the Wilderness of Sin, Dophkoh and Alush[23].

Once more the people became thirsty, but this time they were not faced with bitter water as at Marah but with no water at all. So they cried out to Moses and Aaron, the leaders they could see, *"Give us water that we may drink ..." (Ex. 17:2)* for they had little faith in God in spite of all the miracles He had performed for them. Moses challenged them, *"Why do you strive with me*

---

[22] God Rescues His People

[23] see Numbers or my book The Wilderness Training School

and why do you try the Lord who has thus far supplied all our needs?" After all Moses was also suffering from thirst and needed to drink, but his complete and unquestioning faith was in God, who would supply their needs in due time.

The example Abraham and Moses provided was that once they had trusted in Almighty God, experienced His loving care and committed themselves to His service, they set their minds on seeking and doing His will whatever situations they might meet. That is why Abraham was called God's friend and Moses was a person with whom He talked face to face. Indeed, that is why they were great men in God's service.

Most of the people were followers of others, not leaders, and except for a few, nor were they individuals of character who saw the example of Moses and decide to follow his example by committing themselves to the service of God as He directed them. They were truly like sheep with little to distinguish them from one another, buffeted by the general mood of the camp, following every wind of doctrine that was gossiped about at the time. Fortunately, there was always the remnant, those who have quietly but firmly followed God, setting their spiritual sights on God and who sought only to serve Him, however difficult the way.

These are dire and evil accusations (Ex. 17:3) against a God who had shown them such love and mercy; a God who had demonstrated His mighty power and released them from long-term slavery and then, in the wilderness, demonstrated His ability to supply all their needs from healing bitter water to providing them with flesh and bread to eat. In all the 40 years of their wanderings they would discover that their shoes never wore out. From the miracle of the Red Sea right up to that moment God had been with them and loved them and cared for them.

After all the effort and time given to rescuing them and supplying them with food as He led them through the wilderness with the promise that they would eventually reach a land flowing with milk and honey, what was the point of Him leading them to a place where not only was there no water but He was unable to provide them with water?

Would anyone have trusted Him after that? They were being tested to confirm their faith, but they wanted none of that. A cosy, safe life was more in tune with their mood.

The Israelites could not *see* where water could be found, therefore they believed water was not there to be found. Moses must have wandered all round Rephadim and Horeb as he looked after Jethro's sheep and he was unaware of any water supply being there. The reason that they were there at Rephadim was because God had led them there; therefore, there was a reason for them being there. Moses was not concerned. But the ferocity of the reaction of some of the people made him nervous because he thought they were near to stoning him.

God sometime brings us to the brink to check our trust in Him. We could, like the vociferous Israelites at Rephadim, only believe God when we can see a way forward. But that is not God's way. He asks that we have an implicit trust in His ability to supply all our needs even, or especially, when we can see no way forward. This is what many a wayward man and woman has found when in the depth of despair, they have cried out to God and he has rescued them from disaster and set them on a new path.

Naturally, when faced with a potentially dangerous situation Moses called on the Lord for an answer. Through experience Moses knew that God was with Him and would protect him from harm. Moses trusted God. *What shall I do for these people? They are almost ready to stone me*, pleaded Moses, frustrated at the blind obstinacy of the people.

God told Moses to take his rod and pass before the people posing the question, *Is God among us or not?* (or, *Can the Lord help us or not?*) but were otherwise powerless to hurt him because of God's unseen protection. God's instruction to Moses was, *Behold I will stand before you on the rock in Horeb; and you will strike the rock and there shall come water out of it to quench the people's thirst.* This was God's guarantee that there would be a result to satisfy the people's need.

Moses took with him the elders of the people and went to the rock in Horeb where God was present with him. This was a place that Moses knew well for he had seen the glory of the Lord there and had probably taken the flocks to it many times before in his role of shepherd. This time as leader of the flock of Israel He was to take the rod that had turned the Nile into blood and strike the rock with it. And as soon as Moses struck the rock, out flowed life-giving water, which then flowed down to the people waiting anxiously below in Rephadim. Moses did not know the water was there. It was as much a surprise to him as it was to the elders who were with him.

There are two clear attitudes illustrated here. On the one hand Moses trusted God knowing personally that, as He had directed him before, God would do so again and lead them to water in His own good time, thus 'all would be well'. Many of the people, on the other hand, did not fully trust God because they did not really know Him. They always looked to the immediate, to the one who led them, never remembering and never allowing their faith in God to be built up by past experiences.

It is essential that we take what we are considering to heart because we need to apply what we are learning to our own lives. From the calling of Abraham and his commitment to God, through the life of Isaac and the life of discovery of Jacob to his final spiritual state before God, the remarkable account of Joseph's life that brought his brothers into a new relationship with God and then the period of four hundred years which allowed the population of Israel to grow to form a nation to the remarkable, earth shattering events that led to the birth of Moses, his God directed training for the leadership of his people and the dramatic release from slavery of the

The Training of a Nation

fourth generation from the founding Patriarchs.

Our studies have led us through their initial training in the wilderness to learn to trust God until God directed them to the holy Mount Sinai for a meeting with Him there. This meeting that He organised with the chosen people (and they are still His chosen for God has not and will never abandon His people), is perhaps the most significant moment in their history, for in a moment God tied Himself irrevocably to those through whom a complete understanding of who the Creator God is, how we should approach Him and the development and fulfilment of His plan of salvation is revealed. No other nation or religious group can legitimately make such a claim.

The account of the gradual and systematic development of the nation of Israel, from the initial promises that a saviour of mankind would one day make His appearance and provide, at His own expense, a full and final means of salvation, to the fulfilment of that promise is so intertwined with the history of the nation of Israel that it cannot be separated.

The creator God who provides us with the Way of Salvation is the same God who chose Israel to be the only people though whom He would reveal Himself and to whom He entrusted his word. I am a believer through the word of God as it was delivered to His people. This book is the result of the development of my faith in this very same God through the guidance and inspiration I have received through the work of the Spirit of this same God, through reading and studying the Judeo/Judeo-Christian Bible.

It is important, particularly for Gentile believers, to remember that the disciples were all Jews, born and bred, and it was their realisation that Yeshua was the promised anointed one, through being with Him and listening to Him and seeing the miracles that He performed, that caused them to dedicate themselves to Him.

It was after His dramatic death, prophesied of old, that they received such power from on high that they were enabled to teach the word of God and perform miracles and have knowledge and other gifts, including writing about the Messiah's life and work. This could only have come from God.

The reason I refer to the Judeo/Judeo-Christian bible is that those who wrote the books that are included in what is referred to as the second testament are no less Jewish and no less inspired by God than those who wrote the books that are included in what is referred to as the first testament, for the name Christian came from men and was used to describe those who followed the teachings of the Messiah of Israel, the anointed one we call The Christ. Just as those who do not believe the first testament has any relevance today have no true relationship with the God who wrote it, so those who believe the second testament is a book filled with lies have the same problem of being totally out of touch with that same God.

Please consider this fact very carefully!

Israel Meets Their God at Sinai

Just as God commissioned Abram, Isaac and Jacob, so God needed to commission the new nation of Israel as His representatives in the earth so that they could teach the nations about Him as the Creator God who had chosen them.

It is reasonable that such a meeting and commissioning should be a dramatic event as this extract from God Rescues His People suggests:

Exodus Chapter 19

The people were instructed to prepare themselves for their meeting with a holy and righteous God by sanctifying themselves both outwardly and inwardly. The exceptional awesomeness of the occasion had to be impressed on them, for this rough congregation of people had up until that time only experienced God working, they had never had an audience with Him.

Over three days they were to free themselves of natural urges such as sexual activity and concentrate their minds on meeting a Holy God. They were to wash themselves and their clothes as an outward sign of purification.

God was making them aware of His supreme Holiness. If anyone should but touch the ground that was part of Mount Sinai they would be unable to stand the stress of the comparison between the mighty power of His Holiness and their sinful state. Such was, and is, the gulf that separates us from God. His supreme Holiness, Righteousness and Purity compared to our dirty sinful state.

At the previous meeting the congregation of Israel had with God, it was Moses who had relayed God's message to them. With one voice they had agreed to God's request that they serve him. "Now if you will hearken unto My voice and keep My commandments then you will be My own treasure from among all the peoples; for all the earth is Mine; and you will be unto Me a kingdom of priests and a holy nation", with the response, *"All that the Lord has spoken we will do".*

Now, three days on, with the people having prepared themselves to meet their God we have an altogether different scene because the very presence of God would inhabit the mountain. Because of this God wanted to protect His people from harm. The mere fact of touching the mountain inside the boundary God had instructed Moses to set around it would result in the death of the trespasser because the strain of sinfulness meeting that supreme purity and holiness would be too much of a shock to the human system. So, it is when God's presence has surrounded me my eyes run with tears because of the awesomeness of His love and holiness and my heart is enlarged with joyfulness at His glorious presence. In fact, words are so sterile when trying to describe the experience that it is difficult to pass on to others the amazing impact of a moment when God meets with someone, except to encourage them to seek Him so that they too can experience His presence.

This time the elements rang out a message of salutation to their creator. Dark clouds had accumulated to cover the mountain and much of the sky around it resounded with great peals of thunder and lightning ringing out, accompanied by earthquakes and fire of phenomenal and impressive grandeur shaking the earth beneath. It was an awesome enough sight because of the sheer scale and intensity of the environmental activity. Its purpose was to impress upon the people just who they were to meet with, and prevent them gazing on the unveiled majesty of God as His arrival was announced with the *"voice of a horn that was exceedingly loud"*.

The cloud that took up position on the mountain had become symbolic of the presence of God. What the people were witnessing at this moment was not the presence of an angel who represented God in the cloud that had led them through the wilderness thus far, but the presence of the Spirit of God Himself touching the mountain to cause the eruption of natural phenomena on such a vast scale. This was not the action of a mere man using devices to cause an illusion but the creation reacting to the presence of its Creator. It could not help itself.

The introduction of sin has done man a major disservice by dulling his spiritual senses, preventing him from fully appreciating the awesome holiness, purity, righteousness, love and mighty power of our God and creator. Far from being an asset to mankind as Satan suggested (Gen. 3:5), it has been an insidious despoiler of the true joy and happiness of the spirit as the Creator had intended. Had it not been for the likes of such people as Moses, who had a heart for God and someone God could use to reach out to man to influence him, we would be left in the grip of such unrestrained evil that the world in general and man in particular could not have survived.

No wonder the people trembled, being surrounded as they were by such a volume of noise and violent activity by the elements. It is most probable that many would have been reluctant to congregate on the exposed plain in front of the mountain, preferring to hide away in their tents, in spite of their leader's assurances that they were perfectly safe providing they kept out of the restricted area around the mountain on which the spirit of God had taken up temporary residence.

It was truly an awesome moment as the members of the new nation of Israel gathered before the God who had chosen them the smallest of the nations to be His own people, the God of all creation both Elohim and Adonai. He had personally come down to commission them; a people He was entrusting with His instructions for life for eternity.

Israel was to be the repository of knowledge from God from the beginning of the world to its end; from the creation of all that we see around us today (the understanding of which God gave to Moses), to the end of the world and the creation of a new heaven and a new earth (the vision of which God gave to the apostle John who was a true-born Israelite) as recorded in the book of Revelation[24].

With the mountain seemingly on fire, with billows of smoke surrounding the summit to hide the concentrated presence of God, and the mountain shaking as though it had become a volcanic eruption (Ex. 19:18), Moses was called to ascend the mountain into the presence of God. What is so surprising is that in spite of the ever-increasing sound of the horn (Shofar) along with all the other background noises Moses could hear God calling him; but that is what God is able to do through the noise and distractions that we experience in this life, God is able to break through and speak to our hearts and move us to seek Him. For those wishing to rationalise this event the mountain had obviously not become a volcano or else Moses could not have ascended it, but it was reacting to the presence of God.

God's concern for the safety of the people is clearly evident in His instruction to Moses when He told him to emphasise to the people the penalty incurred if any one touched the mountain. Even the priests, who had the privilege of access to God, were required to be fully and ceremonially sanctified for this special and awesome occasion. God was insistent, despite Moses' protestations; the people must be in no doubt whatsoever, especially the headstrong and daring, about the penalty for touching the mountain.

Once again it was the sheer scale of the activity of the natural elements acting in concert that announced the presence of the Creator God. The people were at that time ignorant of the considerable scale of the universe that we know today. They were ignorant of the true size of the earth and its relatively miniscule size compared to the surrounding universe that we are aware of today. But the knowledge they acquired as witnesses during their release from Egypt and their meeting with God on that day made them far more aware of the unique Majesty and unconfined and unrestricted Power of God than we have today.

---

[24] See my book Seeing Into The Future : Understanding the Revelation of John

The Training of a Nation

For many who still could not fully understand what was happening to them, because their focus was on day to day living, this was a traumatic time. To those with a greater desire to experience things that were greater than this world could provide with all its upheaval and the rule of evil and uncaring men, those who were prepared to try to understand the events as they unfolded and learned from what the message God had given to them through Moses was telling them, this was an experience of the Divine that excited them, however awesome and frightening the experience was to them at that time.

6 NEW LIFE BEFORE GOD

"See, I have set before you today
The choice between life and good
Death and evil ...
To choose life you shall love the Lord your God,
Obey His voice and cling to Him for He is your Life
And the length of your days."
(See Deut. 30:15 – 20)

"Trust in the Lord with all your heart,
And lean not on your own understanding,
But in all your ways acknowledge Him,
As your God and the Authority in your life;
For it is He who shall direct your paths,
In the way of Life and spiritual prosperity.
(See Prov. 3:5, 6)

Hearing God's Voice

U p to this point God spoke to the people through Moses. Now it was time for them to all hear His voice, and for Him to set out the basic principles they must follow for their daily living in His service. Many of them did not realise they were in an incredibly privileged position by being the chosen of God; but we, who have met with God and experienced His immediate love and concern for us certainly do.

The people of the nations around them would remain in their sin and their societies would gradually descend into decadence and ultimately be eternally separated from God. Yet it was this God, the nation of Israel was meeting on the mountain, who could save them and gift to them eternal life. It was, therefore, to be the responsibility of Israel to enlighten the surrounding nations by example and education as the Lord gave them the opportunity and ability.

Their call to holy living was the first step in a remarkable life of eternal hope, if only they would take their eyes off the things of the world, with all its distractions and enslavements, and concentrate on Him and their relationship with Him. In so doing their own lives would become vibrant, even in the most difficult of circumstances, and full of hope. The following is an extract from 'God Rescues His People':

The Founding Principles for Holy Living

In Exodus 20 God immediately establishes who He is:

> *"I Am the Lord thy God, who brought you out of the land of Egypt, out of the house of bondage."*

This is a pregnant statement that should have brought back memories of all that had happened to the people from the time Moses appeared before them in Egypt, to the time they reached the other side of the Red Sea, and then during their wilderness wanderings. There will always be those who will not have, could not have, the mental capacity to understand the spiritual implications of all that had gone on, but they should have accepted what they saw with their eyes, and heard with their ears, about the battle between Moses and Pharaoh, also accepting the obvious fact that Moses was not acting on his own (Ps. 78; cf. Jn 8:47; 10:25-29, 38).

By speaking to the whole congregation of Israel personally, God wanted to impress upon them that:

1. He was eternal, *"I AM the Lord ..."*, and therefore available not just for those present but for those to be born, generation after generation, both Israelite and those Gentiles who had and would come to faith in the one true and eternal God.

2. He was *"... thy God ..."*, that is He wanted to engage with not just the nation of Israel as a whole but with each and every person present. But He was not only the God of the generations represented before Him at that moment but all those who would be born to them. This has been demonstrated throughout the life of recorded scripture and into the present day by God speaking to gatherings and to individuals through angels and through His Holy Spirit to commission, direct, inform and encourage them. And most of all He proved to them that He was all they needed.

3. He was their deliverer *"... who brought them out of the land of Egypt, out of the house of bondage"* who needed no other helper. What more proof would the nation need than the epic events that led to their release and freedom?

4. He, that is this singularly all-powerful God, had a special love for the people He had chosen and wanted to be intimately involved in their daily lives and future destiny. By saying, *"You will have no other gods before Me"*, He set before them the

reasonable and moral claim He had on their lives and the lives of future generations who would now be free-born because of what He had done. Had He not been on their side they would have died out as a people in Egypt without a future or hope (Consider Ezra esp. chs 9-10).

He was their benefactor who had redeemed them, becoming the foundation of their future life, not by reason of that act of redemption alone, but also by His ability to provide for them when all seemed lost. Therefore, how could there be any other god before Him? Especially one so exalted yet one who wanted each and every one of them to acknowledge Him as 'my God'. This, surely, was the beginning of a new and incredible relationship. And what is more, this unique one-to-one relationship was to be available not just to those present but also to their children and to their children's children into eternity. The Almighty Creator God is my God; being both a personal and national God. This and this alone is why Israelis, and those born into the spiritual Israel by virtue of their total allegiance to the Jewish Messiah Yeshua, are unique amongst the nations of the world, and why Satan wants to destroy them.

God's covenant with Abraham was unique in its day. There is no doubt that when he was still Abram and surrounded by the worship of pagan gods, he had a heart searching for the truth for it was only in that state that God was able to speak to him. God, as we are well aware from all that I have written so far, speaks with us Spirit to spirit (Jn. 4:24). By the time God made the covenant with Abraham, the physical sign of which was circumcision, Abraham had been tested and his faith was counted to him as righteousness which had to mean his spiritual awareness of God was extremely high. In the time of Moses, it was Moses alone who was spiritually attuned to God, the majority of the people preferred to hear God speak to them through Moses rather than directly which had to mean their spiritual life was extremely meagre if not dead, being aware of God but not spiritually alive to Him. Moses wanted to inspire individuals to reach out to God themselves by being circumcised of heart (Deut. 10:12 – 11:9) rather than relying on him for he realised that he would not be around forever.

This is why he wanted them to enhance the new covenant of the Law by encouraging them to allow the head-knowledge of the Law to become heart-knowledge; the heart being considered the centre of the will and intellect, to be circumcised of the heart meant that the individual was applying the mental knowledge (what he had experienced through hearing, seeing, touching, tasting, such as the manna) to the will and intellect, thus making it part of his life. This is what our Lord meant when He told those around Him to eat His flesh and drink His blood, not in a physical cannibalistic sense but a spiritual sense (Jn. 6:53 – 58, cf. Jn. 1:1 – 5, 10 – 13).

From the founder of the Hebrew race to the founder of the new, spiritual Israel to whose coming Abraham looked forward with rejoicing (Jn. 8:56) the message was spiritual, the life of the flesh was to be dominated by it so that true believers would not be led into temptation but be trained in the things of God, and fed by the words of God (Matt. 4:4) which are spiritual food.

It must be realised that this is the only sure faith-based belief in God, purely on account of it being a relationship between two living persons, that is between God and each descendent of the first created man and woman who wants to enter into a relationship with Him. And faith is foundational to our relationship with God for it is not merely belief in God but a God inspired total trust in and commitment to God that reflects in the way we live our lives (Heb. 11:4 – 12; Jms. 14 – 26).

If we do not trust God by living our lives as God instructs us to live (particularly in the first and second commandments) and doing things as we are led by the Holy Spirit to do, thus putting what we believe into practice as those mentioned in the Hebrews reference did, then we have no faith and the belief that we think we have is of no practical advantage whatsoever. It certainly will not enable us to draw close to God, nor obtain a lasting salvation.

5. Abraham, Isaac and Jacob had all worshipped God, although not one of them had started out as true believers. They came to believe in Him through an event, an experience in their lives that convinced them of the living reality of God and His desire to enter into a relationship with them. As they grew in faith a relationship developed between them and this amazing God who proved time and time again to be able to do anything and to whom nothing was impossible.

The relationship became a marriage; such was the love and devotion that developed between them. Joseph, having grown up with the knowledge of his father Jacob's rock-solid faith, had a head start in developing his own relationship with God, but still had that faith tested to an extreme through the activities of his non-believing brothers, and his experiences in Egypt before his elevation to supreme command.

You shall not make for yourself a graven image

What could graven images have done to enhance that marriage between each of the Patriarchs and their God? God is a spirit and unseeable and unsearchable but renowned for His love. As soon as an image is made the focus of attention is immediately transferred to that image and away from God. It is a distraction. Therefore, the purity of the human-to-God relationship is broken by a distraction that is in itself completely impotent and potentially dangerous, especially to the young in faith and new believers.

nor any manner of likeness, of anything that is in the heavens above, or that is in the earth beneath, or that is in the sea. The nations around them had all manner of images of things that God had created. What we need to ask ourselves, however, is this, "Were any of these creatures more intelligent than man?" Did any one of them lead the worshippers to the creator? Was Pharaoh, a mere man who was worshipped as a god, greater than the Lord God of Israel? The death of Pharaoh would suggest otherwise. The plagues stand out, announcing clearly, succinctly, that no created thing, living or inanimate is greater than the God who created them out of nothing.

If the universe is God's throne and the earth His footstool (Is. 66:1-2) what would be the practical advantage of an image, whatever it represented? God had shown even by that time that He was looking for those who would worship Him in spirit and in truth (Jn. 4:24). That is the foundation of true worship.

6.   He was not jealous in the normal sense of the word; rather this jealousy can be interpreted as "the justified indignation of a person who has been emotionally injured through the actions of another".

God had showered the Israelis with love and salvation, with a depth of devotional love no human could offer. They were the 'apple of His eye', His chosen vessels, nurtured, transformed and trained from Abram's first call. To be focused on Him, the three founding Patriarchs found that they needed to search for a holiness of mind and character like His, faith and everyday life being bound inseparably together as one single entity. Joseph had this holiness from an early age, which attracted the anger and hatred of his brothers who did not. What Joseph's early life reveals is just how man under the influence of his fallen nature reacts to those who belong to and have much of the nature of God within them that is able to shine and not be hidden (Matt. 5:14-15).

Just as Joseph's life shows us a vision of the Messiah's life amongst His people in attracting jealousy and envy, which so often culminated in violence, it also provides us with a vision of how people, even those in the Christian Church, will react to those who have the imprint of the image of God in their lives in these latter days, before the second coming of the Messiah. Cruelty, impure thoughts and actions (according to God's purity of thought and action), vice and all manner of evil, all these combined to grieve the heart of God.

God had brought Israel to this place to bestow on them the accolade of recipients and guardians of His Holy Word to mankind. They, above all people, needed to follow the example of Abraham, Isaac and Jacob and also Moses in dedicating their lives to Him who had called them to Himself to follow, serve and worship Him, with a singleness of mind and heart, just as Joseph had done.

For the people of today it is clear that such a dedication of life itself will attract opposition both from Satan and his demonic forces and from fellow human beings; even from those of their own family and within the church who do not see or realise what is truth, even though they have the scriptures available to them that provide all the instruction they need to seek Him and find Him for themselves (Jn 5:39). Soon will come the spirit of the anti-Christ and matters will get worse(1 Jn 2:18-23).

7.   When *visiting the sins of the fathers upon the third and fourth generation of them that hate Him* God was not implying that this is what He would do, but making known His understanding of the fallen nature of man, for he knew how children would be influenced by their parents, just as He did not give Pharaoh a hard heart but knew that this would be Pharaoh's state of mind without His purifying influence being received by him.

What must be made clear is that God does not force anyone to seek Him, let alone love Him, and neither does He cause someone to hate Him. Everyone must make up their own mind about their relationship with God and whether to trust Him or oppose Him. What God, knowing the heart of an individual, does do, and this is particularly relevant in the case of the Pharaoh at the time of Moses, is to use him to achieve His eternal ends. God wanted to release His people from their state of slavery in Egypt and to legally rid them of their position of being under Pharaoh's authority. With the rebellious Pharaoh seeking to return the people to slavery, he unwittingly entered into the trap God had laid for Him which is the route of His people's escape.

If a child is brought up in an atmosphere of sin and degradation then, because of the matter of interdependence and role modelling, the chances are that child will acquire the ways of its parents, although this will depend on the nature of the child being accommodating to that way of life. Just as Jacob's sons mostly followed another path, it is inevitable that offspring will go their own way, just like Esau and Jacob, in spite of the teaching of their parents, be it good or bad.

As far as scripture is concerned, Ezekiel makes the point that the person who sins shall be punished, not the parents or the children of that person (Ez. 18:20). Further, in the administration of justice, the scripture makes it abundantly clear that the fathers shall not be punished for sins of the children, nor the children for the sins of the fathers, but every man shall be punished for his own sins (Deut. 24:16).

8.   The enormity of His love, *showing mercy unto the thousandth generation* is far, far greater than the short-term penalty of the sins of the fathers being visited on their children. The whole Bible makes it abundantly clear that God would have no one die, but has continually provided a way of escape, first through the blood of an animal and finally through the blood of His Son Yeshua.

The history of mankind in general and of the Israelites in particular is well stocked with examples of how children have been influenced by their evil parent, yet a few generations later appears one who seeks after the way of truth (2 Kgs 11-13).

9.   By taking His name in vain, *You shall not take the name of the Lord your God in vain* people would devalue not only His great Name in their own minds, but also the special nature

of the relationship God wanted them to have with Him. As God is Holy, so His Name is also Holy.

This commandment was important because of its affect not only on the individual but also on fellow Israelites and the unsaved of other nations. It was directed at the taking of false or flippant oaths, or using that Name that is higher than any other name in casual, or indeed, degraded conversation such as, "O for G's sake". What is the value of using the phrase, "O for C's sake", towards those being told about the salvation God is offering through a living person? There is none. And the use of the Name of either the Father or the Son, or indeed of the Holy Spirit, must be respectful at all times so that others will know that to the speaker God is to be respected and honoured at all times; *You are My witnesses.*

Moreover, we are told there is a sin unto death for which there can be no salvation (that is an unpardonable sin). This sin is a rebellion against the person and work of the Holy Spirit. Why? Because it is He alone who is able to witness to a person within themselves, even to their mind and spiritual selves, and lead them into an understanding of who Jesus is and what He did on the cross, thereby stimulating a desire to love and worship God through the Messiah Jesus Christ (Yeshua). He is the final chance of salvation. Reject Him and a person rejects all chance of salvation.

Take for instance the case of a young lady engaged to be married. She went to the pastor and admitted to having had a sexual relationship with another man. There was no feeling of guilt or shame. Until, that is, the pastor, with her permission, laid hands on her and prayed over her using a Holy Spirit given language (more commonly known in the Christian Church as 'tongues'). Suddenly the young lady felt convicted and burst into tears. Only then was she in a fit state to ask God for forgiveness and with many tears asked her fiancé's forgiveness. The Holy Spirit of the living God is an essential part of our armoury against satanic attacks and just plain temptation. Without the Holy Spirit we are sunk!

What is more God will not leave those who profane His Name guiltless or unpunished, but will protect His great name:

*"Then you shall know that I am the Lord, when I have dealt with
you for My Name's sake, not according to your wicked ways nor
according to your corrupt doings, O house of Israel," says the Lord.
(Ez. 20:44.)*

Truth builds trust and a sense of well-being and
belonging, and gives birth to honesty and justice; whereas
perjury is for the destroyers of human society, for it breeds
fear and uncertainty. For a man believed to be honest,
perjury destroys all respect he may have previously attracted
to himself.

However, there have been times when God has done
something to help the ailing Israelis, not because they had
become especially holy or righteous, but purely for His
great Name's sake and to protect His plan for man's
complete salvation. Similarly, He has also caused them to
overcome obstacles and problems to safeguard His great
Name.

10.   The Sabbath (Hebrew Shabbat means to desist from work),
a day of rest, is part of God's grand design. Six "days[25]"
God laboured on the creation of the heavens and the earth
and on the seventh He rested. By using the word
'remember' it is plain that the seventh day was already
prescribed as a day of rest. By saying to them 'remember
the Sabbath day, to keep it holy' God wanted to impress
upon them that this day of rest was, as His gift to them, to
be a time of concentrating their minds on Him, of
refreshing their knowledge and belief in Him.

It was to be a God-Centred Day with readings from the
scriptures. It is the Word of God that keeps us close to
Him. Neglect that Word and the maintenance of a personal
faith is put at risk, for it is through the prayerful reading of
that Word that we learn of Him and from Him; it also
provides us with a continuing sense of His awesomeness
and ability to provide for our every need, rescuing us from
danger.

The Lord is my shepherd I shall not want.
He makes me lie in green pastures
He restores my soul.
In the valley of the shadow of death

---

[25] Not 24 hour days as we know them (see Appendix B).

I shall fear no evil
For You are with me
Your rod and staff are there to guide me.
(Ps. 23)
Your word is a lamp to my feet
And a light to my path.
(Ps. 119:105)

For the believer, hind-sight is a marvellous thing, because by being in a calm reflective mood and with our minds focused on God it is possible to allow Him to come into our thoughts and fill our hearts with His love; for it is when we are in such a meditative state that God can show us how He has been influencing our lives in the past, and in some cases what He intends to do in our lives in the future. This has nothing whatsoever to do with Transcendental Meditation which is not of God.

Everyone needs a day of rest. By setting aside one day of the week when little is done other than speaking about spiritual things and worshipping God, both as individuals and collectively, God's rule and the effectiveness of that rule within the family and in the community is enhanced. God's originally appointed time of the week was from Friday evening to Saturday evening (1800 – 0600), the Jewish Sabbath, which was part of the covenant requirement God put on Israel. From the last day of the week, after the resurrection of the Messiah the day of rest and worship was changed to the first day of the week, representing a new beginning. The old has passed the new relationship with God has begun.

The anger of the Jews, initially including Paul, displayed by the religious leaders to the active fanatics, over the appearance and the growth of the Way following the resurrection and ascension of the Messiah and the filling of the disciples with the Holy Spirit which emboldened them to preach the good news (Acts 4:17; 5:33 – 42; 8:1 - 3; 9:1 – 9; 12:1 – 3), permeated throughout the Roman Empire causing the disciples and other Christian (Acts 11:2) preachers many problems (also Acts 19:23 – 30) and resulted in Paul, whom God caused to be born a Roman citizen, to be imprisoned (Acts 21:29 – 22:26).

This animosity towards the Gospel of Jesus Christ, Messiah of the Jews, caused God to open up the way for the message of Salvation to spread out to the Gentile nations (Acts 10) and gradually the dominance of the Jews declined. This did not mean that the place of the Jews in God's order of nations changed, only that they were set aside for a time. Paul, an Israelite, born of the tribe of Benjamin (Acts 11:1), pointed out to the Roman believers that it was to Israel that God gave all the instructions concerning His plan of salvation desiring that they should be the vehicle by which He would reach out to all the people of the world and draw all men to Himself.

He had never rejected them for at the time of Queen Jezebel, when the worship of His name was forbidden, God had retained for Himself not only the services of Obadiah a servant of Ahab, but he had helped feed 100 prophets (1 Kngs. 18:7 – 16) and when Elijah went to meet with God, he was told that there were 7,000 who had not bowed the knee to Baal nor kissed him (1 Kngs. 19:18; cf. Ro. 11:2 – 10).

Just because those born of the flesh into Israel thought they had ownership of God's grace and favour, which attitude corrupted the ministry of Israel, there were still those who were chosen of God and still obedient to God.

During this time of the dominance of the Gentiles, it is essential that those who have come to believe in the Messiah of Israel, who were not born into physical Israel, do not demean the position of God's chosen people, for as Paul says, we are but branches from a wild olive tree that have been grafted onto the God cultivated olive tree that is Israel, from the sapling of Abraham which has God at its root, which is still alive today minus those who have rejected the truth of God (Ro. 11). But that does not mean it will be like that forever, for Zechariah tells us that at some time God will pour on the House of David and on Jerusalem (effectively God's chosen nation of Israel) the Spirit of grace and supplication so that they will look upon Me (the Messiah) whom they pierced and realise what happened all those years ago and mourn for the way their forebears murdered Him, piercing His side to ensure He was physically dead, and grieve for Him as though He were their only son, their first born (this will be grieving of the deepest type). Paul never got over the fact that he persecuted the young church which was made up mostly of Jews.

155

This is why I believe it is such a considerable privilege for me to have been welcomed as a brother by two true born Jews who have met with their Messiah and are now His disciples; for I am very conscious of God's grace that has allowed me to be grafted into Israel, an adopted son. As Paul says, there will come a time, prophesied by Zechariah, when Israel will believe and there will be a movement of God's Holy Spirit within the Israeli centred revived Church that will be extraordinarily exciting and fulfilling and powerful.

The emergence of Gentile leaders led to a gradual moving away from the teaching of the Jewish scriptures. Although the letters of Paul and other disciples were read avidly, along with the original gospels and other Christian writings of the time, there arose a growing lack of a strong Jewish influence and understanding of the Hebraic text. Not only did this reduce the Jewishness of the new writings that were to make up what we know as the New Testament but the Gentile dominance also allowed the introduction of erroneous teaching, including the idea that the Church had replaced the Israelites as God's chosen people (known as replacement theology). There was always the problem of deviance even amongst Jewish believers some of whom tried to keep alive the old Jewish teaching such as the need for circumcision which was no longer relevant because of the gift of life through Christ Jesus (Gal. 3:1 – 14).

Today's modern Church has, just like Israel throughout its history, strayed from God, and the stringent sacredness of the Sabbath has all but disappeared, a day that has changed to our Sunday, the first day of the week for that was the day when the Messiah rose from the death introducing a new beginnig. It was the God who created us who, at the end of His work of creation, rested, although we can be encouraged by the fact that our God neither slumbers nor sleeps. In resting from His labours as creator He concluded that we needed one day of rest every seventh day so that we could spend time away from our normal work in meditation and worship, giving us time to concentrate on Him. The six days it took God to create the earth was not 6 x 24 hours but six stages with the seventh stage establishing the 24 hour day. (See Appendix B)

Once the 24 hour day was established the seventh stage which saw God resting could easily be translated into an earth day. All that was required was establishing a first day so that the seventh could then be calculated and set.

What is so important about the manner in which the Lord gave these instructions is that they were for all mankind. Although they were given to the Israelites first, it is interesting that these rules were also for anyone living with the Israelites, including servants and slaves. The fact that an Israeli could desist from work, but still get the work done by someone else doing it for him, made a nonsense of the day of rest; it also prevented the servant or slave joining in this act of worship, for the servant and the slave were, in God's eyes, of equal standing before Him.

The Messiah Yeshua died for all mankind, slave and free, and all those who believe will be of equal standing in His heavenly kingdom. It was also the responsibility of all Israelis to be an example to those of other religious beliefs around them for by that means some might be encouraged to come to faith in the one true God.

11.   The essence of the Sabbath is its emphasis on the family getting together to read the word and to worship their God. It was as a family that the Passover Meal was eaten; it was as a family that the Sabbath was celebrated; therefore, it is logical that God should require the upholding of the family by expecting the children to honour their parents who are given responsibility for them under God. This first tablet contained laws or rules of living that established the requirement of an honest piety towards God.

It is worth considering that initially, apart from the Pentateuch, the scriptures of the first testament as we know them were stories remembered by many people (they had excellent memories in those days). These accounts of events and teaching were passed down from one generation to the next. It was much later in their time in the Promised Land that the remembered word was written down. It is therefore a miracle that God caused the scriptures to be captured and written down for the Holy Spirit to use in the lives of individuals.

In *"Honouring your father and your mother"* (in Leviticus the child is instructed to, *"...fear his mother and his father..."*) it is important that this attitude towards parents extends beyond the grave so that their memory is preserved. Should the parent(s) batter the children and/or teach them to shun God then there is good reason for them to defy their parents, especially where ungodly parents try to dissuade the children from following the Lord. But they should still be respected as parents, however difficult that may be. By throwing a mantle over their father's shame Shem and Japheth showed their father respect and love, unwilling to gloat over him like Ham to degrade him in their own eyes.

What this commandment did was to establish the family as the foundation stone of Israeli society, the true basis of national performance and future prosperity. The scriptures say that in the latter days there will be a tendency towards the destruction of the family where children will report their parents to the authorities and parents their children (Matt. 10:21), if that is they are not already here. In those days, which are to come, Satan will seek to destroy the stability that God brought in with these commandments prior to Him establishing His rule in the earth and Satan being defeated.

Whereas the first tablet contained rules regarding the people's duties towards God, the second tablet contained men's duties toward their fellow men.

12. *"You shall not murder"* emphasises the infinite value of human life and reiterates what God says in Genesis, that man has been 'created in the image of God'. No man can create life. God not only created it but alone has the authority and power to take it away. On a spiritual level Jesus warns us that we should not fear him who can kill the body (Satan and those who serve him both spiritual and physical), but rather Him (God) who can kill both body and soul in hell, (Matt. 10:28) which means that the individual spirit resides in hell for eternity.

The only killing that is permitted is capital punishment (Ex. 21:12) legally imposed by an incorrupt judicial system (be it a judge, judge and jury or tribunal). It is, however, important to distinguish between wilful murder and accidental killing (Ex. 21:13; Deut. 19:4, 5) to save the involuntary slayer from the wrath of relatives and friends of the dead person. When Israel entered into the Promised Land and set up home there, God had them create haven cities for the involuntary slayer to run to for protection.

13. Marriage is a sacred covenant and is to be respected by those entering into that covenant, both husband and wife, and those who are related to them or friendly with them.

Not even suggestive speech or actions can be allowed to contaminate the purity of the relationship between a man and his wife. God set the agenda that a man should leave his parents, cleave to his wife and they shall become one flesh.

This is God's perfect design. It is the sanctity of this relationship, which is totally dependent on trust, on which God based not only the procreation of man but the building of a stable society, and it is this foundation of life that Satan is out to destroy. It is also the man's place to leave the authority of his parents and become the head of a new family (Gen. 2:24).

14. *"You shall not steal"* represents the stability of life. If a man acquires honest wealth by his industrious effort and intelligence then it should not be taken away from him by anyone else by stealth; that is the acquisition of property by dishonest and illegal means such as cheating, fraud, embezzlement or forgery, or by illegal confrontational means such as aggression. There are transactions that are strictly legal but do not possess a pure and honest motive according to God's understanding of purity and honesty. Any transaction that favours one party to a far greater degree than the other is not right in God's sight, and He is our ultimate judge.

This commandment must be viewed and observed in the light of God's holiness for God urges all His people to be holy even as He is holy. Paul made it very clear to the early church that as they had accepted the message of salvation through Jesus Christ they should be employed in useful work, and if they did not work to earn money, they could not eat (2 Thes. 3:12).

15. Everyone has the potential to do their neighbour harm, not only through the physical means accounted for in the previous three commandments, but also in a far more insidious way through word of mouth. In commanding that we must not bear false witness God is requiring the whole person to be honest and true in all that he says and does.

A rumour started by one person can spread like a cancer through a family, village, country and nation. Peoples have gone to war through rumours. Anti-Semitism, which has been used by Satan for centuries to bring grief to God's chosen nation, is as rife today as it ever was for the reasons expounded in this and my other volumes, but it was started through wrong teaching that has got out of hand. It was an accepted belief in some sections of the church for centuries (although now fortunately refuted) that the Jews were responsible for Christ's death and it has been pounced upon and used to considerable effect ever since.

Yet Jesus Himself said that He could call upon legions of angels to save Him, but as the Lamb of God whose duty was first to the house of Israel, He had come down to die not just for the house of Israel but for all mankind. Therefore, I am as guilty of the death of Christ upon the cross as anyone because He died for my sins and He rose to set me free. *"And if the Son sets us free then are we free indeed".* *(Jn 8:36)*

The charge that Jesus was not 'raised from the dead' but that His disciples had taken His body and claimed that He had risen from the dead was perpetrated by the Jewish authorities because they wanted to control events and not allow God to do His will in them. False statements that were cleverly sent out initially became rumours that were then believed as being fact which distorted the truth and the lie is believed, particularly amongst Jews, to this very day (consider Acts 5:35-38).

How can the Christian church be so presumptuous as to believe that God has selected a corrupted church led by men who use 'false witness' to support their cause in place of His beloved Israel? How can it pursue an ungodly agenda when its members, especially its clergy, purport to be servants of God through Christ Jesus? Jesus was specific when He said that salvation is of the Jews (Jn. 4:22). And there is no reference in all of scripture that God has changed His mind and deselected Israel as His chosen nation even though they are hard hearted and so many have rejected their Messiah.

The true Church of the Living God, established by the Messiah, is centred in Israel, for Israel is the foundation of the church, His first-born son. The foundation of the church (Eph. 2:20, 21) have been built upon the prophets and apostles with Christ as the corner stone are of the house of Israel. The church that is established in the world today is Gentile based although there are many Israelite believers (often referred to as Messianic believers) who are members of it.

The Gentile dominated church has, unfortunately, gone the way of Israel by losing sight of the God who is the source of their salvation, and more particularly the fact that Gentile believers have been grafted into the cultivated olive tree that represents the true, God fearing, Israel (consider the place of Israel in the mission of the Messiah – Matt. 15:21 – 28 particularly verse24).

We must be mindful of the fact that it was to the Jews that the Messiah came according to Old (First) Testament prophecy. It was Jews who made up the company of the disciples. The church was founded by Jews who passed the message on to the Gentiles when they were scattered throughout the known world by the persecution that came upon the young church, a persecution led in part by a zealous young 'Pharisee of the Pharisees' called Saul, until he met with the Saviour on the Damascus road.

Christ Jesus (Yeshua) is a Jew (He still lives with the Father) and The Cornerstone (Matt. 21:42; 1 Peter 2:6) of the church. Paul taught the new churches throughout Asia from the then-known scriptures, because the New (or second) Testament had yet to be written. Therefore, we can say that the Christian faith has its routes firmly embedded in Judaism, which is why I am writing about the book of Exodus and relating it to the books concerning the visit of the Messiah to His people when He came to sacrifice Himself for them and all people.

The leaders of the Jews at that time had considerable self-interest in remaining in control of the people, and stirred up the people to condemn the Son of the living God to death, although it was the High Priest of the day who, not realising the implication of what he was saying, spoke the words of God, when he said that it is expedient that one man should die for the nation (Jn 11:50-51). Selective use of the Word of the Living God will not help a person's cause when facing the judgement seat of the Messiah (Rev. 20:11-15).

On a personal level there have been many prisoners that I have visited as a prison visitor who have told me that what had hurt them most at their trials were the lies spoken by witnesses. These were sometimes members of their own family or close friends who, having sworn before God and those present in the court room to tell whole the truth, did quite the opposite. It is wrong before God, it is wrong before men, and it is not acceptable at any time. God says so!

But on a spiritual level people are bearing false witness of God, saying things about God, and teaching things about God that are not true. Such people are not only building up a case against themselves that will bar their way into paradise, but are leading others away from the truth (Matt. 15:14).

All who give witness to the things of God must be sure of what they are saying, or else they may be condemned; those that declare themselves to be teachers of the Word will be judged far more severely. I am very conscious of this as I write and spend much time in prayer asking God to prevent me writing anything that is incorrect.

16. Coveting things that someone else possesses is not healthy because it perverts the life of the covetous person. The potential for that person to break the other commandments regarding murder, adultery, stealing and bearing false witness is that much greater.

Although these commandments were delivered to the Israelites by God Himself whilst they were before Mount Sinai, surrounded by the sound of thunder and with barbs of lightening lighting up the sky, they are directed at all mankind. The whole object of selecting Israel and making them the custodians of the law was to make a people who were God-conscious, and to cause them to be an example of how God can change lives, to show people how much more fulfilling and purposeful life can be with God.

The nations around had degenerated into chaos and sexual deviance, totally against the original God-designed nature of man. However difficult the people of Israel found it to fulfil the observance of the laws of God, and the need to continually offer God sacrifices for sin, they were not, are not, the preserve of Israel, but delivered into Israel's safe keeping, as custodians, for passing on to the rest of humanity.

The Messiah, the only sinless man ever to have lived, came not to dispense with the Law of God but to fulfil it (Matt. 5:17). After all, the first commandment is for man to love God with all his heart, mind and soul and that law above all others must surely stand forever, for we must put our creator God foremost in our lives in order for us to get as close to Him as possible and secure our place with Him in His glory in heaven.

Unfortunately, however good we try to be it is impossible for individuals to abide by the law completely without disobeying it in either a major or minor detail. Paul delighted in the law of God (Ro. 7:22) but realised there were two conflicting laws within him. The first is the law of the flesh (Gal. 5:19 – 21), introduced when Adam rebelled against God and submitted himself and all mankind to Satan. This focuses on the things of the earth and the sexuality of the body.

The second is the law of the mind and the renewed nature which is the Holy Spirit regenerated God focused spirit within those who have been persuaded in their minds and have gained a heart belief in the one true God (Gal. 5:22, 23).

Paul found that within himself these two laws were trying to gain possession of him (Ro. 7:23) for although a regenerated man, because of what the Spirit of Christ had done within him, the fallen man of flesh, which remain in him until after his physical death, was constantly trying to regain control of his members. But Paul is able to rejoice because for those in Christ there is no condemnation.

But why?

Under the law any sin required a sacrifice at the temple. But the temple and the means of sacrifice had gone because the death of the Messiah made the temple and all its functions redundant. In its place is the temple that is Christ's body but added to that the Holy Spirit, who was released into the world at Christ's ascension, is able to work within us (we are temples of the Holy Spirit) and help us overcome, the blood of Christ being available to cleanse us from all unrighteousness.

This means that we should not willfully sin (Ro. 8). Paul recognised that this warring in his members would continue until he put off the corruptible body and put-on incorruption (1 Cor. 15:42 – 57). The law is unable to save us for flesh and blood cannot enter into the kingdom of God but those who have been made spiritually alive in Christ will be saved to the uttermost.

What this occasion did for the Israelites was to confirm them as God's chosen people[26] and brought into sharp focus the enormity of the responsibility of their position in the world. It was undoubtedly a frightening moment, but they were assured of their safety, yet they preferred the more clinical and feel-safe environment of Moses telling them what God wanted to tell them saying to Moses,

---

[26] The laws governing marriage within Israel is that becoming engaged is the first step towards marriage and is as legally binding as marriage. All true believers are therefore engaged to be married to God, but the full marriage ceremony will not occur until the marriage supper of the Lamb in heaven.

Joseph was engaged to be married to Mary. When he found out that she was pregnant he initially sought to quietly divorce her until God told him why she was pregnant.

Many times in the first testament God threatened to divorce Himself from Israel, but ultimately remained faithful to her, because she was central to His plan of salvation.

New Life Before God

You speak with us, and we will hear;
but let not God speak with us, lest we die.

What was the point of God killing them when they were central to His plan of salvation for the whole of mankind? But they did not realise that fact.

Such was their inability to believe in such a mighty God, probably because they had been brought up on a diet of ineffective idol worship that they preferred Moses to be their intermediary. But such a relationship does not last as long as a one-to-one relationship with God Himself. Moses had been with God before and had not died, so why, after all the assurances they had been given by God concerning their safety, should they? This was unbelief in action and revealed their lack of understanding and unwillingness to open up to the knowledge of God that would preserve them in the future.

Just how much of Moses' statement, *Fear not; for God is come to prove you, and that His fear may be before you to avert you from sinning,* the people believed or took to heart we cannot know for sure. But Moses was more and more comfortable with God for he *drew near into the thick darkness where God was,* or where the glory of God was, without protest.

It is that transition from *knowing of God,* which was the state the majority of the people were in, to *knowing God* personally which is the state they needed to be in, is so important for us to understand. For it is one thing to know of God through what people have told us and what we have read in the scriptures, but it is quite another to reach out to God, even in the darkness of our immediate situation, and seek a personal relationship with Him.

Such a change of relationship is only possible if we are prepared to believe not only that God wants a relationship with us personally but also that He will respond to any prayer we might make to Him asking Him into our hearts and lives to bring about that change.

This is the reason both Isaiah and Jeremiah pleaded with the Israelites to enter into a personal covenant with God. Circumcision was the outward sign (a symbol) of the covenant God made with Abraham and his chosen descendants through Isaac and Jacob. But to *circumcise your heart* (Deut. 10:16; Jer. 4:4; Ro. 2:28) they needed to seek a personal relationship with God (as experienced by Abraham and Moses), by asking Him to be their God and King and thereby enter into a personal commitment, a personal covenant with the God of Israel. By turning from their sin and obeying God's will, this new personal covenant would be a spiritual and more intimate covenant, on the lines of the relationship Adam had with God at first.

These rules for holy living are summed up in the declaration of Moses to his people:

"Hear, O Israel: The Lord our God is one!
You shall love the Lord your God with all your heart,
With all your soul, and with all your strength.
And these words which I command you today
*shall be **in your heart**"*
(Deut. 6:4 – 6; also Matt. 22:37 – 40).

This instruction to the people was not to be learned mechanically, but heard with the ears, understood by the mind and become their belief by entering their heart, the centre of the will and intellect. They should have within themselves a desire to obey it and to live a life that was in relationship with the God who wanted them to love Him so that they might experience His love for them in their daily lives and receive blessings from Him.

The Tabernacle – God's plan revealed

What is so important about the Tabernacle is that it reveals to us God's plan of salvation in physical form; from the curtain surrounding the courtyard to the sacredness of the Holy of Holies. What is more, God reveals His character by starting with the furniture in the holiest part of the tabernacle building, and ending with the gate in the outer curtain; whereas man must start at the gate, when starting out on his journey to discover God, and on the way learn how he can enter into a relationship with God through the various areas of the tabernacle complex. The more man progresses through the various sections of God's symbolic tabernacle complex on earth, the closer he gets to God.

Man sees only the outside of a person and then judges them according to his own thoughts and by what he sees them do. God looks at the inner man, into the person's heart to understand their motive for doing things, to understand the truth of their desired relationship with Him. This progressive revelation of the plan of the tabernacle complex also demonstrates to us how God is reaching out to man whilst at the same time guarding His supreme holiness and purity.

The supreme and exalted nature of this structure, which was to be spiritually represented in the body of one man (Jn. 2:19 – 22), is emphasised by the manner of the heavenly model, on which the earthly temple was to be based. This model was shown to Moses.

The glory of the Lord was like a consuming fire to the Israelites
In the cloud that covered the mountain top high above them.
On the seventh day of the sign of God's presence on the mountain,

The day God ordained as a day of rest
and a sign of the completion of His work,
He called to Moses from the midst of the cloud to meet with Him.
Moses was with God on the mountain top for forty days[27] and nights,
Sustained in the rarefied, colder atmosphere,
on the small hard rock area of the summit
by Almighty God.
(See Ex. 24:15 – 18)

It was within the cloud that Moses met with God who was to show him not a blue-print of the plans God had drawn up, but the pattern of the dwelling place God required to be replicated and placed at the centre of the life of the nation. Every part is related to God's plan of salvation, which is why He, through His Spirit, inspired the chosen artisans who designed and built the tabernacle.

To prevent an unauthorised structure being built certain measurements, which were vital for construction but not for significance, were not recorded; in this way God demonstrated that His plan of salvation was the only legitimate means by which man can be forgiven, and made righteous in order to become united with Him.

All the materials used for the structure had to be given as freewill offerings; men and women willingly giving of their substance to God for His work and purpose. Much of it was in fact obtained from the Egyptians before the night of their departure (Ex. 12:35, 36; 25:1 – 9; 35:1 – 29; see 1 Chron. 21:24). But with the call for the Israelites to give their offerings freely and with a willing heart (Ex.35:5) to Him, God also provided the inspiration and skills necessary for its design and construction (Ex. 35:30 – 36:7).

Thus, the Holy Spirit was engaged in the design and construction of this dwelling-place of God to ensure it accurately followed the pattern shown to Moses on the mountain, just as He was with the creation of the earth; this time inspiring and guiding those involved in its manufacture. Every detail had to be exactly as Moses had been shown on the mountain. This surely demonstrates the importance of this building to God and His message through it to man. It also tells us that when God commissions anyone to do something for Him, He will also provide the ability and inspiration to carry it through.

The Centrality of the Ark and Mercy Seat

Note that God starts by giving Moses instruction regarding the most sacred of all the items which was placed on its own in the Holy of Holies.

---

[27] Forty represents the divine order applied to earthly matters.

This is the point where heaven meets with man, for the Ark of the Covenant contained the fundamental principles of living a holy life and it was covered by the Mercy Seat by which God dispensed mercy to the sinner (Ex. 25:10). God ends with the altar of burnt offering in the courtyard and finally the gate through which a man first enters to begin his journey of salvation (Ex. 27:9).

The purpose of the Ark of the Covenant was to hold the tablets containing the ten foundational rules by which the Israelites were required to live by, and these tablets bore testimony to the covenant God had made with Israel, the supreme law. Those who willingly lived by these rules would be of the right mind and heart to meet with God.

The Ark of the Covenant was made of wood, which was of the earth, and covered in pure gold, which represented the purity of the glory of God surrounding and purifying what was of the earth; a meeting of earth and heaven being the agreement between God and the Israelites. It had four carrying rings attached to it; two rings each side, with two fitted carrying poles.

The Mercy Seat, which acted as the lid of the Ark and covered it exactly, was manufactured in pure solid gold, representative of deity, rather than being overlaid with gold, because mercy is God's work throughout; it represented God's willing demonstration of mercy to sinful man, inspired by His own supreme love for man. The cherubim stood at either end of the rectangular lid facing each other, with wingtips touching and faces looking down at the main part of the lid focusing through the gold of divine mercy to the commandments, which was the binding agreement between God and the people He had chosen.

The 'Mercy Seat' was not a seat in the generally accepted sense of the word for no one sat on it. But it was the resting place of God's love for His people and represented God's act of propitiation, His act of allowing appeasement, His conciliatory offer of the forgiveness of sins through the substitutional shedding of blood. The full forgiveness of sin was not to come until the sacrifice of Holy Lamb of God.

The two cherubim, representative of God's spiritual creation and emphasising His eternal spiritual state, have their wings covering the mercy seat emphasising the completeness of this act of mercy. The fact they face towards each other suggests inclusivity and agreement, and by them looking at the mercy seat suggests that it was the focus of their attention which pointed to God's focus on the salvation of man.

It was from between the spiritually representative cherubim, above the testimony God gave to the Children of Israel, that He would meet first with Aaron and then subsequent high priests, once each year, to give commandments to His representative people on the earth. Thus, the ark, with its mercy seat, was central to the relationship between the people and their God. The tablets held secure in the ark contained the law by which those who accepted the authority of God over them were to abide.

Such was the spiritual significance of this item of furniture that once it was made and installed in the Holy of Holies it was not to be seen by ordinary men, only those who were specially chosen as the servants of Almighty God were allowed to see it.

When the Israelites were instructed by God to break camp and move on it had to be covered with holy coverings by Aaron and his sons and their heirs ensuring no one else saw it (Num. 4).

The Ark also indicated the health of the nation. At the time of the high priest Eli and his sons, the people were being misdirected by the priests through the distortion they brought to the sacrificial ceremonies (1 Sam. 2:12 – 36). When the ark was captured by the Philistines, Eli and his sons died through the judgement of the God, because they disobeyed with seeming impunity His instructions regarding the activities which they were responsible for providing, that is the sacred services for the people.

Although the Israelites were concerned about the safety of the ark after it was captured, the Philistines themselves were to realise that the God it represented caused them considerable distress and demonstrated His power over the god statues of these warring people. The events surrounding the statue of their god Dagon when the ark was placed before it gave a graphic illustration of the powerlessness of their gods before the one true God. The priests of Dagon found the statue of their god prostrated before the ark. The problems experienced by the Philistines did not end until they sent the ark back on a cart (1 Sam. 6) with offerings to the God of Israel.

By the time of Jeremiah and the exile, the ark had disappeared without trace. This time however there was no recorded consequence for those who took it, or God caused it to disappear. From God's perspective it had come to the end of its useful life and, through Jeremiah, God told the people that no copy of it was to be made (Jer. 3:16). The purpose of the structure was initially to teach the people of the new nation of Israel the principles of the relationship God wanted to establish with His people. The ark and the mercy seat were symbolic, a physical teaching aid and not an end in itself.

The whole emphasis of God's teaching has always been on the dynamic personal relationship between a person and their God. It is a relationship where a believer cannot earn their salvation through religious observance, for it is a gift of God; the salvation God offers can only be obtained through the believer's commitment to entering into a permanent and loving relationship with God. It is a person to person living relationship, not a relationship that is restricted to religious ceremonial observance. That sort of ceremonial relationship is the prerogative of all the other religions of the world and the worship of non-gods, where what a person does, by their own efforts, in relation to their god is all important.

Having come to the end of its useful life, God allowed the ark with its mercy seat lid to disappear and, through His prophets, called for the commandments of God to reside, not physically in the Holy of Holies, but in the hearts of individuals. Ezekiel, commissioned by God as the watchman of Israel (Eze. 2, 3 esp. 3:17), was filled with the words of God that he might speak to his people which God called a 'rebellious nation' (Eze. 2:3).

Ezekiel speaks of God:

❖ In relation to Deut. 30:3 – 5 God foreknew that, although they would inhabit the land, they would not be perfect disciples but constantly rebelling, just as they were continually rebelling during their wandering in the wilderness. Therefore, there would be times when He had to punish them by allowing another nation to invade the country or take them into captivity, which is why Ezekiel finds himself the watchman to Israel whilst in captivity in Babylon.

The importance of what we are considering at this point is that God did not, will not ever, give up on His choice of the people of Israel to be His people. The message in Ezekiel 36 refers to the future, not just when they returned to their own land from Babylon when there was a purifying of themselves, particularly amongst the priests under Ezra[28].

Sprinkling water is taken from the law and relates to water being sprinkled on the ashes of a heifer (Nu. 19:9 – 18) for when Christ died, becoming a burnt offering, His earthly body (sacrifice) symbolically turned to ashes. His blood cleanses the conscience making the sinner truly deeply clean (He.9:13, 14; 10:22; cf. Jer.33:8; Eph. 5:26). By the sprinkling of water, they would be cleansed of their search for other objects of worship such as idols, which did happen to a greater extent after the captivity, so in this respect this prophecy was partly fulfilled.

❖ changing the heart of stone that was within them for a heart of flesh. A heart of stone is non-receptive for it was representative of the rebellious heart of an unbeliever, or a religious man — ceremonially observant but not having the submissive and open heart of a true believer before God. Consider the contrast between the disciples who saw because of their response to the

---

[28] The books of Ezra, Nehemiah and Haggai in particular give account of the cleansing and redirecting of the people that had returned to Jerusalem and the surrounding land after their time of punishment in exile. Not all the people returned to the land after seventy years of exile, only those truly dedicated to their land and to their God which was in itself a cleansing of the people.

Son of Man in whose company they rejoiced, and those of the people who could not see the Messiah before them because of the dullness of their hearts as identified in Matthew 13 esp. v16, cf. 14, 15.

A heart of flesh — not 'carnal' as that of an unbeliever, but 'spiritual' for it must be attuned to God — is given to man by God, but only when man responds by repenting of sin and turning away from a life of sin, by focusing on God alone, in order that he can obtain a new heart and new spirit that is fully God conscious (cf. Eze. 18:30 – 32; 36:26); therefore, the responsibility for obtaining this new heart is not exclusively the responsibility of either God or man for it is mutual. Certainly, man cannot make or receive the new heart on his own but is dependent upon the grace of God (Phil. 2:12 – 16; Eph. 2:1 – 10 esp. v8).

❖ through the introduction of His Holy Spirit within them they were more able to walk in His statutes and keep His judgements to do them (Eze. 36:26, 27). Although Ezekiel had undoubtedly been blest with the Holy Spirit who revealed to him the things of God and passed to him the words of God that he was to pass on to the people, the Holy Spirit had not been given universally as He was once the Messiah had ascended into heaven after His sacrifice for sin (Jn. 16:7).

This was, after all, the original purpose of the ark and its tablets of stone carrying the inscription of the Ten Commandments; they were not just to be learnt by heart but applied to their daily life. This is what true faith is all about.

It is important to see that God's plan of salvation was progressive for God knew that the sacrifices under the covenant of Moses on Mount Sinai were not sufficient to cleanse the inner man, but were a temporary means to an end until the fulfilment of the plan in the long-promised Messiah. This also allowed succeeding generations to be trained regarding their need to be focused on Him and to be obedient to His laws, laws which were designed to regulate their lives before Him (and this is also surely for our good).

At a time of turmoil, when God was judging them for their waywardness by sending them into exile in Babylon, God introduced to them the prospect of a New Covenant that would have a radical effect on the life of the nation of Israel. When they returned from exile there was a mass turning again to the worship in the temple which the Lord challenged them to rebuild (Hag. 1, 2 esp. 2:9 — Herod rebuilt it and the Messiah entered it which is why its future was to be glorious).

This seeking after God back in their own land brought about a change in them that the nations around them noticed — Jer. 33:8, 9; see also Nehemiah and Ezra. But the real change was to come. Unfortunately, when the Messiah introduced the new covenant at what we know as the last supper, the nation as a whole did not believe for the spiritual leaders rejected Him.

But that did not mean that they (Israel) were finally set aside for God still loved them, *for the gifts and the calling of God are irreversible* (Ro.11:29). But as the deliverer, the Messiah, *will come out of Zion and turn away ungodliness for Jacob* (Ro.11:26, 27; Is. 59:20, 21) it is clear the message of Zechariah (Zech. 12:10 – 14) regarding the realisation that their Messiah had come in Jesus Christ whom they killed would be fulfilled at some future time when the time of the Gentiles has been fulfilled (Ro.11:25).

This means that the turning of the nation to God in spirit and in truth has yet to come, but come it will. In the meantime, there are many in the house of Israel — along with the disciples and Paul and a multitude of other followers — who have come to realise that their Messiah came in Jesus and, although abused by their brethren, they were, and still are witnessing to the truth of the gospel until all Israel is saved. Bringing Israel into the truth is progressive through much suffering, just as all those that believed following the death of Jesus suffered.

Jeremiah speaks of the need of every man to know the Lord (Jer. 31:34), providing each person seeks for God with all their heart (Jer. 29:13). No more the outward observance. No more the mechanical offering of sacrifices to God. Religious observance was to be replaced with meaningful heart-based worship and commitment — see Isaiah 1.

Moses wanted the people to enhance the outward sign of circumcision, which related them to Abraham, by changing the head knowledge of their natural inheritance for heart knowledge resulting in the circumcision of their hearts (Deut. 10:16, 17). This message was echoed by Jeremiah when he says, *take away the foreskins of your hearts (Jer. 4:4)* to become spiritual people before the spiritual God who has chosen you to be His people.

God has always been prepared to listen to those who seek Him with a pure motive and in an attitude of repentance, seeking mercy when they realised their error (Lev. 26:40 – 42). Indeed, such was His love for His people and particularly for His covenant that He made with them, that God was not prepared to destroy them completely (Lev. 26:44, 45). Nehemiah, hearing of the disastrous state of Jerusalem was so horrified that he wept before God, fasting and praying night and day such was his understanding of how terribly his own family had sinned and needed forgiveness (Neh. 1) reminding God of His promise through Moses that if they repented and sought Him then He would re-gather them[29] (v8). Such history is good for the Jewish people and for us also, for it illustrates how successful God and man in action in relationship to each other can be.

In studying the tabernacle, we must not think of the furniture as mere physical objects without considering them as teaching aids, otherwise we will miss the whole point of their careful design.

Perhaps the greatest blot against the people of Israel was their rejection of God so soon after agreeing to the covenant between them (Ex. 24:3). After all that they had experienced of God's mighty power, from the plagues to meeting with God on the mountain with such awesome and spectacular environmental activity, just because Moses was away from them for around six weeks, they persuaded Aaron to make the golden calf and offered sacrifices to it. Because He saw what was happening, God told Moses to get down and sort them out, wanting in His heart to give up on them because of their stiff necked and wayward ways (Ex. 32). Who can be a Jew without being horrified by the things their forebears did against the God to whom they are so intimately attached?

When the tabernacle came to be manufactured and constructed, God gave those responsible the necessary talents and skills to carry out the task starting with the tabernacle structure and covering (Ex. 35:30 – 36:8).

The Tent of the Meeting

From man's perspective he must enter the anteroom of the Holy of Holies; the place of God's dwelling, through the door into the holy structure. However, entry was restricted to those who had been chosen of God to serve Him as priests. The priests were of a certain tribe and family selected by God and had the task of being mediators between God and the people.

Only they could go into the Holy Place and only the high priest could enter into the Holiest Place once a year, according to God's command. Individuals born into one of the other eleven tribes, on the other hand, were only able to gain access to the brazen altar within the outer court when offering their sacrifices to God through the officiating priest.

This meant that the priests were the mediators between God and the individual. Their task was to represent God and keep alive the faith of the people in their covenant making God; which is why the antics of the sons of Eli were so corrosive (1 Sam. 2:12 – 17). The role of the priests was crucial to the faithfulness of the people. It was essential that they of all people had a personal relationship with the God they served; yet throughout the first testament there is a record of the failure of the priests to serve God with a purity of heart before Him.

---

[29] Israel is the only nation that has been able to return to its territory and be re-established in it.

The tent, which was initially physically at the centre of the living faith of the nation, until it was established in Jerusalem, was unique for it had no statues — no statue can represent a spiritual being — but focused on tangible engraved tablets, hidden from their view but which were known to them, containing rules of life that represented the agreed covenant between the creator God and the people who He had chosen to be His sole contact with the rest of the offspring of Adam. A covenant to which the people had agree to abide when they said, *All that the Lord has spoken we will do (Ex. 19:8).*

The structure and coverings were all produced by God-fearing and spiritually inspired individuals from the freewill gifts of the people to the gifted craftsmen. Everything was done to the highest levels of craftsmanship and inspired design that focused on the ethereal aspect of this unique spiritual relationship that God had with His people.

The anteroom of the holiest place on earth, where God met with His chosen, ordained individual, was separated from it by a curtain. The anti-room, called the Holy Place, contained three very important items of furniture, each of which gave a pictorial lesson on how man must approach this holy and righteous God.

Table of Showbread

Golden Lampstand

Altar of incense

Although a brief instruction is given concerning their design, no detail is recorded because the manufacture of each item was down to the inspiration received directly by those handed the position of design authority by God, and the individual craftsmen, who were all at the top of their profession, and open to the guidance of the Holy Spirit.

It is, as we shall learn as we continue our study of this subject matter, no longer required for our understanding of how we can seek after and find the God who is calling us to Himself. The principles underlying the design, manufacture and function of the tabernacle structure and each item of furniture do, however, give us sufficient information that will allow us to understand the method by which we, even in the 21st century, must reach out to and approach this awesome God.

Just as for the Ark of the Covenant, these items were holy and therefore could not be seen by anyone not chosen by God to be a priest in His service. Hangings from the tent were used to cover them before those chosen to carry them could get near them. Just as the priests alone were authorised to administer all the activities in the tabernacle and see the holy furniture, so only certain authorised men could carry them, but without being able to see them or touch them except by the poles.

The Table of Showbread – was constructed to carry the showbread in the Holy Place.

The Table   Represented man looking to God for it was made of acacia wood (from the earth and created from the dust of the ground just like man) and covered in pure (zachar) gold — symbolising Divinity which cannot be reproduced. Gold covered carrying poles of acacia wood went through gold rings secured to the table to make it transportable.

Four vessels were provided for use with the table: dishes for bread, pans or spoons for sprinkling the frankincense, pitchers for liquid offerings and bowls to hold the frankincense.

Showbread   The showbread — meaning 'bread of the face' — was made of fine flour — of the earth but only used for honoured guests — and displayed singly — no hiding — before the Lord. The newly baked twelve showbread was laid out before the Lord and remained in place for a week at a time. The frankincense burning over the loaves of showbread was to be as a sweet smelling savour for the Lord. The loaves were made holy by being in His presence, for the cloud (Ex. 40:34) indicated the Lord's presence in the Tabernacle.

Twelve — representing the twelve tribes — unleavened — meaning purity, uncontaminated with leaven representing sin — loaves of the same size and weight — representing impartiality, were made of fine flour — of the earth — and baked — meaning agony and suffering, were laid out on the table each week before the Lord in the Holy Place.

The previous week's loaves were eaten by the priests (Lev. 24:5 – 9), who were chosen of God and in a ritually pure and holy state before God. These loaves were provided by the children of Israel according to an everlasting covenant, so that they, tribe by tribe, may be permanently in the presence of the Lord (Lev. 24:8 – 9).

To the children of Israel, and in particular the priests, God laid out certain principles that governed their approach to anything that was dedicated to Him. In Lev. 11:44 God said, *For I am the Lord your God. You shall therefore consecrate yourselves to be holy before me; for I am holy.* In Lev. 22 God laid out the conditions for what is dedicated to Him and the physical and spiritual cleanliness required of those coming before Him.

He also gave instruction concerning who may eat consecrated food. The showbread had to be eaten by priests, for only they could enter the Holy Place and prescribed portions of the sacrifices offered to Him.

All these instructions concern His holiness, *for I am holy*, therefore to approach Him, offer anything to Him or dedicate anything to Him, officiate at any of the ceremonies or eat anything that has been made holy by being dedicated to Him or been standing in His presence as a gift or sacrificial offering, everyone concerned must be holy, that is ritually clean, with no uncleanness of body, mind or soul.

The reason for this, and the severity of the punishment set for anyone who disobeyed His instructions in these early days of the people's walk in their covenant relationship with Him, was to emphasise this fact of His supreme holiness compared to their dire sinfulness.

The message to Aaron and his surviving sons clearly sets out the conditions for their approach to God, *'I must be regarded as holy by all those who come near Me'*, and, 'particularly by those who I have chosen to minister at the tabernacle where the cloud symbolises My presence, I must be worshipped and held in awe for My name's sake' - see Lev. 10:3.

Unless the name of God in the minds of the people was held in absolute awe and holy fear, there would not be total respect for Him and His ability to bless them and, through discipleship, use them to ignite respect and the desire to follow Him in individuals of other nations was doomed to failure. This is why, throughout the history of Israel, God has shown His holy anger and fury when they ignored Him, worshipped other gods or tried to live as other nations without any reference to Him as their protector and benefactor.

The showbread is an example, for, having been in the Lord's presence for a week, and therefore made holy by Him, it could not be thrown out with the rubbish but had to be respectfully eaten by those priests who were in a state of 'cleanness' before Him, standing[30] in the Holy Place. The righteousness of God required them — and us — to be in a right attitude with Him when they approached Him and be in His presence.

Frankincense Hebrew 'labonah' meaning to be white: a resin obtained from the Boswellia tree and one of the most highly valued incense gums having a beautiful fragrance of Balsam. The Israelites were required to use 'pure' (tahor) frankincense on the showbread.

Note: the word translated 'pure' used to describe the gold and the frankincense are two different words in Hebrew. Zachar signifies the intrinsic purity of nature in contrast with its uncleanness (e.g. use of animals for offerings and food). Tahor, on the other hand indicates a purity that has been practically developed and manifested through actions. Therefore, zachar symbolises purity of nature, whereas tahor symbolises purity of ways.

The Golden Lampstand – provided light in the dark interior of the windowless Holy Place.

Manufactured from pure gold — divinity — of one piece — complete unity — by divinely inspired skilled designer craftsmen — of God, the lampstand had a central stem which is symbolic of God being light and in Him there is no darkness at all (1 Jn. 1:5; see also Ps. 27:1; Is. 60:19. It had six branches, three either side of the central stem. Let us consider the structure and its purpose, at least my understanding of this remarkable object:

❖ Seven denotes spiritual perfection and is the hall mark of the Holy Spirit, the one who caused the Word of God as we know it to be communicated to man and written down (2 Pet. 1:19 – 21; 2 Tim. 3:14 – 17). It is the number which regulates every period of incubation and gestation in the natural world and in man. It was the seven branch Menorah and the two olive trees either side — prophetic for the two witnesses who would appear in the last days – Rev. 11:3, 4 — which provided an unending supply of oil to the lamps. It gave the message, *Not by might (of men), nor by power (of*

---

[30] To sit before God would be disrespectful as it would have been before a king at that time. Also there would have been no room to sit there.

men), but by My Spirit says the Lord of Hosts. (Zech. 4:6[31], consider vvs. 1 - 14) No man either singularly or nationally can influence the plans God has determined to enact.

❖ Six is the human number, for man was created on the sixth day, the final act of creation before God rested on day seven.

❖ Three is the number of God the Trinity

❖ The central stem, I believe, represents the Lord God who is the central support and light of all life, both physical and spiritual. Nothing exists or is supported without God. The world survives because of God and will end at His command. There is nothing man or his earthly spiritual master Satan can do against either God or the people of God for we are challenged *to fear not those who can kill the body only (Matt. 5:16; see also Prov. 4:18; Is. 26:7; 2 Sam. 23:2 – 4), but Him who can destroy both body and soul in hell. (Matt. 10:28)*

❖ Supported by the central stem and in one piece with it are the six branches representing (I believe) man in his righteous state before God, which means that man united with God can be a light to the world.

But the whole structure is balanced because God is, in Himself, complete perfection. Man is also perfected when he is totally obedient to, and in union with Him as his God. The central theme of our relationship with God must be the first commandment for that instructs us to seek after the most intimate, loving relationship with Him.

The branches are grouped in threes; three being God's number, denoting completeness, representing the triune God. So, within this one symbolic item in the Holy Place, we have the integration of righteous man saved by the grace and mercy of God (Eph. 2:4 – 10) with the Divine and pure God.

The number three is symbolic of Divine perfection and completeness. 'Day' three of creation saw the completion of the fundamentals of the creative work of God, days four to six are completely complementary to the first three and complete in themselves for it was on the seventh day that God rested.

It was on 'day' three that the dry land appeared above the waters and miraculously fruit burst forth on the earth like a day of

---

[31] The English translation Not by might (of men), nor by power (of men), but by My Spirit says the Lord of Hosts, hides the fact that in Hebrew just seven words were used.

bursting forth out of the covering of the waves, and out of the ground.

Significantly it was day three that the stone was rolled away and the Messiah came out of the tomb and out of His earthly confinement when He rose from the dead.

❖ At the top of each branch and the central stem there was a knob and a tip shaped like an open almond blossom. Almond in Hebrew means "the awakening one" because it was the first tree to awake from the sleep of winter and cover itself with blossom. Almonds were sent to Joseph in Egypt by Jacob (Gen. 43:11), and it was the almond tree Jeremiah saw in his vision (Jer. 1:11) which suggested that the Lord was forever awake. Fitting in each of the almond blossoms was an oil lamp which was permanently lit in the holy place to provide light in the otherwise dark place.

❖ Oil, representing the Holy Spirit, and a wick inserted into the oil provided the light for the Holy Place. The oil soaking into the wick allowed it to be lit to provide light when the end of the wick was lit. In the beginning God said, *Let there be light* (Gen. 1:3) so that He could separate the light from the darkness, therefore light is from God for God is light. Darkness has no energy. Light is filled with energy, therefore light is able to overcome darkness, so it can be said that darkness is where light does not exist.

This surely is symbolic of the life of the believer who, when filled with the Spirit of the Living God, is ignited and brought to life by God and therefore able to provide the light of God to the world. But the light must first be uplifted as on a lampstand, and be supplied with oil from a reservoir (Matt. 5:14 – 16; 25:1 – 13) for it to be any use.

In the Golden Lampstand we see God's desire to provide light in a dark world through man's co-operation with, and submission to, Him through a unique and binding marriage-type relationship, for the Lampstand was all of one piece, of beaten gold giving the Divine seal of approval to the Holy Spirit working through man in the world to provide the light of God (Eph. 5:8).

The oil used was to be hand made of olives gently pounded in a mortar with the first drops being of the purest type reflecting the purity of the Holy Spirit and His work.

The Altar of Incense – As with the table of showbread the altar of incense was made of acacia wood — from the earth and created from the dust of the ground just like man — covered in pure (zachar) gold — symbolising

Divinity which cannot be reproduced. Gold-covered carrying poles of acacia wood went through gold rings secured to the table to make it transportable. It had four horns, one on each corner, which symbolised strength, for example, *For You are the glory of their strength, and in Your favour our horn is exalted* (Ps 89:17). The incense offered on this altar, the horns of which received the blood of the sin offering on the Day of Atonement (Ex. 30:10), symbolised the prayers of believers.

Prayer is an essential element in our relationship with God for it is the main means of man's ability to communicate with God. It is through prayer that we seek after God and let Him know we believe He is alive and true, that He is important to us, that we want to get right with Him so that we can have a meaningful relationship with Him, for Him to be active in our daily lives and direct our ways, leading us into an ever deeper understanding of what He wants of us. It is a means of telling Him we love Hm and eternally grateful for all that he has done for us, particularly for dying in our stead.

The summation of the three items of furniture in the Holy Place tells us of the need for the believer to be constantly in God's presence — table of showbread — where God's light shines — golden lampstand, a light we are able to absorb so that we also might shine with His reflected glory, first experienced by Moses (Ex. 34:35), and where our prayers are an essential element in our relationship with Him, prayers said in the secret place (Matt. 6:5 – 8). As only the chosen, those made righteous through the shedding of blood, could enter the Holy Place, it has always been essential, even up to the present day, that only those who have been chosen[32] who would become holy and priestly (Ex. 19:6; 1 Pet. 2:9).

In Matthew 19 and 20 we have some insight into what it means to be chosen of God. For the first priests God chose a family and a particular person within that family who, with his sons, would be ordained as priests. But as time went on and the Israelites possessed the land, and matured in the faith of the Living God, and came to understand through experience what it meant to serve God, God found it necessary to choose individuals to serve Him in particular roles, and not just the prophets who were not necessarily born of the tribe of Levi. Amos was a shepherd.

With the fulfilment of the promises of God in the Messiah we have the matter of Gentiles, such as myself, being brought to faith in the Living God through the Passover sacrifice of the Messiah and the offer of true and conscience cleansing salvation open to all men. The Messiah taught that it was not those who were Jews by birth who were automatically saved; telling

---

[32] Although the chosen priests had to be born into a certain family, since the sacrifice of the Lamb of God, only those who have repented of their sins, and totally committed their lives to Him can be considered chosen of God.

the spiritual leaders of the time that even though they searched the scriptures, their lack of spiritual understanding prevented them from understanding what God was saying through His word and therefore eternal life was denied them (Jn. 5:39, 40).

The experience of Saul after his meeting with the risen Jesus om the Damascus road whilst in his lodgings in Straight Street Damascus, is a good example of the lack of understanding of the religious Jews. He was going to Damascus to put all those Jews who believed in Jesus as their Messiah in prison. But three days of blindness and fasting allowed the Holy Spirit, the only member of the trinity able to enter into people, to open up the scriptures stored in Saul's memory to show that Jesus was indeed the Messiah sent to the Jews. How else would it be possible to transform Saul into Paul?

The same happened to a Jewish Rabbi Aaron, who asked me to write this book. When, through something I had sent to him by email, he suddenly met with his Messiah. His epiphany moment he called it. In a moment, all the years of rabbinic indoctrination suddenly faded away so that when he read the scriptures he saw within the text new things of which he was previously unaware because he had been taught to understand what it meant. He suddenly found the spiritual treasures hidden in plain sight in the word of God. In that moment his life restarted for he had become united in spirit with his Messiah. in that moment he was born again in the Spirit.

The element of choice is important and there are plenty of examples of God making choices. Esau and Jacob were both born of Isaac, but because of their individual attitude of heart, and openness, towards God, Jacob was chosen before birth because of God's foreknowledge (Gen. 25:23; Ro. 9:6 – 13). This means that those who accept that Yeshua, Jesus, is the Messiah, the Christ, the anointed One of God, and reach out to Him in an earnest seeking after faith, will be given sustenance (Jn. 6:35 – 52; 14:6; 3:16). From this we can accept that all those who have a heart for God and reach out to Him will know Him and be heard by Him (Matt. 7 esp. v. 21).

These items of furniture were housed in a tent so that the whole structure and contents could become the physical connection point on earth of the spiritual umbilical cord that God was establishing between Himself and man that centred on the holy of holies. This was a meeting point that had to be separated from the world. Keeping out the contamination of the sight and sound of the sinful world allowed the holiness of God to be experienced by those meeting with Him.

This tent and its contents is a copy of what is in heaven. It is also an essential lesson on how the individual must approach God. Although the elements, from the construction and internal drapes of the tent itself to the furniture it contained, are hidden from the public gaze, the whole speaks of the spiritual nature of our communion with God. He cannot be seen with the naked eye, therefore faith produced from experience of His presence and the blessing received are what confirms to us His reality and love and interest in us as people and as individuals.

It also illustrates the need for individuals to reach out to God in private, for the Messiah told His listeners not to be like the hypocrites praying in public, to the applause of those seeing and hearing them, *but ... when you have shut the door pray to your Father who is in the secret place (Matt. 6:1 – 8).*

The ceremonial acts the priests were to perform were not like plays being enacted for the benefit of an audience, but prayers and acts of dedication, ministering to the God who had saved them from the world to dedicate them and the whole nation to Him.

Having considered the furniture, we also need to consider the covering of that furniture for this Tent of the Meeting was to be a complete whole. The outward show of badger/porpoise skins[33] allowed the tent to blend in with the camp around it. But the internal hangings resounded with the spiritual nature of God,

> *Moreover, you shall make the tabernacle[34] with ten[35] curtains of fine woven linen and blue (colour of the sky representing heaven), purple (representing royalty), and scarlet (representing sacrifice) thread; with artistic designs of cherubim (representing the spiritual nature of God) you shall weave them ... (see Ex. 26:1-14; 36:1 – 37)"*

This is not the place for a consideration of the whole structure which was of fine linen hangings with gold clasps on the inside and graduating through the use of silver and tent covering of ram skins — it was a ram that was caught in a thicket and used as a sacrifice for sin by Abraham for Isaac — which were died scarlet representing blood, to the natural porpoise or badger skins and bronze[36] — which represents judgement — along with

---

[33] Different translations give different type of skin and this is just one of the undefined details that prevent an exact replica structure being produced. All the skin types identified, however, are dull in colour for the glory is within (consider Is. 53:2).

[34] The cost of producing the Tabernacle was met by the gifts the Children of Israel received from the Egyptians before they left Egypt (Ex. 11:2, 3). It is possible there were certain things that they were required to purchase with the treasure they were given by the Egyptians.

[35] The number ten denotes ordinal perfection for having reached 9 the number ten starts the process anew as 20 and so on. The tabernacle is perfection for it is of God's design and speaks of God's dwelling place which is perfection. This is why individuals shall be purified by the blood of sacrifice and why it is essential to be holy as God is Holy, with His help, so that we might remain in His presence. Unfortunately, Nadab and Abihu (Lev. 10:1 – 3) were not the only priests to attract God's wrath and condemnation (Mal. 1 & 2).

[36] Bronze represents holiness and justice and typifies the divine character of Christ who took upon Himself the fire of God's wrath.

fixings which faced the world with all its distractions.

Separating the Holy of Holies from the Holy Place was a veil which only the High Priest could pass through once a year to plead for the life of the whole nation. It is this curtain that is crucial in our identification of the Messiah in a later chapter of this book. The door into the Holy Place through which only the ceremonially clean priest(s) on duty could pass was a screen made of blue, purple and scarlet thread and fine woven linen. It was the door attracting the chosen into the meeting room with God.

God deals with individuals quietly and in secret, that their inner lives may be transformed by the personal application of the shed blood of His Son, our Saviour, on our confessed sin to produce a repentant inner attitude to Him who calls us out of the darkness of this world into His glorious light.

The regenerating power of the Holy Spirit on our spirit means that we might come into communion with the God who created us in His own image. But there is only one way to reach this tent and it is only by travelling that way that we can approach Him.

The Messiah said,

> I am the Way, the Truth and the Life, no man comes to the Father but by Me (Jn. 14:6).

Having dealt with the Tent or Tabernacle, which was symbolic of God dwelling on earth amongst His people, we must move out into the courtyard to understand why it was that the Messiah should come first as a suffering servant, before He could come as triumphant King.

This will be in reverse to our understanding of the furniture in the tent which we considered from God's view-point.

7 GATEWAY TO GOD

"All we like sheep have gone astray;
We have turned everyone to his own way;
And the Lord has laid on Him
The iniquity of us all."
(Is. 53:6)

"Open to me the gates of righteousness;
I will go through them,
And I will praise the Lord.
This is the gate of the Lord,
Through which the righteous shall enter."
(Ps. 118:19, 20)

"Wide is the gate and broad is the way
That leads to destruction,
And there are many who go through it.
Because narrow is the gate
And difficult is the way
That leads to life,
And there are few who find it."
(Matt.7:13, 14)

The Way to the Tent

In chapter 6 we considered the tent and its furniture from God's perspective. It is now important that we approach the Tabernacle complex from man's perspective and consider the courtyard of the Tent of the Meeting and the processes by which the priests prepared themselves to enter the Holy Place.

Surrounding the tent was an area enclosed by a curtain that separated the camp of Israel from the holy tent. The enclosing curtains of fine white linen, symbolising righteousness, were 7.5 feet high, effectively hiding the holy tent, the furniture and all the ceremonial activity in the outer court from the casual gaze of those outside. The cloud, representing the presence of God, which had been the standard since their escape from Egypt and during their initial wanderings rested on the holiest part of the tent, making the whole enclosure sacred, like the holy mountain when God descended to speak with His chosen people.

The purpose of the curtain was not only to separate the things of God from the things of the world, but also to provide a visual barrier that said to the people of Israel,

> *"If you want to enter into a relationship with your God, and commune with Him, you must leave the things of the world behind and enter through the narrow gate at the eastern end (the end of the rising sun) of the enclosure with an offering for sin so that you can first get into a right relationship with God and then walk with Him in the way of righteousness." (Job 29:14; Ps. 24:4 – 6; 119:137 – 144; Prov. 12:28)*

The surrounding curtain also reminded them of the barrier set up around the mountain during their first meeting with God, through which only Moses, God's chosen servant, could pass to go to his mountain top meeting with God.

Anyone entering the enclosure through the single eastern gate had to have a specific purpose for so doing because they were entering into God's domain, His kingdom, and all those who ministered, or were ministered unto, in that area were answerable to God as were Nadab and Abihu (Lev. 10:1 – 3).

It is important to emphasise that there was only one entrance by which a penitent sinner could bring his[37] sacrifice to receive atonement for his sin. There was no other way in. From God's perspective the cleansing of the sinner from his sin when the sinner was seeking to get right with God came first, whether he was a priest or just a citizen of Israel. The cleansing provided by the blood of the sin offering because of repentance by the sinner had to be, and still is, the very first act of anyone seeking to approach God. There was then and still is no other way.

The only difference between then and now is that now we have an all-sufficient sacrifice in the death, resurrection and ascension of the Jewish Messiah, who is the Lamb of God; but we have no choice but to seek after God with a pure repentant heart focused on God, and through repentance and faith, asking that we be cleansed by the blood of His eternal sacrifice.

The sinner could only enter the gate with a sacrifice, the type of sacrifice dependent upon the sin he believed he had committed against God; or an offering depending on how God had blessed him and the wealth of the sinner. This first requirement placed on an individual also spoke of his need

---

[37] Please accept that the references to man or men include wo-man or wo-men. Before God we are equal and are both in need of salvation. Although God had required only men to serve as priests in the tabernacle and ultimately the permanent temple, the principles that govern our approach to God that we are seeing in the layout of the temple complex and its furniture apply to both sexes now that we are no longer under the law but under the grace of God.

to realise that as he had sinned, indeed was a sinner, he had to be prepared to repent of that sin in the presence of God by making the decision to enter through the gate to present himself and his offering to those representing God on earth.

Altar of Sacrifice

The furniture in this enclosed area, which represented the ante-room, or preparation room, of heaven, identifies the altar first, for at the very heart of the Jewish national life was the need to offer sacrifices to God. It is a major problem for some Christians today to understand the need for a continual supply of animals for sacrificial purposes, and from a human perspective it seems to be a waste of good animals. But the animals were created by God and do not have a life after death as we do.

Although Israel became God's chosen people, being commissioned by Him at Mount Sinai as his wife to be — a marriage that would happen at the marriage supper of the Lamb, it is important that we differentiate between the tribes to fully understand God's work of salvation. The priests were all of the tribe of Levi and those who attended to the working of the temple through the prescribed ceremonies and services had to be of the family of Aaron and the offspring of subsequent chosen men. These were the perpetuators of the sacrifices under the Law of Moses.

But Jacob prophesied concerning Levi (Gen. 49:5 – 7) including the phrase, *let not my honour be united to their assembly* partly because of the deception they used to kill a man (Gen. 34 esp. vs. 25 – 30) but also because of the nature of their priestly work. The Levites were scattered throughout Israel when they were settled in the Promised Land. Jacob's prophecy concerning Judah was altogether different proclaiming that Judah would become the dominant tribe because, *the sceptre shall not depart from Judah, nor a lawgiver from between his feet.* Judah means praise and his brothers would praise him (Gen. 49:8 – 12). The name Jew is a derivative of Judah.

But let us consider the matter more closely:

The people God chose to be His people were from the start shepherds.

All men are sinners (Ro. 3:23), not only by inheritance, but, through the change of relationship with God that that first rebellion brought about. Men became sinners in their own right from birth being under Satan's authority.

Away from God they were like sheep without a shepherd, not knowing the Truth of God, which Satan and all his demonic forces tried to hide from them by deception — a fact that is still true today for even intellectuals and prominent men of learning do not know God, nor are they able to see the hand of God in nature and the physical universe. The intrinsic and therefore perpetual sinfulness of man was the main stumbling

185

block to the reuniting of man with God.

The sheep was to be the main, and finally the ultimate symbol of salvation from sin. Each sacrificial animal, which had to be perfect, was burdened with the sin of an individual through the laying of the sinner's hands on the animal's head. The sinner then killed the lamb which died in place of the sinner. This was done in perpetuity until the arrival of the perfect Lamb of God who was to take on the sin, not just of an individual, but of all mankind. According to prophecy the sheep was taken to be symbolic of the suffering servant who, *like a sheep before its shearers is dumb, so He opened not His mouth* (Is. 53:7). He became the Jewish people's Perfect Passover Lamb because of the pure sinless life He led whilst on the earth (1 Cor. 5:7b).

With the altar of sacrifice so prominent immediately inside the gate of the tabernacle complex, and the fact that the fire on the altar was never to go out (Lev. 6:13), God was emphasising to all the people that sin was the main barrier between them and Him and had to be dealt with first before they could progress to a proper relationship with Him.

The sacrificial system was placed by God at the heart of the national life of Israel with the requirement for the perpetual sacrificing of animals that were totally consumed by the fire on the altar; purely because rebellion and unbelief were at the heart of the nation's problems.

The sacrifices put into context their relationship to God and their primary need for their sins to be atoned-for before God through the shedding of blood. For them to become holy and to be able to enjoy His blessings they had to not just believe in Him but put that belief into practice through faith by accepting His rule and authority as central to their lives and trust Him completely. Just as the tabernacle was central to the nation, so God had to be central to their lives.

The altar of sacrifice was the farthest any non-priestly individual was allowed to go in the tabernacle complex. On it were placed the sacrificial offerings, to be burnt to a cinder, which were at the core of the worship ceremonies. If an individual believed they had sinned against God they were required to bring a prescribed animal that was in perfect condition, and to place their hands on the head of the animal in order to transfer their sin to it before cutting its throat, thus releasing its blood which represented its life. The priests then burnt it completely on the altar of sacrifice. This was — and still is — a key factor in a person being cleansed of sin, thereby allowing them access to God. It is the central theme of our relationship with God for without the shedding of blood there can be no remission of sins (Lev. 17:11; Heb. 9:22).

No testament is active whilst the testator is alive. For even the first tabernacle, which we are considering at present, and which had at its centre the tablets of stone containing the covenant God made with the people of

Israel, had to be sprinkled with blood at its dedication (Heb. 9:16 – 22). Therefore, it is the death of the testator that makes the testament legal. The death of an animal as a substitute, and the sprinkling of the blood even on the Mercy Seat (Lev. 16:11 – 17), was an arrangement that was practical only for a while, being limited in its effect, for it had to be repeated on a regular basis and did not cleanse a person's conscience (Heb. 9:13, 14).

This limitation is the main factor for understanding why the first visit of the long promised Messiah had to be as the suffering servant, for it was only when the Son of the Living God became the Son of Man, totally pure and righteous, and offered Himself up as the Passover sacrifice for the sin of the whole world and willingly shed His blood and died on the cross as a fully burnt offering for sin that men, who repent of their sin and accept Him as their Lord and Saviour, can receive eternal salvation.

It is important to realise that although the death of the Saviour provided an all-sufficient sacrifice for us, we continue to sin (1 Jn. 3:3 – 5) because we have a propensity for sin, for we are still living in our sinful flesh (Ro. 7:21 – 25). We therefore need to go before the Lord in repentance and faith to continually seek for the cleansing of the blood. We have been saved, we are continually being saved, but it is not until we are with the Lord in the new Jerusalem (Rev. 21:1, 2) that we will finally receive eternal salvation for, having changed this corruptible body to put on incorruption (1 Cor. 15:50 – 58) and been finally made perfect, we will no longer have the propensity for sin.

Although it was only the priest who was allowed to go further into the holy complex, individuals were still able to communicate with God themselves, even outside the complex, once they had received forgiveness of their sins. Unfortunately, this act of repentance and the offering of a sacrifice was a continual requirement which did not always have the right effect, for to many it was a mechanical exercise because their hearts were not right with God.

When the Messiah came, He spoke with an authority that the people had not heard from any of the religious authorities. So, what of the priests who were supposed to teach the people the truth about God in the days of the tabernacle and early temple building? From what Isaiah says it would appear that the head knowledge — the whole head is sick — and heart — and the whole heart faints — understanding of the priests and therefore the people were at odds with God for there is no soundness in their relationship with God. Spiritual knowledge and understanding were definitely lacking. That is why Isaiah criticised the whole process of burning sacrifices and incense and the ceremonies that were celebrated for they were a sinful nation. (Please read the whole of Is. 1[38] also Mal. 1:6 – 14.)

---

[38] The trees identified in Is. 1:29 were used for idolatrous worship.

With regard to a priest, it was only after offering a sacrifice for sin for himself that he could move onto the laver which was used for washing the hands and the feet to make them ceremonially clean. Only then could the priest perform his duties in the tabernacle compound or in the tent. As a sinner he had to first obtain forgiveness for himself, something the Messiah did not have to do.

The brazen altar of sacrifice, made of shittim[39] (or acacia) wood overlaid with bronze, was 7.5 feet (5 cubits) square and 4.5 feet (3 cubits) high, with a horn on each of its four corners. Numbers are important in scripture. Here we have a perfect square of five cubits; but why five cubits?

God's number is 3, and 3 + 1 equals 4 representing Divine creative works. Add 4 + 1 = 5 and five symbolises Divine Grace; thus God (3) adds His gifts and blessings of His love to the works (4) of His hand which produces the evidence of His grace (5). Five is the leading measurement in the construction of the Tabernacle. (Reference 'The Companion Bible').

The horn is symbolic of both justice and strength. Taking hold of the horns of the altar was the sign that a person claimed sanctuary from their enemy until their case could be properly adjudicated (1 Kgs. 1:50, 51; 2:28). Also the horn, like that of the ram, is symbolically the sign of his dignity, power or strength, for deprive a ram of its horns, its weapon of aggression, and it will become docile, because it realises it has nothing with which to attack another male to establish dominance. (Lam. 2:3; Ps. 75:4 – 10).

The Bronze Laver

The brazen laver, which means a bath or wash basin made of bronze containing water for washing, is the only other item of equipment in the compound surrounding the Tent of the Meeting. Used for cleansing by the priests, it was made from women's mirrors (Ex. 30:17 – 21) made of polished bronze and contained water for washing hands.

This speaks of what people do, their service and work, indeed anything to which they put their 'hands'. As the hands are controlled by the head, which is influenced by the heart, by going through the required ablutions it reminded the priest of his duty towards God and that all that he did must be from a pure heart (1 Pet. 1:16), and feet, which represent where a person is before God and where they go, their lives and ways.

As God is Holy, their walk had to be holy before Him (Lev. 11:44, 45; 1 Pet. 1:16). Moses had ceremonially washed Aaron and his sons only once (Ex. 40:11 – 16), thereafter all they needed to wash was their hands and feet. In this context it is worth considering the action of the Messiah who

---

[39] The shittim tree was remarkably luxuriant in dry places, growing up to 20 feet, with fine grained brownish –orange wood which was hard, very heavy and indestructible by insects. It represents incorruptible humanity and speaks of the Messiah (Ps. 16:10) whose sacrifice as an incorruptible man on the cross was the all-sufficient sacrifice for our sin on the altar of willing service for God.

washed the disciple's feet, but not the rest of them (Jn. 13:3 – 11).

Peter, initially refusing to have his Lord wash his feet, asking for his hands and his head to be washed also, but Jesus told him that, *he who has bathed themselves need only to have their feet washed to be clean* and that although he was clean, not all of them were, referring to Judas, who, even with that washing, was still not clean before God because, through his scheming, his heart was not right with God because he wanted to control God rather than allow God control him.

It is worth mentioning that the priests ministering in the Tabernacle and its compound were required to not only offer a sacrifice on the altar for the forgiveness of sin, but also to wash with water before doing any work as a priest. They had to be of a pure heart and mind when they ministered before God. The disciples were in the privileged position of ministering before the Son of God and, although going through an apprenticeship, needed to be clean in His presence.

A consistent theme in the preparation of priests for their work in the tent and its compound is that they were required to do all they were told to do according to the instructions God gave to His servant Moses. Today, in the atmosphere of more liberal interpretations of scripture it is vitally important that we understand who we are seeking to worship and why we need to reach out to Him and not the other way around.

The altar represents life poured out because of sin, bringing about our atonement with God. The laver represents the next stage in the process of our being brought into a right relationship with God because not only could the priests see themselves through the freshly drawn water in the clean laver because of the mirror surface of the bronze vessel, but the clear, clean, cleansing water itself, was symbolic of God's salvation.

However, when the priests started to wash their hands and feet (they would have been bare footed), sand and dirt and blood and much else would have been added to contaminate the water and distort and obscure the reflection. If we consider that the water represents the word of God through the work of the Holy Spirit (James 1:21 – 25), then it is evident from all that we read, particularly from the extensive experiences recorded in the first testament, that the result of inherent and personal sin muddies the water, often obscuring the received truth.

But we must be careful not to rush ahead of ourselves, for in considering Moses' Tent of the Meeting we are dealing with God's first revelations of His plan for the salvation of mankind. Over the many hundreds of years up to the coming of the Messiah much more would be revealed of that plan and, through the experiences of the people of Israel, how man must approach and relate to God.

It is important for us today to take notice of the experiences of those who have served God through the many centuries since Moses, and to adopt our own intimate relationship with Him that will allow us to experience His presence with us.

We have so much more information concerning cleansing that enhances our understanding than did those first Aaronic priests. God spoke through the prophet Ezekiel concerning their cleansing with clean water and a new heart being given to them (Ez. 36:25 - 27); and to Jeremiah that the people would know Him because He would write His laws on their hearts — God originally wrote His laws on tablets of stone for them to read (Jer. 31:33, 34). Please consider these verses Jn. 15:3; Tit. 3:5; Heb. 10:22 and Jn. 7:38.

Many books and commentaries and articles have been written on every intimate detail of the design the tabernacle and its surrounding compound, giving a far more in-depth understanding of the message God wanted to give to His people than I can afford in this book; for the message I believe God has directed me to give is an understanding of God's whole plan of salvation as revealed to men, from the tragic separation of man from God through its gradual revelation and its development to its culmination in the appearance and obedient sacrifice of the Suffering Servant as prophesied in recorded scripture.

The Covenant

At the heart of the covenant God made with Abram, who had proved to be totally faithful to the God who had called him, was the sign of circumcision. At the heart of the covenant God made at Mount Sinai with the new nation of Israel, that He had rescued from the furnace of Egypt, was the Law which laid the foundation of a completely new and progressive way of life.

The essential ingredient of the new Law of God, the first commandment, was love, for God, who created man in love, wanted the love and dedication of man to be the basis of a new relationship between them. It was to be a relationship that overcame the intrinsic rebellion introduced into man by the action of one man, Adam, and perpetuated by the demonic forces of Satan who now had authority in the world and over man.

The new relationship required individuals to approach Him through the gate in the fence encompassing the tabernacle compound and through the shedding of innocent blood at the altar of sacrifice, leading to a change of heart through the washing of the word that allowed a form of communication between God and man.

At first this communication would be limited in part by the tabernacle services that were an essential part of their life during their wanderings in the wilderness and in the Promised Land. But this process heralded the appearance of the supreme Passover Lamb who would bring about a permanent way to God leading to eternal life.

Thus, the Law starts with the need to have a complete change of attitude to God through love and dedication, and continues with the need for a new way of life. The design of the tabernacle and its furniture showed man just how severe the separation was between man and God and how incompatible were the purity of God and the sinfulness of man. Yet it provided encouragement for men, in illustrating the fact that there was a way back to God by man having a willingness to approach God of his own free will through the gate with a sacrifice for sin.

The shedding of innocent blood and the consuming of the sacrifice by fire allowed man entrance into the kingdom of God[40] within the outer curtain. The design also illustrated the importance of cleansing, through the washing of the word, which alone could alert individuals to their sinfulness, before being allowed through the door into the sanctuary inhabited by God. There the willingness of man to be in the presence of God and communicate with Him through prayer was a foremost requirement. Then the light of God would illuminate the path of the believer. All the while the central theme being the plumb-line of the law of God over which the mercy of God reigned.

What is then the main problem of the law? Its content does not allow for the sinfulness of man, for it describes what man should have been like had he remained righteous and the infringement of one element means that the law as a whole has been broken.

Therefore, the law of God highlights our sinfulness and it is impossible for man to obey it completely. To the Romans Paul, in speaking about the law asks if the law, which identifies us as sinful, is itself sinful.

> *Certainly not! On the contrary, I would not have known anything about sin except through the law. For covetousness would have been unknown to me except the law had said, "You shall not covet." But sin, taking opportunity by the commandment, produced in me all manner of evil desire. For apart from the law sin was dead (Ro. 7:7, 8)*

The law is the basic rule of life that tells man the rule of life God expects all people to live by, but because we have the DNA of sin in our flesh, and therefore man, without the influence of God, lives a life of sin, the law is of no help except to emphasise man's sinfulness. But as Moses demonstrated in his life, living a life dedicated to God provides us with the resources to overcome sin.

The purpose of the Tabernacle was to impress upon man that, even though the law is impossible for him to obey without fault, there is a way of forgiveness but, there are conditions. God is love, of that there can be no

---

[40] God's kingdom is where God reigns and His influence is unopposed.

doubt as far as true believers are concerned, and God wants to enter into a personal relationship with each and every individual born on this earth. There must be a change in not just the way we think but the way we relate to God, and consideration of the covenant that led to circumcision provides us with the best vehicle for us to understand it.

Abraham was a remarkable man who, although a sinner, was chosen by God to serve Him and provide the basis for a new nation through which God could reach out to mankind; in this way it becomes clear that the plan of salvation required time to be revealed and executed.

The sign of the covenant God made with Abraham was circumcision. We can legitimately say that circumcision gave testimony to the willing obedience of a man towards God. We could summarise that by saying the basis of Abraham's life before God was 'personal obedience to a personal God'. However harsh and impossible to obey completely the law might have appeared to those on whom it had been thrust, the Tabernacle pointed out that if a man changed his attitude to God and allowed his heart to be circumcised, not just his flesh, then the impossible nature of obedience to the law could become possible. The message behind circumcision is willing obedience.

Circumcision became a sign for Abraham's male descendants that they were a member of the nation of Israel and belonged to God. The heart was considered by Hebrews to be the centre of physical, mental and spiritual life, the seat of intellect, not human feeling as is accepted in the western world today. Therefore, when Moses challenged the people to circumcise the foreskins of their hearts, he was challenging them to provide a sign that they were willing to bring not just their bodies but the essential centre of their being, the real thinking, situation assessing, decision making, intellectual, rational understanding person under the authority of God, thereby enabling God to influence them for good.

Their journey through the wilderness, their meeting with God and commissioning as His people and times of testing were all part of their God designed training to be His people in the world. They would provide those who followed after them with a progressively clearer understanding of how they should approach God, and how they could become believers, through their recorded experiences in their relationship with God and the surrounding people.

The direct response of God each time they failed to trust Him at the moment of testing, and the healing and salvation God provided when they repented of their sin, provided them and us with a greater understanding of the love and justice of God. This, along with the prophetic messages, helps us to understand the progressive release of information regarding God's plan of salvation.

Consider, for instance, the effigy of the fiery serpent which God instructed Moses to make and erect on a pole. (Num. 21:4 – 9) The relevance of this incident is that sin brought about death by the bite of the fiery serpents let loose among the people. So God instructed that an effigy of the fiery serpent be raised up so that those who were bitten could look on the bronze serpent and live. This equates with what the Messiah told the people, *and I, if I am lifted up from the earth, will draw all people (from all nations) unto Myself.*

Sin resulted in the venomous serpents bringing judgement on the people who then cried out to God for forgiveness; looking at the effigy of a serpent brought salvation from the effect of its bite. Christ, who knew no sin, became sin and was lifted up from the ground to become a curse for us (Deut. 21:22, 23), so that when we seek forgiveness and look unto Him (Zech. 12:10) we will be saved from the effect of our sin.

Just think about it. Sin (rebellion against God) was the result of man accepting the deception put forward by that serpent of old (Satan) and perpetuated by a world dominated by Satan and his demonic forces. It is clear, for history confirms it, that when a person accepts Christ as the Lord of their lives, and as a result becomes an active disciple for Him, then that person becomes an enemy of Satan and will be pursued by him to try and bring him back into his evil fold.

Notice how central the Tabernacle was to the nation when it was camped and where the cloud, symbolic of the presence of God, rested. Also note where the Sons of Aaron were located, for they were camped directly outside the gate into the Tabernacle compound.

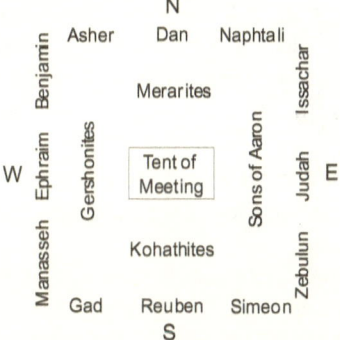

The tent was at the heart of their nation along with those who had been chosen to serve God, the three main families of the tribe of Levi and the sons of Aaron, the first High Priest, next to the Tabernacle (Tent of the Meeting). Surrounding it were the remaining tribes. Notice that the two sons of Joseph, represented by the two half tribes of Ephraim and Manasseh, are accommodated just as Jacob said they would be with Ephraim being the most numerous. The tribe of Ephraim would go on to represent the northern kingdom when the nation was divided, for Israel is often referred to as Ephraim which was the leading tribe. (Is. 7:2-17; Hos. 12-14)

It is worth considering for a moment the materials and colours used for the structure and covering of the tabernacle complex, the garments worn by the high priest and the substances used by him in the holy places. Not only does each speak of aspects of God and pertain to our relationship with Him, but they also give a prophetic understanding of the Messiah who would one day become High Priest, but not a high priest in the line of Aaron. All aspects of the tabernacle spoke of God's plan of salvation that would provide a way for man to get back into a right relationship with Him. Some symbolic aspects are more obvious than others.

As we proceed with our study, we will discover the deeper truths hidden within the structure and materials used in its production, both of which speak of the forthcoming Messiah and the work He was to perform. Although the Levitical tribe was responsible for ministering at the Tabernacle services and carrying it from place to place, its structure and symbolic design described a superior High Priest who was to come, and the offering He was to make on our behalf. It is also clear that such a superior High Priest could not have been of the tribe of Levi, otherwise He would not have been superior to Aaron.

It is interesting that Jacob described Levi, along with his brother Simeon, as *an instrument of cruelty* (Gen. 49:5). Aaron was a rather weak individual being party to the production of the golden calf (Ex. 32:4), for which he would not take full responsibility, and siding with his sister Miriam in her rebellion against their brother Moses. (Num. 12:1 – 16) The Aaronic priesthood had its highs in the persons of Samuel and Joshua (Zech. 3) and others, but mostly its lows, particularly at the time of the appearance of the Messiah — note the attitude of the Pharisees in John. 9 esp. v 34, and that of the priests, including the high priest, who proclaimed Caesar, instead of God, as their only king and incited the crowd to cry, "Crucify".

It is essential that we do not forget that the tabernacle Moses was instructed to make, along with the God-given skills of the artificers who would create it, was modelled on the perfect tabernacle in heaven. The clothes worn by all the priests, and in particular the high priest, which had to cover all the flesh, because it is the spirit of man that communicates with God, the flesh is only the building in which the spirit is housed and is sinful so must be hidden from God (Jn. 6:63), also provided an illustration of the greater message God was giving the people. We would do well to consider and take note of these things for they provide a strong foundation for what we believe today.

The materials used all had a meaning and nothing was done without a purpose and symbolism. In this study we have not considered all the aspects of the construction to prevent confusion. The main reason for this book is to discover the overall objective of God to develop and bring to fulfilment His plan of salvation for man that was established before the creation of the world began.

Metals[41]

Gold	Deity	Throughout the scriptures, pure gold speaks of divinity, that which cannot be reproduced by man. It was the first element presented to the Messiah at His birth when He entered into the life on earth.
Silver	Redemption	Used as redemption money. (Ps. 66:10) The shekel coin was made of silver (Ex. 30:11 – 16) The tabernacle stood on sockets of silver. Both Joseph and the Messiah were sold for silver, Joseph for twenty shekels and the Messiah thirty pieces of silver (Gen. 37:28; Matt 26:14 – 16; see Mk 10:45)
Bronze	Judgement	Used where exceptional strength and heat resistance is required such as the altar of sacrifice. Moses raised the Bronze Serpent during the judgement of God through serpents, and as we had already discussed, the Messiah was lifted up when He took upon Himself the sins of the world and faced the fire of the wrath of God. (2 Cor. 5:21; Matt. 27:46)

Colours

Blue	Heaven	Colour is very important, for people recall things through colour. Woven into or embroidered on the linen of the priestly garments were blue, purple and scarlet threads, these colours being singled out for a particular purpose. Blue dye, which was very scarce even at this time, was then obtained from the excretions of a mollusc (shellfish) found near the coast of Phoenicia.

---

[41] I found the web sight www.bible-history.com/tabernacle a very useful source of information.

Man realised that God was in heaven for He came down to meet with them at Mount Sinai and heaven to them was blue. Indeed, the phrase, "from above" is a Jewish idiom for heaven and was an important point raised by the Messiah when speaking to Nicodemus. (Jn. 3:10 – 13, 31) The blue heaven was also the attractive place to which men would one day go to be with their God.

Purple	Royalty	Obtained from mixing the blue of heaven (that which comes down from above) and the scarlet of sacrifice, it was worn by those of kingly status. (Jud. 8:26) It speaks of the God Messiah who came down from above to die as a uniquely sinless human being for all mankind.
Scarlet	Sacrifice	Derived from a worm that infested certain trees in the East, a brilliant crimson die was produced by drying crushing, and grinding them into powder. Equating to the redness of the blood of animals, scarlet thread was symbolic of sacrifice and woven into every aspect of the Tabernacle and the High Priestly garments.

It is interesting what the prophet David said about sacrifice in Psalm 22 (particularly vs 1 – 18) for it was so prophetic about what was to happen to the Messiah when He came to die. Verse 6 speaks of him being a worm and no man; a reproach of men, and despised by the people.

And did not the religious authorities taunt the Messiah in a clearly sarcastic manner, that mirrored their total unbelief in Jesus being God's anointed, regarding His Godly status, saying haughtily, let Him (God) deliver Him (this impostor) since He (God) delights in him, this man who has set himself up as being equal with God and claimed to be from God? (Matt. 27:41 – 43)

With regard to the final and supreme eternal sacrifice made by the Messiah we are told in scripture that, *"... He has appeared so that He might put away sin by sacrificing Himself ..."* (Heb. 9:26)

Materials

Fine Linen	Purity	Made from Egyptian flax, this linen was finely woven, brilliant white and used for the clothes of royalty and people of rank. In one Egyptian tomb the linen was so finely woven there were found to be 152 threads/inch in the warp and 72 in the woof. White always speaks of purity and righteousness. (Rev. 15:6; 3:5; 19:14) It typifies the Messiah who was pure and completely without sin (1 Jn. 3:3 – 5).
Goat's Hair	Cursed	Apart from its usefulness in providing milk, meat and skins for use as e.g. water bottles, and long, course hair for weaving into cloth, which was worn by the poor – a sign of extreme poverty, the goat was also used for sacrificial purposes (Heb. 9:12; 10:4) The drab colour and coarseness of the hair, in comparison to the fine twined linen, was woven into a covering immediately above the curtain of the tabernacle and speaks of the humility and poverty of the Messiah. (Lk. 9:58).

The Tent of the Meeting was at the centre of the new life of the Israelites as they travelled towards the Promised Land and could easily be contaminated in the minds of the priests and people, becoming less respected, possibly, because of the sameness of the ritual. Therefore, on the Day of Atonement, the high priest was to make atonement not only for himself, his family, and all the priests but also for all the people and, through the sprinkling of blood, the Tent itself.

Of the two goats chosen for sacrifice one was killed within the compound, but on the head of the other the high priest laid his hands, placing on it all the collective sins of the people, and it was released into the wilderness for it was the scapegoat. (Lev. 16:10, 21, 22) Although there are various theories concerning this act of atonement, one that seems sensible is that by sending the goat into the wilderness, the sins of the people were being removed from them. (Mi. 7:19; Ps. 103:12) In Christ our sins are removed from us to be remembered by God no more.

Ram's skins dyed red	Substitution-ary Sacrifice	A ram is a grown male sheep and there were either one or two in a flock of ewes for procreation. Because of the fundamental illustration of the ram provided by God and used by Abraham as a substitutionary sacrifice, that is a burnt offering fully consumed, in place of his son Isaac when his faith was tested (Gen. 22:12, 13), it is considered in the eyes of the Jewish people as the substitute animal, faithful unto death.

The Messiah, the only perfect man to live on this earth and the head of all things (Eph. 1:22; Is. 28:16; Matt. 21:42; 1 Pet. 2:4 – 10), willingly gave up His power to defend Himself (Jn. 19:11) and allowed Himself to be offered for the people by the high priest who, with his ordained colleagues, shouted, *"Crucify, Crucify"* (Jn. 19:12 – 16), thus persuading the governor that it was in his best interests to do as they wanted (Heb. 2:9).

Consider for a moment how hurtful to God it was for the chief priests and religious leaders to cry out loudly to Pilate that they had no king but Caesar? The sacrifice of His Son hurt the Father equally as much as the Son.

Badger Skins	Unattractive appearance	The skins were used for the final covering to make the tent weather proof. They were tough and coarse and plain in appearance and symbolic of the Messiah, for the religious authorities did not recognise in Him someone who was distinctive enough to be from God. This is just as Isaiah prophesied, for he has told us that He would have no form or comeliness that the people should desire Him, indeed there was no

beauty in Him that He should be desired. (Is. 53:1, 2)

But this did not apply to everyone for just as the beauty and holiness of the tabernacle was internal, the same could be said of the Messiah.

Simeon and Anna had to have the right relationship with God for them to be inspired to recognise the promised one in the new born baby being brought to the temple.

Nathaniel recognised Him. (Jn. 1:49) And the disciples were willing to answer His call to be fishers of men because there was something about Him that drew them to Him. (Jn. 1:37 – 45; Matt. 5:1 – 11)

The request of Moses and Jeremiah for the people to be circumcised in their hearts, as a sign that they had had a change of heart to bring them into communion with God, had not been answered by those whose religious pride did not allow them to fully recognise their sinful state before God and therefore come humbly before their God in true repentance and faith.

Condemning the poor man born blind, who was given his sight by the Messiah, as having been born in sin, with such verbal force that suggested that they themselves were sinless, made the point that human sin can remain unrecognised by individuals with a mind and heart blind to God. (Jn. 9:30 – 41, consider verse 31, cf. Jn. 1:10 – 14)

| Acacia Wood | Incorruptible Humanity | The acacia or shittim wood has already been mentioned above as representing incorruptible humanity, speaking of the Messiah (Ps. 16:10) whose sacrifice on the cross as an incorruptible man was the all-sufficient sacrifice for our sin on the altar of willing service for God[42]. As the Son of Man, the Messiah died because He took upon Himself the sin of the whole world. But as the Son of God, He was able to rise again from the |

---

[42] See Appendix A at the end of this book regarding the preparation of the body of the Messiah and for a fuller explanation please read Appendix A of my work, "God Rescues His People"

dead, thereby defeating the death sentence automatically conferred on man because of the sin of Adam. (1 Cor. 15:22)

Aromatic Spices

Anointing Oil — Holy Spirit Anointing

Everything regarding the tabernacle was ordained by God Himself and therefore the copyright was held by Him. It was His trademark on earth, and nothing connected to it could be replicated by anyone without His approval (Ex. 30:31 – 33). Such was the recipe for the holy anointing oil, an ointment compound according to the art of the Spirit inspired perfumer, to be used on the furniture in the tabernacle and its compound to make them 'most holy'. Indeed, such was their holiness that after anointing whatever touched them must be holy; such was the God ordained power of the anointing oil. This same oil was to be used to anoint Aaron and his sons to consecrate them as priests ministering to God because He is Holy in the most sublime sense. (Ex. 30:22 – 30)

The basic ingredient was the 'hin', about 10 pints, of olive oil which speaks of the Holy Spirit, but to make it into a holy anointing oil certain costly sweet-smelling spices were added: 500 shekels of myrrh, half as much each of sweet cinnamon and of sweet calamus, and 500 shekels of cassia — from the same tree species as the cinnamon. The ingredients all have a meaning which we might not understand today, but what is important is the fact that it is a costly sweet-smelling perfume before God, and made the priests holy before God to be able to minister to Him — not to the people.

Notice too that the oil was not to touch the flesh (Ex. 30:32) for the work of the Holy Spirit is with the spirit of man not his flesh, for the flesh will die and decay, becoming like the ground from which it was formed; not so the spirit[43].

Consider the eternal High Priest who, because He was an intrinsic part of the Godhead was filled with the Holy Spirit without measure (Jn. 3:34) Being fully God, He could not be separated from the involvement of the Holy Spirit, particularly during His time on earth, for it was through the work of the Holy Spirit that the Messiah, now become fully human, was able to enjoy unimpeded access with the Father, and it was the Holy Spirit working with the Messiah that caused the dead to be raised to life, the storm stilled, along with healing and the ordering out of evil spirits.

Believers have access to the Father through the Son (consider Jn. 15) through the work of the Holy Spirit making us holy before God so that we can worship Him. It is worth remembering that it was through the collaboration of the Son and the Spirit that the Messiah was able to understand what was going on in the hearts of those who surrounded Him and therefore how to answer their unspoken questions (Matt. 9:4).

It was not until the death and resurrection of the Messiah that the Holy Spirit was given to the disciples (Acts 1:8), who were the first to be commissioned, along with those who later truly believed in Him (Matt. 28:18 – 20) and to all who would call on the name of the Lord of Hosts. For we are told by the messenger, the forerunner, appointed by God and sent before the Messiah, proclaiming that not only was He the Messiah (Acts 1:4, 5) before him — John the baptizer — because of His pre-existence, but that it was He who would baptise with the Holy Spirit.

Why was this? Because up to that time the spiritual leadership was in the hands of sinful

[43] Consider Lk. 11:37 – 44 and the earth-bound flesh-focused Pharisees and Lawyers who removed the key of knowledge which is the Holy Spirit, replacing Him with confusing false religious teaching which hindered others in seeking the truth and a spiritual understanding of God.

men and the Spirit was given to men on an as required, moment by moment basis, such as the proclamation of the high priest that it was expedient for one man to die for the nation (Jn. 11:49 – 52) and the confession of Peter concerning the true identity of Jesus Christ (Matt. 16:15 – 20).

But we are running ahead of ourselves, for at the time we are considering, the initial erection and consecration of the tabernacle, this was unknown and unknowable without special inspiration from God.

Incense sweet A compound made according to the art of the
smelling Spirit inspired perfumer that was to be burnt on the altar of incense as a sweet-smelling aroma to God, representing the prayers of the believers. (Ex. 30:34)

The word frankincense (labonah in Hebrew) means to be white like the snow tipped mountains in Lebanon (which is from the same root) and the moon because of its silvery whiteness. This resin from the Boswellia tree is a highly valued incense gum with a beautiful fragrance of balsam.

The word "tahor", meaning pure, used to describe the frankincense indicates a practical purity that is developed and manifested in man through the inward work of the Holy Spirit. Although the baptism of the Holy Spirit that we can experience now was not available then, it did not mean that the same Holy Spirit was not able to work in the lives of individuals to influence them for good. This is relevant in the lives of the prophets particularly Moses, Samuel and David to name but three. It is worth considering that the Hebrew word used for pure in describing the gold, zachar, speaks of the intrinsic purity of nature as created by God in the beginning, the purity of the Deity.

The "tahor" type purity would suggest that, in considering the burning of the incense, it is not only our prayers that ascend to God as a sweet-smelling aroma, but also the manner in which we live our lives and whether our objective is biased towards selfishness or service.

Consider 2 Cor. 2:15, 16 which expands on this theme for Paul writes to the Corinthian Christians concerning the service of himself, and those with him, as ministers to God before those around them. For in that service, they were to God the fragrance of Christ His Son, their Lord, among on the one hand those who were being saved through the message of salvation, of which they were living witnesses through the work of the Holy Spirit within them, and on the other those who were perishing.

To the latter they were the aroma of death, because they were rejecting their ministry in Christ and therefore heading for eternal death. To the former they were the aroma of life for they were accepting the message of salvation and entering upon the way of abundant life through the narrow gate.

Their self-sacrifice was their service upon the altar, as they drew upon the power of God through the empowering of the Holy Spirit to work in God's service, not counting their lives worth anything (consider Heb. 11, 12), but being focused on the greater prize which is eternal life.

Should we who seek to come close to the one who has given us salvation at so great a cost that we might know Him and be saved from eternal death, not also seek to learn of God, through the word that is available to us, and become teachers of the word (Heb. 5:12 – 14) so that we might spread that word amongst those who are around us?

Empowered by God, and given a voice to speak the words of God before our neighbours, we also could become a sweet aroma before God. Even though we will naturally become the smell of death to those who are perishing, we will have the joy of becoming an aroma of life to those who have been persuaded to taste and see that the Lord is good (Ps. 34:8).

To the frankincense was added three sweet smelling spices: Stacte, meaning a drop, which is a powder obtained from the hardened fragrant resin drops in the bark of the Myrrh bush; Onycha, which is a powder obtained from the horny shell of a mollusc found in the Red Sea that when burnt emitted a penetrating aroma, and Galbanum, which is obtained from the lower part of the stem of the Ferula plant, a thick stalked herb with yellow flowers and fern-like green foliage found around the Mediterranean sea. With a pungent musky aroma, this resin is particularly valuable because it preserves the scent of a mixture of perfumes, allowing its distribution over a long period of time.

Like the holy anointing oil its use was to be restricted to the tabernacle (Ex. 30:37, 38)

None of the spices were cheap to buy, and some were very expensive, but as David said to Araunah, the owner of a threshing floor he was instructed by the Lord to buy to offer a sacrifice, *I will buy it for a price for I will not offer burnt offerings to the Lord which cost me nothing* (2 Sam. 24, esp. v. 24), which is a salutary lesson for us with our easy life style and comfortable style of worship, particularly on a Sunday.

The tribe of Levi was commissioned to minister to God and were to represent God to the people and forward His judgements and commands to the people as He spoke to them. Their state before God became a barometer of the spiritual life of the nation. It is important, therefore to consider the manner in which they were to perform their duties before their God with whom they were to develop a spiritual understanding.

Robes of the High Priest

The description of the production of the garments for the priests starts with those for Aaron the High Priest for it was to be the occupant of that high office who was to become the spiritual head of the nation, even under the kings, with the task of overseeing every aspect of daily routine of the tabernacle. Initially it was Moses who was both priest and spiritual leader with God as King. But on Moses' death it was to be the high priest who would take on his role.

Aaron was to be commissioned as the first high priest by the command of God along with his four sons, not because of any merit of his own for he had singularly failed God most noticeably through his cowardliness when the people pressed him to make a golden calf whilst Moses was with God collecting the tablets on which had been engraved the commandments of God.

The holy garments were for splendour and beauty. Just like the glory of the angels serving God in the spiritual realm so the high priest was to be clothed in glorious robes for ministering before God on earth, clothes that were created by those endowed with creative skills by the inspiration of the Holy Spirit. This emphasises the fact that the high, or Hebrew "hakkohen haggadol" — great priest was chosen of God to minister before Him, although dwelling amongst the people of Israel he was not of the people because he was to be God's representative before them. Just as when a person becomes a committed believer in the Lord Jesus Christ and is filled with the Spirit of God, he is transferred from being in the world to being in Christ.

Therefore, the high priest, more so than the ordinary priests, was to be far more spiritually aware of the things of God than the citizens of the nation of Israel. It is interesting, therefore, that the birth of the fore-runner or messenger who would announce the arrival of the Messiah was not revealed to the high priest of the day, but to a humble priest[44] serving in the Holy Place in the temple at Jerusalem, and it was to a lowly and as yet unmarried maiden that the birth of the Messiah was announced. (Lk. 1). The high priest was totally unaware of what was happening and later even told the Sanhedrin that it was expedient that one man should die for the nation without fully realising the significance of what he had said (Jn. 11:49 – 52).

There were seven elements to the high priest's attire, for of all the priests the high priest had to be in a right relationship with God, particularly when entering the holy of holies on the Day of Atonement. We must never forget the contrast between our sinfulness and His Purity and Holiness which if our physical eyes saw it would lead to our instant death, even

---

[44] Note also that his wife was barren therefore the messenger, John the Baptizer, was their first-born son.

today. Yes we are saved by grace, but we will not be in a right state to be received into the presence of God until God has brought us to that point of perfection that will allow us to see Him.

Through ritual, using the blood of a goat and the holy anointing oil, the high priest was brought to a temporary state of perfection to allow him to enter into the most holy place on earth.

Let us consider the high priest's robes that were so vital to his office (Ex. 28):

Tunic	v39	Made of pure white, fine linen, it was worn next to the skin and reached down to his feet. (Ps. 132:9; Job 29:14; Rev. 3:5, 18; Rev. 4:4) The importance of this foundational garment cannot be overstated, for the essential righteousness of the person presenting themselves to God through the cleansing not just of a ceremonial washing (Ex. 40:12; Jn. 13:10) or works of righteousness which we have done, but of the blood which cleanses the conscience through the regenerative and renewing work of the Holy Spirit (Heb. 9:14; Titus 3:5).
		If we have not got the foundation garment in our relationship with God right, then that relationship is flawed from our perspective not God's. (Consider Matt. 22:11 – 14; Rev. 3:5; 19:8, 9)
Linen Breeches	v42	From the loins to the thighs to cover their nakedness, for those parts which are strictly of the flesh for fleshly purposes have their place in privacy, but have no place when we are worshipping our God.
Robe of Ephod	vs. 31 – 35	A long seamless garment (cf. Jn. 19:23, 24) in blue, symbolic of heaven, God's dwelling place – see above, with an opening at the top with additional weaving around it to strengthen the edge of the opening to prevent tearing, for the garment was not to be torn because it was holy before God. The hem was adorned with balls of richly coloured (blue, purple and scarlet) material

shaped like pomegranates, symbolic of fruitfulness, alternating with golden bells which sounded as he moved to perform his duties. This speaks of testimony, testifying to his ministry before God.

This was particularly relevant on the Day of Atonement when he went into the Holy of Holies, out of sight of the people. During this time, as the high priest met with God on behalf of the people, the people themselves standing in the congregation in the Court would give themselves to prayer and repentance. A total of 36, 70 or 72 items were on the hem, the exact number is disputed.

The blue of the garment speaks of heaven and with the dye being very scarce it could also speak of the Divinity of the one who would come from heaven to become the eternal High Priest.

The reason for the generosity of the Egyptians in giving of their substance to the departing Israelites was an act of God to provide the material ingredients of the tabernacle and the purchase of this dye, for although the people were required to freely give to the work of production, their wealth had been given to them as God's Spirit moved in the hearts of the people of Egypt; thus, all things ultimately come from above (Job 1:21).

Ephod   vs. 5 – 12   The high priest was to wear the robes whenever he ministered before the Lord in the tent, thus the fact that the ephod, which was distinctive of the office of high priest as the spiritual head of the nation, was made of the same material as the curtains and veil of the tabernacle identifying the strong connection between the authority and work of the high priest and the sanctuary (Heb. 8:1, 2), God's dwelling place on earth.
With the linen suggesting the purity of the

forthcoming Messiah, there are clear lessons we can learn from the tabernacle regarding the One who was to come.

Coloured threads of gold — deity, blue — heaven, God's dwelling place and from where the Christ came, purple — royalty for the Messiah was rightly claimed to be King of the Jews but is also King of kings and Lord of lords, and scarlet thread — sacrifice, the central theme of the operation of the earthly tabernacle of Moses and The Christ, the Messiah of Israel and the world.

The ephod, worn like an apron, for the bottom of the breast plate was fitted to the top of the ephod, consisted of two halves, back and front, held up by two shoulder bands connecting the two pieces and a highly decorated waist band which kept the Ephod close to his body — service, see also Eph. 6:14.

On the strap over each shoulder was secured in gold an onyx stone — remembrance stone. In the order of birth, the names of the tribal heads, starting with Reuben and including Joseph, were engraved on them, six on each. The shoulders were a place of strength; therefore, the high priest shouldered the responsibility before God of the spiritual life of the nation. It also spoke of the unity of the nation.

Breastplate   vs. 13 – 30   Called the breastplate of judgement, or decision, it was foursquare, meaning perfection, doubled over creating a pocket, made of the same materials as the ephod and set with four rows of three precious stones, each one engraved with a tribal name according to God's choice. The breast plate was held in place over the heart of the high priest.

The constantly changing meaning of Hebrew words means that the names given to the stones have become obscure making the exact identity of the stones used open to discussion, which is good because although the main purpose of the breastplate can be understood, the lessons gained from knowing the identity of each stone is no longer relevant because the earthly high priest's function is no longer required.

The fact that each stone was engraved meant that the high priest might have been able to use what was engraved on the stones to provide answers to mysteries particularly the identification of Achan (Josh. 7). Some suggest that the stones were illuminated by God to give a message when the high priest asked Him for direction. In David's day such methods were not needed as David sought God for His direction directly, just as Moses had done.

The identity, origin, physical form and working of the Urim and Thummim, literally the Lights and Perfections, and whether or not the twelve stones on the Ephod would light up or not to give God's decision, is obscure and disappeared after David. All that can reliably be said about them is that they were a means of seeking after God's will concerning a national decision such as to go to war or not. But David was able to speak to God directly and received His instructions through various ways.

What is clear is that the breastplate contained precious stones, held in place with gold, deity, thread, with the individual names of the twelve tribes, positioned over the heart of the high priest. Also, like the Onyx stones on the shoulder straps, they were there as a memorial before God and emphasised that the individual parts of the nation had been chosen by God to be His instrument to instruct the world and were held in place by Him.

The failure of the nation to serve God in the way He had intended was a matter of great sadness to God and the cause of much suffering for the people through many judgements.

Take for instance the account of the battle of Ai. It is interesting that when Achan sinned at the battle of Jericho (Josh. 7:21, 22) his sin was only discovered by the Israeli defeat at the battle of Ai. When Joshua went before the Lord after their defeat, even he questioned the Lord as to why they had crossed over the Jordan (Josh. 7:6 – 9), but God knew exactly what was going on (Josh. 7:10 – 13).

After the victory at the battle for Jericho it is interesting that the men sent to spy out the town of Ai (Josh. 7) were so confident that they could easily defeat the town that they told Joshua that only about three thousand men were needed.

Note that Joshua gained such confidence from their report that he did not first seek God's instruction regarding the second battle; had he done so Achan's sin could have been revealed to him by God without any loss of life.

What is revealed here is as much for us as for the Israelites at the time. There is nothing hidden from God that will not be revealed (Ps. 69:5; Matt. 10:26) in due time and there can be no doubt that God will bring us to account for all that we have done during our lives for good or ill. The battle for Ai was only won when they use all the resources God supplied and were in tune with Him.

How the identity of Achan was revealed tribe by tribe, clan by clan, and family by family and then man by man is not revealed. All that can be conjectured is that the Ephod and the Urim and Thummim were used by the high priest of that time to identify the one whose sin had been the cause of the catastrophe.

We are called upon to put on the breast plate of righteousness and, instead of the priestly robes, the whole armour of God that we may be able to withstand in the evil day, and having done all that we can to know and get into a personal, dynamic and right relationship with God, to stand upright before God in the field of battle (see Eph. 6:10 – 18)

Mitre/Turban   vs 36 – 38 God gave us a mind (brain) with which to think and consider what we receive through the various senses, and a heart with which to believe, for it is the heart that is considered to be the centre of a person's will and intellect.

The mitre or turban was the crown of the high priest, and the most important item of clothing that distinguished him from the other priests. He who was in charge of the working of the tabernacle and personally responsible before God for all that was done within the holy rooms of the tent had himself to be pure of thought, with his mind focused on God.

The tabernacle was a tangible emblem of the spiritual ideal, the type of relationship God desired to have with every individual; for if all men received the presence of the Holy Spirit within their bodies then God could rule mightily throughout the world through them. But the fickleness of men, particularly those who call themselves believers, is such that without the discernment given to us through the Holy Spirit we might be fooled more often by the false sincerity of many. (Gal. 1:6 – 12; Acts 20:25 – 32)

The linen used represented purity of thought and was next to the skin. The gold plate, thought to be about 1.5 inches in depth and to extend right across the forehead, held the inscription, "Holiness to the Lord" and was held in place by blue thread. Gold is symbolic of Deity for it is important to remember that Aaron was chosen not for his goodness or any other excellent qualities, for in so many ways he was a failure, but by God's unique and most wonderful Grace, just as we are who have been saved by the Grace of God through the shed blood of Christ our Messiah. (Eph. 4:17 – 32)

To give an idea of the importance of this item, consider the case of king Uzziah mentioned by Isaiah (Is. 6) at the time he, *saw the Lord ... high and lifted up*. In 2 Chronicles 26 we read that, *he [Uzziah] sought the Lord in the days of Zechariah, who had understanding in the visions of God; and as long as he [Uzziah] sought the Lord, God made him prosper."* (v5). But, probably after the death of his spiritual mentor, Uzziah's heart became proud and he tried to take on the role of high priest also by burning incense in the temple.

Not only did the Lord strike him with leprosy (v20), so that he became unclean and had to completely withdraw from society, but the disease erupted in the very place the plate with the engraving "Holiness to the Lord" would have been.

Paul calls on us to put on the helmet of salvation and in another place speaks of love because, *now our salvation is nearer than when we first believed ... and we need to walk properly as in the day ... being each of us fully convinced in our own mind as to what we believe and how we should behave amongst the community in which we live and before the saints who live about us* (Ro. 13:1 – 14:12, esp. vs. 13:11, 14:5, 12).

Indeed, we must make every thought captive to the obedience of Christ (2 Cor. 10:5) that we might become "Holiness to the Lord", not with a plate of gold over our foreheads, but keeping ourselves pure so that our foreheads are free to receive His mark on them (Rev. 7:3; 22:4; cf. Ez. 9 esp. v4 – the foreheads of those sensitive to the Spirit of God, for it was they alone who wept over the abominations within the city).

In chapter 6 we discussed the tent itself which allowed us to view the tabernacle complex from God's point of view. We considered the various items of furniture in the two rooms of the tent into which only the priests were allowed go. The Tent of the Meeting itself was designated holy ground, for it was a totally God centred area within the tabernacle complex into which only those who had been chosen of God to minister before Him were permitted to enter.

The tent is therefore of spiritual significance. Only by passing through the preparation processes within the compound between the entrance gate and the tent, could the individual priest learn how to approach (Prov. 1:7) God in due reverence and speak with Him. But the key factor in all this had to be an honest heart that is open to God. (Ps. 4:3; Ez. 14:4)

Sadly, some who were not prepared to believe but, by having been born into certain Levitical families, went through the preparation process unaffected and not only entered the tent but officiated at the services with a total disregard to propriety before God. Eli and his sons did not honour God in their hearts and submit themselves to Him so that they paid the price of falsehood. (1 Sam. 2:31 – 36 cf. Mic. 6:8)

Occupying the Holy of Holies, God looks towards the entrance gate at the far end of the compound surrounding the tent, and sees those entering His kingdom. He looks into the deep recesses of their hearts to see if they are approaching Him with pure motives and judges them accordingly. No false sacrifice was allowed, such as an animal that was not perfect or an offering that was not of the correct measure. (Mal. 1:7 – 14). No unrepentant sinner was forgiven but remained in his sin, even though he was probably unaware of the fact. The holy of holies was far too small for a God who filled the heavens, but from that place where a portion of His Spirit resided, He knew all that was going on.

In chapter 7 we considered the temple complex from sinful man's point of view. Man is initially faced with the gate of decision because anyone entering the complex must be prepared to approach the first item of furniture, which is the altar of confession, repentance and sacrifice, with the prescribed sacrifice. No man is allowed past this point of decision except with a sacrifice for sin, because God has laid down the rules that operate in the compound — the kingdom of God — and the tent. Even the high priest, who alone could enter the holy of holies one day a year, had to offer a sacrifice for sin on this altar.

As God, who is completely pure and holy, created us we would otherwise not exist. Therefore we must approach God in holy fear and trembling and on His terms because we are the rebellious sinners who have separated ourselves from Him and need to get right with Him in the only way that is satisfactory to a pure and holy God. Only He knows what we must do to bring ourselves to the point where we can start the process of getting ourselves in the right attitude of mind and heart, to prepare ourselves for the work of His Holy Spirit in and on our lives.

It is our decision.

We need to understand the rules governing salvation He has set and the way in which we approach Him and obey them. Only then will God respond to our approach.

Everything about the tabernacle compound and the procedures to be adopted within its precincts is vitally important, and must not be ignored. From our point of view in this twenty-first century, the illustration the tabernacle complex provides regarding the plan of salvation is important purely because it helps us understand more deeply just what the Messiah did from His birth, right the way through to His death, resurrection and ascension.

That God, because of His foreknowledge planned it all in intricate detail before the creation of the world, tells us so much about our loving God. That He laid out His plans before men in the design of the tabernacle according to the original in heaven and then gradually revealed it to man is remarkable enough, but the gradual development of that plan to the original timescale, in spite of the continual difficulties presented by an obstinate and disbelieving people whom He chose, starting with Abram, is altogether miraculous.

The priestly garments and their use of the holy anointing oil and the blood of the sacrifice separated the priests from the lay people; all have a meaning and purpose which helps us understand how we must approach God and how we must be clothed correctly (Matt. 22:1 – 14) in righteousness (fine linen). No other attire will do.

It is essential that we read the details of what God is saying to us through scripture without losing sight of the main picture. Please be sure you understand the collective teaching of these two chapters before moving on to the next chapter.

Through this description of the tabernacle that Moses built at God's command with the aid of Holy Spirit inspired craftsmen, both men and women, we have illustrated for us the way back to God that would steadily be taught to the nation of Israel and developed through their lives before God.

On entering the Promised Land, they were faced with an enemy that on their own they would have found it difficult or impossible to defeat. But providing they were prepared to be obedient to God's word and consult Him in all things, putting Him at the centre of their lives as individuals and as a nation, then no other nation would stand in their way.

8   THE PROMISED LAND

"… this commandment which I command you today
Is not too mysterious for you, nor is it far off.
It is not in heaven for you to ask,
'Who will ascend into heaven for us and
Bring it down that we may hear it and do it?'
Nor is it beyond the sea for you to ask,
'Who will go over the sea for us to bring it to us
That we may hear it and do it?'
But the word is very near you,
In your mouth and in your heart
That you may do it.

See, I have set before you life and good,
Death and evil,
In that I command you today
To love the Lord your God,
To walk in His ways
And keep His commandments …"

I call heaven and earth as witnesses against you today
That I have set before you all you need to know regarding
Life and death, blessing and cursing;
Therefore choose the way of life,
That both you and your descendents may live."
(Deut. 30:11 – 15, 19)

"I have come that they might have life,
And that they might have it more abundantly"
(Jn. 10:10)

Entering the Promised Land

We must now consider Israel under the leadership of Joshua[45] who was trained under Moses to lead the people, and commissioned in that role by God who assured him that, *as I was with Moses so shall I be with you* (Josh. 1:5).

---

[45] It would be useful if you read the book of Joshua as you progress through this chapter.

Joshua was one of two spies who returned from surveying the land of Canaan to declare that the people should go in and conquer the land as God said they could. Unfortunately, the older generation, who had been trained as slaves, were like sheep. They had no vision for the future or ambition to go into and possess a land of their own and were unwilling to believe and put their trust in God and make that all important decision to go into the land. Therefore, God caused them to wander around the wilderness for a total of forty years, continuing to train and test them to provide those who would enter the land with experiences of His ability to provide for them and protect them.

It is important at this point, as the people of that time are criticised for their lack of faith, that we ask ourselves if we are prepared to go where God sends us or whether we have within us a tendency to stay safe?

Moses had pointed out to the people that in the forty years of his leadership neither their clothes nor their sandals had worn out, they had had no need of bread baked in the oven or wine or intoxicating drink, for God had provided all the food and drink they <u>needed</u> for their good health; and when they were attacked God enabled them to conquer their attackers (Deut. 29:5 – 7).

This was a remarkable record. The tragedy was that so many still were not willing to believe that He did that and were therefore unable to put their trust in Him fully. As He is the same today as He was then, we must ask ourselves if we are willing to take God at His word and commit ourselves totally to Him and do whatever He asks us to do? In other words if we had lived at that time would we have sided with those who were willing to go in and possess the land given the opposition we would face trust that God would enable us to achieve victory, or side with those who did not believe God was able to support us against such opposition?

Just two trusted men were secretly sent into the immediate area beyond the Jordan by Joshua to gain the information he needed regarding the terrain and the defenses of Jericho (Josh. 2:1), the first city they would encounter. Rahab, whose inspired perception of the Lord their God and His plan for the land, who was an important factor in their forth coming battle, gave them vital help which enabled their mission to be successful and encouraged them that God was showing them that He was already preparing the way for them. On their return the stage was set for the people to cross over the river Jordan and start the process of possessing the land first promised to Abram.

But purity of mind and heart before God is essential if He is to work successfully through men to achieve His ends. Before crossing the Jordan into the land that had been contaminated with the increasingly depraved sins of the occupying nations, the army of God had to ensure that they were in a right state before Him.

For three days the people camped beside the Jordan to prepare themselves and obtain provisions for their journey (Josh. 1:10), after which they were told to sanctify or consecrate themselves (Josh. 3:5) in preparation for the battles ahead.

The number three is important because it is the number of the Trinity and completeness, for the three members of the trinity are together in all things and without disagreement, illustrating Divine perfection and completeness.

In preparing themselves, they were to take their minds off the things of the flesh, such as sexual intercourse, and spend time washing and meditating on the things of God. The purpose of this was to enable them to purify themselves so that they would be able to do the work of God by removing from the land all those whose sin had become so debased that it had become abhorrent to God. Then, as believers, they were to inhabit the land to purify it. All the fighting men of the tribes, even those of Reuben, Gad and Manasseh who had already been given land on the other side of the Jordan[46], were to be involved in the battles ahead.

The Ark of the Covenant, carried by chosen priests, was to go before the people to lead the way, with a respectful distance of two thousand cubits between them and the Ark, because of the power of God invested in it. The people were going to travel into unknown territory so it was essential they relied on God as their guide.

When they reached the river Jordan to cross over, as soon as the feet of the priests touched the water, they were told that the river would stop flowing from someway upstream, heaping up as though a transparent dam had been erected across it, just as had happened when they had crossed the Red Sea (Josh. 3).

What is this saying to us?

That their way over dry ground was continuous, barrier free, for God was leading them to the place He wanted them to go. At no time could they question whether or not they were going God's way, for He was enabling them (Is. 30:21), even to the conquering of their enemies.

As soon as the Israelites had crossed over the river Jordan, not only was fear put into the hearts of all the nations in the land (Josh. 5:1) but there had to be an accounting.

Some men, born during their slavery in Egypt when unbelief would have crept into the thinking of some families, and many born during their wilderness years, particularly during the frequent rebellions, had not been circumcised. Indeed, there were always those who were uncircumcised of heart among them (Deut. 10:16). This matter had to be dealt with for circumcision was not only an outward sign of their dedication to God and

---

[46] This land is no longer part of Israel.

an integral part of their covenant with God, but was also a sanctification of their sexuality to God.

Many of the people who left Egypt had died in the wilderness because of their rebellious activities, but with the act of circumcision completed, whereby they had re-dedicated themselves to God, God was able to roll-away, which is the meaning of the name Gilgal, from them the reproach of Egypt, the slave mentality and unbelief that had caused them to rebel (Josh. 5:2 – 9). Circumcision was essential to the Passover celebration for only those who were circumcised could partake of the Passover meal (Ex. 12:48).

By celebrating the Passover immediately they had entered the Promised Land, but before the fight for the land got underway, the people were remembering their deliverance from slavery in Egypt on the very day prescribed for that celebration (Ex. 12:6) which shows the accuracy of God's timing. It was a symbolic moment.

The celebration of this feast at this particular moment was not only a sign of the renewal of the Abramic and Mosaic covenants, it also brought together the remembrance of their release from bondage and death over forty years earlier and the promised new beginning that was now before them in the Promised Land.

Although the future was unknown, God had proved Himself to them over forty years and it was He who was instructing them to go forward and possess the land. Therefore, their future was completely tied up with their faith in and commitment to their God.

Following the Passover, the people were able to eat the produce of the land, probably found in the fields of the people who would have fled to the safety of Jericho. On that day not only were they able to eat a variety of fresh food for the first time, but at that moment the supply of manna stopped (Josh. 5:12). Therefore, that day provided a separation from their journeying in the wilderness to the new life in the Promised Land.

Joshua, who had been assured of his place within the plan of God, saw an angel appear before him, when he was surveying the city. The angel appeared as a man with a drawn sword who, when challenged, declared he was the captain of the army of the Lord. It is important to realise, firstly, that this was not a vision but an actual appearance and, secondly, that when Joshua prostrated himself before the man, with his face to the ground in an attitude of profound reverence, the man did not object to him doing so. Such was his position before God, and that He did not object to Joshua prostrating before Him, that it could well have been the Son of God appearing to Joshua, just as He appeared to Abraham as Melchizedek[47].

---

[47] It is interesting how the Holy Spirit has been a part of the creation and development of the world and all it contains from the time is was just a lump of rock so that He alone of the Godhead is intimately acquainted with the world in its entirety, but the appearances of the Son of God on the

Human Legacy Established

Joshua's experience was similar to that of Moses (Ex. 3:5; Josh. 5:15), for he had been told that he stood on holy ground; that is, that he was effectively in the presence of God. With the promises Joshua had received earlier from God (Josh. 1), this meeting with God further confirmed to him that, although he was central to God's plan for His people and their entry into the Promised Land, of which they were to take possession, he was also part of God's command structure in the battle for the land. It was his duty to be obedient to the commands of God, for in chapter 6 Joshua receives strict instructions regarding the battle for Jericho and how the people were to overcome the city. With it came the assurance that the city would be theirs.

This move of God to reassure Joshua not only of his selection by God as the nation's leader, but that God and his spiritual forces were fighting with him, brings into focus the fact that what has been happening on earth throughout the centuries is the physical evidence of a continuing battle in the spiritual realm. After all, who was it who initiated the separation between God and man but the angelic being we know as Satan. And who was it who incited people to seek forms of spiritual worship other than that which focused on God, such as those we have been discovering in this study, but Satan who is working his evil on earth even to this day?

Before the battle commenced, the people were assured that it had already been won (Josh. 6:2), provided they obeyed instructions, even though the king and men of the city were determined and experienced warriors who had frightened ten of the twelve spies sent into the land by Moses. It is important to remember this battle, for what happened here was to affect the outcome of the next battle.

The Battle for Jericho

The number seven is the number for spiritual perfection and is the hall mark of the Holy Spirit who is the author of the scriptures (2 Tim. 3:16, 17; 2 Pet. 1:20, 21), like the watermark in good quality paper. It is the number that regulates every period of incubation and gestation in insects, birds, animals and man. It is also the day on which God rested from His labours after the creation of man.

One other important point is that the treasure trove from this first battle was to be dedicated to God (Josh. 6:17 – 19); after all it was to be God's victory not theirs. Treasure taken by anyone would bring a curse upon them that would affect the whole nation.

The number seven dominates the battle for Jericho. The symbolic processions around the walls of Jericho seemed to be of a carnival nature except that armed men processed before the seven priests, who each blew

---

earth before His coming in human flesh is also significant, for it shows that He was fully acquainted with man before His coming as a babe.

on a trumpet made from a ram's horn, known as the Shofar. They were followed by the Ark of the Covenant, covered with the hangings of the tent, and then the rest of the people. The trumpeters going before the Ark emphasised its power and therefore that of the God it represented. It was the God of Israel the people of Jericho had to fear. The meekness and silence of the people as they followed in the wake of the Ark would have emphasised the power of their God represented by the Ark.

This action, repeated each day for six days, would have put curiosity followed by abject fear into the hearts of even the most experienced mighty men of valour because of the confidence the Israelites displayed in the might of their God. Then on the seventh day the people repeated the parade seven times, building up tension within the people inside the fortified walls before their mighty shout which brought the walls tumbling down and confusion within the now defenseless city. With the walls surrounded by fighting men the battle was won on the grounds of a dispirited population and far too broad a frontal attack.

Apart from Rahab and her family, no one survived the battle. The enemies of God, for they were a Satan worshipping people, had been defeated and annihilated.

The Battle for Ai

False confidence is dangerous. There are a number of factors leading up to the next battle that provide important lessons for us today.

When preparing for the battle of Jericho Joshua sent men out to survey the land and report back and it was no different for the preparation for the next battle (Josh. 7:2). But before the battle for Jericho there had been much preparation that focused the minds of the people on their God and the covenant they had with Him. Now, with that battle successfully behind them, the confidence level of the troops was high; but what about their attitude and relationship to God?

Where was their worship of God in thanks for the victory, and communication with God to ask Him about the future battle? Had they, particularly Joshua and the high priest, gone before God, worshipped Him and thanked Him for their success at Jericho with a new willingness to listen to Him speaking with them concerning their future battle at Ai. It would seem that did not happen, leading to the tragedy that was about to happen.

It is interesting that all through the book of Joshua we mostly read about Joshua and very little about the spiritual leadership of the high priest and the other priests, which could provide a reason for the seemingly complete destruction of the civil and spiritual infrastructure of the nation once it had conquered the land and taken possession of it.

The extent of the land Joshua and the people were to take possession of was from the Nile and the Mediterranean Sea to the river Euphrates. But how much of the land is now considered to be the land of Israel? Tribes to the east of the Jordan seem to have gone the way of all those who lost sight of the one true God. What is known of the tribes of Reuben and Gad and the half tribe of Manasseh who were the first to settle?

When the men returned from spying out the city of Ai they reported that only two or three thousand men were needed to defeat the small town of Ai. There is no mention of Joshua seeking the decision of the Lord as David did when fighting the Philistines (2 Sam. 5:17 – 25). Yet Joshua was not the supreme commander, as his meeting with the 'man carrying the sword' so clearly illustrated. So why does scripture not record Joshua's willingness to seek instructions from God as Moses used to do? False hopes born out of self-imposed ignorance led to disaster and depression, which happened when the battle of Ai was so emphatically lost and 36 men died.

Consider God's reaction to Joshua when he poured out his lack of deep faith before God (Josh. 7:6 – 9), putting the onus on God for their failure. Indeed, there seemed to be a spot of fatalism in his heart, '... *O why were we not content with remaining the other side of the river Jordan* ...'. But why did they cross the river? Whose instructions were they obeying and how spectacular was the crossing that it should be remembered by future generations with the laying of twelve stones taken from the middle of the river Jordan? (Josh. 4 esp. vs8, 9)

When God replied, He told Joshua in no uncertain terms to get up and stop complaining and wallowing in sorrow and reproach before Him.

"Israel has sinned", God declared, because of theft and deception.

It was because Joshua had become mindful of his position as leader and commander-in-chief of the nation that he had forgotten that he was appointed to that position by the God to whom he had suddenly become deaf.

Having been brought back to reality, Joshua set about searching for the person who had been the cause of this disaster, with the assistance of the high priest with the ephod containing the Urim and Thummim.

From nation, to tribe, to family, to man, Achan was identified as the culprit and paid the penalty for the curse that he had attracted to himself, along with all his family (7:20 – 26), and all because he disobeyed the law in relation to covetousness, not against a fellow member of Israel, but God.

For coveting a goodly Babylonian garment, some silver and some gold that had been dedicated to God, the sentence was death. The lesson the people needed to learn was that they were not to abuse God's love and care for them by stealing from Him, after all their future depended upon Him continuing to supply all their needs.

What Achan stole from God were the first fruits of the battle, which means the first of the produce, from whatever activity, belonged to God. It was essential that in all things they remembered that everything they received, both what is considered to be good or bad, came from God, or was allowed by God, and was ultimately for their good. Therefore they had to consider God as their benefactor through the offering of sacrifices and offerings to Him through His servants the priests. This close relationship was also essential for the progressing of God's plan of salvation.

The severity of the sentence at this early stage of their walk with God, which only God could have performed, and particularly as they were taking possession of a land steeped in dehumanising sin, reflected the fact that they were to serve God with due reverence and respect to His mighty power and holiness. What this incident did was to emphasise to all the people that nothing is hidden from God and that *before all the people I will be glorified.* (Lev. 10:3)

With God back in charge (Josh. 8:1, 2) in the minds of the people, and the spoils of war available to the people, <u>all the men of war</u> were required to go up to defeat Ai. Neither the people nor the warriors of Ai would have known that their previous victory against Israel had been because God had not been fighting with Israel. Indeed, they would have been encouraged by their obviously mistaken belief that Israel could be defeated. Notice the strategy for this repeat battle was carefully considered, being faced as they were with more courageous and therefore more determined warriors, their abject fear of Israel having been dispelled by their recent victory.

Now that Israel had been reunited with God and a strategy had been carefully planned, the battle was won. (Josh. 8:3 – 29) Afterwards the whole of Israel presented itself to God through sacrifices and the reading of the word written by Moses (Josh. 8:30 – 35), something the nation, led by the high priest with Joshua, should have done after the battle of Jericho, thereby fulfilling covenant obligations to the God who had enabled them to succeed. Such an action would have allowed God to warn them of the sin that had been committed in Jericho thereby saving lives and the embarrassment of an early defeat.

What this whole episode did was to make the Israelites realise that their entry into the Promised Land was because of God's promise to Abram. They were the beneficiaries of that promise, and it was God's battle they were fighting on earth on His behalf as His human army against the fact that the sin and depravity in sexual and religious matters of the inhabitants of that land had reached a state that God found intolerable. They were guilty of despoiling His creation.

Instead of a repeated judgement of a flood over the whole earth, which God promised not to do through a covenant with Noah and the sign of the rainbow, He had nurtured a nation born of men chosen because of their love and commitment to Him, developing a means of direct communication that would allow them to get to know Him with increasing intimacy. With a direct and developing relationship between God and His chosen people, God's plan was for this nation to go in and cleanse that strategic central area of the world; then, by living a life of obedience and worship in the land, He could demonstrate the reality of the blessings that would come to all those who lived their lives as believers in Him.

The central theme of the Tabernacle of Moses was how man could approach God and experience a new life in Him, and the result of adopting a life with God at its centre would be the enormity of the blessings and protection from enemies that God, who as creator was literally all-powerful, was able to give to them.

The life of Israel, as recorded in the first testament, clearly shows us that where Israel's adherence to His word declined with regard to the Law and statutes, so the promised blessings and protection also declined. They could not succeed, as the episode at Ai so clearly shows, when their lives did not demonstrate a complete and full commitment to, and worship of, Him.

The leadership, both spiritual and secular, failed to focus the nation's attention on the God who had chosen them out of all the nations of the world, and this caused the nation as a whole to fail. This did not mean that there were not those within the nation who did fully believe and were focused on serving Him, such as the two faithful spies sent by Moses.

Such a national disaster comes to all nations and empires that raise themselves up but which God brings down at the appropriate time, for sin ultimately makes the previously successful nation or empire reach the point where it loses the focus and energy the initial leadership brought to it.

If the disaster at Ai was not bad enough, the lack of communication between Joshua and God was to be repeated soon after. The instruction God had given was that all the people in the land had to be slaughtered. The reason for this is that one bad apple in a basket of apples, contaminates the rest. This was the ever-present danger for the nation all the while they were removing the people from the land.

There are some who find the slaughtering of human beings in the first testament distressful, but what we must realise is that there is a spiritual battle raging on earth between Satan and God, and the prize that is being fought over is the offer of eternal life to all men. From the moment he persuaded Eve to rebel against God by eating the fruit of the forbidden tree, Satan has been trying to lure people away from the truth about God's salvation, and generate sympathy for all those who die because they oppose or show indifference to the creator God and His desire to bring all people to repentance.

Consider the vast array of religious groups who today purvey a different gospel to that of the Lord God of Israel and His Christ. They are all trying to attract people away from God through confusion. Yet it is only through our total and unconditional acceptance of the conditions of salvation the one true God is offering, that we can be saved to the uttermost and are therefore able to enter into His rest for eternity (Heb. 2:14 – 3:19; cf. Jn. 14).

All the gods being worshipped at the time of the Israelites' entrance into the Promised Land were a distraction to them and a danger to the progressive development of God's plan of salvation that was able to benefit the whole of mankind. Unless we consider the spiritual along with the physical, nothing in scripture makes sense. It is a case of whether we are serious about eternal life with God or whether an eternity in the fire of hell is acceptable. (Lk. 16:19 – 31)

Let us consider the activities of Balaam (Num. 22), who had special powers (v6) and was called by Balak, king of Moab, to come and curse the Israelites whose victories against their enemies had brought great fear upon them (vs. 2 – 6). Although God initially stopped him from going, God then allowed him to meet with Balak on condition that he only said what God put into his mouth (v38).

In Numbers 23 we find Balaam blessing the Israelites bountifully (v11) because the Holy Spirit was speaking through him. Finding the experience uplifting, he decided to drop the use of sorcery (Num. 24:1), allowing God to speak through him. But Balaam had a secret purpose and that was to ingratiate himself with Balak so that he could receive the worldly riches the king had offered him. What Balaam would not acknowledge was that, if God had such power over nations, He also had power over individual people, which the evidence of him speaking the words of God had demonstrated.

Balaam's willingness to set aside principles in the pursuit of worldly gain caused his downfall. Joshua, during the covenant renewal at Shechem, revealed that God refused to accept Balaam's real purpose in going to Balak, which God stopped by causing the ass to rebel against its master (Num. 22:23 – 35, cf. Josh. 24:9, 10). Peter, writing about false teachers (2 Peter. 2), calls them brute beasts who speak evil of the things they do not understand and includes in their number Balaam who loved the wages of unrighteousness (vs. 15, 16; cf. Jude 11).

But it is in Revelation (Rev. 2:14) that we find out that Balaam encouraged Balak to undermine the Israelite's relationship with God by encouraging the king to get them to eat food sacrificed to idols and commit sexual immorality, for this would sour their relationship with God and, like the hair of Samson which, whilst uncut, was a symbol of his dedication to God, would cause them to become vulnerable like any other nation (see Deut. 13:12 – 18).

This is the problem experienced by all believers who do not read the word of God regularly or spend time in His presence in prayer and meditation. If we are not focused on God in life and do not afford the time and space to personally communicate with Him, how can we possibly expect Him to guide us and bless us or answer our prayers?

In Numbers 25 we read of the effect of Balaam's devious instruction to Balak, for Balak quickly followed Balaam's advice and invited the children of Israel to the sacrifices the Moabites made to their gods. By bowing down to Baal of Peor the people became joined to this god (Num. 25:2), which was harlotry. Hosea was instructed to live his life with a harlot by marrying Gomer. In this way God wanted to demonstrate what they were doing when they should have kept themselves pure because they were married to Him. (Hos. 1:2)

When the Children of Israel offered sacrifices to the god Baal at Peor, becoming joined to him, God's anger was aroused. Indeed, so fierce was His anger that He instructed Moses to hang the offenders out in the fierce heat of the sun and in full view of the people. One young man, a prince among the people, had the effrontery to defiantly take a Midianite princess into his tent to lie with her in full view of Moses and all the congregation of Israel. Phinehas, a grandson of Aaron, saw it and taking a javelin in his hand thrust it through the man and the woman bringing to an abrupt end the plague sent by God on all those who rebelled against Him. We are told that twenty-four thousand died from the plague because of their sin before God. Such is God's attitude to all sin, which corrupts the purity of His creation, is that no unrepentant sinner will experience the delights of His kingdom.

Joshua chapter nine gives the account of a treaty entered into through deception and lack of seeking after the knowledge of God for God knows the hearts and objectives of all men. It is understandable that the people of Gibeon wanted to save themselves because God's instruction to Moses was that all the inhabitants of the land, who all worshipped satanic idols, refuting the existence of the God of creation, had to be destroyed so that the land could be purified (v24).

Working craftily, with old dilapidated clothes and equipment and mouldy food (vs. 4, 5) they appeared before Joshua as those who had come to the end of a very long journey, offering lies about their appearance and the state of their food. The men of Israel made the fatal mistake of not seeking the counsel of the Lord. Using his own judgement, Joshua made peace with them (vs. 14, 15), entering into a covenant with them that was totally against the plan of God for that land. This cost the Israelites dear, for when the neighbours of Gibeon heard of the treaty they had signed with Israel, and fearing for their future, five kings decided to attack Gibeon resulting in the Gibeonites' call to Joshua for assistance. (Josh. 10:6)

The Time of the Judges

To leave such a nation, well grounded in the worship of idols, within the country, even though they were at first treated like slaves, would lead to sin permeating throughout the land. The book of Judges tells of the ebb and flow of oppressive invaders in the land because of the lack of strong, God-focused worship emanating from the Tabernacle which was initially established at Shiloh. Unfortunately, even under the leadership of Joshua, much of the land was still unconquered and we read that, because the Children of Israel did not fully obey the word of the Lord (Jud. 2:1 – 5) some nations would remain and be a thorn in the side of Israel, even to this day, and their gods a snare to them.

Israel is now surrounded by those who worship a god whose name is Allah, once the moon god. The high hopes of gaining full possession of the land were tarnished by sin within the members of Israel, and so it is with the people of Israel today and the members of the Gentile church, so many of whom do not accept the inerrancy of the word of God or, because of errant teaching and leadership, do not worship God in pure spirit and in God's truth.

Such was the lack of faith that when the prophetess Deborah called on Barak to fight against the army of Jabin and its commander Sisera. He agreed to lead the army but only if Deborah herself went with him (Jud. 4 esp. v8).

At a time when it was a matter of considerable disgrace for a woman to achieve a greater military victory than the commander, Deborah prophesied that a woman would overcome Sisera (v9). Their miraculous military success against a formidable, mobile army was God-appointed and engineered. This nation was one of the thorns in Israel's side because of their disobedience before God. With the two armies arrayed below mount Tabor, Sisera chose to be with his chariots of iron on the flat plain by the river Kishon where they would be more effective.

God had also caused a descendent of the father-in-law of Moses to unwittingly position himself in a strategic place (v11) by Kedesh, away from his ancestral home. On the day of the battle, flash floods, caused by a miraculously timed thunderstorm, rendered the iron chariots useless (Josh. 5:4, 5) causing Sisera to flee the battle field on foot in the direction that would cause him to pass the tent of Jael, the wife of Heber the Kenite. Inviting Sisera into her tent she made him comfortable and when he was in a deep slumber, drove a tent peg into his temple killing him (Josh. 4:17 – 24). When they focused on God, they were victorious.

What had happened to the nation? The preparation of the nation, through cleansing and seeking after God before the battle for Jericho, and the significance of their entry into the land with a flooded river Jordan being miraculously dried up for them to cross and with the Ark of the Covenant so prominently announcing God's presence with them, all these dramatic events should have been seared into their memory. The contrast between the victory over Jericho and the initial defeat at Ai, and then the

Achan incident leading to the successful second battle for Ai, should have given them enough understanding of their position before God for them to be persuaded disciples of God.

Unfortunately, this was not the case and the majority of the people continued to lack personal faith and objectivity in their relationship with their God. Joshua's seeming unwillingness to be as subservient to God as Moses was, undoubtedly did not help, and the decisions he made on his own led to on-going problems for them and their descendants.

It is in seeking to understand the actions and lives of these real people that we can gain an understanding of how we need to approach God and relate to Him and, most of all, the need to be completely loyal to Him in His service. Do we tend to make decisions on our own without consulting Him? Have we got so used to asking God for forgiveness of sin, perhaps through the repeated words of the communion service, *Lord we have sinned against you and our fellow men in thought, word and deed,* that the real horror of sin from God's point of view is lost on us?

Is the routine that governs our life in the day to day, week to week, year to year activities we are involved in, and the pattern of work we are engaged in, such that we do not really need God's help?

As a prison visitor I have met with men who have been taken aside out of the normal humdrum existence of life to find out for the first time that they had lost their way. By being taken out of the world for a time, some who had given a commitment to God many years previously, have had time to think about their relationship to God and renew their commitment to Him. Others, whose relationship with God was somewhat precarious, have had time to seek after Him and find Him and be aligned to Him properly.

Some men had a more dramatic change than others; indeed, one man, inside for murder, who had had no contact with God during his life, came face to face with God through a series of connected events that changed him from being godless to being on fire for God.

It is interesting that my working life changed, along with my daily dependence on God, when I went from being a member of staff of a company to being a contractor, when no follow-on work was guaranteed and work could mean living away from home for long periods.

Without strong spiritual leadership many people go astray, as the case of King Uzziah so clearly illustrates. Joshua, who to the end proclaimed his faith in God, clearly told the people that only when they were obedient to the words of the law and the statutes of God, and worshipped and listened to Him, to the exclusion of all other religious propaganda, would they live in peace and prosperity. (Josh. 23, 24)

He declared that, *as for me and my house, we will serve the Lord.* (Josh. 24:15) Unfortunately the people's declared promise to serve the Lord (Josh. 24:21, 22) proved to be false, causing God to bring ever increasing trouble across their borders as promised.

The twelve recorded judges of the people kept the knowledge of God alive. Tragically, such was the transient and fragmented state of the Israelites so newly established in the Promised Land, with everyone living according to their own rules, that only those of the remnant who resolutely focused their attention on God, seeking Him through prayer and worshipping Him with a right heart before Him, maintained some semblance of spiritual life within the nation.

A New Man of God

Such was the belief of Hannah, first wife of Elkanah, who, although barren, still believed in God, was convinced that He alone could give her a child, particularly the son for whom she so clearly craved. Weeping before God in the temple — as a woman and non-priest she would have been confined to the temple outer court, Hannah poured out her soul before Him (1 Sam. 1:15). With Eli's blessing ringing in her ears, Hannah left the temple believing that her petition to God would be granted and putting aside her sadness ate a meal. The boy that was born to her she had promised to dedicate to the God who had removed her shame of barrenness, for she went on to produce five more children.

When the child was weaned[48], she took him to the temple and presented him to Eli the high priest to serve God in the temple, as she had promised (1 Sam. 1:11). Because of the uniqueness of his birth, it is possible that Eli understood Samuel to be someone special before God and therefore allowed him to be his assistant, providing him with accommodation next to his own which might well have been a tent, as in the days of Moses.

The whole purpose of God choosing Abraham, Isaac and Jacob and then developing the nation of Israel was, and still is, that He wants men and women to dedicate themselves to His service, so that He can use them to spread the good news of salvation[49]. His plan of salvation reached its fulfilment in the sacrifice of the Messiah. But unbelief amongst the Jews and the nations and churches of the world, as well as complete ignorance of what is really on offer from God, makes the need for men and women to offer themselves to God as His servants, as Isaiah did, both necessary and urgent. (Jn. 4:34 – 38)

It is true that God speaks to individuals direct and, through the work of His Holy Spirit, many have come into a remarkable vibrant relationship with God; but that does not absolve those who purport to believe to seek such an intimate and dynamic relationship with God that would allow Him

---

[48] Probably at the age of eight.
[49] As the Messiah said: "Therefore whoever confesses Me before men, him I will also confess before My Father who is in heaven. But whoever denies Me before men, him I will also deny before My Father who is in heaven (Matt. 10:32).

through them to bring others into a right relationship with Him.

We need to sow the word just as I am doing now. We also need to reap the reward of the sower in leading the sinner to Christ, which I have also been privileged to do. Such dedicated work, which relies on individuals being totally and consistently open to acting out the will of God according to the direction and inspiration of the Holy Spirit, that will attract its own reward that will be stored in heaven, for where our real treasure is, that will be the true focus of our hearts. (Matt. 6:21)

Hannah's motive may have been the ending of the shame of her barrenness that she had had to endure, particularly from Elkanah's second wife Peninnah, whose insincere and persistent provocations exacerbated Hannah's sense of failure and shame. But her focus on the reality and awesome power of God and her willingness to dedicate her firstborn son to Him, demonstrated a life of commitment to God that shone brightly in an otherwise spiritually dark world and nation.

It is this balance of being in the world but not of the world that we need to adopt for ourselves by placing our trust for our future, both here and after our physical death, in God alone, allowing God to awaken our spiritual lives so that through constant use, our spiritual life might become established and strong.

However strong Eli's faith in God may have been he did not fulfil his responsibility for the proper conduct of the temple services. His sons, ill-disciplined and out of control, did what they wanted; bending the rules and amending the instruction for the offering of sacrifices that God had given to Moses. They were godless sons who were defying God, effectively cursing His Name, and therefore heading for disaster. (1 Sam. 2:12 - 25) Was this because Eli had not given them proper instructions when they were under training on the books of Moses and particularly the book of Leviticus? We will never know for sure.

We are informed that God had not spoken directly to any individual, in a publicly confirmed way that affected the whole nation for some considerable time. By the time Samuel was a young man, possibly 12 years old, and Eli was very old and had diminishing eyesight, God called to the sleeping Samuel. Eli may have called out to Samuel in the night before because, with the call from God being so clear, he automatically thought that Eli was calling him. But it was not until Samuel had come into him for the third time, insisting that he had heard a voice calling him, that Eli realised the divine nature of the call and instructed him how to respond the next time God called.

Eli had been warned of impending disaster by a man of God who revealed to Eli God's anger at the laxity of his disciplining of his sons (1 Sam. 2:29), and that God would only honour those who honoured Him, for the altar was His altar upon which incense was burnt, the sacrifices offered were His sacrifices and the offerings His offerings that were commanded to be offered in His dwelling place.

What Eli knew and his sons seemingly did not, was that they had been chosen by God to minister before Him, which meant they were performing their duties in God's presence on behalf of God and therefore all that they did had to be done in an attitude of utter respect and worship, in spirit and truth. The disaster that would come upon his house was clear; it would be sudden and sure, like an axe at the base of a sapling.

It is no wonder, when the child Samuel came to Eli in the early morning on the third occasion to say that he was definitely responding to his call, that Eli realised this was God speaking to the child. Eli's own experience of God told him that God would reveal something to Samuel concerning the future of his house. Questioning him later, Eli heard the word of the Lord from Samuel concerning his unwillingness to restrain his sons and their vile activities, thus condemning them to an eternal death for neither sacrifice nor offering could atone for their totally disrespectful attitude to, indeed their blasphemy against, the God into whose service they had been ordained and employed.

It is interesting that God, knowing what the heart of Samuel would be, told Eli that He was raising up for Himself a faithful priest who shall do *according to what is in My heart and in My mind.* Such was to be his spiritual sensitivity (1 Sam. 2:27 – 36).

Eli either would not or could not change the lifestyle of his rebellious sons and therefore was expecting judgement to fall at any time. The message God gave to Samuel and which he then relayed to Eli was:

> *11 Then the Lord said to Samuel: "Behold, I will do something in Israel at which both ears of everyone who hears it will tingle.*
> *12 In that day I will perform against Eli all that I have spoken concerning his house, from beginning to end.*
> *13 For I have told him that I will judge his house forever for the iniquity which he knows, because his sons made themselves vile, and he did not restrain them.*
> *14 And therefore I have sworn to the house of Eli that the iniquity of Eli's house shall not be atoned for by sacrifice or offering forever." (1 Sam. 3)*

It is important for us to notice that God did not speak directly to Eli's sons, for as the high priest that was Eli's task. It was also most probable that his sons would not be able to hear God speak to them even if He did try to do so direct because of their total disregard for Him. But God's anger was against Eli, and through him his sons, because of Eli's exalted position as high priest, and minister, before God and before the people.

Human Legacy Established

It is no wonder the people were being put off worshipping God when they saw things being done in the temple that were not according to the spirit of the service let alone the rules governing it, which knowledge was available to all. Eli recognised the proper nature of the sentence against him and his house by saying, *let Him do what seems good to Him.* (1 Sam. 3:18b)

Such will be the severity of the sentence visited upon the heads of all those who perform, and have performed, duties as spiritual leaders of the 'church', particularly in the western world today, in a similar disrespectful manner. A sentence not spoken by God directly to them as there was sufficient information and knowledge available to everyone through the published Word of God as at the time of Eli and Samuel, telling them of how they must approach and minister before God and what they can expect if they do not abide by the instructions provided.

It would seem that, like many ministers and lay leaders today, the priests did not study the writings of Moses to the depths they should have done, nor did they seek after a person spiritual relationship with God which not only meant they were totally ignorant of what God properly required of them, but also they could not have performed their duties with spiritual sensitivity and understanding that would have made the experience of the offeror so much more meaningful.

This book and many, many others also provide plenty of additional explanation, teaching people how they can respond to the calling of God, who is always ready to receive a repentant sinner, who is willing and able to enter into a deep and spiritually vibrant relationship with Him. God has provided the means for man to reach out to Him as the Bible so clearly illustrates, but it is up to the individual to seek after God with all his heart through prayer and a personal in-depth study of the scriptures. Only then will God respond.

By the time Samuel was 30 years of age he had proved to the whole nation that God was with him and that God had established him as a prophet in Israel. During this time Eli allowed Samuel to grow in the Lord and in His service, without obstruction or animosity.

The fall of the house of Eli was dramatic in its execution. Israel, assisted by the excesses of Hophni and Phinehas, had become disillusioned with God. The Philistines[50], their enduring enemy, had defeated them and, on this occasion, having lost about four thousand fighting men the leaders wondered why the Lord had, *defeated us today against the Philistines?* (1 Sam. 4:3) There is no record of Eli making any comment concerning God's accusations against him and his family and their execution of the services in

---

[50] By naming the land Palestine, the emperor Hadrian was insulting the rebellious Jews who had caused such mayhem in that part of the empire following the death of their Messiah, who they did not recognise.

the temple, which might have been the foundational cause of this particular defeat.

If God was not with them in the battle, Eli did not suggest they seek God and offer sacrifices to Him. He was also very, very fat which signalled inactivity. This situation seems to have been a repeat of the tragedy of the first battle for Ai. The Israelites, under Eli's complacent stewardship of the high priestly office, had come to a low point in their spiritual state before God because their immediate reaction was to bring God to the battle in the form of the Ark of the Covenant. As God was to prove in the days ahead, if the hearts of the Israelites were not in tune with Him then no outward show of involving God in their affairs was of any practical use, even if His own holy things were involved.

Although some of the Philistines became fearful of the power of these 'might gods' who struck the Egyptians with all the plagues in the wilderness, there were others who spoke as from God encouraging their countrymen, *be strong and conduct yourselves like men* giving the Philistine army courage to once again defeat the army of Israel (1 Sam. 4, esp. v9 cf. Jud. 7 esp. v14).

The catastrophic capture of the Ark in the battle resulted, as prophesied, in the death of Eli's two sons and his own death devastating Israel. The reason the nation became subservient to the Philistines was because God had left them powerless as a result of the priests' corruption and their faithlessness.

Although the wife of Phinehas named her new born son Ichabod, saying that the glory had departed from Israel for the Ark of God had been captured; in fact, the glory had already departed, for God had withdrawn his protection long before the loss of the Ark. She seemed totally unaware of the activities of her husband and his brother which were partly the cause of the people's hearts being turned away from God. It is no good complaining about misfortunes if we ourselves are at fault because of our lack of commitment, faithfulness and obedience to Him.

The experiences of the Philistine tribes, who were probably glad at first to have the Ark of the Covenant of Israel as a war trophy and which they placed before the statue of their god Dagon in the temple dedicated to it, are interesting in so far as God's power is demonstrated so emphatically amongst unbelievers without the assistance of believers. God does not need the involvement of man for Him to show His undiminished power and authority over mankind. He is more than able to do things on His own. This clearly illustrates the truth of the what the Lord said to Zechariah through an angel, *not by might, nor by power, but by my Spirit says the Lord of Hosts* (Zech. 4:6).

Having said that it is His declared desire to involve those in His work who are willing to totally commit themselves to His service.

Human Legacy Established

The Ark's presence in the temple of their god Dagon (1 Sam. 5) demonstrated the ineffectiveness of pagan gods in general. It was not God who had lost the battle. It was the Israelites who had lost the battle because, through their attitude to their God, He was not with them to enable them to overcome. It was their faithlessness, their spiritual destitution that was the reason for their failure, and so it is for us today. The church in the western world is hemorrhaging members because the leaders and preachers are preaching and teaching a foreign gospel, even an apostate gospel[51].

We, as individuals and as a church, which is two or more true believers meeting together for worship, will only receive power from on high if we are willing to totally surrender ourselves to God and willingly allow Him to rule in our hearts and lives, guiding us according to His plan for our lives.

As the events leading up to the loss of the Ark so clearly illustrate, for God to work in our lives we must be as dedicated to Him as He desires to be dedicated to us. It is a marriage of the most pure order that God desires. Be casual, uncommitted, or part time in our commitment to Him and we will find ourselves at variance with Him and He will withdraw His commitment to us.

With the cry of the Philistines ascending to heaven because of the shame of their god Dagon, brought about when the Ark of the Lord God of Israel was placed in his temple, and the disastrous plagues that they experienced as the Ark was moved from town to town, God guided their pagan priests and diviners concerning the method of how to return the Ark to its rightful home (1 Sam. 6).

The production of the five effigies of each of the tumours and rats, were for a trespass (sin) offering for the five Philistine cities. They were a reminder of the bronze[52] serpent raised up in the desert (Num. 21:8) but this time the effigies were in gold representing deity, for the Philistines had been forced to recognise that they were not dealing with a local god but an all-powerful and almighty God (v3), and it was to Him they were returning the Ark, not to Israel.

The message was quite specific. Give glory to the God of Israel (v5) so that He will lighten His hand from you and from your gods, clearly putting the position of the God of Israel above that of their gods. By using the unfaithfulness of His people who were supposed to be there to demonstrate the blessings of God to those who love Him, and by allowing the Ark of His presence to be captured, God had managed to persuade unbelievers of His mighty power, and that the power of Israel was because of Him, not the people. We must also learn lessons from this incident.

---

[51] A gospel devoid of the true teaching of Christ.

[52] Bronze represents holiness and justice and typifies the divine character of Christ who took upon Himself the fire of God's wrath.

The importance of the first testament is here explained. *Why do you harden your hearts*, asked the pagan priests and diviners under the influence of the Holy Spirit, *as the Egyptians and Pharaoh hardened theirs?* (1 Sam. 6:6; cf. Heb. 3:8) for the history of the plagues God sent against the Egyptians for the purpose of releasing the Children of Israel from the authority of Pharaoh had been so terrible and awe-inspiring that it had been remembered by all the surrounding nations, but so often forgotten about by the Israelites themselves.

For the Philistines, the likeness of the sudden appearance and spread of the bubonic plague to the Egyptian plagues, as they desperately moved the Ark of the Covenant from town to town, was such that they were forced to seek for a way of appeasing the God of Israel and returning the Ark which had been captured with such jubilation but which now no one wanted anywhere near them. Notice that no one amongst the Philistines was actually killed for handling it as happened to Uzzah. (2 Sam. 6:7)

The manufacture of a new cart on which was placed the Ark and a chest containing the 10 golden effigies, and the use of two milk cows that would not willingly leave their calves, showed their seriousness in wanting to not only return the Ark to its rightful owner, but also to appease this all-powerful God who had caused them so much harm.

As the pagan priests and diviners told the people, if the cows took the Ark to its own territory then the plague was of God and if not then it was purely by chance, although what had happened to the statue of their god Dagon had already proved the power of the God of Israel over other gods. The news of this incident must have reached the Israelites and would surely have proved to them their need to fully commit themselves to their all-powerful God.

The contrast between the effect of the Ark on the people of Philistia and on those of the house of Abinadab, where the Ark was housed after its release from captivity, is stark. God was no doubt hoping that His actions against the Philistines whilst the Ark was on its own in, what was for Israel, hostile territory, taught both the Philistines and the people of Israel a very important lesson about the awesomeness and independence of His presence and sovereign power which the symbol of the Ark represented.

The blessings Israel had received over the years since God made a unique covenant with them on Mount Sinai were not because of their goodness to Him, but His goodness and mercy towards them. This same God is supposed to be the God worshipped by Christian churches, but how many of the individuals who make up those churches recognise the power and awesomeness of our God and our responsibility towards Israel with whom we have become joined through the sacrifice of their Messiah? (1 Cor. 3:5 – 17, esp. vs. 10, 11, 16, 17; Eph. 2:11 – 22, esp. vs. 19 – 21; 1 Pet. 2:4 – 10)

Human Legacy Established

Samuel was the firstborn son of Hannah, the barren and despised woman, who trusted in God and was willing to offer up a son given to her by Him for His service. This same Samuel, who was trained from a lad in the things of God, in the course of time, entered into a true relationship with Him, for he heard God speak to him in the early hours of the morning, and his trust in the living God became part of him. This chosen one became God's high priest on the sudden death of the disrespectful and easy-going Eli, who was so careless concerning the things of God.

This was following God's judgement on his sons who showed such a callous indifference towards the God in whom they had such little belief and for whom they had such little respect. Like Nadab and Abihu, the two sons of Aaron the first high priest who died so dramatically within the tabernacle court (Lev. 10), this was surely a salutary lesson for Israel when coupled together with the dramatic events in Philistia, if they had the desire and were willing to search for such truth.

Consider Paul, the ardent Pharisee, who studied under Gamaliel, probably the foremost teacher of the word of God at the time and highly respected by the people (Acts 5:34 – 39). Paul's heart, however misdirected, was for God. Having been trained in the Law, Paul changed after his conversion following the miraculous visitation of Christ on the Damascus road. (Acts 9:1 – 22) In his time of enforced blindness he had time to meditate on the word and was able, through the tuition given to him by the Holy Spirit, to realise where he had gone wrong in his service of God. In his treatise on the more excellent way (1 Cor. 13) Paul itemises the errors that Jews and Christians need to avoid, which can be merely religious exhibitionism, but stresses the importance of spiritual gifts which only God can provide:

Speaking with tongues — pagans enter into trance like attitudes and can speak with strange tongues and make strange and 'other unworldly' noises that pertain to be godlike and pass as spiritual utterances that have no meaning. They also have the potential of being demonic in inspiration. (Acts 8:9 – 24)

But the God given gift of tongues is completely different, for there is no need to enter into a trance like state but a person in their right mind can burst forth in a strange language in a time of worship and prayer on their own or amongst other believers. These tongues can also be interpreted by someone with the gift of interpretation. In fact, Paul says that no one should speak in tongues when in a group of believers without the message given being interpreted.

Gifts of prophecy and understanding — the knowledge of spiritual mysteries was sought by the philosophers of Athens (Acts 17:16 – 33) who spent their time either telling or hearing about some new thing (v21) that did not necessarily change their lives but satisfied their intellectual tendencies.

However, such things feed the mind but not the heart and could therefore be considered as religious through required ritual. Although mentally stimulating for those of a philosophical bent, this was, in fact, a mindless process that did not satisfy the inner man, but often held the people in bondage and was of no practical advantage to them. Promising much, such religious practices gave nothing practical in return.

On the other hand, gifts of prophecy and understanding that are God given can be insightful and edifying to those that believe, as they are to this very day.

Having complete faith — it is possible to have faith that does not connect with others. Eli had faith in God but that faith was of no practical use to others because it was personal and did not influence him or his sons, nor was it passionate in its outpouring, evoking a response from others of a desire for the same knowledge of and faith in God that he had.

Moses' face shone when he had been with God to the extent that the people asked him to hide his face from them once he had spoken the words of God. It seems unlikely that Eli experienced opposition to his faith in God as Moses had done, for the relationship he had with God lacked the intimacy of Moses' relationship with God.

In fact, we are told that God had not spoken to Eli or anyone else for a long time until the boy Samuel heard the voice and Eli guessed that it had been God calling the lad.

But having compete faith is meant to bring about a practical witness to others that will attract them to the God of the faithful one. It is meant to be contagious.

Giving to the poor — such can be construed as a humanitarian gesture with a religious connection, but it does not need to be linked to true belief or intimacy with God.

It is, however, a necessary attribute of those that believe in and serve God, but must be done quietly and without publicity.

Sacrificing the body — religious fanatics have done this since the early days of mankind, but it is done for purely selfish reasons and desires with no particular benefit to others.

In our service of God, we are told not to value our human life to the extent that we are willing to give up our belief in the living God to save it. Indeed, our physical life must be regarded as expendable in His service for, with His rising again from the dead, our life after death in His presence will be far more glorious and last for eternity.

The first commandment says it all. We are to love the Lord our God with all our heart, soul, mind and strength (Matt. 22:37) for God is love (1 John 4:8) and without His love in our hearts we cannot truly or fully know Him. But what does this mean? Love, argues Paul, puts us in a position before God in which we set ourselves aside that God might become dominant in our lives.

Moses learnt to trust God, in spite of his initial reluctance, through service. Although Moses was persuaded to commit himself to God at the start, it was only through experiencing the trials and tribulations in the negotiations with the Pharaoh that he gained confidence in God as a living being who was there consistently. Even through the time of the wanderings in the wilderness when he had to cope with the vagaries of the obstinacy and rebelliousness of the nation of Israel, yet he found God to be his empowerer and unrelenting support, to the point where his personal relationship with God became so intimate that even his thought processes were God-ward continually.

Where did Eli go wrong and what is Paul saying to us about our relationship with God that will prevent us losing faith? When a man lies with his wife they become one flesh. When an individual has spiritual intercourse with God they become one with Him (1 Cor. 6:17). As the influence of the greater affects the lesser, we, if we are seeking the Lord with all our hearts, are in a position to be influenced by Him because the openness of our hearts allows the free and unimpeded working of His Holy Spirit within us. Providing, that is, we are fully aware of the deceitfulness of which the heart is capable and the piercing gaze of God which searches the inner recesses of the heart (Jer. 17:9, 10).

Did not Moses teach the Children of Israel to be circumcised in their hearts? He called for the outward sign of circumcision, which identified the males as being of Israel, to become the true conversion of the inner man (from sinner to believer) and therefore a life-changing conversion of the whole man.

Love, says Paul in chapter 13 of 1 Corinthians, must be the evidence of God being on the throne of our lives for it was love, God's supreme agape love, that brought Moses into contact with God and His glory, and it was God's glory that shone from the face of Moses. It was the understanding Moses had of the amazing love of God for him and the children of Israel and the experience of His pure glory which caused him to be such a humble unassuming man, even though he was a senior statesman in God's service.

We are also able to experience this love and the amazing wonder of God, but we must never allow ourselves to become complacent, as the

Israelites did, and assume that God's love was completely unconditional allowing us to continue in sin. Sin is only overcome by the love of God when we become not only repentant but willing to allow Him to change us into His image from the inside out.

What did Eli do in the way he oversaw the activities in the temple that failed to preach the gospel of God by example? Why were the temple services meaningless to the worshippers? Quite simply, because God was not central to and the focus of the way in which the sacrificial services were conducted. There was no spiritual intercourse with God by him or his sons.

Samuel's first act as high priest was to challenge the people of the house of Israel to, *return to the Lord with all your hearts* putting away the pagan gods with which they had had an affair (1 Sam. 7:3). They played the harlot by 'going with other gods' instead of remaining pure in their marriage to the God of Israel. This turning to God with all their heart was a precondition for them being free of the yoke of the Philistines. Samuel had had a personal experience of God, for God had spoken with him during his apprenticeship with Eli. Such an experience had not only excited the young lad but had made an indelible impression on him that would last throughout his lifetime.

Indeed, such was his conversion from assistant in the temple to true believer that as God spoke to him and through him and in the way he conducted himself within the temple, the whole of Israel got to know about him (1 Sam. 3:19 – 21). It is having God within that matters to all those who truly love Him, for then He is able to shine through them to the world.

But God was their King

As Samuel ministered to Israel, bringing them victory over their enemies, all seemed to be well. There was however a looking outward that was unhealthy. The cry that they wanted to be like all other nations around them and have their own king gradually gathered pace and finally spread throughout the nation, just as God had prophesied through Moses (Deut. 17:14). The fact that they were unique in having Almighty God as their King, who gave them unique laws which kept them holy and who could use His mighty power to protect them (Num. 23:8 – 10; Deut. 33:26 – 29) seemed to fall on deaf ears and, like spoilt children, they said that, as other nations had a visible king to rule over them, so they wanted one too.

In the prophecy of Jacob in Genesis 49, nothing was said about the tribe of Benjamin[53], younger son of Rachael except that he *was a ravenous wolf; in the morning he shall devour the prey and at night divide the spoil* (Gen. 49:27). In other words the men of that tribe were very good fighting men, famous both for their swordsmen and very accurate left-handed stone slingers

---

[53] Saul, renamed Paul was also of the tribe of Benjamin (Ro. 11:1)

Human Legacy Established

(Judg. 20:15, 16). The man God first chose to lead the nation as king was a tall handsome young man of this warrior-like tribe. But it had become the smallest tribe through internal conflict (Judg. 20, 21).

But why Saul of the tribe of Benjamin when the kingly tribe was Judah? (Gen. 49:8 – 12, esp. v10) I believe God wanted to teach Israel a lesson by providing them with the type of leader they deserved, the handsome and worldly warrior king from the warrior tribe of Benjamin, who the people would think would lead them through conflict into a consistently stable state in which they could enjoy success and stability, but without any thought of being dependent upon God for their future (1 Sam. 10:19), for they were a rebellious and hard-hearted people.

The king they really needed, and who they would ultimately be blessed with for a time, would mostly put God first through his commitment to God. Conflict, particularly at that time, was inevitable, because Satan dominated the world and he is the author of chaos and conflict. To enjoy, and fully appreciate the blessings that God would provide them, there had to be a true peace of heart and mind, with a focus on God within each individual and the nation as a whole. There had also to be the acceptance that only when they had complete trust in God could protection from their enemies be assured. It is clear that King David was a one-off, for all subsequent kings failed in one way or another, being unable to emulate his truly God-centred life.

Remember when the Messiah came the people were not looking to God for the Messiah, they needed to free themselves from the practiced ways of sin and godlessness into which they had descended. Rather, as in the case of Saul, it was a warrior King Messiah they sought, being focused as they were purely on the earthly situation. They believed such a king would give them freedom from their enemies by uniting the nation against the Romans under His leadership (Jn. 6:13 -15). But those were carnal thoughts, focusing on the earthly situation not the spiritual because they were out of touch with their God.

Such a king was totally contrary to the illustration the Tabernacle provided which clearly showed the need first for confession and forgiveness of sin before going further into engaging in a personal relationship with the God who inhabited the holy tent.

This subject of who should lead the people would be the defining feature of the future of this nation. It represented a contrast between the people's worldly desire for earthly freedom and peace from those who wanted to bring them into subjection, and God's ultimate purpose for them which was to provide them and the whole world with a way back to Himself by way of His emerging plan of salvation. That was the only way to establish peace on the earth.

Saul did not have the pedigree of either Samuel or David who both entered into an intimacy with God from an early age, Samuel through his apprenticeship in the temple and David through leading his father's sheep. Samuel and David were chosen of God, Saul was chosen by the people at God's suggestion.

The calling and anointing of Saul as the first king of Israel is recorded in 1 Samuel chapters 10 – 31. But it was early in his reign that Saul was tested with regard to his willingness to be obedient to God's instructions through Samuel. Saul had to destroy the Amalekites and all that they had because of their sin against God's people Israel, but Saul and his men repeated the sin of Achan at Jericho by keeping the best of the booty that they were meant to completely destroy (ch. 15). So Samuel challenged Saul, *"Has the Lord as much delight in burnt offerings,* particularly using animals that God had commanded Saul to destroy, *as in those who obey the voice of the Lord? Behold to obey is better than sacrifice, and to heed than the fat of rams"* (see 1 Sam. 15:22).

It was this clear obfuscation of his position before God and his new status as king that was the underlying cause of God's decision that Saul had failed as the king of His chosen people Israel (1 Sam. 13:5 – 15, esp. v13). There must be no confusion of the king's position before God, for, just as with the high priest, the king was appointed by God to shepherd His people Israel on His behalf and not in place of Him.

With Saul's rejection by God as king of His people, a new king of His choice, who would be for the good of the people, would now be selected and anointed. This new man, blessed with the Holy Spirit as he was, would initially be a king in waiting for many years until Saul, from whom the blessing of God's Spirit had been withdrawn, finally died in combat (1 Sam. 31:4).

The calling and anointing of David as king of Israel, when Saul still occupied that position, gave Samuel a major problem because, although he feared the reaction of Saul, Samuel still had affection for him. (1 Sam. 16:1 – 3) But God's instructions to Samuel were specific and he was ordered to proceed with the selection and anointing of a king of God's choice who would provide a strong unifying influence over Israel with an emphasis on the true worship of their God.

It was in David, who was of the tribe of Judah, that God established Bethlehem as the birthplace of the Messiah for He was to be born in the line and lineage of David giving Him a legitimate claim to be hailed as the King of Israel, for, as Pilate stated on a notice nailed to the cross above Him, Jesus of Nazareth was the King of the Jews.

David's kingship established Judah as the kingly tribe for he established a sceptre in Judah that would not depart from it (Gen. 49:10) because of the future coming of the Messiah, first as suffering servant and then as victorious King.

9 HUMAN LEGACY ESTABLISHED

"Now, O Lord God, the word You have spoken
Concerning the house of your servant David,
Establish it forever as You have said.
So let Your name be magnified forever.
Let it be declared that
The Lord of Hosts is the God over Israel.
So let the house of your servant David
Be established before Your presence."
(See 2 Sam. 7:25 – 29)

God Establishes an Identity for the Messiah

It is essential for us to understand that the scriptures were written from God's point of view. We are told that all scripture is *given by inspiration of God* (2 Tim. 3:16, 17) for it is a record of what *holy men spoke as they were moved by the Holy Spirit* (2 Pet. 1:19 – 21)

The whole of scripture is what God wants us to know, therefore it is reasonable to maintain that the only way for individuals to receive it into themselves and to be able to understand scripture is to allow God, through the inspiration of His Holy Spirit who inspired the writers of it, to open it up to them and explain it in such a way that is appropriate to each individual. Added to this we are told by the Messiah Himself that, *man shall not live by bread alone, but by every word that proceeds from the mouth of God* (Matt. 4:4)

Throughout this book the old and new testaments are referred to as the first and second testaments because the word 'old' has the tendency to suggest to some that it is now redundant and the word 'new' as replacing what is old and of no further significance. As far as the scriptures are concerned nothing could be further from the truth. It is like trying to enter the upper story of a two storey building without first entering the building through the entrance door on the first or ground floor.

The first testament gives us a more rounded understanding of the Messiah's character and relationship to God the Father whilst He was on earth. Such study also reveals not only the purpose of His visit to the earth but also the basis and purpose of His life and the sacrifice that He made by hanging on a tree, which we now identify as the cross of Calvary. We read that He was accursed of men, but it is only by considering the reference in

Deuteronomy that we can possibly understand why He became accursed by hanging on a tree – it was God's decree that it should be so because the Messiah, as the suffering servant, was to take upon Himself the sin of all mankind, even though only believers would reap the benefit, and be accursed for us. (Deut. 21:22, 23)

The religious authorities, who did not connect the killing of this Man of God with the scriptures written by Moses so long ago, insisted on the body being removed from the cross because of the forthcoming Sabbath day; but by doing so they were unwittingly obeying that same scripture.

Gentiles who consider themselves believers, and therefore 'Christians', have the same problem those religious leaders had. Why? Because so many either do not read the scriptures for themselves, because their Bible, if they have one, sits on the shelf collecting dust, or by considering that only the second part is 'worth reading'.

Yet the scriptures are only complete and the message clear and unambiguous when both parts are studied as a whole with a good spiritual, prayerful connection with God established so that the Holy Spirit can lead us into all truth (Jn. 16:13), enabling us to rightly meditate on the word of God.

Through the sadly neglected first testament, God gradually revealed His plan of salvation and the two distinct identities of the forth coming Messiah, both the suffering servant, which is illustrated in the diagram below:

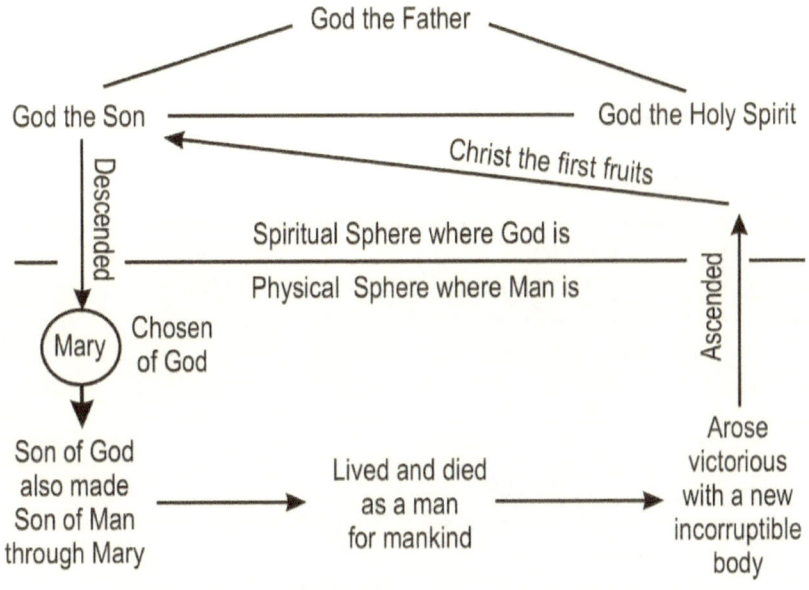

The Messiah as the Servant King who must come first

and the Victorious King, as illustrated below, coming from glory with trumpet sound for, as Paul tells the Thessalonians, the Lord Himself shall descend from heaven with a shout, a military term used for ordering the troops to assemble, that calls the dead in the Lord to life, with the Divine authority being represented by the voice of the Archangel and the shophar[54] of God before those living shall also arise with them (1 Thes. 4:15 – 18).

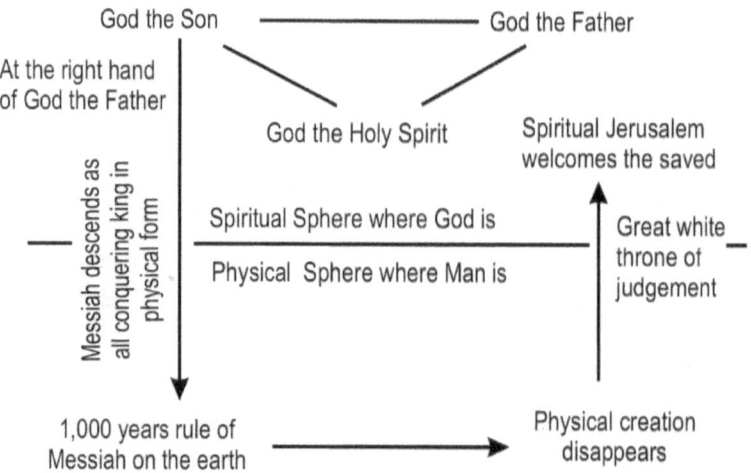

The Messiah as the All Conquering King who is to come in power and great glory

The pattern of the temple complex clearly shows that Christ, the Messiah, as our pure representative and perfect man, could not come as all-conquering King before He had first obtained victory over the sentence of death God issued on all who had sinned from Adam, which meant the whole of mankind.

Because of God's supreme righteousness, the legal issue of man's death, the wages of sin, had to be dealt with first, which is why the altar of sacrifice was encountered immediately inside the gate of decision or enquiry situated at the eastern end of the outer curtain.

Throughout the first testament, God was revealing certain essential truths about what He was going to do to provide mankind with a complete and all sufficient salvation that would enable those who desired to get right with God their creator, to re-establish a spiritual relationship with Him of the type Adam had at the beginning[55]. After all the whole purpose of the creation of man in the image of God in the first place was so that God

---

[54] A ram's horn often translated trumpet it was used for military signals (Jud. 7:18)

[55] It could never be exactly the same because we live in a body that is stained with sin, and as Paul says at the end of Romans 7, that gives us a tendency to sin.

could enjoy a spiritual relationship with Him.

Gradually God revealed a more complete explanation of both the legal and spiritual problems man had incurred through sin which God would overcome for the relationship between man and God to be restored. The whole purpose of this book is to seek an understanding of the plan of salvation God has revealed to us through scripture, for in it there are clear sign posts to the identity of the One who was to come, which were established at various times throughout the Judeo part of the Judeo/Christian Bible.

Consider well that Melchizedek appeared as an established king and priest to Abraham, allowing the Messiah to be appointed a priest according to the order of Melchizedek, being an order senior to that of Aaron. Judah was proclaimed the 'tribe of kings' way before Moses told the people that there would come a time when the people would ask for a king to rule over them at the time of Samuel.

God used that request to establish a kingship that would be everlasting for David, who was loved by God, was born in Bethlehem establishing the kingdom of Israel and also establishing the birth place of the Messiah. The fact that kings disappeared from Israel at the time of the exile to Babylon, made the position of king of Israel vacant for the Son of God to assume and cause prophecy to be fulfilled that it was to be and eternal kingship. As Jesus said to Pilate, My kingdom is not of this world.

He was to be born in the city of David and into the lineage of David so that He could be legitimately called the King of Israel from a human perspective and, according to the prophecy from God, transformed it into an eternal kingship.

The whole matter of the life of obedience that God required of His people, and the marriage-type relationship He desired to have with them, is expounded in a number of prophetic books such as Hosea and Jeremiah. But central is the meaning of the sacrifice of a lamb; from the ram caught in a thicket that Abram used to sacrifice in place of his son Isaac on the very hill on which the Messiah would be murdered, to the Passover Lamb sacrificed immediately before the exodus of the Israelites from Egypt, all of which foretold the type of sacrifice the Messiah would make and the timing of His death within the annual God-imposed calendar.

It was that annually remembered celebration throughout the history of Israel that was the link between their release from Egypt and the Passover Lamb of God who died on the accursed tree and whose sacrifice through the remembered last supper is celebrated by all believers, just as it was celebrated for the first time by a selected group of twelve Jews with the Jewish Messiah present as the host.

Scripture must be seen as a complete homogeneous whole from Genesis 1:1 to Revelation 22:21, with the message being progressive so that the prophetic can be seen to be revealed at a later stage or can be confirmed as being of God and yet to be revealed.

Notice how important God was to David, which is why God chose him to be the next king of Israel, and why he established a kingship that the Messiah would continue so that it became an eternal kingship. It was this continuity from earthly life to spiritual life that was so important to God, for by that means He demonstrated that His original design was that earth created man had a spiritual future through that God breathed spirit within him.

David was still seen as an impudent youth in the eyes of his brothers[56] (1 Sam. 17:28 – 29) and those around him, even though he had been anointed in front of them as God's chosen king by Samuel to replace the rebellious Saul. What set him apart was his absolute belief in the mighty God (v37) who had chosen Israel to the extent that this supreme and eternal being had decided that He was to be known as the Lord God of Israel.

This was a considerable commitment for an eternal God to make in the light of the sinful nature of the people of Israel who He had chosen to be His 'show case' people on the earth. Their wayward and rebellious ways that emulated the life of the other nations instead of being distinctive as God had intended them to be, are still in evidence today because of total unbelief in God. It is interesting that the organisation One for Israel is having success in gradually overturning the teaching of the rabbis which perpetuates the message the religious leadership put out that Jesus of Nazareth is an imposter.

Saul had been the champion of Israel but so enjoyed his position as king that he was not prepared to risk his life in one-to-one combat with an enemy who was 9 feet 6 inches tall and a warrior from his youth. But David, rejecting Saul's armour as being too restrictive, armed himself with five smooth stones from a nearby brook and went out to face this monster Goliath whose derisory assessment of David showed his total lack of understanding of the security David was convinced he had in the God he worshipped. (17:40 - 44)

David's response was to publicly place his future in the hands of that same God (vs. 45 - 47). However frightening Goliath may have seemed to the ordinary infantrymen (17:24), including his brothers, who were members of the army of Israel, to David, who had faced a lion and a bear when looking after his father's sheep, this pagan worshipper was as nothing compared to the might of the God of his own nation, Israel. Through these important events, we are able see the insight into the hearts of men God had in making David king rather than any of his seven brothers.

In full view of both armies David armed his sling with a small stone,

---

[56] Notice from the passage in Samuel that none of his brothers had faith enough to face Goliath.

slung the stone with such force that, with God guiding its passage, the stone pierced the temple of Goliath, bringing him down. David then dispatched the pagan champion with the champion's own great sword before removing his head as a trophy and a declaration of God's victory over the enemy of His armies of Israel.

It is this clear and unambiguous contrast between the people's type of king and God's choice of king that tells us much about the type of person God is looking for as His disciple today and that spoke of the character of the forthcoming Messiah.

Genealogy was extremely important to the nation of Israel (consider Neh. 7:5, 64, 65) during their chequered history and occasional exile, because of their covenant with God. From God's point of view the purity of the nation was essential. When Abram told the king of the country which he was entering that his wife Sarai, who was very beautiful, was his sister, the king was disposed to take her into his harem. (Gen. 12:10 – 20; 20:1, 2) But it was to be through Sarai that Isaac, the promise of the future for Abram to become the Father of many nations, was to be born in their old age, therefore God had to intervene to prevent her going into the king and to ensure that the king did not harm Abram.

This was also important because the lineage of the Messiah had to be clearly demonstrated from Adam through David and Mary, particularly because of the righteousness of God. No contamination was allowed by God to enter the messianic line, for even the two Gentile women, Rahab of Jericho and Ruth the Moabitess, were perceptive in their change of belief to that of the Living God of Israel, and because of their willingness to embrace the things of God were used by Him at the most appropriate time in God's plan.

This latter fact also tells us of the inclusivity of God's plan of salvation that two Gentile women of the 'enemy camp' were included in His human lineage. It is important for us to realise that God never uses people against their intrinsic will and tendencies, just as a carpenter never works against the grain in wood, as this would cause inner conflict within them which would be detrimental to His work of grace. It also demonstrates His inclusivity in that He used Gentiles in the lineage of the Messiah.

Genealogy was particularly important with regard to the two leading tribes of Levi and Judah. For the tribe of Levi it was vital to know which of its families was allowed to serve in the temple, particularly regarding who could serve as high priest, and which were to act as supporters in the temple, for these were God-given roles.

With regard to the tribe of Judah, the kingly and lead tribe, and the tribe into which the Messiah would ultimately be born, the recorded genealogy from Adam through Abraham and David to the Messiah provided a clear line of descent which was essential to demonstrate that He also, in His human form, was under the covenants God had made with His people. He was a Jew and of the tribe of Judah and lineage of David to whom was given an eternal covenant of kingship. Surely it is something to be wondered at that the work of so many inspired authors should be so seamless and connected that the Bible can be studied in depth only to reveal amazing truths and stand up to the most rigorous scrutiny.

It is important to understand about the house of David for, just as the high priesthood established with Aaron was replaced by the greater High Priesthood of the Messiah according to the order of Melchizedek, so the kingship of David was replaced by the supreme and eternal Kingship of the Messiah. (Jn. 18:36, 37) The name David means beloved, and there is no doubt that David, in spite of his sins, was beloved of God because of his inner desire for and focus on God who was to him both Lord and Saviour.

By the time of the Messiah, the house of David had long since fallen on hard times as successive kings after David had not been as God-focused as he had been, allowing injustice and corruption to flourish, under which regime the poor, widows and orphans suffered greatly, attracting the wrath of God. (Is. 10:1 – 5) Indeed Manasseh was a particularly evil king doing evil in the sight of the Lord according to the abominations perpetuated by the Canaanite nations they had cast out of the land when Israel went in to possess it according to God's instructions. (2 Kgs. 21:2)

Therefore, by the time the Messiah visited the earth, there was no king of the house of David sitting on the throne of Israel; the tree representing the house of David, son of Jesse, having been felled by the rod of the Assyrians to become a stump. Isaiah, through his prophetic utterances, warned those of his time, who were perpetuating the injustices in the country, that the Assyrian invader, by God's decree, would take away their ill-gotten gains. (Is. 10:6, cf. Lk. 19:8 – 10)

It is worth noting that although God used the surrounding pagan nations to carry out His acts of judgement on Israel, their subsequent boasting that it was either by their own strength that they were able to invade Israel, or by the power of their own god(s) over the God of Israel brought upon them that same wrath of God, such that today, of them all, only Israel is still a nation.

Although God passed judgement on Israel, He had no intention of ever obliterating their name from the face of the earth given their central role in His plan of salvation. To the encouragement of Israel God promised a God-focused remnant would always be present within the nation through which He would work to save the nation from total extinction, and that the real but temporary wrath of God would end with the removal of the yoke of the invader. (Is. 10:20 – 27)

It is important for us to differentiate between the spiritual and human birth of the Messiah. Scripture clearly tells us that He was begotten, not made (how He was begotten is a mystery of God) and is declared the Son of God although He is, to all intents and purposes, equal with God. What differentiates Him from the Father is that only the Father knows the time when the Son will return victoriously to the earth (see Appendix H).

The Messiah also made it very clear publicly, whilst on the earth, that He was about His Father's business, speaking and doing only what the Father had instructed Him to say and do. His visit to the earth enabled us to see the differences in the person and function of each member of the Trinity, and their total unity of purpose that was demonstrated in the supreme acts of selfless service and sacrificial death of the Messiah.[57]

We are told that flesh can only give birth to flesh and Spirit to spirit (Jn. 3:6), that it is the Spirit who gives life, conversely there is no benefit for man in the flesh (Jn. 6:63), and that, of all mankind, it was only the Son who was filled with the Holy Spirit without measure[58]. (Jn. 3:34, 35) When the Messiah came as a Spirit into the body of a child, we know that sin held man in the grip of spiritual death, *for all have sinned and fall short of the glory of God* (Ro. 3:23) and because, *the wages of sin is death* (Ro. 6:23a), that is except, as we have already seen, where men were prepared to seek atonement for their sins through the sacrificial death of a prescribed animal.

Because of the manner of its birth[59], the Spirit of the Son of God, with all His knowledge and power, demonstrated by the authority of His speech (Lk. 2:46 – 50) and the miraculous power He displayed even over natural things such as the lives and conditions of people, the weather and food, dwelt within the body produced by Mary with full spiritual communication through the indwelling and measureless impact of the Holy Spirit.

For how else was He able to accurately know the thoughts of those around Him and able to walk through the middle of a hostile crowd without them attacking Him except the Holy Spirit told Him and hid Him from the crowd? This is the Trinity working on earth as our example. The Son, in obedience to the Father, clothed Himself with the body prepared through Mary and was filled with the Holy Spirit without measure (Jn. 3:34, 35) so that the three members could communicate easily with each other.

As the Messiah was confined to a human body like us, He was not able to read the thoughts and hearts of those around Him; that was the job of the Holy Spirit, for He, being spirit, was able to know what was going on in the minds and hearts of those around the Messiah.

Perhaps one of the greatest misleading doctrines of the western church today is the belief that the Messiah came to the earth fully human in the sense that He became like one of us, divesting Himself of all His

---

[57] See my book A Fresh Look At Easter

[58] In fact because God cannot be changed, or the three members become separated, the Messiah and the Holy Spirit worked together all the while He was on the earth.

[59] The body of the Messiah was without sin (refer to Appendix A)

supernatural power and knowledge. That is impossible given the intricately made plans God, in Triune-unity, revealed through all the prophetic utterances about the coming of the Messiah, the need for Him to be completely sinless and the nature of the task that was put before Him. His arrival on earth was merely the fulfilment of the plan that has gradually been unfolding before us; although the Messiah did experience less immediate communication with His Father than He had been used to, finding it necessary to go aside to a quiet, uninhabited place to pray.

The time in the Garden of Gethsemane was an exception, for the actual time of suffering, the full horror of what He knew He had to experience, was immediately before Him, therefore the severity and intensity of the suffering He was to experience was vividly present in His mind. At that moment He experienced a human moment of fearful anticipation to the extent that He sweated great drops of blood, yet He resolved to continue with the task set before Him by submitting to the will and purposes of God, His Father. Many martyrs of the faith have accepted His example, and the example of some of His disciples, to suffer torture and death rather than be deprived of their eternal glory.

Even when He chose the disciples the Messiah knew who would betray Him, just as He knew Nathaniel when he was under the fig tree. (Jn. 1:50) We have been privileged to gain an understanding of the technicalities of the superior High Priesthood of the Messiah that is above that of Aaron, and the superior Kingship that is above that of David, which He was to receive from His Father after His triumphal victory on the cross, because He was from eternity and above the earth and was directly involved with all that was made that was made. (Jn. 1:1 – 5)

He was, therefore, never human like us even though He was tented amongst us as we are in this life (2 Cor. 5:1) because the eternal Spirit within Him was the 'Word that became flesh' whose glory, that of the only-begotten of the Father, full of grace and truth, (Jn. 1:14, 15) was actually seen and experienced by those who believed in Him and followed Him closely as disciples, having their spiritual eyes opened by the same Holy Spirit who filled the Messiah without measure (Jn. 16:5 – 15; Acts 1:7, 8)

But what of the body He received from Mary? Ours, received from our parents in the usual way, returns to the dust from which it was made; but not so the body prepared for the Messiah, for it was nowhere to be found after His resurrection. This is because He is the first fruits (Prov. 3:9) of all those believers who have fallen asleep and whose bodies have disintegrated, returning to the earth from which the first man was created. (1 Cor. 15:20)

But what do we mean by this? Christ the Messiah came to present Himself to men to be killed, slaughtered as a sacrificial animal on the cross by the very people He came to save, knowing precisely what He was doing (Jn. 18:36, 37), and that He would rise up on the third day before ascending to His Father. His body did not lie in the ground to return to the earth for the Psalmist wrote, *For You will not leave my soul in Sheol, nor will You allow Your Holy One to see corruption* (Psalm 16:10), but His body was preserved and placed in a tomb, and in the three days of being in the tomb was changed from the corruptible body that He had before, into a spiritual, incorruptible body (1 Cor. 15:35 – 54) that He might precede us, as the first-fruits, in returning to His Father and our Father.

We must wait for the second coming of the triumphant King Messiah for first the resurrection of the death and then the bodily resurrection of the living. Therefore, just as God required His people to present to Him the first fruits of the harvest (Ex. 23:19; 34:26) for the benefit of the priests (Num. 18:12; Deut. 18:4) along with the ritual to be used (Deut. 26); so the Messiah, in rising first from the dead, became the first fruits before His Father (1 Cor. 15: 20 – 23), followed at His appointed time by those who have committed themselves to the Saviour prior to His return.

Humanly speaking, He was born into the line and house of David, which meant that the birth of the King of kings was according to the lineage of David: but the Royal House He would establish when uniting the roles of priest and king was not.

The Messiah was greater than David for He existed before him. Therefore, according to the prophetic word God gave to Isaiah, the Messiah was represented by a branch that grew not out of the tree of David but out of the root (see Appendix G) of Jesse, the father of David.

Although the tree of David had been hewn and only the stump was left just above the roots, which were of God, it was out of that stump that the new eternal royal house would be established which would maintain God's relationship with not just the nation of Israel, but the eternally respected royal house of David.

In the Messiah the roles of priest and king were to be united for He is now both Priest and King. However, it is important that we emphasise the point that, as with the high priesthood, where a greater priesthood than that of Aaron had to be established that would be eternal in nature, so God needed to establish a greater kingship than that of David who, although chosen of God and dedicated to the worship and service of God throughout his life, failed in five aspects of the Law of God in that he lusted after another man's wife and coveted her, obtaining possession of her through murder.[60] From then on David experienced terrible conflict within his disjointed family, and even the choice of Solomon to succeed him was an afterthought to prevent another son taking the throne. (1 Kgs

---

[60] The five aspects of the law David broke were: lust, covetousness, bearing false witness, theft and murder. God's prophet Nathan advised David of his sinful acts through a parable (2 Sam. 12:1 – 14) and David wrote Psalm 51 as a confession.

Human Legacy Established

1)

How did the Messiah's lineage from King David allow David's throne to continue?

The Messiah was physically descended from David, born into the line of David, but He was not a direct descendent spiritually in the sense that He was alive before David. This is why it is essential to understand the information contained in chapter 11 of Isaiah. But first in chapter 10 we read of God taking account of the judges and magistrates of Israel who, with the approval of the kings and rulers, decreed unrighteousness and unjust decisions (vs.1, 2). But what protection did they have when God removed His protection from them and used the rod of Assyria in His anger (vs. 3 – 6)? God reduced the nation to an obedient remnant whose heart was with God like that of Jacob from whom they were descended (vs. 21 – 23). Because of their boast that it was by their might and their gods that they had taken over Israel, God had to deal with the Assyrians, bringing them low (vs. 7 – 12).

Now God's prophet Isaiah deals with the future, and not just of the first, but also the second coming of the Messiah. *There shall come forth*, focusing on the future, *a rod[61] from the stem of Jesse,*, and to emphasise the point *and a Branch shall grow out of his roots.* (Is. 11:1)

But notice that the rod/branch does not grow out of the tree of David, which was to be reduced to a stump when Zedekiah (597 – 587) the last king of Judah was toppled by the Babylonians under Nebuchadnezzar, but out of the root of Jesse, David's father. And the root is God who created all things. To put things in perspective, the Messiah in His glory tells us that He is the root of David and also his offspring, emphasising the importance His human birth (Son of Man) is to the Messiah. (Rev. 22:16)

Such confirmed heritage gave the Messiah, particularly because of His virgin birth by which He proved that He had come from God, a legitimate calling to:

1. introduce a new covenant that not only ended the sacrificial offering of animals for sin, but also allowed Him, by way of an oath from God (Ps. 110:4; Heb. 7:21, consider vs. 11 – 28) to replace the human high priest with an eternal (Heb. 7:16) and supreme High Priest[62], superior in every way to the succession of human high priests established with Aaron.

2. claim the covenant given to David regarding the eternal nature of his kingly descendants in His physical form, particularly by being born of the house and lineage of David, in Bethlehem the city of

---

[61] Rod: a shoot that grows out of a tree stump.
[62] Heb. 7:21 and references to Melchizedek in this book

David. But He was also able to claim that His kingdom was not of this world (see Appendix G) being far greater than any worldly kingdom. That was because it is a spiritual kingdom.

Indeed, this is the incongruity of the Messiah's position. He was able to claim to be descended from King David yet at the same time claim He was superior to David in every way, for even David declared that, *the Lord said to my Lord [the Messiah], sit at My right hand, until I make Your enemies a footstool* (Ps. 110:1), a relationship revealed by David through the influence of the Holy Spirit but a complete mystery to the Pharisees who were unable to answer the question posed to them by the Messiah concerning whose Son the Messiah was (Matt 22:34 – 45). The key question is this, *if David calls Him 'Lord' how can He also be his Son?* (v45) The answer has to be that the Son of God came to earth as the Son of Man in the line of David, yet as the Son of God He was before David and therefore his superior, his Lord.

The choosing of David is interesting for the following reasons:

❖ David was to be God's choice for the benefit of His plan of salvation; as opposed to the person the people deserved because of their rebellious, self-centred ways, (that is Saul), who was chosen to satisfy the aspirations of the people; that they might be like the surrounding nations, led by a visible king and be secure within their borders. By desiring a human king, they were rejecting God as their king[63].

The reason the people gave for wanting a king was that Samuel was old and his sons did not walk in his ways, seeking after dishonest gain and taking bribes (1 Sam. 8:1 – 5) just like the sons of Levi who Samuel succeeded, but in reality it was God they were rejecting because of their world-focused ways (v7).

However, as God instructed Samuel, their kings would be no better than the priests who rejected God, because they would all be sinners in need of salvation (vs. 8, 9) with the propensity to go the way of all flesh, as we know from the historical events of the first testament.

❖ He was the youngest of Jesses' eight sons (1 Sam. 16:10 – 13) and despised by his brothers (1 Sam. 17:28, cf. Jn. 7:1 – 9), just as the Messiah was rejected of men. It is a salutary lesson that we all need to heed, which is that we have no say in the position we hold in God's sight for we are told that it is not only possible for the first to be last and the last first (Matt. 20:16),

---

[63] But the sovereign succession came to an end with Zedekiah at the time of their exile in Babylon

but we should not put ourselves up to be better than others (Lk. 14:7 – 11), rather we must be prepared to accept the instruction that *he who would be great among you must be the servant of all* (Matt. 20:26; cf. Lk. 17:10)

❖ He was chosen for his willingness to be obedient to God, submitting himself to the authority of God over him, even though he was king of God's chosen people Israel.

❖ He had received the training of a shepherd, just like Moses, having to look after his father's sheep to the point of defending them against a lion and a bear which he overcame in the sure knowledge that it was by the power of God. Indeed, such was his confidence in the God of Israel that he, even though still a youth, was willing to face the mighty Goliath with just a sling and shot (1 Sam. 17:32 – 37, 45 – 51).

❖ He was gifted, being able to both lead the armies of the Lord and order the worship of God with singing and play the harp. (1 Chron. 15:16; 16:7; ch. 23, 25 - cf. 1Chron. 25:8 and Lk.1:8, 9)

❖ He was a prophet, recording many statements that ultimately referred to the Messiah.

❖ He fully united Israel, and for the first time, with God taking him from the sheepfold and tending the sheep to being the ruler over His people, a shepherd king, (Ps. 78:70 – 72) providing a prophetic picture of the type of Servant King the Messiah was to be, the good shepherd who would give His life for the sheep. (Jn. 10:11)

He established Jerusalem as the capital of the united Israel, however the union of tribes was brittle for under Rehoboam, son of Solomon, the union fractured with the ten tribes breaking away from Judah because of an unwise decision the king made regarding his treatment of the people (1 Kgs 12 esp. v16) and the begrudged, although prophesied, supremacy of the tribe of Judah.

Under Jeroboam Israel returned to its pagan ways (vs. 27, 28) even though God had made promises to Jeroboam that he was not prepared to believe. (1 Kgs 11:29 – 39) Thus Israel walked away from God.

When David established Jerusalem as the City of God, it became the centre of the worship of God with the Ark of the Covenant being brought there (2 Sam. 6). Jerusalem and the temple were to become central to the work of the Messiah.

David also provided all the elements and funding for the first permanent temple being built because of the treasure he accumulated and the plot of ground he purchased that would soon accommodate the Temple of Solomon.

The purchase of the land was the result of an ill-considered numbering of the people. David wanted to know the number of men he had at his disposal should he need to go to war, but God needed David to trust Him at all times so that if there was a need to mobilize there would be enough men for God's purposes (Jud. 7:2). Only God could command a census to be taken, and David did not seek God's permission first (2 Sam. 24:10). Therefore David was given a choice of three punishments which only ended when David had offered the sacrifices required by God on the place where the temple was to be built (vs. 11 – 25). This was on Mount Mariah where Abraham had almost sacrificed Isaac.

Although it was David who wanted to build a temple for God to replace the tent structure David had erected in the city that followed the design of the tabernacle Moses had built, God prevented him from doing so, instead allowing his son Solomon to build it. However, over many years David worked hard to accumulate all the finances and building materials necessary for its construction. (1 Chron. 22:1 – 5; 29:1 – 20)

A sinner he may have been, but Moses murdered an Egyptian and Paul, as Saul, imprisoned many believers of 'The Way' who could well have died there in prison because of their belief, however David's heart was right with God and it was this God focus that caused his legacy of an eternal kingly rule in the tribe of Judah to be established (1 Kgs. 11:34 – 36). Such was David's love for God and His word (Ps. 119:97 – 104) that when he was told of his sin or became aware of it himself, he immediately went before God to ask for forgiveness, but this was not so with his son Solomon (2 Sam. 12; Ps. 51 cf. 1 Kgs. 11:34 – 36).

Sins have consequences. However able he was to unite the tribes of Israel under his leadership, David was no family man, and failed over the years to apply the discipline, guidance and cohesion for which a father is responsible in order to develop a well-balanced and unified family. Following the example of the kings of that day he acquired many wives, yet it was forbidden for kings to have many wives lest they turn his heart away from God as happened in the case of Solomon (Deut. 17:17).

The children the various wives bore him were obviously not united because of the matter of divided loyalties. However, God provided relative peace in David's family, because of his love for God through the influence for peace that He alone can provide, until towards the end of his days his sons anticipated the prospect of acquiring the throne. Then family animosity became prevalent with their succession foremost in their minds.

255

Human Legacy Established

The particularly evil affair against Uriah the Hittite, which David would not have been able to keep secret and did his reputation amongst the people no good at all, resulted in his disconnected and dysfunctional family being left by God to its own devices, with particular sons having no compunction but to seek to succeed their father without his permission even when he was alive, due to their seniority by birth (e.g. 2 Sam. 15). Only at the last minute, through a plan concocted by Nathan the prophet and Bathsheba, did David decide that Solomon should succeed him as king. (1 Kgs. 1)

Through David, therefore, the notion of a God-chosen, God-centred King of Israel, albeit one prone to sin, was established; a righteous king who could establish supreme rule over the nation and all the surrounding peoples and who would bring peace to the people of God. This was David's legacy that God established, leading the way for the establishment of a kingly Messiah who would rule the nations, having first established a way for man to get in tune with God and becoming righteous through His sacrifice.

Solomon was a completely different king to his father David. His relationship with God was remarkable at first, in so far as his request for discernment in ruling the people of God (1 Kgs. 3:9) was the premier skill he required, coming fresh to an established throne as he did. At no time previously had Solomon sought to take over the kingdom from his father David, and this could have been due to the influence of his mother Bathsheba. His big mistake, which is understandable given the tendency of the kings of the surrounding nations and his father David, was to marry many women from pagan backgrounds, just like Esau. However, this was totally against all the commands of God and had earlier caused Esau to lose his inheritance.

Solomon organised his government to rule not just Israel but the surrounding nations and to keep them in submission. With twelve governors, one for each of the twelve designated areas, to ensure he always had plenty of food on his table, and various other officials, including one over the labour force, Solomon ruled the nation with strictness and a large army, with chariot cities in strategic places. Indeed, as soon as the building of the temple got underway it must have seemed like Egypt all over again, with the exception that the Israelites were not classed as slaves, just dutybound to provide their labour free of charge. The doubtful honour to provide slave labour was given to the descendants of all those Canaanite nations that were not annihilated when the Israelites went in to possess the land. (1 Kgs. 9:20 – 22)

The stores of treasure and building supplies provided as a legacy by King David gave Solomon a remarkable store of materials for the major task of erecting a notable temple to the Lord God Almighty. David was insistent that it should be a magnificent building, showing how great God was. And so it was, for along with the greatness of David, who is remembered and admired as Israel's greatest king, even today, the temple Solomon built using the treasure David accumulated is still, even though it was destroyed by Nebuchadnezzar, considered as the greatest of all the temples built for the worship and honour of the God of Israel.

Like Moses, Solomon was assisted in the work by skilled craftsmen, including 'Huram of Tyre' who was born to a Jewish mother of the tribe of Naphtali and a Gentile father of the city of Tyre. Huram was skilled in the working of all types of bronze. (1 Kgs. 7:13, 14) The temple took seven years to build from the laying of the foundations (1 Kgs. 6:37, 38). During its dedication, Solomon declared his faith in God saying that,

> *there is no God in heaven above or on the earth below like You who keeps Your covenant and mercy with Your servants who walk before You with all their hearts ..."* (1 Kgs. 8:23)

Although Solomon could not believe that the God who inhabited the heavens and the heaven of heavens would be able to inhabit this lowly temple build by human hands, yet he asked God to consider his prayer, during which he focused the people's attention on the temple as a reminder of the God they served. When the people sinned, if they looked towards this place and called out to God in repentance and faith, Solomon asked God to forgive them and bring them back into fellowship with Him turning His cursing into blessing (1 Kgs. 8:22 - 56 Chron. 6). When Solomon had finished praying fire came down from God and consumed the sacrifices (2 Chron. 7).

It is recorded that God appeared twice to Solomon, first at the start of his reign when he needed the skill of discernment (1 Kgs. 3:5) and then after he had dedicated the temple (1 Kgs. 9:1 – 9). The key message God gave Solomon was that he and his descendants had to walk before Him in integrity of heart as His servant David had done (v4). But far more significant is the record in 2 Chronicles 7 where the verse that has been greatly used in the western churches is included in what God said to Solomon:

> *"If My people who are called by My name*
> *Are willing to humble themselves,*
> *And pray and seek My face*
> *And turn from their wicked ways,*
> *Then I will hear from heaven,*
> *And will forgive their sin and heal their land.*
> *Now My eyes will be open and My ears attentive*

Human Legacy Established

To prayer made in this place."
(2 Chron. 7:14)

When the ark was installed by the priests in the Holy of Holies there were within it just the tablets of stone put there by Moses. (2 Chron. 5:10) Gone was the rod of Aaron and the jar of manna. When the Ark of the Covenant was installed in the temple and the priests were singing and glorifying God the priests were suddenly ejected from the temple by the cloud of the glory of the Lord which filled the building. (2 Chron. 5:11 - 14; 7:2)

Thus, just as He did at the dedication of the Tabernacle of Moses, so He did at the dedication of this new and far more glorious temple. God symbolically entered and blessed the building that it might be used to His praise and glory. In so doing God established not just the temple but Jerusalem as the place for His great name. Hadrian, in calling Jerusalem by another name as an insult to the Jews, just as he renamed the country Palestine after Israel's constant enemy the Philistines, said that the name Jerusalem would never again be used for that city.

But Hadrian was a pagan emperor who had no knowledge of the supreme power of almighty God. God is greater than all humanity and the name Jerusalem, at the centre of so much world news today, still brings to mind the name of the Lord God of Israel because Jerusalem is God's city and anyone who tries to decide what should happen to it without reference to Him will find that they have taken on more than they can cope with for Zechariah tells us that God Himself will make His city of Jerusalem a cup of drunkenness to all the surrounding peoples (Zech. 12:2). Some of those involved with the Oslo Peace Accord (1993) have experienced a shortened life.

Although God followed up His promise to Solomon with considerable blessings, to the extent that the Queen of Sheba proclaimed to him that he exceeded the fame of which she had heard (2 Chron. 9 esp. v6), on his part Solomon did not pursue the life of faith that was required of him. Unfortunately, with the riches and fame, came focus on the things of the world and looking at life from a worldly perspective and thus a falling away from God, mainly because he allowed his heart to be influenced by his many pagan wives and concubines (Deut. 17:17), which he accumulated against God's strict instructions.

Solomon's departure from the ways of God that his father had followed so assiduously, sealed the future of the line of kings from David. The fading out of the human kings of Israel, through their own sin and the reflected sin of the people, was inevitable but not unpredicted; the people had forgotten that it was God who gave the victory, and without God, even though they had a king, the battle was lost (1 Sam. 8:10 – 20).

The prophecy God gave to Solomon came to pass under the rule of his son Rehoboam who listened to his peers rather than the wise men in the court. (1 Kgs. 11:9 – 12:24) Unfortunately Jeroboam set the seal for the ever-changing rulers of the ten tribes by introducing the worship of the Golden Calf in Bethel in the south and Dan in the north, which was in direct conflict with the promise God made to him (1 Kgs. 11:37 – 39).

Through sheer human desire for position and power, the umbilical cord of dependency on God was severed and Jeroboam gave birth to a nation with a very violent history in the arena of power struggles, but it could never escape being influenced by God who ultimately had the final say over the future of the nation, just as He did over its birth (1 Kgs. 14:1 – 18).

Solomon's legacy was the temple that was built in Jerusalem to the glory of God when he was pursuing a life of faith and listening to God. Our focus must therefore be on the people and the temple in the tumult that defined the next stage of the history of Judah.

Thus we have these two strains that we must consider further: the position of the King of Israel that was to come and the role of the Temple and its High Priest in the lives of the remnant that was preserved by God.

Warning of Exile

Such was the fall from grace of the children of the fractured Israel that had been divided off from Judah, that they fell victim to the war-like nations around them. Devoid of God's protection because of their lack of faith and turning to other gods as Moses prophesied, they were at the mercy of the more belligerent nations God used to punish them. But such was their obstinacy to even try to understand their position before God that they even refused to listen to the warnings being given to them by both Isaiah and Jeremiah, and also the message of the life and message of Hosea. Indeed, Jeremiah was considered a traitor by telling even the people of Judah and Benjamin to accept exile in Babylon. The choice was plain.

> *"'If you will return, O Israel," says the Lord,*
> *'Return to Me*
> *And if you will put away your abominations*
> *Out of My sight,*
> *Then you shall not be moved.*
> *And you shall swear, 'The Lord lives,*
> *In truth, in judgement and in righteousness;*
> *The nations shall bless themselves*
> *in Him*
> *And in Him they shall glory.'"*
> *(Jer. 4:1, 2)*

Human Legacy Established

See again the role Israel as a whole should have accepted; the God-given role of attracting mankind to Himself as their God also. As it is, we will see how God used their obstinacy and unbelief to draw the Gentiles to Himself through their faith in the Messiah to the Jews, for as it is recorded, *I, if I am lifted up from the earth, will draw all men unto Me* (Jn. 12:32) and in contrast, *We have heard out of the Law that Messiah abides forever; yet you are saying, 'The Son of Man must be lifted up?', Therefore, tell us, who is this Son of Man?* (Jn. 12:33, 34)

This message through Jeremiah is directed to Judah, the central tribe in God's work amongst men. If the people of Judah (Jews) returned to Him and acknowledged Him as their Lord, and that their Lord lived and was the source of truth, judgement and righteousness, not only would they be saved from exile in a foreign land but they would also bring blessing to the nations around them.

The warnings God announced through Jeremiah were numerous. Standing in the gate of the Lord's house he warned the people of Judah to amend their ways if they wanted to remain in Jerusalem. (Jer. 7:1 – 3) Sadly they did not heed his warning, for God was in their mouth but far from their hearts (Jer. 12:2b). The message was changed. The warnings were not heeded so the seventy years of exile became the new message which left the land desolate (Jer. 25 esp. vs. 9, 11; 29:11).

No expense had been spared in building Solomon's temple, dedicated to the worship of Almighty God who had chosen Israel as His people, through whom He would teach mankind not only the truth about their relationship with Him, but also the means by which He would provide a way of salvation. It was by that Way alone that individuals, if they chose to do so, could once again be united with Him in spirit. The temple was the most glorious of its day, far exceeding all other temples erected to the worship of lesser, ineffectual gods.

The ten tribes of Israel[64] were the first of the tribes to enter exile because of their blatant following after the golden calves Jeroboam created, together with gods of the surrounding nations. These were the very gods the tribes were charged with eradicating, through the judgmental slaughter of all the inhabitants, when they first went in to possess the land under Joshua. Therefore, the tribal lands of Judah, centred in Jerusalem, were surrounded by a hostile invader.

Jeremiah did not have an enviable task. How was he, single-handedly, even with God supporting him, going to change the minds and hearts of such stubborn-minded people as the Jews so that they refocused their attention on their God? Corruption was rife. The king and the princes were more interested in their own comfort and retaining power than in being concerned with the pronouncements of a single, seemingly errant Levitical

---

[64] See my book Law & Grace.

priest.

The autobiographical account of the life of Jeremiah is a remarkable account of how God, loving His people as His did, tried desperately to redirect them from their blind, lemming-like run towards death, destruction and exile through this one man who was so in love with God that he was willing to serve Him no matter what the circumstances (Jer. 20:7 – 13).

It is essential that we see this book from God's point of view. How does He guide the people to a path of faith and security rather than the separate ways they had chosen that would lead to the dangers Moses warned them about, the cursings instead of the blessings (Deut. 28); yet also the promise of restoration when they came to their senses (Deut. 30; cf. 29 esp. vs. 17 – 19). The choice of life required them to love the Lord their God and obey His voice and cling to Him, for He alone was able to give them life. (Deut. 30:19, 20)

God was like the potter Jeremiah was directed to see (Jer. 18). The potter tried to make a vessel of beauty but the vessel was marred, not because the skill of the potter had deserted him, but because the clay in his hands was not malleable or fine grained enough for him to make a vessel of beauty. There was no consistency in the texture of the clay due to the lumps and imperfections it contained, such problems as sinfulness, rebelliousness and obstinate unbelief dictated the type of vessel the potter was able to make with it. An everyday pot for use in the home, not for display or boasting about, or one to use for special occasions.

The Lord is unwilling to change the way men behave for He made them with a free will, hence the two trees in the centre of the Garden of Eden illustrating the way of faith and the way of sin. But it is clear that their choice would lead to Him being able to reward them with either life or destruction. Where a nation turns from its evil, God will relent of the disaster He thought to bring upon it, (Jer. 18:8) but conversely the reverse is also true (Jer. 18:10).

Spiritual blindness resulting in their total ignorance concerning the truth of the power and authority of Almighty God was a key factor in the fall of the Jews into the hands of Nebuchadnezzar. Even when the word of the Lord was written down and spoken before the king, such was the belief that only words of encouragement rather than those proclaiming the certainty of disaster should be heard by the people at a time of political turmoil that the king cut up the word of the Lord and burnt it, thinking he could stop the promised destruction from happening by so doing (Jer. 36).

But Jeremiah gave another scroll to Baruch to again record the words of the Lord (Jer. 36:27 – 32. Man cannot silence God however hard he tries. Even confining the prophet in prison, or in the mire at the bottom of a dried up well, could not silence God's word (Jer. 37, 38). What the king failed to recognise is that there was nothing that he could do to prevent

God doing exactly what He needed to do for the sake of the future of His people (Jer. 32).

It is interesting that when the Jews tried to trick the Messiah at the time of the accusation of the woman caught committing adultery (Jn. 8:1 – 11) He challenged her accusers by replying that the one who was sinless should cast the first stone (v7), and continued writing in the ground. We are not told what He wrote in the dust, but by looking at Jeremiah 17:13 we discover the significance of this activity. *All who forsake You shall be ashamed* Why? Because *those who depart from Me shall be written in the earth*. With these two references saying the same thing. The older men would have known the significance of the Messiah's action and, realising that they had no basis in believing they were without sin, were therefore the first to leave the scene.

Even though Jeremiah's task was to speak good things to the Lord on behalf of the people of Judah they sought to repay evil for good, seeking to destroy his life through their schemes (Jer. 18:20, 23).

What is also significant throughout this remarkable and illuminating book are the prophetic words that the old order of the first covenant God made with the people of Israel on Mount Sinai did not work; not because God's covenant was a failure, but because the lives of those it was designed to change and make new were not being changed through their unbelief and rebelliousness. God had chosen Abram, then Isaac and then Jacob. He had also been behind the choice of Jacob's wives, particularly Leah to whom was born the two main players in the life of the nation of Israel, Levi and Judah.

It was as the God of Israel that the 'I Am' wanted to be known. His whole plan of salvation was to be revealed through these chosen patriarchs and the nation that sprung from them. The scene was therefore set with Israel, and particularly Judah, taking centre stage. The rebelliousness of the people and their stubborn unwillingness to put their trust in God was a major cause of concern, requiring God to search out men and women who could be trusted to challenge the people, warning them of disaster if they persisted in neglecting His word which forecast so much about their errant ways and less than distinguished life in His service.

Israel was central to God's plan for the fulfilment of His permanent way of salvation for mankind. Therefore, any waywardness was to be dealt with firmly and in such a way as to awaken within some sensitive souls the sense of sinfulness and departure from the covenant God had made with them that would encourage them to seek Him afresh, just as Nehemiah did (Neh. 1). Just as Israel could not survive without God, so God could not pursue His eternal plan of salvation without them.

As God had committed the gradual revelation of His plan of salvation, through the illustrative Tabernacle and through life-training of the nation, of Israel, He could not suddenly employ another nation so late in the process. God was committed to Israel, and because of Satan's antagonism of Israel, they were in turn, whether the people liked it or not, committed to God. There was no turning back for either party.

What God wanted was a marriage-type relationship with His people, where the wife submits herself to her husband as Leah did to Jacob. Israel had become like Rachel who could not leave her father's earth gods behind and surrender all to her husband's God. This was so with the Israelites. They were instructed to remove all the Canaanite nations from the Promised Land because God knew that even one tribe or even one person left alive would corrupt the people. And this proved to be true.

Israel, under a number of evil kings, finally felt the wrath of God by being invaded by the Assyrians who believed it was by their own strength and the might of their gods that they had conquered the land of Israel. Sadly, because Judah did not learn the lesson of her sister Israel (Jer. 3:7 – 10) and went blithely on worshipping idols who could not save her, God brought them low by employing the Babylonians under Nebuchadnezzar to conquer them. Although the Babylonians destroyed Solomon's magnificent temple, God had no objection to seeing the back of a construction that had lost its meaning for the people.

God needed a voice in Judah to speak for Him because He had a problem. He needed to warn His people that if they persisted in their ignorance of Him and continued to go their own way, listening to men rather than Him, then they would be following the ways of Satan and His offer of salvation would fail. Therefore, He called the very young Jeremiah[65] into His service by touching his mouth, symbolising God's word being placed in his mouth (cf. Is:6:7), with the only assurance that whatever the people tried to do to him, God would protect his life (Jer. 1:8).

He was to write about the trials he was going through in God's service

> 7 *O Lord, You induced me, and I was persuaded;*
> *You are stronger than I, and have prevailed.*
> *I am in derision daily;*
> *Everyone mocks me.*
> 8 *For when I speak, I must shout out,*
> *"Violence and distruction!"*
> *Because the word of the Lord was made to me*
> *A reproach and a derision daily.*
> 9 *Then I said, "I will not make mention of Him,*
> *Nor speak anymore in His name."*
> *But His word was in my heart like a burning fire*

---

[65] He was possibly aged about 17 when he was first called.

Shut up in my bones;
I was weary of holding it back,
And I could contain it no longer.
10 *For I heard the whispering and mocking:*
"Fear on every side!"
"Denounce him! Let us denounce him"
All my friends and relatives watched for me to fail, saying,
"Perhaps he can be persuaded and deceived;
Then we will overcome him,
And we will take our revenge on him."

Then in self encouragement he adds:

11 *But the Lord is with me as a mighty, awesome One.*
Therefore my persecutors will stumble, and will not prevail.
They will be greatly ashamed, for they will not prosper.
Their everlasting confusion will never be forgotten.
(Jer. 20:7 – 11)

It is true that nothing is impossible for God, and nothing is outside His knowledge or sovereignty. So why do I say God had a problem? God does not have to work through individuals or nations; it has been His choice to do so. The whole purpose of the creation was the contact and empathy God wanted to enjoy between Himself and those He had created in His image. When we live in line with His designed way of life then all goes well and we are able to live in union with Him. Rebel and He leaves us to our own devices which leads to eternal destruction.

When we sin and go our own way, then our relationship with God is put under strain and it is up to us to change and seek Him again through repentance and faith. However, when we cut ourselves off from God, He has to find ways to bring us back to Himself which, had we been true to Him, He would not have had to do. God wants to reach out to all those who are lost. In the case of Israel, God wanted to work through them for the benefit of the whole of mankind.

Over the course of our study so far, we have learned how God wanted to establish on earth a full and free way of salvation that would allow anyone to be reunited with Him after Adam's sin had caused that catastrophic separation. Every time the nation of Israel was rebellious, God had to find another way of bringing them back to Himself so that He could continue with the development on earth of His plan of salvation.

It was these 'problems', resulting in interruptions to the God/Israel relationship, that were caused by the rebellion and unbelief of the people of Israel to which I am referring. They were not unsolvable for God, but they did mean that God had to make additional plans to bring His work of establishing salvation through the nation of Israel back on track. God has the same 'problem' with us when we get lazy or turn a deaf ear to His requests for us to do a work for Him.

Jeremiah's task of going to whomever God sent him and speaking God's word to them was not an easy one, for the people misunderstood the message. Yes, God was accusing them of duplicity and rebellion, but He also wanted them to re-engage with Him so that He could bless them. Jeremiah was that lonely voice, the person standing in the busy city street calling out to the people as they rushed by that God was real and wanted to save them, wanted to change their lives for the good.

But such was their focus on where they were going and the business in which they were involved, imprisoned within their busy-ness and the things of the earth, that they were deaf to the preacher's call. Speaking from the steps of the temple Solomon built from such accumulated wealth that it was glorious in its appearance and renowned for its beauty and splendour (Jer. 7), Jeremiah had to try and convince the people that even though God had blessed this building with His presence when it was dedicated by Solomon, it was not the building that was sacred, it was God who made the building sacred.

The Messiah emphasised this matter when He criticised the scribes and Pharisees concerning the oaths they allowed. To them swearing not on the temple but on the gold of the temple meant that the oath stood, yet it was the temple that sanctified the gold (Matt. 23:16, 17). The same applied to the altar and the sacrifice, for was it not the altar that consecrated the sacrifice (Matt. 23:18, 19)? Those who made out that they knew more than the people about their religion knew less than they thought they did because their concept of what was holy made no sense whatsoever.

Did not God dwell in the temple? Therefore, surely, if anyone swore by the temple, did they not swear by it and Him who dwells in it? In all their boasting and the rules and regulations they put upon the people they themselves were like whitewashed sepulchres which contained dead men's bones (Matt. 23). Unfortunately, because the name of God was in their mouths but far from their mind (Jer. 12:2b) and heart, their witness was false, just as it is in the established church today. Man, so full of sin as he is, has not changed.

Just because the building was there representing God's presence among them (Jer. 7:4), it did not mean that if their hearts were not right with Him that He would save them.

Is it any wonder that My anger is so great against this people when children collect wood, the men kindle the fire and the women knead dough to make cakes for the Queen of Heaven and they pour out drink offerings to other gods?" (see Jer. 7:17, 18).

Worshipping other gods, relying on lying words to direct their lives that cannot profit and then going into the Temple of God having been contaminated in such a way, was an insult to the God who had done so much for them in the past.

It was no good for them to rely on the temple being in the city when all along God had commanded the people to be pure before Him by obeying His voice alone and to walk in the ways He commanded them to walk so that He could be their God. (Jer. 7:23; 17:5, 7 – 10) In that way alone could they ever hope to be His people and all would be well with them.

The corruption of their worship and their duplicity in mechanically worshipping both their acquired gods and the God of their fathers clearly advertised that their hearts were far from having true belief in Him and Him alone. The name of God may have been present in their mouths but He was far from their hearts. (Jer. 12:2b) which is why Jeremiah, who had been married to God in the strictest sense, took God to task about the prosperity of the wicked whilst He suffered rebuke and attracted only animosity and harassment from his family and the authorities.

> *1 You are Righteous, O Lord, when I plead my case with You;*
> *Yet let me discuss issues of justice with You.*
> *Why does the way of the wicked prosper?*
> *Why are those happy who deal so treacherously?*
> *2 You have planted them, yes, they have taken root;*
> *They grow, yes, they even bear fruit.*
> *You are honoured by their lips*
> *But far from their heart and mind.*
> *3 But You, O Lord, know my devotion to You;*
> *You have seen me,*
> *And You have tested my heart toward You.*
> *Pull out the faithless sheep for the slaughter,*
> *And prepare them for the day of slaughter.*
> *(Jer. 12:1 – 3)*

When God brought the people out of Egypt, He did not speak to them about burnt offerings and sacrifice, rather He taught them through various experiences primarily to trust Him (Jer. 7:22). Throughout their wilderness wanderings God was able to demonstrate His ability to provide them with all they needed, both in terms of food, by supplying them with manna and, when they complained bitterly, with quail and water by making bitter waters sweet and providing water out of a rock.

It was this total trust in and obedience to the word of God that was the most important element in their life of blessing and service. *"... man shall not live by bread alone,"* said the Messiah, *"but by every word that proceeds from the mouth of God"* (Matt. 4) It was in the wilderness that the people were able to experience, undistracted, the wonders of God.

The temple services came later when they had already experienced the practical abilities of God which had refined their faith. First came trust and obedience, and then came the sacrifices for sin and an established, movable temple to train them for when they were settled in the Promised Land and no longer so immediately and obviously dependent on His guidance and supply. Yet unwittingly they were dependent upon Him for the former and latter rains to provided water for their crops.

The tabernacle complex, as we have already seen, teaches us much about the long-term message God wanted His people to learn without unlearning their need to trust Him and be obedient to His commands. Indeed, without intrinsic obedience and faith, all the services of the temple were pointless. Isaiah raised this point in the first chapter of his book. The sacrifices were for when they were spiritually attuned to Him.

The forgiveness of sins at the altar and the study of the word at the laver, which is why the Sabbath[66] was so important, were in addition to, not apart from a life devoted to obeying His voice and walking in the ways in which He had commanded them to walk as written down in the Law and statutes He had given to them.

It was David who brought out the important truths in his psalms such as Ps. 51:

> *"Create in me a clean heart, O God,*
> *And renew a right spirit within me ..."*

Surprisingly this was a new way of thinking, where obedience and faith go hand in hand with repentance and seeking a personal relationship with the God of Israel. Far too many church-going believers today rely on the fact that they attend church. The phrase so often used is, "I am a Catholic", or "I am Church of England", or a Methodist or Baptist or any other of the myriad denominations, as though that particular organisation can save souls.

Through their services and the preaching of the word of God some people receive the vital knowledge of the saving grace of Christ Jesus that

---

[66] The purpose of the Sabbath was for the family to get together for quality time, and for the reading and study of the Word of God within the family. In this way the family as a whole was able to focus their attention on God and the parents instruct the children on the truths of their faith. Families also got together in the temple or synagogue to worship God as a community. There were no one-parent families, except through the death of one parent, but then the greater family group absorbed them so that they would not be on their own.

changes lives. But not one of those organisations can actually save people from the condemnation of their sins. Only total belief in the sacrificial death and resurrection of the Lamb of God can do that. It is the Holy Spirit who cleanses us from all sin by the application of the sin-cleansing blood of the Saviour which gives our consciences a deep clean so that we are in a fit state to enter into that life-changing, personal and dynamic spiritual relationship with Christ Jesus the Lord.

Through Jeremiah God challenged the people to think about their relationship with Him:

> *what injustice have your fathers found in me that they have gone far from Me and followed idols and have become idolaters (Jer. 2:5).*

He challenged them to tell Him of any other nation who had dared to trade in the gods of their fathers for new gods, illustrating that other nations were far more dedicated to their gods than Israel was to their mighty God who had demonstrated to them power over all the other gods they had ever encountered, particularly in Egypt. He had been to them a fountain of living water.

In an area where water is in short supply it had a significant impact on the lives of the population. The farmers were particularly dependent upon the former and latter rains for their crops, to the extent that the rains were considered to be a sign of God's favour. Imagine then a fountain of living water that cannot be polluted.

The Messiah told the Samaritan woman at the well that He was able to supply her with living water. How could that be, she asked, as He had nothing with which to draw water. (Jn. 4:10 – 26) But the water that He could supply would become a fountain of spiritual water springing up from within the believer to eternal life. This speaks of the supply of God's blessings and spiritual refreshment that the Father supplies through the Holy Spirit, for we need to receive from God continually; this is the sustenance that comes from the mouth of God.

The alternative to the plentiful and inexhaustible supply of spiritual refreshment was the provision of broken cisterns. These pits dug in the rock were dependent upon what could be received from the surrounding land. Porous or cracked rock allowed the water to leak away. In times of conflict the cisterns were targets for the enemy to pollute. Any drought would result in empty cisterns.

By applying the matter of water supply to God's endless and inexhaustible care and blessing of His people and their willing dependence on other gods which are powerless; Jeremiah was trying to persuade them to understand just how ridiculous their actions were. Fancy calling a tree 'my father' or a stone 'my mother', which is what the chosen people of God were effectively doing in worshipping carved wood and stone statues. 'Let these gods you have made save you', is what God was saying to them.

It is essential that we never forget that we are dual persons, that is we are spirit beings living in earthly bodies, created by God Himself, and it is the spirit being within us that will live for eternity in a place of joy and laughter, provided we ensure that through our communing with God in spirit and in truth our relationship with Him is cemented. It is He who applies regeneration and sanctification to us so that we not only become spiritually alive in Him, but by it our spirit is held secure and sustained by Him until we reach His rest in glory where all our spiritual needs will be met (Jude 24, 25). Jeremiah's desperate plea to his people was:

> *'Rededicate yourselves to Me by circumcising not just your bodies but your hearts also (Jer. 4:4), make yourselves clean in both body, mind and spirit, with a complete change of heart that will allow the seed of God's word to fall on good fallow ground and grow',* (Matt. 13:23)

These were important times. The drift of the people of Israel, and in particular Judah, towards the gods of the surrounding nations was destroying their special relationship with God. Their dependence on the temple, standing as it did so prominently in Jerusalem, meant it had become a lucky charm to them, just like the Ark at the time of Eli. But bringing the Ark to the battle when their hearts were so far from God was a waste of time because God had left them to their own devices although He showed His power to the Philistines through the Ark of the Covenant.

At this time, with the Jews reliant on God defending His temple which had become polluted and corrupted with what was going on there, and which they thought would save them from disaster, Jeremiah told them that they would be doomed if they continued to believe that they could go after other gods and still be saved from disaster by their own God of gods.

What is far worse is what was happening in the temple itself out of sight of the non-priestly worshippers. Ezekiel, who had not entered into full service in the temple by the time he was taken into exile, had a vision of the abominations that were taking place in the temple courts that incited God to jealousy and to decree that the people of Judah would not only endure exile for 70 years, the length of sentence being given by God to Jeremiah, but that they would also be bereft of any word from God until the appearance of the Messiah 400 years after their return and the temple was rebuilt.

In Ezekiel chapter 8 we have recorded for us the vision Ezekiel received from God in the presence of the elders of Judah. In this way God revealed to him the hidden idol worship in the sanctuary of the temple which had been dedicated to the worship of Almighty God. Although Ezekiel was never able to serve in the temple, he was called by God to be His prophet in exile. God enabled him to witness firsthand, by taking him in the spirit to the temple as it was before its destruction, the abominations in which the king and priests, and particularly the priestly elders, had been involved.

Without a temple in which to worship and celebrate the Sabbath and the other events in the ceremonial calendar of the temple, the elders were meeting with this prophet of God which meant that, having heard what God showed Ezekiel concerning the sort of abominations they had been involved in, they had no complaint against what God had done in sending them into exile. Sat before the elders Ezekiel experienced not just a vision, but was taken up in the Spirit to the spiritual realm in which God lives.

The form of God Ezekiel saw when he was 'in the Spirit' could have been the Messiah who was beginning to take centre stage prior to His appearance on the earth in human form, and through whom God was to manifest Himself to men. It certainly gave authenticity to the vision (cf. Ez. 1:26; Jn. 1:18). The flames from the waist down (v27) symbolised both the vengeance of God against those wicked Jews who had incited Him to jealousy and the purification of those believers who owned a true heart before Him, and through whom He was able to continue to work as He revealed His plan of salvation which was so crucial to the future of mankind as a whole. In contrast the brightness of the upper part of the body speaks clearly of God's unapproachable majesty. (1 Tim. 6:16)

What is particularly pertinent about the vision is that the Spirit carried him away to Jerusalem, although not bodily, so that what he was able to describe to those sat before him would have had the greatest possible impact.

There were three sections to this vision:

1.   God showed Ezekiel just what had been going on in the temple prior to the nation being exiled.

2.   The door of the North Gate (vs. 3 – 6), also known as the 'Altar Gate', gave access to the king's palace, so the king would know what was going on in the area of the temple immediately inside this gate. Here, in the inner court, an area restricted to priestly activity, the image of an idol was set up (2 Kgs. 21:1 – 5; 23:4, 7), possibly Astarte or Asheera. The Syrian Venus, and supposed "Queen of Heaven" and wife of the Phoenician god Baal, was worshipped with licentious rites. It is possible that there were separate proofs of Jewish idolatry rather than being restricted to just one idol. It was the erection of this idol in His temple that provoked God to jealousy. God had, as we have already heard, declared that He was not willing to give His glory to another.

3.   The plagues in Egypt proved beyond doubt God's mighty power over all creation. Through His personal covenant with the Children of Israel, established on Mount Sinai, God made it very clear to the Israelites that only He had the power to provide them with blessings and protection from other nations, provided that He had their full attention at all times. Time and again in their history God proved this to be the case. So why this incomprehensible yet persistent urge to seek after other totally ineffective idols to worship which led to untold suffering as prophesied by none other than Moses?

It was in that magnificent temple God showed His presence through His Shekinah glory; but how could His presence remain with them when they were filling His sanctuary with these abominations? How could truth live with lies and how could it be the centre of worship to Him if their hearts were so rebellious? And this amongst the very men who should be directing the people to worship their God and Him alone so that they might become righteous in the same way that Abraham was righteous. Not only did God's glory leave the temple but the people were forced out of the land and the temple destroyed.

In a hidden room within the temple complex (vs. 7 – 12) seventy-seven priestly elders had been worshipping idols depicted on the walls of the room which were particular abominations in God's sight. (cf. Acts 10:9 – 16) These priests thought that God could not see them hidden away in this inner room, but there is nothing on earth which is invisible to God, even the deep recesses of the heart.

Ezekiel was urged on by God who was keen that he should be aware of all that His ordained priests, Ezekiel's own relations, had been guilty of and which had caused Him so much pain and sadness. For Ezekiel there were greater abominations for him to see than those He had already seen (vs. 13 – 18). He saw before him twenty-five priests standing at the door of the holy place where only those chosen of God to minister to Him were allowed to enter; the inner sanctuary of their spiritual and almighty God.

Ezekiel saw that these priests, instead of having their hearts and minds focused on their God and the spiritually based ceremonial activities in which they should have been engaged, standing with their backs to the sanctuary of God's presence, which was in itself an insult to Him, worshipping the sun (Egyptian god Ra) which was rising in the east. In this century we are fully aware that the sun is just a planet that is ablaze sending light and warmth to us on earth. But to those priests it was a mystery but still part of God's creation to be admired but not worshipped.

In looking towards the sun with their backs to the presence of God they were both physically and symbolically turning their backs on the God who had done so much for them in order to worship just an element of God's mighty creation. With the presence of God comes peace. By provoking God to anger through the abomination of their worship of the gods of the nations around them, the priests, even those who should have been teaching their younger brethren of the deep spiritual truths of the law and worship of God so that they too could become united in praise of God, were allowing violence to enter the land because of the withdrawal of God's protection and the peace of His presence through their profound blindness to His presence and glory along with their reckless rebelliousness.

With his bodily presence before them, the priestly elders of Judah and Jerusalem were hearing a running commentary from the lips of Ezekiel whose spirit had been carried back to Jerusalem to witness their activities in the last days before they were taken into exile in Babylon. The clarity of God's accusations against them meant they had no excuse for being the cause of the nations present predicament. They were being condemned by God from the lips of His servant for the despised, anti-God activities in which they had been engaged. What greater witness and what greater condemnation could there be?

With the erection of abominations, particularly those within the temple area, which led to their exile, the gradual decline of the God-designed temple was, by this time, well established. The Ark had already gone from the Holy of Holies leaving a bare room and, according to Jeremiah, the ark was not to be reproduced (Jer. 3:16).

The purpose of its mysterious disappearance was that God wanted the people to consider their individual relationship with Him according to the ten commandments that were now imprinted on their hearts through repetition, just as the majority of people in the UK know most of the words of the Lord's prayer. Rather than the collective understanding that everything connected with God had to be through the Temple and the priests, they were to seek after God individually.

It is very sad that many of those who believe themselves to be believers in The Christ and call themselves Christians are following the same path as the Jews of Jeremiah's day. The reason for this is because they are denying themselves a personal faith and personal walk with God by relying totally on the minister of the church they attend to provide them with all their spiritual food and direction.

However good or bad the minister or leader of that church may be, they are still sinners before God and make mistakes, unintentional or intentional. It is clearly the responsibility of every individual to work out their own salvation (Phil. 2:12) before God with fear and trembling and to seek God for themselves. Although we are all guided and supported by others, our personal relationship with God will always be our own personal responsibility and no one else's.

Gradually God wanted to wean the people away from the strictly ceremonial towards a personal faith and relationship with Him. Marriage and divorce feature heavily in the text. Even though they had sinned by going after other gods that were no gods[67], with God issuing them with a certificate of divorce, unlike in a normal human relationship God was willing to receive them back (Jer. 3).

In Israel, God had planted a noble vine, a chosen seed of the highest quality, yet they had turned it into a degenerate plant (Jer. 2:21). Abram, so blessed by God because of his indomitable faith and remarkable giving of himself to God, was followed by a dedicated Isaac, and then by Jacob who searched for God and found Him when he was alone. These represented the seed of the highest quality which was refined in Egypt to produce the cultivated vine that was Israel.

Such was the blind ignorance of the tribe of Judah, from the king and princes, judges and leaders down to the people and their willingness to play the harlot with other gods, making treaties that meant nothing in a time of crisis in spite of God's warning through Jeremiah, exile became inevitable.

With the kings of Israel and Judah now a thing of the past, at the end of their exile the people once more had to rely on the priests and the temple, but in a totally different way as we shall see in the next chapter.

---

[67] We ned to be very clear about this matter of the gods being worshipped around the world were non-gods. This is because as creator of all that is only the God of Israel had absolute power. Not only had He created all things, but He was also the sustainer of all things. Indeed, He has consistently had complete and absolute power over His creation which has, according to Peter (2 Peter 3:10, 11) a limited life span and will disappear as miraculously as it appeared. Therefore, He is the only God who should be worshipped and to whom we owe our very being and life, both here and in the world to come.

"O come, let us worship and bow down;
Let us kneel before the Lord our Maker.
For He is our God,
And we are the people of His pasture
And the sheep of His hand."
(Ps. 95:6 , 7)

"Not unto us, O Lord, not unto us,
But to Your Name give glory,
Because of Your mercy,
Because of Your Truth.
Why should the Gentiles say,
Where is your God?
Our God is in Heaven;
He is able to do whatever He pleases."
(See Ps. 115)

"Be doers of the Word,
And not hearers only,
Deceiving yourselves."
(Ja. 1:22)

Exile brings self-examination

What was particularly devastating for the Jews about going into exile was what happened not just to their glorious city of Jerusalem, called the City of God, but to the even more glorious temple Solomon had built from such a treasure trove that David had carefully accumulated for that purpose.

When Nehemiah heard about the destruction whilst serving the king in Babylon, he wept and mourned for many days, fasting and praying before the God of heaven, confessing both his own sins and the sins of his fathers (Neh. 1). Such was the sense of despair amongst them that one Psalm records that the captives sat down by the rivers of the magnificent city of Babylon and wept when they remembered Zion. *"How,"* they asked, *"shall we sing the Lord's song in a strange land?"* (Ps. 137) But it was the people as a whole and not just the leaders who had so angered the Lord with their errant and rebellious ways that they had attracted this major disruption to their lives.

What was so significant, as far as God was concerned, was that the time of the appearance of the Messiah was drawing near. The promise of His visit to the earth was the golden thread woven into the tapestry of not just human history but the history of God's chosen people from the beginning of time. It was a visit that was central to the ultimate salvation of all mankind, not just the chosen people of Israel alone, a fact the Jews themselves found very hard to accept and still do.

Although salvation is offered to all mankind, it is only those who accept that gift of salvation through repenting of their sin and accepting the fact that salvation only comes through the sacrificial death of the Messiah in their place, and surrendering their hearts and all that they have and are to that Saviour whose lives can be changed. After all by dying on the cross the Messiah was buying back mankind to Himself. Thus, having created us, He then had to die for us to have us return to His authority.

Many believe that by going through the motions of being baptised as a child and through the process of confirmation at an older age they are saved. This is not necessarily the case, for as we have discovered God looks into the heart of a person, and the heart process must be right before Him. Mechanically following the words on a printed page has no meaning before a Holy God.

Even though God had protected His chosen people, nurtured them and become married to them for the specific purpose of reaching out to all mankind through them, through rebellion and a total ignorance of spiritual things they had tried to completely disrupt His plans. This was in spite of all the messages he had sent to them through His servants the prophets, and particularly the warnings they had received through Jeremiah and Isaiah.

But what was their attitude towards His servants the prophets? As the parable of the landowner who planted a vineyard and set a hedge around it, dug a winepress, built a tower and leased it to vinedressers who did not want to pay their dues (Matt. 21:33 – 44). To avoid parting with any money:

35 And the husbandmen took his servants, beat one, killed another, and stoned another.

36 Again, he sent other servants more than the first: and they treated them in the same manner.

37 Then last of all he sent his son to them, saying, They will respect my son and have regard for him.

38 But when the husbandmen saw the son, they said among themselves, This is the heir; come, let us kill him, so that we can seize his inheritance.

39 So they caught him, cast him out of the vineyard, and slew him.

Re-establishing the True Worship of God

This was perceived by the chief priests and Pharisees as being directed at them, but feared taking hold of Him for fear of the multitude who rightly believed he was a prophet, although he was more than a Prophet.

The priests and the people had only themselves to blame for the predicament they were experiencing. Even the priests in the days of the Messiah, who thought they were wiser and more righteous than their forebears, were found to be no better. In fact, they were found to be far worse because rather than merely seeking to kill the prophets of God, they were guilty of seeking to kill God's Son.

Although God had not been able to work through His chosen people in the way that He had wanted, He was not prevented from fulfilling His ultimate plan of salvation, for He was able to broadcast other lessons to mankind particularly regarding the spiritual nature of the relationship men needed to adopt if they wanted to enter into a meaningful dialogue with Him.

This was achieved either through the individuals He chose, like the prophets, or those who chose to reach out to Him, like Hannah the mother of Samuel. In obedience to God's instructions, Hosea actually lived his life in such a way that Israel's rebellious ways before God and the disruption that it caused to their relationship with God was dramatised daily before the people.

The treatment of those prophets, particularly by the religious leadership, was used by the Messiah as a condemnation of the leadership of His day for they were perpetuating the sins of their fathers (Matt 23:29 – 31).

Solomon was unsparing in the construction of the temple, with much gold on surfaces and for utensils and even solid gold ceremonial shields for his personal bodyguard. The magnificent temple building, so admired by the people and those of other nations, and which had become their 'lucky charm' against invasion, had been reduced to a pile of rubble with the precious vessels used in the worship services being taken as booty by the invading force (Dan. 5:2).

The religious and civil leaders had focused their attention on the temple building itself and not on the God it directed the people to worship and who had blessed it by demonstrating His presence in it through the witness of the cloud at its dedication. The lessons of the exile were not learned by the scribes and Pharisees for they focused on the wrong things, believing that the temple itself was less important than the gold that covered it (Matt. 23:16 – 23).

The presence of the temple within their midst was to be a constant reminder to the people of their God and His power and glory, not an object of worship in itself. They had forgotten that the Word the nation had received at Mount Sinai, of which they were so proud and possessive, had been delivered direct to them by a God who could not be seen because He was/is spiritual not physical. This was totally opposite to the worship of the idols they had made and had come to be assimilate into their worship.

Here was a clash between the worship of an eternal and spiritual God, who was jealously protective of His rightful place as their sole spiritual leader, and the worship of dumb physical creations of men. The first commandment of the covenant God made with them on Mount Sinai focused on their need to love Him before all others. Yet their physical senses were redirecting them to powerless physical objects causing them, through superstition, to become blind to the things of God just as Adam and Eve were made blind when looking at the fruit on the forbidden tree

Through their obvious fall from grace in having to enter exile, no longer independent and ruled by their own king as they had requested, God had brought the arrogant, power-hungry leaders and corrupt judiciary down, along with the people who were so intent on following the 'pleasures' of their own hearts through the earthly pleasures prescribed in the worship of other gods, even though such activities were known to be an abomination to God. Such deviant activity signalled the divorce and separation God had promised through His prophets who were so despised by the people for their words of correction which challenged the people's alternative way of life.

Such was the decay of the religious and spiritual life of the Jews over a long period of time that the Book of the Law was totally ignored. It is astonishing that in the time of King Josiah the Book of the Law was found in the temple! (2 Chron. 34:15) How could they observe the Law of the Lord by ignoring the study of that Law? King David claimed that he had to meditate on it night and day to remain obedient to that Law (cf. Ps. 1:2).

What this shows is just how far from God the priests had wandered because of their ignorant attitude towards His laws and statutes, taking the rest of the nation with them. Yet it was through this nation that God wanted to reach out to the people of the world[68]. If they had treated their relationship to God with contempt, how was the rest of the human race to understand what they needed to do to get right with Him, the God who created them?

Daniel Identified

There were some who entered into exile refusing to bow to any god except the Lord God of Israel. Just as at the time of Jezebel, the wife of the weak king Ahab who banned the worship of the God of Israel, Elijah

---

[68] Israel took on a persecuted attitude with regard to the rest of the world because other nations were used to punish Israel, whereas God's plan was that they should be an example to them. God wanted to demonstrate how He could love and care for them, protecting them from attack and giving them bountiful harvest and causing them to be successful in every sphere of life. It was their rebelliousness which caused them to be persecuted in the way they were, even to the present day.

learned that God had reserved for Himself 7,000 who did not bow their knee to Baal (1 Kgs. 19:18). So at the time of the Babylonian exile there were those of the remnant who were determined, at whatever the cost, to worship God alone.

Daniel, a prince of Israel, made a stand by refusing the food sent to him by the king, choosing to eat only the food prescribed by God in His word (Dan. 1:8 – 16). By being obedient to God in spite of all the pressures to conform to the local customs, Daniel and his friends were able to influence those who ruled over them because by doing so God blessed them.

God brought the children of Israel into exile both as a punishment and as a time of training away from their normal life of freedom in their own land. God did not stop working in and through them. Indeed, as we shall see, during this time out of their own country and environment, God was able to work amongst the rulers of other lands through those of His own people who were prepared to believe and trust in Him, letting pagan rulers into the mysteries of the spiritual realm which were to denied the sorcerers and magicians who were mere ignorant men, boasting that they knew about these things.

Daniel tells us of the selection of four noble young men of Israel to be trained in the ways of the court of the king, one of them being himself, to whom God gave knowledge and wisdom and skill in all literature. Daniel also had the additional ability to understand all visions and dreams (Dan. 1). Thus through His involvement in their lives, God could influence the king by them demonstrating that the power of God was not confined to the land of Israel nor was it intended to be confined to the people of Israel, but was for the benefit of all mankind through them. (Dan. 1:17 – 21)

A moment of testing came when Nebuchadnezzar had a dream but would not tell the dream to the usual wise men and sorcerers, possibly because he had forgotten it, as some of us do on waking, or more reasonably because through it, God wanted to demonstrate the power of His Spirit to speak through those dedicated to His service.

Concerned that the usual wise men and sorcerers would play for time and then lie to him, when the men told him that they could not decipher his dream without knowing what it was he sentenced them to death (Dan. 2).

When Daniel found out that the king had decided to kill all the wise men, which would have included himself and his three companions, he asked the king for time to find out what his dream meant. After seeking God, Daniel was given the knowledge required so that he was able to go before the king and describe the dream and then give him the interpretation, but not without acknowledging that there was a God in heaven who revealed secrets (v28).

This gave the king the clear message that there was an all-knowing God in the heavenly places who was far above all other gods worshipped in his kingdom; a God who was able to give the king dreams with a message. This incident was God witnessing to His existence and, by giving this dream to a pagan king who was not anti-God, just ignorant of Him, God was showing the Jews that He retained the power and the right to work directly within nations through those Jews who were true believers in Him, wherever they happened to be and whoever they happened to be with.

As it happens this dream was prophetic, for it foretold of the kingdoms that were to come. The king was seen as the golden king at the top of the figure in his dream. He was followed by the Medo-Persian Empire led by Cyrus and Darius, then the Grecian Empire led by Alexander the Great and the four generals who took over and divided his empire into four parts, and then the Roman Empire under various emperors.

However, in chapter 11, Daniel was given a revelation of the power struggles between Egypt and the area now called Syria with powerless Israel trapped like a pawn in the middle and suffering as a result. Finally, after many rulers had come and gone and before the Romans took control, a usurper, Antiochus, took power as king of Syria, calling himself 'Antiochus Epiphanes'.

Antiochus, the 'little horn' of Daniel's vision and undoubtedly the most tyrannical ruler of the first testament, ruled the whole area, including Egypt, through successful battles. During the contraction of his empire, however, he took vengeance on the Jews, killing tens of thousands and selling as many into slavery. His major act of defiance against the God of Israel was to 'take away the daily sacrifices and the place of His sanctuary was cast down' (Dan. 11:11), for this king sacrificed a pig on the temple altar and erected an image of the god Jupiter in the temple.

According to the prophetic knowledge God gave to Daniel, the timing of all these events was set at 2300 days, after which time the sanctuary 'shall be cleansed' (Dan. 8:13, 14). Remember that the majority of Jews had, at the time of Nebuchadnezzar's defeat of Jerusalem and the sacking of the temple at the time of the second exile, lost all knowledge of and respect for their God. Many Jews had gone into exile willingly before the final defeat of the city in obedience to the command of God through His prophet Jeremiah, but it remained the responsibility of the true remnant, like Daniel and Nehemiah, to maintain a personal relationship with Him and thereby maintain the faith and true purpose of Israel.

Throughout all this turmoil it is clear God was still in control, for it is made clear through reading Daniel's account of his spiritual awakening (Dan. 1:17) and the angelic activity he experienced, that the spiritual realm God inhabited was far greater and more glorious than all that he saw or experienced on the earth. Indeed, it can be said that the main battle between God and Satan was spiritual, being fought in the heavenly places, occasionally spilling over into the physical world. Daniel's prayers were being heard by God, but the fallen spiritual angels were doing battle with God's messengers who were trying to reach God's earthly disciples (Dan. 10 esp. v13).

But how did Daniel come to see spiritual things? Because in chapter 9 we read that he was willing to

- humble himself before his God (v3),

- make confession of the sins of his nation and himself (vs 4 – 9),

- recognise that they had not obeyed the voice of God

- walk in His ways according to the words of His prophets (vs. 10 – 15; cf. Matt. 23:29 – 39),

- ask for forgiveness (vs. 16 – 19).

It was the earnestness with which he focused his attention on God, and the way in which in a personal and heartfelt manner he directed the words of his mouth to God, recognising the special covenant relationship they had with Him which attracted a remarkable response from God, for none other than Gabriel, the angel later sent to Mary to announce her pregnancy with the messianic child, appeared to him to announce that he, Daniel, was greatly beloved of God (v23).

Daniel sees into heaven

In Chapter 7 we read that Daniel saw thrones being put in place and the Ancient of Days was seated with garments white as snow and hair like pure wool, purity, His throne was a fiery flame, judgement, and its wheels a burning fire (vs. 9, 10). At the end of these verses is a pertinent phrase about the court being seated (v10d) and books being opened.

This is dealt with in more detail in chapter 20 of Revelation, where we are told of a gathering of the small and the great before God (v12) to witness the books being opened in which their every action for good or ill is revealed.

The separate Book of Life containing the names of all true believers is also opened. These two books provide all the evidence required for God to judge justly the actions of all who have lived and died. So what does this tell us about God and His character that the nominal Israelite, who did not seek after their God as Daniel had, would not, could not, have appreciated because of ignorance?

The whiteness of His garments and His hair represented righteousness of the purest quality. Fire purifies and is a symbol of purity and holiness. The fire on the altar was never to go out for it was used to consume the sin offering which took away the sin from the person seeking forgiveness. Fire from God consumed the sacrifice (Lev. 9:24), destroyed the two rebellious sons of Aaron (Lev. 10:2) and the murmurings of the people brought upon them the fire of God (Num. 11:1). It also proved to the people that the God proclaimed by Elijah as the true God of Israel was the only one to be worshipped (1 Kgs. 18:38).

Fire also represents the divine presence and power. God appeared to Moses through the burning bush and Moses was instructed not to get too close and to take off his sandals because the ground on which he stood was holy ground (Ex. 3:5). God descended to the summit of Mount Sinai in fire (Ex. 19:18). The appearance of God's glory was described as being like a devouring fire (Ex. 24:17), His presence among them was manifested by a pillar of fire (Ex. 13:21) and even in the Psalms God's angels are described as spirits and flames of fire (Ps. 104:4; cf. Heb. 1:7).

Although the Israelites were in exile on account of their sins against God, how many of them knew God personally enough to relate their experience to the condition of their own relationship with God, as Daniel did?

Thus did Daniel experience spiritual things in the heavenly realm; but such an experience was made possible only because of His willingness to submit himself completely to God through repentance and faith and his dogged determination to keep himself separated from worldly contamination in order that he might be open and pure before his God. Therefore, he was loved of God (Dan. 9:23; 10:11).

To Daniel's vision of the Ancient of Days is added the presentation of dominion and glory and a kingdom to *'One like the Son of God'* who all peoples, nations and languages would serve and whose dominion is everlasting. His kingdom, unlike the earthly kingdoms of the world Daniel saw represented in his visions as strange beasts, would never pass away. Is this not the kingdom that is 'not of this world' that the Messiah told Pilate about? (Jn. 18:36) With what we are learning about the Messiah, the Son of God[69], is it any wonder that the temptations of Satan in Matthew 4 were rejected by the Messiah?

Also, should we not now be far more positive about our rejection of what Satan has to offer through the worldly attractions that surround us and accept with greater enthusiasm what God has to offer through the work of the Holy Spirit?

It was the Messiah who brought to the people's attention the fact of the heavenly kingdom, mentioned throughout scripture, which was not of this world but which has existed alongside the physical creation since the

---

[69] This might help in further understanding the relationship of the Son of God with the Ancient of Days (or Fatherhood of God that the Messiah kept talking about) and His transformation into the body of the child we know as Jesus Christ, Messiah of the Jews which is detailed in Appendix A.

creation, and more prominently in connection with this world since His resurrection and ascension, through His believers.

This has not been achieved by the conquering of vast areas of land but by the changing of hearts. This re-emphasis of the Kingdom of God was illustrated by the stone that was cut out of the mountain without hands that felled the image Nebuchadnezzar saw and which grew into a mountain that filled the earth.

But although the Kingdom of God came down to the earth to fill it, for the disciples were directed to *make disciples of all nations* (Matt. 28:19), confirming them as members of that kingdom by *baptising them in the name of the Father and of the Son and of the Holy Spirit*, it was not a kingdom in the human sense of ruling the world, as illustrated by the statue the king saw in his vision.

The reason for this is that there have been many human empires since then. Indeed, it is interesting that the first coming of the Messiah was timed to coincide with the Roman Empire, based in a city rather than a country, which enabled ease of travel across vast areas with a common language. This joining of various nations into one empire allowed the disciples and believers, including Paul, to spread the Gospel of Christ to the then-known world.

After many and various empires had come and gone, an empire was established over many centuries based on a small island off Europe which brought in a single language to a world of many languages to enable the ease of communication throughout the world in the end times before the second coming of the Messiah is announced. The remarkable rise, and eventual fall, of the British Empire, which at one time covered a fifth of the earth's surface and involved two thirds of the world's population, established the English language as the main commercial language of the world which also allowed the Word of God to be spread more easily.

The rise of the USA from the restrictions of being ruled by a small island to dominate the world as it does today, finally established the English language as the dominant world language, even though other languages can claim to be the first language of a far greater number of people[70]. It is worth remembering that empires have come and gone, countries have risen to dominance and fallen to obscurity throughout history according to God's will, and no country, however big (in land area) or powerful in military strength can think they will continue in that role for all time. The Roman and British empires are clear examples. The history of the world is undoubtedly according to the will and purposes of God (Dan. 4:34, 35; cf. Ps. 2:1 – 5; Is. 40:17 – 31).

---

[70] Chinese and Spanish are two such languages.

The Eternal Spiritual Kingdom

But what does this tell us of the mountain that filled the earth in Nebuchadnezzar's vision? Although in his vision the king saw the mountain fill the earth, it did not take over the world in the normal sense, for other empires followed that of Babylon as identified by the various materials of the image and the further visions that Daniel saw as recorded for us in chapter 11. So how can we understand this vision of future events if the mountain relates to the Kingdom of God on earth? As we have been discussing, there were to be two visits by the Messiah. The first was to settle once and for all the problem of sin which, however minor a sin it might be, is anathema to God.

Therefore, as sin was getting in the way of the relationship between man and God, it had to be legally sorted out to God's satisfaction. This matter was dealt with by the first appearance of the Messiah of which plenty of warning was given. Only then could the second coming of the Messiah be permitted. But as we know there is a longtime delay from man's point of view between the first and second appearances of the Messiah. Indeed, the Messiah told us that the timing of His return in glory is known only to the Father and we would be foolish to try to hazard a guess as to when it would be as it will come without any warning:

> *'For as in the days before the flood,*
> *People were eating and drinking,*
> *Marrying and being given in marriage,*
> *Until the day Noah entered the ark,*
> *And did not know until the flood came*
> *And took them away,*
> *So also will the coming of the Son of Man be.*
> *Then two will be working in the field*
> *And two grinding at the mill:*
> *One will be taken and the other left.*
> *Watch, therefore,*
> *For you do not know*
> *What hour the Lord will come. "*
> *(See Matt. 24:36 – 44)*

As there is this long gap of thousands of earthly years between the first appearance of the Messiah and when He will return *coming on the clouds of heaven with power and great glory* (Matt. 24:30), we have the problem of how we can accept this illustration of the mountain in the king's vision. As the mountain must be assumed to be symbolic of the coming of the Messiah, what Daniel described could not have been the complete mountain, given there are to be two visits of the Messiah to the earth.

Re-establishing the True Worship of God

Therefore, there must be two peaks to this mountain, with the nearer peak representing His first appearance as the suffering servant at the time of the Roman Empire, being lower than the main peak which represents His second and more glorious coming. This can best be seen as a crudely drawn illustration[71] below. It is like viewing a mountain with two peaks where the first peak is lower than the second with a saddle section connecting the two peaks in between, but when viewed as shown the first peak merges with the one behind it.

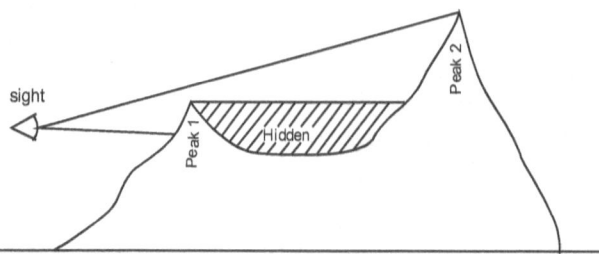

The two-peaked mountain that looked as though it filled the whole earth had a dip (or saddle) between the peaks which could not be seen, so that the foremost peak merged with the peak behind it. The fall of the Roman Empire soon after the visit of the Messiah was followed by other lesser kingdoms of men that existed in the world as the Kingdom of God was being established on the earth by the Holy Spirit who was sent by the Messiah to rule in the hearts of those who were, and are, prepared to believe in Him.

What we must be clear about is that the Kingdom of God is a spiritual kingdom, reigning in the hearts of individuals who were once alienated, and enemies of God through the sin which worked in their minds to encourage them to do those things which are abhorrent to God (Eph. 2:1 – 9).

Such people are reconciled to God through the Messiah's physical, sacrificial death on the cross and the shedding of His blood as required at the altar of sacrifice. In that way believers, who are prepared to remain grounded and steadfast in the faith through the work of God's Holy Spirit within them, are presented holy and blameless in the sight of the spiritual God (Jude 24, 25) to become members of His eternal spiritual kingdom, which does not have a physical land mass to call its own.

This is because its members come from many countries, tribes and ethnic groups scattered around the world, their unity centred on their belief in and commitment to the Messiah; and their vision is a place in the

---

[71] Recommended reading: In "Unlocking the Bible Omnibus" David Pawson summarises the various books of the Bible. His insights are worthy of consideration. No direct textual quotes have been included here from that book, as far as I am aware.

spiritual home He has gone to prepare for them (Jn. 14:2, 3). The main part of the mountain will appear when the Messiah comes the second time in victory when all the kingdoms of the world will become subject to Him.

By providing the king with the dream and its interpretation, Daniel was now propelled from being a captive, who spent time being trained in the things of the Chaldeans and receiving the God given *knowledge and skill in all literature and wisdom, and ... understanding in all visions and dreams* (Dan. 1:17), through to being elevated to supreme authority under the king. This was a remarkable achievement, similar to that of Joseph, that could not have happened without God's involvement in the life of this faithful believer.

The witness of the fiery furnace

Three of Daniel's fellow countrymen who were trained with him[72] were also to have their faith tested when they refused to bow down to a golden image set up by the king (Dan. 3). Even when challenged by the king before their presumed death, they boldly told him that they would not bow down to his god but were prepared to trust in their own God (vs. 13 – 18).

Their punishment was to be thrown into a furnace heated seven, spiritual perfection times hotter than normal. How this was achieved in the crude arrangement for heating a brick kiln that they would have had at the time is not known and could be a figure of speech meaning to be very hot, with the significance of the seven times being that it represented the work of the Holy Spirit who was undoubtedly employed at this time to save these fervent believers from suffering harm in such a fierce and extreme environment.

Nebuchadnezzar, seated in a prime position before the mouth of the furnace, suddenly noticed to his astonishment that there were four men walking unharmed in the fierce heat, one being like the son of God. We have already discussed at length the appearance of the Messiah to Abram in the form of Melchizedek, the priest of the Most High God.

It is, therefore, not impossible that Nebuchadnezzar had a vision of the Messiah as the Saviour of these three fervent believers and that the utterance of this man was God-inspired (cf. Jn. 11:49 – 52). This would not be out of place, given the vision the king had had of future kingdoms on the earth and the eternal kingdom that was to come.

We might think we are a sophisticated people living in this so-called modern and enlightened age. But in that we deceive ourselves for we are no different from those who lived at the time of Daniel. People today might know more about the world on which we live, and live in a time of technical innovation, and engaged in inter-planetary travel, but we are still fallen men and women in need of a Saviour.

---

[72] We know them with their exiled names as Shadrach, Meshach and Abed-Nego.

True, those of us who believe are no longer under the Law but under Grace, but, as we have been discovering, we still need to refresh our minds concerning how we came to be in need of being reborn spiritually and the legal implications for us of the altar of sacrifice and the cross of our Lord and Saviour Jesus Christ.

We might be sceptical about the account of these three men being thrown into a furnace, but this was a recognised means of punishment which was confirmed by the Huguenot Chardin, known as "The Traveller", who travelled to Persia in the 1670's. If we doubt God's ability to save these men from being affected by the heat, then we doubt God.

The writer of the book "From Witchcraft to Christ" admitted that at the height of her powers as a witch she went into the middle of a raging bonfire with no ill effects whatsoever. How much more then did God have the power to save those who loved Him and were prepared to put their lives on the line?

What is interesting about the book of Daniel is that spiritual things began to happen to some Jews once they were away from the restrictive, organised and corrupted, religious activities in the temple building in Jerusalem. What we learn from Daniel and Ezekiel ought to be part of the true believer's way of life in their walk of faith. Now separated from the temple, many of the priests and people started searching for God. It is evident that there was the desire in many hearts to understand the true reason for their predicament.

This new focus on God, with the willingness to experience the spiritual nature of God, would suggest that the temple and its solemn, ritual services had become an impediment to them. Deprived of a view of the imposing edifice, the priests and people were gaining a greater understanding of God. In which case, surely the temple had become of no practical use either for ensuring the priest were kept close to God, they had after all become wayward whether it was there or not, or for providing the majority of the people with a focus on their spiritual God, which, after all, was what the temple and its services was meant to do. The timing of the arrival of the Son of God and the ending of the temple's practical use was therefore perfect.

From parts of the Middle East even today come tales of crudely horrific torture and death that would not have been out of place at the times we are considering. Therefore, the people of that time were not so different to the people of today given that distorted religious belief is driving the perpetrators of those horrors. The three young men who looked directly at the tortuous death in the fiery furnace were driven not with false bravado but by such a compelling knowledge of God that they could not deny Him whatever the physical cost to themselves.

Have we, as sophisticated believers, particularly in the comfortable

West, become so satisfied with our lives and so far from the spiritual God we purport to worship and adore that we prefer to live and bow down to the gods of this world, even though it is not a physical act of obeisance, in order to keep our lives?

If that is so, another question needs to be put before us. Why are believers in the modern era so frightened of spiritual things that were recorded so long ago? The book of Daniel is undoubtedly and unashamedly spiritual, just like the book of Ezekiel and the Revelation of John. But does that mean these personal records of three servants of God are out of place in a book about God who is Spirit?

The scriptures are a record of God speaking to men and men reacting to God; therefore, if it were not of a spiritual nature then God is not an eternal Spirit. The madness of Nebuchadnezzar recorded for us in Daniel chapter 4 tells us how God is able to have a significant influence on the affairs of men, even in the case of great leaders. The obvious and devout faith of Daniel and his companions, and the public display of Daniel's ability to far exceed the skills of the professional magicians and soothsayers of the day in Chaldea, must have made a considerable impression on Nebuchadnezzar, turning him from his pagan ways to believe in this versatile, demonstrative and all-powerful God of Israel.

God challenges a king

Belshazzar's abuse of the holy vessels taken from the temple (ch.5) in an open display of insult to Almighty God, reminds us of the Ark of the Covenant being taken triumphantly into Philistia only to become such an intolerable burden to the Philistine people that it was quickly returned to Israel. In this case, as the result of his blasphemy, the king and all his guests saw a dismembered hand writing on the wall of the banqueting hall. This was a frightening experience, particularly to superstitious people. When the hand had finished writing the message and disappeared as quickly as it had come, the words written by the hand were left as a cold, spine-chilling reminder that the experience had not been a dream.

Daniel was called to interpret the message left by the hand which signalled the end of Belshazzar's reign. What Belshazzar failed to do was to learn from his father Nebuchadnezzar who came to realise that because pride caused him to think more highly of himself than he ought, he was driven from his high position to eat grass like an animal until he recognised the supremacy of Almighty God (Dan. 4). What is particularly significant is the immediacy of God's punishment following Belshazzar's sin, as though his sin was anticipated. The timing is undoubtedly extraordinary.

We cannot be ignorant of the fact that, if we read the word of God then the greatest lesson we have to learn is that God is Spirit and not of the earth and earthly as we are. How can we account for the miracle of the creation if we are unwilling to accept the infinity of God and His ability to do whatever is in His mind to do in the vastness of His universe? As there is nothing that God is unable to do, we must accept the spiritual dimension that allows God to open up the spiritual realm to individuals who seek Him, as Daniel did, and to work miracles through and for believers even in today's modern and sophisticated world.

The reason many parts of the book of Daniel are unacceptable to some is because they are either spiritually dead, or spiritually very immature, or even spiritually deformed. Our growth in spiritual matters depends not just on a superficial belief in God, as with Nicodemus, but a willingness, after our acceptance of the salvation God offers us through His Son, our Lord, to seek after spiritual union, spiritual marriage, with God as a member of the Bride of Christ, for if God wanted Israel to be married to Him in an eternal spiritual marriage, how much more does He desire all believers in the Messiah and His full and complete salvation, both Jew and Gentile, to be fully married to The Christ, the Son of the Living God?

Return from Exile

It seems inconceivable therefore, with such an incredible display of God's mighty power in the affairs of men that, after the first returnees arrived in Jerusalem with such a positive command and funding from Cyrus to rebuild the temple, that the slightest opposition should have caused them to stop working on it to focus on their own houses. With offerings of gold and silver and priestly garments (Ezra 2:68 – 70), work started on the temple with the rebuilding of the altar and the offering of sacrifices to God (Ezra 3:1 – 4).

Is it not interesting that this should happen in the seventh month during which the festival of the Day of Atonement was celebrated (day 10), which had not been celebrated for seventy years, was significantly the day the whole of Israel was to be conscious of their national sin and the one day of the year that the high priest entered the Holy of Holies to meet with God and implore Him to be merciful to the nation? (See Heb. 7:22 – 28) This was followed by the feast of tabernacles on the fifteenth day which celebrated the provision of shelter by God for the Children of Israel during their wandering in the wilderness following their release from slavery in Egypt[73].

The timing of these particular festivals immediately on their return to their beloved land, and to the city of Jerusalem in particular, was immensely significant, particularly to those sensitive enough to the work of God amongst them. During the noisy celebrations for the laying of the new temple foundations, many of the old men remembered the glorious nature

---

[73] All these ceremonies that God instructed the Israelites to celebrate at specific times during each and every year were reminders of their past and what God had done for them at those times.

of the temple Solomon had built; but those who had not seen it in all its splendour, celebrated this new beginning. Thus, did the weeping of the old, who looked back to what had been, and the shouts of those who were looking to the future mingle together to be heard far off. (Ezra 3:4 – 13)

The commencement of temple services brought a sense of fear upon them, for they were surrounded by those that were hostile to their return, and they were conscious of possible repercussions from them (v3). With continued offering of money, food, drink and oil, the work of the temple and its reconstruction was started.

Inevitably it was not long before the opposition came to offer their services in the rebuilding of the temple, but the governor Zerubbabel and heads of the houses of Judah rightly refused their request, for it was by working too closely with those opposed to the work of God that had got them into the mess in which they found themselves in the first place.

The advice Balaam gave to the king of Moab to offer a welcome to the Israelites when they worshipped their gods caused the Children of Israel to sin, and having come through 70 years of exile and separation from their precious Jerusalem, they were not about to make the same mistake this time. In retaliation for the snub the surrounding people believed they had received with this rejection of their help, they did all they could to disrupt the work of rebuilding the temple.

The Jews needed, in this instance, to renew their national covenant with God with the erection of God's house before entering into a work of witness to the surrounding nations; just as new believers must first allow God to establish His presence within them before they seek to witness to others concerning their new-found faith. However, such was the progress on the building of the temple that their opponents, frightened that it would be completed quickly, sought higher authority to stop them.

Any work of true God-focused believers will be opposed by those people who are in tune with Satan. Satan is not concerned with those believers who are inactive and impotent in God's service, but those who are a danger to him and his cause because they are on fire for God and willing to show their faith in the way they live their lives.

Appealing to the king by letter, and receiving a reply supporting their appeal, the opposition boldly stopped the work on the temple through force of arms (Ezra 4:24). Their willingness to crumble before such opposition and not fight their corner, trusting in the might of their God, was not what God wanted them to do.

If we have a command from God to do something then we need to pursue it whatever the cost. God then spoke to His people through two prophets, Haggai and Zechariah to urge the people to continue to rebuild the temple in the name of the God of Israel (Ezra 5:1, 2,). But what did these two prophets say that inspired these people to continue their efforts in rebuilding what would be a shadow of its former glory, and that caused some to resort to tears? (Ezra 3:12, 13)

Message from God

The message the prophet Haggai received from God was directed to Zerubbabel the governor and Joshua the high priest. It was a challenge to the people concerning their readiness to down tools when faced with opposition, even though they had received a command from Cyrus, as prophesied by Isaiah, to rebuild the temple. Why were they so willing to respond to the command of men rather than that of God?

The people were saying that it was not time to rebuild the house of God. But without any personal focus on God or desire to do His will there was little satisfaction in their lives because, as the people of God and central to His salvation of mankind, they were not fulfilling the purpose of their existence. *Is it time for you to dwell in your panelled houses, whilst leaving this temple to lie in ruins?* God was saying to them. Yet there was little satisfaction in their own lives for, *you have sown much but harvested little, eat but do not have enough ... and even your wages disappear as though your pockets have holes in them* (Hag. 1:1 – 7, also vs. 9 – 11). God told them to get back to work and start putting Him first and rebuild the temple *so that I may have pleasure in it and be glorified* (1:7). Thus were the leaders inspired and the people responded to restart the rebuilding. It is no less true today than it was then.

Individually we are temples of the Holy Spirit. Therefore, is our house/temple in order? Is the focus of our lives on God or on the things of the earth? Are you living for God or are you more concerned about living your daily life amongst the people you meet? Are you trying to please God or are you more concerned with not upsetting those around you who do not know God or who are, like the priests of old who just went through the motions of being priests of God, nominal believers?

These are profound questions that each and every one of us must answer before God. We cannot look down on these Israelites without ensuring we are not making exactly the same mistake. Of one thing you can be sure and that is that God knows the state of your heart before Him and will judge you accordingly!

The message the prophet Zechariah received was altogether different. The challenge God presented to the people through Zechariah was that their fathers had totally ignored the word He had spoken to them through the prophets, and had done evil in His sight, which had resulted in the exile from which they had so recently returned. Although their fathers and the prophets were long dead, the word God spoke was still alive and relevant, as we are now finding out for ourselves (Zech. 1:1 – 6).

Throughout the history of Israel after the time of David, Jerusalem has been central to God's plans. Mount Moriah was the site of the saving of

Isaac's life with the substitute ram; it was where the city of Jerusalem was established, which King David conquered and made the capital of a united Israel. It was where David bought the threshing floor to sacrifice to God in order to stop the plague (2 Sam. 24:21 – 25), and where Solomon established the first permanent temple building which was now in ruins. At the appropriate time it was to be the site of the sacrifice of the true Passover Lamb of God.

It is no wonder that God proclaimed that He was *jealous for Jerusalem and Zion,* which most probably relates to the hill on which the temple stood, *with great zeal* (Zech. 1:14). Even though God had centred His plan of salvation on that city, His chosen people had not understood just how important the purity of the city, and in particular the temple, was to their God. Just as the sanctity of believer's lives, because we are temples of the Holy Spirit, is so important to God.

It is understandable that the surrounding nations, who served Satan rather than God, were always as happy as the one they worshipped when the city was in difficulty. It is why the forces of Satan are so adamantly focused on wresting the city from the hands of the Israelites today, for it is to that city that the victorious Messiah will return, bringing in the judgement on all men.

What Zechariah was able to tell them was that, once again, God was returning in mercy to Jerusalem so that His temple could be rebuilt in it (Zech. 1:16 – 20). For the encouragement of the people at this difficult time, God told them that the opposition would be overcome so that they would be able to complete the rebuilding.

It is interesting that the opposition, wanting to bring the rebuilding to a complete halt to the point where it was totally abandoned, believed that by asking the Chaldean king to look into the archives, he would find enough evidence to bring that about. But they had not reckoned on the fulfilment of Gods' prophetic word. The king found the command of Cyrus and ordered the rebuilding to be authorised to the point where the surrounding nations had to assist with various provisions (Ezra 6).

But there was more to Zechariah's prophecy concerning the rebuilding of the temple. The reason the people were sent into exile was due to the worship of other gods by the senior priests within the temple complex completely corrupting it. This had to include the high priest in some way or, at the very least it had been allowed to take place by him, for images had been set up inside the temple, as we discovered in the previous chapter. Which is why the temple had to be completely destroyed

But it was not only the sins the priests perpetuated in the temple that was of concern to God, but the sin in the hearts of the whole population. In the presence of some of the elders of Israel who were visiting him, God spoke to Ezekiel concerning the idols these men had set up in their hearts and the spiritual temperature of the priest was reflected in that of the population as a whole (Ez. 14:1 – 4). Yet the first commandment clearly required that God should have taken up residence in their hearts, not idols, therefore it can be said that their hearts were far from the God they purported to worship. God wanted to seize the hearts of the people of Israel (v5), calling them to repent and turn away from those idols (v6); but if they did not do so then God Himself would cut them off from the midst of His people (vs. 7 – 8).

It was because of the enormity of their sin, and the standing of those leading the liberalisation of worship in the temple, which had been dedicated to the God of Israel alone, that prompted God to stop speaking to them through His prophets. As the priests and the people had totally ignored what the previous and present prophets were telling them, and at times abusing His prophets, there was little point in God sending others to be ignored and treated in the same way (Matt. 21:33 – 46).

Purity was the key word now that they were back in the land, therefore the purity of both the leaders and the people involved before God was paramount. Zechariah witnessed the purifying and rededication of Joshua the high priest before the angel of God. It is worth spending a few moments considering the name Joshua for it will give us further insight into the importance of names in scripture. There are three men with this name that we will consider:

1.   The first Joshua was trained by Moses after the Exodus from Egypt and went on to be chosen by God to lead the Children of Israel in their conquest of the Promised Land. His original name was Oshea, or Hoshea in many Bibles, of the tribe of Ephraim, which was to become the lead tribe of the ten separated tribes of Israel, but he was renamed Jehoshua, by Moses [Joshua is a shortened form of the name used in much of scripture]. (Num. 13:8, 16) The name Jesus is the Hellenized version of Jehoshua which means "Yahweh is salvation". Jehoshua as an Ephraimite was descended from Joseph who was the only son of Jacob who truly believed in the God of his father Jacob from the start and demonstrated that belief throughout his life. He was the head of the army under Moses

2.   The second Joshua, of the tribe of Levi, was the high priest at the time of the rebuilding of the temple after Israel's release from Exile in Babylon.

3.   The third Joshua, or rather Jehoshua, is of the tribe of Judah and the fulfilment of "Yahweh is salvation" for He is the Messiah to Israel. This last Jehoshua combines the lay and priestly roles of

the first two leaders of Israel.

As Joshua the high priest stood before the Angel of the Lord, with Satan, the accuser of the brethren, at his right hand, the twice repeated rebuke, *The Lord rebuke you, Satan* and *The Lord who has chosen Jerusalem rebuke you*, emphasises Satan's powerlessness before God, for God now wanted Jerusalem to once more become the centre of His attention because of the impending visit to the earth of the Messiah, and no matter what Satan tried to do he would be unsuccessful. This is exactly what happened when the reply from Darius to Governor Tattenai was received which confirmed that authority had been given by the king to the Jews to rebuild the city and the temple.

The return from exile and the instruction to rebuild the shattered temple was the Lord's doing. God had purged His people through exile using Ezekiel to challenge them concerning their relationship with their God. God wanted to put within them a new heart and new spirit so that He and they would be able to communicate again (Ez. 36 esp. vs. 26, 27). Their change of heart was a precondition of their future relationship, for only *then shall you dwell in the land I gave to your fathers; you shall continue to be My people, and I will be your God. I will deliver you from your uncleanness* (Ez. 36:28 – 32). This surely is what Ezekiel's vision of the valley of the dry bones so clearly illustrated (Ez. 37).

In the vision Ezekiel saw a valley filled with the dried bones of the people. The valley was probably in Mesopotamia where the spirit of the proud independence of the people died. God asks Ezekiel the question, *Can these bones live?* (v3) Because there is nothing that God is not able to do (Deut. 32:39) the answer to that question had to be, *you know Lord.* As believers in the Lord Jesus we, through that same faith, believe in the resurrection of the dead even though, to all intents and purposes in this life, it is physically impossible.

Our experience of God, however, because it is spiritual rather than physical, causes us to have confidence in God's ability to raise us up, not in our decayed physical bodies, but in new spiritual bodies that will be able to survive in the spiritual realm with Him in glory (Jn. 5:21; Rom. 4:17; 2 Cor. 1:9; 4:13 – 18; 1 Cor. 15:50 – 53). This does not preclude God's ability to heal us and even extend our life on this earth as He so clearly demonstrated miraculously during His life on earth.

The promise of God is new spiritual life, even though the situation the people found themselves in persuaded them that there was no hope. The animated vision illustrated to the prophet that the desperate situation could be retrieved by God, not only with the bones coming together and being clothed with sinews and flesh so that once more they looked like people, or the bodies being able to stand up and move about, but He had the ability to cause them to become fully alive (v14) both physically and spiritually.

The four winds would bring the people together again as a nation and give them breath which would enable them to live physical independent lives; but true life would come only when God's Spirit came upon them, for it is the Spirit who gives true life, as God had intended (v14, cf. Jn. 6:63). The whole purpose of the creation of man was for him to be in fellowship with God who is Spirit. The life of flesh and the birth of carnal man, came after the rebellion of Eve and Adam; and the carnal mind of Cain and those who followed him was at odds with God, being against the Law of God and all that is spiritual.

Sadly, by the time of the arrival of the Messiah, the Jewish religious leaders were no further forward in understanding the spiritual truths of God, for even when the Son of Man was just twelve human years old the so-called wise men were amazed at His knowledge of the things of God.

The purification of the high priest was the first act of God to purify His people (Zech. 3) but always there was the condition that he had to *walk in My ways and keep My commands* (v6). The promise was the arrival, at some future date, of God's servant the BRANCH about whom Isaiah and Daniel had prophesied. The filthy garments that were stripped away from the high priest represented the heinous sins which had contributed to the imposition of God's judgement that had so disrupted their lives. But those who returned leaving many of their countrymen behind in Babylon, particularly those that had been assimilated into the lives of the other peoples there, were now feeling God's direct influence on their lives after their imposed separation from the Promised Land and the retraining they received which gave them time to consider their relationship with their God.

The prophetic BRANCH is dealt with differently by each of the four Gospel writers. (See Appendix G)

In Matthew, the converted tax collector, the Messiah is presented as Jehovah's KING using two references from the first testament, *Behold Your King is coming to you* (Zech. 9:9) *Behold I will raise unto David a righteous BRANCH, and a King shall reign and prospe.* (Jer. 23:5, 6; 33:15) It is to emphasise this aspect of the Messiah's role before God the Father that the royal genealogy from Abraham through David to the arrival of the Messiah is included at the beginning of the gospel.

Also, by inspiration of God for He wanted His Son acclaimed to be the Messiah, and King, the notice on the cross written by Pilate declared Jesus to be the King of the Jews. Matthew takes a more formal and deeply Jewish prophetic line in his gospel, emphasising the Kingship of the Messiah and all the prophecies concerning His arrival and life. It is Matthew who includes the coming of the wise men and their remarkable, God inspired gifts.

In Mark, believed to be the recorder of the preaching of Peter, the

Messiah is presented as Jehovah's SERVANT, *Behold! My Servant whom I uphold.* (Is. 42:1) *Behold I will bring forth My Servant the BRANCH*[74]. (Zech. 3:8) The subject matter of this gospel presents the Messiah as the ideal servant, entering immediately into His ministry without any introduction concerning His birth and upbringing.

In Luke, the Gentile physician, the Messiah is presented as Jehovah's MAN emphasising the humanity of the Messiah, *Behold the Man whose name is the BRANCH! From His place He shall branch out, and He shall build the temple of the Lord.* (Zech. 6:12 – Joshua and Zerubbabel were both a type of Christ and would build the physical temple but it was the Messiah who alone could build the spiritual temple of God – Eph. 2:21, 22) For this reason the genealogy produced by Luke traces the Messiah's lineage back to Adam the human son of God, identifying the Messiah as the ideal, the perfect man because of the manner of His conception and birth.

In John, the spiritually attuned disciple, the Messiah is presented as JEHOVAH HIMSELF, *Behold Your God* (Is. 40:9 to end). Although all flesh is like grass that withers, the prophet exclaims that *the word of God stands forever* (Is. 40:8). The beautiful feet on the mountains of him who brings good news, who proclaims peace, who brings glad tidings of good things to Zion and in particularly to Jerusalem saying to Zion, *Your God reigns* (Is. 52:7). *In that day the BRANCH (Messiah) of the Lord shall be beautiful and glorious* (Is. 4:2). This is the Word made flesh that dwelt among us. There is no need for genealogy for John starts before the creation of time and leads us directly into the ministry of the Messiah, omitting His entry to the earth in human form to avoid distractions.

These four aspects of the character of the Messiah are essentially separate for they provide us with a rounder and more inclusive picture of the person of the Messiah and His ministry to His own people and ultimately to the whole of mankind.

The angel who had taken the prophet into the spiritual realm to witness the presentation of Joshua to the Angel of the Lord once more showed him new things. This time it was the turn of Zerubbabel who was the governor of Judah and, being a descendent of David, was in the lineage of the Messiah (Matt. 1:13). The prophet saw a golden lamp-stand supporting seven lamps (Ex. 25:31, 32), each of which was supplied through an individual tube from a central reservoir. Beside the reservoir and overhanging it were two olive trees.

Two represents difference but, with two agreeing, a partnership is

---

[74] Isaiah 11:1 explains the Branch more fully: "And there shall come forth a Rod out of the stem of Jesse, and a Branch shall grow out of his roots." The Branch, from a human perspective, descends from the line of Jesse, the father of David. Jeremiah 23:5 and 33:15 both refer to "a Branch of righteousness" of Davidic lineage, and in Revelation 22:16 Jesus himself affirms, "I am the Root and the Offspring of David."

formed. Therefore, in this vision we see the constant supply of oil from the olive trees to reservoir to lamp to maintain the seven[75] lights. By this means God was telling the people through the prophet that God would supply all their need and that the Judean governor, Zerubbabel, need have no fears regarding his weakness for neither might nor power were any match for the Spirit of the living God.

The combined forces of the surrounding nations were no match for Israel's God. Because God was with him, no mountain — opposition — however high — powerful — could thwart Zerubbabel's work to restore the temple, completing it with the shout that it had been achieved only by God's grace and mercy. Indeed, God was guaranteeing that as Zerubbabel's hand had laid the foundation stone, so he would be enabled to finish the task. That was a wonderful and encouraging promise.

But what of the inglorious nature of this building compared to its previous glory, built as it had been from the stored treasure of David with the ability of Solomon? (Hag. 2) In the eyes of those who had known the former structure it was as nothing, causing many to weep (Hag. 2:3). But God calls on the leadership of both Zerubbabel and Joshua, telling them to be strong because the Lord's presence was with them, and that the glory of this latter temple would, in the future, be greater than the former and in it He would give peace (v9). Why? Because the Messiah would personally bring the glory of God into it as the Son of Man so that it would no longer be dependent on the created treasures of the earth and the skills of man to promote it, but on God and His glory.

God then focused His attention on the priests for, like the sons of Eli, they were directly responsible for ensuring the worship services in the temple were God-focused and God-exalting; something from which they had previously so clearly deviated, bringing upon themselves and the people the judgement of God (Mal. 2:7, 8). Now back in the land of Judah, the priests had to be rededicated, as we shall see when we consider the work of Ezra.

Here Haggai had a word from the Lord for the priests (Hag. 2:10 – 19) which challenged them regarding their previous activities when through their corrupt behaviour nothing was as it seemed, for twenty ephaphs were properly ten and fifty measures of wine turned out to be only twenty. The need now was for them to consider their behaviour before Him, for from the day the foundation stone of the temple was laid, He wanted to bless them because of the progress they had made in responding to His call to rebuild the temple.

However, there was to be no immediate harvest (Hag. 2:19) to which they could look forward. Although the harvest would come, they would

---

[75] Seven represents spiritual perfection.

have to wait for it. But this also meant that, during that time of waiting, they had the responsibility of being faithful to their calling.

The final proclamation by God through His prophet Haggai was directed to Zerubbabel, the Jerusalem Governor. Declaring His power over the nations and their armies, God told Zerubbabel that he was to become His signet ring, for the governor was chosen and would succeed in all that he did; which we know to have been the case.

The signet ring was used by a king or nobleman to put an impression in the security wax seal of a document which signalled ownership and authority. It was handed to a trusted official of the court as a sign of delegated authority. Ultimately, out of the loins of Zerubbabel would come the boy child, Jesus, who would save both His own people and the whole of mankind from their sins.

During this time Ezra arrived in Jerusalem with a letter and authority from Artaxerxes to offer sacrifices to the God of Israel and to set up a legal system for judging the people (Ezra 7). But Ezra was immediately faced with a problem for the priests and people who had remained behind in the land, and some who had returned from exile, had intermarried with those of the surrounding nations (9:1), in direct contravention of the Law of God (Lev. 18:1 – 5; Deut. 7:1 – 6; 2 Cor. 6:14). The putting away of these pagan wives and their offspring (Ezra 10) illustrated yet again how the sins of Israel were to cause them problems in the future because of the hatred generated in the hearts of the rejected and discarded wives and children, who had no hope of salvation, just as happened with the rejection of Ishmael.

Nehemiah wept when he heard the news of the devastation of Jerusalem (Neh. 1), and at great danger to himself appeared before the king in a depressed state. Because God's hand was upon him Nehemiah not only avoided immediate execution but was given permission by the king to return to the city and rebuild the walls.

Once again, he and those who returned with him experienced opposition (ch. 4) from the surrounding nations, to the extent that they had to build with weapons beside them in case of attack. Remarkably there was injustice among the Jews themselves, even though they were in a parlous state of insecurity (ch. 5 esp. vs. 3 – 5). There was also a plot by their enemies to kill Nehemiah (ch. 6).

Nehemiah not only built the walls of the city and hung its great doors, but purified the inhabitants to ensure only true-born Israelites were registered (ch. 7).

The book of the Law of Moses was read out publicly by Ezra the scribe, standing on a specially erected platform (ch. 8), with others explaining the text to the people as he spoke so that they could understand it (v7). Then, separating themselves from the foreigners, they made a public confession of their sins (ch. 9) and reestablished a covenant with God (9:38; 10 esp. v29).

Thus did the people re-establish Jerusalem, the city of God, and the temple of God, purifying themselves and getting right with God, establishing the temple services and sacrifices and the annual festivals, cleansed of past sins and refocused in mind and heart on the God who had enabled them to get back to their homeland. But after all this intervention by God through several prophets, and a great homecoming, there was to be 400 years' silence before the last of the first testament prophets proclaimed the coming of the Messiah.

11 THE SERVANT MESSIAH

'Who has believed our report?
And to whom has the arm of the Lord been revealed?
For he shall grow up before Him as a tender plant,
And as a root out of dry ground.
He has no form or comeliness;
And when we see Him,
There is no beauty that we should desire Him.
He is despised and rejected by men,
A man of sorrows and acquainted with grief.
But He was wounded for our transgressions,
Bruised for our iniquities;
The chastisement for our peace
Was upon Him
And by His stripes we are healed."
(Is. 53:1 – 3, 5)

Exile brings self-examination

We have now reached the point where what we have been studying is fulfilled. The layout of the Tent of the Meeting complex built by Moses had the single purpose of illustrating God's remarkable plan of salvation. Throughout our studies we have been seeking to understand how this could be. We are now at the point where that plan is realised and acted out.

Previously it was only the high priest who could start at the altar of sacrifice and end, once a year, in the holiest place. But all previous high priests had to offer sacrifices for their own sins along with the sins of those they represented before God. Now we will see illustrated before us the only high priest who has the authority and position to go all the way without having to offer sacrifices for Himself. Instead, he had to offer the sacrifice of Himself for the sins of those who would believe in Him as the all-sufficient sacrifice.

Throughout His life the Messiah had to fully abide by the Ten Commandments and the statutes God had given to His people. From the start Mary and Joseph observed the sacrifices required by scripture after the birth of the first born when they presented Him to God at the temple, and for the 'cleansing' of Mary. The Messiah even went so far as to be baptised by His messenger John, even though He was no sinner.

Just as in the tent and temple complex, all had to be done in order and with decorum, according to the rules God had laid down, so now with the arrival of the Son of God to the earth's stage, where every move would be witnessed, recorded and analysed, which is, after all, what we are doing in this book, to illicit vital information that will be food for our souls.

Prophecy Being Fulfilled

The Tent of the Meeting and its surrounding compound, or Tabernacle as we shall refer to it, provides us with the complete illustration of God's plan of salvation. With the building of the permanent temple structure, which included within its boundaries the screened compound called the outer court, the worship services became more sophisticated within the elaborate structure. The importance of keeping in our minds the structure built by Moses is because, through of its simplicity, it gives us a better visual aid of God's plan of salvation.

Throughout the first testament, the activities of the priests and the people, first in the Tent of the Meeting and its surrounding compound and then in the temple first built by Solomon, were a practice-run for the real thing. The reason for this is that the sacrificing of animals had to be continually offered because they did not atone completely for the sin of the one offering the sacrifice. High priests and their assistant priests came and went according to the pattern of all flesh. The people were not perfect and therefore the law required them to offer sacrifices for their own sinfulness.

Now that we have reached in our study the boundary separating the first and second testaments, we must understand that we are entering not the tabernacle of Moses or the temple of Solomon, but God's tabernacle on earth. The reason for this will hopefully be made obvious as we proceed in our study of the life of the Messiah of Israel, the Jehoshua, "Yahweh is salvation", who was to come, promised by God through His prophets throughout the preceding centuries.

We need to remember throughout this next part of our study two principle facts: Prophecy and Lineage. God not only told His people what would happen, but also when it would happen, and He chose the people through whom it would happen. This will hopefully become more apparent as we proceed. As far as lineage is concerned there are two genealogical lists for the Messiah in the second testament. In Matthew 1:1 – 17 the genealogical list starts with Abraham and ends with the Messiah, but the list in Luke 3:21 – 38 starts with the Messiah and goes back to Adam who is referred to as the son of God[76]. The first Adam was the created son of God, whereas the second Adam was the true born Son of God, and intrinsic part

---

[76] Adam was the human creation of God and therefore God can be referred to as his Father, and conversely Adam as His son.

of God, who became Son of Man.

The ending of the centuries of God's silence was announced by a priest in the Temple. Zacharias was a priest in the temple division of Abijah (1 Chron. 24:3, 10) who, with his wife Elizabeth, were righteous — blameless — before God. But Elizabeth was barren and the couple were well advanced in years. One day Zacharias was chosen by lot, which was controlled by God, to burn incense on the altar of incense, trim the lamps and offer the shewbread in the Holy Place within the temple in what had been the Tent of the Meeting. Being blameless before God, Zacharias was a true, faithful believer and in a fit state to meet with God, or at least with an angel sent by God. In the confined space with the six branched, seven light candelabra, the table of showbread and the altar of incense there suddenly appeared an angel standing on the righthand side of the altar.

Zacharias will have been a priest from the age of 30 and during all that time nothing of note had happened. His life had been ruled by the routine of the temple services. Now that He was old and without any children, he and his wife did not have a great deal to look forward to in anticipation, such as the progress of their children and the arrival of grandchildren. Indeed, their lives as a childless couple had been wrapped up in routine and disappointment of what might have been. The arrival of the angel would have been quite a shock to this elderly priest. (Lk. 1)

After all those years of praying for a son, they would have finally surrendered to their misfortune, accepting that it must be the will of God for them. Indeed, by those who knew them Elizabeth was called the 'barren one'. At their age couples did not produce children. It must have been an incredible shock, therefore, to the elderly priest when an angel of God suddenly appeared within the confined space of the holy place as Zacharias was about his temple duty. Even more remarkable was the angel's announcement that Zacharias and his wife would have a son after all. *Do not be afraid, Zacharias, for your prayers have been heard; and your wife Elizabeth will bear you a son and you shall call him John* (Lk. 1:13, 14.

It is interesting that Zacharias' duty on that occasion should have been the burning of incense, the smoke from which represented the prayers of believers.

He was told that the characteristics of the child's stature and life were to be that:

1. He would be great in the eyes of the Lord.

2. He would drink neither wine nor strong drink.

3. He would be filled with the Holy Spirit even in his mother's womb.

4. He would turn many Israelites back to the Lord their God.

5.   He would be God's forerunner, going before Him in the spirit and power of Elijah who, through his willingness to stand up and be counted even though his was a lone voice, became the voice of God amongst an unbelieving and rebellious people, like a beacon in a dark land.

In the power of the Holy Spirit John was to be the voice of one crying in the wilderness, as prophesied by Isaiah. He would remind an oppressed and godless people that the God who had chosen them as a nation was still the true Almighty and all-powerful God who was calling them to Himself. Through his ministry this, the last of the first testament prophets (for he was under the law not under grace) was to turn the hearts of the people, fathers and children, to prepare them for the coming Lord.

6.   His name was to be John, which was a complete break with tradition in the family.

As a priest Zacharias would have known the scriptures which were full of God sending messengers to various individuals in various forms and through various agencies with promises of what was to come. Yet in the holy place, going about his God given duties, when an angel appeared in close proximity to him, Zacharias was so astonished by what he was seeing and hearing that he almost impulsively asked the question, *How shall I know this? For I am an old man and my wife is well advanced in years.* So where was his faith in God, given that the angel had given him such a detailed and specific message that should have warmed his heart, for at last, God was answering their prayers regarding an offspring? It is a problem for all of us who believe.

It is easy to believe in God if we have to do nothing apart from follow a routine, particularly if our life is lived within a protected and protective comfort zone. Such an existence, at least outwardly, indicates that we are a believer, but it does not challenge our faith by asking us to do anything that is outside our experience or understanding of the Judeo/Christian faith. We will be fine, provided we are not directly involved with God in a specific and singular service that makes us unique, causing us to stand out from the crowd, for it is only in such situations that our faith is really tested.

I have been blessed with an amazing ministry. Alone with my computer, with various translations of the Bible and a few reference books readily to hand, I type away and text appears before my eyes on the screen. It is true that my hands are tapping the keys, but what I have been privileged to experience is the undeniable influence of the Holy Spirit and prophetic promises that are gradually coming to pass which were given to me at various times in my life.

The inspiration I have received to understand a certain incident or statement in scripture, and the specific guidance to look up a certain reference or read a certain book, has been humbling. It is like being in a lone tutorial with God, for I have learned so much about scripture that I had not known before. I am forthright, I cannot deny it. Some find my attitude a little too positive, and yet were not the prophets of old, when speaking up for God as He directed them, also forthright? Consider Elijah, of whom we have learned much in these last two chapters; had he not been positive in his ministry he would have been totally ineffective and would not be remembered even to this day.

True, believers have not only to believe in the Lord Jesus, but also to have a desire within them to confess His name with total confidence, which to me means to be forthright — straight forward, plain spoken, but we do need a humbleness of approach to ensure that those to whom we witness realise that we also are sinners who have benefitted from experiencing the work of the Saviour of whom we speak. If we, as professing believers in the Lord Jesus and God the Father, speak in such a way that suggests there is some doubt in our minds, then what does that do to our witness to unbelievers? Surely our witness then becomes ineffectual.

I have found that it is no use being dogmatic. Rather, it is best to seek to persuasively put over what I want people to know and particularly that *'I know whom I have believed and am persuaded that He is able to keep that which I have committed to Him against the day of Judgement'* (2 Tim. 1:12). There is no doubt in my mind or heart concerning this eternal truth. My experiences of the presence and guidance of God during my writing have been far too strong and His influence on my life far too specific for me to doubt His hand upon my life. I have kept the faith, and I trust only to include in my writing that which is strictly according to God's word.

So if some passages sound a bit presumptuous I make no apology, for God is too strong upon me and my prayer far too persistent and insistent that I might be prevented from writing anything that is not true. In these days when the coming of our Lord Jesus draws ever closer — the signs of the times emphasise this fact — and the 'established churches' are clearly erring towards apostasy, where the word of God is modified to accommodate people's desires rather than true belief, God is looking for those who, with a true and certain belief, are willing to boldly stand up and be counted as so many ordinary saints have done in the past.

However, we must always be mindful of what the Lord said as recorded in Luke 17:10, *So likewise ye, when ye shall have done all those things which are commanded you, say, We are unprofitable servants: we have done that which was our duty to do.* It ensures that those of us, whose work is seen by so many people, keep our feet well and truly on the ground, acknowledging that, as sinners, we also need not only the salvation our Lord is offering to all mankind, but to also totally commit our lives to Him so that He can use us in His service.

Announcing himself as Gabriel who stands in the presence of God, the angel told Zacharias the priest that because of his unbelief, and as a sign that these things would come to pass, he would be mute until the arrival of his son. Such a condition had a dramatic effect on those waiting outside the temple; believers who would have been praying to God, thus emphasising the importance of the sweet aroma of the burning incense rising up to God from the small golden altar of incense in the holy place.

Routine dictated that the task Zacharias was performing should only take a certain time and the people were expecting him to reappear within that time frame; but there seemed to be some delay and therefore their expectancy turned into curiosity. When Zacharias finally appeared and indicated that he could not speak, they immediately presumed he had experienced a vision, which would have been something for them to talk about, thus initiating rumours that would have swiftly permeated the tight-knit priestly community and those known to them.

It was not until his son had been born, and at the time of his circumcision when the child was named that there arose some speculation about the future of this child. The assembled company of family and friends had naturally assumed that the child would be given his father's name according to tradition. So, when Elizabeth said that his name was to be John, Zacharias had to confirm his wife's statement in writing and it was only then that his tongue was loosened and he was able to speak to them again.

This caused consternation because those present must have experienced some apprehension concerning the future of this child. Filled with the Holy Spirit, Zacharias the priest proclaimed the fact that according to prophecy God was taking action to visit His people Israel and perform acts within the nation that would transform it. He declared (Lk. 1:68 − 79) that his son would be called the prophet of the Highest for his son was commissioned to:

1. go before the face of the Lord to prepare His way.

2. give knowledge of salvation to God's people, concerning the remission of sins.

3. introduce the tender mercy of God, in spite of their waywardness, through the visit of the Messiah. The Dayspring refers to the springing up of the Branch (Is. 11:1 − 5; Jer. 23:5; Zech. 3:8) but it also means light, for the Messiah was the light of God amongst His people.

Six months after Gabriel's meeting with the old priest Zacharias, the archangel met with Mary who lived in Nazareth. The reaction of this young girl to the sudden appearance of the angel was altogether different. Mary was troubled by it. It was a somewhat flamboyant greeting the angel gave *Mary Rejoice highly favoured one, the Lord is with you; blessed are you among women.* (Lk. 1:28) For a young girl more used to being about the house and household chores, it could be considered rather embarrassing. But more was to follow, for the angel told her that she would be made pregnant by the Holy Spirit and would bear a son whom she would name Jesus. Being pregnant out of wedlock was a matter of considerable disgrace and a punishable offense (Jn. 8:4, 5). It was, therefore, not unreasonable for her to question the angel, *How can this be, seeing I do not know a man?*

For Mary it was the practicalities of how she could become pregnant without being with a man that she did not understand. The angel then told her that her pregnancy would be caused by the Holy Spirit and that the child born to her was to be the Son of God. Remarkable! Being devout, Mary gave herself unreservedly to God saying, *Behold the maidservant of the Lord! Let it be to me according to your word.* (Lk. 1:38)

It was a considerable honour for this young woman to have the Son of God, albeit briefly, live within her body as the body of the male child developed within her womb. But Mary was still a human being born in sin who needed what the Son had to offer, as much as anyone else. For her to bear this child was undoubtedly a considerable honour, but that is no reason for worshipping her alongside, or even at times in place of, the Saviour. (See Appendix A for a full understanding of the Virgin Birth.)

Notice how God so easily fooled the religious elite by choosing a couple, already engaged to be married, but who had not co-habited, living in Nazareth but both of the house and lineage of David into whose home the Messiah would be born. Both were true believers and living according to God's word at that time. There would be no public and overt rejoicing at the birth of the One who was to come, or a royal welcome with the priests taking centre stage. God chose the humble, him being a humble carpenter, and insignificant to provide the means of welcoming of His Son to the earth.

It took a pagan ruler to ensure that Mary gave birth in Bethlehem, the City of David. Only God could have ensured the timing. The parables the Messiah used to pass on the message of love from His Father started with the parable of His birth in Bethlehem and early years in Nazareth. These events were not according to the will of the leaders of the people but according to God's will and purpose. Out of the ordinary God's power is revealed, just as it had been throughout the history of His people and continues to this day.

Engagement (betrothal) for Jews was legally binding and was

automatically followed by full marriage when the couple came together to become one flesh. When Joseph heard that Mary was pregnant, being a righteous-man he naturally did not want to complete the process of marriage until, that is, an angel of the Lord appeared to him in a dream to tell him that his future wife's pregnancy was of God. It was then essential that Joseph had no sex with Mary until the child was born. Thus the prophecy would be fulfilled, *Behold the virgin shall be with child, and bear a Son, and they shall call His name Emmanuel,' which is translated, 'God with us'* (Matt. 1:23).

The characteristics of the child's stature and life were:

1.   He was to be called Jesus — Jehoshua in Hebrew, but Yeshua is used.

2.   He was to be called the Son of the Most High, for that is what He was, the Son of God.

3.   The Lord would give Him the throne of His human father David, which was the throne of the united Israel, all twelve tribes including the tribes of the two sons of Joseph, Ephraim and Manasseh. David was His earthly fore-father because Mary was descended from him, as in fact was Joseph. Mary was not nor could she be the mother of God, only the mother of His human body.

     Because within the body of the child she bore was the Spirit that was the Son of God, who existed from before the foundation of the earth. All Mary did was to provide that Spirit with a human body so that He could become Son of Man, and in doing so she was blessed above all women, because she needed to be pure of heart along with Joseph who was also honoured in being required to parent the child as He grew up into adulthood.

     The perfect, holy, Son of God actually dwelt within her body during the development of the feotis, which is why Mary was blessed above all women. A considerable honour.

4.   He would reign[77] over the house of Jacob[78]. Jacob ruled the tribe founded by Abraham and sustained by Isaac, the first two believers in the eternal creator God who called Abraham out of the rebellious world of paganism.

---

[77] God was the ruler of Abraham, Isaac and Jacob because they all owed allegiance to Him as their God. It was when Israel demanded a king to rule over them that they lost that connection with God being their King. Here we see that Jesus reintroduced the Kingship of God over His people.
[78] The name Jacob refers to the whole of Israel and by referring to the house of Jacob all those ruled by Jacob were included, even the servants and slaves. Jacob's name was changed to Israel.

The tribe included family, servants and slaves, and after their meeting with God as a nation at Mount Sinai the tribe was not to be so exclusive that they rejected the stranger; thus this description of Him being ruler over the house of Jacob is a more inclusive description of the Messiah's role for anyone who seeks Him will be welcomed.

5. There would be no end to His reign and kingdom because it was not to be an earthly kingdom over which He was to rule. He was far superior to all men born of women[79], for at His human birth He was still a full member of the Triune God and has remained so.

The law, which once governed the behaviour of the citizens of Israel, precluded Gentiles from being part of Israel unless they became proselytes and were circumcised. When the Messiah died on the cross, although He did not abolish the law received by the children of Israel at Sinai, He did introduce the new covenant of grace through His blood, overseen by the Holy Spirit. The law of the Spirit, under which all those who are spiritually 'born-again' are now obliged to live, is far more searching than the Ten Commandments.

The previous law was weak in that it required individuals not to sin without providing them with the necessary support to avoid those sins which so easily entrapped them. By condemning sin in the flesh when He died and then rising again (the first man ever to do so), the Messiah made available essential support, not only by His example of sinless living but by demonstrating the essential part the Holy Spirit has to play in the lives of all born-again believers.

The Messiah did not live His life alone, even though He was ultimately responsible for His actions in the most testing of circumstances. In His human form He was filled[80] with the Holy Spirit without measure and maintained contact with the Father through the support of the fullness of the Holy Spirit. It was also the Holy Spirit who gave Him information regarding what was going on in the hearts and minds of those He met so that He was able not just to speak to their needs but also to challenge those who opposed Him[81].

---

[79] See Hebrews chapter 1

[80] In saying that He was filled with the Holy Spirit, it was not an initial filling, for being part of the Godhead He was at one with the Holy Spirit and the Father, and had been ever since His birth as an eternal member of the trinity.

[81] See Romans 8

The Messiah condemned sin in the flesh for those prepared to accept His sacrifice on the cross, firstly by immediately declaring the forgiveness of their past sins so that they would be considered sinless before God. They would be saved from the condemnation of sin. Secondly, those who were thus 'saved' would also be able to receive the gift of the Holy Spirit, the comforter, who would enter the lives of those who accept the Messiah as their Lord and Saviour. It is up to the individual to say to God how far they are willing to give themselves up to Him, but the degree of surrender is equal to the assistance the Holy Spirit is able to give them.

There is no doubt that the Holy Spirit has a significant part to play in our lives, often without our being aware of it, except, that is, when we use the gift of hindsight in being able to look back over our lives to see the pattern of His influence there. In a sense we dictate to the Holy Spirit how much we allow Him to work directly in our lives both through our free will that we retain, even when we ask God into our lives, and through our understanding of the scriptures or in our service to God.

One woman who did not respond to the Spirit calling her to go to the mission field was burdened with guilt until she was in her 80's when she realised, during a service at her church, that God had long ago forgiven her. If we want to lead an ordinary life, then that is up to us. However, if like Paul and many others throughout the centuries we are willing to say as Isaiah did, *Here am I; send me* and do what you want with me', then God will do just that. The degree of our commitment to God and His work and the degree of intimacy of our working relationship with Him is entirely up to us. It is our free will that dictates to the Holy Spirit just how much control of our life we want to give over to Him.

At least nine months before Gabriel's meeting with Zacharias some astrologers[82] living far to the east of Israel witnessed a remarkable star in the heavens. Its appearance was discussed by three wise men, astrologers, as they studied it. They came to the conclusion that this star was announcing a great event which was most likely to be the birth of a very important king. They prepared themselves for a long journey (approximately 2 years) and set off to follow the star.

---

[82] Consider the time scale. These men needed to be in Bethlehem soon after the Messiah was born. Mary met the angel Gabriel six months after he had appeared to Zacharias. Jesus would have been born nine months later. This equals fifteen months. If the star appeared two years before the birth (Matt. 2:7, 16) then they must have seen it at least nine months before the angel met with Zacharias and decided to set off sometime after that.

What remarkable heavenly event, the result of God's handiwork, caused this star to appear, or indeed what sort of star it was, we cannot be sure, but the fact that it caused the reaction it did in the lives of these three men is now a matter of historical and spiritual significance.

Let us consider the events and people surrounding these three wise men[83] and their visit to the land of Israel:

❖ the magi were not kings but astrologers/wise men, possibly of another religious persuasion, who recognised the sudden appearance of a unique star in the heavens as a sign that a momentous king was to be born. From the text, it suggests that from the time they had collectively decided on the meaning of the star, it took them approximately two years to get ready and then travel from their home to Jerusalem. As they were following the course of the star they would not have known their destination. Such a journey at that time would not have been entered upon lightly, so they will have been sure in their own minds that what they saw was significant enough for them to go and see what was due to come to pass.

❖ Through 'subjective' thought, rather than just following the star until it stopped, they naturally went to see the king of the country in which they were travelling to tell him of their travel plans. This accounts for their meeting Herod in his palace in Jerusalem. As the reigning king, Herod wanted to find out more details of this king who would have been born by now, according to their calculations.

It might have been a matter of etiquette at that time for such prominent individuals to go to the ruler to announce their arrival in his city. It might also have been that they assumed this new King would be born in the palace.

Had they followed the star without following their normal customs, many male children would have been saved from an untimely death.

❖ Consider Herod. One night he received three wealthy, foreign visitors asking where a king had been born. Explaining the circumstances of their enquiry, Herod would have changed from being curious to being very concerned, encouraging him to glean from them the exact time of the star's appearance so that he could calculate the age of the child and take action to quietly dispose of any opposition should their quest be true.

---

[83] Just like their gifts, even the number of the magi (3) is significant.

Men of such obvious wealth and stature did not set out on a long journey of this type unless they were sure of their objective. Undoubtedly such a display of heavenly activity witnessed by the three men meant that something of very great importance had occurred. Herod would have been totally unaware that God had allowed for the travelling time of the men so that the child was likely to have only recently been born by the time they arrived in Bethlehem to see Him.

Herod's natural instinct was to seek advice from the religious leaders and those who studied the scriptures to find out where the promised Messiah was to be born, for it is thought that His possible imminent arrival had been talked about by the scholars for a year or so. As soon as he heard that the Messiah, promised by God, was to be born in Bethlehem, he happily sent the wise men on their way, asking them to let him know the exact place where the child was living so that he too could go and worship Him, although he had alternative plans for the child's future.

This not only demonstrates the depth of Herod's unbelief in the existence and power of the God of Israel, but indicates that he was being used by Satan to rid himself of a threat, not realising that God would protect His own self.

The fact that a King was to be born who was to be of such stature that a sign appeared in the heavens to announce His birth anything up to two years before His arrival was, from Herod's point of view, a severe threat to his position. Even though this new born King was promised by God, Herod, focused as he was on the practical human implications of this event to his future position and power, set a course to annihilate the opposition. In this we are reminded of Pharaoh's unwillingness to recognise God's call to release His people from slavery and Saul's attitude to David after David had been anointed to replace him.

But this King was to inherit a kingdom that was a spiritual kingdom, with no claim on any territory and no threat to Herod's position. After all, the people were to learn from this King that the earth had a limited life-span and therefore territorial gain would be of no value to an eternal kingdom.

Tragically, when Herod realised that the foreigners had left the country without informing him of the child's exact whereabouts, he sent in the troops to kill all male children in Bethlehem of two years and under, for he could take no chances as to when and to whom the child had been born.

This was an event unconsciously prophesied by Jeremiah

when he spoke of a current event during his lifetime where he saw Rachel — the wife of Jacob who died on the way to Bethlehem - then called Ephrath – giving birth to Benjamin - Gen. 35:16 – 20 — weeping from her grave just outside the city for her sons Joseph and Benjamin then in exile in Babylon (Jer. 31:15). This further tragic prophetic fulfilment (Matt. 2:16 – 18) demonstrates just how Satan uses godless men to do his dirty work, which again was unsuccessful, for the Messiah had already been taken to Egypt with Mary by Joseph, out of harm's way, having been warned by God of the danger to the child's life.

❖ Consider the religious leaders and those who studied the scriptures. When called to the presence of Herod that night, they were to learn about the possible arrival of the long-expected Messiah. Yet we do not hear about them again! No excitement at the possibility of the arrival of their Messiah, no enquiries on their own behalf to find out for certain if what the wise men had told Herod was true, no desire to go with the three visitors to see for themselves what had happened. Nothing!

True, the wise men were strangers and despised Gentiles, but mention of the coming of the King of kings so long prophesied, surely that should have sparked an enquiry? However, just as Herod planned to deny life to the new born King of kings, so they totally ignored Him.

The three wise men left Herod to continue to follow the star until it led them to the place where the holy child lay, and there, we are told, they rejoiced with exceeding joy. Three non-Jews who responded to a sign in the skies announcing the Saviour's birth, travelled a very long distance to offer Him costly gifts of:

❖ Gold — representing deity — the Ark was covered in gold and the Mercy Seat was of pure solid gold, as was the light-giving candelabra in the holy place.

❖ Frankincense — an ingredient of the holy incense to be used only in the tabernacle (Ex. 30:34), on the meal offering of first fruits (Lev. 2:15, 16) and on the showbread (Lev. 24:7).

❖ Myrrh — used in the holy anointing oil (Ex. 30:23) and as part of the preparation for the burial of the bodies of royal and distinguished people (Jn. 19:39).

The gold and both the frankincense and myrrh, which were very expensive resins, could only be afforded by the very rich. This says something about the three wise men. Moreover, that these foreign men should choose gifts that speak of the holiness of the One who had arrived from God, as illustrated by the Tent of the Meeting, tells us much about this moment. Their journey completed, and being warned by God in a dream to leave the country without informing Herod of the child's whereabouts, they set off home by a different route; but this divine intervention would have further confirmed their original conclusion, that this birth was something extra-ordinary.

In chapter 6 of this book, we considered the tent and its furniture from God's perspective, where we noted that God starts by giving Moses instruction regarding the most sacred of all the items which was placed on its own in the Holy of Holies. This is the point where heaven meets with man, for the Ark of the Covenant contained the fundamental principles of living a holy life, the contract between God and man, covered by the Mercy Seat by which God dispensed mercy to the sinner (Ex. 25:10). God ends with the altar of burnt offering, the courtyard and finally the gate through which a man has first to enter to begin his journey of salvation (Ex. 27:9).

The life of the Messiah reflected that approach, for on His arrival as the babe in a manger the Messiah was worshipped as God, for the Spirit within the child was the Son of God, begotten of God and now miraculously clothed in human flesh. He was the fulfilment of the Ark of the Covenant for the words on the tablets of stone were from God and the Messiah came as the word made flesh. Indeed, God had produced the first set of tablets with their inscription without human interference. But, through the sin of His people in worshipping the golden calf made by Aaron, those tablets were broken by Moses. The next set of tablets was carved from the rock by Moses, with God making the inscription.

But now, God had Himself come, through Mary, to announce a new and better covenant (Lk. 22:20; Heb. 8:6, 8, 10, 13). He was also the mercy seat for He came to provide the way of salvation (Heb. 9:14, 15; consider v28). The wise men gave holy gifts to a holy God because the Holy Spirit had directed them so to do.

Although God has the power to accomplish all that He purposes to do alone, and does from time to time, He has willingly restricted Himself to using individuals and groups to do His will; which is why it is so important for those who truly believe to make a definite commitment to serve God as Isaiah and the other prophets of old did. God wants men and women to witness for Him and, in conjunction with the work of the Holy Spirit within them, lead individuals to salvation.

God wants to empower individuals to persuade others of the reality of God and for believers to build each other up in their walk with God. How many readers have been brought into a relationship with God, or even a renewed and more intimate and more dynamic and truthful relationship with Him, through the work of others? Although God could do it all Himself, and at times must step in when He meets reluctance on the part of believers to do His will, like the prophet Jonah, we must not allow ourselves to believe that that is His preferred way of working. Why then does He desire the closest and most intimate relationship with those who love Him, like the relationship He had with the disciple John 'whom He loved'?

Physical and Spiritual Life United in One Body

The promise to Zacharias was that his son John, born of human parents with a holy task (Jer. 1:5), was to be filled with the Holy Spirit's assistance even when he was in his mother's womb. Consider then the arrival of Mary, only recently made pregnant by the power of the Holy Spirit, on a visit to her cousin Elizabeth. Mary herself was of the royal line of David and had been told by the angel that her relative Elizabeth, who was called the barren one, was then six months pregnant. As soon as the voice of Mary was heard by Elizabeth, the child developing in her womb leapt for joy.

Filled with the Holy Spirit at that moment, Elizabeth proclaimed the blessedness of Mary as the mother of her Lord, confirming to Mary that all that she had been told by the angel Gabriel would be fulfilled. It is interesting that the women selected to bear the children for this remarkable drama were related. The old priestly couple gave birth naturally to the fore-runner, or messenger, of the Messiah; a man who would normally have become a priest. John was to announce the ending of the Aaronic priesthood. Whereas Mary gave birth to a boy child without her fiancé's involvement.

Mary, inspired by the immediate events, burst into the song of praise that is known as the Magnificat because of the introductory words, *My soul magnifies the Lord* (Lk. 1:46 – 55). What is significant in this celebration of what God was doing within their family is that God did not employ the proud, the rich, the mighty, nor kings or the leaders of men. Rather God regarded the lowly estate of His maidservant and His mercy is on those who fear Him, filling the spiritually hungry with good things. He had helped His servant Israel in remembrance of His mercy. Mary left to go to her home with Joseph in Nazareth just before the birth of John.

In preparation for the birth, Mary had to travel to Bethlehem, the acknowledged city of David and the place God had planned for His Son to arrive on earth (Matt. 2:6). God caused this to happen by command of the Roman Emperor Caesar Augustus. The command involved the world under Roman rule being registered, which meant that Joseph, with his now heavily pregnant wife Mary, had to travel from Nazareth (consider Jn. 1:46) to Bethlehem. It was a journey of some fifteen kilometers as the crow flies.

The Servant Messiah

Because of the difficult terrain Joseph would have had to walk, leading the donkey on which his wife sat. When the couple arrived in the town there was nowhere to stay except with cattle, possibly in a cave.

The birth of the Messiah was a very low-key private affair. No noisy celebration by family members, or enquiries from friends and relatives because they had been separated from them through circumstances. Just as the Ark of the Covenant was separated in the holy of holies so the Messiah arrived in silence and was unseen by people except those God chose to look after Him in the early years of His physical development, and those He chose to worship His Son's arrival on earth.

It would have come as a complete surprise to both Mary and Joseph when the three wise men suddenly arrived one night after the birth of the Saviour, who was still bound in swaddling clothes, particularly when the couple saw the richness of their attire and the gifts that they bore, gold, frankincense and myrrh, which were so symbolic, speaking as they did of the splendour of the Tent of the Meeting and the worship of God and the characteristics of the future life of the child.

Then the shepherds arrived, again at night, speaking of the visit of an angel of the Lord to them whilst they were in the fields tending their flock. Even though it was well into the night, the glory of God shone around the whole area, making it like day. The angel told them of the arrival of the Messiah and explained how they could find Him. Then, no doubt excitedly, they spoke of the angelic host in the sky praising God. The shepherds were symbolic of the sacrificial lambs which they were responsible for providing. After all, the child they had come to worship was the Lamb of God who would die on behalf of His people. Although the shepherds made their discovery widely known, the news did not seem to cause much of a stir, leaving Mary and Joseph in peace with their new child.

The timetable for all these events is difficult to work out. Certainly, after eight days the parents were required to have him circumcised, at which time He was named Jehoshua, Jesus to us. Then when the days of her purification according to the Law of Moses were completed (a further thirty-three days) they took the child to Jerusalem to present Him to God, as it is written, *Every male child who opens the womb shall be called holy to the Lord.* This is because it was the firstborn who were saved by the blood the angel of death saw on the outside of the house around the door at the time of the Passover in Egypt (Ex. 13:12; 22:29; Num. 3:13; 8:17).

Because they were too poor to offer a lamb, a pair of turtledoves or two young pigeons had to suffice as a sacrifice for Mary's purification (Lev. 12:6 – 8). At the same time they offered the Messiah to His Father and it was at that time two people, who had focused their attention and worship on God, saw Him.

First was Simeon, described as being just and devout who was waiting for the consolation of Israel. It was revealed to him by the Holy Spirit who was upon him (Lk. 2:25, 26) that he would not see death until he had seen the Messiah. What a promise and certain hope! The Spirit led him into the temple at the time Mary and Joseph were about their business there, and seeing the child he took Him into his arms for he knew, in that moment, that here was the precious Messiah of Israel. At last, he could leave this life knowing that the salvation, prepared in the face of all peoples, the light that would bring revelation to the Gentiles and the glory to God's people Israel had arrived and was resting in his arms. These revelations were being added to the memories Joseph and Mary had accumulated since the angel Gabriel's meeting with Mary and God's message to Joseph all those months ago.

Anna, a prophetess, of the tribe of Asher, who had only been married seven years before being widowed, was then about 85 years old. Therefore, for about 60 years she had dedicated her life to God, living in the precincts of the temple, serving God with prayers and fasting. Meeting Mary and Joseph when they were in the temple, she also spoke publicly about Him to all those who were looking for redemption in Jerusalem. But there was still no reaction from the religious leaders or scribes, even with such publicity from two remarkably dedicated individuals!

We cannot tell how old the Messiah was when the Magi and shepherds arrived to worship Him, how long it took Herod to realise that his foreign visitors had decided not to return to him, or how long it took Herod to organise the forces necessary to carry out his cruel orders; but about eight weeks from the day of His earthly birth, Joseph was directed by God to take the child and His mother to Egypt out of harm's way.

On their return from Egypt, it was logical, for safety reasons, for them to return home to Nazareth where they would be known. Nothing was recorded of their lives until the Lord had been on the earth for twelve years. Certainly, to be called a Nazarene was not something of which people would be proud (Jn. 1:46). This fact also confused the authorities who accepted that Jesus could not be the Messiah purely on account of Him coming from Nazareth not Bethlehem.

At the age of twelve the Messiah became so engrossed in debating with the learned elders of the day in the temple that he forgot about his 'earthly parents'. All who heard Him were astonished at his understanding and answers, but the Spirit within the child was the Son of God, the Word made flesh. He had been willing to leave His omnipresence behind and confine Himself to a human body, starting life on earth as a baby and had to be allowed to grow to maturity before He could do what He had been sent to do, which was to speak the words and work the miracles and live according to the instructions He had received from His Father, knowing from the start of His untimely and cruel death. Such is the patience of God.

The Servant Messiah

What the scholars were seeing was not a twelve year old boy, but the eternal Son of the Living God, housed in the body of a boy which had been living on the earth for twelve years. How could He be the Word made flesh if at that moment He was just a twelve year old child? At such a young age, how could He have gained such in-depth knowledge of the scriptures that He could amaze the scholars of the day? It is nonsensical! If, according to John 1 verse 1 and 14, He is the Word that was from before time began made into human flesh, then the boy before them had to be the eternal Spirit we can identify as the only begotten (born) Son of the Living God.

We have to consider this appearance of the Son on the world stage in the light of the tabernacle of Moses from God's perspective. Starting in the Holy of Holies, as soon as the tent was erected and dedicated the spirit of God descended in the cloud which filled the tent, just as He filled the temple when it was built by Solomon. Now we have the Son made flesh dwelling amongst us first in the form of the baby as witnessed by the wise men, shepherds, Simeon and Anna, who all experienced great joy in His presence; then as the child of twelve and then the man of thirty.

Although, from the human point of view, the child was only twelve at the time of His stay over in Jerusalem, the Spirit within the human frame was the Son of God from eternity who had issued all the words that the learned men were reading and studying. It is essential that we distinguish between the purpose of the Son (Israel's Messiah) and the Holy Spirit.

The Son is the declared Word of God; the Holy Spirit is the active power of God who puts the word into action. In the beginning it was the Holy Spirit who brooded over the waters and caused the creation to happen according to the Word proclaimed by the Son at the direction of the Father. It is this eternal and consistent nature of God who came to the earth as a human being that can be difficult to comprehend. *"Did you not know"*, He asked His human mother, *"that I must be about My Father's business?"* (Lk. 2:49)

Unfortunately, at that time, they did not understand what He had said to them, for Mary and Joseph must have been routinely treating Him as their son along with His step brothers and sisters. Although He willingly remained subject to His earthly 'parents', He was merely biding His time until His ministry could start.

Ministry of John the Baptiser

John was the first to appear on the scene as an itinerant preacher when the word of God came to him to initiate his ministry. The words of the prophet Isaiah were fulfilled where he talked about the voice of one crying in the wilderness *'Prepare the way of the Lord ...'.* This was to be accomplished by individuals removing all obstructions to their full understanding of the salvation of which He spoke.

The obstructions would include such things as their religious baggage, which is what they had been taught by tradition and by the polluted teaching of the scribes and Pharisees, and their own preconceived ideas about God and His relationship to Israel, which would have caused many objections to John's message to be raised in their minds.

Only those who heard John teach with an open and receptive mind — fallow ground — would be able to receive the true message, which is the seed scattered by the sower he was there to pass on to them. John came for a witness to the Light of God, although he was not that Light, he was there to announce and be a witness to the light who was the Messiah born of Mary. That was his preordained task as the last of the first testament prophets. The fulfilment of all the Messianic prophecies.

We have already seen that the religious leaders were nowhere to be seen when the Messiah was born in humble surroundings, even though there were signs that they should have picked up on. Now that John had gone public and was baptising those who wanted to get right with God, suddenly they started to come out of the woodwork. Sceptical to the core they questioned John about his identity and the authority by which he was baptising people. He openly confessed that he was not the Messiah, nor Elijah nor the prophet who had been spoken about by Moses (Deut. 18:15, 18). A popular Jewish tradition was that Elijah would return before the arrival of the Messiah[84].

"Why then do you baptise if you are none of those people", they asked. John's answer was probably confusing to them for he told them that he only baptised with water but there was one among them, whom they did not know, who was preferred before him and was of such a stature before God that John could not even loose His sandal strap, the work of the lowest servant in a household.

We know that John was filled with the Holy Spirit from his conception in his mother's womb. It was this Holy Spirit who spurred him into action at the start of his ministry, who gave him words to say when challenging those who were coming for baptism without having a change of heart, but merely going through the motions of repentance. *"Brood of vipers!"* he cried out, *"Who warned you to flee from the wrath to come?"* It is by our fruits that we are known, and a bad tree does not produce good fruit, nor a good tree bad fruit. If anything was to guaranteed to anger the authorities it was statements such as those.

The people were warned not to rely on their ancestry, by saying that Abraham was their father, which is what they tried to do, for God would not pay any attention to it. People had to know God personally for themselves as individuals. It was up to each and every individual to respond to Him; to be seen to live godly lives with a clear concern for others,

---

[84] John came in the spirit of Elijah, not Elijah himself who remained in heaven.

particularly the poor, the widow, the orphan and the homeless.

John did his job as the messenger by denying he was the Christ, but proclaimed to all those prepared to listen that One was on His way who would baptise not with water, as he did, but with the Holy Spirit and fire. It was a baptism that would differentiate between the true and the false believer, saving the wheat but burning the chaff (Lk. 3:15 – 17).

As soon as John saw the Messiah, even from a distance, the Holy Spirit enabled him to recognise the Lamb of God as the One who was to take away the sin of the world. *"This is He"*, proclaimed John in his role as the forerunner, the messenger who went before the King of kings to announce His arrival, *"of whom I said, 'After me comes a Man who is preferred before me, for He was before me.' I did not know Him; but that He should be revealed to Israel, therefore I came baptising with water"* (Jn.1:15).

What a remarkable proclamation! John was conceived naturally six months before Mary became pregnant by the Holy Spirit. Therefore physically, John was before Jesus. But Mary's pregnancy was not completely natural; it was caused by the creative skills of the Holy Spirit for she was to bear no ordinary child. Mary was *highly favoured*, which means that she was chosen by God from all the virgins then living for she was to give birth, not to a new human being in the normal sense, but to the body of a male child that was to be inhabited by the Eternal Spirit of the Son of God. And who was the Son of God? He was part of the trinity of Father, Son and Holy Spirit.

Let us spend a moment to fully grasp the wonder of this moment which Charles Wesley described in a hymn as:

> "Our God contracted to a span.
> Incomprehensibly made man."

This was a miracle to surpass all other miracles. The only begotten Son of the Living God, who, as a spiritual being, was like His Father, omnipresent and eternal, yet He came to earth to be confined within the body of a developing fetus in the womb of a woman, to be born in the tent of human flesh and then for His human body to grow into an adult male. Here, spiritual and physical life was united in one body.

King David had said,

> *'The Lord said to my Lord, 'Sit at My right hand,*
> *till I make Your enemies Your footstool.'*
> *The Lord shall send the rod of Your strength out of Zion.*
> *Rule in the midst of Your enemies!*
> *Your people shall be volunteers*
> *In the day of Your power;*

In the beauties of holiness,
From the womb of the morning,
You have the dew of Your youth.
The Lord has sworn and will not relent,
'You are a priest forever
According to the order of Melchizedek[85] *.'''*
(Ps. 110:1 – 4)

Long before the arrival of the Messiah, David, under the influence of the Holy Spirit, spoke of the relationship between the Messiah and His Father.

The Lord, [the Father of our Lord Jesus Christ] said to my Lord, [God's Son, the One who would be born in the line of David (Mary was a direct descendent as was Joseph)] "Sit at My right hand until I make your enemies subservient to you" (cf. *Acts 7:35; Ro. 8:34*).

The Messiah was God's Son, participating in the power of the Godhead, which was implied by being welcomed to God's right hand (Heb. 1:3; Jn. 1:1 – 3). God was the Son's Father for He was able to say, *I and My Father are one* (Jn. 10:30).

But how could the Messiah make such a statement if He had been conceived in the same way that John the baptiser had been? He could not. Therefore, His unique conception and birth were the only means for the Spirit of the Son of God to become Son of Man. Indeed, He said to those who listened, *You are from beneath, I am from above. You are of this world; I am not of this world* (Jn. 8:23).

It is also interesting that the outbursts of the old priest Zacharias, his wife Elizabeth and Mary when she came to them, being by the inspiration of the Holy Spirit which gave them much joy because there is an incredible depth of beauty in the holiness that is imparted by the Holy Spirit to those He influences.

The Messiah demonstrated His power to rule in the midst of His enemies in both works and speech to those around Him, with knowledge and an ability to do a work for God that far surpassed that of the so-called spiritual leaders of the day. He was surrounded by volunteers for the disciples were called as unpaid followers and adherents, but because they had met with the Messiah, the Holy One of God who had been promised, they experienced a calling, an attraction to follow and serve Him which they probably could not have adequately described at the time. Is it not interesting that it was fishermen and ordinary people who recognised the

---

[85] This has already been dealt with in great detail.

Messiah, rather than those who studied the scriptures and thought they knew God?

The womb of Mary was the starting point of His vigorous ministry on earth. *'The dew'*, an essential means of liquid refreshment for many plants in dry and dusty lands, *'of His youth'*, would characterise the freshness and energy of this King, for He increased in wisdom and stature, and in favour with God and men during His adolescence before taking up His preordained ministry at the time of His baptism.

When Mary visited her cousin after her meeting with the angel Gabriel, Elizabeth, under the influence of the Holy Spirit, spoke out this message to Mary with a loud voice, such was the sense of overwhelming spiritual power she felt within her,

> *"Blessed are you among women,*
> *And blessed is the fruit of your womb!*
> *But why is it granted to me,*
> *That the mother of my Lord*
> *Should come to me?*
> *For indeed,*
> *As soon as your voice was heard*
> *Announcing your arrival,*
> *The babe in my womb leapt for joy.*
> *Blessed is she who believed,*
> *for there will be a fulfilment of those things*
> *which were told her from the Lord."*
> *(Lk. 1:42)*

The presence of the Holy Spirit with which the fetus of John was blessed from the moment of his conception, caused him to 'leap for joy' in his mother's womb in recognition of the presence of the eternal Son of God within Mary; the eternal and previously omnipresent Spirit that was the Son of God in the spiritual realm but now in the body of a woman within whom was being created the body that He would use for His ministry on earth. At the time of the Lord's baptism, God the Father spoke from heaven these words, *This is my beloved Son in whom I am well pleased* (Matt. 3:17).

There is no other way to understand the process by which the eternal Son of God, who appeared on earth in the appearance of human form as a priest after the order of Melchizedek, and possibly at other times also; but now, He was provided with a human body so that He could become one of us. Our God contracted to a span, incomprehensibly made man, a man, in the fullest sense, who was completely without sin.

He was born not of the seed of man but born of God, for the Messiah was God's Son, which is why we refer to God as Father, and of a woman that He should become also the Son of Man in order that He could become the Lamb of God to die as our full and sufficient sacrifice.

There was no other way but for Him to become human flesh. To Nicodemus the Messiah explained that there was no compatibility between the spiritual world and the world of the flesh (Jn. 3). Angels cannot marry humans and produce offspring. It is impossible. Therefore, the miracle of the virgin birth remains sublime in its complexity and central to the arrival of the Son of God on earth as a human being.

Public Ministry of the Messiah

It was a surprise to John when the Messiah, who it was his duty to announce, came to be baptised by him. John had been preaching the message of repentance in line with acknowledging that he was the messenger calling on the people to repent of their sins, for the spiritual kingdom of God was at hand. They were to get ready for the arrival of the 'One' who was preferred before him and able to not only forgive them their sin (consider Mk. 2:5 – 12 particularly v7) but also to baptise them with the Holy Spirit.

Sin is to rebel against God in word or deed and as the Messiah was God, which the scribes were unwilling to accept in spite of their great learning, it was fully within His power to forgive sins, especially as it was to be He who was to die for the sins of men and ultimately be the judge on the great white throne to judge all mankind. It was a new way of life, the way of the Spirit, a new beginning in man's relationship with God.

Therefore, for Him to have any credibility with the people, Jesus also needed to be baptised, saying to John, *Permit it to be so now, for thus it is fitting for us to fulfil all righteousness* (Matt. 3:15). It was immediately after the baptism, by which means the Messiah dedicated His human life to His Father, that the sign of the dove coming down assure John that He was indeed the Messiah, the Son of God who was joined to the Holy Spirit in an unbreakable love triangle with the Father.

From the initial relationship of Abraham with the God who spoke to him and attracted him to serve Him, through the individual relationships with God of both Isaac and Jacob, the nation became a reality through the suffering of the children and offspring of Jacob in Egypt. It was in Egypt that the relationship between those born to Abraham, Isaac and Jacob, who was renamed Israel, changed through the leadership of Moses. The Israelites witnessed the mighty power of God when He rescued them from Pharaoh. But it was against the back drop of Mount Sinai that their relationship with God who had chosen them from Abraham, became formal, with the introduction of the Ten Commandments and the Tent of the Meeting with the accompanying spiritually based services.

The gradual changes in the worship of God came as the people became established in the Promised Land, with the building of the temple of Solomon followed by its destruction, the disappearance of the Ark of the Covenant from the holy of holies during the exile in Babylon and the building of a far less glorious replacement temple under Zerubbabel by which God promised to glorify Himself, for as His arrival on the earth established, God does not require great and splendid introductions as rich and famous people do, for His glory is all around us. During the exile there was considerable emphasis on the individual's spiritual relationship with their God through the teaching of the Prophets as established by the quiet faith of the remnant which kept the light of God burning in Israel.

With the appearance of the long-awaited but unrecognised Messiah, God was introducing another element in His plan of salvation which was to do away with the need for a central structure in which He was worshipped. The synagogues played a part in this education, for although they could not replace the temple as the main place of worship because of the essential sacrifice, particularly for sin, that was performed there, they provided an alternative for congregational worship.

With the appearance of the Messiah, however, God wanted to establish the spiritual essence of the individual's relationship with Himself, for He came to establish that 'mountain' on earth that would not demand territory but promote the spiritual life of individuals with the God of all creation. This was and is the kingdom of God to which those who believe in the Lord Jesus ascribe. We are part of the Kingdom of God providing we have gone through the entrance formalities as laid down in scripture and enumerated in this and other books.

"I did not know Him; but that He should be revealed to Israel, therefore I came baptising with water" (Jn. 1:31). In baptising the Messiah, John was revealing the Messiah to Israel. For when the Messiah came out of the water after His baptism, the Holy Spirit descended in the form of a dove and the Father spoke to and of His Son, in whom He was well pleased. This was confirmation that the carefully planned and partially executed plan of salvation was on course, and to the Father's satisfaction. How wonderful. But who, particularly amongst the learnèd leaders of the Jews, would understand who this Holy Spirit was, for the majority did not seem to have any notion of spiritual matters whatsoever, as the incident with Nicodemus so clearly illustrated.

Here was the messenger, the Father, the Son, and now the Holy Spirit together to announce the start of a ministry that was to have such a profound effect on the spiritual life of so many on the earth. Indeed, just as the Tent of the Meeting was filled with the Holy Spirit in the form of a cloud, and the temple of Solomon was filled with the Shekinah Glory on its dedication by Solomon, so that the priests were forced to evacuate the temple building, so, too, in this new temple of flesh, the living example of what God wanted to happen originally with Adam and Eve, the Holy Spirit came, filling Him without measure, for the Father and the Son and the Holy Spirit needed to work closely together without restriction to their means of communication.

This could not have happened to someone who was a complete human being at birth; the Spirit within the body had to be familiar with and at one with the spiritual realm of God, and at one with the presence of the Holy Spirit. How else could He impart the Holy Spirit to others, except they were equal in the Trinity?

The Spirit was to be the information gatherer for the Son of God, who was made Son of Man, and indwelt the restricted temple that was His body, to be His spiritual eyes and ears and senses. This was the Tent of the Meeting, particularly the Holy of Holies, being established on earth in human form as an example of God's means of entering into the lives of individuals in the future.

Consider the candelabrum in the holy place: Jesus is the light of the world. The candelabrum has a central stem with six branches making seven lights and the number seven represents spiritual perfection. The term seven spirits of God denotes the work of the Holy Spirit. Could it be that as the Son was filled with the Holy Spirit throughout His ministry and it was the Holy Spirit who witnessed His death, the candelabra illustrated the work of the Son and the Holy Spirit giving light to the world during His ministry on earth, including His death? (Heb. 9:14)

The enlightening Word made flesh broadcast with the power of the Holy Spirit because it was the Spirit who was able to sear the word onto the hearts of those willing to receive it. Indeed, today it is the Holy Spirit who works in our hearts under the instruction of the Messiah who is now victorious in heaven.

The imperfections in sinful men would be the underlying problem with regard to the ease or difficulty with which the personal relationship between them and God would develop and prosper. This is so, particularly where a person seeks for an ever deeper and more intimate spiritual intercourse with God in order to become a true temple of the Holy Spirit as God desires. But in the case of the Son of God, there was no inherited sin to cause those difficulties that could either disrupt His work or the intimacy of the working relationship between Him and the Holy Spirit.

But why was the Holy Spirit's presence within the Son of Man so vital? As a man, the Son of God willingly restricted Himself to the limitations of the human body. As a spiritual being, He had been omnipresent and able to know what was going on in men's minds and hearts; these were all open to Him. But as a man such insights were denied Him. The Holy Spirit at no time experienced those limitations. Therefore, it was the Holy Spirit who, knowing what was in men's hearts and minds, was able to pass that information to the Messiah (Consider Mk. 2:8). It was the Spirit who had brooded over the waters to cause the thoughts of the Father, and the Word of the Son to become reality, in order for all that we see today to be created. The Father had the plan, the Son was the Word and the Holy Spirit displayed the practical power of the Godhead.

The person of the Messiah was the new temple which, when destroyed on the cross, was rebuilt in three days (Matt. 26:61; 27:40; Jn.2:19), not into a new body but into an incorruptible body that the disciples could recognise (1 Cor. 15:42 – 53), and that could enter into the immortal spiritual realm of the eternal Kingdom of God.

From the beginning, in the Garden of Eden, God wanted to prepare man for His eternal Kingdom. Flesh and blood could not inherit that kingdom (1 Cor. 15:50), only the spiritual could do that. Had Adam eaten of the fruit of the tree of life things would have been entirely different; but by corrupting himself with sin, a far more drastic measure for man's salvation and preparation for the heavenly realm had to be brought to play.

Although man is made of dust, the Messiah, the second man, who was from heaven (1 Cor. 15:47) was originally and eternally spiritual. The Spiritual Man entering into a body made from the dust of the ground physically died on the cross, and in the tomb His body of dust was transformed into a spiritual body so that it did not see corruption (decay) (Ps. 16:10), a totally different operation to the transformation that we will have to go through after our death. For we will be provided with a new incorruptible body.

The Messiah was the first-fruits. In dying for us, and being of a spiritual birth before His appearance on the earth, the Messiah was able to take on the sin of mankind and die a human death[86], then, through the powerful work of the Holy Spirit, He was able to rise again in a body that had been transformed from being purely flesh, the tent He had occupied during His life on earth, into a spiritual body that made Him fit to return to His Father.

From unrestrained Spiritual being to earthly body that was transformed into a spiritual body, made the changes that occurred to the Messiah unique in human history and explains why no body was discovered in the tomb after His resurrection, and why the disciples could not have removed what was not there for them to remove.

We, on the other hand, were created as tents of flesh which house a new spirit which is the real us. Our spirit must be regenerated through the new birth that only true belief in the Messiah can bring about. When we die our

---

[86] The Spirit of the Son of God within the body did not die because He yielded (gave) up His Spirit (Matt. 27:50), meaning His Spirit left His body so that it could die, for the Son, being an intrinsic part of God could not die.

souls and spirits leave our body and our physical body decomposes and returns to the dust from which we were made (Gen. 3:19). That means we shall be without a body from the moment of our death, when we shall 'sleep' until the last trumpet is sounded to announce the return of the Messiah when those in Christ shall be provided with new incorruptible bodies (1 Cor. 15:51 – 53), to become like the Saviour, the life-giving Spirit, who preceded us (1 Cor. 15:49). All others will be eternally separated from God.

The temple built of stone that the Jews were so passionate about had, for the past 400 years, been but a dead symbol of what had been a means of focusing the people's attention on God. The emphasis of the message of the last of the first testament prophets before the appearance of John the Baptizer, was the need for all true believers to become acquainted with their God as a spiritual God not confined to the physical restrictions of the temple and its services.

The new 'temple' in the person of the Messiah of Israel, who was not built with the hands of sinners, but pure born, was to be symbolic of the new relationship God wanted man to have with Him. This new spiritual relationship would allow individuals to be in the presence of God like the showbread on the table, and regularly in prayer, as illustrated by the altar of incense in the holy place, because, through the indwelling of the Holy Spirit the individual would become a temple of the Living God just like the man-built tabernacle and temple of old.

Although we cannot be filled with the Holy Spirit without measure as the Son was, yet to become a temple of the Holy Spirit (1 Cor. 3:16) all we have to do is to focus on God and worship Him in spirit and in truth (Jn. 4:21 – 24). This is a whole new concept which, even with the advantage of the complete scriptures available to us, many in the church find difficult to understand.

The religious leaders of the day had no chance of understanding the message of the Messiah because they were hampered by much religious baggage with which their forebears had conspicuously burdened them. Yet this was the whole purpose of the simple illustration God had given them in the Tent of the Meeting, which they had either not seen or ignored. We cannot be lights in this dark world unless the Holy Spirit dwells in us as He did in the Messiah. We need to be conscious of our place before God and be regularly in prayer so that we can be totally open to God and with God. It is we who need to make ourselves available to Him for God is always available to us.

The Word made flesh that had come to dwell among them was unknown to them. The glory of the holiness of God that was in His face, which men could not see and remain alive (Ex. 30:20), was attenuated by the tent of human flesh that He wore. He became like us, therefore they could not recognise Him, and their pomposity and opinionated sense of self-importance barred them from the simple love for God that was required of them, and prevented them from having that loving relationship with Him which John experienced (Jn. 1:10 – 13).

They were totally focused on the man-built temple and its accumulated ceremonies and procedures and laws that had to be strictly observed if they were to be considered righteous[87], not in God's sight but in the eyes of men. The appearance of the Messiah as their example specified a new birth into all things spiritual that replaced the formal observance of rules and regulations. The spiritual example of the Messiah was the goal they were meant to achieve through the instructions God had given them through His servants the prophets and through the quiet example of the remnant. For although they were born of the flesh, that is of blood and the will of their parents, to be temples of the Holy Spirit they also needed to be born of God, in a rebirth of the spirit within them. This immediate, personal, spiritual relationship with the supreme God was to many, including Nicodemus, a completely new concept; yet it was what God had wanted them to enjoy in order for them to become a true Israelite, a true member of the eternal Kingdom of God.

But how can this be? Is it necessary for us to enter our mother's womb again and be born a second time as Nicodemus asked the Messiah, demonstrating, even as a leader of Israel, just how little he knew about the things of God? (Jn. 3:1 – 21) No. We must make the decision to enter through the gate of decision into the kingdom of God, be baptised in the name of the Father and the Son and the Holy Spirit and, in repentance and faith, make our peace with God, seeking His forgiveness so that He is able to baptise us with the Holy Spirit. That is being born of God. It is that willingness within ourselves to seek after God that will allow Him to meet with us and enter our lives so that He is able to dine with us and be our God (Rev. 3:20). That is how we can become a new temple of the Holy Spirit; the Messiah, who came down from heaven (Jn. 3:12 – 15), being the first of its type.

After His baptism in water and joined with the Holy Spirit, Jesus, our example, was led of the Spirit into the wilderness for 40 days and nights. 40 is the Divine order as applied to earthly things. With regard to numbers, it is interesting that the four perfect numbers are 3, 7, 10 and 12. Their product is 2520, which is the Least Common Multiple of the ten digits covering all numeration. It can be divided by each of the nine digits without a remainder. It is the number of chronological perfection (7 x 360). It is exciting to see the importance of these four numbers, so widely used in

---

[87] This is surely a picture of the established churches, particularly the Roman Catholic and Church of England with its annual calendar of events and ceremonies that have become an end in themselves.

scripture. Moses was on the mountain top for forty days and nights (Ex. 24:18) and Elijah went in the strength of the food given to him by an angel for forty days and nights (1 Kgs. 19:5 – 18).

This was a time for Jesus to be alone with His Father in this new situation of being a mature man at the start of His earthly ministry that was to end with His physical death which, with His resurrection, gave Him final victory over Satan and the enslaving sin he had introduced into the world for his own advantage. Just as God gained victory over Pharaoh who had enslaved the children of Israel for his own ends.

The Father was in heaven which the Messiah had left to become fully human on the earth. This could be likened to astronauts on the moon speaking to mission control on earth. After all the planning and gradual rolling out of that plan over the centuries, now had come the moment of final teaching and example before the consummation of the plan of salvation when the ultimate sacrifice for sin was to be offered at such enormous cost.

It was also a time for Satan to try and thwart the Messiah's work by tempting Him as he had tempted the first man and woman. The three recorded temptations are worth considering for the teaching they provide.

1. **Concerning food** – we are created spiritual beings in a human frame, although unlike the Messiah, each person that is born is a completely new physical and spiritual being. As humans we need to eat to live; but as both spiritual and human we need two types of food. Therefore, it is important to learn from the Messiah's response to Satan's first temptation.

   After the Messiah had gone without food and water for 40 days and nights, He was obviously physically hungry and thirsty. Satan suggested that if He was the Son of God, He should enact a miracle by turning the stones on the ground into bread to satisfy His human hunger. There was no doubt He was the Son of God but to misuse His power in such a selfish way was not what He was on earth for, therefore the Messiah told Satan:

   Man shall not live by the physical food of the earth alone
   But also by the spiritual food of the Word of God.
   (See Matt. 4:4)

   This was the food of which the disciples had no knowledge (Jn. 4:32 - 34). It is the spiritual food applied by the Spirit which gives life to the inner man (Jn. 6:63). It is in the spiritual sense that we are allowed access to the Son for there has to be within our hearts a fervent desire to know God; it is only spiritual food that can feed and satisfy that fervent desire. It is certainly what satisfies me in my daily walk with God. It is the Holy Spirit who looks into the inner man, and it is the Father who knows those whose seeking is genuine (Consider Jn. 6:65; Matt. 5:6).

2. **Concerning the will** – defiance has always been a characteristic of man since sin entered into him. Obduracy is a problem for all of us. What Satan was asking the Messiah to do was to demand proof of God's intentions towards Him. Yet from an early age, particularly when He was twelve, He knew what God's intentions were for Him, after all had He not willingly come from the bosom of the Father to the earth and, moreover, as part of the Godhead, did He not have the witness of the Holy Spirit within Him confirming to Him God's intentions towards Him?

    Not only did He have unlimited access to the Holy Spirit, but they were working as one even to the point of His death for we read that He was to shed His blood with the cognisance of the eternal Spirit (Heb. 9:14). The reference the Messiah used was a statement used to counteract Israel's constant demand for God to prove His presence with a miracle (Ex. 17:1 – 7; cf. Jn. 4:48).

    You shall not tempt the Lord your God.
    (Matt. 4:7; cf. Deut. 6:16)

3. **Concerning power and status** – Satan rebelled against God because he wanted to take God's place, however impossible that objective was to a created being. The temptation he used to persuade Eve to eat of the forbidden fruit was to lure her into thinking she could be like God, knowing good and evil (Gen. 3:5), although, unbeknown to her, it would be knowledge gained from the point of view of evil not good.

    In this last of the triune temptations, Satan took the Messiah in the spirit to an exceedingly high mountain and showed Him his domain, Satan was known as the prince of the power of the air and the reference in Job means that he walked over his territory – Job 1:7. Then the temptation:

    "All these things I have the power to give You,
    If You will fall down and worship me".
    (Matt. 4:9)

    The whole purpose of the arrival of the Son of God on earth was to free men from bondage both to Satan and the sin he peddled. The Messiah's reply is again instructive.

With single-mindedness of purpose,
you shall both worship and serve the Lord your God.
(See Matt. 4:10)

These temptations and the responses of the Messiah are a lesson for us in this life, backed up as they are by so much scripture in both testaments.

Why the Passover Lamb of God?

The sheep was domesticated from the start of man's independent existence on earth. Because of its totally defenseless nature, but often independent and obdurate spirit, God chose the sheep to be symbolic of the man He had created. Therefore, it was Abel's sacrifice of a lamb and the shedding of its blood which met with God's approval. The self-centred nature of Cain's offering of the product of his own efforts was rejected. The scripture clearly tells us not only that we are like sheep, but that like sheep we have strayed from the will and purpose God had for us (Is. 53:6).

It was John, the forerunner and announcer of the Messiah, who called Him the Lamb of God as he was guided by the Holy Spirit. But it is also interesting that the Messiah is much more than just the Lamb of God, for the sacrifice He gave of Himself was for a moment in time, taking three hours to die on the cross, and three days before the victory of the resurrection. The Messiah also came as the shepherd of the flock of God (Ez. 34:23; Jn. 10:11), which included not only Israel but all who choose to willingly accept the gift of salvation; for the Messiah stated clearly that there were other sheep that were not of the fold of Israel for whom He had to care because God's plan was for there to be one flock and one shepherd. (Jn. 10:16)

Pharaoh chose not to believe what Moses told him, believing himself to be a god who was to be worshipped in his own right. When he said that he did not know of a Hebrew God, he was telling the truth. What God did, in spite of what the Biblical text seems to say in its translated form, was to use Pharaoh's obstinacy to His advantage. Likewise, God did not impart to King Saul an evil spirit, for God is pure and holy and incapable of imparting to anyone anything that is evil. Rather when Saul showed contempt for Him, God withdrew His Holy Spirit from the king thus removing His protection, allowing Satan free access to him.

On the other hand, there have been a number of individuals God has particularly chosen to do a work for Him knowing that their heart was right: which is why Jacob was chosen and Esau rejected, David was chosen and Saul rejected. Paul, just like the twelve disciples, was also chosen to be his disciple because of the Pharisaic training and a heart on fire for God, whereas Judas Iscariot, on the other hand, was also chosen for a far different reason. It must be accepted that salvation is a gift offered to all who are willing of themselves to accept it, and God will accept as His, those who desire a new life in Him.

What predestination refers to is the way the true and fully committed believer naturally behaves after he has been baptised in the Holy Spirit. This is because the believer allows the Holy Spirit to guide and direct him and willingly follows His direction in a predestined manner.

Is it not interesting that all the three main Biblical characters chosen of God to look after His people, Israel, were all shepherds? Consider Moses whose 80 years of training for the first forty years included instructions in the accumulated word of God known up to the time of him being handed to the Royal Family of Egypt where he was trained in diplomacy and Egyptian royal etiquette. Then, after his escape from Egypt, Moses received about 40 years training as a shepherd in the area where he would lead the people of God.

What about David whose elevation to the throne of Israel to become the greatest of all her kings was because he was knowledgeable in the word of God, had trained as a shepherd and was willing to fight against all those who would try to harm first the sheep and then the people? Then the Son of God came full of the knowledge of the word of God, because He was the Word of God incarnate. King David stated clearly, *The Lord is my shepherd therefore I will not want* (Ps. 23). The Messiah Himself publicly claimed to be the good shepherd who, unlike the foolish shepherds (Zech. 11:17) who had had no concern for the flock of God, would lay down His own life for the sheep as the Lamb of God (Jn. 10:11).

This means that God, as the Messiah, was not only the shepherd of the flock, but also the access and the door, for all those wishing to enter into the sheepfold of the Kingdom of God to enjoy the protection offered to all true sheep[88]. He was willing to protect those committed to Him from those who would do them harm, even to the point where He was prepared to lay down His own life for the sheep. (Jn. 10:7 – 17) This is, after all, the reason He came.

The sacrifice of the Passover Lamb was first held the night before the people of Israel were released from slavery in Egypt (Ex. 12). The lamb was slain and the blood painted on the front door surrounds, to stop the angel of death killing the first born of the people of Israel, that is so that the angel would passover that home. The lamb was to be roasted and eaten with unleavened bread and bitter herbs. The Passover festival was to be celebrated at the same time every year in perpetuity.

Jesus was the Passover Lamb because he was to be sacrificed at Passover. It was the night before Passover that Jesus wanted to celebrate

---

[88] That is all true believers – consider Acts 20:29

the Passover meal which He changed from celebrating the release of the Israelites from Egypt into the first communion service[89]. He was crucified exactly on the day of Passover.

The Son of God Tells Us About the Messiah

Isaiah 53 is the chapter most closely associated with the Messiah. It is essential that, as we read that chapter, we realise the words we are reading were given to the prophet by the Son, the Word of God, through the Holy Spirit, that is the same person who came down to the earth and lived out His life on earth as described by Isaiah. Sadly, the attitude of the Jews was, throughout their history as the chosen nation of God, one of unbelief.

Indeed, it will not be until they see the Messiah coming in glory that they will realise who it is that they crucified, and for centuries have despised. The cry of, *who has believed our report, and to whom has the arm of the Lord been revealed* (Is. 53:1; Jn. 12:37 – 41) is desperate because unbelief had blinded their eyes so that in seeing they saw not and in hearing they heard not, (Jer. 5:21) even though they had witnessed the mighty arm of God throughout the life of their nation. But it was the personal seeking after and experiencing their spiritual God through the circumcision of their hearts that would have allowed God to reveal Himself to them individually.

When Isaiah was spiritually uplifted at the time he saw the Lord high and lifted up in the temple, and dedicated his life to God, the Lord told him to proclaim to the people that they, *keep on hearing, but do not understand; keep on hearing, but do not perceive*, (Is. 6:9) which resulted from their attitude towards Him, from the high priests right down through the nation to the ordinary citizen.

The veil Moses was asked to put over his face because of the fading reflected glory of God the people saw (Ex. 34:33), is still in place when it comes to the reading of the word, the first testament scriptures. The Messiah told His hearers to walk whilst they had the light of His presence with them, for the light would be snuffed out and they would return to darkness. (Jn. 12:35; cf. Jer. 13:16)

The Jews, even today, seek for the King who would come to reign and set them free militarily, humanly speaking. Yet, as we have discovered from the beginning of our studies, they had first to be released from inherited sin and then have their personal sin forgiven, before the victorious, all conquering Messiah could come.

There was nothing about the look of the Messiah that distinguished Him from anyone else of His age; rather He fitted in easily and seamlessly with the humanity around Him, undistinguished, with no 'form or comeliness, or special beauty that they should desire Him'.

---

[89] For details see my book A Fresh Look At Easter.

The Servant Messiah

Those who heard Him preach and perform miracles were divided about who He was; mostly either rejecting or being sceptical about His word and even the miracles themselves. Certainly, He was rejected by the leaders, those who considered themselves wise in the things of God. As Isaiah spoke the words of God, *He is despised and rejected of men* (Is. 53:3a) so it came to pass, as we also read, that He was despised by the religious authorities during His time on the earth because they saw Him as a threat to their falsely exalted pious position in society and rejected Him as a trouble maker (Lk. 18:10 – 14).

As *a Man of sorrows and acquainted with grief*, (Is. 53:3b) because of the rejection He experienced, He nevertheless continued to deliver the true message He was there to broadcast the message about the love of His Father. He experienced such a level of grief that He instinctively wept over Jerusalem because He knew what their ignorant rejection of Him would mean to their future life there (Lk. 19:41 – 44). The people had, *hid as it were their faces from Him; He was despised, and they did not esteem Him* (see Is. 53:3c & d).

If only the people had known that it was their true King entering the city on the donkey's colt, on which no one had ridden, they would have known peace. Sadly, because of their blindness to the things of God, after His death the Roman occupying force would establish siege mounds and destroy all that they held dear; particularly the temple which, after 46 years in construction, would once more be destroyed as at the time of Nebuchadnezzar. They were repeating the mistakes of their forebears. What structure man builds up God can so easily knock down.

But the whole purpose of His visit to the earth was to teach the people of the love of His Father and, in loving commitment, take the place of the Passover Sacrifice which the people had been routinely celebrating according to God's instructions received through Moses, without realising its full significance (Jn. 12:23 - 26).

This is what Isaiah was seeking to relay to the people. But the message was not just for the people of his day, as the prophecy concerned the task of the future Messiah. This message was also given for future generations to consider. *"Surely"*, said the prophet, *"He has borne our griefs and carried our sorrows; yet we esteemed (regarded) Him stricken, smitten by God, and afflicted"*. (Is. 53:4)

Just as the sacrificial lamb was chosen and taken unceremoniously to the altar of sacrifice, so the Messiah would be treated without ceremony and abused before being executed in order to bear our sin. But this was for a purpose. *He was wounded* (v5), that is, He was physically injured, pierced in hands and feet and side, His back being severely torn to bits by the whipping He received at the hands of pagan soldiers, not because of His own sins and rebelliousness against God, as He was without sin, but *for our transgressions*, because of the blind and ignorant accusations of the priests who were supposed to be ministers and servants of God, the Father of the Messiah.

The prophet then provides us, even today, with this explanation of what the Saviour came to the earth to do, not just for Israel, but for us today; in fulfilment of Genesis 3:15, when God said to Satan, *He shall bruise your head, and you shall bruise His heel*, causing Him grief but not terminal damage. *He was bruised*, that is, crushing inward and outward suffering, not for His own sin but *for our iniquities*. Even though He came to His own people He was rejected, and is still being rejected by them as a nation, and suffered verbal abuse and antagonism even from His half-brothers and sisters until after His death and resurrection when they came to realise just who He was[90].

A further aspect of His work on earth was to be chastised; which is the correction inflicted by a parent on children for their own good (Heb. 12:5 – 8, 10, 11). Because our Lord, in taking our place, was sinless, there could be no aspect of punishment in what was to happen from His point of view. Even though we deserve the full condemnation and eternal punishment of the supreme law of God, in taking our place He was not punished by the Father in the same way that those who reject salvation will be punished by suffering the second death, but was chastised for us so that He, having carried our burden on the cross, was able to rise again and be restored, not to the position He had before, but to the position of a victorious King and High Priest having defeated not only Satan and the sin he introduced, but also the finality of death.

In the words of the prophet, *the chastisement for our peace was upon Him*, which means He bore for us, along with the griefs and sorrow (Is. 53:4), the chastisement, punishment, reprimand, of His Father so that our peace, which is our reconciliation with the Father, and the cleansing of our consciences, may be made available to us if we are mindful to accept the salvation of our God in its totality (Rom. 5:1; Eph. 2:14, 15, 17).

In the well-known verse John 3:16 we are told that, *God so loved the world that the Father gave His only begotten Son, that whoever believes in Him should not perish but have everlasting life*, the key words are *'whoever believes in Him'* should not perish. This is confirmed in verse 18 where we read, *but he who does not believe is condemned already*.

It is essential that we realise that for the gift of salvation to be of any value at all to us personally, we, individually, must accept the whole package of salvation and give ourselves completely to God, who we are, what we do, what we have. If God has saved us from eternal death by His sacrifice, then He has bought us with the price of His earthly life which gives us no alternative but to surrender ourselves completely to Him so that He

---

[90] Read the letters of James and Jude.

becomes king and lord of our lives and we come under His complete and absolute authority in love.

We have no right to devalue His salvation by entering into a half-hearted and casual relationship with Him through the leaders and facilities of the church/synagogue we attend, or of which we are members. It is no good believing we are saved when all we are really doing is attending church and entering into a ceremonial, procedural relationship with our Lord Messiah merely by going through the requirements of that particular church solely to become a participating member of it.

We must, individually, get real with God in a one-to-one direct and personal relationship with Him through the working of the Holy Spirit. Only by enjoying two-way communication with God, Father, Son and Holy Spirit, and by demonstrating our commitment to Him will we be assured of our personal salvation in Christ Jesus.

Many in the church and synagogue will be devastated when they realise too late that they did not secure for themselves the salvation they believed they had. It is our personal responsibility alone to read the whole of scripture for ourselves and pray for revelation from God so that we can make the right decisions from the position of knowledge and understanding whilst we are able. That is what this book is all about.

There is no doubt that we can become spiritually alive and enter into an active, indeed vibrant, relationship with God to the degree and depth that we desire. If we only want to experience being saved and no more, then God will not insist that we enter into a deeper commitment with Him. But, at the other end of the spectrum, if we want to be totally absorbed into an ever deepening, spiritually enhanced relationship with our God, then He is more than willing to draw us ever deeper into Himself with the result that we will experience the truly deep things of God which will, like on the face of Moses when he had been with God, shine forth in our lives and affect the way we live and relate to others.

Lastly, we are told that it was, *by His stripes we are healed,* which prophetically spoke of the excruciatingly painful scourging He willingly endured for us (Matt. 27:26; 1 Pet. 2:24; cf. Jn. 12:27, 28). The healing is spiritual (Ps. 41:4; 103:1 – 4; 147:3; Jer. 8:22) allowing for the acceptance by God the Father of the believer's penitential confession, particularly that of the people of Israel in the last days (Zech. 12:10).

"All we like sheep have gone astray;
we have turned, everyone, to his own way;
And the Lord has laid on Him
The iniquity of us all."
(Is. 53:6)

What this is telling us is that on our own, away from God, we have strayed into the godless wilderness of the Satan-controlled sin-filled earth; the creation as corrupted by Satan and his demonic forces. The whole creation may continue as God had desired, but the corruption of man has infected his stewardship of it to the extent that the beauty of this earth is being despoiled by evil men (Ro. 8:22).

However, the reverse of all this is that although by our very nature we are prone to wander, driven headlong, lemming like, to our destruction, which is the behavioural effect of the inherited sin nature within us, known as the sheep effect; yet in the Messiah, the shepherd of the sheep, we are drawn together as a separate people into the flock of God being led to the door of the sheepfold which is the entrance to the kingdom of God, the gate that opens to the difficult way that leads to life. Incredibly, however, Isaiah tells us that, in spite of the fact that it is we who have gone astray, it is the Lord Messiah on whom the Father has laid our iniquity.

This is the fundamental teaching of the Tabernacle of Moses. The door into the compound surrounding the holy tent leads directly to the altar of sacrifice. Before ever we reach the laver, the word of God, it is necessary for us to hear and understand, probably through the work of the Holy Spirit, the basic fact that our sin, our rebelliousness against God, must be dealt with first through a blood sacrifice. This is crucial to any understanding we may acquire concerning the theology which enables us to understand the spiritual God who created all things and from whom we have been separated by our sin.

We must then accept that it is the Jewish Messiah, who is central to all understanding of the Word of God, who alone can reunite us with our creator God through His coming to earth, dressed in the fleshly clothing of a man, specifically to be sacrificed for our iniquities. That is what the Word of God, as relayed by Isaiah, is telling us.

At no time in His entire ministry and trial did the Messiah, the Lamb of God and spiritual Shepherd of the sheep, cry out in complaint. Yes, He challenged those who thought they knew all about the God who had chosen their nation. Yes, He accused them of hypocrisy. Yes, He responded to the high priest when challenged before God to admit to being the Messiah (Matt 26:63, 64), but He never complained about the injustice that was being perpetrated in order that they could kill Him, even though He had done nothing wrong and had every reason to appeal over their treatment of Him (see Is. 53:7, 8). The oppression He underwent refers to having a debt aggressively exacted, and the affliction He suffered He bore patiently.

Thus, was He taken from the prison, from out of the earth, being held below ground, and from the judgement of those who will one day, with horror, find themselves before this same Man to be judged by Him as the supreme judge sitting on the great white throne when the book of life and the book containing a record of all that they did in life are opened.

The whole of Isaiah chapter 53 is dedicated to the commitment of the One who would come, the Messiah, the suffering servant who was willing to accept the condemnation incurred by man, by taking upon Himself the iniquities of the whole of mankind. *"It pleased the Lord"*, said Isaiah, *"to bruise Him"* Why? Because His soul, His body and person, the tent in which He lived on earth, was made an offering for sin, for the major purpose of seeing His spiritual posterity become numerous.

That is, you and me as believers. But more than that, by willingly dying physically for the sin of the world He was to see length of days by being elevated to the right hand of Power (Mk. 14:62; consider Matt. 26:63 – 68), which the spiritual blindness of those who considered themselves righteous (see John 9 esp. vs 24 – 34, 41) prevented them from understanding or believing. By doing the will of His Father He would be rewarded for eternity, far above all the rewards of the earth. His reward was the accolade He received from his Father, 'well done thou good and faithful Son in whom I am well pleased' (See Matt. 3:17).

The Centrality of the Passover Lamb of God

We have already discussed at length the fact that the Spirit that was the Son of God became the Son of Man simply by being tented in the body of a human being supplied for Him in Mary's womb (Jn. 1:1, 14). It was this immediate intimacy between God the Son and the body provided by this young woman that made her gloriously blessed among women. The temporary dwelling of the truly Holy and Righteous God within the body of a human being is beyond the imaginings of the most spiritually minded person who ever lived.

There was no doubt in anyone's mind that He was fully human; indeed, the problem was that those leaders who met with Him could not understand that the Spirit within the body was that of God's eternal Son. He displayed His credentials through His knowledge of the Word of God, for no one could outwit Him nor speak with the same level of authority as He was able to do so fluently; which was because it was the Word He had delivered to man in the first place.

The miracles He performed were outstanding because no one had performed such feats since the limited miracles of the prophets of old or so many or such a variety of miracles in such a short time. But the experience of hearing the word He spoke and witnessing the miracles He performed justified many at the time, and justifies many even today because of belief in Him.

Such was the victory the Messiah achieved that one day He will come in the clouds of glory to gather to Himself all believers. Having poured out

His soul unto death by being numbered amongst the transgressors, even on the accursed cross (Lk. 23:34); by bearing the sins of many, He was able to intercede for those same transgressors; not just for the thief who sought for His forgiveness, himself rightfully hanging on a cross alongside the Lord, but also for those who put Him there and everyone who has lived since.

His cry *Father forgive them for they do not know what they are doing* (Lk. 23:33, 39 - 43) was because they really did not know what they were doing, but inadvertently fulfilling prophecy. Now, as we know, He is in the original Holy of Holies in heaven (replicated on earth by Moses) to intercede for us as our advocate before the Father (Is. 59:16; Heb. 4:14 – 16; 9:24; 1 Jn. 2:1).

The central character that we have been concentrating on is the lamb, the key sacrificial animal for sin. From the first Passover, and annually thereafter, the Passover Lamb was offered as required by God in remembrance of that first offering in the land of Egypt prior to their being freed from slavery. Egypt represented the world and Israel the people of God. Blood around the door represented a covering for sin.

The slaughtering of the sacrifice, releasing its blood, represented the pouring out of the life of the lamb being offered as a substitute for the sinner for atonement (Gen. 9:4 – 6). When the angel of death saw the blood around the doorway of the home, he passed over that dwelling leaving the firstborn alive. This action was the final act of God on the Egyptians, a mighty judgement to demonstrate His power over life and death, an action that would initiate the release of His people from their slavery of Egypt. It was the death of the Pharaoh as he defied God, by trying to recapture God's people at the Red Sea, which finally destroyed his satanic-type power over God's people.

When God sees the blood applied to those who have sought for forgiveness from God the Father in the name of the Lord Jesus in repentance and faith through prayer, He is not able look at their sin which has been washed away by the blood of the Lamb. Therefore, though others in the world will be condemned, as the unbelieving Egyptians were, believers will not be condemned.

What was the whole purpose of the sacrificial death of the Perfect Man of God? For this we must compare what happened at the time of the first Passover, and the lesson it provides, with what happened at the last Passover hosted by the perfect Passover Lamb. As we consider the comparison it is important that we realise that God was, at the birth of the nation of Israel, setting the scene for the final Passover meal to be hosted by His Son who would use the occasion to introduce the New Covenant, the culmination of His plan of salvation, and the revised Passover meal, which was translated into the Holy Communion by which the new born Church of Israel was to remember His death until His future gloriously public earthly visit which is to be announced not only by the trumpet, the shofar, but by the glorious nature of that coming.

From the beginning God made the Passover central to His mighty work of salvation and we need to remember that His plan is consistent throughout His word and human history. Indeed, as some have said, human history is in fact His-story.

I have referred to the church that came into being after the death of the Messiah as the 'Church of Israel' because the church is of Israel, it being the primary fold into which other sheep would be brought that were previously not of that fold. The church is founded on the nation of Israel, which God chose to be His nation, His first-born son. Indeed, the new-born spiritual Church of the Living Christ seamlessly continues on from the physical nation of Israel through those Israelites who believed that Jehoshua, Jesus, was and is the long-promised Messiah.

The disciples and other Jewish believers were the first members of the Church created by the Messiah, and it was through their willingness, even at the cost of their own lives, to broadcast the good news of the gospel in the power of the Holy Spirit, and as taught by the Messiah, that other Jews and Gentiles have been able to believe in Him and be saved to the uttermost.

The fragmented western 'church' is but a part of the Church of the Living Lord, not the one and only Church. There is not a man on earth who can claim to be specially chosen of God to lead the whole church on earth for, just as God was the one and only true King and God of Israel, so there is only one head of the true Church on earth and in heaven, and that man is the Messiah to the Jews, the only Son born to the Living God, Jehoshua/Jesus, to the Jews He is known as Yeshua..

At the time of the first Passover, God demonstrated His power over life and death and over the spiritual kingdom of Satan, in order to have His people released from the slavery of both the sinful world, represented by Egypt, and the spiritual being who had tricked them into slavery, represented by its ruler Pharaoh. To achieve this a yearling lamb, perfect in every way, was killed by families, according to the instructions given to them by Moses (Ex.12), and the blood of the lamb painted around the outside of the doorway of the house in which they lived. God gave strict instructions that not a bone was to be broken, because not a bone of His Son's body would be broken.

The angel of death passed over the houses so marked for the blood was a sign; a sign that told the angel that those inside belonged to God. The blood was therefore a sign; it provided protection for the first-born as the angel of death was commanded to kill only the first-born of each household, both slave and free.

At the time of the second Passover, again God demonstrated on earth His eternal power over life and death (Matt. 10:28), over Satan himself and over the Satan-introduced rebelliousness and sin which has permeated the world and men, particularly rebellious and hard-hearted Israel. He was able to do this by being born into the world as a perfect man and an Israelite of the tribe of Judah, living a perfect life and then willingly dying for the eternal spiritual lives not only of the first-born of Israel as at the time of the exodus, but all mankind by taking upon Him the sin of the world. This included the sin already committed, that was being committed and would be committed in the future. So, for all those that believe and have been cleansed by the blood of the Lamb of God, the Father sees the blood of His Son upon them and knows that they are pure and holy.

This glorious Passover Lamb of God died at the hands of His own chosen people, at the specified time of the sacrificing of the nation's Passover lamb. But, unlike the animal sacrifice, this Passover Lamb of God was to rise again from the grave, finally establishing a sacrifice for sin that was so thorough, because it cleansed the conscience of the repentant sinner, that no other lamb need be slain.

Because the Sabbath that year immediately followed the sacrificing of the Passover Lamb it was essential that the body of the Lord was removed from the cross according to God's requirements (Deut. 21:23). This is why it was necessary for the bones of those still alive to be broken to hasten their death, and why it was necessary for the Son to have already given up the life within His human body by His Spirit leaving the body (Matt. 27:50; Lk.23:46; Jn. 19:30). Thus, just as not a bone of those lambs sacrificed at the first Passover was to be broken, so not a bone of the final Passover Lamb was to be broken.

Let us now consider the events leading up to that momentous sacrifice.

The timing of the arrest of the Messiah was crucial. Knowing that the Jews were out to kill Him, the Messiah avoided a public entry into Judea where the enemy's efforts were concentrated around Jerusalem and the temple, which was so central to their religious life. His brothers taunted Him concerning the publicity they thought He needed (Jn. 7:3 – 5) because they did not believe in Him being the Messiah either. He was their human brother after all, the son of their mother, so how could He be God? Ignorance always accompanies the lack of the knowledge of the Truth.

Although their time was their life time, His time of offering Himself up for sacrifice had not yet 'fully' come; therefore, He had to become inconspicuous until that time arrived (Jn. 7:3 – 13). It is interesting that when He did make His presence known, showing an outstanding knowledge of the scriptures even though He had 'never studied' during His earthly life (Jn. 7:15), the authorities could not arrest Him as they had wanted to because God's power prevented them from doing so. God's power was so much greater than theirs (Jn. 7:30).

It is important for us to realise how the service of Holy Communion that we celebrate in churches became a continuation of the Passover Meal. As the time of the Passover drew near, when His body would be sacrificed as the Lamb of God, He had made arrangements in preparation for His last Passover meal with His disciples (Lk. 22:7 – 14). With Judas having received the blood money for his betrayal of the Messiah, but not knowing anything about the arrangements for the last celebration of the Passover meal, which prevented him from alerting the authorities too early, the final Passover was celebrated by the host, the Messiah, and His disciples. After His death no Passover celebrations were appropriate.

The Messiah told His disciples it was with 'fervent desire' that He had wanted to celebrate this particular Passover with them before His death because it was to be the transforming Passover that introduced the New Covenant and the celebration of His death until He comes. Just as the celebration of the Passover reminded the people of the death of a lamb that saved their first born from death and triggered the release of the nation from slavery in Egypt, so this new meal of bread and wine would enable adherents to celebrate His death, and in consequence the new covenant of salvation which released them from the slavery of sin and the world, until He comes again to call the saved into the place He has gone to prepare for them (Jn. 14:1 – 3) in the spiritual realm of His Father (Lk. 22:15 – 20; 1 Cor. 11:23 – 26).

As He was to be the final and far more glorious Pascal Lamb, at that meal he was not able 'to eat of the (final part of the) Passover meal until it is fulfilled in the kingdom of God' (Lk.22:16), because the final part was for us to remember His death through the sacrifice of His body, represented by the bread, and the shedding of His blood, represented by the wine – redemption, that was shortly to take place[91]. What was to be fulfilled was eternal salvation through His death on the cross; salvation that was open to all who wanted to accept it.

The Passover, celebrated to this day by observant Jews who do not accept that the Messiah has already come in Jehoshua, is called the Haggadah. It is a symbolic meal with a narrative, interspersed with quotations from the first testament, which explain why they celebrate the Passover. The purpose of the meal was to remind those well-versed in this celebration, and for them to give instructions to the young and newly observant participants regarding what had happened in Egypt that had turned the twelve tribes into a nation and released them from slavery. All males involved in the celebration had to be circumcised.

During the celebration four cups of wine were provided. The first three were all to do with the celebration of the remembrance of God's mighty action in Egypt that brought about their release from bondage. The fourth

---

[91] For a more in depth explanation see my book A Fresh Look At Easter

cup of wine had been introduced, at some stage in their history, as part of a desire to look ahead towards the Passover meals of the future, and the redemption that was to come. It became the belief amongst Jews that at a Passover in the future the undying prophet Elijah the Tishbite, who had been taken up to heaven in a fiery chariot, would come again as the messenger of God to announce the arrival of the long-anticipated Messiah.

As we have already discovered, John had already come in the spirit of Elijah, but not as Elijah, to do exactly that, but they are unwilling to understand this fact. John was not Elijah, for he was born normally to a childless couple.

In Luke 22 verses 17 and 18 we read that the Messiah took the third cup of the Passover meal, the cup of redemption, and blessed it and pronounced the end of the Passover celebration as they had known it from their youth. *For I say to you I will not drink again of the fruit of the vine until the kingdom of God come*". He then took the unleavened bread, gave thanks and broke it and gave it to them saying, *This is My body given for you; do this in remembrance of Me* (v19). This was the body He willingly offered up to be slaughtered on the cruel cross, the altar of sacrifice.

As blood represents the life of the flesh to God (Gen. 9:4), it was given for atonement (Lev. 17:10). The blood of the Saviour represented the out-flowing of His human life. Therefore, as the Messiah took the third cup, called the cup of redemption, He said, *"This cup is the new covenant in My blood ..."* (v20), and through Paul we are told that, *as often as you eat this bread and drink this cup, you proclaim the Lord's death until He comes* (1 Cor. 11:26). This means that just as the Jews were told to remember the Passover annually because of the freedom they received through the power of God unto salvation, so we are asked to remember the Lord's death and the eternal salvation available to us which is implicit within that selfless act of surrendering Himself to die on the cross and to rise again on the third day.

It is important, therefore, that we differentiate between the Passover lamb that was forcibly sacrificed, and the perfect Passover Lamb who offered Himself as the eternal sacrifice (Heb. 9:14). It was that offering of Himself and who He was which transformed His death into the New Covenant in His blood that entirely replaced the now Old Covenant God had made with the Children of Israel on Mount Sinai through Moses, for the Messiah is greater than Moses. This made the claims of the priests, scribes and Pharisees to be the disciples of Moses so tragically pathetic (Jn. 9:28).

The Messiah not only brought to the attention of the disciples the fact of His forthcoming death, but also their need to be humble in His service by taking on the role of the lowest servant in the house to the extent of washing their feet (Jn. 13:1 - 20; cf. Lk. 22:23 – 27). However, knowing that His death was imminent and knowing about the horrors of the tortuous death by which He was to die, the insults and degradation He was to face and the treatment He was to receive from the leaders of His own chosen people, He, in His human form, was understandably deeply troubled as He sought peace and quiet in the Garden of Gethsemane the night before His crucifixion.

It was natural for Him to pray that the horrendous cup that was before Him to drink be taken from Him, but He also knew that was why He was in the world; He had to face what He had been expecting since the start of His ministry, and which was now almost upon Him, in order to do not His own will, but the will of His Father who had sent Him. This did not lessen the horrors He knew He had personally to face (Jn. 13:21; Lk. 22:39 – 46). The time had now come when He had to voluntarily offer Himself up for sacrifice.

Having been thwarted in his attempt to kill the Messiah when he was a baby, Satan saw his next hope in killing the Messiah as a man, cutting Him off in His prime through the betrayal of Judas Iscariot. It is clear that truth is not a subject Satan knows too much about, for he had no idea of the substance of God's plan of salvation or how imminent was his own final sentencing. This ignorance of the things of God is a state in which far too many people have found themselves over the history of mankind, as we have discovered.

The focus of Judas Iscariot was not wholeheartedly on committing himself to the Messiah and learning from Him the words of the Father. Rather, it was to try and manipulate the Messiah and get Him to do what he wanted Him to accomplish in his personal very restrictive desire for the future of Israel. Thus, Satan was able to entice that troubled young man, Judas Iscariot, into betraying his Master secretly, so that the arrest could be made away from the public eye because the authorities were not able, in the normal course of events, to convince the general population that He was worthy of death. The Lord knew exactly what was going to happen and even identified His betrayer at the Passover meal; but He did nothing about it because the time of His death had come.

The authorities had a healthy respect for the man so many in Israel worshipped as the Messiah because of the miracles He had performed, miracles that should have alerted them to who He was. This uncertainty of what He might do when they seized Him is the reason they sent such a large force of soldiers to arrest Him. Apart from the unfortunate effect of Peter's untrained use of a sword, all went smoothly for the authorities, causing the disciples, who thought that their dream of a new future for Israel under the rule of the Messiah had suddenly come to an end, to flee just as the Messiah had prophesied (Mk. 14:27; cf. Zech. 13:7b).

It was a moment of testing that they would look back on with shame, but it was a natural reaction at a time of intense spiritual and emotional activity. They had previously been told by the Messiah that all of them would be made to stumble, according to a prophecy given by Zechariah which said that when the shepherd was struck, the sheep of the flock would be scattered (Matt. 26:31). The teaching they had received, however, coupled with the work of the Holy Spirit in their lives meant that the sheep would once again be brought together in order for them to receive further teaching and instructions for their future work.

The way the Messiah prepared His disciples for the traumatic events that were to see Him tried, convicted and murdered on the cross was crucial to their future service when they witnessed it happening as He had foretold; after all they were the future messengers that He wanted to send out with the message of salvation which they were to broadcast around the known world. The timing of these events was crucial. The now well-established Roman Empire had made travel around the then-known world relatively easy through the road systems, and reasonably secure through the army bases scattered throughout the empire.

> *"A little while, and you will not see me;*
> *And again a little while and you will see me,*
> *Because I go to the Father".*
> *(Jn. 16:16)*

The Messiah had impressed upon them the important message that what was about to happen was not the end but the beginning of something new. He was to die at the hands of evil men, but they would see Him again because death had no power to hold Him. Their present circumstances may have seemed to be dire, but the disciples, and those who had faithfully followed Him through both the joyous and the difficult times, had to look beyond the immediate and into the future. The Messiah Himself had come from the Father into the world, and was now on His way back to the Father (Jn. 16:28). This meant that, what he was establishing was a continuing process of which they had now become an essential part.

The Messiah needed to bring them a message of comfort just before the cruel and intensely upsetting events started that He knew would soon be upon them. The atmosphere would dramatically change in the frightening and mentally draining pressure of the spiritually charged turmoil that would soon envelop the whole of Jerusalem and the surrounding area.

"I am the true vine and My Father is the vinedresser", the Messiah told them, *"every branch that does not bear fruit He takes away; and every branch that does bear fruit He prunes that it may bear even more fruit"* (Jn. 15:1, 2). The underlying message that the Messiah was trying to give His disciples was that their relationship with Him was to change dramatically.

Yes, He was to leave them, but the word that He had spoken to them in their period of training had made them clean, the laver, was filled with water cleansed by the presence of the word made flesh, giving them access to the Tent of the Meeting, in particular the Most holy place, which, unbeknown to them at that moment, was to become their individual bodies for the Holy Spirit was to be transferred from the Most Holy Place in the temple to their bodies. They were to be the light in a dark world, just as the candelabra was in the Holy Place, to remain in the presence of God, just like the bread on the table of showbread, and establish a pattern of prayer with their Messiah, just as He had done with His Father, represented by the altar of incense.

He told them to abide in Him, which had to be of a spiritual nature because of His physical absence. Therefore, just as He had inspired and directed them when He was present with them, so through an intimate spiritual relationship that was to be developed between Him and them on His death through the baptism of the Holy Spirit, they were to experience an abiding presence and relationship with Him that would enable them to bear fruit in the future.

Just as God had endeavoured, throughout their history, to instruct the people of Israel in spiritual things so that they could develop a spiritual sensitivity and relationship with Him that would lead them into a deeper and far more meaningful and relevant relationship with Him, so now the time had come to take that spiritual relationship and experience in trusting Him a stage further, as, the prophets had done, but with the new gospel of salvation of the Messiah. They were to preach and teach the message of salvation through the shed blood of the Messiah Jews and Gentiles alike. Unlike the prophets of old they were teaching this new gospel, not prophetic words, but the message of salvation that would immediately connect those willing to accept their message directly with God so that they could go and do likewise; passing on the news of the gospel of salvation to others, thus creating the ripple effect.

The uniqueness of the holy of holies within the Tent of the Meeting was emphasised by the severe penalties that would have been incurred by the high priest if he did not prepare himself strictly according to God's instructions for a meeting with God on the Day of Atonement each year. The possibility of death was ever present during the high priest's visit to that room because of the awesome nature of God and the dire state of man. However, over time the importance of the holy of holies had been steadily downgraded with the disappearance of the Ark of the Covenant and the Mercy Seat which provided the Ark with its lid and the holy of holies with its true purpose.

It is clear that the first covenant was a temporary measure to give time for God to reveal His plan of salvation to a nation biased to unbelief. The working of the services in the Tent of the Meeting and its enclosing compound relied on fallen man to strictly obey the rules laid out by God which, because of his immature spiritual development, were mostly a mystery to him.

There were the exceptions, such as Moses, Samuel and David, who led more devoted lives than most. The history of Israel, interwoven as it is with clear evidence of God's loving involvement, revealed the intrinsic waywardness of the nation in general caused by inherited sin coupled with a potentially weak faith that succeeded or failed according to the prevailing conditions.

"If", wrote the writer to the Hebrews, *"the first covenant had been faultless then there would have been no need for a second"* (Heb. 8:7 – 13). Spiritual development was the key element of God's training programme for the Jews to prepare themselves for the arrival and teaching of the Messiah. Unfortunately, those involved in the leadership of the people, particularly the supposedly 'spiritual' priests, scribes and Pharisees, were ignorant of such things, being focused on the earthly and physical things as the witness of Nicodemus so clearly indicated (Jn. 3:1 – 17).

The first temptation illustrates the essential nature of the Messiah's ministry against the teaching of the evil one who had had such a major success over the years in weaning the religious elite away from the spiritual things of God. The reaction of those investigating the miraculous healing of the blind man thought they were in possession of all knowledge in the things of God (Jn. 9:24, 34). The message of the Messiah warned them of their error, *"If you were blind, you would have no sin, but because you are telling people, and believe within yourselves, that you see your sin remains ..."* for it demonstrated that they were not seeking after the things of God and were therefore spiritually blind; they were not asking God to reveal Himself to them so that they could see spiritual things and thereby be drawn close to Him.

Rather they preferred to believe that of themselves they were knowledgeable and fluent in the things of God, thus completely severing themselves from any chance of God influencing their thoughts (Jn. 9:41). Intellectually, through their scholarly pursuits, they were at the top of their chosen profession, but their profession should have been spiritual, not confined to learning using the abilities of the mind. Their studies should have been mainly focused on the Word itself, in self-study and a self-seeking after the knowledge of God, not learning what others had written and considered important and agreeing with the accepted doctrine of the day.

Sadly, the de-spiritualising influence of Satan has impregnated many of the so-called ordained clergy of the Western Christian Church of all denominations, just as he had with the so-called religious elite of Israel at the time of the Messiah.

The Servant Messiah

The apostate church, which is the product of the steady corruption of the true message of Christ, is already alive and flourishing in villages, towns, cities, and nations, led by the pioneering and vociferous wolves Paul warned the Ephesians about. These include the liberal-minded students of the word. True believers often find it hard to challenge such people who seek devious means to get their own way and publicise their own teaching, using those imprisoned by apathy to get their own way. Consider the challenges to the congregations of the churches identified in Revelation chapters 2 and 3.

It is no wonder then that the Jewish leaders could not understand anything of the teaching of the Messiah, but believed that He was a heretic and therefore believed it was their responsibility to silence Him, ignorantly warring not against an enemy of God, but against God Himself (Acts 5:33 – 42). The introduction of the new covenant by the Messiah, privately in that upper room with His disciples, was in stark contrast to the introduction of the previous covenant before all the people at the base of Mount Sinai, with the presence of God evidenced on the mountain top by the dramatic environmental activity on the summit. Faith in God had changed from being the faith of the nation in the God who had chosen them, to the faith of individuals who were prepared to believe God, and personally worship Him in spirit and in truth. (Jn. 4:21 – 24; cf. Matt. 18:20; 2 Cor. 3:12 – 18) Of such is the kingdom of God.

The new covenant that the Lord would establish with His people was to involve individuals who were not dependent on the authority of the priestly tribe of Levi, for the new covenant would be directly between the Lord and all those individuals who were willing to respond to Him (Ro. 9:6 – 8). They were, as living spiritual stones to be built together to become a spiritual house for God (Eph. 2:19 – 22; 1 Peter 2:4, 5), in place of the temple in Jerusalem, and a holy priesthood appointed by God to offer up not animal sacrifices, but spiritual sacrifices; this was to be firstly the giving of themselves completely to God, for we cannot give anything of worth to God unless we have first given of ourselves completely and unconditionally to Him; only then can we offer praise and worship to God for we are no longer seeking after the temple in which to serve God, for we are the temple in which God dwells if indeed the Holy Spirit of God dwells in us. That is what the word temple means, the dwelling place of God (1 Pet. 2:1 – 5; Eph. 2:19 – 22; Rev. 1:5, 6).

It is clear that God knows those who will respond to Him, as with Jacob and Esau, so although the offer of salvation is open to all, and it is an entirely individual choice, there are those who will be more likely to believe than others (Act 2:39; 13:48).

Only in the case of an individual who possesses a responsive attitude to

God is the Lord able to write His laws in their minds and on their hearts (Lk. 18:9 – 14), for the working out of a covenant requires the willing commitment of two people: God and the individual (Jer. 31:31 – 34). Only those who owned a pure and willing heart were able to experience forgiveness at the altar of sacrifice in the compound of the Tent of the Meeting (Is. 1). This changed relationship between the individual and their God allowed them to progress to the laver to obtain a full understanding of the salvation that they had received through the tutoring work of the Holy Spirit in the word of God. Only then was the door into the Tent of the Meeting and the close presence of God available to them.

Although, spiritually, believers can have confidence to enter the most holy place, which is now in heaven, by the blood of the Messiah, because we have all become priests to our God (Heb. 10:19 – 20; 1 Pet. 2:4 – 10), we will not actually enter into it until we are clothed with our new incorruptible bodies. The reason the Messiah is described as the first-born from the dead is because He alone received an incorruptible body whilst in the grave and entered heaven as He ascended through the clouds.

We will have to wait, as we shall see in the next chapter, for from our physical death, although some will be living at the time of the second coming, we will enter a time of sleep (1 Cor. 15:51) until the time of the Messiah's second coming. The throne room of heaven, the heavenly Holy of Holies will only be available to those who are saved to the uttermost when they pass from this corruption to incorruption at the time of the second coming of the Messiah (1 Cor. 15:46 – 58). Only when all have passed before the Judgement Seat of Christ will access to the New Jerusalem and the immediate presence of God be available to us.

The veil of the temple, which was far more than a man's height, had separated the holy of holies, where God met man on earth, from the holy place, where the priests ministered daily, within the temple itself from the beginning. On the death of the testator of the new covenant, the Son of God/Son of Man, that veil was torn in two from top to bottom for it was an act of God. This one action removed the uniqueness of this room as the sole meeting place of man with his God.

The new high priest became the true spiritual head not just of Israel, but of the Church of Israel, which was populated first by Jewish believers in their Messiah, followed by all believers in the Messiah, and established Himself not in an earthly temple, as had happened with the priests of Aaron at the consecration of both the tent in the wilderness and the temple of Solomon, but in heaven where He went to be with His Father, and where the original holy of holies is situated. This is our final destination when we will be with the Messiah for eternity (Rev. 22:3 – 5).

In this way was a new, non-earthly, relationship introduced where man met with his God in a spiritual sense continually, moment by moment, through the sending of the Holy Spirit into the world by the Messiah (Jn. 14:26). Gone was the man-made physical structure of the temple with its ordained priests. In its place was the person of the man and woman, within their human frame, who willingly received the Holy Spirit witnessing with their spirit.

Previously the cloud had come down on the Tent of the Meeting at its dedication; the Shekinah glory had entered the temple of Solomon at its dedication, driving out the priests from the building. But how was God going to demonstrate His dedication of the millions of Tents of the Meeting that would replace the Herodian temple soon to be destroyed? The first to receive the in-dwelling Holy Spirit as individual believers were the disciples who had tongues of fire appear above each of them as the Holy Spirit entered into them.

For the Messiah it had been the dove of peace which signalled that He was united with the Holy Spirit in His earthly form, although the Spirit is unlikely to have been far from Him during His human growth from babe to adult. When the time of His ministry had come, the full power possessed by the Holy Spirit entered into Him without measure so that the Messiah could display the power of God as He did at the time of the creation (Jn. 3:33 – 36).

Although He was going to be absent from them in physical form, the Messiah insisted that the disciples should not allow their sorrow at this prospect to retain a hold on them, for His departure brought with it an advantage to them which they would not at first understand. Providing they were prepared to obey the commandments He had taught them, which were not grievous (1 Jn. 5:3), they would naturally abide in Him and His love, just as He had been abiding in the love of His Father through His obedience to the commands of His Father which had enabled Him to remain in the Father's love throughout His ministry. This is the example we must all follow.

But how strange it must have seemed to them for their Messiah, in whom they had invested so much faith, to one minute warn them of His imminent departure, which would completely disrupt their lives and destroy the dreams they had originally entertained of a new and glorious time for their country, and the next tell them the reason He was telling them about it was so that His joy may remain and that their joy might be full!

How could they possibly understand that His departure would herald a completely new and far greater relationship with Him and His Father, and bring an exciting purpose to their lives? Their heavy hearts, compounded by the spiritually charged atmosphere in which they were living at that time, did nothing to encourage them, but then they were not yet in possession of the encouraging and uplifting power of the Holy Spirit.

Love was the key to their future. The Messiah told them that *Greater love has no one than this, than for a Man to lay down his life for his friends* (Jn. 15:13). It would take them time to fully realise the importance of all that He was telling them. He knew what was going to happen. All He could do in preparation was to warn them of what was to come, emphasising the love they must by then have known He had for them, so that during the emotional and spiritual turmoil that would ensue, which would see them scattered and lead to Peter's dramatic and emphatic threefold denial, their underlying knowledge of being loved by God would protect their still fragile and childlike faith to provide an anchor and some stability for them in the impending spiritual storm (Matt. 26:31).

To sustain them after His departure, not only was He going to provide them with a comforter, but the comforter He was to send them was to be none other than the Holy Spirit, the third member of the trinity. He had worked with and within the Messiah Himself to ensure the work the Father had instructed Him to do was done, and the message He was to give to His own chosen people was delivered in such a way that not only would those who saw and heard Him, and were receptive to His teaching, more fully understand His message, but so also would those, like us, who were to follow and were receptive to His message be able to understand more fully the person and power and, most importantly, the intense love God (Jn. 15:9; 17:20 – 26) has for all those who were born of Adam. As far as the disciples were concerned, they were to love and support each other just as He had loved and supported them, no matter how difficult at times that might seem to be.

Just as the Holy Spirit provided an essential service to the Messiah, particularly in telling Him of the heart-thoughts of those around Him and being the power to still the storm (Gen. 1:2), so that same Holy Spirit would do a number of things through them. Far from being a consolation prize, the Messiah told them that it was to their advantage that He should leave them, because he was walking a path, as the perfect Lamb of God, along which they could not follow.

By the giving of Himself to those whose only desire was to murder Him, and by dying in man's place for the sins of mankind, the disciples and all believers would receive eternal salvation. By rising again, He would signal complete mastery over death which would enable them to rise spiritually after death, ready for their entry into heaven and the place He was going to prepare for them (Jn. 14:1 – 3).

If the Messiah did not complete the task the Father had given to Him and return to heaven where He had been before His human birth (Jn. 17:24), the Holy Spirit could not have been released into the world to provide them with inspirational spiritual support in the ministry into which the Messiah was commissioning them (Matt. 28:18 – 20). Whilst the Messiah was alive on earth, the prince of the power of the air focused the attention of all those who did not have a heart for God, as Abel had had, on total hatred for His person because love and salvation had no part in Satan's world.

When the Messiah had completed His work in successfully fulfilling God's plan of salvation, thereby securing a way back to God for all those willing to find it and walk that way (Matt. 7:13), He would leave them to return to His Father. They would then be exposed to Satan's anger, particularly as he had lost the battle at Calvary, and would therefore be the target for the hatred he inspired in men's hearts to the things of God, even those whose outward show suggested that they were God-fearing people, such as the leaders of synagogues and other 'spiritual' leaders (Jn.16:1 – 4).

For example, the Holy Spirit would:

❖ Convict the world of sin, because of its unbelief. As all sin is based on unbelief (Acts 20:27 – 31), the Spirit's task is to direct man's thoughts to the person and message of the Messiah (Jn. 16:13, 14).

❖ Convict the world of righteousness, for those who passed by the place of crucifixion blasphemed Him (Matt. 27:39 – 43), quoting Him out of context concerning the rebuilding of the temple in three days, which we know to be His body. It is unlikely that the Lord was crucified on an isolated hill as some have imagined because it is said He was crucified just outside the city wall. Therefore, the crucifixion was most likely to have happened at the side of a busy thoroughfare just outside old city wall of Jerusalem which we know was built on a hill, possibly quite near to an entrance gate (Matt. 27:39).

Sadly, the leaders and scholars who missed the signs of His birth, and misunderstood His message by announcing to those witnessing this event that although He saved others, He seemed incapable of saving Himself, looked very silly because the evidence clearly showed they were empty vessels calling out in complete ignorance. How sad it was that because of their ignorance of spiritual truth they could not 'see' that He was fulfilling what had been illustrated in the design of the tabernacle of Moses and spoken about by the prophets, and all that we have been learning about in these pages.

The scriptures tell us that all have sinned and fallen short of the glory of God, steeped in unrighteousness and maintaining hearts full of rebellion against God. Surely this act of murder and the verbal hatred directed to Him as He suffered in the place of those whose voices were raised against Him, clearly illustrates for us just how volatile man in slavery to Satan is towards the righteousness of God.

The final act of rebellion by the priests and 'spiritual leaders', concerned His resurrection. The question they faced, not realising that it was Satan's problem they were seeking to solve, was how could they confuse the people concerning the fact of His resurrection, which they were not prepared to accept as a spiritual act of God?

Their plan was to announce that the disciples had stolen the body of this troublesome man to feign His resurrection. It is in this way that even in the 21st century so many observant Jews have not been able to accept Jehoshua as their Messiah, even though centuries after the prophetically promised coming of the Messiah they are still with patience waiting for it to happen.

In this way the servants of Satan have sought to undermine the message of God concerning His Son and the eternal salvation that is on offer to us (Matt. 27:62 – 65; 28:11 – 15). The Spirit of Truth the disciples were to receive would provide them with the words to counter these lies, just as He is able to assist us today, and just as He has enabled me to write this book, for it is only by the Inspiration of the Holy Spirit that I have been able to write all that you have been reading. But one day the people of Israel will also realise who it was who died all those years ago so that the time of the Gentiles will give way to the enlightenment of Israel.

❖ Convict the world of judgement, for by rejecting God and the salvation the Saviour of the world offers all mankind, people remain under the curse issued to Adam after his rebellion; that because of his sin he would surely die. Only the price paid in blood by the Saviour can remove that judgement from individuals.

Having done all He could to encourage those the Father had given to Him (Jn. 17), He knew that what He had come to do, had been accomplished. It is finished!

Spiritually we are regenerated people to the degree that we allow God to regenerate the spirit within us. There are some who do not seek after God in order that they might grow spiritually in Him and therefore their spiritual relationship with God is of an immature type, mere babes in Christ, even though our Lord has provided us with every opportunity to be completely united spiritually with Him, which is what regeneration is all about. It is up to each of us individually how spiritually involved we are with our Saviour and to what extent the Holy Spirit gets involved in our lives. If we are happy with just being saved and staying as immature babes in Christ then so be it (Heb. 5:12 – 14).

However, at the other end of the spectrum, if we have within us a desire to be continually growing in the Spirit, a continual hunger for an ever-greater spiritual intimacy with God, then God will continually draw us closer to Himself through the work of His Holy Spirit. As one having a consistently increasing spiritual hunger for the presence of God, although far from being mature in spiritual things, I have, several times now, experienced the presence of demonic forces in my house which have brought me to wakefulness in the darkness of the night and clearly indicated to me that my desire for God is not appreciated by Satan and his forces of evil.

During those times I had to ask God to apply the cleansing power of the blood of Christ to me and my family before ordering Satan and his forces out of the house in the supreme name of Jesus. The unnerving physical effects of these events made it difficult at times to focus the mind on what I had to do, but there was sufficient spiritual strength within me to demand the departure of whomever, whatever was taking up spiritual room within my house. Because of the authority we have in Christ Jesus over the evil one, 'they' left and I regained sufficient peace in my spirit to be able to go back to sleep. On one occasion it took nearly an hour to do it.

It is impossible for us to imagine the increasing physical and spiritual pressures on the Messiah in first the days and then the hours leading up to His arrest, particularly as He tried to tell His disciples about what was soon going to happen. First there was the realisation within His mind and Spirit of the physical and spiritual trauma He would have to endure when He set aside the authority He had had over events during His ministry, calling on the power of the Holy Spirit to save Him from those attempting to harm Him before His time had come.

As the time for the final events of His earthly life began to unfold, He would have been increasingly aware of the build-up of the spiritual forces of evil and their impact on the Jewish leadership, much of which represented the physical arm of Satan's loyal forces. The population would have known that something was going on by the charged atmosphere, particularly within Jerusalem, but were divided in their understanding; possibly believing within themselves one thing concerning just who this thirty-three year old man was, but being told quite another by the religious elite.

Satan was determined not to fail this time, not realising that his 'victory' would be stolen from him when he realised too late that he had helped seal his own death. Here were God and Satan battling it out on the earth that Satan considered his domain. It was a battle he could not win because of the Messiah's focus on finishing the work God had entrusted into His hands, with the encouragement and empowerment of the Holy Spirit who would enable Him to give up His human life before any bone in his body would have had to be broken to enforce His early death (Ps. 34:20).

The Father had to turn His back on His Son for He is unable to look upon evil. Therefore, it was left to the Son, who through the Eternal Spirit offered Himself without spot to God on the cross, so that together the Son, ably assisted by the Holy Spirit, ensured that what happened on the cross was according to the prophetic plan laid out in the Hebrew scriptures (Heb. 9:14).

One point worth considering is the response of the Messiah to the high priest and the reaction of his officials. The high priest asked the Messiah, who he did not realise was the Messiah, about His disciples and His doctrine. The Messiah asked the high priest why he had asked Him such a question when he should be asking those who had heard Him teach openly. When one of the officers of the guard struck the Messiah He challenged the officer over his action (Jn. 18:22, 23). How different to the response of Paul to being struck, (Acts 23:1 – 5) which shows the difference between the Master and the servant.

Finding men willing to give false witness concerning the Messiah, the priestly leaders were determined to secure a guilty verdict. When put under oath by the high priest, the Messiah had no option but to admit, *it is as you said. Nevertheless, I say to you, hereafter you will see the Son of Man sitting at the right hand of power, and coming on the clouds of heaven* (Matt. 26:64). To the high priest this was blatant blasphemy because he was so far removed from the God he purported to serve, having no understanding of spiritual things. The trial was a sham. Pilate was disturbed by a message from his wife advising him to have nothing to do with 'that righteous man', for she had suffered many things in a dream that day because of Him. Pilate believed it was through envy that they had handed the Messiah over to him (Matt. 27:18).

After so many failed attempts to arrest Him, the Jewish authorities were determined not to fail this time in ridding themselves of a major problem to their authority and dominant control of the people. Stoking up the desire for blood amongst the crowd, now greatly increased because of the Jewish and proselyte visitors who had come from various parts of the empire and beyond to celebrate the Passover in their beloved Jerusalem, the Jewish authorities brought to fever pitch the demand for the Messiah's death, putting immense pressure on Pilate to sign His death warrant.

Even Pilate's feeble attempt to divert the crowd's obsession with the Messiah by offering them a choice between a notorious criminal, who had killed many innocent people, and the Messiah failed because of the manipulation by the Jewish authorities who claimed that they had no king but Caesar, thereby putting a pagan emperor before their God. This was undoubtedly Satan demonstrating his power over those whose spiritual life was dead.

The Servant Messiah

The scourging by the pagan soldiers would have caused the Messiah excruciating pain and sapped His human strength. The crown of thorns biting into the thin flesh of His head would have been an even more directly painful burden. But the worst pain He had to bear was the knowledge that, even though it was necessary for Him to die for the people, He had been denied by His own people and given into the hands of unbelievers, to pagans.

The cross He had to carry to His own execution, which in itself caused intense and almost unbelievable pain and suffering, in His wearied state and on a back which would have been like a ploughed field, merely added to the sense of hatred against Him that filled the atmosphere, and confirm His humanity. Knowing the events in Jerusalem that would follow His death, He warned the women who mourned and lamented His situation to weep for themselves and their children, for if the authorities could do such a thing to the spiritually living wood, what would they do to the spiritually dry and guilty 'wood' of Israel (Lk. 23:27 – 31). To put it another way if the fire of judgement tested the living wood that resisted it, how would the fire of judgement affect the dry and lifeless wood that abounded in Israel?

The authorities may have thought at that moment that their efforts to rid themselves of an evil man had succeeded and that they were now back in control of the country and religious life, not realising the turmoil that was about to be unleashed upon them and the nation which they would be powerless to control and which would leave their nation fragmented and dispersed for almost two thousand years, and the target of their enemies for much longer.

Yes, they had their moment of triumph when the Messiah was nailed to the cross and they were able to jeer at Him suffering the curse of being hung on a tree (Deut. 21:22, 23). But such was their spiritual blindness, they could not have realised at the time that their problems were just about to start. By having the power through the Holy Spirit who was there to assist Him, the Messiah was able to end His own earthly life by releasing His Spirit from His human body, having achieved the goal of dying in the place of individuals for whom He had paid the ultimate penalty for sin. This was the culmination of God's plan of salvation, the supreme act which confirmed its successful conclusion.

In this one act, that was confirmed when, on the third day, He demonstrated once and for all His total power over life and death by rising from the dead, the Messiah overcame the powers of subjugation in the earth Satan had assumed in the beginning when Adam surrendered himself to the power of Satan.

We are told that a number of things happened when the Messiah Himself ended His human life on the cross, which prevented any bones in His body being broken, as prophesied in scripture (Ex. 12:46; Ps.34:20;

22:14 – 18; Jn. 19:31 – 37):

❖ The veil in the temple, separating the most holy place from the holy place, was torn in two from top to bottom, removing the uniqueness of that room, which was by now empty because of the disappearance of the Ark of the Covenant and the Mercy Seat at the time of the exile to Babylon when the people were directed to a spiritual relationship of the individual believer with their God.

This act of God signalled the end not only to the status of that meeting place, where the Jewish high priest alone was required to meet with God once per year on the Day of Atonement, but also of the position and authority of the Jewish high priest, the descendent of Aaron. In opening up this room God Himself decreed that there was no unique activity for the human high priest to perform any more thus sealing the end to the earthly priesthood.

Indeed, there was no further practical use for the man-built temple, a copy of that which is in heaven. The destruction of the temple by the Roman army did not cause God to immediately encourage His people to rebuild it as He had done previously through prophets such as Haggai. The old-style prophets had now been replaced by the disciples trained by the Messiah, and those chosen by Him, both Jew and Gentile, to teach and write things concerning His truth, just as I am doing here (Matt. 27:51).

❖ There was an earthquake which destroyed many graves, including those of the saints who were raised to supernaturally witness in Jerusalem to the person of the Messiah whom the people and their leaders had just killed on the cross. The events were enough to persuade the soldiers that the person they were guarding was the Son of God as He had admitted publically.

But why was it that these humble and practical soldiers could come to a realisation of who He was through these events, and not the authorities? Surely this emphasises the degree of the leaderships' spiritual blindness. Sadly, that spiritual blindness is now endemic in the Western Church today, for there have been many public challenges to the divinity and authority of the Son of Man, the Messiah to the Jews, and the meaning of His sacrifice on the cross by clergymen; even bishops (Matt. 27:51 – 54).

❖ The soldier who pierced the side of the Messiah saw blood and water[92] coming out of the wound, which proved He had died physically (Jn. 19:33 – 37).

Throughout the events of His arrest and crucifixion it is clear that the authorities had determined that the work of the Messiah should not succeed and that His ministry, and the fulfilment of prophetic utterances recorded in the first testament, should not gain any public recognition. Without realising what they were doing, as Jesus said, *they do not know what they do* – Lk. 23:34, their ultimate aim was that the successful accomplishment of God's whole plan of salvation for mankind, from its launch in the beginning to its fulfilment in the person of the Son of God, should be made ineffective.

Their denial of His divinity and accusations of blasphemy, their dismissal of the miracles He performed and their consistent and constant challenge to the teaching He had given, even though it was far superior to their own, signalled an entrenched attitude to any change in their situation, even though they purported to look for the coming of the Messiah.

But their hardness of heart towards the things of God was clearly demonstrated in their unwillingness to investigate His birth to see if His claims of being the Son of David were true or false, and in their unwillingness to accept Him as their Messiah even though the events surrounding His birth and the miracles he performed during His ministry, clearly signalled His supernatural credentials.

These actions were all the work of unbelievers who were acting as gods just as Satan had promised Adam and Eve. However, even though man proposes, it is God who disposes, because He has the greater power to fulfil all His good pleasure. Whatever they did they could not thwart the plans of God.

It seems incredible that the authorities were not challenged by the witness they received from those they had employed to stand guard over the tomb in which He had been laid (Matt. 28:2 – 4, 11 – 15). However, such was the extent of their blindness and determination to settle this matter to their own apparent advantage that they focused not on the information they were receiving, but on how they could maintain their control over the situation as it evolved.

The lie they perpetrated at that time, through the guards, that the disciples stole His body whilst they slept is alive and well to this day in the minds of those Judaic believers who are willing to accept the teaching they receive from ordained rabbis, who are subject to concentrated learning over several years. But as we are well aware, teaching and learning is all very well but it is what we are taught, and from whom, and what and how we learn

---

[92] Suggestions for an explanation https://www.gotquestions.org/blood-water-Jesus.html

that matters. Are we to just accept what we are taught or do we need to be inquisitive enough to ensure what we are being taught is the truth through our own research, that confirms whether or not we have the right knowledge?

It is important for us to accept the teaching of our Lord who told the disciples that He had overcome the world (Jn.16:23; see also 17:12 – 19) of Satan (Jn.17:15) and men. It mattered not what the Jewish authorities did to try and nullify God's work through His Son, nor their attempts to suppress the message of salvation the disciples were inspired to broadcast, as they had been commissioned to do. (Matt. 28:18 – 20).

They were no match for the Holy Spirit with whom the disciples had been baptised after the Lord's resurrection (Acts 2:3, 4). Since that time millions have owed their salvation to the sacrificial efforts of the first Jewish believers and the Gentiles who followed them in sacrificial giving of themselves throughout the generations. If Satan, with all his powers and experience could not disrupt God's work of grace, how much less can individual men stand in God's way? Surely the dramatic increase in the Christians in China and Russia, in spite of the efforts by the authorities to crush the church, stands as an example of the power of God unto salvation.

Israel has not, nor will it ever be, abandoned by their God, as Paul teaches us in Romans chapters 9 – 11, in spite of all that the people of Israel have done to alienate God and man; all Gentile believers need to accept that fact. Although there have been many Jewish believers in their Messiah over the course of time, for there has always been a remnant who have believed because of their desire to be right with God, the time is still in the future when a greater number of the children of Israel will come to true faith and understand the truth concerning the Living God, when God will pour out the Spirit of grace and supplication (Zech. 12:10). There will come a time when the Jewish people will have their eyes opened to realise that the suffering servant, who they pierced, had to appear first before the nation could be restored to its true place in God's eternal kingdom.

The emphasis of the leaders of the Jews at the time of the Messiah, and what they wanted their Messiah to achieve, was their total freedom from occupation, being totally ignorant of their need to be first cleansed of their sinfulness. Personal dominance over physical territory, however, was not what God had taught them. The crusades were a disaster and demonstrated a total misunderstanding of the role of the believer on earth. From time-to-time various organizations have been bent on violence have had, as their sole aim, to secure territory for a particular religion, or section of the 'Christian' church. There have been and will always be those whose belief is that they are the only true chosen of God and therefore have a total right to be His army on the earth, to kill and maim according to their own judgement and desire. But God says to us, as He did to Zerubbabel, *not by might, nor by power, but by My Spirit', says the Lord of Hosts* (Zech. 4:6). Such is God's way of doing things.

Not only is God's kingdom not of this world, but neither are His people, even though they are in the world, for they have been born into that spiritual Kingdom which the Messiah came to establish on earth. This was the mountain that Nebuchadnezzar saw in his dream (Dan. 2:44), which one day will cover the whole earth but, unlike the earth, will last forever, for it is an eternal kingdom.

The question is, when they had dominance over the Promised Land and over other nations under their kings, particularly King David, were they concerned about passing on the spiritual knowledge and understanding of God, and His salvation through sacrifice, that they were supposed to enjoy?

It is certainly incumbent on all believers in the Saviour today to pass on the knowledge of salvation and the new life in God they have come to know through the indwelling of the Holy Spirit they are supposed to have experienced when they became believers, that is if indeed they allowed Holy Spirit to enter into them as He had with the Messiah (Ro. 8:9). Jesus said:

> *Therefore, whoever confesses Me before men, him I will also confess before My Father who is in heaven. But whoever denies Me [does not confess me] before men, him I will also deny [not confess] before My Father who is in heaven (Matt. 10:32, 33).*

12   HE WILL COME AGAIN

"Christ is the image of the invisible God,
The first-born over all creation.
By Him all things were created
Both in heaven and on the earth,
The visible and invisible,
Thrones, dominions, principalities and powers.
All things were created through Him and for Him.
He is before all things, and in Him all things consist.
Christ is the head of the body which is the church.
He is the first born from the dead.
In all things He is preeminent."
(See Colossians1:15 – 18)

"Be filled with the knowledge of His will,
In all wisdom and spiritual understanding;
That you may walk worthy of the Lord,
Fully pleasing Him,
Being fruitful in every good work
And increasing in the knowledge of God;
Strengthened with all might,
According to His glorious power,
For all patience, longsuffering and joy;
Giving thanks to the Father who has
Qualified us to be partakers of the
Inheritance of the saints in light.
He has delivered us from the power of darkness
And conveyed us into the kingdom
Of the Son of His love,
Through the power of His blood,
Which is the forgiveness of sin."
(See Colossians1:9b – 14)

Supremacy of Christ

As much as the Tent of the Meeting built by Moses provided the clearest illustration of God's Pan of Salvation, so the Passover, which was to be remembered annually, was the vehicle for providing the key element of that salvation; the sacrifice for sin that would one day completely release the true believer from the slavery of this sinful world. Although believers in the Messiah are in the world, they are no longer full and obedient members of it. For just as the Children of Israel were released from slavery in Egypt because of the death of the Passover lamb within their house, by the protection of the blood evident around its door, which saved the first born from death, so all those who believe on the Lord Messiah, and accept that the blood shed on the cross has the power to wash away their sin, are released from the sentence of death imposed on Adam and his offspring, freeing them from the oppression of the world.

By the sacrifice of many lambs amongst the children of Israel on that first Passover night, and their release from their slavery in Egypt through the exodus, they were introduced to the possibility of a new life with their God on the earth. By this one sacrifice the possibility of a new relationship between God and the believer was made available to all those involved. How much more by the shed blood of the Messiah has a far greater opportunity of a new life in the almighty and eternal God been provided not just for the children of Israel, but for all mankind?

We have discovered throughout our studies on the layout of the Tent of the Meeting complex that to reach the tent where men met with God, the self-confessed sinner had to enter into the kingdom of God on earth, represented by the area surrounding the Tent and enclosed by curtains of fine white linen, symbolising righteousness, with an animal sacrifice, and had to be involved in its sacrifice on the altar of sacrifice.

Since the death of the Messiah, to enter the Kingdom of God the self-confessed sinner only needs to accept the sacrifice of the Lamb of God already offered on the cross to enter the Kingdom of God. The repentant sinner on the cross alongside the Messiah was welcomed into His kingdom because of his confession. The physical altar of sacrifice has therefore been made obsolete.

We are told that the Messiah loved the church to the extent that He gave Himself for her, sanctifying and cleansing her by the washing of water by the word. Paul puts it in perspective when he asks the believers in Rome how people are able to call on God if they have not believed in Him? Equally, how shall they believe in Him if they have never heard of Him?

Surely for them to hear about Him requires a preacher, and a preacher has to be inspired and sent by God. Quoting from Isaiah he recalls, how beautiful are the feet of those who preach the gospel of peace. Not any peace however, but the peace of God which passes all understanding. These preachers of the word also bring glad tidings of good things which only become evident the more the hearer and doer of that word allows that word, through the Holy Spirit, to work its work.

The Children of Israel provide us with an example of what not to do, which we need to take to heart. Paul continues by telling the Romans that not all the Israelites obeyed the gospel that was preached, for Isaiah asked the Lord to tell him who had believed those who reported the gospel of peace, or the glad tidings of good things. Faith, says Paul, comes through hearing, and hearing by the word of God (Ro. 10:14 – 17). Paul then goes on to explain how Israel will, because of their unbelief, be provoked to jealousy because of the acceptance of that same gospel by Gentiles of many nations, not any particular one.

Surrounding the tent was an area enclosed by a curtain that separated the camp of Israel from the holy tent. The enclosing curtains of fine white linen, symbolising righteousness, were 7.5 feet high, effectively hiding the holy tent, the furniture and all the ceremonial activity in the outer court from the casual gaze of those outside. This was symbolic of the kingdom of God on earth in which the priests, who were supposed to be ministers of God, were able to go about their daily tasks.

The fact the priests failed as the spiritual leaders of their people is clear from the record of scripture. We who believe today must be in no doubt that if we fail to grasp the opportunity of the new life in Christ that is on offer to us, God will deal with each one of us in like manner. For as the remaining verses of Romans chapter 10 tell us, God is no respecter of those people who ignore His overtures to mankind.

There is no doubt that, for a time, the leaders of the Jews must have considered their efforts to silence the Messiah to have been successful. The Sabbath went ahead as usual, once His body had been removed from the cross and hidden in a cave tomb. Agreed, the veil in the temple was inexplicably torn, but the news of that event could be kept quiet, with only those immediately involved knowing what had happened. In spite of the fact that they were now obsolete and totally without meaning, the services in the temple could continue as they had done down through the centuries. On the third day there were various, curious happenings; such as an earthquake and sightings of the saints of old talking about God to the people, and the incident of the watchmen at the tomb. But nothing the leaders were unable to handle.

However, it was the persistent witnessing of those who had been the Man's disciples which caused the most irritation. On the day of Pentecost Peter spoke powerfully about the Man, Jesus of Nazareth, who had proved He was of God by the miracles He performed; indeed, such was His position before God that He was made both Lord and Messiah[93].

Being convicted of sin, the people gathered before Peter wanted to know what they had to do. Peter told them that it was necessary to be baptised in the name of the crucified Man and in so doing they would be

---

[93] anointed one – the Christ in Greek

baptised in the Holy Spirit as the disciples had been (Acts 2). Three thousand believed, giving their hearts to God, and were baptised.

It is interesting that the Jews in Alexandria in northern Egypt had the Hebrew Scriptures translated into Greek. With the death of the Messiah those same scriptures were to become far more widely available in the languages of many people around the world. With the establishment of the English language as the language of the world brought about by the progressive growth of the British empire over centuries, the movement of the Word of God gained greater freedom, as it has done to this day.

Following this remarkable event, given the previous fear of the disciples as they hid away from the reach of the authorities, there was a great rush of people wanting to hear from the disciples and to know what this new Way was all about, with five thousand more being added to the church.

This was the power of God which the Jews had declined to know anything about even when the man born blind had been brought before them, a man who had been healed of the blindness he had had from birth, by the Messiah. The man linked his healing to the fact that only someone totally in tune with God could have done such a thing, but the Jews found the whole matter beyond their comprehension and therefore contemptible and beneath them (Jn. 9:24 – 41).

Those who tried to make out that they were superior, because they considered themselves chosen of God, were ignorant of the things of God purely by their unwillingness to become different, to break out from the mould into which they had been poured as children and in which they grew up through their formative years. Strict conservatism and tradition was an imprisonment without bars and without any possibility of release; rigidly binding them to the understanding of men.

At the Gate Beautiful Peter and John healed the crippled man in the name of the crucified Messiah, later explaining to the crowd that it was through faith in the name of Jehoshua of Nazareth, whom the people and their rulers had crucified in ignorance, that this man had been healed and through no other name. The leaders found this public display of the miraculous most disturbing for it flew in the face of all their teaching and belief. Called before the Sanhedrin, the highest religious court in the land, Peter, again filled with the Holy Spirit spoke as from God (Acts 4:1 – 22).

This was what the Messiah had warned them would happen, for if the world hated Him then it would hate them also. It was because He had come and preached the truth of God, which the priests and religious elite had received from God through His word but were unable to pass on to the people because of selfish rebelliousness and spiritual blindness, that now allowed them no excuse before God for their attitude towards Him. In this way their sin was exposed. (Jn. 15:18 – 27; 9:41)

The disciples took their arrest and questioning and warning about further preaching in His name as an honour, for they were willing to suffer in that way. Indeed Peter's boldness before these rulers of the people and elders of Israel was because he was filled with the Holy Spirit, and even though he was uneducated man and untrained in the scriptures (Acts 4:13), he was able to speak with authority about things that he would not have been able to speak about otherwise. That is what the Holy Spirit was able to do then, and is still able to do even in this modern sophisticated world.

Such was the power given to the disciples to heal that people found that even by Peter's shadow passing over the sick and demon possessed that they were healed. Many who were spiritually hungry were willing to commit themselves to this new movement, not just because they saw the miraculous signs, but because they found that they were being fed spiritually by the teaching of the disciples as never before and came to believe in the Messiah through experiencing the power of the Holy Spirit. However, we must not forget that within the young church, the Holy Spirit moved to demonstrate the importance of truthfulness with the death of two deceivers, Ananias and his wife Sapphira (Acts 5).

The disruption to the life of the city worried the authorities because they had no answer to what was happening, even though it had been prophesied (Acts 2:14 – 39). Thinking with earthly minds, the authorities believed they had to find some excuse to arrest the disciples again, without causing a commotion, for they feared the people, not realising that God was at work in the city through these disciples and therefore they were unknowingly seeking to extinguish God's new work of salvation, which was now in its infancy, through the newly released power of the Holy Spirit.

The authorities wanted to persuade the disciples to stop their activities. But from the perspective of the people, if miracles were being performed that they had never seen or heard about before, except when the Messiah was preaching and teaching among them, they wanted more of it, for this work was answering their inner spiritual and daily needs which the religious elite had never been able to do because of their spiritual deadness. At a time when violence was the order of the day, here was a ministry provided by ordinary men who seemed to have gained supernatural powers; a work that did the people a great deal of good without the accompanying violence.

The leaders still did not get the message. Gamaliel, a well-respected teacher of the law who taught Saul, who was to become the apostle Paul, warned them that previous leaders, such as the man Theudas who had been recently crucified, had come and gone and their disciples had finally dispersed and nothing was heard of them again. If the authorities continued to try and suppress the teaching of these men, who continued to witness even though their leader had been killed, they might find themselves fighting not individuals, but God (Acts 5:33 – 42).

But the degree of blindness and separation of these leaders was such that when Stephen was brought before them, they were cut to the heart by what he said (Acts 6:8 – 7:60). During his defense, Stephen explained to them the spiritual nature of God. Even though Moses had been instructed to build the tabernacle followed by Solomon building the first temple, the Most High does not dwell in temples made with hands for He had made the heaven, which is His throne, and the earth, which is His footstool, and was therefore superior to both. Stephen's accusations of being stiff-necked directed at these pompous, self-opinionated men, an accusation God had directed to His people often enough through His prophets, that they were uncircumcised in heart, in direct disobedience to the instructions of their mentor Moses, punctured their pride and exposed their inner insecurity and evil minds.

So crazed had the minds of these normally upright and respected leaders been made by the obvious comparison of their godlessness and sinfulness deep within them to Stephen's true godliness and true understanding of the scriptures, that they collectively passed the sentence of death by stoning him. But they had no legal authority to pass such a sentence. It was for this very reason that they had had to get the governor Pilate to pass such a sentence on the Messiah.

Such was the crazed state of their collective minds that, probably without realising what they were doing, they led Stephen away to his execution in a totally disorderly manner, driven by the intense hatred that filled their hearts. This was the earthly-minded coming face to face with the Holy Spirit and being found wanting.

Saul became involved in fighting this new Way because of his formal training in Jerusalem under Gamaliel. Although born in Tarsus of the tribe of Benjamin and a Roman Citizen, he was sent to Jerusalem to receive formal instructions in the Jewish law. God had His hand on this fervent man in seeing to it that he received training in the scriptures that he would eventually use to write the most important foundational doctrinal documents that the Church owns. They provide the apostolic and prophetic foundations which promote the Messiah Jehoshua, Jesus Christ, as the chief corner stone, the essential ingredient in all godly and spiritual teaching (Eph. 2:19 – 22).

The new temple is not that which is built from what is dug out of the earth, but what is born spiritually. Believers are the result of God's workmanship, created in the Messiah for good works which God prepared beforehand that we should walk in them (Eph. 2:10). Most importantly, every believer is a 'living stone' just as the Messiah was the first 'living stone' which was rejected by men but made precious by God and head of the corner (1 Pet. 2:4, 5).

The need was specified by Moses for a spiritual experience through the commitment of each individual to God. They were not to rely on the act of the circumcision of men. But by each person, both male and female, willingly reaching up to God in order to be united with Him, God was able, through the spiritual work of the Holy Spirit, to circumcise the heart of each individual, for it is the heart which expresses the individual's wholehearted and willing commitment of themselves to God (Ro. 2:28, 29).

The circumcision of the body, in which the women were unable to take part, was physical and therefore of the earth and merely signified that they were a member of the Hebrews. The circumcision of the heart was altogether a different matter for it was spiritual and therefore of God and dependent on the power of God to perform it. Circumcision of the heart speaks of the willing personal consecration of the whole inner person to God which could lead them through the spiritual, saving power of God into a personal spiritual relationship with God. Gone is the earthly focus on the flesh and in comes the spiritual focus on their spiritual God.

Paul, speaking to Gentile believers, tells them that they are no longer strangers and foreigners, shunned by the isolationist Jews (Eph. 2:19). Yet it was those same Jews who had, through their hardheartedness towards God suffered much hardship over the centuries. But, because of the Gentile believers' acceptance of the salvation offered by the Jewish Messiah, they had become fellow citizens with the saints and members of the household of God.

Why the change in relationship? The Jews were still Jews and the Gentiles still not born of the seed of Abraham, Isaac or Jacob. But as we have seen a Jew is not a true Jew unless they have received the circumcision of heart which changes his relationship with Abraham from being purely physical to being both physical and spiritual.

For Gentile believers the new relationship is that we, like them, have become spiritual sons of Abraham. Through the salvation that all believers, both Jew and Gentile, have received through faith in the Messiah, we have become built on the foundation of the Apostles and Prophets because of the word we have heard and accepted.

We have all become the spiritual offspring of Abraham, and are now built on the truth of the Messiah who had become the chief corner stone of the new living church, for He became the Mediator of a better covenant, established on better promises (Heb. 8:6). Having received Him, we are all taught to walk in a manner in which we are focused on Him as the ultimate word of God, and established in the faith by being rooted and built up in Him so that we abound in that teaching in our daily lives with thanksgiving (Col. 2:6, 7).

Believers, both Jew and Gentile, are described as living spiritual stones (1 Peter 2:5) which, because of their universal love of the Messiah, coupled with the bonding of the Holy Spirit, fit comfortably together (Eph. 2:21) to grow into a spiritual and holy temple in the Lord. The whole purpose of this temple of people whose central focus and cementing force is the Lord Jehoshua is to be a spiritual temple for God. If, as individuals, we are individually temples of the Holy Spirit, then together we are the one single temple of God because we are not divided into fragmented groups by the doctrines and divergent ideas of men, but have become one by the unifying force of the Messiah through the powerful work of the Holy Spirit.

Peter had been trained to have nothing to do with Gentiles, however sympathetic to Judaism they might be. It took a vision of God to change that ingrained attitude (Acts 10). *"You know,"* says Peter to those assembled waiting to hear what he had to say, *"how unlawful it is for a Jewish man to keep company with, or go to one of another nation. But God has shown me that I should call no one common or unclean,"* admitting that for centuries the Jewish law-makers had got it so very wrong. Israel was God's vehicle to reach the rest of the world and had no business isolating themselves in that way.

On hearing the prayers of Cornelius, God had to first change the ingrained attitude of Peter before He was able to send His senior disciple to the household of Cornelius, an Italian centurion, to explain His plan of salvation.

The next challenge for Peter arose when the Holy Spirit stepped in and baptised the people present at this private gathering (Acts 10:44). Baptism by total immersion had to follow, Peter had no choice. Peter then had to explain why he went to the house of the Gentile Cornelius in the first place and what had happened there to the leading Jewish believers in Jerusalem. This was the first big lesson for these isolationist Jews; that God's gospel, as delivered by the Messiah, was for all mankind as had always been intended, not just for the Jews.

Those Jews who had recognised in Jehoshua their Messiah (consider Jn. 1:45 – 51), still had much to learn about the task God wanted them to perform. They were to present no preconditions and have no reliance on what they thought should be done, just complete trust and faith in God and a willingness to be a servant of God in the new way.

Saul had been trained in the mould of the Pharisee. Seeing the whole daily routine in Jerusalem being totally disrupted by this new teaching, he decided that firm action was necessary, so he started to imprison those who were considered deviants to the traditional Jewish way (Acts 8). Men, women and children were thrown into prison because of their belief that the crucified man was the long-awaited Messiah. With growing passion Saul asked for written permission to go to other places where this errant teaching was breaking out to try and stop it spreading. God knows us and is able to decide whose heart is changeable (Acts 9:15).

On the way to Damascus Saul met with the Messiah. One minute he was with his supporters travelling towards Damascus with an angry heart, the next he was blinded by an intensely bright light and challenged by a voice that only he fully understood regarding his personal relationship with the God of his fathers who he had so passionately worshipped but so clearly misunderstood.

The Messiah challenged him, not about the persecution of His followers, but Saul's persecution of Himself. *Why are you persecuting Me?* Any persecution against one of His followers was persecution directly against Him. What could Saul do, faced with such a charge? *What do you want me to do?* was his reply.

During the three days and nights Saul was blind in lodgings in Straight Street, Damascus, the Holy Spirit instructed him, using his vast knowledge of the Hebrew scriptures stored in his memory, to convince him that Jehoshua, Yeshua, the name of Jesus used by Jews today, of Nazareth was the Messiah. It was that personal tuition by the Holy Spirit that so convinced him that he ended this time of separation and fasting having been transformed in his thinking.

God's next problem was to persuade a reluctant Ananias to go to Saul, in spite of his reputation, and lay his hands on him. We may think we are totally surrendered to God and willing to do whatever He wants us to do, but this is not necessarily the case. God wanted to restore Saul's sight, but needed one of His servants to go and lay hands on him so that he knew there were other believers in Damascus loyal to Him, and Ananias was reluctant to put his life at risk unnecessarily (Acts 9:10 – 19).

During the three days and nights Saul had given to meditation and fasting, he was able to sort out in his mind what had happened to him, and in particular the vision of the risen Messiah whom he had thought, as he had been persuaded to think by the religious leaders of the Jews, was an imposter and blasphemer and a worthy candidate for the cross on which He had died.

A blasphemer glorified by God? Yet we read that worthy is the lamb who was slain to receive power and riches and wisdom, and strength and honour and glory and blessing; and again, blessing and honour and glory and power be given[94] to Him who sits on the throne, and to the Lamb forever and ever (Rev. 5:12, 13). But nothing is heard of those who led the cry, *"Crucify"*.

After the three days and nights of solitude, fasting and prayer, Ananias came to Saul with the words, *Brother Saul, the Lord Jesus who appeared to you on*

---

[94] God does not have problems as we understand them. However, through the centuries God has had to work round man's waywardness and lack of spiritual understanding as He seeks to use individuals in His work. In this case Ananias was not convinced in his own mind that Saul had been changed and had become a believer; therefore, God had to convince him through His authority over Ananias as a believer that it was safe for him to go to Saul. How much persuasion do you need to do a specific work for God? How sure are you that it is God speaking and do you foresee all the difficulties without being sure that God is able to overcome them all? Trusting God and living in obedience to Him is not an easy thing to do, particularly for the first time.

the road as you came, has sent me that you may receive your sight and receive the Holy Spirit. This is the work of the Holy Spirit, demonstrating to Saul the power of God and His ability to use others in His service. Immediately Saul could see; he arose and was baptised in the name of the Father and of the Son and of the Holy Spirit as prescribed by the Messiah.

God approaches every person in a unique way that is suitable to them. This one event transformed brother Saul and set him on the road of ministry to the Gentiles, proclaiming the Messiah he once denied, which ultimately led to his death in Rome. Using the learning and knowledge he had gained in the University of Jerusalem where Gamaliel was a teacher of the law, and now inspired by the Holy Spirit with whom he had been baptised, Paul was able to explain the prophetic word in great clarity to show that Jehoshua the crucified One had to be the long-awaited Messiah. This new message, delivered by a one-time opponent of the gospel of the Messiah, caused many to be saved to the uttermost and many today to come into a practical and fulfilling knowledge of the Saviour we call, using the Greek form, Jesus Christ.

God had accomplished His work in training Saul in the knowledge of the law and the prophets, allowing him to live as a Pharisee and develop that knowledge through practical application, before he was baptised in the Holy Spirit. Then, just as with the disciples, it was the Holy Spirit who brought to his mind the truth of God's plan of salvation which was hidden in the treasury of the Word of God, the first testament, that he had studied so meticulously under the greatest teacher at that time.

This was the work of the Holy Spirit, for just as He passed on instructions and encouragement from the Father to the Son and from the Son to the Father when the Messiah was on earth, so He is working in us and around us to the glory of God of whom He is part. He is the instructor and guide and the One who empowers God's people.

No matter what the authorities tried to do, God undid it. But because of their refusal to accept the truth, God saw to it that those who believed in Him, to the extent that they were willing to witness to the truth of the new gospel no matter what the personal cost, were scattered abroad, so that the Gentile nations were told that eternal salvation was offered to them also.

Jerusalem, including the temple in which the Jews had such pride, was once again destroyed by a foreign, pagan force. But even today the Jews have not been able to relate the reason for the sacking and burning of Jerusalem by Nebuchadnezzar to what happened when the Roman army did the same thing.

Thus started the work that we read about in the 'Acts of the Holy Spirit', which is a more appropriate title for the book of Acts; for in it we are told how He worked in the lives of the disciples and others, bringing to life the spiritual dimension of God's relationship with those who truly believe in

Him. This was the beginning of the spiritual work of God through the lives of men and women who aspire to spiritual things in the Lord Jesus, who have willingly been circumcised of heart as Moses taught and which has continued through the centuries and has been recorded in many books (Jn. 21:24, 25). It is they who have truly served God by distributing the good news of salvation throughout the world through His power at work in their lives.

But this continuing process is not the end but the beginning. This earth has a limited time to remain before it gives way to what is to come; and the promise of the Messiah was that He would come again. The disciples had to wait in Jerusalem for the promise of the Father concerning the baptism of the Holy Spirit, first spoken about by John the Baptizer.

Asking about the restoration of Israel, the disciples were told that it was not for them to know the plans of the Father but that they would receive power when the Holy Spirit had come upon them, elevating them to a new spiritual experience in their relationship with the trinity of Father, Son and Holy Spirit.

This was the whole purpose of their three and a half years of training with the Messiah, for now they were required to be His witnesses not just in Jerusalem, Judea and Samaria, but to the ends of the earth. They would be empowered by the indwelling Holy Spirit through whom they would be reminded of all that they had been taught throughout their lives, but particularly during their intensive training in the presence of the Messiah, Yeshua of Nazareth. It is this same Holy Spirit who can teach us the deeper truths of the gospel.

As they witnessed the ascension of their beloved Messiah rising up through the clouds, two men in white asked them why they were staring into the heavens, informing them that this same Jesus who had ascended into heaven would come again in like manner as they saw Him go into heaven, confirming what the Messiah had told them, that the Son of Man would appear in heaven, when all the tribes on earth would mourn for they would see the Son of Man coming on the clouds of heaven with power and great glory (Acts 1:10, 11; Matt. 24:30, 31).

But more than that, angels will be sent, just as they were to the shepherds at His human birth, to the sound of a great trumpet, the Shofar, as used to rally the troops for war, announcing a time of a great gathering of those who had died in the Lord from all parts of the heavens and the world. The dead, that is those who sleep in the Lord, would rise first and then those still living (1 Cor. 15:52; 1 Thes. 4:16, 17). The warning the Messiah gave was that there would be no warning of His coming, for He will come like a thief in the night, therefore we must be watchful, always abounding in the works of the Lord so that our hearts are continually in a right attitude to Him who has called us out of the world into His kingdom of light.

Secret Revelations from Heaven[95]

We are blessed in our Judeo/Christian Bible with complete end to end teaching. There is teaching covering events at the beginning of creation when everything we see around us came into being, particularly the spherical earth and the heavens in which the earth is suspended. There is also instruction concerning prophetic utterances of what is to happen at the end of the life of the earth. Finally, we have knowledge of the new creation of the heavenly Jerusalem which will be provided for those who have received God's offer of eternal salvation.

The prophetic and spiritual books of Daniel, Ezekiel and the book of Revelation are not regularly read by most Christians because these three books contain images and language that are, at times, difficult to understand. It is, however, essential that these books are not neglected for they contain important information which is for our good and encouragement.

If we accept that the word has been written as the result of the work of the Holy Spirit inspiring the writers, then we have the key to understanding the contents of these books. If the Holy Spirit was at work in the authors, surely He can be with the readers and interpret the message according to our way of thinking and degree of spiritual development. All that is required of us is that we must be of a sufficiently spiritually mature mind to be able to receive teaching from the Holy Spirit. Many can't or won't seek His teaching.

The book of Revelation was essential reading at the time that it was written because the believers were going through various degrees of persecution and needed the assurance of the continuing power and authority of the Son of God in whom they had put their faith, and in whose name they were suffering. It was just like the prophetic messages being given to us today as we experience the demise of the preaching of the true gospel in churches for a comforting gospel.

The gospels, when they appeared, provided accounts of the Messiah and His ministry that included His teaching and miraculous signs. These provided instruction for unbelievers and believers alike. The gospels were supported with the appearance of the apostles' letters which were pregnant with encouraging instruction and teaching.

The Revelation of John provided confirmation not only that the Messiah was alive, but gave warning of the tumultuous events that would occur prior to His return in glory. Encouragingly it included news of the preparation and promise of the place of His rest to which believers will eventually go to be with Him.

The truth and authority of the message John received from God needed

---

[95] For a fuller understanding of the book of Revelation please read my book "Seeing into the Future"

to be established to provide confidence amongst the readers of its reliability, particularly as some of the language was unique and the description of the creatures at times bizarre. During a time of great turmoil and with many of those who had 'been with Jesus' having been killed or having died a natural death, it was important to bring stability and authenticated instruction to the churches that had been established, particularly those in Asia Minor; an instructional message that would encourage them to look to the future with confidence however dire their personal circumstances had become. Some were to be described as having the misfortune of living where Satan was strong, causing them much grieving of spirit and a severe testing of their faith in God.

John was known to have been a disciple of Jesus and his gospel and letters had been accepted and widely read because of that knowledge. It was also the spiritual nature of the message that inspired many. When he published these revelations after his return from Patmos, they were also accepted as authentic by the church leaders of the time.

The fact that the Bible as we know it starts with Genesis, which informs us of the creation of all that we see around us, and ends with the Revelation given by God to John, that informs us of the things that will happen in the future, including the eternal death of Satan and the appearance of the new Jerusalem, makes the Bible a complete whole.

The Jews had been established for thousands of years and their policy, in obedience to the instructions God had given them, of teaching their children the tenets and historical foundational truths of their faith from the earliest age, along with the overriding love and protection of God, ensured their uniqueness and continued presence and cohesiveness as a people even during the times they were deprived of a homeland.

The new believers in Jesus were not all Jews, although Jews initially dominated the new church of 'The Way' established after the death of the Messiah. The danger came when a greater number of Gentiles were converting to this new message and giving their hearts to the Lord Jesus. In the expanding church the Jews were gradually outnumbered by Gentiles.

Thus the 'time of the Gentiles' (Lk. 21:24) was brought in; but the Gentiles, did not have, and still do not have, the knowledge, or the accumulated baggage of Judaism and the Law to help them. One Jew told me that the heavy duty theology of my books helped him overcome Judaism, for to a Jew there is no theology as God is unknowable because Judaism is the history of God. Unfortunately this lack of continuity enjoyed by the Jewish believers caused decisions to be made that had the potential to lead the Gentile converts away from the truth, which is why Paul had to write to the believers in Rome, from which city most of the Jews had been expelled by an emperor, to inform them that God had not abandoned the Jews (Ro. 9 – 11) but was giving the Gentiles the opportunity to get to know and accept the salvation originally offered, and still on offer to the Jews before the Jews themselves would come to realise the truth of His visitation and finally accept Him as their long awaited Messiah. It was also at this time that the animosity of the Jews towards this new Way, as they called it, became a real threat to the church.

There was the danger that the new leaders of the church, who were without the years of training and knowledge that has since been accumulated, would concentrate on the present. With their vision deflected from the spiritual to earthly things in trying to establish themselves in the growing church organization, which happened, there was the potential for them to lose their spiritual way and thus wander away from the truth that had been given to them at such great expense by the original Jewish believers (see 2 Cor. 11). The apostle Paul himself had been no stranger to hardships, torture and imprisonment.

What many experienced in the early years of the church, and even today, was a true conversion with a spiritual rebirth but, like the seeds that did not fall onto fallow ground, the cares of this world, or the dryness of the teaching or a lack of understanding during personal studies of the scriptures or Satan removing the seed from their hearts, many quickly became carnal Christians — Christians of the flesh.

The key passage regarding the carnal believer is Paul's letter to the Romans and chapter eight where he explains that the carnal mind is one where the person lives according to the flesh, whereas the spiritual believer lives according to the Spirit. The test is whether or not the Spirit of God dwells in the believer and each believer can only be sure of that by the Holy Spirit distinctively witnessing with their spirit that they are children of Go. (Ro. 8:4 – 17) .Only then can we say, *I know whom I have believed* (2 Tim. 1:12) and just as Paul knew of a certainty that God was with him through the witnessing of the Holy Spirit with his spirit, so do I!

Paul accused the Corinthians of still being of a carnal mind because of the envy and strife that was among them. Their focus was not on the things of the Spirit but the flesh; that is, what they saw and felt within their fleshly vision (1 Cor. 3:3). Therefore, even though they were supposed to have been converted and been born again in the Spirit, the reality was that that conversion did not result in a Spirit-filled life because, like Rachel, their hearts were never united with God but remained with the things of the earth and its gods.

Be in no doubt whatsoever that our walk with God is not dependent upon God alone! For just as the Children of Israel went astray in spite of all the miraculous events they experienced and the blessings God had showered upon them, so believers of today are quite capable of going astray and walking out of the will of God.

What Paul wrote to the Philippians concerning God's work in the believer that *He who has begun a good work in you will complete it* (Phil. 1:6) only refers to those who intend to give God their full mental and spiritual attention and serve Him alone, allowing Him to train them to be His true disciples. Just as the decision to seek for and receive His salvation is up to us — our freewill, so is the continuing of that process into a full Holy Spirit based marriage to God through Christ Jesus our Lord.

It is known that some 'Christians' have been 'converted' to Buddhism and Islam and other religions, thus denying all faith in the saving power of God through the shed blood of the Messiah which means that the gospel message had no deep effect on them.

It was to ensure that the increasingly scattered population of believers were given a focus on the future, and to establish the fact that although He had risen from the dead and ascended into heaven, Jesus Himself was alive and well, that the Revelation was given to John. Jesus was in glory with His Father and the triune God was in control of events; all the believers had to do was to be firm in their belief, to be attuned to God speaking to them and to overcome all problems and adverse circumstances through the power of His Spirit within them.

A Revelation from Whom? (vs. 1 – 4)

It was John who told the believers to test the spirits (1Jn. 4:1 – 6), therefore at the beginning of his record of the revelation he received from the Lord Jesus are the credentials of the source of that revelation. It was a revelation given by the Son, which He had received from the Father, concerning things that must shortly take place that was passed on to John by an angel or, to put it another way, information regarding things that would soon take place was given by the Father to the Son who passed it on to John via an angel.

To confirm the truth of this significant revelation, John says that he bore witness to the fact that what he received was the word of God and the testimony of Jesus Christ and everything he saw was truth. His reputation for being particularly close to the Messiah during His three and a half years of ministry and that the Messiah loved John, just as Jacob loved Joseph because they were of like mind, provided sufficient assurance for the believers of the time, and for us today, that what John wrote IS TRUTH in its absolute sense.

Many have tried to downplay this book as being too difficult or too open to various interpretations to be of much value. But John is quick to say that those who were able to read and those who listened, possibly because they were illiterate, to the reading of this Revelation that he received from God would only be blessed if they kept the message contained within it and their Godly understanding of it within their hearts, because the time was near when things would start to happen.

He Will Come Again

It is important to remember that to God a day is like a thousand years and a thousand years like a day (2 Pet. 3:8) for He exists outside of time and is therefore unimpeded by it; which is why everything is eternally present to Him. What has passed He cannot forget – apart from those sins we have confessed and He has forgiven – and what is, as far as we are concerned, in the future is of no surprise to Him. Therefore, things promised could happen the next day, in a week or even the next year, decade or century.

So what did John, the brother and companion of those experiencing the tribulation and the kingdom and patience of Jesus Christ see whilst he was exiled on the Island of Patmos (Rev. 1)? He was in the Spirit on the Lord's Day, Sunday, the first day of the week. The Jewish day started in the evening (around 1800hrs) of one day to the same time the next day. Their Sabbath day was celebrated from Friday evening to Saturday evening. Saturday was considered to be the last day of the week, the day God rested from His labours of creating all things. With the death and resurrection of the Messiah, the chosen of God, the day of worship was changed to the first day of the week which could be because the birth of the church announced the start of the final chapter of the work of God on the earth.

On this day set aside for the worship of God, as John was praising and worshipping God, he was filled with the Holy Spirit, thereby entering into a state of spiritual absorption resulting in an overwhelming desire to exalt the person of God, lifting his spirit out of the normal, daily, mental and spiritual state to become entirely enveloped and sensitive to the presence of God, an unforgettable experience for those who have been privileged to have been elevated to that state.

This was how John recalled the experience:

1.   He heard a loud voice confirming the position of the Messiah as the Alpha and Omega, the first and the last, and all that we need in this life and the next for He is our all-in-all. He was born of God before the world was created as an eternal being, indestructible. He was also the firstborn from the dead for not only did He rise from the dead to be seen by His disciples after His physical death, even eating food with them, He also entered heaven in a miraculously transformed incorruptible body to be with His father after His physical death before the arrival of all believers.

We will follow Him, after we have slept and He has made all things ready for us, but He was the first to be resurrected. It is interesting that the Messiah told the Jews that He was not only able to lay down His life, He also had the power to take it up again; this is because he had the power in the Spirit to lay it down and take it up again.

It is essential that we accept that although His body died His Spirit remained all powerful and alive for Satan was only able to kill the body not the Spirit of the Messiah (Matt. 10:28). By describing Himself as the first and the last our Lord is proclaiming that He is the all-sufficient one, for He was born before the world began, He was the first to live a completely sinless life, He was the first to die and then rise again totally of Himself. He is the last insofar as He is the all-sufficient one whose sacrifice does not need to be repeated.

2. He was instructed to write down what he saw, and send it to the seven churches which represented the whole of the Christian church at the time for the letters were for the surrounding churches also. The number seven when used in scripture is the number of perfection the hall mark of the work of the Holy Spirit, for it was He who provided the writers, both prophets and disciples, with the inspiration to write what they did. It is the water-mark in all scripture such as is seen in all quality manufactured paper. It is the number central to creation for it regulates every period of incubation and gestation in insects, birds, animals and man. It is the number of the stage of creation at which God rested from His labours.

3. He saw, in place of the candelabra in the holy place with its central stem and six attached branches, seven separate golden lampstands. The candelabra in the holy place had represented the unity of the nation of Israel in God providing light in that windowless space. Although the plan of salvation was to be for all mankind, God's focus during its development was on that one nation to ensure the teaching He was providing would be complete.

Involving other nations would diversify and confuse that teaching. The ceremonial services were all held in the one temple and the whole aspect of Israel's relationship with its God was one of tight unity centred in that temple and the high priest who oversaw the prescribed services and ceremonials celebrated by the priests of Levi.

With the demise of the central temple building with its centrality of service, because of the fulfilment of God's plan of salvation in the person of the Messiah, the Lamb who was slain, God's light given off by the candelabra in that spiritual place was now fragmented as the church was established in various places, with each assembly of God's people being independent, yet all having the same dependence, not on an earthly high priest, but a heavenly one in the person of the risen Lord.

Christ is the light of the world. Individual believers are bearers of that light to those around them but not the source of the light itself. The churches are the combined light of the believers who gather for worship. The lampstands are of gold, meaning that they are precious and of divine origin, for it is only when Christ reigns in the life of the individual believer that they can assume the role of disciple, and through them, light the church of which they are part.

4. In the midst of the lampstands stands one like the Son of Man, the familiar figure of the Messiah on whose breast John rested at the last supper, but who was now transfigured, not temporarily as on the mountain with three of His disciples, of whom John was one, but for eternity; not just as King of the Jews, rather in His new role as the risen and ascended King of kings and Lord of lords, the priest after the order of Melchizedek.

What is more, no longer are priests restricted to the tribe of Levi, but in Christ we are made a kingdom of priests, a royal priesthood with the Messiah at the centre of our lives. Having become saved by the blood of the Lamb and therefore under His authority, we are authorised to be His witnesses, confessing the name of our Saviour so that others may come to the cross and be saved; to the fountain and be cleansed and fed with spiritual food that will not decay.

The Messiah is seen at the centre of the church, the chief corner stone rejected by the earthly builders but to God, the spiritual builder, priceless. It is this Messiah who must be at the centre of all our activities as individuals and of the church, for He is at the centre of our understanding of God. It is He who gave us the clearest example of a loving God because He loved us and loosed us from our sins by virtue of His own blood.

Just as the Aaronic priesthood went through a symbolic cleansing, not only of themselves but their garments also, so we also must pass through that act of cleansing so that deep within us our conscience can be cleansed by the blood that never loses its power.

In this way, by virtue of our having gone through the gate of decision, and accepted His sacrifice for us on the altar of sacrifice, we are able to enter the kingdom of God to be made His priests. The kingdom is opened to us, enabling us to partake of the word of God, the laver and enter the holy place to enjoy the light of God, the candelabra, and be a light for Him as we are supplied with the oil of the Spirit, and so to be continually in the presence of God, bread of the presence, and to communicate with Him in prayer, altar of incense.

An Essential Overview

There are a number of factors that we need to consider at this point before we proceed to look into what John was instructed to write down and distribute to the believers when he was released from exile in Patmos. It is interesting that both Ezekiel and Daniel experienced spiritual encounters and instructions on the spiritual world whilst in exile in Babylon.

1.   It is clear that it was essential for a member of the triune and spiritual God to have come down to earth. The Son was trained by the Father in what He was to do whilst on earth, including suffering and dying for mankind in accordance with the Passover festival. Everything had to be done according to the rules already established through God's word that had been given to His selected servants.

Therefore, the Son knew all that had been done, not only at the time of the creation, but also during the gradual unfolding of God's plan of salvation and in particular what awaited Him when He returned victorious to the spiritual realm of His Father. All this is evident from the text of the second testament.

Numerous Biblical references testify to the fact that the Son not only came down from heaven, but then rose again to return to His Father, with some of these references coming from the Messiah Himself. We have spent time considering the need for a perfect man to die for the sins of man, but now we need to consider the position to which that Man attained when He ascended; the first man to have His body transformed from the corruptible body that was His dwelling on earth to what became incorruptible when He rose from the dead in order for Him to become the first fruits from the dead.

Everything about the Messiah was exceptional; the manner of His entering the earth as a baby to the manner of His departure. All those who have been saved, however, must first sleep before being raised at the second coming of the Messiah. But even being asleep we will have the confidence of being totally secure in the Lord.

We must remember what the Messiah said to His disciples as recorded for us in John chapter 14. *I go to prepare a place for you and if I go to prepare a place for you I will come again and receive you to myself* (vs. 2b, 3), and clearly that has not happened yet. Paul speaks of those believers who had died being in the state of asleep, although there will be some who will still be alive at the coming of the Lord – 1 Cor. 15:51, until the Lord comes to take all believers to Himself, and we have a passage in Revelation that speaks of those who had been martyred for their faith in Christ being given a white robe and told to *'rest a little while longer'* (Rev. 6:9 – 11).

First must come the judgement seat of Christ (2 Cor. 5:10), and this is confirmed with the opening of the books seen by John (Rev. 20:12), before the appearance of our new home in the new heaven and earth (Rev. 21:1, 2). We must not be deceitful in thinking that as soon as a believer dies they will immediately be transported to a new 'home in the skies', the new heaven and new earth that are yet to come. But when our new home is ready after our moment of judgement then we will enter it and truly rejoice with unspeakable joy.

The Messiah is the only man to rise from the dead of His own volition because not only was His spirit, which had descended from heaven for His birth as a human, still alive when His body died, for He yielded up His Spirit so that His body could die, the presence and power of the Holy Spirit was with Him continually, even in the grave. The Spirit never left Him from the moment He was born to the time He was acknowledged to be filled with the Holy Spirit without measure in His human frame and even when He had ascended to be with His Father.

Although Lazarus was raised from the dead by the Messiah, he later died a physical death, his spirit fallen asleep along with all other believers who had left this temporary earthly existence. The Messiah, however, rose from the dead; not purely a physical resurrection but a spiritual resurrection, for although the Spirit of the Son of God within the body never died, it was necessary for His earthly body to be transformed to become incorruptible, which is the only form acceptable in the heaven realm, before His Spirit returned to His body.

His body was of the earth, although He was born without sin, but the Spirit was from heaven. When the Messiah rose from the dead to appear to Mary and the disciples His body was no longer the body He had when alive in the normal sense. He told Mary not to touch Him for He had not yet ascended, and he was able to walk through a closed door into the room in which the disciples were hiding. The remarkable thing is that He was able to eat the fish presented to Him. All this is well within the power of God to perform, but a mystery to us.

In his vision (Rev. 1:13 – 20) John saw the Son of God, and

such was His body, made incorruptible in the grave, that John recognised Him from the time of ministry and the agonised Man sweating great drops of blood in the Garden of Gethsemane, and painfully impaled on the cross.

He was now in glorified form, confident of His position before His eternal Father, the ruler of kings (Rev.1:5) which was a far greater position than that offered by the tempter if He would only give him homage. Now can be seen the reason the Messiah answered the tempter in such strong terms, knowing the greater and eternal position to which He was to aspire, and that the earth and all the kingdoms within it was to become no more.

John saw His Messiah whom he loved:

a. Clothed with garments down to His feet, a sign of high rank and kingly dignity; the garment and the pure gold band were probably emblems of His priestly position after the order of Melchizedek. (Aaron wore a robe and girdle for glory and beauty - Ex. 28:2; 29:5).

b. In the midst of the lampstands; this alluded to the temple and the candelabra and of higher priestly things. This points to His role as king-priest to which only a member of the triune God can aspire.

c. With the whiteness of His head and hair signifying purity and glory. Man cannot look upon the face of God and live. The Son is part of the Godhead yet the disciples beheld His glory (Jn. 1:14) which meant that His earthly body attenuated that glory for men to see Him and live.

Now in heaven, and with John transformed both by the work of the blood of the Messiah and the Holy Spirit in transporting him into the heavenly realm, there was no longer any need for His body to attenuate the brightness of His presence as it once did. Moses was only able to see God's back, not His face lest he die. Yet here is the record of John, transported in his spirit into heaven, seeing the risen Saviour's face. How? Because his conscience had been cleansed through the power of the Messiah's sacrificial blood. (Is.1:18).

d. With eyes like flames of fire; searching eyes with the power to discern the motives of people's hearts, searching out abhorrent sin in judgement and burning away the dross of men's facade. Eyes capable of righteous judgement because they belong to the King of kings and Lord of lords (Rev. 19:11 – 16), a far more glorious title than the one Pilate put on His cross that the chief priests and leaders of the people objected to so strongly (Matt. 27:36).

With feet like burnished brass. That which is precious is able to withstand intense heat. We are told that all our works will have to endure trial by fire. (1 Cor. 3:12 – 14). Brass is obtained through melting certain metals in a furnace which reaches white heat, refined by fire.

The Messiah told His disciples that they only needed to have their feet washed and they would be clean; the priests in the tabernacle complex went about their duties bare foot. Here we have the Messiah with righteous feet, thus the whole of His person was pure and holy, fit for His duties of both king and priest (cf. Ez. 1:7; Rev. 10:1).

e. With his voice was like the sound of many waters (Ez. 43:2; Dan. 10:6), like the voice of a multitude which is threatening to His foes, in stark contrast to the loving tones of the beloved in Song of Songs 2:10 and 5:2.

f. With seven stars in His right hand. The time of separation between man and God had come to an end because the servant Messiah had come and through His death brought in the possibility of a new spiritually attuned relationship between the Children of Israel and their God; and even Gentiles are also brought near by His blood enabling us also to enter into a new spiritual relationship with the God of Israel (Eph. 2.13).

What is the promise of the position to which we can aspire? Nothing less than a crown of glory in the hand of the Lord; a royal diadem in the hand of your God (Is. 62:3). This is for all believers for we who are of that other sheepfold have been bought with a price and are now one with Israel.

g. Out of His mouth went a sharp two-edged sword. This is the Word of God which is not wielded in the hand but by the mouth and the written word. God's word is omnipotent in its primary role of conviction when applied by the Holy Spirit, the Spirit of Truth to the hearts of men; for He does not speak on His own authority but whatever He hears He speaks (Jn. 16:8 – 11, 13).

In this respect we need to consider for a moment what the prophets revealed concerning the robe of the Messiah who comes from Edom with dyed garments from Bozrah who speaks in righteousness, because it is described by John in Revelation 19 verse 11: (Is. 63 esp. vs 1 – 6).

Edom epitomised the enemies of the Lord, those who take counsel together against the Lord and His anointed (Ps. 2) but does not exclude those who think of themselves as being His but have not truly received His salvation.

Sin is abhorred by God and He will deal with those who refuse His salvation in vengeance because sin in all its forms is rebellion against God who, in creating man, is man's eternal parent. Because the word of God is a two-edged sword, piercing even to the division of soul and spirit, it is also the discerner of thoughts and intents of the heart (Heb. 4:12). It is able to condemn those who, like Cain and Esau, refuse to surrender to the God of salvation, yet save to the uttermost those who hear or read and accept that word; which illustrates the possibility of the blood on His robes also being some of His own which He shed on the cross.

The time for judgement has come because He had fulfilled all righteousness on earth through His ministry and sacrifice; therefore, we see the Son of God in His role as King of kings and Lord of lords, clothed in a robe (Rev. 19:11 – 16) dipped in the blood of His enemies slain by the word of His mouth.

h. If Nathanael recognised Yeshua as the Messiah merely because of what He said to him (Jn. 1:45 – 51), how much more would he have recognised Him as the Son of God through the eyes of John in his spiritually enhanced state, when he saw the Messiah with a countenance like the sun shining in its strength?

We know that to stare at the sun in its strength would render us blind. Here is John seeing the risen

Saviour in His perfect glory without dying or going blind. How awesome is the cleansing power of the blood of the Lamb of God by which we shall be saved?

i. Who is worthy to open the scroll in the right hand of power of the Almighty? (Rev. 5) Written on both sides, the scroll had been sealed with seven seals since it was written at the beginning of time. It held details of the final stages of earth's history, including the punishments that would be released onto the earth because of the sinfulness of man. The seven seals prevented anyone but the most pure from opening the scroll.

For some reason John, caught up in the emotion of the moment, cried because there seemed to be no one to open the seals which meant the contents of the scroll would remain unknown. Then one of the elders encouraged John by saying that there was one who could open the seals of the scroll, and He was the Lion of the Tribe of Judah (Gen. 49:9), the root of David and the Lord who was and is his senior (Rev. 5:5).

In the midst of the elders stood a Lamb as though it had been slain, and to emphasise the essential presence of the Holy Spirit with the Son, it is revealed that the Lamb has seven horns and seven eyes which are the seven spirits of God. (5:6) When He took the scroll into His hands, the elders acknowledged His supremacy by worshipping Him (Matt. 26:64).

Here the twenty-four elders[96] had harps and golden bowls full of incense which represent the personal devotional prayers of believers to their God in recognition of His awesome power and authority.

The truth of the Messiah's position in heaven, so disdained by the religious elite during His ministry, is now revealed to John. The song sung by the elders gives emphasis to the position of the risen Messiah and in particular the fact of His sacrifice, so essential for Him to accede to His new role in heaven, which is not just as the Son of God, but also the crucified Saviour.

---

[96] Twenty-four is a higher form of 12 which is Governmental Perfection.

Death where is your sting and grave where is your victory? It is gone because of the victory of Messiah, the Son of the living God.

> *"Worthy are You to take the scroll,*
> *And to open its seals;*
> *For You were slain,*
> *And, moreover, You have redeemed us*
> *To God by your blood*
> *Out of every tribe and tongue*
> *And people and nation,*
> *And have made us kings and priests to our God;*
> *And we shall reign on earth."*
> *(Rev. 5:9, 10)*

The song is now taken up by many others (v11):

> *"Worthy is the Lamb who was slain*
> *To receive power and riches and wisdom,*
> *And strength and honour and glory"*
> *And (v. 13)*
> *"Blessing and honour, glory and power*
> *Be to Him who sits on the throne (the Father),*
> *And to the Lamb, forever and ever!"*

What now of the dungeon where He was held after His arrest, the place of torture where He received lashes so cruel, the accursedness of the cross on which He hung racked with pain, or those who blasphemed Him as they passed by unfeeling, unsympathetic as He hung there in agony and all because of their sin and ours?

Where now are the chief priests and scribes with their godless inflated sense of importance, the Pharisees and elders sitting arrogantly in the Sanhedrin? All will find themselves bowing down to the Lamb on the great white throne just as He told them.

The consequences of opening the seven seals, the coming of the antichrist and what would happen to him are recorded in the pages of Revelation[97]. Just as

---

[97] See my book Seeing Into the Future

in the book of Daniel, people under the power and motivation of Satan are described as beasts of various kinds. Satan himself is identified as the dragon who seeks to present himself as God, having seven heads but ten horns, and seven diadems.

The Arch-Angel Michael and the angels he commands fight the dragon. The dragon, finding no place in heaven is sent tumbling to the earth where the last spiritual battles will be fought, as we have seen from the conflicts on the earth particularly in the Middle East around the nation of Israel, which is despised because Israel belongs to God (Rev. 12 – esp. vs. 3, 7; 13 – esp. v4; 20 – esp. v2).

j.   The encouragement for us is the assurance of the power of God, that the battle against Satan is already won. But we are to maintain our purity before God and not allow ourselves to be deceived so that we receive the mark of the beast on our forehead instead of the mark of God. Just as the high priests from Aaron wore the turban which had over their forehead the plate on which was inscribed 'Holiness to the Lord', so we must avoid any mark on our forehead other than the mark of the Lamb (Rev. 9:4; 13:16 – 18; 14:1; 9 – 13; 20:4; 22:4). The head is the centre of our thoughts and the control centre for our bodies therefore it must be sacred, hence the need for the helmet of salvation.

There are the martyrs, those who were killed because of their commitment to the Messiah (Rev. 6:9) and those who had been decapitated (Rev. 20:4). Many have died because of their love for the Messiah and many more will follow in their footsteps, but they and we have the assurance, provided in this remarkable book, that in Christ alone we have the victory.

The pseudo-message of Satan will have no lasting power, therefore whatever disasters we face we have the assurance of eternal victory in the Messiah.

2.   The earth was to be the place where people were born and trained in the things of God and prepared for heaven. Adam and Eve were told to multiply on the earth and fill it, but the earth is of a finite size therefore there would come a time when the

multiplication of people would have reached a number whereby the earth could no longer sustain them.

We will never know what would have happened had Adam not sinned, but we do know that, because of the contamination of the earth by sin (Ro. 8:22 – 25), there is to be a new heaven and a new earth where sin is not known and only those born anew will have right of entry. This was first prophesied by Isaiah (65:1) and confirmed by Peter in his second epistle (3:13 – 18) with the warning that we must be diligent in maintaining a relationship with our Saviour, through the work of the Holy Spirit, so that being at peace with God we remain without spot and blameless (See chapter 2 regarding false teachers).

Why the new heavens and new earth? Because the earth, as we know it, will be burned with purifying fire (2 Pet. 3:10), both it and all the works that are in it, leaving the people of the earth without a home at the appearance of the great white throne on which sits the One rejected by the chief priest and the religious leaders of the people in Jerusalem (Rev. 20:11). The people of the earth, both those living and those who have died will come to face the judgement of the Messiah against their entry in the two books, of which one is the Book of Life in which is recorded the names of the saved and the other contains a record of the works of every individual, both good and evil, throughout their life.

The removal of the first heaven and earth before the judgement, and the appearance of the new heaven and earth after it, prevents the new from being contaminated with the sin of the previous world because all who have died enter into a spiritual sleep[98] between their death and the moment of judgement, except, that is, those who are alive at the second coming.

John sees the new heaven and new earth in place of the first earth and its surrounding cosmos, and then, in its refined glory, John sees the holy city, the New uncontaminated holy Jerusalem coming down to the new earth out of the heavens from God, prepared as a bride adorned for her husband.

3.   Satan appears in the first part of Genesis to tempt Adam and Eve away from the tree of Life to focus on the fruit of the tree of the Knowledge of Good and Evil, and thus to rebel against God and to come under Satan's power and authority. Throughout scripture we have seen Satan's unsuccessful efforts to derail God's plan of

---

[98] Those who have died before the second coming of the Messiah sleep, waiting to be awakened for the judgement and the appearance of the new heavens and earth in which only believers will live for eternity.

salvation. In Revelation, the concluding book, we read of his demise, first prophesied by God in Genesis 3, *and He shall bruise your head.*

Daniel threw light on the heavenly places in his book, and included some rather bizarre descriptions of animals that were symbolic of the leaders who were to come, and become distinctive people like the Pharaoh at the time of the exodus; individuals who through their actions in their role as leader became identified by the description of the beasts in the text, as we have already seen.

The beasts in Revelation are individuals that are to come and are described by John according to the type of character they will be and the actions for which they will be responsible. These are anti-God leaders bent on doing damage to God's people, such as Stalin and Mao of China and many others like Mugabe who have ruled others with ungodly cruelty with seeming impunity. Some believers are put off by such language, preferring to ignore the book rather than to try and understand its implications as applied to life in the world today. By thinking of the individual beasts as symbolic of the type of people who would rule on earth, rather than deformed beasts, they would find the book of Revelation far more revealing.

4. God's supremacy over everything that was created and exists according to our knowledge is here emphasised. We are allowed to see through the eyes of John the spiritual world first introduced to the Jews in Exile by Ezekiel and Daniel. Always there is the vision of the Ancient of Days on His throne above the shaking of the earth and heavens which were applied to show how temporary and fragile they are, and yet how permanent God is in His place of rest.

What is so important about the book of Revelation is that it is written by the disciple the Messiah particularly loved because of his spiritual inclination, and contains word from heaven itself. It was an important book at the time it was written because it gave the believers the encouragement to know that their Saviour was undoubtedly alive, and that the future was in the capable hands of the trinity.

The letters God had John write to the seven symbolic churches and the challenge He gave them so that they could change to comply with His desire for them, are also important for us to analyse so that we can ensure we do not fall into the same trap which Satan might have laid for us.

What John was instructed to Write

It is interesting that the Messiah held the seven stars in His right hand, the hand of power.

The following brief assessment of each church has been taken from my work "Seeing Into the Future".

Church at Ephesus (2:1)

To: The angel, messenger and overseer of the church at Ephesus.

From: The One who is providing you with support and is in your midst.

Where they were: *"I know your works, labour, patience and abhorrence of evil, your detection of liars through testing, your patient and unwearied perseverance in labouring for My name's sake."* Notice how our Lord puts forward their attributes, what they are doing before notifying them of the problem in their walk of faith.

The problem: *"You have lost the love you originally had for Me."* Paul speaks about their faith in this way:

> *"In Him you also trusted, after you heard the*
> *word of truth, the gospel of your salvation; in*
> *whom also having believed, you were sealed with*
> *the Holy Spirit of promise ..."*
> *(Eph. 1:13 see also vs. 15 – 21).*

What is the message of salvation that they had heard and believed?

The letter Paul wrote to the Ephesians is a remarkable in that it contained much about the spiritual maturity of the believers at Ephesus at the time. It contains perhaps the clearest presentation of Christian theology, covering the new covenant introduced by the Lord Jesus, in the Second Testament (although it is possible that the letter was not primarily for the church at Ephesus, because all the chief manuscripts that have been preserved have either a blank space or the name Ephesians inserted in what was the blank space and there are no personal greetings included in the letter, it is interesting that the only manuscripts to be found with a name inserted have the name of the Ephesian church.)

Ephesus was after all the chief city on the west coast of Asia Minor and had been the centre of Paul's work in that area for two years. During that time he had provided the believers with intensive training, so it may well have been the church to which the letter was first sent. It is certainly interesting that this church is the first to receive a letter from Paul.

The message first received by the Ephesians concerned the message of John the Baptizer which, simply put, was that they were to, *"Repent for the kingdom of heaven is at hand".* It was focused particularly on the Jews, many of whom, like those in Israel at the time of Christ, would have realized that their nation had drifted away from God, which meant they needed to not just repent but also be cleansed of their sin through baptism. This is how John (the old style prophet) got his name as 'The Baptizer' (see Nehemiah 1). However, many Jews were bound by the shackles of the teaching of the Talmud (Jewish rabbinical law which seemed to take precedence over the Word of God – the first testament) and interpretations of it; the intellectuals amongst them were so entrapped by learnéd argument over finite details that they could not, would not see the whole truth contained in the writings of the prophets concerning the future appearance and work of the Messiah.

John the Baptizer's challenged to the religious leadership of the day was uncompromising, *"Brood of vipers (poisonous snakes)! Who warned you to flee from the wrath to come? Therefore bear fruit worthy of repentance ..."* and, *"... but He who is coming after me is mightier than I ... he will baptize you with the Holy Spirit and fire (for purification) ..."* (*Matt. 3*). This message, which would undoubtedly have been understood by those born and raised in Jewish families, had gone throughout the Jewish communities of the dispersion (those living outside Israel) attracting some Jews who had minds that were open to the message, some proselytes (those who had come to believe in the God of Israel) and non-Jews. It was not until Paul arrived that they were able to receive the full message and the gift of the baptism of the Holy Spirit (Acts 19).

The Ephesians had first received the persuasive message of salvation concerning the Messiah Jesus from Apollos, an eloquent Jewish speaker who knew the scriptures; but he only knew about the baptism of John (Acts 18:24, 25). When the Jewish couple Aquila and Priscilla, who had been expelled from Rome by the decree of Emperor Claudius, which required all Jews to leave the city, heard him preach they quietly took him aside and explained to him the way of salvation more accurately. This was because they had lived in Corinth for a time when Paul was there and it was Paul who taught them about the way of salvation through the Messiah who had died on the cross for the forgiveness of sins. Then Paul was able to provide them with in-depth teaching concerning the salvation offered by Christ the Messiah over a period of two years. The message was clear. Although *"... all had sinned and fallen short of the glory of God ..."* the good news was that whoever believed in the Lord Jesus Christ would be saved and enjoy everlasting life. This news was accepted by many Jews who gradually left the synagogue and dedicated themselves to learning this message of the fulfilment of Biblical prophecy (consider Acts 18:5 – 11).

Thus they received the message that changed their lives for, with their consciences cleansed, they were transformed through the empowering of the Holy Spirit, which they received when Paul arrived in their town to preach and to teach them of the things of God. The remarkable letter to the Ephesians that followed, provided them with first a clear understanding of the nature of the church established by the Christ. It emphasized that salvation came through faith, it could not be gained through works, and the objective of that salvation was not only to make us all one in Christ, but also enable us to build one another up into a spiritual building and to fight not the physical but spiritual forces by using the whole armour of God (Eph. 6:10 – 18). This was their first love that bound them to the risen Lord.

So where had they gone wrong?

Unfortunately they had got established and were concentrating so much on serving Christ and on every day living that they had forgotten their personal walk with Him; that personal, private Holy Spirit based intimacy with God through personal prayer and meditating on His word. It would seem that by trying of themselves to live the new spiritual life in Christ, they had forgotten to allow Him to enter their daily activities and decision-making. In that way they had lost their dependence upon Him. Neglecting their prayer life and their focus on Him, they were relying on themselves to gain salvation and serve God. This is so clearly the problem of the church today.

I have recalled in an earlier work that the 'chance' reading of a book encouraged me to tell my wife that I loved her. This got me thinking that if I needed to tell my wife that I loved her, should I not apply the same principle to my relationship with the Lord? What if I told the Lord that I loved Him? So that is what I did. As I walked to the shop to buy the newspaper early each morning, I repeated the phrase "Father I love you", and "Jesus I love you", and also "Holy Spirit I love you". As I told the Lord that I loved Him the more I wanted to let Him know that I loved Him. "Father I really love you", "Jesus I really love you", "Holy Spirit I really love you". My love for the Lord has increased consistently since then, and He has responded by drawing me ever nearer to Himself, which has introduced a spiritual intimacy between us that is active and getting ever deeper. How else could I have written the books I have produced that have touched so many lives if He had not been with me?

The relationship we have with our families is dependent upon our actively engaging with each one and demonstrating our love and concern for them, not just once but continually. For a man and his wife divorce threatens if they do not consider each other and daily demonstrate their love one for the other in positive ways that each will understand. Signs of affection that are meaningful, however small, encourage deepening affection. My wife and I had been married 50 years at the end of 2011. It has lasted because we have made it last and we are happier with each other now than we have ever been. The marriage was undoubtedly the work of God as it was He who miraculously brought us together, but it was up to us, with His help, to make sure it worked.

It is exactly the same with our relationship to Christ our Saviour. Unless we are actively engaged with Him every day then we too could loose our first love and grow cold, and in that way cease being a vessel fit for the Master's use.

The solution: They were to remember what it was like when they first believed, to go back to what it was like for them at the beginning when they were excited about what they were hearing and wanted to know more. They would sit for hours listening to Paul teach the truth about salvation and as a result seek God for themselves (an example of Paul speaking at length – Acts 20:7 – 12). There was a hunger and desire in their hearts for God when they heard the word of truth.

There is always the danger that people will not move on, preferring the comfort of the baby's milk bottle or feeding from the mother's breast. The writer to the Hebrews wrote, *"For though by this time you should be teachers of the word, you need someone to teach you again about the first principles of the oracles of God, still requiring milk rather than solid food. For everyone who can only take milk is unskilled in the word of righteousness, like a babe at the breast. Solid food belongs to those who are of full age, who have exercised their senses to discern both good and evil" (Heb. 5:12 – 14).* Many of those to whom Paul was writing had stood still, not thinking about growing in Christ, just enjoying themselves, listening to others preach and teach the word. They preferred the easy life rather than the life of a student and disciple.

The problem with the Ephesians, however, was not immaturity but spiritual infidelity. They allowed orthodoxy to creep in and take them over, and that led to a loveless ritual of a faith. The one thing about the God we worship is His love for us as demonstrated in the sacrificial service of the Lord Jesus, *"I have not come to be served but to serve, and if I your Lord and Master serve you, you must also serve others and show My love for you to them through that service".* It was that emulation of our Lord's service to others, whilst remaining focused on God and having a dynamic relationship with Him, that was so important because it meant that in their daily lives they involved God in their service for Him. As soon as orthodoxy and formality of service crept in, God's love and involvement with them left.

Not only has God declared that the whole basis of our faith is founded on Love, *"You shall love the Lord your God with all your heart, soul, mind and strength ..."*, but Paul tells us that His love is the basis of our faith for without it we become unprofitable, *"... so abides faith, hope and love, but the greatest of these three is love" (1 Cor. 13).*

In the middle of the first testament is a love story

(Song of Solomon), which says much to us about the wonderful beauty, purity and security that can be found in a love that is pursued with honour and integrity. It encapsulates the patient and remarkably unwearying love God had (and still has) for His people. Hosea lived out that love through his love for a wayward and promiscuous wife in order to demonstrate God's love in a practical and pragmatic way. Here in this first letter God is calling the Ephesians back from their promiscuous ways.

The Ephesians quickly learned of the spiritual elements of their faith. Paul prayed that from His limitless resources God would give them mighty inner strength through His Holy Spirit and that Christ would be more at home in their hearts as they trusted Him. He called on them to always keep themselves united in the Holy Spirit, no longer living as the ungodly that are far away from the life of God with selfish earthly desires.

But, importantly, Paul ended his letter with a warning, which was emphasized by the pagan rituals that were prevalent all around them. He told them that they were to be strong in the Lord and in His mighty power, a power far greater than anything the Devil and his forces could rage against them. Because of their new found faith in Almighty God, they no longer wrestled against flesh and blood but against the evil rulers and authorities of the unseen world, and the mighty powers of darkness who rule this world, and even the wicked spirits in the heavenly realms. Therefore, they needed to put on the whole protective armour of God not only to resist the enemy in the time of evil but to also be able to stand throughout the battle and remain standing to its end (Eph. 6).

On his way to Jerusalem where he knew he would be put in chains and imprisoned for his faith, Paul spoke to the elders of the church in Ephesus warning them that false teachers, human servants of demons, would, like vicious wolves, come among them and not spare the flock. Even some of the leaders themselves would distort the truth they had learned in order to gain a following of the believers (Acts 20:22 – 36).

Now that they had lost their first love, this letter from God to John was calling on them to remember from 'where you have fallen', or to put it another way, realize just how far you have deviated from the intimacy you had with Me when you first believed, when you were sealed with the Holy Spirit and joy filled your heart. Repent of your sins, your deviant ways, and return to the way you were and live the life and do the works you did then.

The penalty: *"I will come quickly and remove your lamp stand from its place"*, which meant that God would no longer recognize them as His, so that when they finally stood before Him sitting on the great white throne He would say to them, *"Assuredly, I say to you, I do not know you." (Matt. 25:12; Rev. 20:11)*. Let us not fall into the teaching that God's love is so powerful and overwhelming that it neither recognizes sin nor immediately reacts against it. That is deception and is of Satan. When Eve said to him that to eat of the fruit of the forbidden tree would lead to her death, Satan immediately replied that she would not die.

We must not be deceived. To Satan, during His time of temptation, Jesus said, *"Man shall not live by bread alone but by every word that proceeds from God's mouth"*, and to those who followed Him to receive His teaching He said, *"You are truly my disciples if you keep obeying my teaching"*. So what does that tell us? That we can interpret the word of God as we see fit? No. This is because it is God's word, and when the Christ, who came to save us from our sins, sits in judgement on the great white throne, He will judge us by that same word, not by our interpretation of it but by His knowledge of what it means (don't forget that He was responsible for having it written). For this reason Jesus told His disciples He was sending the Holy Spirit to them to tell them all about Himself (Jn. 15:26 see also 27), to convict the world of sin and the coming judgement and to guide them into all truth (Jn. 16). Having warned the disciples that they would experience hatred (Jn. 15:18) for if the world hated them, and the world is ruled and kept in deception by Satan and his demonic forces, it had hated Him before it hated them.

Now God's word clearly tells us that God sent His Son into the world, not to condemn it but to save it, for the Christ, the second sinless man to be born but the first man to remain sinless throughout His life, came to die as our Passover Lamb, in our stead, and taking onto Himself our sins so that all those who believe in Him should not die but receive eternal life (Jn. 3:16, 17). Now that clearly informs us that all human beings that have lived, are living and will live in the future, have sinned and come short of the glory of God (Ro. 3:23), because all the offspring of Adam (the whole human race) have been condemned by his sin and therefore we are all under the penalty of death.

However, the glorious news is that if we believe in and accept that the Christ was able to take upon Himself the sin of the whole world so that through His death, we can receive forgiveness and therefore bring an end to that condemnation. (The reason we can accept that news is because Christ Jesus can be considered a second Adam because, by being born sinless and remaining sinless throughout His life, He alone could die for the sins of others). It is true that the forgiveness we receive is so strong that when the sacrificial blood of Christ is applied to us by the Holy Spirit, it not only purifies our hearts from deeds that lead to death, but more importantly frees our spirits from condemnation so that we are able to worship the living God in spirit and in truth.

We can be assured of one thing. What God says, He does! Therefore it is required of us to listen and learn of him and obey. Why? Because God alone knows what is best for us. After all He made us what we are. From the moment our mother became pregnant with us He knew each and every one of us.

An asset:

They hated the Nicolaitans, who would seem from the text to be particularly evil people, whom God also hated. The Nicolaitans were variously described by the early church fathers as both lovers of pleasure and given to spreading malicious gossip in order to ruin the reputation of others; as corrupters of their own flesh, living lives of unrestrained indulgence; of eating things sacrificed to idols and fornication. These are but some of the wolves Paul warned the Ephesians about during his last brief meeting with them at Miletus - Acts 20:29, and fortunately the church at Ephesus would not tolerate them. It was the almost natural adverse reaction of the Ephesians to the teaching of these people (or sect), so clearly contrary to God's word, and their intrinsic desire to do what was right in God's sight that allowed the Lord to warn them of where they were going astray, for He knew of their willingness to correct their error once they had been warned. (It is interesting to note that Ephesus is now part of Turkey, which is a Muslim country.)

The recovery: *"He who has an ear let him hear what the Spirit says to the churches."* This is a clear message for the 'modern believer' too, because it is only by a true believer focusing their attention on constantly seeking after God that they can follow Him along the way He has planned for them. It is up to the individual believer to seek Him with all their hearts, to reach out to Him, asking Him into their lives and committing their lives to Him daily that will enable them to keep to the narrow way that leads to life (read Matt. 7:13 – 24). The moment they do not make Him the centre and purpose of their lives is the moment they walk straight out of His will, and away from Him, thereby missing the goal which is the prize of eternal life in Christ Jesus our Lord (Phil. 3:14).

We also need to be aware of what God is saying to us, for He is not inactive or uncaring in regard to the way of life His followers are pursuing, as these letters so clearly indicate. Rather, He is alive and fully aware of what is going on in the hearts and minds of those who believe in Him and are trying to serve Him. And His constant desire is always to strengthen and sustain those believers in their daily walk with Him. God does not change.

"He who has an ear let him hear". But hear what? A message that was sent from God by the Spirit of to John for the believers of the day; a message that is particularly relevant today because we are that much nearer the end of days than when this letter was written. Now I have been seeking the Lord for very many years and have been steadily growing in the Spirit so that God has been able to speak to me direct. These messages have never been audible in the normal sense of the word. When God asked me the question, "Do you trust Me?" in 2001 I 'heard' the question very clearly, but not with my physical ears. However, there was no doubt in my mind what the question was, or from whom it had come, because I answered the question. But I did not 'speak' to the questioner using my mouth, but my mind; the best way to explain it is I thought the answer in my mind, just as you think about a situation and how to reply to a questioner.

But could I have heard that question from God and then given Him my answer if I was on a different wavelength or speaking a different language. The people in the days of Noah could understand what Noah was saying, because he was speaking to them in their own language, but either they did not, could not, or would not understand its relevance to them. They did not believe that what he was telling them was of any practical significance to them whatsoever. Surely this is exactly what is happening today because so many have shut their ears, for whatever reason, to the truth of the Gospel.

Here the Ephesian believers were being asked to hear and believe what the Spirit was telling them through John. However, it was because they were not switched on to the voice of the Spirit that God was using another means of communicating with them. Being sensitive to the Spirit of God, John was able to hear and write down the message in the form of a letter, which the members of the Ephesian church were then able to read, understand and act upon if they were mindful to do so. This is another reason why, as individuals, it is essential that we keep in contact with the Lord to maintain our spiritual faculties that were made alive when we received the baptism of the Spirit when we first believed.

The reward: *"To Him who overcomes I will give to eat from the tree of life, which is in the midst of the paradise of God"* (see Gen. 2:9). This is the tree from which Adam and his wife were allowed to eat the fruit, until, that is, their sin caused them to be evicted from the garden.

It is the tree that sustains us for eternity and beyond in the paradise of God (Rev. 22:2), but access to it is restricted to those who have an ear to hear what the Spirit says and using that knowledge to then go on to overcome. Following Christ is a life commitment requiring us to be hourly, even moment by moment conscious of God and doing those things that are pleasing to him, for such living is immensely beneficial to us. Not only does it enable us to live our lives to the full (Jn. 10:10), it also leads us to be with the God who loves us so very, very much that He was willing to suffer horrendous pain and anguish of soul so that we might live that new life in Him.

Our God is a person to whom we can relate (Jesus

suffered temptations just as we do – see Rev. 4:14 – 16), and with whom we can converse. He is not some remote being who keeps himself to himself. Our Lord during His time on earth said to those prepared to listen, *"Come unto Me all you who labour and are heavy laden and I will give you rest for your souls" (Matt. 11:28)*. The heaven, or paradise that the Bible speaks of, is not some place provided for us to enjoy the lusts of the flesh as with one religion, indeed quite the opposite, for having put off corruption that we might put on incorruption (1 Cor. 15:42 – 58) we will see and meet with the righteous God we now worship in the spirit.

Being 'in the flesh', we would not have been able to even hope for such a prize because there is no prospect of us changing our situation for ourselves. It is because Christ, being first a Spirit, took on human flesh and then returned a victor to the spiritual realm that the prospect of such a new sublime life has been made possible. He has demonstrated to us the abundant life He has promised to us. This is because life with the indwelling Spirit of God brings meaning and purpose, and a sense of His perfect peace to our lives to sustain us through particularly difficult times so that we can be obedient to His will and purpose for us according to His word. In that way we can be fully confident that the promise of eternal life is not a vague possibility but a certainty, this is because He has told us that He has gone to prepare a place for us where we can be at peace and enjoy His presence forever. It is this fact, and this incontestable and irrefutable fact alone, that makes our faith in the Lord God of Israel totally different from all the religions of the world. Notice I did not say "all other religions".

Religion is a form of life that requires strict adherence to a set of rules and regulations, with all the effort being required by the observant follower, with no assistance whatsoever from the object of their worship; whereas our 'faith' is a true faith, based on truth, and directed at someone who is alive and who is able to help us. All the promises that He has given, which have been published, are just as certain and sure as He is.

Heaven is where we will enjoy His actual presence, rather than just His Spirit in us; and greater still is the knowledge that we will be able to enjoy that situation for eternity and beyond, a never ending inner supreme joy and profound peace.

So what is the alternative?

Falling into the hands of evil men and, after living through turmoil and anguish of spirit, facing the prospect of it continuing after this life into a never-ending existence of the same in the next, but in an environment of complete darkness and godlessness. This is because hell is where God is completely absent; a place there is no light at all. Just the sound of weeping and gnashing of teeth (Matt. 13:50) because of the overwhelming evidence and constricting effect of oppressive evil and horror, for this is where Satan and his demonic angels have been sent for eternity.

In the world there is evidence of God, for His Holy Spirit is presently working in it amongst those that are His. We are the salt of the earth, the savouring essential to life itself. But in hell there is the prospect of being suspended with nothing to see and nothing to do, without any evidence of God or the people of God (Matt. 8:12). This is the reality of hell.

It is essential for us to remember two things:

1. the Love of God has provided all men with a way of salvation that is free to all who accept that salvation according to the terms of that salvation according to the word of God.

2. the judgement of God is based on His truth and will be applied to all men according His standard of righteousness. This means that not all men will enter the kingdom of heaven. This is because it is reserved for all those who have committed themselves to being obedient servants of God according to His word that they have received.

The Church at Smyrna (2:8)

To: The angel, messenger and overseer of the church at Smyrna.

From: *"The First and the Last who was dead and has come to life"*. This was of tremendous comfort to a church where persecution had led to martyrdom and much suffering (1 Thess. 1:6). It meant that because Christ had lived and died but is alive again (a Spirit that was dressed in a human body for a while but has returned to the spiritual realm, although restricted to human form) it meant that they too had the prospect of resurrection and could not be separated from God at any time, that is all the while they remained strong in their faith in Him.

What an encouragement that statement must have been to the individual members of this suffering church. To have received such a letter from their Lord clearly informing them that, not only did He know exactly what was going on, could warn them personally of what was soon to happen, but also encourage them with the knowledge of the prize of the high calling of God that awaited their continued faithful witness, meant that they would have been filled with a new vision of hope.

What a wonderful example these dear, poverty stricken believers have left us. And they are not alone. There have been many who, throughout the intervening years, have followed their example, even in more modern times, throughout the world. Those believers who have been willing to give up all worldly possessions, and even their freedom, to suffer imprisonment, deprivations, separation from their families, even torture and death, purely because they loved the Lord Jesus and enjoyed a relationship and intimacy with the one true God that they could not deny or surrender whatever they were threatened with (Matt: 10:16 – 39 esp. v28). The cost to them in this life was very high, but for them the suffering was worth it for the sure and certain promises God had impressed upon their hearts concerning the peace and joy of life in the next. He who is the object of our worship will be central, seated on the throne surrounded by a multitude of worshippers (Rev. 19:5 – 8) all filled with the love of God and focused on the One who made all things and has brought us to into His perfect rest to be with Him. No other 'faith' or religion promises such an eternal goal.

Where they were: *"I know your works, tribulation and poverty (but you are rich); and I know the blasphemy of those who say they are Jews but are not, for they are of the synagogue of Satan".* (cf. Jn. 8:42 – 47)

Paul says to the believers in Rome that one who can confirm his lineage as true born a Jew with the mark of circumcision is not necessarily a true Jew. Why? Because Moses called for them to believe not outwardly but inwardly, thus converting the outward mark of their Jewishness into an inward mark. This meant that they had to be circumcised in their heart , thus confirming that the message of God he had received with his physical ears had been established in his mind thus bringing him under the authority and will of God (see Deut. 10:12 – 22; Jer. 4:4). It was, therefore, being a Jew in the Spirit that confirmed his true Jewishness, for it meant that his acceptance of and belief in God was complete, not a mere outward physical sign (Ro. 2:28, 29).

After all, the outward sign was received by a man as a baby of eight days old when he was not in a position to make a decision for himself. The mark was merely to identify him as having being born of Jewish parents and therefore of the lineage of Abraham, Isaac and Jacob (Gen. 17:10 : 14; Rom. 4:11, 12). When the boy became a man and was able to make a personal decision it was then that he needed to confirm the mark by acknowledging God as his personal Lord and Saviour (Deut. 10:12, 13, 16). In exactly the same way those born of Christian parents who were dedicated to God is some way as babies or children, need to enter into a covenant relationship with God themselves by publicly acknowledging Christ Jesus as their Saviour and Lord, often through baptism by immersion (or full baptism). The decision is personal. No one person can make that decision for another.

The Jews that were troubling these believers at Smyrna did not have the mark of the Spirit, only that of the flesh, for they had sold their souls to the Devil. Like the leaders seeking the death of the Messiah, God was not their King of kings and God of gods for they had *"no king but Caesar" (Jn. 19:15)*, indeed they threatened Pilate that if he let 'their Lord Messiah' go then he was not Caesar's friend. This above all else identified their true master and lord as the Devil.

The problem: Unlike the church at Ephesus it was not God who had a problem with this church, but this church that had the problem of suffering. God knew about their works, tribulation and poverty. It is often the rich churches that have trouble in trusting God because their riches focus their minds on the things of the earth, for that is where their treasure is (Matt. 6:19 – 21). But here we have a congregation of people living in poverty who were suffering at the hands of Jews, but by their works they declared their undying faith in the Lord Jesus (see Heb. 11:32 – 40; James 2:14 – 26). It is interesting to see how the Lord describes them? *"But you are rich!"* (James 2:1 – 13) In one translation this comment is in brackets suggesting that it was almost an aside, a complementary comment that gives the true facts of the case.

They were rich!

But how could they be rich if they were poverty stricken?

Because their treasure was with the Lord and that had precedence over their earthly state because it lasts into eternity; it is an eternal inheritance (Matt. 6:19 – 21). These faithful believers were servants of the living God, and of them it could be said the world is not worthy of them (Heb. 11:38). A Nigerian once said to me that he had moved from the countryside into the capital city of Lagos and looked around for a church to attend. During the first four or five weeks he visited a number of churches, although they seemed to be prosperous, none of them had that spark of the Spirit. This was because they had attained a degree of sophistication and the message from the preacher was muted. Finally he found a church where the message was unadulterated and its full power could be felt.

The solution: How can there be a solution to a non-problem? But here the Lord is warning them of what was to happen in the near future, and the attitude they were to adopt when it came.

This letter was to warn these dear folk that more suffering was on its way. *"Do not fear"*, says the Lord, *"what you are about to suffer."* They were warned that some of them would be thrown into prison as a result of the work of the Devil, which God was allowing for the purpose of testing and refining them. The time over which they were to experience tribulation was to be limited to ten days. But they were not to be afraid of what they were going to face because the One who was far greater than their opposition was there to support and sustain them in their agony (after all He had also suffered and knew their plight). They were to let go and allow God to provide for them, giving them an inner peace and assurance that whatever they went through the prize of the high calling of Christ was worth everything that they would encounter, even death (Matt. 10:28).

"Be faithful unto death AND I will give you the crown of life." The greater we emphasize the importance of the life we lead here on earth the dimmer the life after death becomes. Yet it is the life we will be able to enjoy with the Lord after our physical death that should be the object of our desire, for there will be no more pain or weeping or any of the traumas like those we experience here on earth. Why then do we seek a path of well being in this life, whatever the cost to our spiritual walk with God? We should never put our ambitions before God's plan for us. *"Seek first the kingdom of God and all the other pertinent things pertaining to this life will be provided" (Matt. 6:24 – 34).* What is better, to be successful here on earth in the eyes of men, or to receive the crown of life from God? That is the question that we must ask ourselves.

Did not The Christ (how blessed and glorious is the Name that is above every name that is named because it is the only name through which we shall be saved) come and suffer throughout His life for us? Was that not the essence of His life of service that of suffering? Therefore should we not also focus our attention on serving God and putting all else aside, looking unto the author and finisher of our faith and follow in His footsteps, denying ourselves that which would hinder our life in Him, and work for Him?

We can say with confidence that the dear believers of Smyrna had the right attitude. It did not matter to them what happened to them in this life, this was because their true and lasting reward was being held in trust by God in heaven (Matt. 6:19 – 21). Their task here on earth was to seek Him with all their might, love Him with all their being and serve Him in any way that was open to them. Indeed, ignoring the temporary discomfitures in this life, they were prepared to be faithful unto death, just like their Lord (Lk. 22:42).

The penalty: The difference between the believers in Smyrna and those in Ephesus is startling to put it mildly. Here we see a contrast between the simple folk living in poverty and trusting fully in their Lord, and the sophistication of the Ephesians who needed to be told that they had strayed from the relationship they had had with God at the beginning. As the people of Smyrna had no problem with their relationship with God, there was no need for a solution to that problem and therefore no penalty.

An asset: Their life of faith and complete dedication was an asset.

The recovery: To ensure the continuation of their perfect life of service they were to hear with their ears the message that the Spirit was giving to the churches; not to be puffed up with pride, but to be prepared for the impending suffering and even the moment of death they had been told was to come, and just to trust God completely that what He said He would do for them He would carry out to the letter.

The reward: That the second death, that is an eternity in hell (see under Hell in the introduction), would not affect them, for they were assured of a place with the Lord in heaven (Jn. 14 esp. vs. 2, 3) providing, that is, they took their suffering with fortitude and kept their eyes on their future life with Christ in heaven (Rev. 6:9 – 11). Do you who read these words not rejoice at the thought of being with the Lord for eternity, in a place where the streets are paved with pure gold and where there will be no more night because the light of God (the Father, the Son and the Holy Spirit) will provide our light and be our joy continually? This is heaven, to be where God is, in His home in a never-ending rejoicing of our spirits, with new incorruptible spiritual bodies. No more pain and suffering. No more medical problems.

Nothing in this life is truly long term. It is temporary. Empires come and empires go. Leaders come and leaders go. BUT the Lord our God is far greater than all those who would assume power and control over others. He was alive, then He was dead, but now He is alive for evermore.

The message of the example of the people in Smyrna is that faithfulness to the calling of the Lord Jesus is by far the most important principle of life that we should adopt, for it is far above all other considerations of life, and though it might bring suffering and death at the hands of others in this life, it will inevitably bring eternal life in the Spirit in the life to come.

The Church at Pergamum (2:12)

He Will Come Again

To: The angel, messenger, and overseer of the church at Pergamum.

From: *"He who has the sharp two-edged sword."* (The heavy two-edged broad sword used for fighting, which when swung with force against an enemy could amputate limbs, is held in his mouth to give a perfect picture of the power of His word for reproof, punishment and condemnation (Heb. 3:11,12; Eph. 6:17; 2 Tim. 3:16, 17; 2 Pet. 1:19 – 21) when used against sinners).

Where they were: *"I know your works, and that you dwell where Satan has his throne. You hold fast to My name and did not deny your faith in Me even when Antipas became My faithful martyr when he was killed among you where Satan dwells."*

The problem: *"You have there those who hold to the doctrine of Balaam, who taught Balak to put a stumbling block before the children of Israel, to eat things sacrificed to idols and to commit sexual immorality. In this way you also have those who hold to the doctrine of the Nicolaitans, which thing I hate."*

The problem with this church was compromise.

In our dealings with God it is essential that we realize that it is man that sinned against God and therefore God is the injured party. The fact that He has always loved man, His supreme creation, to the extent that He was willing to provide a means whereby man could be spiritually reunited with Him, according to His rules, if a man so desired, then it is not open to any man to change or modify those rules for that reuniting to happen. Accept your state of sin and God's way of salvation and you will be saved. Reject it, or modify it in any way, shape or form, then there can be no salvation. Break God's rules and you remain in your sin and a godless future awaits you after your physical death. I can put it with no greater clarity than that.

This allowed those to remain within the fellowship of the church that did not hold strictly to the uncompromising doctrines of the church that had been built up by the prophets, the disciples (including Paul) over the years. Those doctrines held that the word of God, contained in the first testament and writings by those who had been with Jesus, were truth and should be strictly adhered to. Deviation was not an option.

"I marvel", writes Paul to the church at Galatia, *"That you are turning away so soon from Him who called you in the grace*

of Christ Jesus, to a different gospel, which is not another; but there are some who trouble you and want to pervert the gospel of Christ." *(Gal. 1:6).* There only needs to be one vociferous and dominant person who has a 'different' view on what the scriptures say, someone with an opinion of their own which is not backed up by scripture, along with some who are easily led to accept his teaching and you have the problem experienced at this church at Pergamum.

This is exactly the problem that is tearing the western churches of today apart. We have the orthodox and the liberal fighting it out regarding practicing homosexual priest, women priests and bishops and much more (most recently the possible marriage of so called 'gays' in the church). It must be emphasized that the problem is not about the orthodox or liberal point of view. It is, however, about what Almighty God is saying in His Word! A Methodist minister, ministering as a prison chaplain divorced his wife of many years and started living with another man in a homosexual relationship. He taught that everyone would go to heaven. In subscribing to that doctrine he is living a deception, and in so doing serving Satan rather than God, which will end in him experiencing the second death (this could also mean permanent death of the human spirit, although there is no definite scriptural teaching on this – Rev. 20:6 – also see under Hell in the introduction). It is interesting that he took his male partner into the prison for the morning service one Sunday, but the prisoners objected to the authorities that he had done so. He had to immediately end his service to the prison.

Go back to the account in Genesis where it is recorded that God made the first man and from his the first woman and God's instruction to them to be fruitful and multiply and fill the earth (to procreate according to God's design). In fact there is a clear statement of God's intention for mankind in Genesis 2:24, that man shall leave his parent's home and be joined to his wife so that they became one flesh.

Does it say anything about two men or two women being united to produce offspring? The problem of homosexuality was prevalent in Paul's day. In his letter to the Romans, Paul recalled that women discard the natural way of sexual relations to indulge in pseudo sex with each other, and that men did the same (Rom. 1:22 – 32). Although the key point in Paul's epistle is that such people refuse to acknowledge God, the problem today is that the church has drifted so far away from the truth of God's word, that those who subscribe to a relaxation in the church's rules governing sexual relationships are being allowed to have a voice and encourage changes that declare their unwitting and dangerous rebellion against God. This deviation from God's word is in line with Satan's efforts to lead the church away from God, just as Balaam did in regard to the Israelites, and the Nicolaitans were focused on continuing.

The sin of Balaam (Num. 22 - 25), which cost him not only his life but earned him a reputation of notoriety throughout scripture, was his pursuit of his own agenda. Called by Balak to curse the nation of Israel for a rich reward, Balaam could not take his eyes off the earthly reward of a human king even though God had shown him, very clearly indeed, through the prophetic words he had uttered whilst under the power of the Holy Spirit, that He had to bless them, *"... Balak calls me to come and curse Jacob, and come execrate (that is express or feel abhorrence for) Israel . How shall I curse those whom God has not cursed or express or feel abhorrence towards those for whom God does not express or feel abhorrence ..."* (see my book "The Wilderness Training School : Powerful Lessons in Numbers").

The revelations of God to John reveal the secretly liaison between Balaam and Balak where Balaam, having allowed himself to come under the authority and power of Satan (after his pronouncement of God's prophetic word), explained to Balak that the only way he could defeat the Israelites was by encouraging sexual immorality amongst them and the worship of his national gods. In that way the Israelites would be separated from the God who was empowering them to conquer the nations (Rev. 2:14), thus rendering them powerless.

With all the proof of God's power having been shown to him, Balaam still blindly went and taught Balak ways of undermining the essential fellowship the people of Israel had with their God in total and resolute defiance against the One who had called him to His service. God's anger blazed against the tribe of Israel and it was only pacified when a faithful priest put an end to the illicit sex between a prince of Israel and the daughter of a Moabite princess by thrusting a spear through their joined bodies (read Num. 25:1 – 9). This shows that it is not only the Israelites who were obstinate and pigheaded and rebellious towards God.

This is Satan at work in the heart of one who was supposed to be God's prophet on earth. Just as Judas Iscariot thought he was doing the right thing when he betrayed the Lord, because although he knew 'of God' he did not in fact have a personal intimate relationship with God, and therefore could not be sensitive to the guidance of God so that, influenced by a demonic spirit, he betrayed the Lord thinking he was doing the right thing. So also others, who are in the same way completely out of touch with God, seek to teach the things of God in their own way, according to their own agenda with disastrous results. I have heard many a preacher who obviously did not have any knowledge of God whatsoever, but spoke empty words that did not satisfy the spiritual hunger of those who listened. I have debated with such people at meetings that should have been spiritually charged with the Holy Spirit but were not. Shame on such people!

John himself in his first letter wrote, *"These things I have written to you concerning those who try to deceive you." (1 Jn. 2:26)* which is why I insist on including the following statement at the beginning of everything that I write for scripture proves scripture:

It is essential that you assure yourself of the truth of what is written here by checking up everything and confirming it with scripture (1 Jn. 4:1).

You will have noticed that I use many scriptural references, for most of them I provide the book, chapter and verse reference so that you can look them up and read them for yourself, not forgetting to understand the 'context' of the reference by reading what goes before it and after it. What is important, however, is that although you might have gained confidence in my credibility as a 'man of God', it is still important to get in the habit of checking everything using scripture. This is also the way you learn to appreciate and prayerfully interpret scripture; it also helps to bring you nearer to God. No one can be spiritually joined to God if they do not prayerfully read and study the scriptures.

There is no doubt, and I am forced to admit it, that without the inspiration that I have received from God I could not have written this or any of the other books in the style and to the depth that I have (sometimes, as I read what I have written, even I am amazed and inspired by it). But it is necessary for me to insist that without my desire to dedicate my life to God, without my taking the trouble to read the Bible from cover to cover many times over the years, and without my seeking God with all my heart, and being receptive to His voice coupled with my desire to obey His commands, I would not have been able to write these books at all.

Jesus proclaimed that he was about His Fathers business. But it was He who delivered the message from God, it was He who was willing to serve His Father unto death and by that death provide the way of salvation God the Father had planned from the beginning. Without His involvement and dedication we would still be in our sins. In the same way these letters to the churches are clear evidence that we must follow the lead of our Lord and Saviour in being obedient to God the Father in our service to Him as believers as influenced by His Spirit inspired word.

Our relationship with, and service for, God is a two way process. He calls us and we respond, but we do not all respond in the same way, nor does He call us in the same way, or to the same type of service (1 Cor. 12). God invested in me the talent to write. I have responded by seeking to be obedient to God's call and write as He directs, just as John did.

God brought Derek and I together and, over the years, we have become far more than just friends for we have both grown together and in the Lord and in our desire to serve Him. God suggested to Derek that he ask me to write my thoughts on the book of Genesis (I needed that prompting especially as it was from a Jew, because I have a tremendous love for the Lord's people). God arranged for me to be made redundant. With time on my hands I started to write.

A great number of people over the years have praised my writing skills (remember this is the talent that God has given to me – Matt. 25:14 – 30). Also I have gained an enjoyment for writing, and for training people in classrooms and in the work place, more than any other type of work that I have been engaged in throughout my working life. Couple the appreciation others have for my style of writing with my love of writing and you can understand the mind and heart of God, for He is able encourage people to serve Him purely because He alone knows what they are really capable of doing.

By the time I finished writing my thoughts on the book of Genesis, Derek had already suggested that I write my thoughts on the book of Exodus. During this time God has spoken powerfully to me through His word and in a practical way through my changing circumstances, both of which have a bearing on my future work with and for Him. The result of this study and writing is that not only have I been incredibly blessed myself, but also many people have told me that they have also been helped by what I have written.

Although I have needed that feedback, that response from people concerning the helpfulness of my books, as indeed all writers do, I cannot get puffed up with pride because my relationship with Christ is like a marriage, the deeper the love and intimacy of the union and the greater the dependency the more effective the relationship is.

Had He not:
- provided the way of salvation,
- called me,
- provided me with the necessary writing skills, and then the inspiration that I have definitely received and am receiving from Him,

Had I not:
- responded to His call,
- been prepared to be active in the work to which He had called me (I also served as a Methodist Local Preacher for over 20 years in my younger days, although I am no longer a Methodist),
- been willing to read His word and seek Him with all my heart,
- been willing to put my writing skills to work to produce all that I have produced,

then:

the inspiration that God was willing to provide me as I wrote would not have been used, and you would not have been able to receive and study these books. All this is underwritten with the all-embracing love of God, which has also affected and infected my heart.

Who knows, some might even have perished in their sin had I not been obedient (I do not know the use God has made of these books because only He is able to utilize them to the full for He knows the hearts of men and is able to engineer circumstances in which the books can reach the people who need them and for the words to touch their hearts).

What then can I claim concerning all that I have written? That I have the joy of knowing that God has used me in His service to save and build up those that could not (or might not) have been reached by any other means. Surely that is a reason for rejoicing not boasting? Thanks be to God, to whom all praise shall be directed for He is the giver of talents and the inspiration for their use.

Compromise caused the death of truth for the believers of Pergamum. Their downfall was probably caused by an overriding desire to keep the church together, whatever the cost. They allowed those who not only followed the teaching of Balaam but also that of the Nicolaitans (see under the church of Ephesus) freedom to teach their deviant doctrine within the church when the leaders should have put a stop to it and even band the perpetrators from entering the church. This is clearly happening today in many churches and causing the death of many because as soon as errant teaching becomes acceptable God withdraws the Holy Spirit from that church for His name's sake.

These variant teachings were potential stumbling blocks, especially amongst new believers and those whose faith was weak (the wolves Paul warned the Ephesians about during his last brief meeting with them at Miletus - Acts 20:29).

I was told of a believer who was taken on as the pastor of a church of about a hundred souls (the actual number is immaterial). Within a few months of her arrival 80% of the regular members had left. Some years on it became a thriving church full of the Spirit of God.

It is not the number of believers who attend a church that is important, but the quality of the God focused teaching and faith of each individual member, along with the reality and intimacy of their personal relationship to the Lord Jesus that is most important. If there is not within each member of the church that active and vibrant personal relationship with Christ Jesus, however simple their faith, then each of them, especially the leaders, needs a spiritual health check or the church will suffer.

And prayerful study of the scriptures is the foundation of that personal relationship with our Lord, for how do we fully know how we are to approach and relate to Him without studying His instruction book?

An inner city church held a Christian convention. The large church was full of believers and the Spirit of God was seen to be working amongst them with many gifts of the Holy Spirit (including the gift of tongues – that is speaking in an unknown tongue through the direct inspiration of the Holy Spirit and healing – read 1 Cor. 12, 13 and 14) being in evidence. The following day the leaders of that city centre church went around the building exorcising what they thought were demonic spirits, when what they had witnessed the day before was the work of the Holy Spirit. Remarkable. Unbelievable. Unforgivable. And these were church leaders!

But the Christian faith of such people is not real; their relationship with the Lord was not active or intimate. Indeed they were as far away from the Lord as unbelievers outside the church! A Spirit filled believer, whom I know very well, gave me this account of what had happened.

The gospel of Christ is living, but it is only effective in the lives of those who receive it with joy and take it to heart and study it prayerfully and apply it to their own lives.

So the problem being pointed out to the church at Pergamum was that they had allowed in amongst them those who propagated deviant teaching which, if not corrected, could lead them away from the Lord and into the arms of the evil one. The elders had not remained true to God's Word, had not kept the sheep separated from the goats but had allowed the church to deviate from the truth.

The solution: Repent. This is the simple process for all who stray from God's word and will. But it must be followed up with an inner desire to seek God with greater fervour and a renewed commitment to being obedient to Him. In the case of this church it was essential that they got back to the pure unadulterated teaching of the word of God and to get rid of all those who were not willing to align themselves with that word and come under its authority. The same thing must happen to all those who teach that homosexuality is alright in God's sight. It is not! (see Belief & Faith : Understanding the Essentials – a full chapter is given over to the Marriage Covenant)

Compromise and the unwillingness to accept the fact of his holiness and justice and that the covenants and laws God laid down at the beginning will be interpreted by Him and not modified to suit the desires of men are undoubtedly Satan's two greatest strategies against the church.

He wants to remain hidden from view; the anonymous enemy. He loves it when people treat him as a joke, for that allows him total freedom to work with his forces of evil in the world, and in particular within the church, with impunity. How can a person fight an enemy they do not believe exists? Sadly, few members of the church, and in particular members of its various ruling bodies, are willing to believe in the existence of Satan (Devil), let alone the world of demonic forces arrange against the church. The teachings of Jesus and his disciples are glossed over, and Paul's insistence that believer's arm themselves with the whole armour of God treated so casually and with such disregard that it is basically ignored.

Repent means to turn (or return) to God. Isaiah puts it this way, *"Seek the Lord while He may be found, speak to Him while He is near and in your thoughts. Let those who have turned away from the Lord by neglecting His word and have stopped speaking to Him through prayer, those who have allowed His word to be corrupted and His teaching compromised for the sake of human unity instead of unity in the Spirit, turn (or return) to the pure teaching of His word and become obedient servants of God and all His commands. Let them banish from their minds any thought of subverting God's truth and seek with purity of heart and an openness to the work of the Holy Spirit to understand God's word by inspiration from God Himself. Let them turn to the Lord so that He may have mercy on them. Yes, turn to our God for He will abundantly pardon". (My interpretation of Is. 55:6 – 7.)*

We must realize that God's thoughts are not our thoughts, neither are His ways our ways, for as the heavens are higher than the earth so are His ways higher than ours, and His thoughts higher than our thoughts (Is. 55:8 – 9). As our creator, it is essential that for us to fulfil His desires for us, it is essential that we focus our attention on Him and submit ourselves to His will and purpose for us.

Satan's thoughts and plans are anchored to the earth, which will one day disappear, so that all those whose focus is on the earth and earthly things are is worthy servants. What God is doing is to call upon all those prepared to listen to enter into a higher relationship with the higher power that is God, and completely turn from their previously devious ways.

The penalty: *"I will come quickly and fight against them with the sword of My mouth."*

This is a terrifying thought to those who have had and spiritual experience of, and have known the power of God.

Christ has the responsibility as our Lord and King not just to save but also deliver judgement. (The word of God is referred to in the letter to the Hebrews as living and powerful and sharper than any two-edged sword, piercing even to the division of soul and spirit, and joints and marrow, and is a discerner of the thoughts and intents of the heart.)

The quote above refers to what John saw earlier. The heavy two-edged broad sword used for fighting which, when swung with force against an enemy, could amputate limbs, is here seen being held in His mouth giving us a perfect picture of the power of His word for reproof, punishment and condemnation (Heb. 3:11,12; Eph. 6:17; 2 Tim. 3:16) when used against sinners, that is those who have followed the way of the wicked and the spiritual enemy, which is Satan.

It is also a reminder of what happened to those Israelites who defied God and joined the Moabites in their worship and sexually biased and debased ceremonies after Balaam had instructed Balak on what to do to disempower these people whom Balak wanted Balaam to curse but could not (Num. 22 to 25). The leaders of the rebels were hanged and others killed by the sword (Num. 25:4,5). One prince who blatantly took the daughter of a Moabite chieftain into his tent in the Israelite encampment to lay with her was killed by Phinehas using a spear which he thrust through both of them (Num. 25:8) to stop the plague God had sent (see 2 Peter 2:15; Jude 11).

Once again we need to remind ourselves that the power of God to do what He says He will do is undiminished and unstoppable! We do not know what happened to this church in Pergamum and whether or not they obeyed this instruction. What we can say is that if they had not, and if those who followed the deviant teaching persuaded the other believers that all was well when it was not, then there is no doubt whatsoever that God would have acted in the way He said He would.

An asset: There were none in this case, which says little about the individual 'believers' in that church.

The recovery: *"To him who has (spiritually attuned) ears to hear let him hear what the Spirit says to the churches."* Let him hear and be aware of what the Holy Spirit is saying, not just to the church mentioned but also to what He is teaching the churches around about, in this case the other six churches, for we can all learn from the experiences of others. Where individuals or churches are growing or declining.

The reward: *"To him who overcomes (that is he who resolutely decides to follow Christ whatever the cost) I will give some of the hidden manna to eat."*

Whilst Moses was leading the Israelites in the wilderness they collected the manna that appeared on the ground every morning, which God had promised as food for them. It is on record that God never failed to provide it. But that manna was for their physical need of food (Jn. 6:31 – see Ex. 16:11 – 18 esp. v18) and Christ wanted to get them to feed on the spiritual food that was His Word (Jn. 6:63 – cf. Matt. 4:4).

Here, however, Christ was offering the believers in Pergamum the provision of hidden manna, or rich spiritual food, that would sustain them in the particularly difficult circumstances they were experiencing as they wandered through this life, for they were not permanent residents but transient, travelling towards their goal which was to be with Christ in the glory of the New Jerusalem.

It is no good speaking in human terms here, for that is what the Jewish religious leaders did. They constantly wanted physical signs from Christ to demonstrate that God was with Him (Matt. 12:39). They always talked about the physical signs of God's involvement with them, harping back to the time in the wilderness when God gave their forebears manna to eat (Jn. 6:31), never about their own relationship and experiences of God. But Christ had come to give them the true bread from heaven (Jn. 6:32 – 36), which would bring them into a new, dynamic relationship with Him, if only they were to believe in Him. The word of God, the Second (New) Testament revelation, is just a means to an end, for it leads the individual seeker into that inner sanctuary where God dwells. It is only by individuals reading and accepting the teaching of the word, believing it as truth and applying it to their lives, and at the same time reaching out to God, asking Him to come into their lives to transform them, that the truth and power of that word can become an effective force within them.

That is why the temple curtain was torn in two from the top to the bottom. It signified that it was God's plan to make the innermost sanctuary, where previously only the High Priest could meet direct with God once per year on the day of atonement, redundant. The holy of holies in the temple was, after all, but a copy of the true holy of holies in heaven. The new High Priest, Jesus Christ, after His resurrection and ascension had entered the eternal holy of holies in heaven to be a priest forever after the order of Melchizedek. The physical place of meeting had now been replaced by the spiritual. The earthly holy place, on the other hand, had become the bodies of individual believers. Paul told the Corinthians that their body was a temple of the Holy Spirit *"who is in you"* (1 Cor. 6:19, 20). Therefore the individual believer has become the holy place of the temple, the separating curtain into the holy of holies physical death, and the holy of holies has returned to the original in the heavenly spiritual place where God lives.

Jesus Christ Himself declared that it was the Spirit who gave life (Jn. 6:63), for it was the Spirit Himself who interpreted the Word that Christ the Son brought to His people from the Father that they might live (Jn. 16:13). Unfortunately, the Jewish religious leaders did not have the Spirit because they were unwilling to believe in Him, even though they studied the scriptures (Jn. 5:37 – 40) and without the Spirit they could not understand what Christ was speaking about. It was as though He was talking to them in a strange language that they did not understand.

The progress of the tabernacle from travelling tent to its demise is also the work of God. A sample of manna was placed in a container which was then put into the Ark of the Covenant (Ex. 16:32) to be kept with the tablets of the testimony (the Ten Commandments that under pinned Israel's relationship with their God even to this present day) before the Lord in the holy of holies, the most holy place on earth at the time.

In order for them to progress their with faith in Him, God allowed the ark with the tablets of stone to be 'lost' because the laws would in future be written on their hearts (Jer. 31:33), that is their conscious and self-determining self (something living rather that dead, for stone is tied irreversibly to the earth), to become personal and to raise them up to new heights. Their stony hearts would be taken away and hearts of flesh (which would be malleable) implanted into them (Eze. 36:26).

With the death of the Messiah on the cross of sacrifice, the curtain, which separated the holiest place from the holy place within the temple, was removed, meaning that the temple was no longer relevant. To those who truly believed, the holy of holies had not disappeared, but was transferred to heaven (with the ascension of our Lord who is the new High Priest), elevating still further the spiritual integration of the faithful with their God. The temple in Jerusalem is currently no more. But Jerusalem is still the Holy City of God where He has placed his name. The Jewish people (that is the whole of Israel led by the tribe of Judah as prophesied by Jacob – Gen. 49) are still the chosen of

God, but they have been joined by all those Gentiles who have come into the knowledge of the Messiah, the Saviour who is Christ the Lord, so that only those, both Jew and Gentile, who truly believe and have been baptized in the Holy Spirit can claim membership of the true Israel.

So what about the portion of manna that was deposited in the Ark of the Covenant by Aaron the first human high priest? God had provided it every morning for the physical needs of the Israelites. But like the Ark itself it is what it represented that is important. The commandments written on the tablets, that were the basis of God's covenant with Israel, were transferred to the hearts of believers as the basic principle of their life as an Israelite (often referred to as Jews). The manna, or bread from heaven became the Word of God (Matt. 4:4; Jn. 6:33). Aaron's rod or staff that blossomed to prove that he was God's chosen, was transformed into a cross, that is because the new high priest, who is of the tribe of Judah rather than Levi, was raised from the dead having provided His own body for the ultimate sin offering.

The hidden manna is, I believe, a higher form of spiritual food provided to satisfy the spiritual hunger of those who earnestly seek to enjoy an ever-deeper intimacy with God. It is a richer spiritual food that can only be digested by those whose walk with God has led them into a life of total commitment. Just as the manna supplied to the Israelites during their journey in the wilderness provided them with the assurance of the reliability of God's promise to sustain them, so the physical food was raised to the spiritual food of the Word made flesh that led to a new life in Christ (Jn. 6:63). There is no doubt that we must progress from the word that teaches us the first principles of the Christian life (Heb. 5:12 – 14), to the solid food that helps us to maturity and leads us into the deeper things of the Spirit, even as John experienced whilst he was on the island of Patmos. That is the food that God provides us today, personally, individually, as we are able to digest it. But the closer a believer gets to God, the deeper the truths and the richer the spiritual food that is required.

The reward God wanted to give to the believers in Pergamum was a white stone inscribed with a new name which no one would know except the person to whom it is given. White is the colour of heaven for it represents, in its truest form, total and absolute purity throughout.

The white stone is considered to be a glistening diamond, the hardest, purest, brightest and the most desired of the precious stones. The Urim (meaning lights), which with the Thummim (meaning perfections) (Ex. 28:30), was held in the pouch (the breastplate of judgement) worn by the high priest when He went into the Holy place to consult with God regarding some matter of concern. It was only the high priest who knew the name that was written on the Urim and saw the hidden manna to remind him of the how God supplies our practical needs and only he was originally intended to be the final source of direct revelation and guidance from God.

In this case, the stone being presented to the believer who overcomes is inscribed with a new (heavenly and completely new) name.

What this reference to the hidden manna and Urim stone indicates is the elevation of every overcoming believer to a similar position in the new dispensation to that of the high priest of old who had direct access to the revelation and guidance of God, for the Aaronic high priest alone was able to enter into the holiest places in the tabernacle and near where God dwelt between the heavenly bodies (cherubim) sculptured in gold on the cover of the Ark of the Covenant.

This then is the reward promised to the believers of this church and those who would hear what the Spirit says to the churches and overcomes through the support and inspiration of the Holy Spirit. But the warning is that if the world did not love Christ, it will not love us; if the Jews did not love their Messiah when He appeared, they will not love us now, until that is the time of their salvation comes.

The Church at Thyatira (2:18)

To: The angel, messenger, and overseer of the church at Thyatira.

From: The Son of God who has eye like flames of fire *(v 23 "I am He who searches the minds and hearts")* and feet like fine brass (representing strength – v27 *"He shall rule them with a rod of iron; they shall be dashed to pieces like the potter's vessel."* (from Ps. 2:9).

Where they were: *"I know your works, love, service, faith and your patience. As for your works, the last are more than the first."* That is they had increased their efforts to serve God and had the results of the increased effort to show for it.

The problem: *"You allow that women Jezebel, who calls herself a prophetess, to teach and seduce My servants to commit sexual immorality and eat things sacrificed to idols."*

Just like Jezebel, the wife of Ahab (1 Kings 16:31), whom he married against the will of God. It was this Jezebel, who led Ahab into greater sin with the brutish seizure of Naboth's vineyard (1 Kings 21 esp. v7), who promoted the worship of Baal. It was her priests Elijah slaughtered after the dramatic contest on Mt Carmel (1 Kings 18). This modern Jezebel, a self styled prophetess had beguiled the believers in Thyatira and seduced them by her charms into sexual immorality. A deviant lifestyle to that which our Lord had taught and the disciples had written about; just as the previous Jezebel had encouraged the people of the northern tribes to deviate from all that God had taught them and the prophets had written about all those years ago.

The essence of these letters and their subject matter must be to challenge all believers throughout the centuries, and most definitely in this modern age, to look to their own activities and see how they match up to the Word of God. Ask yourselves the question, "In all that I do is there anything that is contrary to the high calling of God in Christ?" Or to put it another way, "Am I living the life of believer, or is my life really no different to those who do not believe, with the sole exception that I attend church services?"

How are you matching up to what you are learning about being obedient to the teaching of our Lord as revealed by what you have learned so far?

There is much 'liberal' theology at large in the church today, which allows a personal interpretation of the word of God to influence their walk with Him. But, and it is a very big BUT, it is not the will of God that we should stray from a strict adherence of His will and purpose for us as it is revealed to us through the Holy Spirit, if, that is, the Spirit of God dwells in us..

So what is the true will of God?

1. to do justly and to love mercy (towards our fellow man). We must consider our fellow men for God loves them all just as much as He loves us as individuals (read Lk. 10:25 – 37). If we want God to be merciful to us how can we not show, in like manner, mercy towards others (Matt. 18:21 – 35)?

2. to walk humbly with our God (Micah 6:8). Something that is not thought about in our churches today is the need for each one of us to be totally committed to God. If God in Christ paid such a high price for us, should we not be prepared to offer Him our all as a sign of appreciation for His sacrifice?

It is easy to be concerned about the things of this life. Martha had this problem when Jesus came to call (Lk. 10:41, 42). But what are we required to do? Focus on God by walking in the Spirit, for then the things of the flesh will not be able to distract us (Gal. 5:16). There is a chorus I remember singing as a child:

Turn your eyes upon Jesus
Look full in His wonderful face
And the things of earth will grow strangely dim
In the light of His goodness and grace.

This is what the believers at Thyatira were not doing!

So what of this woman Jezebel who had seduced some of the men (and possibly some of the women) into sexual immorality and eating things sacrificed to idols? Many of those who were converted would have been idol worshippers and prone to that way of life.

Remember that they did not have the second testament scriptures chosen and collected together and a printed in a book as we have them today. There was also other literature of a deceptive nature freely available in a volatile environment of a confusion of language and nationhood (Rome was the occupying force at the time) and many would be poor and illiterate, so it is important that we do not judge them unjustly.

But it is still the degree of impact that the message of the salvation offered by Christ had upon the life of ordinary people in that area at that time. From the rich to the poverty stricken, like the people of Smyrna, some, having heard the message of salvation, believed. But with the young church came immature leaders who would have found it hard to make the necessary changes in their own lives from that of pagan to Christian. It certainly meant that they would become vulnerable to the deceptive advances of those who worked for the evil one. Having responded to the gospel message, did they then earnestly seek the confirmation of that salvation through the infilling of the Holy Spirit?

To the believers of that day it was all very new. No established churches or church hierarchy to sustain them, or easily purchased Bibles in various translations in the shops. But the people were converted and gave themselves whole-heartedly to worshipping God and serving Him, and we are the beneficiaries of their struggles.

When Paul reached Ephesus he asked some believers if they had received the Holy Spirit when they believed. But they had not even heard about any Holy Spirit. Just as the disciples had not been empowered until they were baptized in the Holy Spirit (Acts 1:6), so too the Ephesians Paul met were not empowered and given to understand the scriptures without receiving the filling of the Holy Spirit. It is the reason Jesus spent time teaching the disciples about what they had to prepare themselves for after His death and the essential nature of the work of the Holy Spirit (Jn. 15, 16, 17).

The reason why the word of God has been effective and survived all these years of the history of mankind since the ascension of our Lord and Saviour, is because of the work of the Holy Spirit in the lives of those believers who were willing to open up themselves to Him, and the power He has been able display in the life of individuals (male or female). Jesus had told His disciples that they would receive power when the Holy Spirit had come upon them, and this is as true today as it was then. We have no spiritual power, no real or dynamic spiritual relationship with the spiritual God of our salvation unless the Holy Spirit takes up residence in our bodies. In all the chaos of human history the Holy Spirit has been active in the lives of individuals and many have been saved to the uttermost. It is He who has overseen the writing and compilation of the second testament and the combining of the two testaments into today's Bible.

If there are things that you do not quite understand you need to ask God about it. Don't just offer a quick prayer, "Lord I do not understand what is being said here, please enlighten me". First seek God and mean it, after all He alone knows what you are thinking in your heart better than you do! Then don't just ask God to open your eyes (Ps. 119:18, 27), but keep on asking, indeed pester Him for an answer by continually asking and open the Word of God and read the scriptures frequently until you have an answer. Have you been baptized with the Holy Spirit? Do you know what being baptized in the Holy Spirit is all about? You don't know? Then don't be worried but seek God by constantly asking Him as you would ask a friend to give you understanding (Lk. 11:5 – 13), and if you realize you have not received the Holly Spirit, then ask God to fill you with His Spirit. But be ready as much to listen to His voice, as you are to ask Him.

On the question of the baptism of the Holy Spirit, we have only to look at what happened to the disciples at Pentecost. The Holy Spirit filled them, occupied their bodies and minds and hearts. Did that mean that they were filled with the knowledge of God continually and never went wrong? Unfortunately no! They continued to make mistakes, but God was undoubtedly with them and guided them with regard to where they went, what they did and what they said so that His message got told to those they met and to those who received their letters.

God has been remarkable active in my life in recent years. But that does not mean that He was not active before, just in more subtle ways, sometimes without my realizing it. The first principle is for you to believe that, whatever the circumstances, or however you 'feel', God is with you; that is what faith is all about (Fantastic Adventure In Trusting Him even when things seem to be going wrong). It is then up to you to trust Him to do what is right in spite of any tendency you might have to make wrong choices or decisions; this is what I have had to do, so what I am writing to you is from my experience.

Surely the situations experienced by the members of the early church are the same as those we are experiencing today, although perhaps in a more sophisticated way. Even in this modern environment there is the same sense of confusion with such a mix up of peoples and languages, wars and rumours of wars, bombings and other terrorist activities, all perpetrated by those who are obedient to the evil one and therefore far from the knowledge of the truth of our creator God.

We too must be convinced that we are sinful and in need of a Saviour; that we need to hear about Christ who is able to save to the uttermost. We then we need to confess and repent of our sins and ask God to be merciful to us and forgive us, washing us in the blood Christ shed upon the Cross at Calvary. It is then that the Holy Spirit applies that conscience cleansing blood to us (Heb. 9:14). After that we need to seek for ourselves a relationship with Christ that will sustain us; it is not a one-way process!

Just as in a marriage, it is the man and the woman getting involved with each other, determined to enable the love affair between them to grow deeper in order to sustain the marriage; so it is the individual's determined response to God's love for them that seals their individual marriage to the Lord Jesus. He will not fail anyone who wants to experience a deepening relationship with Him. But those that do not respond and seek Him with all their hearts, that marriage will founder because of their failure not His.

The marriage of some of the believers at Thyatira to their Lord was failing. This was because they took their eyes off the Lord Jesus and allowed themselves to become interested in this alternative gospel, which was in fact not a gospel of life but of death. It bore no relationship to anything taught by the apostles and other true believers.

God gave this woman time to repent (v21) but she did not repent because she was far too worldly focused. The promise of God was that He would cause her to become ill, along with those who followed her teaching. Children born from their activities would die. This would be taken as a sign by the churches round about, particularly because of what John had written, of God's judgment; it would also clearly emphasize the fact that God searches minds and hearts not just the outward appearance and works, indeed they would be rewarded according to their works (v23).

It is important to note that there are varying degrees of believers, even today (Matt. 13:3 – 9, 18 – 23). There are those who, having received the message of salvation have been saved but do not advance beyond babyhood, remaining as babes at the breast (Heb. 5:12 – 14). There are those who move on and grow into adults, but who do not have that spark of the Holy Spirit within them that would take them deeper into the things of God because the pull of the world and their integration in it is too important to them. Finally there are those who seek not just the taste for spiritual maturity but cannot get deep enough into the spiritual life of the Lord for they are in a constant state of being hungry for more of Him. We will all be rewarded according to our works (1 Cor. 3:12 - 23).

It will have been a relief to those who were upset by this woman's activities that they would not be tainted by her activities (v24) and no other burdens would be placed upon them. However it would undoubtedly have made them determined to follow the Lord even more circumspectly than before. This record of events must impact upon our lives also, because what happened then is bound to happen today in some gatherings of believers, for such is the fallen nature of men. What is very clear is that there has never been an excuse for anyone to fall by the wayside.

The teaching of nature is towards the existence of God, however much those who have followed Darwinian type ideas deny His existence by their doctrine of the mystical Big Bang theory (how it occurred or if there was someone engineering it seems not to have been investigated too thoroughly, possibly in case the truth is revealed which would undermine Satan's efforts in promulgating confusion).

There have always been those in the world (the salt of the earth) who have been beacons for God and His Christ (Jew and Gentile). They are the ones who have, through their life and witness in the world, directed those who showed an interest in God to God, giving them the knowledge of God (His address if you like), so that they can contact Him themselves.

At the time of John's letters, and now his Revelation, the message of the gospel was spreading like wildfire throughout the Roman Empire and beyond. The English language (and for a time the now defunct British Empire), plus the missionary activity entered into by inspired individuals and organisations during those years of greatness, helped the spread of the Gospel of Christ around the world. And even today the universal use of the English language is providing a means of the further spreading of the word.

A hare once challenge a tortoise to a race. The course was agreed and officials appointed to ensure fair play. From the start the hare forged ahead leaving the tortoise far behind, but the tortoise undismayed plodded on towards the finishing line. Half way round the course the hare, realizing he was way ahead of the tortoise, decided that he would have a rest. Unfortunately he fell asleep and whilst he slept the tortoise passed him. On waking the hare looked at his watch and realized that he was in danger of loosing the race. Running towards the finishing line as fast as his legs would carry him he began to realize that he had indeed lost the race for there in the distance beyond the finishing line was the tortoise.

This is a tale that I heard many, many years ago. So why have I included it here? Because it can highlight a principle that is an essential element in the believer's walk.

The essence of the messages contained in this book relates to the degree of dedication of the believers to the Word of God and His will and plan for them. Apart from the church at Smyrna all were found wanting in one-way or another; hence the need to highlight a problem and a solution.

In the case of the Ephesian church they had lost their first love and for the Pergamum church they had made unacceptable compromises. To both God offers a solution. But what does this mean to us? In the story above the hare thought he was so far in front of the other participant that he had timed to have a rest.

Paul speaks about the Christian life as a race, taking the symbolism from the Greek and Roman games that would have been a feature in many major cities of the empire. "I press towards the goal," writes Paul, "for the prize of the high calling of God in Christ Jesus." (Phil. 3:14).

What is the prize a runner in a race most desires? To win! The tortoise in our strange story had one objective. Whatever the ability of the other competitor, he wanted to finish the course and cross the finishing line. As it happened the hare focused on his own ability to run fast, not on the importance of running to win. The hare was so full of his own ability to run fast that he failed the test of the race, which was that he should run without slacking, focused on that goal which was the finishing line. It was a very uneven race, for the very fast was set against the very slow. But in the Christian race this matters little for all who complete the race win. It is the way we run the race and ensure we finish it that matters.

In the Christian life our aim must be to finish the race by reaching the goal, which is the high calling of God in Christ Jesus – that is Heaven. It is possible to slacken; to take things easy. But we need to remember there are dangers on the way, for the Devil is seeking to divert us (I Pet. 5:6 – 10), to encourage us to slackening or take things easy. That is why our determination to run the race to win is so crucial. The tortoise plodded on determined to finish the race, never slackening his pace, for he knew his limitations. We are sinners saved by the grace of God. It is therefore essential that we do not allow ourselves to become proud or conceited; to think at any time that we are better than anyone else. In fact, because we all need the cleansing blood of the Saviour, no believer is any better than another.

At the start we need to ensure we go through the right gate and travel the right path for wide is the gate and broad the way that leads to destruction but narrow the gate and difficult the path that leads to life, and there are few that find the gate (Matt. 7:13,14). What does that mean in normal language? We need to know the true Saviour from all the religious imitations of Him that are put before us in this world. This means a decision. If we do not make a definite and decisive choice to follow Christ, unable to make up our minds as to which the saviour actually is, then we will mistake the entrance gate (Ps. 118:19, 20; cf. Jn. 10:7; see 1 Cor. 16:9). But once we have identified the Christ, or He has made Himself know to us, then we must remain focused on following Him and travelling that difficult way as all His disciple have done previously (Jn. 14:6).

What Jesus said to each of the disciples was very simply, *"Follow Me" (Matt. 9:9)*. But how can we follow someone we do not know? That is why it is so important for each and every one of us to seek the Lord while He may be found (Is. 55:6; Matt. 7:7). Andrew was so sure he had found the Messiah that he immediately went and told his brother Peter (Jn. 1:41), and we also need to be sure that we have found the Christ before we attempt to follow Him and travel on the Way that leads to life, for it is difficult.

We also need to be determined, once we have made the decision to follow Christ, to continue to the end. Those in Thessalonica followed the Lord after receiving the word in great affliction. But the word had come to them in power and in the Holy Spirit, that is the word was applied to their hearts and minds by the Holy Spirit in such a way that they were so convinced of its validity that they were willing to suffer, having received this life giving message with joy (1 Thes. 1:5, 6). Jesus did not hide the fact that because He attracted opposition, all who followed Him would meet the same opposition (see Mk. 8:34 – 38), which is why His followers had to be prepared to surrender their earthly lives and expectations in order to gain the eternal life that was on offer. The Thessalonians were willing to do just that, purely because of the impact the message they received had on them and the way the Holy Spirit opened that message up to them.

In the letter to the believers in Pergamum we read of the martyrdom of Antipas. Did he follow after the Lord Jesus expecting to lose his life? I doubt it. But the fact that he was willing to give up his life, rather than deny the Lord Jesus, tells us that he valued his human life as nothing in order to obtain the greater prize of being with his Lord in heaven.

We who live in the 21st century might not have to face martyrdom, but we do have to make the decision of whether or not we are prepared to follow God's plan for us whatever the personal cost, and remain faithful to Him until we are called home.

The solution: The solution for the woman prophetess was to repent, but this she failed to do.

The penalty: She and those who aligned themselves with her were to perish.

An asset: Those who did not follow her teaching, who did not plumb the depths of Satan's alternative teaching and abominations, on them would be put no other burdens.

Is it not interesting that there were some, who did not have any leadership role in the church, who refused to accept the teaching of this errant woman and kept the focus of their attention on the Lord and His word? These remarkably steadfast believers clearly demonstrate that every individual believer has the option of accepting or rejecting what they are taught by others. It is as individuals that we are saved; it is as individuals that the Lord wants to enter into a marriage type relationship with us; it is as individuals that we will be judged; it is as individuals that we will enter heaven or hell.

Individual believers have no excuse. If they fall by the wayside it is their responsibility. The ten spies may have given the people a biased report, but it was up to each individual to make up his own mind and not go along with the crowd. Narrow is the gate that we are to go through to enter upon the way fraught with difficulties and dangers. But it is that way alone that leads to life.

Unfortunately there was not the variety of different types of 'church' organisations in Thyatira at the time John was writing, so they were stuck with the only church available. In that situation these dear focused individuals, who refused to accept her teaching and kept themselves to the truth they had first received remained steadfast, and it was that steadfastness that led them to the joy of being named by the Lord Himself and told that they would have to endure no other burden.

The recovery: *"But hold fast to what you have till I come."*

That is they were to hold fast to the belief and faith that had sustained them and the teaching that had been the basis for that faith.

The reward: *"He who overcomes and keeps My works to the end, to him I will give power over the (enemy) nations (Lk. 19:17), as also I have received power from My Father; and I will give him the morning star. He who has an ear let him hear what the Spirit says to the churches."*

Those who use the gifts, the talents that God has given them, and remain faithful to Him even though they have not met Him in the flesh, no matter what the opposition does to deflect them from the way, to them not only will God give responsibilities in His kingdom but will give them Himself (for He is the morning star – consider 2 Pet. 1:19; Rev. 22:16) that they also might shine brightly as evidence that they belong to God in Christ.

To him who has (spiritually attuned) ears to hear, let him hear what the Spirit says to the churches. Let him hear and be aware and mindful of what the Holy Spirit is saying, not just to the church mentioned, but also what He is teaching the churches around about, in this case the other six churches. There is no doubt that we can all learn from the experiences of others, particularly where individuals or churches are growing or declining with regard to their faith and walk in the Spirit.

Clarity, assurance and conviction of belief must be the foundation stones for the individual Christian's life, for the simple reason that that is the only way their walk with God will allow their relationship with Him to become increasingly more spiritually intimate and ultimately grow to maturity. Those who deceive others will definitely receive the appropriate reward for their actions, make no mistake about it. What makes our understanding of the situation in the church at Thyatira so important is that not all the believers in the church at Thyatira went along with the teaching of this Jezebel. This means that for those that attend a church where there was errant teaching, providing they remain faithful to the God of their salvation and His word to them, they would be sustained in their spiritual life, for this letter tells us that those who remained faithful would be rewarded, not those who followed after the deception.

We so well to treat this study seriously! Indeed, cannot stress enough that it is the responsibility of each and every believer to pursue their own walk with God. There will come a time when each and everyone of us will be required to give an account of our actions and whether our work has been for good or evil (Matt. 12:35 – 37; Rom. 14:12; I Cor. 3:9 – 20; Rev. 21:11 – 15), and teachers of God's word, like myself, will be judged with greater severity than those who only receive the word. It is the responsibility of all believers to listen to what the Spirit is telling us through God's word and act upon it, for these things will happen, of that there can be no doubt. Let everyone be assured that not every one will enter into God's rest (Heb. 3:7 – 19). And it is on the day of judgement, when we individually stand before the great white throne, that the sheep will be separated from the goats (Matt. 25:31, 32). It is your personal responsibility to ensure you will be among the sheep.

If you personally have not read the Word of God often, or with a searching mind, asking, nay pleading with the Lord to open up its real meaning to you, and then applying what you have learned to your own life, or if you personally, on the strength of all that you have read and understood to be your state before God, have not sought with all your heart and mind and strength for the Holy Spirit to lead you into a deeper and more intimate spiritual relationship with Him, then your state before Him could well bring a reprimand from Him.

The believers in the church at Sardis (next letter) thought they were true born again Christians. That is what they honestly thought. Indeed they were happy in that state, believing they were saved to the uttermost. It is all too easy if we do not seek the Lord with determined passion, even as a drowning man seeks with all his might to grab hold of anything floating on the surface that will sustain his life, to be lulled into a false sense of security. But so many in the churches today have no idea whatsoever that through their lack of searching the Bible for truth, without any preconceived ideas, and spending time in prayer asking God to speak with them, to show them the way of truth, to fill them with the Holy Spirit to ensure that they keep to the path He has planned for them, then it is possible that they will walk straight out of the will of God. (The disciples asked the Lord to teach them to pray. They were learning new things from Him. Things that had the authority of the Father behind them, for our Lord only spoke what His Father had told Him to speak about. Things that they had never heard before, because the spiritual deadness of the Scribes and the Pharisees prevented them from knowing the truth that would set them free.)

You may think that I am labouring this point too much. My friends that is not possible because it is vital that you accept what I am saying and ensure you do what

I am advising you to do. It is your decision. If you want to meet with the Lord in the paradise of heaven, then you have no alternative but to seek Him with all your heart and mind and soul and strength. That is the condition God set for us to enter into a relationship with Him. The first commandment says it all, *"You shall love the Lord thy God with All thy mind and with All thy heart and with All thy soul and with All thy strength"*. If that isn't a total giving of oneself to God, I do not know what is.

One of the greatest compromises the church is allowing today is that of same sex relationships and marriages. This IS an abomination to the Lord and always will be. Be assured that He will not change His mind because He made us Male and Female. No other relationship produces children. Anyone who accepts compromises must accept that God will disown them. That is not to say that we should treat those that are that way inclined with hostility of any kind. We must pray for those we know about, and love them into the kingdom, that is if there is any chance that we might change their minds. We are not allowed by God to judge them (Matt. 7:1, 2), only to warn them with loving gentleness of the consequences of their activities.

God is waiting for each and every one of us to respond to Him for He desires that no one should perish (2 Pet. 3:9). Be assured that only those who either reject His call out right, or live their lives according to their own desires, will find themselves in hell.

Do you believe me to be too harsh and uncompromising in what I have written? Then let me ask you some pertinent questions:

- Who sinned, the Lord the creator of all that is seen and unseen or Adam?
- Who has not only inherited sin, as the descendents of Adam, but has also acquired personal sins?
- Who designed the way of salvation?
- Who was prepared to leave His home in Glory, surrender His spiritual existence and clothed Himself with a human body?
- Who was then prepared to suffer the indignation of being despised, slandered and falsely accused of sin by the very people He had chosen to be recipients of the first and second covenants?

- Who paid the price of sin, even thought He was sinless, so that we might be saved to the uttermost?
- Who is dependent upon whom for their salvation?
- Who can set the rules concerning who can be saved?
- Who has the authority to say who will be saved and who will not be saved?

If your answers imply that it is we who are the sinners and it is the Lord God of Israel who has provided the sacrificial Lamb and the way of salvation, then you must also agree that He has the power in His own hands to save whom He will and reject whom He will.

Whether or not I am uncompromising is not the issue. The real issue is if you desire to be saved then you shall accept the conditions attached to that salvation. And the conditions are that you obey the word of the Lord, not the word of the Lord as interpreted by you or any other human being.

In all that I have written thus far, the Lord has impressed upon my spirit the essential nature of the importance of the vibrant spiritual life of the individual. The basis of this is that right from the start of the existence of Israel as a nation, the Lord wanted the sign of circumcision to be not just an outward sign of membership, but for that outward sign to be converted into a circumcision of the heart (which for the Israelite meant the centre of their thinking process not the emotions) because of their reaching out in their minds to the Lord to desire not just a physical understanding of that special relationship, but a spiritual understanding of the deeper things of God. So important is this matter that I believe the Lord would have me explain the importance the example Israel is for us who have been grafted onto Israel, through our own spiritual birth, which has been brought about by the Spirit of God.

The message is consistent and we need to take it to heart:

> He who has an ear, let him hear what the Spirit
> says to the churches.

The Church at Sardis (3:1)

To: The angel, messenger, and overseer of the church at

Sardis.

From: *"He who has the seven Spirits (representing the work of the Holy Spirit) of God and the seven stars (representing the seven churches)".*

Where they were: *"I know your works, that you have a name that you are alive, but you are dead."*

The problem: They were spiritually dead even though others thought from their outward appearance that they were alive.

God does not look at the outward appearance of anyone. His eyes are described as a fire for He is able to search the hidden depths of a man, the thoughts of the mind and the intents of the heart. Nothing escapes His critical gaze. The praise and worship within a church could suggest a fellowship of believers who are on fire for Him; whereas in truth it is all an outward show, a joyous time of music and words that has little depth of meaning to those who sing them because of a complete lack of inner personal commitment to the Lord Jesus. Anyone can sing the right songs, anyone can say the right things as they pray, but no one can fool the understanding and wisdom of the Lord as He looks into their spirits and hearts.

Indeed in this case the believers in the church in Sardis gave a show of being full of the Spirit of the Lord. Everything seemed right. The appearance was enough to fool those who looked on. But the Lord saw only spiritual deadness. Something Paul was most concerned about when he wrote to the church at Colossae and Laodicea (Col. 2). He wanted them to attain to all the riches of the full assurance of understanding of the Godhead, and to know about the mystery of God, both of the Father and of His Christ, in whom are hidden all the treasures of wisdom and knowledge (Col. 2:2, 3), rather than being cheated through philosophy and empty deceit, according to the tradition of men, according to the basic principles of the world (as written by Satan) and not according to Christ. (Col. 2:8).

It is only in Christ that the fullness of the Godhead dwells bodily. And these letters emphasize very strongly that Christ is not fooled and does not tolerate mediocrity before Him. Who suffered? Was it us? Or Christ? Surely it was Christ who endured three hours of agony during which time His father, with whom He had been intimate from eternity, turned away from Him? And this was for us, not for Himself! Who then can set the rules for those who would be saved that we shall abide by and walk in? Is it not the Christ who showed us the way of the cross by example?

I remember being invited back to a local church I had left because of guidance from the Lord. During the evening's activities (a party to say goodbye to the minister who was retiring and moving away from the area) I felt very strongly in my spirit the spiritual deadness of the people of that church. Even those I thought were alive were in fact spiritually dead. I am now very cautious when attending the worship in a church I am visiting about making a judgment of their state before God unless God enlightens me. It is so easy to take things at face value.

The believers of the church in Sardis (and at my previous church) had been deceived, cheated through philosophy and empty deceit, according to the tradition of men, according to the basic principles of the world (as written by Satan) and not according to Christ. What is particularly sad is that they did not at any time seek the truth for themselves through earnest prayer and the study of His word, for the truth was available to them at all times. Unfortunately they wanted to be spoon-fed. They wanted to take the easy path. What is so dangerous is that by thinking they were saved to the uttermost, they might find themselves barred from the joys of heaven because the Lord might tell them that He never knew them? The only way God can know you is by you seeking Him with all you heart, mind, spirit and strength and opening yourself up to the work of the Holy Spirit.

Even though we are saved by the grace of God and that it is the Holy Spirit that applies the blood of Christ to us, salvation is still the gift of God and if we do not of our own free will accept the gift, it is of no use to us. It is a matter of the will of an individual making the decision to accept that gift that dictates whether or not a person gets to know the Lord on a personal basis and He gets to know them.

The solution: *"Be watchful and strengthen the things that remain but are ready to die, for I have not found your works perfect before God. Remember therefore how you have received and heard; hold fast and repent."*

Such was their walk with the Lord that there were still some aspects that were just alive, but only just.

Do you see the importance of getting back to basics that start with the cross, and include going back to the time when you first believed and came into that knowledge of God that opened your eyes to the truth of the gospel; that brought you to repent of your sins so that you might enjoy the reality of the presence of God?

It will have made the difference between your continuing to live your life as you had before and making a decision to follow our Lord Jesus Christ. Then, having made that decision to follow God, you first received the gift of the Holy Spirit and your life was transformed. This is exactly what the believers in Sardis where being advised to do, "remember therefore how you have received and heard the message of salvation and hold fast to the gospel you have received and repent of your sin of falling away from following after the Saviour."

What is of particular concern, of course, is the question of whether or not you received the Holy Spirit when you first believed. When you made the decision to accept Christ into your life, did you then study the scriptures for yourself (hopefully with spiritual guidance from someone who was filled with the Holy Spirit) to find out how you could receive the baptism of the Holy Spirit, which affects different people in different ways because we all receive different gifts according to the tasks God has for us to do in the body of the church.

The penalty: *"If you will not watch, I will come upon you as a thief and you will not know the hour of my coming."*

It is our responsibility to seek after the Lord. He can call us to repentance. We can respond and receive that repentance which is of faith. But it is then up to us to continue to respond to God. As the Lord has touched my spirit and drawn me to Himself, I have had a desire in my spirit to pursue Him with my whole being that I might obtain more, much more, indeed very much more of Him. The more I receive the greater my hunger for even more of Him.

Our relationship with God must be progressive or it will stagnate and die. The Psalmist cries out, "Oh taste and see that the Lord is good; blessed is the man who trusts in Him!" (Ps. 34:8). But then, having tasted the good word of God, there is a very great and real danger that we might fall away with the possibility, or rather the probability, of our not renewing that repentance day by day, as we are required to do. In such a situation we would of all men be the most foolish, regretting not holding on to what we had when we come face to face with an eternity in the wrong place. This is what the believers of Sardis were in danger of experiencing.

God will not chase after us. The offer of salvation is freely available to all. It is, however, a gift and not ours by right, even if we received it at some time with joy. A future life bound up in Christ is ours if we want it, but be of no doubt whatsoever it is also ours to ignore, reject or neglect with tragic consequences. He will not implore us to accept what He has to offer, or for us to follow Him. If, as is the case with this church, we first believed and then went cold, there is the potential for Him to tell us, when we stand before the throne of judgement, *"Depart from Me for I never knew you!"* What terrible words to hear when you are expecting to be greeted with welcoming arms.

Are we not in a battle? (Eph. 6) Are there not deceivers who, having gone out from the church but were never of the church, are trying to encourage us to renounce our salvation? (1 Jn. 2:19). Is not the Devil likened to a lion prowling around seeking whom He may devour? (1 Pet. 5:8).

This is not a game but a life and death spiritual struggle!

Be in no doubt whatsoever. When you least expect it, Christ will come (Matt. 24:32 – 51; 2 Pet. 3:10 – 18 esp. vs. 17, 18) and remove your candlestick; the wild olive branch will be unceremoniously 'broken' off the cultivated olive tree and, without the root (which is Christ) supplying you with sustenance, you will die in your sins (Ro. 11:16 – 24; 1 Cor. 9:24 – 27). It is the truth! I do not lie! God is my witness that I pray before, during and after writing these things that God Himself will protect me from error, so that far from leading you astray I will lead you into such truth that it will inspire you to seek for the truth yourself.

An asset: *"You have a few names even in Sardis who have not defiled their garments; they shall walk with me in white for they are worthy."*

436

This statement, more than any other, emphasizes the responsibility for every individual to pursue their own path to salvation.

One cannot say to another, "You led me astray". They will have gone astray of themselves. It is when they allow themselves to be persuaded by others to pursue and alternative course, or when the attraction of the things of the world in which they live have a greater impact on their hearts and minds than the attraction of the things of God, that their spiritual eyes will grow dim and they will look away from Him (Matt. 14:22 – 32, esp. vs. 30 – 31). Peter, on seeing the Lord walking towards them on the water of the lake, desired to go to Him even on the water. But he started to sink as soon as the reality of his situation dawned on him, causing him to look away and see the water rather than keeping his eyes on Jesus from whom his strength came. Be in no doubt whatsoever that there is no situation that an individual will ever face in His service over which God does not have full and complete control.

The Word is there for all to read and God is always within praying distance to provide an understanding of the word to all those willing to take the trouble to find out about the truth of who God really is, and why the message that He is trying to give to men is so vitally important.

Those who attend church have far less excuse than anyone else of being ignorant of the things of God. Sadly, there are many within the church unwilling to give the personal commitment to God that He demands. Such unwillingness to get spiritually involved with God will cause them to grow cold, even to become spiritually dead, if, in fact, they ever allowed the Holy Spirit to regenerate their spirits in the first place. Others have believed they have been saved to the uttermost even when they were still dead in their sins and even though they went on to take up leadership and preaching roles within the church.

Unfortunately, the lack of spiritual regeneration leads individuals to teach the word through ignorance, and that allows them to be at the mercy of Satan. It also allows more unregenerate believers to be produced. Surely the parable of the sower and the seed highlights this situation so very clearly (Matt. 13). Unless the seed falls on good fallow ground that has been well prepared and fertilized, it will not survive. It is only those in whose heart the seed is sown (so that they understand it) and it takes root and is allowed to grow, even in all the storms (trials and tribulations) of life, that it will reach maturity to produce a crop (fruit) of a hundred or sixty or thirty fold. It is only such people in whom the seed has taken root and flourished who can possibility attempt to be like the man who found the treasure in a field or the merchant who found the pearl of great price (vs. 44, 45).

I feel incredibly burdened about this matter. God has taken the trouble to reach out to us. Yet many of those who say they believe are in fact unbelievers (Lk. 18:9 – 14). This is because their belief consists of practical, visible things that others can see, not the things of the Spirit that only God can see. Regularly meeting with other believers, singing the right hymns and spiritual songs, praying the right kind of prayers and serving others are all good in their own way, but unless there is within them that burning desire to know God, and to love Him with passion, to have Him (the God of Love) come and take up residence within them and to transform them into the vessel He wants them to be, then all the outward signs of a believer are a facade, a sham, a clanging cymbal (Matt. 15:8, 9; 1 Cor. 13 – chapters 12 to 14 should be read as one). When it is without substance, the Christian faith does no one any good; indeed it does the work of the Gospel of Christ great harm.

The question you must ask yourself is, "Am I alive in Christ?" If you are in any way unsure of how to answer, then pray and keep on praying until you are sure in whom you have believed. Ask God, no implore Him to reveal Himself to you, demand an answer, and do not stop praying until there is no doubt in your mind that you have been united with Christ, with the Holy Spirit witnessing the truth to your spirit.

We have the example of those spoken about in the second testament that met with the Messiah. They thought they knew the truth, proclaiming that they were true descendents of Abraham and disciples of Moses. Outwardly, they seemed to be respected, true believers in the same God whose existence Abraham and Moses gave witness to through, and throughout their lives. But even though they assumed leadership roles and preached in the name of God, they were far from the truth (Jn. 5:39 – 47; 8:31 – 40).

Did Caleb or Joshua follow after the people when the ten spies told the people that the mighty men and the fortified cities in the Promised Land were too strong for them? No. Emphatically No! Both did their best to dissuade the people from rebelling against God. This was because they realized their future was also on the line and they did not know what God would do in response to the people's cry of frustration and bewilderment and their rejection of His certain promises to them (Num. 14:6 – 9).

The statement above also provides a clear message of hope to those who are alive, but find themselves amongst those who are dead in Christ within the church they attend, unable to meet with others who are of like mind. These faithful few remained resolute in their love for and knowledge of God, believing in all His sure and certain promises, entering into a living and vibrant relationship with Him which sustained them and kept them from spiritual death.

The situation is not unknown to me. I have met with lay preachers who clearly had not that spark of Divine fire, that measure of the Spirit that identifies them as being born anew and aware of the things of the Spirit. Ordained and lay, the members of the meeting seemed blind and dead to the things of God. The meeting of those who had taken on the responsibility of teaching the people the truth of the Gospel, which should have been a spiritual power house with time for praise in the Spirit (Act 16:25) and prayer for the people and for the preaching of the Word in power, could better be described as a spiritual morgue, full of dead men's bones.

Do not be misled. God will do all that He says He will do; separating the good from the bad, the edible from the inedible (Matt. 13:47 – 50), the sheep from the goats, so that only those who believe with all of their hearts and minds will be chosen. God requires thinking men and women, who firmly and actively believe that:

- He truly is the Christ of God,

- through Him alone can salvation be obtained
- committing their lives fully and whole heartedly to His service is the only way to properly follow Him and be His own.

Such people will be (not maybe or could be) saved to the uttermost, entering into the joy of their Lord (Matt. 25:21, 23). But let us be in no mind to soften God's word by saying that everyone will eventually go to heaven. The Word of God, that is the anointed of God, the Christ, says otherwise. Those that say to rebels against God that all will be well are preaching an alternative doctrine.

The recovery: *"He who overcomes will be clothed in white garments and I will not blot out his name from the book of life; ..."*

In the ancient church, those who would be baptized were dressed in white identifying them as those who have been washed in the blood of the lamb and made whiter than snow (Is. 1:18). It was in those garments that they were subjected to the waters of baptism, symbolically dying to self and rising up to life eternal. Those who have truly overcome, and therefore not allowed the filth of sin and rebellion to defile and soil their garments, will continue to wear white garments.

Let us be very clear about what this means. It states categorically that he who does not overcome will, in consequence, not be clothed in white (purity, saved to the uttermost), nor have his name written in the book of life. This is a serious business. The generally accepted saying of 'once saved always saved' does not necessarily hold true. It is possible to lose ones state of being saved. But how many of God's people are aware of this fact?

The reward: *"... but I will confess his name before My Father and before his angels."*

Does the Father know about you? Have you been saved? Are you being saved? Will you be saved in the future because of your commitment to follow Christ Jesus and become His disciple? Will you be one of the faithful who will enter through the gates of pearl (Rev. 21:21) into the New Jerusalem?

It is only the man that:
1. is spiritually aware,
2. has spiritual ears actively listening to what the Spirit says to the churches,
3. takes those things to heart, applying what he

hears to his life and thereby overcoming the
pitfalls and dangers of the Christian life
who is able to reap the rewards being promised.

The Church at Philadelphia (3:7)

To: The angel, messenger and overseer of the church at
Philadelphia.

From: *"He who is holy and true, who has the key of David so that what
He opens no one can shut and what He closes no one can open."*

David, a man after God's heart, became king of the
nation of Israel, an absolute ruler. It was he who had the
power to allow men to enter or require them to leave the
capital city, to maintain life or to deny it to those who
opposed him and the nation he ruled.

In those days anyone who held the keys to the city
had the authority to open or close the gate, and no one
else could overrule him, except the king of that city. It
was also between the inner and outer gate into the city
where the government of that city met. So in every
respect the gate was vital to the city both in the day-to-
day activity of entering, leaving and governing and for its
defence (Matt. 16:18).

Christ is called the Son of David for, in His human
state, He is in the direct line of descent from David. He is
of course superior to David (Matt. 22:43 – 45), having
been born before David, and ruling the spiritual as well as
the actual kingdom of Israel. It is He who has the
ultimate authority over the keys to the Kingdom of God,
the new city of Jerusalem that is being prepared for all
true believers. He also has the keys (that is the authority
over the entrance) to hell and death for he has the
authority to decide who lives and who dies, who has a
place prepared for them in heaven and who has not and
is therefore 'persona non grata' (Matt. 10:28).

Where they were: *"I know your works, see I have set before you an open door which
no one can shut for you have little strength, you have kept My word
and not denied My name."*

In witnessing to their faith in Christ they were
resolute. But it was a strain. In spite of considerable
opposition from the Jewish community they refused to
give up their study of the word of God, their search for
truth or to deny the name of the Lord Jesus Christ. These
were essential to their daily lives because they fully

believed in the God of their salvation and had committed themselves to Him.

These words of our Lord must give each one of us, especially those who have served God through many difficulties, much encouragement, for the Lord is saying here that because they had been faithful witnesses but were tiring, He was giving them an open door to ease their burden, enabling them to continue to believe and evangelize through their determined witness to the truth, thereby preventing those opposing them the opportunity to overcome and silence them. It would seem it was a critical time for them, and the Lord's intervention was crucial to their continuing survival and work as His servants.

The problem: They had but a little strength remaining because of the ferocity of the spiritual battle. Unyielding in their dedication to the Lord Jesus, for they had not only been obedient to His word but had also not denied His Name, or follow a deviant gospel. They had faced the considerable animosity and opposition from the Jewish community, the members of which, like their fellow Jews in Israel, thought they owned an exclusive right to God (Jn. 8:44). But it was those that opposed them that were far from the God, and in fact they had crossed over to serve the adversary of all true believers, Satan.

The Philadelphian believer's stand for God was so consistent and resolute that God moved some (how many we are not told, although it is unlikely to have been all of them, just the remnant) within the Jewish community, whose hearts were not so hard, into realizing that these Christians had something to which they felt drawn. These Jews came to the embattled believers and knelt before them to seek for their forgiveness and to learn of them (see Ps. 115:9 – 13).

In this way their hearts were made malleable (Eze. 36:26) and they were able to discover that their God, the God they thought they had worshipped and served, had been blessing these believers because of their acceptance of their Messiah, Jesus Christ.

The members of the church had taken the Lord at His word, for they had accepted in faith the full and free salvation that He offered to them and as a result God had blessed them. As they had witnessed to their faith and the blessings they had received, in spite of the tactics that had been used in cruelly opposing them, some of the Jews began to realize that these Gentile believers were closer to their God than were the members of the Jewish community. It was that realization that finally persuaded some of the Jews to meet with the Gentile believers.

Although this conversion of some of their Jewish persecutors was not offered to the believers at Smyrna, who were in a similar situation regarding the local hard line Jewish community, it is important not to make comparisons. This is because God deals with us as individuals in the circumstances in which we find ourselves. He ultimately knows what is best. It would seem the believers at Smyrna were going through far harsher trials, against a more determined foe, which included imprisonment and death, than were these believers at Philadelphia, which is why such comparisons should be avoided.

It is abundantly clear, however, that throughout its history the church has been purified by times of trial. It is then that believers must make the stark choice: suffer or deny the Lord. On one occasion when Russia occupied Hungary, believers had gathered in a large church in a Hungarian city. During their time of worship a Russian soldier entered and went to the front of the building. Facing the congregation and pointing his gun at them he told those who did not want to die to get out. When the remnant was left sitting in their seats the soldier lowered his gun and apologized to the remaining congregation. "I am sorry that I had to do that, but I also am a believer. But I could not tell you that in front of those who would go and tell the authorities."

The solution: Because they had kept God's command to persevere He will keep them from the time of trial, which shall test all who live on the earth. It is not as though God is expecting them to do something He is unwilling to do, for Christ is our example in perseverance. However, as they had been faithful and were getting weary, so God would be faithful in protecting them, preventing them from being tested more than they were capable of withstanding (1 Cor. 10:13).

It is interesting that temptation brings out the fidelity in those who believe, but hardens the reaction of unbelievers and the criminally inclined.

"Behold", says the Lord, *"I am coming quickly! Hold fast to what you have, so that no one can take away your crown."* The true believers at Philadelphia had suffered much, were promised much and the crown of life that they would receive was all but theirs. Providing they maintained the same stance that had brought them such commendation from God, then the crown of life would be theirs.

Although they still had to remain faithful until death whilst the battle continued to rage around them, they were assured of God's support and encouragement.

The penalty:	There was none.
An asset:	They had assets aplenty.
The recovery:	There was nothing from which they needed to recover.
The reward:	*"He who overcomes, (rather he who continues to overcome) I will make them a pillar (or permanent fixture) in the temple of My God and he shall go out no more (rather he shall have no reason for leaving it). I will write on him (that is on his forehead) the name of My God with the name of the city of My God (the New Jerusalem), which comes down out of heaven from My God. I will also write on him My new name."*

What a wonderful reward, one that all believers seek. That we should have the mark, the stamp of God on our foreheads for it is His way of declaring to all that we belong to Him. With the name of the Father and the Son and the name of the place where we will enjoy eternity and a peace and joy that far exceeds anything that we are aware of today on earth, our reward is certain and sure.

How wonderful for these dearly beloved brethren in Christ who, in spite of their suffering at the hands of disgruntled, rebellious and hardhearted Jews had, with considerable faith, tenaciously remained faithful to their calling in Christ Jesus. Having heard the truth of the Gospel, possibly from an itinerate preacher of the word, they had not just believed their report but accepted Christ as their own and were determined to remain faithful to their calling whatever the consequences. And that without the written word and theological knowledge that we have available to us today. As such they have become an example to us all, especially the believers in the affluent countries of the world of today.

Regarding the one, or ones, who took the good news of the Saviour to them, surely it can be said, "How beautiful … are the feet of them who bring good news, who proclaim peace, who bring glad tidings of good things, who proclaim salvation, who say to Zion Your God reigns." (Is. 52:7).

They were willing to abandon all to follow Him, taking up their cross; they were willing to count their lives as nothing (Matt. 10:38, 39) in order to gain the prize of the high calling of God (Phil. 3:14).

The Church at Laodicea (3:14)

To: The angel, messenger and overseer of the church at Laodicea.

From: *"The Amen, the Faithful and True Witness, the Beginning of the creation of God."*

Here Christ refers to Himself as the Amen at the beginning as He did when making an announcement (verily, verily I say to you) to certify what followed was of God. In Hebrew the noun 'āmēn means "firmness" and is derived from the verb root 'āman meaning "to believe" (Abram believed in the Lord and said "Amen" to God's promise). He is the Witness who was and is both Faithful and True to the Father in everything He has done, is doing and will do in the future. He is also the Beginning of the creation of God because He brought it into being.

These titles are particularly important because they relate to the accusations that follow.

Where they were: *"I know your works, that you are neither hot nor cold. I could wish you were either hot or cold. So because you are lukewarm I will vomit you out of My mouth."*

"Because you say that you are rich having become wealthy and are not in any need, you have no idea that in fact you are wretched, miserable, poor, blind and naked."

These piercing accusations were received by a church that thought they were perfectly in tune with God, just as the Jews of the synagogue thought they were the chosen of God and therefore special in His sight. But the problem for them was not to do with outward appearances but matters of the heart and the spirit.

The problem: Human kind needs to display their wealth for all to see. The large houses dotted around the United Kingdom with huge acreages of land surrounding them, are testament to the affluent men who had them built. People of today display their wealth in the clothes they wear, the cars they drive and the location, value and size of the houses in which they live.

The believers of Laodicea were just such people. They were not troubled by Jews from the local synagogue, because their belief did not threatening the Jews standing as God's chosen people; in fact it might be that they did business together. Indeed, they were in the unfortunate position of not being cold towards the Spirit of God, but not being hot either. Satan only attacks those who are on fire for the Lord because he wants to extinguish the flames. This means that by being lukewarm it was not possible for a dynamic relationship to be established between them and their Lord and therefore He was unable to use them in His work. In fact they could have been considered an embarrassment to Him, because they were giving the wrong messages to the unsaved regarding the power of salvation that He wanted to publicize through them.

In the state they were in, probably living comfortable lives at ease with the local population, and with no problem affording all that they required to live a comfortable life, they were no threat to Satan and therefore no good to God. They were living lives independent of Him. That is not how our God works. We have to be dependent on Him because without the salvation He offers us we are dead men, and without His constant support and strength we will fail in the battle. Paul realized from experience that it was when he was physically and spiritually weak that he was at his strongest because he was then not relying on his own feeble strength but that of God (cf. Joel 3:9 – 12; 2 Cor. 12:10; Eph. 6:10; Heb. 11:33, 34).

I have always said that those who have continuous well paid jobs are more likely to not want to cause problems than those who have little or nothing and have therefore little to lose. The first have no desperate need of God because, from a worldly point of view at least, they have everything they need, whereas the latter have a desperate need for support. The young ruler was rich in worldly terms and was comfortable in his wealth, but spiritually he was not satisfied. It was for this reason that he went to the Lord searching for an answer to his keen sense of emptiness in his inner self; why else would he have come to the Lord Jesus and asked the question, "What must I do to inherit eternal life?" (Mk. 10:17 – 31, esp. v24). He had followed all the teaching of the scriptures, obeyed the commandments and all the dogma and ritual of the outward life of a Jew, and attended all the services in the synagogue, but these activities had done nothing to satisfy the inner man. It is the Spirit alone that gives true life.

"Sell all you have and give to the poor", says Jesus, *"so that your treasure is transferred from earth to heaven and then come, take up your cross (of service) and follow Me (listen to what I have to tell you from the Father and follow my example of total commitment to Him that you might realize for yourself a personal and vibrant relationship with us and in that way you will be made alive in the Spirit – for My words are Spirit and they are life – which will give you peace in the inner man)."* But his worldly wealth was more important to him than his spiritual needs. And such was the situation in the Laodicean church.

The message to the church from God was, "I will vomit you out of My mouth." Although they had accepted the Lord when they first believed, they were unwilling to fully leave the things of the world behind and follow God; they tried to keep a foot in both camps. But God's standard of decision making is all or nothing. Because they were unwilling to fully leave the benefits of the world they could have no part in His salvation.

Please do not get this wrong, for not all rich men are to be banished from the kingdom of our Lord. It is only those who are unwilling to commit their wealth to God so that it can be used in His service and for His glory so that they can become personally dependent upon Him. The true and lasting riches of the kingdom of heaven are available to all who are willing to commit their lives to God and submit to His authority over them; it is they that will enjoy the benefits of the kingdom now and then enter into His eternal rest. To all those who prefer to put their trust in temporary riches now, the prospect of an eternity in the glorious new heaven and new earth, which have already been prepared for us, could well be denied them.

Unfortunately the Laodiceans had got the idea that not only were they saved, but they also had spiritual abilities; believing, as did the Jews at the time of the Messiah, they understood the scriptures and were doing what was necessary to secure their salvation. But their spiritual eyes were sightless. Not willing to accept, or not realizing the critical nature of their state before God, the Lord is here challenging the members of that church to change their ways.

What is so important here is that our Lord wanted to reach out to them, to tell them that their state before Him was not as they thought; in fact it was quite the reverse. However, He was willing to help them make the changes necessary by making available to them all that they needed to achieve that change. He was even using their own business style language, of buying and selling, to convince them to take advantage of this offer.

Paul had written a letter to the church at Colossae, that was also to be read out to the believers at Laodicea, desiring their hearts to be encouraged to attain to all the riches of the full assurance of understanding God's secret plan, which is Christ Himself. This was because in Him were hidden all the treasures of wisdom and knowledge (Col. 2:1 – 3). Paul, who had never met them, was focusing his effort in one way, which was that they should gain a complete understanding of who Christ was and what He did, both through His teaching and His sacrifice. Now God through John was emphasizing their need to take this matter seriously because they had focused on other things. At no time could they say they had not been warned.

The solution: Laodicea was known for its great wealth; but what they needed was to purchase spiritual wealth fresh from the fire, gold in its highest state of purity with its surface like a mirror (as faith tried in the fire of adversity). And what was the price of this gold that they were advised purchase? *"Ho! Everyone who thirsts"*, wrote Isaiah, *"Come to the waters; and you who have no money, come buy and eat ..."* *(Is. 55 esp. v1)*. This is because there is no charge. To buy we need to accept the price Christ has paid for us through His death on the cross, and then pay the price He asks of us, which is total commitment to Him and to His service (take up your cross and follow Me), and then feast ourselves on Him.

There is no time to delay, no time to wait for parents

to die (Matt. 8:21, 22), or for our careers to get started, or for us to achieve a certain goal we have set ourselves, or for this or that to happen. God is saying that the time is now (2 Cor. 6:2). As soon as you have believed! Do not wait for that prospective new life to wilt but respond immediately to His call to follow Him.

Laodicea was known for its textile industries; but what they needed was to acquire clothing to cover up their nakedness; robes made white by the blood of the Lamb (Rev. 6:9 – 11; 7:13, 14).

Laodicea prided itself on its precious eye ointment that healed many eye problems; but, having received no commendation whatsoever, what they needed was to use eye-salve so that they could see the truth (Jn. 9:39 – 41) so that through repentance they might regain the inner sight of the spirit. Without spiritual sight how would they be able to see their spiritual state and be able to fully and purposely repent and seek to make the necessary changes to receive commendations like those received by the other six churches?

However harsh and ruthless we believe God's decisions are, such as His condemnation that because they were only lukewarm 'He would vomit them out of His mouth', we also need to recognize that this was done in love for He also says, *"As many as I love, I rebuke and chasten (Job 5:17, 18), therefore be zealous and repent."* Out of His love for them He was prepared to challenge them to repent and change. Let us be clear about God. He has two sides, Love and Righteous Judgement. No one can expect one without the other.

Here was the Laodicean's opportunity to change their ways and reposition themselves under God's authority and guidance to ensure their continued salvation.

The penalty: To be rejected by God.

An asset: They had none. What a terrible condemnation.

The recovery: *"Behold I stand at the door and knock. If anyone hears my voice and opens the door, I will come in to him and dine with him, and he with Me."*

How loving! How gracious is our God! He knocks at the door of every individual's heart, pleading for permission to enter (Jn. 6:56) and enjoy an intimate meal with them, and what better meal than the last meal He had with the disciples, which we call the Communion, with the bread and the wine – do it in remembrance of Him. It is a meal of repentance and faith. The One invited becomes the host, for He was and is the Bread of Life and it was His own blood that He shed for the forgiveness of our sins.

"With fervent desire I have desired to eat this Passover with you before I suffer ..." (Lk. 22:15). "Then their eyes were opened and they knew Him ....did not our hearts burn within us while he talked with us along the way ..." (Lk. 24:31, 32).

The reward: *"To him who overcomes I will grant to sit with Me on My throne, just as I also overcame and sat down with My Father on His throne."*

Instead of immediately spewing the lukewarm believer out of His mouth, He is inviting them to repent and return to the intimacy of the fellowship they had with Him when they were originally saved to the uttermost; for then the repentant sinner, the one who overcomes, will be able to sit with Him in glory on His throne (Is. 42:3).

But do not be misled. If they did not take the opportunity to repent and change their ways to His satisfaction, then he would go ahead and 'vomit them out of His mouth' and their names would not be recorded in the Lamb's book of life and, therefore, they would no longer be known to the Father.

The message to the churches is consistent and we need to take it to heart. *"He who has a spiritually active ear let him hear what the Spirit says to the churches."*

13 IN CONCLUSION

97 O how love I your law!
It is my meditation all the day.
98 Through your commandments you have
made me wiser than mine enemies:
For they are ever with me.
99 I have more understanding than all my teachers:
For your testimonies are my meditation.
100 I understand more than the ancients,
Because I keep your precepts.
101 I have refrained my feet from every evil way,
That I might keep your word.
102 I have not departed
From your judgments: For you have taught me.
103 How sweet are your words unto my taste!
Yes, sweeter than honey to my mouth!
104 Through your precepts I get understanding:
Therefore I hate every false way.

9 Wherewith shall a young man cleanse his way?
By taking heed according to your word.
10 With my whole heart have I sought you:
O let me not wander from your commandments.
11 Your word have I hid in mine heart,
That I might not sin against you.
12 Blessed are you, O LORD:
Teach me thy statutes.

105 Your word is a lamp unto my feet,
And a light unto my path.
(Ps.119)

Deuteronomy contains the teaching of Moses which was there to keep the nation in a right relationship with God. Unfortunately, only the few who were determined to remain faithful and seek after God with all their might were sustained by God as part of the remnant. Saul was of the earth and earthly, blind to the things of God, whereas David was spiritual seeking after the ways of God, which is why

In Conclusion

His reign succeeded and Saul's failed.

The book of Revelation, containing teaching given to John by God, is for our instruction also, and we do well to study and take to heart, being obedient even unto death, which is easy to say but difficult to do.

Be Inspired to Read and Learn

It is essential that we allow no part of scripture to be outside our focus of study, because we will be the loser. Just as we have considered Genesis to Malachi in the first testament, including Ezekiel and Daniel, so we need to consider the second testament from Matthew to Revelation to ensure we understand fully the message of the plan of salvation with which God has provided us. And the consequences of personally not believing in the Messiah and accepting that salvation.

The Messiah has come and fulfilled that plan by His death and resurrection, but there is much to come in the form of the fulfilment of prophecy; prophecy given initially in the first testament, concerning the Kingdom of God that is to come in the form of a new heaven and earth in the New Jerusalem that is to come down from heaven.

We wait with patience for the second coming of the Messiah, the Lord Jesus Christ in whose name we have been baptised, to be taken up into heaven in glory, and there to dwell with God the Trinity in joy and peace. Not until that happens will God's plan of salvation be completely fulfilled.

Let us consider some of the things that will happen in the future to gain an understanding of what is to come so that we can be encouraged by future events rather than being upset and discouraged.

The Eternal Passover Lamb

The sacrifice of the Passover Lamb, before their exodus from Egypt to become a free nation under God, was the first collective religious act carried out by the Children of Israel as a new nation. It was to become a tradition, and the focus of the nation's religious leaders in their earthly rather than their spiritual state, a tradition that blinded their eyes to the arrival of the supreme Passover Lamb who became the final Passover sacrifice. They were outwitted by God in the way the Messiah arrived and how He conducted His ministry, and the objective of His work on the earth.

With the sudden and inexplicable demise of the temple as the central place of worship so clearly signalled by the rending of the curtain from top to bottom, and the obstinate refusal of the religious leaders to realise that God's plan of salvation, not just for them but the whole of mankind, had been completed with the sacrifice of the Messiah, the focus on Jerusalem as the centre of the worship of the God of Israel was necessarily distracted for a while. But it is important to accept that Jerusalem is still central to our focus on God for it is to Jerusalem that the Messiah will return in triumph, hence the unwitting renewed importance of that city in the minds of people throughout the world today. It is the focus of political and media attention for very good reason, because that is where the final moments of the present political systems will be overturned

The sacking of the temple emphasised the fact that it was no longer needed by those whose heart was drawn to Almighty God through the message of salvation now being preached by the disciples and those they trained to be leaders of the dispersed church of the Messiah throughout the known world. Those who have been inspired by the Holy Spirit have gradually taken that message to the ends of the world, although there are still some remote people who have yet to hear the gospel.

The finality of the progressive plan of salvation in the sacrifice of the Messiah is clearly stated by John in the first chapter of his book of Revelation which we have already considered. We need, therefore, to conclude this study by considering the actions taken by the Messiah in the throne room of heaven as described in Revelation chapter 5.

The Lamb and the Scroll

In chapter five John's attention is once more drawn back to the throne and the one seated on it. In His righthand John sees a scroll with writing on both sides of it and sealed with seven seals. All attention is now drawn to this scroll by a mighty Angel with a loud voice shouting out the question, *"Who is worthy to break the seals of this scroll and reveal its contents?"*

Three aspects of the scroll are important:

1. It is full, with writing on both sides, declaring completeness, there being nothing else to add to what has been written. It is the mystery which God, who created all things through Christ Jesus (Eph. 3:9, 10), planned and recorded concerning what was to happen in the end times, knowing full well what would happen to His creation. And this record was kept hidden from the beginning of all ages (Heb. 1:2, 3), the title deeds if you like to the inheritance He wanted to make available to all those who would become worthy, because of their willingness to become His committed servants.

   It is essential that we are not misled. God is able to work in our lives and do great things in us and through us, and the glory for that must be directed to God (Lk. 17:10). However, if we are not willing servants and, like the Israelites of old, keep putting obstacles in God's way as He seeks to do a work within us and through us, then God has to abandon us to our own devices just as He did to the Israelites. We are entirely responsible for putting ourselves fully at God's disposal and maintaining a dialogue with Him. He does not do it alone.

This is His will and Testament to those who are still alive after judgement, the manifold wisdom of God that He wanted to make known to the church, and through its members to the world, and the principalities and powers in the heavenly places. This is the eternal purpose God accomplished in Christ Jesus; for this was the moment when what was planned is united with what has been achieved, for the plan and the conclusion of the action are to be married together, being a perfect match. As the salvation of man and future status of man have been achieved through the cross, the way is now clear for the revelation of the conclusion of God's plan.

2. It is held in the right hand, which is the side of power and authority, of the One sitting on the throne, God the Father — the One who has all knowledge. The whole universe was His idea; the creation which He created without help from anyone for, as He is the only non-created being, He did it entirely on His own.

> *'Have you not known?*
> *Have you not heard?*
> *Has it not been told you from the beginning?*
> *Have you not understood from the foundations of the earth?*
> *It is He who sits above the circle of the earth ...*
> *Who stretches out the heavens like a curtain*
> *And spreads them out like a tent to dwell in.*
> *"To whom then will you liken Me,*
> *Or to whom shall I be equal?"*
> *Says the Holy One.*
> *Lift up your eyes on high, and see*
> *Who has created these things,*
> *Who brings out their host by Numbers;*
> *He calls them all by name,*
> *By the greatness of His might*
> *And the strength of His power;*
> *Not one is missing.*
> *Why do you say, O Jacob*
> *And speak O Israel:*
> *"My way is hidden from the Lord,*
> *And my just claim is passed over by my God"?*
> *Have you not known?*
> *Have you not heard?*

The everlasting God, the Lord,
The creator of the ends of the earth,
Neither faints nor is He weary,
His understanding is unsearchable.'"
(see Isaiah 40)

It is the Father who knows what is to happen in the future and the only one to know the timing of those events (Matt. 24:36). On the scroll is God's plan for the future which He has known from the beginning. Not only is He able to make plans for the future, He also has every right to set out His plan.

"Remember the former things of old,[99]
For I am God and there is no other;
I am God and there is none like Me,
Declaring the end from the beginning
And from ancient times things
That are not yet done
Saying, 'My counsel shall stand,
And I will do all My pleasure.'"
(see Isaiah 46, also
Deut. 32 esp. vs. 7, 8)

What we must accept is that the supreme God, who is both creator and Lord of all that is, knows what is best for us for He loves us with a love far in excess of the love we are able to show. Jesus, speaking to the Jewish leaders, knowing their sinfulness and hardness of heart, spoke of the highest and purest love that He could when He told them, *but I know you, that you do not have the love of God in your hearts.*

It is He alone who is pure and holy and has the supreme and unchallengeable authority that can deal with all the evil in this world; that is both the symptoms, which we see through the action of unbelieving men and women, and the cause of it which is Satan, even though this fact is hidden even from those who consider themselves to be wise, as we shall see as we continue the study of this book of Revelation[100].

What is very important to understand, and why the study of Ezekiel is so revealing, is that the scroll John has seen is

---

[99] It is for this very reason that we need to read the first testament. Without the knowledge we are able to gain from all that God did in the beginning we will never be able to fully (or even partially) understand the truth of what God is saying here.

[100] See my book Seeing Into the Future which is study on Revelation.

completely different from the one seen by Ezekiel. This is not just because of who was is holding it but also because the one Ezekiel saw was not sealed, emphasising just how world history has moved on. Ezekiel saw that the unsealed scroll, written on both sides in the same way, was full of woes. He was called upon to eat it so that it became part of him, enabling him to speak the word of God with the authority of God as we considered in the last chapter.

It was unsealed and was quickly revealed because it contained a message that was for that time, filled as it was with lamentations, mourning and woes. The message was not secret but urgent; that the exiles might learn from the mistakes of the past and change their ways, returning to God with repentant hearts and a willingness to seek God afresh.

3.   It is sealed with seven seals[101]. Not only does it have the authority of the Father because it is He who is holding it, it is also for the future and the message it contains is therefore restricted. Only the one authorised by the Father, who is pure and holy and of the same standing with the Father is able to break the seals and open the scroll at the time chosen by the Father to reveal its contents, just as the Son was the only one able to die in our stead because He was not created and was holy and pure.

The call goes out challenging all who could hear the projected voice of a mighty angel calling out, *Who is worthy to break the seals of God and open the scroll?*

Remember that John had entered through the door into heaven by invitation, as an observer, for all on earth were prevented through sin from entering heaven, although we are told that the dead also heard the challenge uttered by the angel. There was silence. That no one in heaven or alive on the earth or among the dead was able to answer the call causing the emotions within John to well up inside him as though he was terrified that the essential revelation of God's word would be hidden forever.

He must have felt like someone who needs to urgently obtain some vital documents from a safe but finds that the safe cannot be opened and is thus made fearful for the future. He wept, sobbing that there was no one to break the seals and reveal the contents of the scroll that had been sealed from

---

[101] As seven denotes spiritual perfection, this is the work of the Holy Spirit under the authority of the Father

before the foundation of the earth.

It was necessary to utter the challenge to the whole of heaven and earth and to the dead to emphasise that there was no one who was found worthy, no one who dared approach the throne of God to be given the chance to attempt to break the seals God had put in place.

This was done to emphasis the uniqueness of the Lamb who had died, exalting Him to the highest place of honour. The vast numbers of created beings who had died were not only unworthy but knew they were unworthy; in contrast to the One who was God made man, who was by birth and behaviour supremely worthy. None of the saved who had received the cleansing of the blood and the healing of the stripes Christ received on His back, because they were willing to approach the throne of grace and seek forgiveness and surrender themselves to the authority of the Christ, were in any way tempted to put themselves forward because their standing before God was purely on the basis of Christ's sacrificial act.

There are some words of a hymn which I often use which puts things in perspective, "Nothing in my hand I bring, simply to thy cross I cling."

Once the challenge had been proclaimed and no one had come forward, for such was the awesome nature and aura of the mighty God who sat on the throne that no one dared approach Him, one of the twenty four elders informed John that his weeping was unnecessary for he was to see the Lion of the Tribe of Judah[102], the root of David, who had conquered and had alone proved Himself worthy to open the seals and open the scroll to reveal its contents.

It was Jacob who prophesied that the tribe of Judah would be the leading tribe and would rule because of the one who was to come, *The sceptre shall not depart from Judah until the one who was to come who was worthy to claim it.* (Gen. 49:8 – 12; see also Is. 63 esp. vs 1 – 6). Without the teaching of the first testament, we would be ignorant concerning the true role that Jesus played in our salvation, and all the legal transactions which were necessary for God's abhorrence of sin to be assuaged.

Then John looked and saw a Lamb standing before the twenty-four elders and before the throne of the Almighty, His Father, and the four living beings. The wounds that Thomas saw and was told to touch, that he might be sure of the presence of the risen Christ, were there for all to see. No more the flow of blood from the Lord's side where the spear had

---

[102] In blessing Judah, Jacob referred to him as a lion's whelp, but through the history of the nation that lion matured into the Messiah, who came from above and assumed membership of the tribe of Judah in being born of a descendent of David, to become the exalted Lion of the Tribe of Judah, the king amongst beasts. The sceptre shall not depart from Judah because the Messiah became the king of spiritual Israel. (Gen. 49:8 – 12)

pierced the skin, for the blood had been shed as required. But the scars from the wounds were there: the nail prints in the wrists and in the feet where the nails were driven through into the wood of the cross gave evidence that this was the Christ (Heb. 9:11 – 22) who had died and had risen again.

We must be careful as we read the symbolism here. The lamb as being central to the gospel that God was revealed from Abraham (Gen. 22:13) until now. Our Lord acted like a lamb, for as a sheep before its shearers opens not its mouth to defend itself but submits itself to the shearer's scissors, so our Lord opened not His mouth in defense when He was before the Sanhedrin and Pilate.

The seven horns and seven eyes represent the Spirit of the living God with whom Jesus was filled without measure. It was the Spirit who was with the Lord on earth, being his piercing eyes which saw into the hearts and minds of men telling the Lord what they were thinking and believing. Nothing was hidden from the Lord Jesus. In Zechariah the Spirit of God is represented by a candlestick with seven branches with olive trees supplying the oil for the lamps, a living supply to ensure continuous light (Zech. 4:2 – 6, 10).

The Lord appeared to John as a lamb for it was as a lamb without blemish or spot that He presented Himself to be tortured to death on the cross for us. A lamb that was slain but now is alive for evermore. But this Lamb was also where He said He would be, in the presence of the Mighty Power.

Rejected by men of power in this world, Jesus stands as the centre of attention in the world that never ends. It is important for us to keep a sense of perspective whilst here on earth. The charge of blasphemy sealed the Lord's death even though He had not blasphemed. The high priest and those around him erupted in accusing our Lord of blasphemy when Caiaphas demanded in the name of the living God that the Lord Jesus say whether or not He claimed to be the Messiah, the Son of God (Matt. 26:63). At such a moment the Lord Jesus had no option but to declare His true identity,

> *And in the future you will see me, The Son of Man, sitting at the right hand of God and returning on the clouds of heaven.*

At that farce of a trial there was uproar. Goaded on by their complete lack of faith and understanding of the things of God these statesmen tore at their clothes shouting at the top of their voices, *Death, Death, Death!*. They thought that they had got this usurper where they wanted Him; that they would kill Him and all would be well again. But all that they had done was to do Satan's work for him very effectively and they would one day stand trial themselves before this Man whom they so cruelly treated and against whom they administered such gross injustice.

As the Lord stepped forward to take the scroll from the hand of His Father, so the twenty-four elders fell down before the throne and the Lamb, each with a harp and golden vials which held incense which was the prayers of the saints sent up to heaven as a sweet-smelling savour. God uses all His 'senses' when accepting our worship. His 'ears' hear our voices raised in verbal praise, thanksgiving and prayer. His 'nose' smells the incense of sacrificial offering of submissive, repentant prayers just as He smelt the smoke from the animal sacrifices that were offered in true repentance and faith. With His 'sight' he sees our activities which are another form of sacrifice and worship; but His sight does not look at the exterior alone but is able to penetrate to the hearts and minds of men to see if there is truth in them. We are able to hide nothing from God.

Heaven erupted in singing a new song of worship to the One who sacrificed Himself for the whole of mankind; that sacrifice which bought repentant sinners as gifts for God, man returning to the position he had before God, previously enjoyed by Adam before the fall. They are gathered into a kingdom as priests before our God. O, the rejoicing there is in heaven because of the victory of Jesus.

John witnessed the elders singing a new song that was only possible because of the mighty sacrifice made by the Messiah, for only now could the plan of God, kept sealed with seven seals from the eyes of all but the Father, be revealed and experienced. *"You are worthy,"* sang the elders, *"to take the scroll and have the authority from the Father to break open the seals with which He sealed it, for You were slain, Your blood has bought people from every nation as gifts for God."*

What other religious movement can match the majesty of Almighty God and the exaltation of the Lamb who died? Who else can promise you a future in glory for doing nothing other than accepting your sinful state and repenting of your sins, to be promised a place in heaven where moth and rust do not corrupt nor thieves break in and steal your treasure? What other faith can give cast-iron promises that you will join with the heavenly hosts in praising the Lamb in thankfulness for His sacrifice which has saved you?

The worship John witnessed gathered apace to involve millions of the heavenly host and the living creatures and the elders, who all joined in the heartfelt praise of the Lamb who was slain, for He is worthy to receive the power and the riches and the wisdom and the strength and the honour and the glory and the blessing.

He who steadfastly set His face to Jerusalem to offer Himself as a willing sacrifice for the whole of mankind, suffering incredible pain and agony of spirit, knowing what was to be the final outcome but still having to go through the humiliation and tortuous death of the cross and ultimately the rejection by His Father. He fulfilled his mission in full and now He was reaping the rewards of that loyal and steadfast service. We must do likewise.

Finally, the whole of heaven and earth and those who had died took up the theme and joined in the worship of the Lamb. The blessing and the honour and the glory and the power belong to the One sitting on the throne and to the Lamb for ever and ever. And the four living creatures repeatedly said Amen. And the twenty-four elders fell down and worshipped Him.

O my friends, there will come a day when we too will be able to worship Him with the whole of heaven rejoicing in the adulation of the One who is worthy, both the Father and the Son through the enabling power of the Holy Spirit. How wonderful that time will be.

Look no further. The answer to all life's questions lies with the Trinity of Father, Son and Holy Spirit. Whatever men might say, God holds the truth against which all other knowledge is pure lies. So, seek The Messiah, our Lord and Saviour Jesus Christ, with all your heart, all your soul, all your strength and all your mind whilst he may be found and do not let up in your worship of Him who is worthy.

There is More to Come

If John's sight of the Lamb that had been slain being acknowledged to be the only one worthy to take the scroll from the hand of His Father who sat on the throne of heaven was not enough, the opening of the seven seals by the Lamb of God, the Messiah of Israel, signalled the start of the events that will eventually lead to the disappearance of the world and its surrounding cosmos, the judgement of all people before the great white throne on which the Messiah will sit, and the appearance of the New Jerusalem, the new creation of God in which no sin will be found, for it will be populated by all those who have totally committed their lives to the Messiah.

There were two things the Messiah said when giving witness to the one who sat in judgement on Him during His initial trial in Jerusalem,

1. you will see the Son of Man sitting at the right hand of the Power,

2. coming on the clouds of heaven.

Consider what was known of the Son of Man before His arrival on earth (Dan. 7:13, 14). Consider the return of the Messiah, according to the angels, as the disciples watched their Messiah return to heaven (Acts 1:9 – 11) and what the Messiah told them about His return (Matt. 16:27; 24:29 – 31). He has gone to prepare a place for each and every believer, and He will come again to take us to be with Himself, for He made that promise and God is incapable of lying (Jn. 14:1 – 3).

The task rabbi Aaron gave me in the year 2009 was to write about the Tent of the Meeting. With God the Holy Spirit as my inspiration, I have sought to fulfil that task to the best of my ability. The Tent of the Meeting made by Moses and Spirit-filled inspired artisans that produced it and those commissioned to dismantle it, move it and re-erect it each time they moved camp site, finally became the glorious temple of Solomon when the people were settled in the Promised Land.

Sin took the people into exile and caused the glorious temple to be demolished. A pagan king ordered it to be rebuilt, becoming the less glorious temple of Zerubbabel, which temple God glorified because of the promised arrival of the Messiah. It was first the tent and then the temple that provided the venue for the daily services of worship and sacrifice.

But it was the Passover which became the main theme of the final earthly revelation of God's plan of salvation. The shed blood of the Lamb of God became the signature on its certificate of completion. It is the blood of the Lamb of God that cleanses us and our consciences from the contamination and imposed slavery of sin, and also gives us power over Satan and the temptations that we face from the attractions of the fallen world.

We look for the coming of the Messiah in glory, just as He promised, in faith; a faith that only God can provide and sustain.

No single book can provide a comprehensive study on Holy Scripture, nor can all the books collectively give you all the answers. Although it is my hope and prayer that this book will help some seeking souls to come into a detailed knowledge of God, it is only through regular prayerful reading of the word of God that we are provided with the true spiritual food that we need every day to keep us close to the Saviour and to enable us to be certain of our salvation.

Amen

APPENDIX A   THE ESSENTIAL NATURE OF THE VIRGIN BIRTH

No one, not even the very rich or any king,
Can by any means whatsoever,
Ransom even his own brother
From the penalty of sin.
God's forgiveness is not available by such means.
For a soul is far too precious to God
To be ransomed by the mere
Temporary worldly wealth of men;
Indeed, there is not enough wealth in all the world
To purchase eternal life
For just one soul
To prevent it from entering hell."
(Consider Ps.49:7 – 13)

"For God so loved the world
That He gave His only begotten Son,
So that whoever believes on Him
Should not perish but have everlasting life."
(Jn.3:16)

"Beloved, let us love each other,
For love is of God.
In this act of love, we observe,
Not that we loved God of ourselves,
But that He loved us to the extent
That He sent His Son
To satisfy God's anger that was stirred up,
Against us because of our sin
(Consider 1 Jn. 4:7-10)

Preparation

I have called the first few paragraphs of this appendix 'Preparation' because it is important for you, the reader, to realise that the thoughts recorded here have enabled me, and many others, to better understand the legal technicalities of this fundamental subject. They are, however, not for everyone. But it is hoped that these thoughts might initiate a train of thought in the minds of individual readers that will be helpful to them. As one called of the God of Israel to write on His word, I am completely at peace in my spirit before Almighty God regarding the entire contents of this book, and in particular this appendix.

The scriptures are complex and fully known only to God Himself, who is infinite and all-knowing. They represent God speaking to man messages of spiritual truth which means that we must contemplate them with a spiritually attuned mind, not one that has its emphasis on the things of this earth and its carnal thinking and understanding.

God gave the message not of a bodily, but of a spiritual salvation, for it is all about our rising again after death to meet with God in His spiritual environment. It is also all about how we must approach Him and was delivered to finite men in manageable chunks throughout the history of mankind.

The whole of scripture is available to us today, providing us with a complete picture so that we, through the work of the Holy Spirit sent by the Messiah into the world after He had ascended to His Father, can understand for ourselves the spiritual message it contains as He enlightens us. As individuals we can only know in part, until, that is, we meet with God when we will fully know even as we are fully known. (1 Cor. 13:12)

I have approached this task, which I and my Jewish friends believe was God given, as an experienced technical author who is used to writing accurate instructions on the operation of industrial equipment and processes and producing training material in a nuclear power generating environment. The scriptures are not as rigid as industrial equipment and processes, because it is a living spiritual word that has involved individuals, along with their relationship with each other and with God. As we know we are all individually formed. Therefore, each one of us is unique and thinks uniquely.

One Jewish friend once said, "Get two Jews together and you will have three opinions", but such differences are not restricted to Jews alone. In the West there is a separation of churches because of different emphasis on Biblical thought.

Consider, for instance, the use of the words 'soul' and 'spirit' which are dealt with in this appendix. These seem to be clear one minute but then become muddled through becoming interchangeable when written about by others in scripture. They have been pondered over and expounded by countless authors through the centuries without any firm consensus.

Regarding references to the words, 'flesh' and 'body', the Messiah spoke about the difference between the flesh and the spirit. The flesh is reasonably considered to be the physical life of a person on the earth and their reaction to the various influences in it, and is aligned to the body

463

which is made of the dust of the ground. The spirit, on the other hand, comes from God and is not of the earth but separate from it, being part of the spiritual realm in the kingdom of God. That which is of the flesh is flesh and that which is of the Spirit is spirit, and seemingly the two are totally incompatible, much like oil and water. Certainly, angels in the spiritual realm cannot co-habit with humans, or create offspring between them. But do references to the flesh refer solely to the body? In the following text, a possible explanation is given as to how the body and the spirit, which are completely separate elements within a person, communicate with each other through what is known as the soul of man, which is the person's individual character, that which identifies them as a unique individual. What is certain, is that physical breath, which is the natural function of our bodies, and the 'breath' a spiritual God breathed into the nostrils of the first man are not the same thing as we shall discover.

Even though I have set things out specifically, as though what I have written seems to be absolute truth (which is not necessarily so, but another way of looking at the subject matter), there are bound to be some who will challenge my thoughts because they will not see these things exactly the way I see them. But that is not to say I am wrong and they are right or vice-versa. But how many students of scripture cling on tightly to what others have set down over the years concerning their understanding of scripture as though it was established truth, instead of just the thoughts of men?

But did not the religious leaders at the time of the Messiah cling to what was then considered established 'truth' as though it was God's truth but was contrary to the teaching of the Messiah who came directly from the Father to teach us about what God the Father wanted us to know? That 'difference of understanding' led to the death of the Messiah.

It is essential, therefore, that we prayerfully meditate on these things and not reject them out of hand, seeking through the wisdom of God's Holy Spirit to understand new ways of seeing revealed truth, without bending to, or being swayed by, every wind of doctrine however old and established it appears to be. It is not easy being a seeker after Divine truth because our sin contaminated nature often gets in the way.

The explanation contained in this appendix is unlikely to be suitable for everyone, which is why it should be read prayerfully, for God alone is our inspiration. But please meditate on these thoughts without prejudice, or preconceived ideas and either accept or reject them as you desire. To someone else they might be the path to a fresh understanding that will bring them into a deeper understanding of the gospel of Christ Jesus who alone is the Word of God and absolute truth.

The whole basis for this act of virgin birth was God's love for mankind in general and the lives individuals in particular. Mary was loved of God and blessed because of the role she played in helping the Son of God enter this earth as a human being uncontaminated by sin. Through that selfless service to God she is undoubtedly blessed, but as an ordinary child of God she must not be worshipped.

As a writer who has been called by God through others[103] to write on His Word, I have a responsibility before God to be both approved of Him and to rightly divide the word of truth (2 Tim. 2:15); which is what I have done. With these thoughts in mind please read on:

An Explanation of the Virgin Birth

Central to the Biblical text is the love of God, man's sin and the mercy of God. The bias of the message is that God has not only created us but done everything He can to avail us of the means to keep us in tune with Him. It is man alone that has seen fit to be rebellious and to support Satan in his bid to usurp the throne of God.

Through sin the first man, and through him the whole human race, became separated from God. This did not serve the purposes of God who had created man for His good pleasure, that He might lavish blessing upon him. The one redeeming feature is the remnant; that is those of the minority of the population of the earth who, individually and collectively, seek after the at-one-ment (atonement) God offers to all men so that they can get in tune with the living God in order to serve Him in whatever capacity He sees fit.

From before the world began, God, through His foreknowledge, knew what would happen regarding man and his sin. Therefore, before one element of the creation was initiated, God prepared a plan, with the full knowledge and acceptance of His Son, to enable those who, through their own free will, desired to enjoy a relationship with Him to do so. God's desire and love for man knows no bounds which is why He was willing to create man, even with all the difficulties and challenges man would introduce into the relationship.

This book is all about the gradual revelation of the plan of salvation God prepared before the earth was formed through the teaching that is available in God's Word from the beginning of man's existence to that point in the history of man when the eternally Perfect Man (God's true son) came to earth to suffer and die for mankind.

It is true we can only properly understand the second part of the Bible for it is there that we learn that the Messiah was not a mere man, only if we are prepared to relate it to the first part of God's Word, for it is there that we learn He had existed before the world began and appeared to a number of people before His appearance as a baby in a manger. Indeed it was he who gave the written word to the prophets through the Holy Spirit.

---

[103] For further information please read "A Tale of Three Men"

The Essential Nature of the Virgin Birth

Those of us who have believed Jesus Christ to be the Messiah to the Jews have understood just who He was (and who He still is) by confirming what we have read in the second testament by what is recorded in the first.

But how can we be sure? Ultimately by God's Spirit witnessing with our spirit that we are His child (Ro. 8:16) and then by that same Spirit opening up to us the scriptures, which were written at God's behest (Ex. 34:27; 2 Tim. 3:16, 17; 2 Pet. 1:20, 21), to reveal to us the inner secrets of God (Jn. 5:31 – 47). There is just so much that we do not know; indeed, cannot know about God and particularly the complexity of the triune God. We know that it was the Son of God who came down to earth, taking on a human body to become the Son of Man. The title 'Son of God' was one that the Messiah accepted for Himself. Therefore, we have the members of the triune God listed as Father, Son and Holy Spirit. If we have a father and a son then, as the Messiah spoke to us in human terms, it is reasonable that somehow the spirit Son was born to the spirit Father.

How and when this occurred, we have no way of knowing, except that it was before the physical creation came into being. But we do need to accept that they had a Father/Son relationship purely because of the way the Messiah spoke about His relationship with His Father throughout His short ministry. It is after all only the Father who knows when the Son will return in glory to the earth, and it is to the Father the Son will hand over all control when He has the final victory over all that is evil.

But consider this. According to scripture (Jn. 5:39), One born of God before the world began (Jn. 1:1 – 3; 1 Jn. 1:1 – 4)[104], and therefore Divinely equal with God (Son of God), entered the world (Son of Man) after many prophetic utterances (Deut. 18:15, 18, 19; Jn. 8 esp. vvs 28 – 36), with such a fanfare (Lk. 2:8 – 18) at the behest of His Father (Jn. 4:34; 5:30; 6:35 – 40; 8:23) and witnessed to the truth from the age of 30[105], came to suffer and die for mankind (Jn. 8:28), being lifted up, 'crucified', to save people from the scourge of sin, just as those who looked at the fiery serpent lifted up by Moses were saved from the poison of the serpents God had let loose among them because of their sin (Num. 21:7 – 9; Jn. 3:14, 15). Man sinned because of the attractions of the world in which he lived that was ruled by that old serpent called Satan.

The crucified Christ, by being lifted up from the earth (Jn. 12:23 – 50) would draw to Himself all those who believed on the name of the Son of God (who also, through His human birth, became the Son of Man). Those believers are told that they shall be saved from sin and eternal spiritual death. But it was not sufficient for the Christ to just die on the cross. If that had been the case then death would be victor for no one could live after

---

[104] 1 Jn. 1:4 - How can we enjoy true Joy if it is not of God?

[105] This was the age a priest first entered the temple to minister before God.

death. No. This second Perfect Man (Phil. 2:5 – 8) was not a living being created by God as Adam was, but a life-giving Spirit who became man (1 Cor. 15:45), a Spirit eternally begotten of the Father (Jn. 1:14, 18; 3:16, 18; Heb. 11:17; 1 Jn. 4:9); a man the grave could not hold onto for it was His rising from the dead that ensured our future life when we who were made from the dust of the ground will put off this corrupt body and put on incorruption (1 Cor. 15:46 – 57).

How do we know this? Because of the promised Comforter, the Holy Spirit who, as promised (Jn. 16:7 – 11) came to abide with all those who confess the name of the Lord, but only after the Lord's departure from earth to return to His Father, having achieved all that He was commissioned to do (Jn. 16:5 – 15). It is the Holy Spirit who leads us into all truth (Jn. 16:13, 14). It is this same Holy Spirit who inspired Peter to speak with such boldness at Pentecost (Acts 2) and Stephen to witness to the Sanhedrin (Acts 7).

Thus, God's plan to legally save man from the penalty of eternal death (that is complete, eternal separation from God), so that His righteousness and purity would not be compromised, was established before the world was created with the willing acceptance of the Son of God. This plan was gradually revealed to man over the course of human history and finally fulfilled with the appearance of the Son who arrived on the earth in human form.

God initially introduced the sacrificing of lambs, defined by God at the time of the first Passover as lambs one year old, without blemish. The shed blood of these animals would provide temporary atonement for man's sin. The continual sacrificing of animals as a sin offering was a perpetual requirement, until the time came when God would send to earth the perfect man who was born without sin and who lived a sinless life. That man would need to be falsely accused of sin and die at the very moment the Passover lamb was slaughtered in the temple. For the message He gave to man had to be clear and consistent throughout His word.

The purpose of this appendix is to highlight the central theme of salvation which is the means God employed to avail men and women of the way of salvation. The Messiah said that He was the Way, the Truth and the Life, the only way to the Father. By that He meant that He was specifically sent to the earth by His Father to not only teach men about the truths of God but to be the one sufficient sacrifice that would allow those who believe in Him to not just be cleansed of the accusation of sin, but be sanctified[106], to become God compatible, so that they may enter into a relationship with God the Father through the offices of the Son. He is the only way to reach the Father.

---

[106] To sanctify means "to make holy.

The Essential Nature of the Virgin Birth

Man and Woman in God's Order

According to scripture man was created out of the dust of the ground and, like all the animals, had physical breath that allowed his body to function. There was also within him a soul which is the character of the person. However, when God breathed into man's nostrils the breath of life, He was taking man out of the purely physical realm of his earthly existence and giving him an eternal spiritual gift, which brought man into the realm of the eternal and into communion with Himself.

By the time the Messiah arrived on earth to witness to His Father's love for man, man's life span had been reduced from the hundreds of years to tens of years. Death, which signified the end of a man's life, was all too common particularly amongst the poor, often restricting their life-span to just a few years. Even the rich could not guarantee longevity of life, or be able to take their accumulated wealth with them, as the tombs of the Egyptian Pharaoh's so clearly illustrate.

Thus, the message the Messiah gave regarding the poor value of physical life was significant. Indeed, physical life is of little value whereas the Spirit gives true life for it is eternal as He is eternal (Jn. 6:63). This is the message of the 'God breathed life' which He breathed into the nostrils of the first man.

The Messiah went on to tell the Jews that the words He spoke to them were both spirit and life because they taught them the true meaning of the Father and the plan of salvation that He had prepared for them from the foundation of the world. Had the religious elite read the word of God, as given to them in the scriptures, prayerfully, opening their hearts to God in their search for the truth, and then obeyed the word that they had so studiously read, they would have recognised Him because the scriptures spoke of Him (Jn. 5:29).

> *whoever hears my word and believes in Him who sent Me has eternal life*
> (Jn. 5:24)

It is essential that we differentiate between physical and spiritual life when we read the scriptures, otherwise much of what we read will be confusing. The breath God breathed into the nostrils of Adam is a prize example of this, because it was something He did not do to any other creature on earth. And to illustrate the fact that God only needed to do it once; when God created woman from the man's rib He did not breathe life into her nostrils because she received spiritual life from the man.

Indeed, all their heirs have also received it from Adam. Sadly, the sin committed by the first man broke-off the immediacy of the spiritual relationship he had had with his creator in the beginning, thereby introducing the need for men and women to reach out to God as individuals so that they could have their spirits reborn in order to reactivate that immediacy and gain eternal life. Sadly, even though we are saved by the grace of God, such intimacy Adam had with God in the beginning can never be our experience. It can never be to quite the same level of purity because of the inherent sin within us, although we are able to enter into a special relationship through the Holy Spirit to get close to God and be assured of eternal life.

What differentiates man from the rest of creation is his special relationship with God, for it was into the man's nostrils alone that God breathed the breath of life for man to become a living, spiritual being. The breath of life from a spiritual God into the body of the man did two things:

1. It created in the man a living spirit which was able to communicate with God's Spirit, which is the Holy Spirit. This took man to a higher level of spiritual existence above that of the rest of the natural world that God had created. As God is spirit the only way we can communicate with Him is through the spirit, which is a specific living entity within us.

    It is important that we differentiate between the first man, who received the breath of life and ourselves who were born of man with inherited sin. It is true that Jesus said to Nicodemus that he had to be born again, that is of water and the Spirit, but that is because the first man lost that spiritually active intimacy with God because of his disobedience and every individual born from him must seek after God through repentance and faith, believing in the shed blood of the Messiah for our salvation and rebirth in the Spirit.

    Adam received a spirit within his body that was not only alive and fully responsive to the Spirit of God but a spirit that would not die, which means that his soul and spirit would live on even after his physical death. It was only after his ejection from the garden that he, and therefore all his offspring up to the present day, and into the future, became spiritually dead in trespasses and sins (Eph. 2:1 – 5) in the sense that he was no longer able to fully relate to and communicate with the Spirit of God as he once did.

    Man became 'carnal' (sensual, fleshly - Ro. 7:14). This meant that when Christ became the ultimate sacrifice for sin, those who accept the way of salvation thus offered have been born again spiritually, that is their spirits are once again able to communicate with the spiritual creator God. The spirit of the new believer has been made alive through the work of the Holy Spirit.

    It is true that flesh gives birth to flesh and the Spirit gives birth to the spirit within man (Jn. 3:6 – 8). It is only when we, sinners that we are, are reborn spiritually through the vital work of the Holy Spirit that we will be like Adam was at first, able to receive instruction from God and thereby understand the deep things of God, although not meet with God face to face as Adam did (1 Cor. 2:10b – 16).

It is also essential that we do not confuse our understanding of what happened to the first man before he was forced to leave the garden as recorded in the first testament and what the second testament tells us about the state of our fallen nature which we received at birth.

2. The spirit created in man cannot communicate directly with the body of man for one is formed from the dust of the earth and the other is a gift from God; therefore, the two are, on their own, incompatible. Indeed, our Lord said, *that which is born of the flesh is flesh and that which is born of the Holy Spirit is spirit* (Jn. 3:6) which means that they are as different as water (flesh) on the one hand, and oil (Spirit) on the other, unable to mix without a mixing ingredient which is in our case is the soul, or life, of man that is able to combine the body and the spirit to make within the body one whole man. To put it another way, there is a need for an intermediary that is able to communicate both with the spirit and the body to enable those two elements of man to communicate with each other through that intermediary.

Therefore, by the very act of breathing into man's nostrils the breath of life, God also created the soul for scripture says, *and the Lord God formed man from the dust of the ground and breathed into his nostrils the breath of life; and man became a living soul* (Gen. 2:7). The man created from the dust of the ground was a living, breathing being just like the animals. The result of that breath God breathed into this living being, however, was to create within him a spirit within his body and at the same time produce a living soul, nephesh in Hebrew, which means life of a living being and is translated as such in the NKJ and other versions. In this way God made man compatible with Himself.

The soul must not be confused with the spirit as it is a completely different element in man and as such has a particular part to play within the body of man. Therefore, in the physical form, the true man is the product of the God-given spirit, the soul produced when the spirit entered into the body, and the body made of flesh. In this way the God breathed, created spirit, in entering into man, brought spiritual life to the earthly tent of the body so that it became someone others could see and with whom they could communicate but, even more important, could communicate with God. From that initial living being God created an individual who was independent and cognisant and able to live on the earth yet communicate with Himself who is not earthly but spiritual.

One way the makeup of man after God breathed into his nostrils the breath of life can be illustrated, according to my understanding, is shown below although this might not suit everyone's vision of man. However, it is essential that we remember to separate the things of the earth, which are temporary, and the things of the Spirit, which are eternal and represent real fulfilling life according to the teaching of the Messiah.

Understanding the Structure of Man

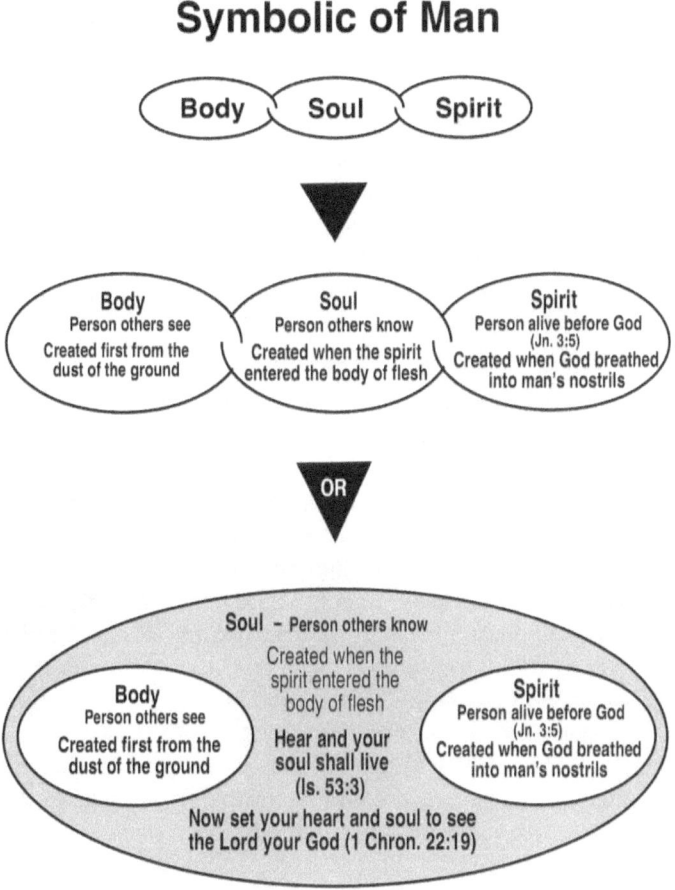

Symbolic of Man

Body The word body describes the material element in humanity which provides the individual with the ability to live and move on the earth, and the facility to see, hear, smell, touch and speak. It is the house or tent (1 Cor. 5:1) that others see and by which we are recognised.

The body is a living, breathing being suitable for living on this earth, but in relation to the spiritual God who created it, it had no spiritual life in it. Indeed, the body that we have on earth must eventually die, because that is the way of human flesh. But we are not just a body.

Because of the breath of life, uniquely given to man from God and to no other creature on earth, we are spiritual beings living on the earth in a physical body; that is the spiritual us has been put by God into the human body (which is the house or tent in which we live) to live on the earth. What is also uniquely human is: if we have accepted the gift of salvation then we are promised eternal life with God when we leave this earth on the death of our physical body.

But what sort of body will we have after our physical body dies when we stop living on the earth? The truth is we do not know because it will be God given. Paul speaks of bodies in the heavens and bodies on earth with the glory of one being different to that of the other. But we are promised a more glorious spiritual body because we will exchange this corruptible body for one that is incorruptible because it will be an eternal spiritual body that God will provide us with. (See 1 Cor. 15)

Spirit The word spirit describes the immaterial element in humanity which provides the individual, the real person, with the ability to have an intimate relationship with God, who is Spirit. (Jn. 4:24).

When God, being entirely spirit, breathed into Adam's nostrils the breath of life, it was spiritual life that man received; life that would enable him to communicate with his Spiritual creator God. (Jn. 3:6; 6:63). What makes man so unique on the earth is that it is he alone who can communicate directly with his creator God, because it is the God given spirit in man that allows us to communicate with God, and the spirit of man never dies (1 Pet. 3:18 - 20).

However, the spirit is incompatible with the body (Jn. 3:6) in which it lives, for the body is of the earth and dies to return to the earth. That is when the spirit leaves the confines of the material earth.

Soul The word soul describes the essence of humanity's being; it is who we are. It was the Messiah who told us that flesh and the spirit are incompatible for the flesh can only give birth to flesh but the Holy Spirit gives life to our spirit which is eternal (Jn. 3:6; 6:63).

Therefore, when the Holy Spirit causes the spirit within us to take on new regenerated life, there needs to be something that enables the body and spirit to unite and for the spirit to dominate and overcome the lusts and fleshly tendencies of the body. With a regenerated spirit within us the predominant element within us must be our spirit, for it is the spirit that communicates with the God who is life to us.

Therefore, the body, that is the flesh, the carnal earthward part of us, must come under the authority of the spirit to enable us to lead a higher spiritual life with God, with the soul acting as the communicator between them. It is therefore, through the soul that we exhibit the knowledge, understanding and intelligence that identify who we are.

God's Test

We are all tested in one way or another throughout our life by the situations we meet and the problems we experience where we need to make decisions. God also uses tests for two reasons:

1. to strengthen our faith

2. to ensure that our hearts are with Him and our outward show of commitment is not just a facade. This is as much for our benefit as for His.

In the beginning God told the first man that he could eat freely of every tree in the garden but not of the fruit of the tree of the Knowledge of Good and Evil. Then, using a rib taken out of the body of the man, God created the woman. Notice that God did not breathe into the woman's nostrils, for the rib of the man had all the requirements (the DNA of life) to make the woman into the same Body, Soul and Spirit type person as the man but different to the man.

It is important for us to realise that although in the horizontally (within the area of human relationships) the man is senior to the woman, vertically (within the area of an individual's relationship to God) the woman is exactly the same as man, indeed when we reach heaven, we will be exactly the same. (Matt. 22:23 – 31)

The purpose of the creation of the woman was for her to be a helpmeet (Gen. 2:18), a comfort for the man and to bear children. She was Adam's responsibility, for he had authority over her as far as God was concerned

The Essential Nature of the Virgin Birth

(see Eph. 5:22 – 33).

When Satan met with Eve at the tree of the Knowledge of Good and Evil and persuaded her that the fruit was good to eat, Adam could either have stopped her doing so if he was sufficiently close at hand, or, if he was at a distance and came to her at her call, did not have to follow her in eating the fruit of the tree she gave him to eat; the scripture says that he ate it freely and willingly.

In this instance, therefore, it was Adam who sinned, not Eve who received the lesser charge of being deceived[107]. Sin is rebellion against God and is abhorrent to Him. It was to man that God said the fruit of the tree was not to be eaten, not to Eve. Therefore, Adam, who had the full responsibility for ensuring both of them obeyed the command of God, was directly disobedient to a command God gave to him personally.

Notice that both were driven out of the garden, for both, in their own way, and according to the responsibility accorded to them by God, had rebelled and therefore sinned against Him. But the importance of the manner of their conviction is that sin is passed down the male line, for it was Adam who was judged to have sinned directly against God, but Eve was deceived.

When the Son of God was born through Mary as the Son of Man it was essential that He was not contaminated with sin. Although the Virgin Mary was born in the normal way, being the offspring of her parents, and therefore born in sin, according to the judgement of God on the first woman (she was deceived) Mary could not contaminate her offspring with her own sin.

Because Adam sinned, it was only when Mary went with a man to produce offspring that they would be born in sin. Therefore, when the Messiah was born to Mary when she was a virgin through the creative work of the Holy Spirit, He was born sinless. However, when Mary gave birth to sons and daughters by Joseph, they were sinners at conception because Joseph was their father. Mary and Joseph 'knew' each other only after the birth of the Messiah.

If Mary was able to contaminate her offspring with her own sin as a virgin, then the Messiah would have been contaminated with sin at His human birth and could not have remained sinless and would therefore not have been able to die for the sin of mankind whatever His Divine nature and state before-hand.

It is essential that we understand that the Messiah came to earth as a

---

[107] The reason for this is that it is possible Adam did not tell her about the warning God had given to him about eating the fruit of that tree, or did not stress its potency. Be that as it may, Adam as the senior had the responsibility to ensure she did not eat of the fruit of that tree, This meant that sin was passed down the male line allowing the Messiah to receive a human body from Mary that was without sin.

man, a human being, to live a sinless life (human as well as Divine) and to die as a sinless man, a sinless physical human being, therefore what happened at His human birth is an essential element in His life and sacrifice.

It is only by studying the first and second testaments carefully that the rules (legal issues) behind God's plan of salvation can be properly understood. Adam was created first and Eve was created from him as his helpmeet. The full responsibility of obeying God's command to not eat of the fruit of the forbidden tree was therefore Adams not Eves for it was up to Adam to prevent Eve from doing so; in which responsibility he was clearly found wanting, for the scriptures tell us that it was, *as in Adam all die*, his disobedience led to the death of all men (not the deception of Eve which is also a mystery that only God can explain).

Because of this, sin is the responsibility of the man not the woman (although women, including Mary the mother of Jesus, are also sinners because they are born of man) because of God's judgement naming Adam as the one who had sinned.

It is essential that we understand the underlying legal argument that if Mary could have contaminated her offspring with her own sin, then the virgin birth would have been impossible, for the body of the baby boy made available for the perfect, sinless Son of God from heaven would have been contaminated with sin. If the Messiah had been contaminated with sin from His birth on earth through Mary, He could not then have been the perfect sinless Son of Man that He was and He would therefore have been unable to die for the sins of the world.

We are clearly told that it was through one man that sin entered into the world (Ro. 5:12) and spiritual death through that sin. Because all mankind has been born of Adam, we are all convicted with Adam (1 Cor. 15:22) for that one act of sinful rebellion against the specific command of God. As it was God's intention to create man to be like Him, *let us make man in our own image* (Gen. 1:26), it is clear He had done so with the objective that we would become united with Him in eternal spiritual life.

Indeed, God had wanted Adam to eat of the tree of life which would have given him eternal life through obedience, and this by the very fact that he would not have eaten of the fruit of the other tree of testing.

The tree of life survives to this day and those of us who believe shall see it for ourselves one day. (Rev. 22:2) But as we all died a spiritual death with Adam, which separated us from the One who created us, God was left with having to provide the means by which we can once again be reunited with Himself in such a way that His purity and holiness is not compromised.

The Essential Nature of the Virgin Birth

Fully God Became Fully Man

Let us further consider the remarkable birth process of this baby. The birth of every baby heralds the birth of a new person (Body — Soul — Spirit[108]). But Mary was told that the child born to her would be called the Son of God, therefore the child would not be a 'normal' child in the accepted sense. Furthermore, the Messiah, the promised anointed one, who was to be born of the virgin Mary, was not a new person for we are told that the Spirit within the body was not only present before the world came into being, but part of the triune God who created the world and all that surrounds it,

> *"In the beginning was the Word …*
> *He was in the beginning with God …*
> *without Him nothing was made*
> *that was made …"*
> *(Jn. 1:1 – 5).*

So how do we link this knowledge with the birth of a baby boy born to a virgin chosen of God? Simply by accepting that, through the miraculous and creative work of God, the Spirit that was the Son of God at the time of the creation somehow fitted into the body of the baby developing in the womb of the virgin.

It is essential that we do not confuse the spiritual with the physical. The Messiah as the Son of God is an integral part of God the trinity and a Spirit being. Therefore, He needed a human body to be born as a man on earth. The scripture tells us that, *a body You have prepared for Me.* (Heb. 10:5 – 7)

The Spirit that is the Son of God had to enter the body that was prepared for Him in Mary, who was told by the Angel that she would be delivered of a son even though she was a virgin (Lk. 1:26 – 38) by the power of God. There is no other way to understand the transfer of the spirit that was the Son of God in the heavenly realm into the body of a child on earth so that He could become the Son of Man, for there is no doubt that He became a true human being even though He retained His divinity, which was demonstrated by the power he had over nature as well as the infinite knowledge of the scriptures and the authority of His speech and teaching (Matt. 7:29).

---

[108] For a fuller and deeper understanding of this subject please read "The spiritual Man" by Watchman Nee.

Thus, instead of:

for the 'normal' baby, in the case of the Messiah we have:

Symbolic of Son of Man

One hymn writer put it this way:

> Our God contracted to a span
> incomprehensibly made man.

It is possible for us to understand the soul of man but the soul of the Messiah is a mystery, for even His body did not rot in the grave (Gen. 3:19 Ps. 16:10) but in His earthly body, by rising again and ascending to heaven He became the first fruits of all those who believe. That is, when He rose His body was transformed into a spiritual body, the first man to take on incorruption. (1 Cor. 15:35 – 57) Even though He had an earthly body yet He was born of God and was wholly spiritual, never carnal.

When the soul was originally created in man it was under the authority of the spirit that God had breathed into man. Man became a living being before God and able to communicate and relate to Him because the spirit took charge of the soul, which ensured the man showed the attributes of God in whose image he was made. Unfortunately, after man had sinned and the spirit in man had become dead because it was no longer able to communicate with and therefore relate to the Spirit of God, the soul started to take orders from the body and became earthly or 'carnal', which means to be sensual, fleshly. (Ro. 7:14)

All flesh has a soul. The original meaning of the word for soul 'psuche' is given in the Greek lexicon as "animal life". As far as fallen man is concerned, it is the person we are before our regeneration when God the Holy Spirit causes the rebirth of our spirit. (Jn. 3:3, 6)

The Essential Nature of the Virgin Birth

The whole process of a repentant sinner being saved and going on to enter into a spiritual life depends on the inner change that retrains the soul to come under the authority of the spirit not the body. (Ro. 8:9) That is, we change from a life focused on the flesh to that focused on the spirit.

But this is dependent on a realisation within the saved person of the importance of the new life he has been given through the Spirit of God that was made available through the sacrifice of the Lord Jesus Christ (Heb. 8:14; Ro. 8:14, Jn. 16:13, 14). This requires him to leave his old earthly-focused life and pursue a spiritual life focused on God that will lead him into a spiritual union with God that will enable an individual to get deeper and more spiritually aware if they are willing to leave their interest and desire for the things of the earth to focus their attention on the things that will involve them in the things of God through their relationship with the Spirit of God. (Ro. 8:6 – 8, 10, 11)

Without this willingness of the individual to allow God, through an inner refocusing of the purpose and direction of his life, to bring about that all important transforming inner change (Ro. 8:12 – 13), then their regeneration into a renewed spiritual being will not progress for they will retain a life which has an earthly or carnal focus. (Ro. 8:14 – 16) which will either mean that person is accepted into heaven by the skin of his teeth, or will miss out on the spiritual future with God that they could and should enjoy. (Ro. 8:17 - 30) (Watchman Nee in his book "The Spiritual Man" considers this matter in depth; it is a valuable resource for the believer who wants to gain a greater understanding of how we can grow ever closer to God.)

Thus, the Messiah, who was fully divine, being the true born son of God the Father (begotten not made), became fully human through the reproductive services of Mary without His eternal spiritual nature being compromised. The body the Messiah received from Mary had been initiated in her by the unique and eternal creative power of the Holy Spirit (how the third person of the Trinity did this is beyond our understanding, but so is the creation of all that we see around us and all that is hidden from our sight). Even the miracles performed by the Messiah are beyond our understanding.

To provide a more complete understanding of this miraculous event we need to consider other scriptures that will hopefully make things clearer. Consider this abridged extract from 'Appendix A' of my work 'God Rescues His People':

"Sacrifices and offering You did not desire,
But a body You have prepared for Me.
In burnt offerings and sacrifices for sin
You had no pleasure.

Then I said, 'Behold, I have come -
In the volume of the book, it is written of Me -
To do Your will O God.'''
Heb. 10:5-7; Ps. 40:6-8)

Verse 5 of Hebrews 10 is not a direct quote from Psalm 40 for the line

'My ears you have opened'

which was achieved through persistent effort, has been changed to,

'but a body you have prepared for Me'

which was necessary for the statement,

'behold I have come'

to become a reality, for it tells of the coming of the Messiah in human form. This is the obedience of the One who is written about in the volume (the whole of the scriptures). But why should we accept this interpretation of the verse in the Psalms? Because of the reality of the Messiah who lived on this earth and gave witness to the fact that the Father had sent Him saying, *And the Father Himself who sent Me has testified of Me.* (Jn. 5:37)

With the Jewish leaders wanting desperately to kill Him because He broke the petty Sabbath rules, many of which they had created and imposed on the people themselves, and proclaimed that God was His Father, the Messiah told them clearly that they were unwilling to accept Him because they did not have the God they purported to worship abiding in their lives; they were in effect spiritually dead.

The fact that they searched the scriptures diligently was pointless, because they were spiritually dead and therefore unwilling to seek after the true spiritual knowledge of God and thereby understand that those scriptures spoke of Him (Jn. 5:39), which is why He spoke in parabolic form.

The Son from before the world began came that He might impart spiritual life to those who were willing to believe (Matt. 4:4) because He was Spirit and therefore spoke of the truth that existed in the beginning because He was there at the beginning. The Messiah was speaking from first-hand knowledge when He said that, *It is the Spirit who gives Life; the flesh profits nothing* (Jn. 6:63) for God gave the spirit, that is life, to man when He breathed into his nostrils the 'breath of life' (that is the spirit) which man then totally ignored because he allowed his body through his eyes to lead him into sin; therefore it is the flesh that carries in it the sentence of death through sin. The flesh is only for a limited time, a time on this earth for testing the suitability of the individual for eternity with God. It is the spirit that is eternal.

It is the body of the Messiah that people saw that made Him the Son of Man and therefore suitable for sacrifice and that was killed, murdered on the cross, held there by His obedience to the commands of His Father and the love of His Father for the chosen race; but it was the spirit of the Son of God that rose triumphant, undefeated, taking with it the transformed body of the Son of Man so that nothing was left behind. The body might have died but the spirit that was the Son of God (Lk. 1:35) did not die but went into hell to preach to the spirits there (1 Pet. 3:18 – 22; cf Jn. 5:25) and then ascended to where He had been before, accepted by His Father because of the marks on the hands of His physical body, now made into a spiritual body, received from men during the crucifixion.

There must be no doubt in anyone's mind that the Messiah, the anointed of God, suffered the full force of the physical agony incurred by the stripes and barbarism of the crucifixion whilst hanging there on the cross until He gave up His own spirit so that the body died. The suffering was real and altogether what any one of us would suffer in a similar experience with the additional fact that spiritually He was separated from His Father because the Father could not look upon Him as He carried the burden of our sin. Such suffering is beyond our imagination or comprehension.

The cleansing we receive because of the blood He shed does nothing for the filth of the flesh, for flesh and blood cannot inherit the Kingdom of God which is spiritual, but it transforms the spirit within us which is made alive to the Messiah because of the work of the Holy Spirit (Jn. 6:63), giving us a clear conscience (Heb. 9:14, 15). The time will then come when we will put off the corruption of this body and put on the incorruption of the body that we will receive (1 Cor. 15:42 – 58).

As we have seen as we studied the pictorial message of the tabernacle Moses produced at God's command, and the references to God's plan of salvation throughout the scriptures, there is within it the prospect of the coming of a Messiah who would save from their sins not only those of God's people Israel who were and are willing to believe in Him, but all who would trust in Him for salvation, and then rise again in glory.

The sin offerings and sacrifices were offered according to the law, but were not always offered with the right attitude of heart for them to be genuine (Is. 1; Mal. 1). The visitation of the Messiah was according to the Love of God and was completely genuine.

According to prophetic utterances the Messiah was born into the world to do the Father's will and demonstrate, for us all to see, what God has always meant by willing obedience. We know from the writings in the second testament that the, Messiah throughout His life, did not sin but did the will of God His Father (Matt. 3:17; 17:5; Jn 12:28). Therefore, being without sin from the beginning, being born through the Virgin Mary without any contamination from sin, and being able to live a life without sin, the Messiah was able to take on the sin of the world and die in the place of Man at the time of, and in the place of the Passover Lamb.

The body provided by Mary was the instrument God used to provide the perfect sacrifice for sin. It was the spirit of the Son of God who wore that body through obedience to His Father, assisted by the Holy Spirit[109], and carried through to completion God's plan of salvation.

---

[109] This is the Divine Trinity working together as a united whole to fulfil God's Plan of salvation as progressively revealed in the scriptures.

APPENDIX B   A JEWISH UNDERSTANDING OF THE CREATION

By Gerald Schroeder - Edited by Peter Russell-Yarde

One of the most obvious perceived contradictions between the Torah and science is the age of the universe. Is it billions of years old, like scientific data, or is it thousands of years, like Biblical data? When we add up the generations of the Bible, we come to 5700-plus years. Whereas, data from the Hubbell telescope or from the land-based telescopes in Hawaii, indicate the number at 15 billion years.

In trying to resolve this apparent conflict, it's interesting to look historically at trends in knowledge, because absolute proofs are not forthcoming. It is interesting to see how science has changed its understanding of the world over the years, but the record in the Torah remains fixed because the Torah doesn't have the option of changing. (I refuse to use modern Biblical commentary, because modern commentary is already too influenced by modern science.)

The only data that can therefore be used with any degree of safety as far as Biblical commentary goes is ancient commentary. That means the:

- text of the Bible itself (3300 years ago),

- translation of the Torah into Aramaic by Onkelos (100 CE),

- Talmud (redacted about the year 500 CE),

- three major Torah commentators.

There are many, many commentators, but at the top of the mountain there are three, accepted by all:

- Rashi (11th century France), who brings the straight understanding of the text,

- Maimonides (12th century Egypt), who handles the philosophical concepts,

- Nachmanides (13th century Spain), the earliest of the Kabbalists.

This ancient commentary was finalized hundreds or thousands of years ago, long before Hubbell was a gleam in his great-grandparent's eye. So there is no possibility of Hubbell or any other scientific data influencing these concepts. That's a key component in this attempt to keep the following discussion objective.

A universe with a beginning.

In 1959, a survey was taken of leading American scientists. Among the many questions asked was,

"What is your concept of the age of the universe?"

Now, in 1959, astronomy was popular, but cosmology - the deep physics of understanding the universe - was just developing. The response to that survey was recently republished in Scientific American - the most widely read science journal in the world. Two-thirds of the scientists - an overwhelming majority - gave the same answer which was,

"Beginning? There was no beginning. Aristotle and Plato taught us 2400 years ago that the universe is eternal. Oh, we know the Bible says 'In the beginning.' That's a nice story, it helps kids go to bed at night. But we sophisticates know better. There was no beginning."

In 1965, Penzias and Wilson discovered the echo of the Big Bang in the black of the sky at night, and the world paradigm changed from a universe that was eternal to a universe that had a beginning. Science had made an enormous paradigm change in its understanding of the world.

It is essential to understand the impact of that dramatic and far-reaching change of thinking. Science, which had said that there was no beginning, now said that our universe had a beginning, proving that the first words of the Bible *In the beginning* were correct after all. The importance of that scientific "discovery" cannot be overstated. Evolution, cave men, these are all trivial problems compared to the fact that we now understand that we had a beginning.

Of course, the fact that there was a beginning does not prove that there was a beginner. Whether the second half of Genesis 1:1 is correct, we don't know from a secular point of view. The first half is "In the beginning;" the second half is "G-d[110] created the Heavens and the Earth." Physics allows for a beginning without a beginner. I'm not going to get into that today, but my new book, "The Science of G-d," examines this in great detail.

It all starts from Rosh Hashanah.

The question we're left with is:

"how long ago did the "beginning" occur?"

---

[110] Many Jews are unable to fully pronounce the name of God omitting the vowel, just as Yahweh and Jehovah can only be used without the vowels because of their respect for His uniqueness and awesomeness. To the true Jew God is unknowable and so mighty and hugely complex that He is indescribable, so they prefer to leave out the vowel when using His name in the text. As this is not my work I wish to show respect for the author by using his text, taken from the web and sent to me by a friend, with as little alteration as possible.

A Jewish Understanding of the Creation

Was it, as the Bible might imply, 5700-plus years, or was it the 15 billions of years as is accepted by the scientific community?

The first thing we have to understand is the origin of the Biblical calendar. The Jewish year is figured by adding up the generations since Adam. Additionally, there are six days leading up to the creation to Adam. These six days are significant as well.

Of course, what the question would be is where we make the zero point. On Rosh Hashanah, the Jewish New Year, the Shofar is blown three times during the Musaf service. Immediately upon blowing of the Shofar, the following sentence is said:

"Hayom Harat Olam - today is the birthday of the world."

This verse might imply that Rosh Hashanah commemorates the creation of the universe but it doesn't. Although Rosh Hashanah does commemorate a creation, it is not the creation of the universe.

The Shofar is blown three times to commemorate the last of the three creations that occurs in the Six Days of Genesis. First, there is the creation of the entire universe and the laws of nature. Then on Day Five, there is the creation that brings us the Nefesh, the soul of animal life. Finally, at the end of Day Six, there is a further creation that brings us the Neshama, the soul of human life.

Rosh Hashanah commemorates not the first or the second of the creations, but the third only, that is the creation of the Neshama, the soul of human life. This means that the counting for the 5700-plus years of Jewish history starts from the creation of the soul of Adam. Thus the clock that begins with Adam is separate from the six days. This means that the Bible has two clocks.

This might seem like a modern rationalization, if it were not for the fact that Talmudic commentaries 1500 years ago record this information. In the Midrash (Vayikra Rabba 29:1), an expansion of the Talmud, all the Sages agree that Rosh Hashanah commemorates the soul of Adam, and that the Six Days of Genesis are separate.

Now 1500 years ago, when this information was first recorded, it wasn't because one of the Sages like Hillel was talking to his 10-year-old son who said, "Daddy, you won't believe it but we went to a museum today and learned all about a billions-of-years-old universe," and Hillel says, "Oh, I better change the Bible, let's keep the six days separate." That wasn't what was happening.

It is essential in this situation to use the mind frame of 1500 years ago, when people travelled by donkeys and electricity or even zippers were yet to be invented. Why were the Six Days taken out of the calendar? At the time, there was no need to make them separate.

The reason they were taken out was because they came to realise that time is described differently in those Six Days of Genesis. To say, *There was evening and morning* is an exotic, bizarre and unusual way of describing time even at that time.

From Adam, the flow of time is clearly in human terms. Adam and Eve lived 130 years before having children! Seth lived 105 years before having children, etc. From Adam forward, the flow of time is totally human in concept. But prior to that time, it is an abstract concept: *Evening and morning.* It is like looking down on events from a viewpoint that is not intimately related to them.

Looking deeper into the text.

In trying to understand the flow of time here, it is important to remember that the entire Six Days of Creation in Genesis are confined to 31 sentences! This has given people so many headaches in trying to understand science and relate it to the Bible. At MIT, in the Hayden library, there were about 50,000 books that dealt with the development of the universe: cosmology, chemistry, thermodynamics, palaeontology, archaeology and the high-energy physics of creation. Up the river at Harvard, at the Weiger library, they probably have 200,000 books on these same topics. Yet the Bible gives us just 31 sentences. So don't expect that by a simple reading of those sentences it is possible to know every detail that is held within the text. It is obvious that there is a need to dig deeper to get the information out.

The idea of having to dig deeper is not a rationalization. The Talmud (Chagiga, ch. 2) tells us that from the opening sentence of the Bible, through the beginning of Chapter Two, the entire text is given in parable form, a poem with a text and a subtext. Now, again, think according to the mindset of 1500 years ago, the time of the Talmud. Why would the Talmud think it was parabolic? Is it possible that 1500 years ago they thought that G-d couldn't make it all in 6 days? It was a problem for them? People have a problem today with cosmology and scientific data. But 1500 years ago, what's the problem with 6 days? No problem.

So when the Sages excluded these six days from the calendar, and said that the entire text is a parable, it wasn't because they were trying to apologize away what they'd seen in the local museum. There was no local museum. No one was out there digging up ancient fossils. The fact is that a close reading of the text makes it clear that there is information hidden and folded into layers below the surface.

The idea of looking for a deeper meaning in Torah is no different from looking for deeper meaning in science. For those who get up early in the morning, look over and there comes the Sun, rising in the east. Wait a few hours and the Sun sets in the west. The simple "reading" is "there's the Sun again going around the Earth." But there is much more to it. How about the Earth rotating on its axis? And neglecting the rest of the universe and just considering the Sun-Earth system, it is not the Sun that is moving, although that is every perception of human perception.

In the Sun-Earth system it is the Sun that is standing still, and the Earth that is rotating on its axis which means that at this moment, even sitting down, people are moving about 800 miles an hour. There go the clouds. Look at them zooming by. No, that's not what's happening, because we're all moving together. It cannot be felt it because it is inertial motion, there is no acceleration. So it feels like we're standing still. But in fact we are moving at 800 miles an hour as we rotate around to get a day and a night out of that one 24-hour day.

The Earth is moving around the sun at about 20 miles a second. And the entire Solar System is moving around the centre of our galaxy at about 250 miles a second. That is per second. Do we feel any of it? No. So when Galileo argued and claimed that Earth is not standing still, he got put under house arrest.

Just as we look for the deeper readings in science, we need to look for the deeper readings in text. Thousands of years ago we learned that there are subtleties in the text that expand the meaning way beyond. It is those subtleties we need to see.

Natural history and human history.

There are early Jewish sources stating that the calendar is in two parts (even predating Leviticus Rabba which goes back almost 1500 years and says it explicitly). In the closing speech that Moses makes to the people, he says that if you want to see the fingerprint of G-d in the universe, *consider the days of old, the years of the many generations* (Deut. 32:7). Nachmanides, in the name of Kabbalah, asks, "Why does Moses break the calendar into two parts -

'The days of old, and the years of the many generations?'
Because,

'Consider the days of old' is the Six Days of Genesis.

The years of the many generations' is all the time from Adam forward.

Moses says it is possible to see G-d's fingerprint on the universe in one of two ways. Look at the phenomenon of the Six Days and the development of a . universe which is mind-boggling. Or if that doesn't impress, then just consider society from Adam forward - the phenomenon of human history. Either way it is possible to find the imprint of G-d.

I recently met in Jerusalem with Professor Leon Lederman, Nobel Prize winning physicist. We were talking science, obviously. As the conversation went on, I said, "What about spirituality, Leon?" And he said to me, "Schroeder, I'll talk science with you, but as for spirituality, speak to the people across the street, the theologians." But then he continued, and he said, "But I do find something spooky about the people of Israel coming back to the Land of Israel." Interesting.

The first part of Moses' statement, "Consider the days of old" - about the Six Days of Genesis - didn't impress Prof. Lederman. But of the "Years of the many generations" - human history - that impressed him. Prof. Lederman found nothing spooky about the Eskimos eating fish at the Arctic circle. He found nothing spooky about Greeks eating Musika in Athens. But he finds something really spooky about Jews eating falafel on Jaffa Street. Because it shouldn't have happened. It doesn't make sense historically that the Jews would come back to the Land of Israel. Yet that's what happened.

And that is one of the functions of the Jewish People in the world. To act as a demonstration. We don't want everyone to be Jewish in the world, just to understand that there is some monkey business going on with history that makes it not all just random. That there's some direction to the flow of history and the world has seen it through us. It is not by chance that Israel is on the front page of the New York Times more than anyone else.

What is a "day?"

Let's jump back to the Six Days of Genesis. First of all, it is known that when the Biblical calendar says 5700-plus years, to that must be added "the six days."

A few years ago, I acquired a dinosaur fossil that was dated (by two radioactive decay chains) as 150 million years old. (If you visit me in Jerusalem, I'll be happy to show you the dinosaur fossil - the vertebra of a plesiosaurus.) So my 7-year-old daughter says, "Abba! Dinosaurs? How can there be dinosaurs 150 million years ago, when my Bible teacher says the world isn't even 6000 years old?" So I told her to look in Psalms 90:4. There, you will find something quite amazing. King David says, *"1000 years in Your (G-d's) sight are like a day that passes, a watch in the night."* Perhaps time is different from the perspective of King David, than it is from the perspective of the Creator. Perhaps time is different.

The Talmud (Chagiga, ch. 2), in trying to understand the subtleties of Torah, analyses the word "choshech." When the word "choshech" appears in Genesis 1:2, the Talmud explains that it means black fire, black energy, a kind of energy that is so powerful you can't even see it. Two verses later, in Genesis 1:4, the Talmud explains that the same word - "choshech" - means darkness, i.e. the absence of light.

Other words as well are not to be understood by their common definitions. For example, "mayim" typically means water. But Maimonides says that in the original statements of creation, the word "mayim" may also mean the building blocks of the universe.

Another example is Genesis 1:5, which says, *"There is evening and morning,*

A Jewish Understanding of the Creation

Day One." That is the first time a day is quantified: evening and morning. Nachmanides discusses the meaning of evening and morning. Does it mean sunset and sunrise? It would certainly seem to.

But Nachmanides points out a problem with that. The text says *"there was evening and morning Day One... evening and morning a second day... evening and morning a third day."* Then on the fourth day, the sun is mentioned. Nachmanides says that any intelligent reader can see an obvious problem. How do we have a concept of evening and morning for the first three days if the sun is only mentioned on Day Four? We know that the author of the Bible - even if you think it was a bunch of Bedouins sitting around a campfire at night - was smart. He or she or it produced a best-seller. For thousands of years! So it is not possible to attribute the sun appearing only on Day Four to foolishness. There is a purpose for it on Day Four. And the purpose is that as time goes by and people understand more about the universe, you can dig deeper into the text.

Nachmanides says the text uses the words "Vayehi Erev" - but it doesn't mean "there was evening." He explains that the Hebrew letters Ayin, Resh, Bet - the root of "erev" - is chaos, mixture, disorder. That's why evening is called "erev", because when the sun goes down, vision becomes blurry. The literal meaning is, "there was disorder." The Torah's word for "morning" - "boker" - is the absolute opposite. When the sun rises, the world becomes "bikoret", orderly, able to be discerned. That's why the sun needn't be mentioned until Day Four. Because from erev to boker is a flow from disorder to order, from chaos to cosmos. That's something any scientist will testify never happens in an unguided system. Order never arises from disorder spontaneously. There must be a guide to the system. That's an unequivocal statement.

Order cannot arise from disorder by random reactions. (In pure probability it can, but the numbers are so infinitesimally small that physics regards the probability as zero.) So you go to the Dead Sea and say, "I see these orderly salt crystals. You're telling me that G-d's there making each crystal?" No. That's not what I'm saying. But the salt crystals do not arise randomly. They arise because laws of nature that are part of the creation package force salt crystals to form. The laws of nature guide the development of the world. And there is a phenomenal amount of development that's encoded in the Six Days. But it is not included directly in the text, otherwise creation would be in every other sentence!

The Torah wants people to be amazed by this flow of order, starting from a chaotic plasma and ending up with a symphony of life. Day-by-day the world progresses to higher and higher levels. Order out of disorder. It is pure thermodynamics. And it is stated in terminology of 3000 years ago.

The creation of time.

Each day of creation is numbered. Yet there is discontinuity in the way the days are numbered. The verse says: "There is evening and morning, Day One." But the second day doesn't say "evening and morning, Day Two." Rather, it says "evening and morning, a second day." And the Torah continues with this pattern: "Evening and morning, a third day... a fourth day... a fifth day... the sixth day." Only on the first day does the text use a different form: not "first day," but "Day One" ("Yom Echad"). Many English translations make the mistake of writing "a first day." That's because editors want things to be nice and consistent. But they throw out the cosmic message in the text! Because there is a qualitative difference, as Nachmanides says, between "one" and "first." One is absolute; first is comparative.

Nachmanides explains that on Day One, time was created. That's a phenomenal insight. Time was created. I can understand creating matter, even space. But time? How do you create time? You can't grab time. You don't even see it. You can see space, you can see matter, you can feel energy and you can see light energy. I understand a creation there. But the creation of time? Eight hundred years ago, Nachmanides attained this insight from the Torah's use of the phrase, "Day One." And that's exactly what Einstein taught us in the Laws of Relativity: that there was a creation, not just of space and matter, but of time itself.

Einstein's Law of Relativity.

We look at the universe, and say, "How old is the universe? Looking back in time, the universe is about 15 billion years old." That is our view of time. But what is the Bible's view of time? How does it see time? Maybe it sees time differently. And that makes a big difference.

Albert Einstein taught us that Big Bang cosmology brings not just space and matter into existence, but that time is part of the nitty gritty. Time is a dimension. Time is affected by your view of time. How you see time depends on where you're viewing it. A minute on the moon goes faster than a minute on the Earth. A minute on the sun goes slower. Time on the sun is actually stretched out so that if you could put a clock on the sun, it would tick more slowly. It's a small difference, but it's measurable and measured. If you could ripen oranges on the Sun, they would take longer to ripen. Why? Because time goes more slowly. Would you feel it going more slowly? No, because your biology would be part of the system. If you were living on the Sun, your heart would beat more slowly. Wherever you are, your biology is in synch with the local time.

If it were possible to look from one system to another, time would be seen very differently. This is because time, depending on factors like gravity and velocity, is perceived very differently.

A Jewish Understanding of the Creation

For example: One evening we were sitting around the dinner table, and my 11-year-old daughter asked, "How could you have dinosaurs? How could you have billions of years scientifically - and thousands of years Biblically at the same time? So I told her to imagine a planet where time is so stretched out that while we live out two years on Earth, only three minutes will go by on that planet. Now those places actually exist, they are observed. It would be hard to live there with their conditions, and you couldn't get to them either, but in mental experiments you can do it. Two years are going to go by on Earth, three minutes are going to go by on the planet. So my daughter says, "Great! Send me to the planet. I'll spend three minutes there. I'll do two years worth of homework. I'll come back home, no homework for two years."

Nice try. Assuming she was age 11 when she left and her friends were 11. She spends three minutes on the planet and then comes home. (The travel time takes no time.) How old is she when she gets back? Eleven years and 3 minutes. And her friends are 13. Because she lived out 3 minutes while we lived out 2 years. Her friends aged from 11 years to 13 years, while she's 11 years and 3 minutes.

Had she looked down on Earth from that planet, her perception of Earth time would be that everybody was moving very quickly. Whereas if we looked up, she would be moving very slowly.

Which is correct? Is it three years? Or three minutes? The answer is both. They're both happening at the same time. That's the legacy of Albert Einstein. It so happens there are literally billions of locations in the universe where if you could put a clock there it would tick so slowly that from our perspective (if we could last that long) 15 billion years would go by... but the clock at that remote location would tick out six days. Nobody disputes this data.

Time travel and the Big Bang.

But how does this help to explain the Bible? Because the Talmud and commentators seem to say that Six Days of Genesis were regular 24-hour periods!

Let's look a bit deeper. The classical Jewish sources say that before the beginning, we don't really know what there was. We can't tell what predates the universe. The Midrash asks the question: Why does the Bible begin with the letter Bet? Because Bet (which is written like a backwards C) is closed in all directions and only open in the forward direction. Hence we can't know what comes before - only after. The first letter is a Bet - closed in all directions and only open in the forward direction.

Nachmanides the Kabbalist expands the statement. He says that although the days are 24 hours each, they contain "kol yemot ha-olam" - all the ages and all the secrets of the world.

Nachmanides says that before the universe, there was nothing... but then suddenly the entire creation appeared as a minuscule speck. He gives a dimension for the speck: something very tiny like the size of a grain of mustard. And he says that is the only physical creation. There was no other physical creation; all other creations were spiritual. The Nefesh (the soul of animal life) and the Neshama (the soul of human life) are spiritual creations. There's only one physical creation, and that creation was a tiny speck. The speck is all there was. Anything else was G-d. In that speck was all the raw material that would be used for making everything else. Nachmanides describes the substance as "dak me'od, ein bo mamash" - very thin, no substance to it. And as this speck expanded out, this substance - so thin that it has no essence - turned into matter as we know it.

Nachmanides further writes: "Misheyesh, yitfos bo zman" - from the moment that matter formed from this substance-less substance, time grabs hold. Not "begins." Time is created at the beginning. But time "grabs hold." When matter condenses, congeals, coalesces, out of this substance so thin it has no essence - that's when the Biblical clock starts.

Science has shown that there's only one "substanceless substance" that can change into matter. And that's energy. Einstein's famous equation, $E=MC2$, tells us that energy can change into matter. And once it changes into matter, time grabs hold.

Nachmanides has made a phenomenal statement. I don't know if he knew the Laws of Relativity. But we know them now. We know that energy - light beams, radio waves, gamma rays, x-rays - all travel at the speed of light, 300 million metres per second. At the speed of light, time does not pass. The universe was aging, but time only grabs hold when matter is present. This moment of time before the clock begins for the Bible, lasted about 1/100,000 of a second; a miniscule length of time. But in that time, the universe expanded from a tiny speck, to about the size of the Solar System. From that moment on matter exists, and time flows forward. The clock begins here.

Now the fact that the Bible says there is "evening and morning Day One", teaches us time from a Biblical perspective. Einstein proved that time varies from place to place in the universe, and that time varies from perspective to perspective in the universe. The Bible says there is "evening and morning Day One".

Now if the Torah were seeing time from the days of Moses and Mount Sinai - long after Adam - the text would not have written Day One, because by Sinai, millions of days had already passed. Since then there was a lot of time with which to compare Day One, it would have said "A First Day." By the second day of Genesis, the Bible says "a second day," because there was already the First Day with which to compare it. You could ask on the second day, "What happened on the first day?" But you could not say on the first day, "what happened on the first day?" because "first" implies comparison - an existing series. And there was no existing series. Day One was all there was.

Even if the Torah was seeing time from Adam, the text would have said "a first day", because by its own statement there are six days. The Torah says "Day One" because the Torah is looking forward from the beginning. And it asks, "How old is the universe? Six Days" (that is just taking time up until Adam). Six Days. We look back in time, and say the universe is 15 billion years old. But every scientist knows, that when we say the universe is 15 billion years old, there's another half of the sentence that we never say. The other half of the sentence is:

"The universe is 15 billion years old as seen from the time-space coordinates that we exist in."

That is Einstein's view of relativity.

The key is that the Torah looks forward in time, from very different time-space coordinates, when the universe was small. But since then, the universe has expanded out. Space stretches, and that stretching of space totally changes the perception of time.

Imagine in your mind going back billions of years to the beginning of time. Now pretend way back at the beginning of time, when time grabs hold, there's an intelligent community. This is totally fictitious. But, for the sake of this experiment, let us imagine that the intelligent community has a laser which is going to shoot out a pulse of light every second. Every second -- pulse. Pulse. Pulse. It shoots the light out, and then billions of years later, way far down the time line, we here on Earth have a big satellite dish and we receive that pulse of light. On that pulse of light is imprinted (printing information on light is called fibre optics - sending information by light), "I'm sending you a pulse every second." And then a second goes by and the next pulse is sent.

Now light travels at 300 million metres per second. So the two light pulses are separated by 300 million metres at the beginning. Now they travel through space for billions of years, and they're going to reach the Earth billions of years later. But wait a minute. Is the universe static? No. The universe is expanding. That's the cosmology of the universe. And that means it's expanding into an empty space outside the universe. There's only the universe. There is no space outside the universe. The universe expands by space stretching. So as these pulses go through billions of years of travelling, and the universe is stretching, and space is stretching, what's happening to these pulses? The space between them is also stretching. So the pulses really get further and further apart. Billions of years later, when the first pulse arrives, we say, "Wow - a pulse!" Written on it is "I'm sending you a pulse every second." You call all your friends, and you wait for the next pulse to arrive. Does it arrive another second later? No! A year later?

Maybe not. Maybe billions of years later. Because depending on how much time this pulse of light has travelled through space, will determine the amount of stretching that has occurred. That's standard cosmology.

15 billion or six days?

Today, time is observed looking backwards, that is 15 billion years. Looking forward from when the universe is very small - billions of times smaller - the Torah says six days. In truth, they both may be correct.

What's exciting about the last few years in cosmology is we now have quantified the data to know the relationship of the "view of time" from the beginning, relative to the "view of time" today. It is no longer a matter of science fiction. Any one of a dozen physics text books all use the same number. The general relationship between time near the beginning and time today is a million million. That's a 1 with 12 zeros after it. So when a view from the beginning looking forward says "I'm sending you a pulse every second," would we see it every second? No. We'd see it every million million seconds because that is the stretching effect of the expansion of the universe.

The Torah doesn't say every second, does it? It says Six Days. How would we see those six days? If the Torah says we are sending information for six days, would we receive that information as six days? No. We would receive that information as six million million days. Because the Torah's perspective is from the beginning looking forward.

Six million million days is a very interesting number. What would that be in years? Divide by 365 and it comes out to be 16 billion years. Essentially the estimate of the age of the universe. Not a bad guess for 3000 years ago.

The way these two figures matchup is extraordinary. I'm not speaking as a theologian; I'm making a scientific claim. I didn't pull these numbers out of a hat. That's why I led up to the explanation very slowly, so you can follow it step-by-step.

Now we can go one step further. Let's look at the development of time, day-by-day, based on the expansion factor. Every time the universe doubles, the perception of time is cut in half. Now when the universe was small, it was doubling very rapidly. But as the universe gets bigger, the doubling time gets exponentially longer. This rate of expansion is quoted in "The Principles of Physical Cosmology," a textbook that is used literally around the world.

(In case you want to know, this exponential rate of expansion has a specific number averaged at 10 to the 12th power. That is in fact the temperature of quark confinement, when matter freezes out of the energy: 10.9 times 10 to the 12th power Kelvin degrees divided by (or the ratio to) the temperature of the universe today, 2.73 degrees. That's the initial ratio which changes exponentially as the universe expands.)

A Jewish Understanding of the Creation

The calculations come out to be as follows:

- The first of the Biblical days lasted 24 hours, viewed from the "beginning of time perspective." But the duration from our perspective was 8 billion years.

- The second day, from the Bible's perspective lasted 24 hours. From our perspective it lasted half of the previous day, 4 billion years.

- The third day also lasted half of the previous day, 2 billion years.

- The fourth day - one billion years.

- The fifth day - one-half billion years.

- The sixth day - one-quarter billion years.

When you add up the Six Days, you get the age of the universe at 15 and 3/4 billion years; the same as modern cosmology. Is it by chance?

But there's more. The Bible goes out on a limb and tells you what happened on each of those days. Now you can take cosmology, paleontology, archaeology, and look at the history of the world, and see whether or not they match up day-by-day. And I'll give you a hint. They match up close enough to send chills up your spine.

APPENDIX C   SATAN'S ATTEMPTS TO DERAIL GOD'S PLAN

There is clear evidence that at strategic times, by working through individual leaders and the people in general, Satan tried to stop or end God's plan to bring salvation to mankind after he had successfully broken the spiritual bond between God and the man and woman He had created in His image in the Garden of Eden.

The following are just general thoughts on the main events that we would do well to consider:

The decay of man's morals before the Flood (Gen. 6:5 – 8)

With the death of Abel, and Cain's unwillingness to repent of his sin against God and his brother, there came a decay of men's morals because Cain established a society without God (Gen: 4:16). Although there were exceptions, for we are told that after the birth of Seth men began to call on the name of the Lord (Gen. 4:26), and a man named Enoch was so in-tune with God that God took him (Gen. 6:24), the majority went the way of Cain.

As the opposite of love is hate, and the opposite of order is disorder, it is clear that without God's direct influence in mankind, where the light of the life of faith had been switched off and therefore the right-ness of those whose only desire is to live in harmony with God could no longer exist without considerable difficulty, man went the way of deception and evil which is the way of Satan. (Jn. 8:44) Such was the fall of mankind into a very deep and unrestrained decadence that God had to step in and order the flood. Only godly Noah and his immediate family were sufficiently close to God that they were saved.

Pharaoh's Attempt to Kill All the Male Babies of Israel (Ex. 1 – 12)

God had chosen Abram because, in a land where paganism was rife, He saw in him a heart that was open to His voice and receptive to His involvement in his life. Isaac learned the lesson of God's practical involvement in his life through his father's demonstration of faith in God and through the ram caught in a thicket that saved his life by being sacrificed in his stead.

Jacob, as we have seen, was a God-seeker and, because of that, was chosen of God to succeed Isaac as the man in whom the promise He gave to Abraham would be secure and through whom He would work for the good of mankind by at first revealing and then establishing His plan of salvation through the promised Messiah.

In the crucible of Egypt, where God wanted to develop a nation from the twelve separate tribes, Satan saw a chance of ending the development of that nation through which God could work to bring about salvation for all mankind. We know that those who do not worship God worship Satan, whether knowingly or in ignorance matters not. Pharaoh confessed to Moses that he neither knew nor accepted the reality of the God of the Hebrews and therefore he was vulnerable to the will of Satan.

Pharaoh through purely personal reasons wanted to retain the services of the Hebrews as slaves to work on his great building projects, but to prevent them growing in numbers to the point where they could pose a threat to his and Egypt's security, he wanted to assimilate those people into Egypt by arranging for all the male babies within the Hebrew nation to be killed. By continually frustrating and bringing to nought all God's efforts in providing that way of salvation that we now enjoy, Satan would have been able to continue to rule the world as the prince of the power of the air.

Fortunately for mankind, God is infinitely more perceptive and powerful than any spiritual or human power, which means that Satan's efforts will never succeed.

Balaam's Advice to Balak (Num. 22 – 25; Rev. 2:14))

In the account of Balaam's call to assist Balak king of Moab to curse the Israelites we read the account of a duplicitous man. (Chapter 6) Outwardly he has all the appearances of a man of God willing to only do what God wanted him to do.

Balak wanted Balaam to come to his aid and curse the Israelites because of the threat they were to him and his country, but God prevented him from doing so. (Num. 22 - 24) However, in his heart Balaam wanted to receive the earthly riches Balak promised him, so out of the public gaze Balaam gave Balak advice on how to attack Israel's weak spot, which was for them to eat food sacrificed to idols and engage in sexual immorality. (Rev. 2:14) This meant that those who engaged in such activity were 'joined to Baal of Peor', the god they worshipped. (Num. 25:5) Such a stumbling block, achieved by friendly means, caused the death of many Israelis, even the death of the son of a Simeonite leader and the daughter of a leader of the Midianites who publicly sinned against God, when God carried out a cleansing operation to purify the nation. (Num. 25:5 – 18)

It is this undermining of the righteousness of the people of God that is still going on today through all the distractions of the world around us which deflect our attention and wholesome and pure worship of the God of our salvation. It is important for us to remember the promise of eternity for we will enjoy the peace and joy and purity of heaven for ever, whereas our life on earth is very short in comparison.

We are all offered the choice of life or death, as explained in this book, but it is up to us whether we choose eternal life or eternal death.

Jezebel's Attempt to Stop the Worship of God (1 Kgs. 16:29 – 19:18)

The account of the witness of Elijah is a salutary lesson for us all. Evil rulers will come and go but those who love God must be steadfast for their reward is eternal. What is certain is that all evil rulers will face the judgement of God, if not during their lifetime on earth, then certainly when they appear before the great white throne when the Messiah of Israel will come to judge all mankind. (1 Kgs. 22:34 and 2 Kgs. 9:30 – 37; Rev. 20:11 – 14)

The attempt by the servants of Satan to remove the worship of the God of Israel to replace it with substitute gods ultimately fail for those who are true to God will not give up, even when faced with imprisonment and death as, for example, the witness of Russian and Chinese Christians so clearly illustrated during the reign of the religion called Communism in those countries.

When Ahab became yet another evil king of Israel, by degree he was the worst up to that time, like Esau he married a pagan princess, Jezebel, and in so doing became an enthusiastic servant of the god Baal. The worship of the God of Israel was banned. God sent Elijah to bring a famine to the land that lasted for two and a half years before confronting the priests of Baal on Mount Carmel, where he proved beyond doubt that the God of Israel was the only God. In killing all the priests of Baal in the valley by the brook Kishon he incurred the anger of Jezebel but she was powerless against God and finally met her death according to prophecy. (2 Kgs. 9:30 – 37)

To many the first testament appears brutal, but we must all realise that we only have our life span, (which, because of the violence and dominance of others, might not be three score years and ten), to find and give our hearts to God, and it is God alone who has the power and authority to choose who enters heaven and who does not (Matt. 10:28).

It is not up to any of us make a judgement on others whose hearts we cannot possibly know. True, it is by the works of others that we will be able to see their 'fruit', but we will never know their inner heart at the moment of death. Therefore, anyone who seeks to promote the worship of Satan through the worship of many gods in the guise of a variety of religions is depriving poor souls of the knowledge of God that could enable them to enjoy salvation and an eternity in heaven with Him. It is only by being with God for eternity that we will enjoy the light of His presence, where there will be no more night. Indeed, the spiritual city of Jerusalem has no need of the sun for the glory of the Lord will illuminate it. (Rev. 21:23)

Satan's Attempts to Derail God's Plan

Haman's Attempt to kill all the Jews *(Queen Esther — Esther 1- 10)*

The account of Haman's rise and fall in the book of Esther is another example of how Satan used individuals to disrupt the work of God amongst men. Haman, by manipulating the king's decree, was able to signal the death of all Jews. (Est. 3:13) But God had already pre-empted his actions by having a Jewess, Esther, chosen as queen, and Mordecai to do the king a great service. (ch. 2)

Hearing of the decree written by Haman, Mordecai persuades Esther to take action. (ch. 4 – 9) Through a series of well-planned events by the Queen, and God's personal intervention to the king one night, Haman was first made to show respect to Mordecai, whom he had planned to publicly hang (6:1 – 4), and then brought to ruin. (6:13; 7:1 – 10) The Jews were not annihilated (ch. 9) and Mordecai was elevated (ch. 10).

King Cyrus, who released the Jews from their exile and gave money for a rebuilt temple (2 Chron. 36:22 – 9) is believed to have been the son of Esther.

Satan's Attempt to defile Joshua and stop the rebuilding of the temple

A large number of Jews returned to Jerusalem to find the wall broken down, the gates burned. Nehemiah managed to get permission from the king to return and rebuild the city which he did with much opposition from a Horonite, Ammonite and an Arab, all enemies of Israel, who heard that the Jews were rebuilding the walls of Jerusalem and laughed at them, despised them and then challenged them concerning their allegiance to the King of Babylon.

Nehemiah's reply was that they relied on the God of heaven Himself who would prosper them. (Neh. 2:19 – 20) The anger of these senior officials of Samaria took root when they saw the fortifications of the hated city of Jerusalem taking shape. Anger is often translated into mockery with reference to feeble Jews, fortifying themselves and reviving the stones from the heaps of rubbish. Sandstone when burned crumbles, hence the jibe that the weight of a fox could bring all their work tumbling down. (Neh. 4:1 – 3) The people had a mind to work and raised the wall up to half its previous height, but then they heard that their enemies wanted to attack the city (Neh. 4) so the people armed themselves and continued to build the walls, ready at a moment's notice to defend themselves and their city.

As Jerusalem was central to God's work of salvation it was a worthy target for Satan who would have preferred for it never to have been repopulated. Anything he could do to disrupt the rebuild he would do, using the enemies of the Jews as his tools.

Two men returned to lead the people of Jerusalem, Zerubbabel as governor and Joshua as high priest. In Zechariah 3 the prophet in a vision sees Joshua standing before God with Satan present who is accusing Joshua of many things but God had a mind to forgive Joshua (vs. 1 – 4). Zerubbabel was faced with the task of rebuilding the destroyed temple and in Zechariah 4 it is Zerubbabel's turn to receive encouragement (vs. 6 – 10).

Haggai spoke to the people who were distraught by the state of an iconic building which they had either known or been told about (Hag. 2:3). What God is saying to them is that however poor the new temple might look in comparison to the previous grand temple of Solomon, they were not to look on it from man's perspective but from God's perspective and believe that He was able to transform the new less glorious building, which may look a shadow of its former glory, into something mighty for He would fill it with His glory (Hag. 2:4 – 9) just as He did with the original tabernacle built by Moses and that built by King Solomon.

However fine or simple a building appears it is what God is able to do with it that matters. It is the same with people, for the poor and less glorious person can often have a far more glorious testimony to tell of God's work in their lives than those who are richer, more beautiful and fashionable and publicly more acceptable. As it happens it was to this temple, enhanced by Herod, that the Messiah came to worship.

Whatever man says or does matters not for power belongs to God which is what God was saying when He said, *not by might nor by power but by My spirit says the Lord of Hosts*. (Zech. 4:6) Zerubbabel may have been faced with an apparently impossible task of erecting a building to Almighty God out of the ashes of the old, but if God was with them then the task was no longer impossible. Just as they were able to rebuild the walls without the attack from their enemies taking place, so they would be able to erect a temple that God could use for His glory and good pleasure.

Herod's Attempt to Kill the Messiah as a Baby

When Herod realised that the three wise men were not going to return and inform him of the whereabouts of the new born child, but knowing the city in which He was born, Herod cast the net wide when he sent troops to kill all male children of two years of age and under because he was not sure of His exact age when the wise men visited him. Not one of the leaders of the Jews or the religious scholars who provided Herod with the details of the prophecy tried to persuade him not to do such a thing, because they were not at all excited by the news of His possible arrival.

Satan tempts the Messiah

Satan's attempt to derail God's plan of salvation in its moment of supreme fulfilment through the three temptations put to the Messiah had to be a non-starter from the start. As the Son of God, the Messiah knew Satan from the moment he was created, so that even though He had fasted for forty days and nights He had the spiritual strength to overcome the physical feelings of hunger and desire for restricted and temporary earthly glory.

Satan's Attempt to Kill the Messiah

Throughout the years of human history Satan used many people in his attempt to fight God and stop the onward march of the development of His plan of salvation. None of his attempts had worked yet there was within this fallen senior angel an obsession with his goal of trying to achieve parity with God, the creator of all things, and sadly he did not care who else he took with him to hell, his final destination.

Through their lack of sensitivity to God because of their unwillingness to seek after Him that they might receive a new enlivened spirit by which they could enter into a new and living hope through the work of the Holy Spirit, the proud and arrogant religious leaders of the Jews became obvious prey for employment in the service of Satan. As the inherent goodness of the Messiah exposed their godlessness, such a sense of hatred was generated within them that they sought to not just oppose the Messiah but to actively seek His death, in spite of all the good He did and the power of His oratory.

With the help of Judas, who wanted the Messiah to do what he wanted Him to do (i.e. be the warrior Messiah they were in fact expecting), the final achievement of the religious leaders was seeing Him hanging on the accursed tree. Totally ignorant of God's plan of salvation, they believed His death was something to be celebrated. Mocking Him they called out, *if He is the King of Israel, let us see Him come down from the cross, and we will believe Him. Let God save Him if He is the Son of God.* (Matt. 27:39 – 43) Yet that was the whole purpose of His first visit to the earth.

Even though they sealed the stone across the entrance of the tomb in which His body was laid to rest and set a guard on it, the resurrection of the Lord made them use lies and deception to say that the disciples had stolen the body; a deception still accepted by many Jews today. If Satan lost the battle to end the human life of the eternal Son of God, then he could stop many souls from being saved, nullifying their opportunity for full salvation and keeping them under his power. (Matt. 13:3 – 33; 1 Pet. 5:6 – 11)

Satan's attempt to stop the spread of Salvation

Until his meeting with the Lord on the road to Damascus, Saul was part of the war the religious leaders were waging against God as they sought to crush the onward and upward march of the salvation of men and women through the witness of believers in the Way. After his conversion, Paul met with considerable opposition that finally led to his appeal to Caesar and ultimate death by beheading.

Satan is still actively seeking to put people off the message of salvation on offer to everyone, perverting the word through liberal theologians who are prepared to alter the word to suit their own lifestyle and convictions. Although they will receive their reward, sadly they will take with them many others who were not prepared to seek God for themselves.

In Nigeria there is the continuing problem of Moslems who seek out and kill Christian believers. Recently a Nigerian Christian spoke of his concern about this on-going problem. Unfortunately, all those who do not put their faith in the Jewish Messiah, who do not accept that it is only through Christ Jesus alone that we are saved to the uttermost, are potential servants of Satan and his demonic forces.

The reign of the ayatollahs in Iran fighting all those who do not subscribe to their version of Islam are a case in point for they want the eradication of Israel.

Satan hates anyone who stands out as a believer in the Son of God and Son of Man and will take whatever action he can to silence them according to the restricted freedom he receives from God. This is why the message of the book of Revelation is so important to understand, even in part.

But we do have the victory, those who have been born again in the Lord Jesus, for even though the servants of Satan kill our physical body, we will rise with an incorruptible body and rejoice with unspeakable joy in heaven where our Lord has gone to prepare a place for us. Death, where is your sting and grave where is your victory? Our victory is in the One who died and rose again, and now reigns in heaven with His Father for eternity.

APPENDIX D BIBLICAL INTERPRETATION

Whose word is it?

Perhaps we should start with the question, "Whose world is it?" for at the very beginning of the Hebrew Bible we have the statement,

In the beginning God created the heavens and the earth.
(Gen. 1:1)

We then have a whole series of 'God said and it was done according to His word'. Indeed, as we read further, we find that there is no possibility of divorcing God from what happens in the world for ultimately it is His world for He created it and He has never lost control of all that happens in its environment. In some situations, He causes things to happen and in others He allows things to take their course.

As this is so certainly true it is imperative that when we look into this Word of God and seek to understand what it is saying to us it is essential that we seek inspiration from the author and not merely accept the interpretation of others without question, for there have been many false prophets throughout the history of mankind.

Take for instance the prophet Micaiah who was called to the presence of the king of Israel (1 Kgs 22). The king's messenger called on Micaiah to encourage the king, that he would be victorious in the forth coming battle, as the other prophets were doing (v13), but the prophet was adamant that he could only say what God told him to say (v14).

The problem for Micaiah was that the king was expecting a contrary prophecy from him but was determined to go ahead with the battle anyway. As Micaiah was before the king a 'prophet' named Zedekiah struck him on the face demanding to know which way the spirit from the Lord went from him to speak with Micaiah (v24), for Zedekiah was fully convinced that he spoke the word of the Lord. As it was, the prophecy of Micaiah was the correct one as Zedekiah was soon to find out (v25).

God had the same problems with false prophets in the days of Jeremiah:

'For both prophet and priest are profane;
Yes, in My house I have found
their wickedness,"
Says the Lord.

"Therefore, their way shall be to them
Like slippery ways ..."
(Jer. 23:11, 12)

Just like Micaiah, Jeremiah had problems with the reaction of his fellow Jews when he spoke the word that God had given him:

O Lord, You induced me, and I was persuaded;
You are stronger than I and have prevailed.
I am in derision daily;
Everyone mocks me.
For when I spoke I cried out
I shouted, "Violence and plunder!"
(Jer. 20:7, 8)

Jeremiah was wearied by this constant opposition to the word that God had given him to speak to the people, so he decided not to make mention of the Lord God who had called him to that prophetic ministry, nor speak anymore in His name. Unfortunately, this action did Jeremiah no good for he found that God's word was in his heart like a burning fire shut up in his bones so that he wearied of holding it back and had finally to release the word that God had given to him (Jer. 20:9).

So what does this tell us, these references from the word of God; these experiences of the prophets of God who were not chosen by man but by God Himself?

Surely it is a warning that we must not meekly go along with everything other people say, but seek the truth of God for ourselves as individuals. Just because the interpretation of a passage in God's word has been accepted over centuries does it have to mean the same to us today as it did then?

At the start of the commentary in the Pentateuch and Haftorahs on Genesis chapter 3 is says "According to Rabbinic legend ..." which immediately says to me, "Is the legend correct?", for at some time someone had to have made that statement about the serpent and they could well have been a Zechariah, not believing that the spirit of the Lord had gone from him; if indeed the angel of the Lord had ever been with him in the first place.

If we play about with the interpretation of God's word then surely we are playing about with the Creator God Himself, and I do not think that is such a very good idea at all.

We are dealing with a book that has been written by those who have been personally and directly inspired by God to write down the message God wanted the people of that time to hear. This is confirmed to us by two men who were themselves chosen and inspired:

> *knowing this first, that no prophecy of scripture*
> *Is of any private interpretation,*
> *For prophecy never came by the will of men,*
> *but holy men spoke as they were moved*
> *By the Holy Spirit.*
> *(2 Pet. 1:20, 21)*

And

> *All scripture is given by inspiration of God,*
> *And is profitable for doctrine, for reproof*
> *For correction, for instruction in righteousness,*
> *That the man of God may be complete,*
> *Thoroughly equipped for every good work.*
> *(2 Tim. 3:16, 17)*

Let us consider certain details within those verses together, for they tell us that all scripture is given by inspiration of God.

Does this not suggest to all of us that when we handle the word of God we must do so with complete respect for Almighty God and open our hearts to Him, allowing Him to speak to us through it? Malachi had some serious words for the priests who had little respect for God:

> *"And now O priests, this commandment is for you.*
> *If you will not hear, and if you will not take it to heart,*
> *To give glory to My name," says the Lord of hosts,*
> *"I will send a curse upon you..."*
> *(Mal. 3:1, 2)*

Did not Nadab and Abihu suffer through their attitude to the living God? (Lev. 10). No one is safe from God's wrath if they persist in treating God and His word with contempt; surely it is said somewhere that it is a fearful thing to fall into the hands of the living God and David spoke of his flesh trembling for fear of God and His judgements (Ps. 119:120). Surely the God, who called Abraham, Isaac and Jacob and gave to them eternal promises, who called Moses, who through his total submission to God's call and because of all that God inspired him to write and relay to the people became the great-law giver and led His people out of the slavery of Egypt (representing the world) to a land flowing with milk and honey must be the focus of our attention all the while we remain on this earth.

Therefore, as we study God's word in our search for truth, we must treat it with the very greatest respect and open our hearts to the revelation only He is able to give us concerning its meaning for us as individuals.

Man's relationship to God

What does our consideration of the author and copyright holder of the word of God tell us? Surely it tells us that there is a special relationship between man and Creator which is not found in any other created being!

Just as God is three (Father, Son and Holy Spirit), so man is within himself threefold.

Man is world conscious, in so far as through his senses (feeling, smelling, taste, hearing and sight) that are exercised through the physical organs of the body (nerves, nose, palate, ears, and eyes) he senses the reality of the world about him.

Man is ego conscious for he is a self with volition (decision making ability) and an individual personality that identifies each individual from all the others. We are each a unique individual with the ability to steer ourselves through life and relate to those around us.

Man in his original created state is God conscious, because there is a space within us that God created in which He alone could fit. *"Behold,"* says the Lord, *"I stand at the door and knock, if anyone hears my voice and opens the door, I will come into him and dine with him and he with Me."*

But, as we have been seeing in the verses quoted above, there is an additional element within us that is unique to man and that is a spirit so that we can be spirit conscious. For how can we relate to the Holy Spirit, the Spirit that brooded or hovered over the waters, unless we have within us a spirit consciousness?

Now it is said that no man has seen God at any time, indeed certain men have been warned in scripture that no man could see God's face and live. The reason for this is the contrast between the intense purity of God and the corrupted level of man since his fall from the surrounding environment of righteousness that existed at the beginning. Such a contrast would prove too much for man to cope with and he would die; immediately.

God has not changed for He is the same yesterday and today and forever. Man, on the other hand got to such a level of degradation that God almost started His work of creation all over again; had He not found a man named Noah whom He saved from the waters of the flood (judgement) by the waters of the flood (judgement).

The uniqueness of man is therefore, firstly, that he has been made in the likeness of God, and in God breathing into the nostrils of the first man the breath of life he not only received life with the potential for immortality but a spirit residing within the body that is unique to each and every individual[111].

This is the reason why we are able to communicate directly with God but we must do it with complete respect for Him who created all things and in whom we exist.

Can We Pick and Choose What We Believe?

If it is God's word then the answer must be a very decisive no!

Since I started my writing career I have found the need to leave no book within the complete Bible alone as though it has nothing to give.

Many years ago I went to hear an itinerant evangelist. When he got up to speak he started by asking us these questions:

"How many of you read?"

"How many of you read a book from cover to cover?"

"How many of you believe the Bible is the most important book in the world?"

"How many of you have read the Bible from cover to cover?"

As you can imagine many hands went up in answer to the first three questions but very few went up in response to the last question. Certainly mine didn't.

This challenged me to the extent that I set out to read the complete Bible from cover to cover, which I have now done several times.

As believers, both Jew and Gentile alike, we are dealing with the Almighty creator God who is also called the Lord God of Israel. Yes, Jews and Christians worship the same God. But we have a problem.

There are some Jews who adamantly refuse to believe that the Messiah has come in (Jehoshua) Jesus of Nazareth. Yet the Second testament was written by Jews who were convinced, ultimately through experience, of the authenticity of that Man, having met Him and lived and worked with Him over three and a half years and then experienced the power and guiding ability of the Holy Spirit promised by that same Messiah.

We must not forget that the Messiah was a man the Jews were expecting at the time of His arrival but because they were divided as to what sort of messenger from God He would be, they did not realise He had come, and after over 2000 years many are still waiting expectantly, even though He said that He had not come to destroy the Law or the Prophets but to fulfil all that the Law represented and that the Prophets had relayed to the people from God.

Was it not the people, particularly those in authority both priestly and kingly, who rejected the prophets and in many cases killed them because of what God was saying to them through those prophets? How many times

---

[111] A useful book on this subject is "The Dawn of World Redemption" by Eric Sauer ISBN 0 85364 012 2

has God accused the nation of Israel and the Jews of being a stiffed-necked and rebellious people? Is that not true today? From what stand point then are their descendants accusing those who follow their Messiah of deception?

It is interesting that this Son of God who also referred to Himself as the Son of Man used the scripture of the first testament (particularly during His time being tempted after 40 days and nights in the wilderness) as any devout Jew (and Eve) should have done by saying, *It is written.*

The Jewish leaders could not make up their minds about Him, so on one occasion He said to them:

> *You search the scriptures for in them you think you have eternal life;*
> *And these are they which testify of Me.*
> *But you are not willing to come to Me that you may have life*
> *(Jn. 5:39, 40)*

There was a resistance within them because they studied the scriptures from an intellectual standpoint, arguing principles and ideas, but not from a spiritual point of view. Yet we read when the magi came to find the 'man born to be king', the religious scholars quickly identified Bethlehem as being His place of birth.

I need the inspiration of the Holy Spirit to write on scripture and the only reason my writings have been a success, particularly as I use the words of the first testament in harmony and collaboration with those of the second, has to be that the Holy Spirit of the Living God has inspired me to the extent that people are learning new things about the Word of God.

During a debate on the witnessing of Jehoshua's disciples after His death the highly respected Gamaliel gave this advice to his colleagues on the Great Sanhedrin, the supreme court of the Jews:

> *And now I say to you, keep away from these men*
> *and let them alone;*
> *For if this plan, this work is of men*
> *it will come to nothing;*
> *But if it is of God you cannot overthrow it -*
> *Lest you even be found to fight against God*
> *(Acts 5:38, 39)*

And I am among those who have been drawn to that same Son of God, rejected by men but raised by Almighty God to the highest heaven being convinced, just as they were through the work of the Holy Spirit, that He is the Messiah (Jn. 1:43 – 51) and He has changed and is changing my life because my heart has been captivated by Him and I desire His presence more than that of any other.

A rabbi I heard of admitted that at one time he could open the Bible and know the meaning of the text; he then met with the Messiah and enjoyed a moment of total surrender. Since when, each time he opens the Bible, he learns new things; for he changed from believing he knew it all to a voyage of discovery as God speaks to his spirit.

Men look at the outward appearances of others and take note of what they say and the way they live their lives which they then measure against what they believe and what is acceptable to them. God on the other hand does not look at the outer but the inner man for He looks at the heart.

In directing the prophet Samuel in His search for a king to replace Saul, whom He had rejected, the Lord said to Samuel:

> *Do not look at his appearance*
> *Or at his physical stature*
> *Because I have refused him.*
> *For the Lord does not see as man sees;*
> *For man looks at the outward appearance,*
> *But the Lord looks at the heart.*
> *(I Sam. 16:7)*

Hear what the Psalmist says:

> *My heart is steadfast O my God ...*
> *I will praise You O Lord among the peoples;*
> *I will sing to You among the nations,*
> *For your mercy reaches into the heavens,*
> *And Your truth into the clouds*
> *(See Ps. 57:7 – 11)*

> *I will praise the Lord*
> *with my whole heart,*
> *In the assembly of the upright*
> *(Ps. 111:1)*

And Paul says to the Romans:

> *let God be true and every man a liar*
> *(Ro. 3:4)*

Are those the words of an unbeliever? I think not.

Many of the Jewish leaders, those of academia and the priests thought they knew the Bible and some over the centuries have undoubtedly been

508

inspired by God. But many, particularly those still waiting for the coming of the Messiah at the time of His appearance, were searching the scriptures to find the truth but then putting their own interpretation on what they read so that it was clear they were not reading it with a desire to learn the truth from God. Their spiritual ears were closed to the true word of God, listening to their own thoughts and desire instead.

I have gained an understanding of Genesis chapter 3 that many believe is totally wrong. But I seek after God and have desired most urgently to understand the Word of God as God wants me to understand it praying earnestly that God will actually prevent me from writing anything that is not truth. I have no interest in perpetuating an interpretation some respected sage gave for a passage if it is not the truth. That is the key to any study of scripture, to personally seek after God with a heart that desires to hear His truth, that is open to Him and that is willing to wait for it.

There is no doubt that since I was challenged by that evangelist I have enjoyed the interplay of the message of God in both testaments, how each supports and embellishes the other; indeed even though I was initially asked not to use references from the second testament in this work, I have singularly failed because scripture backs up scripture. Leave one of the testaments out and you have only half the information required to understand what God has been saying to man through the nation of Israel since the time of Abraham and right through Moses and His books of the Pentateuch containing the Law. None of it can be termed as being of no use or a deception; rather, and far better still, all of it is essential to bring us close to God.

I am a Gentile yet I am writing on things particular to the Jews and peculiarly Jewish. How could I do that with any acceptability unless God was guiding my thoughts? How could I feel the power of Almighty God if God was not speaking to me through the power of His Holy Spirit? For what I write to be effective in God's work it must be inspired by God and not be of my own interpretation.

Like all men, God is my judge too; so that if I want to enter heaven after my time on earth has come to an end, then I have to be careful about how I interpret scripture. And whether reading, writing, teaching or in every day conversation we must all do the same.

Gateway to God

This is a passage from the letter of Jude:

Now to Him who is able to keep you from stumbling,
And to present you faultless
Before the presence of His glory with exceeding joy,
To God our Saviour, who alone is wise,
Be glory and majesty,
Dominion and power,
Both now and forever.
Amen.
(vs 24, 25)

Who is brave enough to categorically tell me that that is not of God, or about the Lord God of Israel?

APPENDIX E THREE FOUNDATION STONES

Abraham, Isaac and Jacob

These three patriarchs are clearly different characters with different roles in the initial stages of God's clear plan of salvation; that is the process we must observe if we desire to get right with God by ridding ourselves of the stain and stench of both original and personal sin through repentance and faith; a process by which God applies the cleansing power of the blood of sacrifice that started with the temporary sacrificial blood shed by submissive sheep to atone for man's sin.

This held true until, at the appointed time, God sent His Son into the world to die as the ultimate Passover Lamb. His sacrifice of blood, shed on our behalf, is never to be repeated because after His physical death He rose again from the dead and ascended into glory to be with His Father and, for those who have decided to leave the world and cling to Him, our Father also (He created us).

From the time when Abram was first called until the time of John, the messenger for the Messiah, God progressively revealed how His plan of salvation worked and all that we needed to do to profit from this escape route from the prison of sin into His glorious Life.

This death sentence, the judgement of God incurred by the first man, applied to all men *for all we like sheep have gone astray, we have turned everyone to his own way*; we are collectively and individually all sinners before God because we are all the descendants of Adam and Eve. Even the patriarchs (each and every one born a sinner) needed to offer sacrifices to God to atone for their sin, and however remarkable Job's life was, and however total and pure his faith, we still read of his need and willingness to seek atonement through sacrifice, that he might receive forgiveness of sin from God. (Job 42:1 – 6)

It was only when a man, a perfect man who was inherently and entirely without the blemish of sin before the pure and righteous God, died in our stead, shedding His life blood (the life of the man is in the blood) in such a way that His death could legally be accepted by the God of justice as effective against the sin all mankind.

It was that death, that shedding of life blood, which made it possible for man to obtain complete forgiveness of sin. This forgiveness was so thorough in its cleansing power that it would cleanse the individual, so that even his conscience would be free of all sense of guilt before God. Such a deep cleansing of inherited and personal sin was God's objective and would be provided to all those who approached the one true God in repentance and faith no matter whether they were Jew or Gentile; for this Way of Salvation was not exclusively for the Jews, but they would initially be the messengers of this Way to the whole human race.

But this goal is at the end of the road we are on that will enable us to understand clearly what this Way of Salvation God is offering us is all about and how it was declared and provided. It is also essential that we realise that it is God's plan, God's way and that it is He who has been the power and authority behind all the decisions that have been made and the events that have occurred.

This makes my task in writing this explanatory book all the more critical for I must continually stand before this same God and ultimately be judged for all that I have done. If I fail to put before you, the reader, the Truth of God, then His judgement against me will be severe.

We need to have at the back of our minds at all times the fact that our ways are not God's ways neither are our thoughts God's thoughts. This is the principle that requires us to submit ourselves completely to God; something I have done over a long period of time and which has ultimately led me to write this book.

Abram

Abram was born and brought up surrounded by paganism, first in Ur of the Chaldeans, and then in Haran. But Abram was a seeker. Dissatisfied with worshipping useless idols that could not speak or do anything, he was in a state of questioning if there was a God out there.

Just as with Saul, who was passionate about protecting the Jewish religious way of life and sought to punish anyone who was deviating from the laws and rules of life, God met with him on the Damascus Road and caused him to go blind. Then, during three days and nights of fasting and prayer, the Holy Spirit opened up his vast knowledge of the Hebrew scriptures to point out to him that Jesus of Nazareth really was the long promised Messiah. Saul became Paul the apostle to the Gentiles.

Through the Holy Spirit, who spoke to the prophets, God introduced Himself to Abram, causing Abram to believe in His existence, to the extent that he was willing to trust Him completely.

Thus was Abram chosen by God to be the founder of the race that would be the channel God would use to transmit the information necessary for us to understand how we can not only approach Him, but enter into communion with Him. It is the record of this information, contained in the Bible and available to all, that is the basis of all that you have read and will read as inspired by the Holy Spirit of the One True God who willingly took upon Himself the title of the Lord God of Israel.

God put Abram through a number of tests which he passed, one of which was the birth of his son Isaac when both he and his wife Sarah were passed child producing age. Therefore, Isaac was born not because of the will of man but the will of God. Then followed the greatest test, when God called on Abraham to sacrifice his only, miracle son Isaac. Not only was it a test for Abraham, but it presented to us the first indication of a substitute lamb to be slain on Mount Moriah on which the temple and Jerusalem were built

In Abraham God found a man who was prepared to be completely obedient to His voice and instructions and in doing so would become a trail-blazer who laid the foundations of a new way of life and understanding of the Most High. Abraham was a doer; our eternal example of true, self-effacing commitment to God.

God called and he responded, believing God to be true and His promises sure. It is undeniable that his faith faltered at times but the central theme of his obedient service to God was never in doubt, particularly when it is realised that the land through which he travelled would never be his but was reserved for his descendants.

It was this determination to serve the God who had called him, no matter what the cost, that led Abraham to set out as God had directed him, and even to the extent of later being willing to sacrifice his only son Isaac. It was this intrinsic faithfulness that led God to choose him to be the founder of the Hebrew race, for Abraham was the first of that Semitic tribe, the first to be called a Hebrew.

Isaac

Isaac was not technically Abraham's first born son. Ishmael was. But Ishmael was not of God. Isaac was. Ishmael was the product of human doubt and determination to do something God appeared to be unable to do Himself which was to provide Abraham with a son and heir.

It was Sarah's idea and depended on a human tradition that the first wife could allow her husband to take a second wife to provide a son who would technically be her son, but not physically or emotionally; added to which Ishmael was the son of a slave woman and the objective of the plan of salvation was to make men free (Gal. 4:22 – 31). Ishmael's birth ultimately complicated the work God has been doing right up to the modern age.

The unbelief of Sarah at the suggestion that she would bear a son in her old age caused her to laugh at God's promise (Gen. 18:10 – 15); hence the name Isaac, meaning laughter. But what Isaac's birth clearly demonstrated was that God had not lost His creative and controlling power.

Isaac's role in God's plan was to submit to his father Abraham. As a young lad he had the strength to oppose his father when he realised that he was to be the sacrifice on mount Mariah, but he did not oppose him.

Bound and placed on the wood for the burnt offering it was he who experienced first-hand the sight of the knife poised above him ready to be plunged into his chest. It was Isaac who also heard the voice of the angel restraining his father from carrying out God's instruction and thereby realising the importance of being faithful. (Gen. 22:1 – 19) The result was the finding of the ram in the thorn bush which was used in his place, a God-provided sacrifice once He realised the faithfulness of His servant.

Isaac himself was also to realise the blessings that resulted from that faithfulness. But he was not central to the working out of the progressive relationship between his father and the God who had called him to service. At the death of his father, Isaac took on the leadership of the tribe and became the father of Jacob. Isaac was undoubtedly important because it was his obedience to his father Abraham on Mount Mariah that allowed God to demonstrate His ability to provide a lamb for the sacrifice when Abraham's faith had been tested.

But it was the birth of the twins, Esau and Jacob, and God's selection of Jacob by seemingly devious means (Isaac favoured Esau) who would provide the foundational structure of the nation through which God has been able to reveal Himself and His ways to all men. The tribe of Israel was to receive by Divine authority the rules governing man's approach to God and the way of life he was to live to gain access to and maintain his relationship with God.

Although Isaac was the father of Esau and Jacob, it was his wife Rebekah who was central to the events in which God's chosen received his blessing. Isaac's choice was contrary to that of God, for the older was to serve the younger in God's plan.

Jacob

Jacob was not the older twin, Esau was. But the battle for supremacy between God and the evil one began in Rebekah's womb. The twins were born of the same parents yet one centred his life on the pleasures of this world and the other, more contemplative son, sought to understand the things of God. It was Jacob who became aware of the relationship with God engendered through his experiences with his father Isaac, and the accounts he heard about Abraham's life in God's service.

It is interesting how God led Abraham's servant to choose Isaac's bride. Canaan, as we know, lost the knowledge of God so that men looked to pagan influences for their spiritual diet. This is what man did prior to the flood but God found that merely getting rid of those who followed such a path and selecting a holy man to begin again did not work because of man's inherited sin. It was not that God did not know that that would happen, but it is recorded as an instruction to us that man has a tendency without Him to seek the ways of the earth, which is ruled by Satan since the fall of Adam.

It is man blind to God who seeks after demonic and increasingly decadent ways.

Abraham's servant was therefore sent back to where Abraham started his walk and where his original family lived. As has been seen, the ease with which the servant found the bride for Isaac clearly identified her as being chosen of God. It is only in understanding the reason why Jacob received Isaac's blessing rather than Esau, that her timely and believing service can be properly understood. It is pointless understanding that God led Abraham's servant in his search for a bride for Isaac if we then ignore her part in God's plan, particularly after understanding why the twins fought so hard whilst in her womb.

It is not that God hated Esau in the human sense of the word; rather that Jacob was preferred. Why? Simply because Esau focused on going out and enjoying himself in the outdoor pursuits that pleased him, but God had a greater purpose for the leader of the Hebrews as part of His plan of salvation. God had carefully chosen Abram[112] to found a new people (Hebrews) He would develop for His own purposes. He did not initiate this plan only to have the whole focus of that tribe in the third generation deflected from His purpose for it by a leader who was more interested in the things of the world, and the worship of gods, rather than serving God. That purpose, that objective was to further His Way of salvation. Thus, the selection of Rebekah was critical to His plan.

Isaac saw in Esau the sort of person he would have wanted to be, carefree and living an exciting and gregarious life. It was also Esau's birthright to receive the stewardship of the tribe from Isaac on his death. Isaac was therefore intent on passing on the blessing he had received from Abraham to Esau. But God had laid on Rebekah's heart a love for Jacob.

This can be understood because Esau's rebellious spirit was totally contrary to that required by a man of God. Esau had, totally against the will of God and his parents, married two girls of a Canaanite tribe; the very people God would later replace with His own people to whom would be given the land in perpetuity as promised to Abram.

When Esau lost the blessing of his father, Isaac, to Jacob he showed his true rebellious spirit by going to his uncle Ishmael, to obtain two additional wives, women from Canaan, where God was not honoured and worshipped as Lord. This meant that, in the future, there would be war between the descendants of the brothers with God on Jacob's side.

It also demonstrates that just because parents are believers it does not mean that their offspring are automatically believers; rather each and every

---

[112] The use of the names Abram and Abraham throughout this work is dependent upon whether the reference relates to before or after the occasion when God changed his name from Abram, literally exalted father, to Abraham, literally father of a multitude, when he was 99 years old. (Gen. 17:5)

individual offspring must make their own choice of what or whom they are prepared to believe and serve, and the degree of their commitment to that service.

Although Jacob had gained Esau's birthright, which meant that technically he was now the eldest son, it was the blessing from Isaac that was important to confirm that birthright. Jacob on his own would not have had the courage to have gone to his father to gain that blessing, but in Rebekah he had an ally who could pass the deception off.

Notice that Isaac had become virtually blind which was essential for the deception to succeed. Had he been able to see then it would not have been possible for Jacob to have received the blessing, so Isaac's senses were reduced to smell, taste, touch and hearing, for he detected that the voice was not that of Esau. It is always interesting how God prepares the ground first before any action happens.

Rebekah was in the right place at the right time and of the right mind and with the right organisational skills and determination to do what was necessary. She heard Isaac instruct their son Esau to go and obtain venison and make his favourite meal so that he could bless him. Whether she had already had a plan in mind we will never know, but she very quickly galvanised Jacob into action and with his assistance produced the meal she knew her husband would appreciate. She proceeded to fit the deceptive goat skin to Jacob, promising to accept any cursing from Isaac herself. Jacob was a reluctant deceiver.

Jacob's interview with his father was not plain sailing. Right up to the moment of giving the blessing, Isaac was not completely sure the right son was before him. At any time he could have found him out by feeling Jacob's neck and arms to discover the edges of the goat skin, but as God was behind this activity this did not happen and Jacob received the blessing which God wanted him to receive.

Once again it was essential that a wife be obtained for the future leader of the tribe, not from the Canaanites (who would at some time be destroyed because of their rebellion against God) but from their own family in Haran.

We have already studied the progress of Jacob from his youth to his returning to meet with Esau, who had by then lost all thought of killing his brother. At the time of the deception and stealing of the blessing, Esau reacted in a natural way. God made sure that by the time of the burial of their father he had calmed down, being the leader of his own tribe. It is, however, important to identify certain aspects of his life to bring to the fore the essential features of God's way in Jacob's life.

Of the two wives of Jacob one was the wife of deception (Leah) and the other the wife of love (Rachel). But beauty on the outside is not the beauty that God sees, for God looks into the heart. Leah gave her husband her all, for when she married Jacob in her eyes he was her lord and she was there to serve him fully and also the God he served. Rachel, on the other hand, needed to retain the gods of her father (Gen. 31:34, 35) and did not want to fully commit herself to her husband, Jacob. Her cry to Jacob when she realised that she was not bearing any children (Gen 30:1, 2) clearly showed that having a child was her concern and not seeking the God of her husband as Leah had done. As it is, Rachel only bore two sons and only one of them was a significant player in God's work for of all Jacob's sons (before the arrival of Benjamin[113]) it was Joseph who was, like Jacob, God-sensitive[114]. She is, however, remembered as a mother (see Jer. 31:15; Matt. 2:18).

It was Leah, the unloved but truly devoted wife and mother of six sons, who bore Levi, leader of the priestly tribe, and Judah, leader of the kingly tribe and the tribe into which the Messiah, King of kings and Lord of Lords, was to be born.

These are important factors in God's plan in providing mankind with a Way of salvation that enables us today not just to reach out to God but to come into a personal and intimate relationship with Him.

---

[113] King Saul and the apostle Paul were both from this tribe.
[114] For a full understanding of Jacob's life please refer to my book The Origin of Life

APPENDIX F JOSEPH AND JESUS – A COMPARISON

Edited from a document by Elhanan ben Avraham

Copy of an appendix in "The Origin of Life"

To begin with there are statements made by Rav Jesus that call to mind the Talmudic reference quoted earlier (Brachot 34B: "All of the prophets prophesied only of the days of the Messiah") "These are my words which I spoke while I was still with you, that all things which are written about me in the Torah of Moses and the Nevi'im (prophets) and the Tehilim (Psalms) must be fulfilled." (Luke 24:44), and "You search the scriptures, because you think that in them you have eternal life; and it is these that bear witness of me." (John 5:39).

These are bold statements indeed for a son of Israel to make, and yet this one born in Beit Lehem (Bethlehem) from the tribe of Yehuda (Judah) and the house of David, raised by Joseph the carpenter and his wife Miriam (Mary), did make them. But there is more to this confirmed human being that is important to our understanding.

1.   Before the world was Jesus existed (John 1:1) for He was able to tell the Jews, "before Abraham was I AM" (that is I have existed, I am existing and I will exist).

2.   God is spirit and they who worship Him must worship Him in spirit and in truth. Therefore, if Jesus is begotten and not made, He too must have been entirely spirit when he was with His father before the world began.

Thus:

A.   the Father sent Him

B.   a body was prepared for Him (Hebrews 10:5), see Appendix A.

C.   Jesus had to come down from heaven and restricted Himself initially to the body of a baby, taking on the form of a human being. In the words of one hymn writer, "Our God contracted to a span incomprehensibly made man".

1.   Jesus came to earth a sinless man and remained a sinless man

until He took on the sin of the whole world at His crucifixion – see Appendix A

2. He was the only eternal spirit (and therefore Divine because only God is eternal), made truly human who has been filled with the Holy Spirit without measure. By that means there was a continuous collaboration between the Word made flesh and God's power for miracles such as the stilling of the storm, the knowledge Jesus had as to what was going on in men's hearts and minds and His ability to cast out demons.

3. Sent by the Father with full instruction for His ministry, empowered by the Spirit, the Word gave utterance.

I have, over many years, studied scripture and God in His goodness has revealed much to me to the benefit of some. All that has been written in this The Origin of Life has been by reading and inspiration. Unfortunately, I am not a Biblical scholar and my understanding of the Word of God is limited both in detail, scale and scope. In the life of Joseph, however, I have been led to see the need for a far more profound, Jewish understanding of the text than I am able to provide. I cannot do better than to use the major part of the text on Joseph provided by Elhanan ben Abraham who, in my humble and ignorant Gentile opinion, has dealt with the account of Joseph with such sensitivity and insight that it has inspired me.

Let us now turn to the ancient texts to see if there may, or may not be, some validity to such claims. It will be beneficial to read the Genesis text along with following information.

Ref	Joseph	Jesus
37:2	A special relationship had developed between the father and this one son even as he brought bad reports about his brother.	In several discussions with His brethren, the children of Israel, He brought before them the issue of their sins, *"Those of the Pharisees who were with him heard these things and said to him, 'We are not blind too are we?' Jesus said to them, 'If you were blind you would have no sin; but since you say we see, your sin remains'"* (John 9:40-41); and, *"If I had not come and spoken to them they would not have sin, but now they have no excuse for their sin"* (John 15:22). Jesus also said, *"But whoever shall deny me before men, I*

Ref	Joseph	Jesus
		will also deny him before my Father who is in Heaven" (Matthew 10:33)
		At the age of twelve Jesus declared to Joseph and Mary, when they finally found him in discussion in the temple in Jerusalem, *"Did you not know that I had to be about the affairs of my Father?" (Luke 2:49).*

These words and acts of both Joseph and Jesus could not be, indeed were not received by their brethren without exacting a strong reaction

Ref	Joseph	Jesus
37:3	*"Israel loved Joseph more than all his sons."* In the Torah (Deuteronomy 14:1) we are told that the God of Israel has many sons: "You are the sons of the Lord your God." In Genesis 22:2,12 God tells Abraham, "Take now your son, your only son, whom you love, Isaac, and go to the land of Moriah, and offer him there as a burnt offering ..." But what of Ishmael? Therefore an "only son" here speaks of one who is chosen for a unique purpose, the only one of his kind, one through whom the covenant would be established. (Genesis 17:18-21).	In Matthew 3:17 and 17:5 it is reported that the same Lord pronounced, *"This is my beloved son, hear him."* Again, the picture of the one favoured of his Father.

Joseph was the son of Jacob's wife Rachel, who was buried by Bethlehem, which is where Jesus was born (Matthew 2:1).

Ref	Joseph	Jesus
37:4	Joseph, being favoured over his brothers by their father caused envy and jealousy to turn to hatred, and they could	(Psalm 69:4) *"But this came to pass that the word might be fulfilled that is written in their Torah, 'They hated me without cause.'" (John 15:25).* The

Ref	Joseph	Jesus
	not speak well of him, nor address him with shalom. It could be said that they hated him without cause.	Rabbis have also declared that God allowed Jerusalem and the Temple to be destroyed in the first century for this same reason.
		The majority of Jewish religious authorities, both in the first century and now, cannot seem to bring themselves to speak well of Jesus of Nazareth
37:5 - 10	Joseph recounted his dreams to his brothers, and they hated him even more. Yet the dreams were prophetic, given him by God.	Jesus made equally bold announcements before Israel: *"Behold, there is one here greater than Solomon" (Luke 11:31); "But I say to you there is one here greater than the Temple" (Matthew 12:6); in order that all may honour the son, even as they honour the Father" (John 5:23);* and Jesus said before the Sanhedrin, *"hereafter you will see the Son of Man sitting at the right hand of Power, and coming on the clouds of heaven" (Matthew 26:64),* for which his elder brethren mocked, beat, spat at him and pronounced him worthy of death.
37:11	*"And his brothers were jealous of him."*	*"For he (Pilate) was aware that the chief priests had delivered him up because of envy" (Mark 15:10).*
37:12- 17	Joseph sent by his Father to his brothers, the children of Israel who were tending the sheep at Shechem.	*"I have been sent only to the lost sheep of the house of Israel" (Matthew 15:24);* and, *"...the Father has sent me" (John 5:36)*
37:18	His brothers saw him from afar, and before he came close, plotted to kill him.	To this day Jesus is seen from a distance by the children of Israel through a fog of prejudice and misunderstanding, through the sins of an idolatrous religious system which misused the name "Jesus", even attempting to erase his Jewishness, and at that name

Ref	Joseph	Jesus
		(Yeshua) the Jews, for the most part, think negatively, linking it with the sufferings of the centuries, wishing to "kill" even the memory of it, that it might not come close to them, to be objectively examined (as the anagram "Yeshu", which is the common pronunciation of his name in Hebrew, is intended by some to mean "may his name and memory be erased.")
37:19-20	They mocked Joseph and plotted to kill him.	Then the chief priest and elders of the people were gathered together in the court of the High Priest, Caiaphas, and they plotted together to seize Jesus by stealth, and kill him." (Matthew 26:3-4).
37:21	Reuben rose to Joseph's defence.	Nicodemus arises in defence of Jesus (John 7:51).
37:23	They seized Joseph and stripped him of his tunic still with the intent to destroy him.	Jesus' garments were stripped from him before his execution, the seamless, woven tunic being of one piece, (John 19:23-24).
37:24-25	They threw Joseph into a pit, and they sat down to eat a meal.	Jesus was arrested and imprisoned when Israel reclines to eat the Passover.
37:25-30	Here we have the picture of Judah, one of the twelve, suggesting the selling of their brother for monetary gain.	Judah (Judas), one of the twelve disciples sold him to the religious authorities.

In both cases

1. they were turned over to the Gentiles: Joseph to the Egyptians, Jesus to the Romans (Matthew 20:18-19).
2. the intended sellers of their brother were unable to retain the desired money, the Midianites stealing Joseph before they could sell him, and in Judas returning the thirty pieces of silver (Matthew 27:3-7).

Ref	Joseph	Jesus
	In the prophesy of Zechariah (11:13) it is written, *"Then the Lord said to me, 'Throw it to the potter, that magnificent price at which I was valued by them,' so I took the thirty shekels of silver and threw them to the potter in the house of the Lord."* This sum was the value of a slave gored by an ox (Exodus 21:32).	
37:31	They slaughtered a male goat in Joseph's stead, dipping his tunic in its blood. (It is noteworthy that there is no account of Joseph, uttering a single word.)	*'For this is my blood of the covenant, which is to be shed on behalf of many for the forgiveness of sins."* (Matthew 26:28) *"Behold the lamb of God who takes away the sin of the world."* (John 1:29).
37:32-35	It was reported to Jacob/Israel that Joseph was dead and he was to remain with that belief for many years, until a much later revelation, when he would again see him.	Jesus has been considered dead and separated from the house of Israel for two millennia. Jesus spoke a number of parables referring to a distant journey and a long passage of time, "for the kingdom of heaven is as a man travelling into a far country, who called his own servants, and delivered unto them his goods. ...Now after a long time the master of those servants came and settled accounts with them" (Matthew 25:14-19); *'For I say to you, from now on you shall not see me until you say, 'Blessed is he who comes in the name of the Lord'."* (Matthew 23:38-39).
38	This chapter is a breaking away from the account of Joseph and turning attention to Judah, who has played, and will continue to play, a key role in the fate of Joseph. This chapter essentially leads us to the birth of Peretz *("breach")*, from whose line would come King David, and Zara ("he has shined"), sons of Judah and Tamar. In the name Peretz we have a remez[115] regarding the later	

---

[115] remez = "hint" the interpretation of Scripture at the level of allusive implication. For instance, Pidyon Haben - redemption of the first-born - is alluded to by an acronym of the letters of Bereshit,

Ref	Joseph	Jesus

prophesy found in Micah 2:12-13, which speaks of one called "the Breaker" (poretz) who would open the way for the remnant of Israel to "break forth". It reads thus: "I will surely assemble all of you, Jacob, I will surely gather the remnant of Israel. I will put them together like sheep in a fold; like a flock in the midst of its pasture they will be noisy with men. The breaker has gone up before them, they break out, pass through the gate and go out by it, and their king goes on before them, and the Lord at their head."

This passage is reminiscent of Pesach and of the coming out of Egypt under Moses but is of course a later work, prophesying a later, yet not dissimilar, event.

39:1-6 And Joseph was brought down to Egypt.

Egypt in the Torah stands as the antithesis of the Promised Land, Eretz Israel. It is a land of little water and plentiful sand, filled with false religion and idolatry; an oppressive regime and a house of bondage.

It is from here that God was to deliver His people and bring them back to the land that He had promised to their fathers, "a land flowing with milk and honey," where they were to learn to serve the Living God in truth, by His Torah. They were to be "brought up" from the Land of Egypt, to go up (to make aliyah) to the land promised to Abraham. Aliyah is the same word used today for immigration to Israel. They were not to go "back down" to Egypt (Isaiah 31:1).

In John 6:38 Jesus declares, *"For I came down from heaven not to do my own will, but the will of him that sent me." According to his words, he had left his Father's house and the glory (kvod) therein, to seek out "the lost sheep of the House of Israel" (John 14:2; 17:5).*

In the first century, though Israel was in the land promised to them, yet they were under the oppressive hand of the pagan Roman Empire, and occupied by the Roman army. Religious leadership in Jerusalem was no longer truly established according to the Torah, but with those willing to compromise with the Roman authorities. The evident corruption in the religious system was stated in the records of the Jewish sect of Qumran (Dead Sea Scrolls).

---

which spell "ben rishon acharei shloshim yom tifdeh" - the first son you shall redeem after thirty days.

Ref	Joseph	Jesus
		It was to this background that Jesus came and stated, *"If you continue in my word, then you are my disciples indeed, and you shall know the truth, and the truth shall set you free."* To this the reply came that they are Abraham's seed and in bondage to no man. *"Jesus answered them, Truly, truly I say to you, Whosoever commits sin is the slave of sin. And the slave shall not abide in the house forever: but the son will abide forever. If the Son therefore shall set you free, you shall be free indeed"'* (John 8:31-36).
	It is written of Joseph in Mitzrayim, "that the Lord was with him, and that the Lord made all that he did to prosper in his hand." This describes a relatively short period that Joseph was a servant doing many good works in Potiphar's household, before his arrest.	And it is written of Jesus, concerning the three years before his arrest, *"... all they that had any sick with various diseases brought them unto him; and he laid his hands on every one of them and healed them"* (Luke 4:40); and, *"Go your way and tell John what things you have seen and heard, how that the blind see, the lame walk, the lepers are cleansed, the deaf hear, the dead are raised, to the poor good tidings are announced"* (Luke 7:22, Isaiah 29:18-19). Jesus also announced, *"... the Son of Man came not to be served, but to serve ..."* (Matthew 20:28).
39:7-19	Joseph was tempted by Potiphar's wife, which temptation he was able to overcome, resisting a series of opportunities; unwilling to compromise and to "sin against God."	Matthew 4:1-11 gives the account of Jesus' encounter with Satan (accuser, tempter), who tempted him to compromise and break the commands of God, to which Jesus resisted on every point.
39:20	For his moral and spiritual integrity, and refusal to	It is recorded in Mark 14:55-61 that many false witnesses were

Ref	Joseph	Jesus
	compromise, Joseph was falsely accused and cast into prison. Again it is important to note that there is no record here of Joseph opening his mouth in his own defence before his accusers.	brought to the trial of Jesus, and that he spoke nothing in his defence, other than answering in the affirmative when asked by the High Priest as to whether he was the Mashiach. In Matthew 27:12-14 we find, "And when he was accused of the chief priest and elders, he answered nothing. Then Pilate said unto him, ' do you not hear how many things they witness against you?' And he answered him not a word, inasmuch that the governor marvelled greatly."

The above is reminiscent of the prophesy of Isaiah (53:7-8), "He was oppressed, and he was afflicted, yet he opened not his mouth: he was brought as a lamb to the slaughter, and as a sheep before her shearer is dumb, so he opened not his mouth. He was taken from prison and from judgement, and who will declare his generation?" and, (53:12), *"he was reckoned among the transgressors."*

Ref	Joseph	Jesus
		Jesus said, *"For I say unto you, that this that is written must yet be accomplished in me. And he was reckoned among the transgressors: for the things concerning me have an end"* (Luke 22:37, Isaiah 53:12).
39:21-23	The Lord was with Joseph in prison and the prisoners were given into his hand. "And whatever he did the Lord made to prosper."	The reference in Isaiah (53:10), *"Yet it pleased the Lord to bruise him; He has put him to grief ... and the desire of the Lord shall prosper in his hand."*

The prophesy of Isaiah (61:1) reads, "The spirit of the Lord is upon me, for he has anointed me to proclaim good tidings to the humble, he has sent me to bind up the broken-hearted, to proclaim liberty to the captives, and the opening of prison to them that are bound."

Ref	Joseph	Jesus
40:1-	Here Joseph as interpreter of	

Ref	Joseph	Jesus
22		

dreams, was able to see, not by the sight of his eyes, but discerning the judgement of God concerning who shall live and who shall die.

Isaiah 11:1-4 reads, "And there shall come forth a rod out of the stem of Jesse, and a branch shall grow out of his roots: and the spirit of the Lord shall rest upon him, the spirit of wisdom and understanding, the spirit of counsel and might, the spirit of knowledge and fear of the Lord; and shall make him of quick understanding in the fear of the Lord: and he shall not judge out of the sight of his eyes, neither reprove after the hearing of his ears: but with righteousness shall he judge the poor, and reprove with equity for the humble of the earth, and He shall smite the earth with the rod of his mouth, and with the breath of his lips shall he slay the wicked."

Jesus taught, *"Judge not according to the sight of your eyes, but judge righteous judgement"* (John 7:24) and, *"And yet if I judge, my judgement is true: for I am not alone, but I and the Father that sent me"* (John 8:16).

Simon Peter said of Jesus, *"And He commanded us to proclaim unto the people, and to testify that it was he which was ordained of God to be judge of the living and the dead. To him give all the prophets witness"* (Acts of the Apostles 10:42:43). All of the accounts of Jesus' arrest tell of the presentation of Bar Abba and Jesus before the crowds, that by choice one would live and one would die - a reflection of this account of the butler and baker.

40:23		

The chief butler did not honour Joseph's request, but forgot him when he was released, leaving Joseph imprisoned. Again we see the

Barabbas was released and Jesus left in prison. Peter denied knowing Jesus three times the night of Jesus' arrest (Matthew 26:69:75). And it is written of his

Ref	Joseph	Jesus

picture of one rejected and one abandoned, though he is righteous and correct in his judgements.

disciples at the time of his arrest, "And they all forsook him and fled" (Mark 14:50).

41 This chapter gives us the picture of a Hebrew who is able to bring a solution to an unsolvable problem, to open a way before kings and wise men of the nations who were unable to find a way.

Here is the prophesy of Isaiah (52:13-15), *"Behold my servant shall deal prudently, he shall be exalted and extolled, and be very high. As many were astonished at thee, his appearance was so marred more than any man, and his form more than the sons of men: So shall he sprinkle many nations; kings shall shut their mouths at him: for that which had not been told them shall they see, and that which they had not heard shall they consider."*

41:14 The highest power (in Mitzrayim) sent and called Joseph hastily from out of the pit (the Hebrew word for pit is the same as that used to describe the hole which his brothers threw him into; it is also the same word used in the Nevi'im and the Tehilim for "the grave").

Joseph *"shaved himself and changed his clothes, and came unto Pharaoh,"* is a remez[116] to the messianic prophecy of Avid Tzemach (*"My servant the Branch"*) in Zechariah chapter 3, *"And he showed me Joshua the High Priest standing before the angel of the Lord, and Satan standing at his right hand to accuse him. And the Lord said unto Satan, "The Lord rebuke you, Satan, even the Lord which has chosen Jerusalem rebuke you: is not this a brand plucked out of the*

On the third day after the execution, the Most High revived Jesus of Nazareth from the dead, and brought him forth from the tomb. *"He is not here, but is risen: remember how he told you when he was yet in the Galilee, saying, 'The son of man must be delivered into the hands of sinful men, and be crucified, and the third day will rise again'"* (Luke 24:6-7).

In Luke 10:18, Jesus said, *"I beheld Satan as lightning fall from heaven."*

It is described in Matthew 17:1-2, *"And after six days Jesus took Simon Peter, James and John his brother, and brought them up to a high mountain apart, and he was transfigured before them: and his face did shine as the sun, and his clothes as white as the light."* (see: Isaiah 61:10, *"for he hath clothed me with the garments of salvation, he has covered me with the robe of righteousness"*).

---

[116] remez = "hint" the interpretation of Scripture at the level of allusive implication.

Ref	Joseph	Jesus

fire?"

"Now Joshua was clothed with filthy garments, and stood before the angel. And he answered and spoke unto those that stood before him, saying, Take away the filthy garments from him. And unto him he said, Behold, I have caused your iniquity to pass from you, and I will clothe you with a change of clothing". And he said, Let them set a pure mitre upon his head, and clothe him with garments. And the angel of the Lord stood by. And the angel of the Lord testified unto Joshua, saying, Thus says the Lord of Hosts, if you will walk in my ways, and if you will keep my charge, then shall you also judge my house, and shall also keep my courts, and I will give you places to walk among these that stand by. Hear now, Joshua the Chief Priest, you, and your friends that sit before you: for they are a sign: for behold, I will bring forth my servant, the Branch." (Zechariah 3:14-16).

Ref	Joseph	Jesus
41:15-16	*"And Joseph answered Pharaoh, saying, It is not in me; God shall give Pharaoh an answer of peace."*	Jesus said, *"The son can do nothing of himself, but what he sees the Father do: for what things so ever He does, these also does the son likewise. For the Father loves the Son, and shows him all things that He does: and He will show him greater works than these, that you may marvel" (John 5:19-20).*

Joseph and Jesus claimed to speak for God (*"the word which you hear is not Mine, but the Father's which sent Me"* - John 14:24).

Ref	Joseph	Jesus
41:17-36	Joseph *"the dreamer of dreams,"* again correctly interprets dreams, now doing that which the magicians and wise men could not. According to Jewish sources, the Mashiach is to give correct interpretation to the Torah (Genesis Raba 98.9.), which is to fulfil the Torah.	In Matthew 5:17, Jesus said, *"Think not that I come to destroy, but to fulfil."* The Mashiach was to unlock the mysteries of the Torah and the Prophets.

An event is described in Isaiah 29:9-14, *"For the Lord has poured out upon you the spirit of deep sleep, and has closed your eyes: the prophets and your rulers, the seers has he covered. And the vision of all is become unto you as the words of a book that is sealed, which men deliver to one that is learned saying, Read this, I plead: and he says, I cannot, for it is sealed; and the book is delivered to him that is not learned, saying, Read this, I plead; and he says,*

529

Ref	Joseph	Jesus

I am not learned. Wherefore the Lord said, For as much as this people draw near with their mouth, and with their lips do honour me, but have removed their heart far from me, for their fear towards me is taught by the commandments of men; therefore behold I will proceed to do a marvellous work among this people, even a marvellous work and a wonder; for the wisdom of their wise men shall perish, and the understanding of their sages shall be hidden."

Jesus, in discussing the resurrection with the Sadducees, said, *"You err, not knowing the scriptures, nor the power of God"* (Matthew 22:29), and of the state of the Scribes and Pharisees, he said, *"You blind guides"* (Matthew 23:16) – [for they were spiritual blind and could therefore not know God as they should have known Him – editor]

41:37-38

Here the Gentile king declared that the Spirit of God was in Joseph: but had not his brothers, the children of Israel, mocked him for his visions?

Much the same has occurred during the last millennia, with many from among the Gentiles declaring that the Spirit of the Lord is in Jesus, while much the opposite has been said by the people of Israel.

Jesus had said, *"The Spirit of the Lord is upon me."* But the Pharisees said, *"This fellow does not cast out demons but by Ba'al Zevuv, prince of the demons"* (Matthew 12:24); and *"Then answered the Jews, and said unto him, Do we not say well that you are a Samaritan, and there is a devil within you?"* (John 8:48).

41:39-41

Joseph, the insignificant servant, was brought forth from the prison and obscurity and raised above the heads of both the Gentiles and his own brethren, to sit at the right

Jesus lay in the confines of the tomb and death, utterly defeated in Israel's eyes and in that of the Romans (the Egypt of its day), suddenly brought forth from obscurity and raise up from death,

Ref	Joseph	Jesus

hand of power of the king, Pharaoh. The king said to him "according unto your word shall all my people be ruled," giving him full authority.

conquering the most unconquerable of all in resurrection. He was raised up to the right hand of the throne of power (g'vurah) of HaShem HaMevurach. Psalm 110:1 states, *"The Lord said unto my lord, Sit at my right hand, till I make your enemies your footstool"* (Yalkut interprets this as "King Messiah"). Jesus stated, *"All authority has been given unto me in heaven and on earth ,"* (Matthew 28:18) and, *"Henceforth you shall see the son of man sitting at the right hand of power, and coming on the clouds of heaven" (Matthew 26:64).*

The prophet Daniel thus describes the Mashiach (as interpreted by Rashi and Metzudat David, this is Melech HaMashiach). *"I saw in the night visions and behold, one like unto a son of man came with the clouds of heaven, and came unto the Ancient of Days, and they brought him near before him. And there was given unto him dominion, and glory, and a kingdom, that all people, nations, and languages should serve him: his dominion is an everlasting dominion, which shall not pass away, and his kingdom that which shall not be destroyed" (7:13-14).* From the Talmud we have described one called "Metatrone" (i.e. one next to the throne), in the story of "Four entered paradise" and saw there one seated next to the throne of the Most High (Hagiga 14:B).

41:42 — Again here the image of the changing of garments; Joseph was adorned with the outer garments and symbols of Egyptian royalty - certainly styled from head to foot - in Gentile garb. He became totally unrecognisable to his Hebrew brothers.

After the first century CE, Jesus was to be taken and as it were, made "King of the Gentiles," wrapped in the garments of foreign custom, and in time even hidden under the heavy accoutrements of idolatrous religion (which would turn his light to darkness) which essentially forgot that "King of the Jews" was written above the execution stake upon which he suffered death. All the above helped serve to blind the eyes of

Ref	Joseph	Jesus
		his own nation and brethren, Israel, who have even lost sight, to a high degree, of his being indeed a Jewish rabbi of our own.
41:43-44	Joseph had been called by the king himself to reign with him over all the land, giving Joseph equal authority. They cried before Joseph, "Bow the Knee."	In John 5:23 Jesus said, *"He who honours not the Son, honours not the Father who sent him."* The King Messiah would reign over the earth with God: *"It is a light thing that you should be my servant to raise up the tribe of Jacob, and to restore the preserved of Israel: I will also give you for a light to the Gentiles, that you may be my salvation unto the ends of the earth,"* (Isaiah 49:6), and, *"Yet have I set my king upon my holy hill of Zion. I will declare the decree: The Lord has said unto me, You are my Son, this day I have begotten you. Ask of me, and I shall give you the nations for an inheritance, and the uttermost parts of the earth for your possession"* (Tehilim [Psalm] 2:6-8 which Yalkut and Metzudat David interpret as referring to Mashiach).

Joseph, rejected by the children of Israel, became king over Mitzrayim; Jesus, officially rejected by Israel, became king over Gentiles.

Ref	Joseph	Jesus
41:45	Joseph received a new name, of the Gentiles.	Jesus received, through translation, the Greek name "Yesous," becoming "Jesus" in English; losing its original Hebrew meaning of "salvation" (Matthew 1:21). In the Revelation to John 3:12, Jesus says, "and I will write upon him my new name." (In Jeremiah 23:5-6, the name of "Branch" - Messiah - is to be "the Lord our Righteousness".
	Joseph married the daughter of the Gentile priest.	

Ref	Joseph	Jesus
		Jesus' "bride" (Revelation 19:7-9) would also be those Gentiles called out from and cleansed of idolatry, being taught of the God of Israel and His Torah ("until the fullness of the Gentiles be come in" - Paul's letter to the Romans 11:25).
41:46	Joseph was thirty years old when he stood before Pharaoh. This is the age according to the Torah (Numbers 4:3) that a man may begin priestly service in the Tabernacle.	Jesus, when he began his works in Israel, was *"about thirty years old" (Luke 3:23).*
41:50-52	Two sons were born to Joseph, Menashe (Manasseh) and Ephraim. When Jacob blessed the two children, he laid his right hand on the head of Ephraim, the younger, again the reversal of roles with the first born, and declared that *"his seed shall become the fullness of the goyim (Gentiles)"* (Genesis 48:19). He also said that Joseph's two sons were as his own two firstborn sons, Reuben and Simeon. Thus these two were later to become half-tribes, numbered among the twelve in the inheritance of the Land of Israel, causing the name of Joseph to rest in a separate and unique position, further fulfilling Jacob's prophesy over him that he would be *"separate from his brethren"* (Genesis 49:26).	Jesus chose twelve intimate Talmidim (disciples) according to the number of tribes of Israel, himself separate, the thirteenth.

Ref	Joseph	Jesus
41:55	*"and Pharaoh said unto all Egyptians, 'Go unto Joseph, what he says to you, do."* In Deuteronomy 18:15 Moses states, *"The Lord your God will raise up unto you a prophet from amongst you, of your brethren, like unto me; unto him you shall hearken."* Also in 18 and 19 of the same chapter, the Lord confirms, *"I will raise them up a prophet from among your brethren, like unto you, and I will put my words in his mouth, and he shall speak unto them all that I shall command him. And it shall come to pass, that whoever will not hearken unto my words that he shall speak in my name, I will require it of him."* (Later we shall see what the Talmud says regarding this passage).	In the new testament, the Lord declares of Jesus, *"This is my beloved son, in whom I am well pleased, hear him"* (Matthew 17:5). And Jesus clarified, *"The words that I speak unto you I speak not of myself, but the Father that dwells in me ..."* (John 14:10). Again in 5:46 of the same book, *"For had you believed Moses, you would have believed me; for he wrote of me."*
41:56-57	Joseph was able, through the intercession of the Lord's spirit of wisdom, understanding, counsel, knowledge, and the fear of the Lord (Isaiah 11:2) to save the land from starvation, from lack of bread.	In Matthew 14:15-21, Jesus blessed five loaves of bread and two fish, which were then passed out and fed five thousand people.

The Torah tells us, "Man shall not live by bread alone, but by every word which proceeds from the mouth of God" (Deuteronomy 8:3). In the book of Amos 8:11 it is prophesied, *"Behold the days come, says the Lord, that I will send a famine in the land, not a famine of bread, or a thirst for water, but of hearing the words of the Lord."*

In the days of Jesus, it had been over four hundred years since a prophet of God had been in the land, to bring forth His word. Malachi had been the last. The nations of the world at that time were immersed in all forms of idolatry.

Ref	Joseph	Jesus

Jesus told his disciples, *"But you will receive power after the ruach hakodesh (Holy Spirit) is come upon you: and you shall be witnesses unto me both in Jerusalem, and in all of Judah and Samaria, and unto the uttermost part of the earth"* (ACTS 1:8); and, *"Go therefore, and teach all nations"* (Matthew 28:19).

In Isaiah 55:2-3 it is written, *"Wherefore do you spend money for that which is not bread and your labour for that which does not satisfy? Listen diligently unto me and eat that which is good, and let yourself delight itself in fatness. Incline your ear, and come unto me: hear, and your soul shall live; and I will make an everlasting covenant with you, even the sure mercies of David."*

Jesus said, *"I am the bread of life: he that comes unto me shall never hunger, and he that believes in me shall never thirst"* (John 6:35).

Thus Jesus would save the land from spiritual starvation, and bring the knowledge of God to the goyim, to a starving world; who then, knowing the ways of life and death, could choose accordingly (as it is written in the Torah, *"I call heaven and earth this day against you, that I have set before you life and death, blessing and cursing: therefore choose life"* - Deuteronomy).

42 The completely natural and essential phenomenon of hunger was used here to draw Israel out to Mitzrayim toward the fulfilling of God's overall plans. Yet this speaks of a hunger of the spirit, perhaps unbeknown to them at the time.

In Matthew 5:6 Jesus said, *"Blessed are they that hunger and thirst after righteousness ..."*; and *"Truly, truly, I say to you, Moses gave you not that bread from heaven; but my Father gives you the true bread from heaven. For the bread of God is he which comes down from heaven, and gives life to the world"* (John 6:32,33).

42:6 Here is the eventual fulfilment of Joseph's prophetic dream, after many years; though the children of Israel did not know that they were bowing before their

Ref	Joseph	Jesus
	brother, and would not have admitted to the fact; *"they worshipped him."* It is the same gesture of bowing down before kings or God, as in the case of King David's dedication of Solomon in I Chronicles 29:20, *"And all the congregation blessed the Lord God of their fathers, and bowed their heads and worshipped the Lord and the king."*	
42:7	*"And Joseph knew his brethren, but they knew him not."* Joseph did his best to maintain that distance of non-recognition, being in full control of the situation, though his brothers were completely ignorant of the fact. In the prophet Ezekiel 39:23 it is written, *"And the nations shall know that the house of Israel went into captivity for their iniquity: because they trespassed against me, therefore hid I my face from them, and gave them into the hand of their enemies ..."*	We are reminded again of Jesus' words, *"You shall not see me again until you say, Blessed is he who comes in the name of the Lord."* So it was to be, that Jesus' identity would be hidden from Israel, yet they would be known of him, as it is written in I John 4:19, *"We love him because he first loved us,"* and Paul's word in Romans 5:8, *"But God commended his love toward us, in that while we were yet sinners, Mashiach died for us."*
42:17-18	Joseph imprisoned his brothers for three days, on the third day calling them forth. This recalls the passage in Hosea 6:2, *"After two days he will revive us: in the third day he will raise us up, and we will live in his sight."*	Jesus was raised up, according to his word, on the third day, from death. In John 11:25, *"Jesus said unto her, I am the resurrection and the life ..."*
42:21-22	The brothers began to associate their predicament with what they had done to Joseph, though they in no	(There has been an awakening of interest of a positive sort in Jesus among a number of Jewish writers and scholars, including

Ref	Joseph	Jesus
	way recognised him.	Martin Buber and Rabbi Eliyahu Solevitchik, who for the most part have not recognized him as the promised Messiah.)
42:23-24	*"And they knew not that Joseph understood them, for he spoke to them by an interpreter. And he turned himself about from them, and wept ..."* Joseph wept upon hearing his brothers' conversation.	*"And when he was come near, he beheld the city (Jerusalem), and wept over it, saying, If you had only known, in this your day, the things which belong unto your shalom (peace) but now they are hid from your eyes." (Luke 19:41-42)*
42:25-34	Joseph indeed answered their supplication by supplying their needs, loading their donkeys with grain, even returning their money in their sacks. This being a fine illustration of chesed (grace), that they would know that what they had obtained had not been deserved or purchased by their own earnings.	Though many in Israel do not recognize the validity of the Torah, nor the portion in the Rambam's statement of faith regarding the coming of Mashiach, yet is HaShem faithful to his word, *"for his chesed endures forever."* It is written in the prophet Ezekiel 36:22, regarding the regathering of Israel to the land, *"Thus says the Lord God, I do not this for your sakes, O house of Israel, but for my Holy Names sake ..."*
42:35-38	Israel saw no good coming from this situation, but evil only, and fear.	This was the deduction of the leaders in Jerusalem in the first century, *"If we let him thus alone, all will believe on him, and the Romans shall come and take both our land and our nation" (John 11:48).* A condition that exists for the most part in Israel and the Jewish people today, regarding our relationship to Jesus and the Brit Hadasha.
43:1-7	Joseph had told them, *"You shall not see my face, except your younger brother be with you."* He would eventually gather all his brothers together before him,	

Ref	Joseph	Jesus
	while his true identity was yet hidden from them. It is thus prophesied in Ezekiel chapter 39:28-29, *"Then shall they know that I am the Lord their God, which caused them to be led into captivity among the nations and I have gathered them unto their own land, and have left none of them any more there. Neither will I hide my face any more from them: for I will pour out my spirit upon the house of Israel, declares the Lord God."* The reader is given to understand that Joseph knows more about the children of Israel than they know of him, as they are completely in the dark regarding him. Today the average Jew knows little or nothing of Jesus of Nazareth, other than distortions and preconception.	
43:11	Offerings were to be given to this unknown "man", the same who had angered them when told that they would make obeisance to him. At that time, had they known that it was Joseph to whom they were offering mincha, it would have been a mighty shock to them.	
43:14	Here Israel called for God's mercy in the situation, neither knowing nor understanding that Joseph is in fact God's instrument of mercy.	This according to the Brit Hadasha account, is the exact parallel to the work of God in Jesus towards Israel (see Paul's letter to the Romans chapter 11). For God has concluded them all in unbelief, that he might have

Ref	Joseph	Jesus
		mercy upon all."
43:15-16	This is the second time the brothers appeared before Joseph, the king. He commands, "Bring these men home and slay an animal, and make ready, for these men shall dine with me at noon."	In the period of the second national return to the Land of Israel (the first being from Egypt, the second from Babylon), which is the time of the second temple, Jesus appeared to Israel, in fact dining with his brethren. In Luke 22:15 Jesus says, *"How greatly I have desired to eat this Passover with you before I suffer."* In Isaiah 53:7 it is written, *"He was brought as a lamb to the slaughter."* It is the same Hebrew word used in Joseph's command. As Joseph fed his brothers, so Jesus said, *"I am the bread of life: he that comes to me shall never hunger, and he that believes on me shall never thirst,"* (John 6:35).
43:18-25	*"And the men were afraid, because they were brought into Joseph's house."* The closer they came to Joseph, the more uncomfortable they grew, in effect experiencing their transgression (as we shall see later), though not yet knowing why. In 43:23 the fact is here spoken that Joseph's generosity, which put fear in their hearts, was the work of the God of Israel. Though his brethren had betrayed him and cast him out, yet did he repay them with goodness, in fact fulfilling Jesus' teaching, *"But I say unto you, love your enemies, bless them that curse you, do good to them that hate you ..."* (Matthew 5:44). In 43:18 we	Jesus said, *"If I had not come and spoken unto them, they had not had sin: but now they have no cloak for their sin,"* (John 15:22). Jesus' ultimate function was to deal with the matter of sin: *"For this is my blood of the new covenant, which is shed for many for the remission of sins"* (Matthew 26:28).

Ref	Joseph	Jesus
	see that Joseph's generosity has been interpreted as malicious, and as yet is Jesus' kindness often spoken evil of amongst our people.	
43:26-28	*"And bowed themselves to him to the earth."* Again we see the literal fulfilment of Joseph's dream, confirming the prophetic nature of it.	It is written in the revelation of John 5:12, *"Worthy is the lamb that was slain to receive power and riches, and wisdom, and strength, and honour, and glory, and blessing."*
43:13-31	We witness the depth of Joseph's feeling, expressed in tears hidden from his gathered brothers, along with his identity.	Jesus wept over Jerusalem, and said, *"O Jerusalem, Jerusalem, you that kills the prophets, and stones them which are sent unto you, how often would I have gathered your children together, even as a hen gathers her chicks under her wings, but you would not"* (Matthew 23:37).
43:34	Joseph fed his brothers in his own home.	In Luke 22:30 Jesus said, *"That you may eat and drink at my table in my kingdom ..."*
44:1-12	Again Joseph provides sustenance and returns their money, the picture of chesed (grace). But this time by design, he will use another tactic to make them aware of that chesed. A false accusation is levelled against them as a means of drawing out the nature of their actual transgression: hardness of heart and unbelief and hatred expressed those many years earlier. As God, the righteous judge, will not allow transgression to go undealt with at some point, so are the children of Israel taken in this trap, arrested and hindered	As we shall see shortly, the betrayal and turning over of Jesus to the Roman authorities for execution was not in the essence of crime, for his death was of Divine intention, for the highest purpose. Jesus said concerning his life, *"No man can take it from me, but I lay it down of myself"* (John 10:17-18). The transgression according to the prophets, including Moses, was hardness of heart, unbelief and "hatred without cause."

Ref	Joseph	Jesus
	from returning to the Land of Israel. A parallel to this is the accusation often levelled at Jews: "Christ killers."	
44:13-34	Here the sons of Israel tear their garments in dismay as their worst fears come upon them and all hope of success appears to be lost. The above principle is well illustrated in Judah's expression of his deep guilt (it was he who had wished to murder and later sell Joseph), realising that, "God has found out the iniquity of your servants." He confessed, "What shall we say unto my lord? What shall we speak? Or how can we clear ourselves?"	

We may recall the words of Isaiah 53:8, *"And who shall declare his generation?"* Judah brings forth to Joseph his long harboured anguish of spirit for his crimes against Joseph himself (as yet unrecognised) and the pain which this had caused to their father; wishing now to repent by laying down his own life for the sake of his younger brother Benjamin. It is noteworthy that the rejection of Joseph had caused such profound grief to Israel, the father, as Jesus' rejection has been the anguish of Israel.

But it is in the return, the repentance of Judah here that we see before us the

Ref	Joseph	Jesus
	prophesy, *"For the redeemer shall come to Zion, and unto them that turn from transgression in Jacob, declares the Lord"* *(Isaiah 59:20)*. (It is from his name, Judah, that we get the word, Yedhudi, or Jew.)	

Jesus declared, *"Greater love has no man than this, that a man lay down his life for his friends"* *(John 15:13)*. At that moment, Judah, in his desire to cover his own sin against Joseph and his father by laying down his life for Benjamin, did not understand that Joseph's life had already been given to redeem not only Judah, but all his brothers and their families. This is much the same principle seen in the Akeda that God himself provided a life in the place of Yitzhak's on the sacrificial altar. This is also seen in the sin sacrifices in the later temple system ("A life for a life").

45:1-2 It is Judah's broken-hearted confession that finally tears the curtain of separation and their redeemer is revealed before their eyes. *"The sacrifices of God are a broken spirit: a broken and contrite heart, O God, you will not despise"* *(Telehim 51:17-19 in Hebrew)*. Here is the essence of t'shuva shlemah (perfect repentance). How deep is the feeling in the breast of Joseph and the love he had for his brothers. He can no longer contain the feeling and cries aloud. The Gentiles hear the weeping, though he has sent them out, making this a private family matter. Is not the gathering of Israel back to the land again, in our days, separating them from the nations, for a purpose?

In Ezekiel 36:24-26 it says, *"For I will take you from among the nations, and gather you out of all the countries, and will bring you into your own land. Then I will sprinkle clean water upon you, and you shall be clean from all your filthiness and from all your idols, will I cleanse you. A new heart will I give you, and a new spirit will I put within you, and I will take away the stony heart out of your flesh, and I will give you a heart of flesh."*

Jeremiah, describing the gathering of Israel to her land, brings the prophesy, *"Behold, the days are coming, declares the Lord, that I will make a new covenant (brit hadasha) with the house of Israel, and with the house of Judah, not according to the covenant that I made with their fathers in the day that I took them by the hand to bring them out of the land of Egypt, which my covenant they broke, although I was a husband unto them, declares the Lord. But this shall be the covenant that I will make with the*

Ref	Joseph	Jesus

house of Israel, after those days, declares the Lord, I will put my Torah in their inward parts, and write it in their hearts, and I will be their God, and they shall be my people. And they shall teach no more every man his neighbour, and every man his brother saying, "know the Lord, for they shall all know me, from the least of them unto the greatest of them, declares the Lord, for I will forgive their iniquity, and I will remember their sins no more" (31:31-34).

By design this, the third time that his brothers appear before Joseph, he chooses to reveal his identity to them. Today is the third national gathering from exile of the Jewish people back to the Land of Israel. As stated earlier, the first was from Egypt, under Moses; the second, the return from Babylon; now the third, from all the nations of the world. The prophesy in Jeremiah 16:14-15 states, *"Therefore behold, the days come, declares the Lord, that it shall no more be said, the Lord lives, that brought up the children of Israel from the land of Egypt; but, the Lord lives, that brought up the children of Israel from the land of the north, and from all the lands where he has driven them: and I will bring them again into their land that I gave unto their fathers."* The intent here, is to gather Israel

Ref	Joseph	Jesus

together again to speak to them privately, in their own language.

45:3 *"And Joseph said unto his brethren, I am Joseph; does my father yet live? And his brethren could not answer him, for they were troubled at his presence."*

Allow me again to refer here to the passage which the Rabbis state speaks of "Mashiach ben Joseph", Zechariah 12:10-14, *"And I will pour upon the house of David, and upon the inhabitants of Jerusalem the spirit of grace and supplication: and they shall look upon me whom they have pierced, and they shall mourn for him as one mourns for his only son, and shall be in bitterness for him, as one that is in bitterness for his firstborn. In that day there shall be a great mourning in Jerusalem, as the mourning in Hadadrimon in the valley of Megiddon. And the land shall mourn, every family apart; the family of the house of David apart, and their wives apart; the family of the house of Nathan apart, and their wives apart; the family of the house of Levi apart, and their wives apart; the family of the house of Shimei apart, and their wives apart; all the families that remain, every family apart, and their wives apart."* Here is one presumed dead by Israel, torn by a wild beast, suddenly appearing alive in the most unexpected form, time and place, asking if his father Jacob lives, the answer to which he already knows.

Joseph's brothers cannot answer his question, for they are deeply troubled, as the tribes and families of Israel shall mourn, husbands and wives not able to look into each other's eyes, or speak, as they behold the Mashiach ben Joseph.

In Matthew 24:30 Jesus states, *"And then shall appear the sign of the son of man in heaven: and then shall all the tribes of the land mourn, and they shall see the Son of Man, coming in the clouds of heaven with power and great glory."*

45:4-6 Mourning is for a limited period of time, as Joseph speaks kindly unto them, *"Please come unto me"*. Jesus said, *"Come unto me you who are weary and heavy laden, and I will give you rest"* (Matthew 11:28).

Ref	Joseph	Jesus

In another place, John 5:40, he says, *"And you will not come unto me, that you might have life."* Joseph tells them, *"I am Joseph, your brother whom you sold into Egypt."* He comforts his brothers with great love and tenderness, explaining that this was all the work of God, for the salvation of their lives (and of course the lives of the Gentiles, who would receive his counsel and teachings), literally *"to bring to life"*.

45:7 *"And God sent me before you to preserve you a prosperity in the earth, and to save your lives by a great deliverance."*

Joseph was God's tool used in fulfilling the promise to Abraham of making his seed a great nation (Genesis 12:2).

Joseph had gone before Israel as a shepherd before his flock, bringing them to food and water, even if his sheep were reluctant (*"Give ear, O Shepherd of Israel, you that leads Joseph like a flock"* - Tehilim 80:1).

In John 14:2-3, Jesus' words are, *"In my Father's house there are many dwellings ... I go to prepare a place for you. And if I go and prepare a place for you, I will come again, and receive you unto myself, that where I am, you may be also."* He speaks here of his death and its special significance, that his provision would not be only a temporary one, but an eternal place of glory in the kingdom of heaven.

Jesus, who declared, *"I am sent to the lost sheep of the house of Israel"* (*Matthew 15:24*), also said, *"I am the good shepherd: the good shepherd gives his life for the sheep ... No man takes it from me, but I lay it down of myself"* (*John 10:11, 18*). Unlike Joseph, here is one who has voluntarily

Ref	Joseph	Jesus
		taken the role of outcast, for the salvation of the flock of Israel.
45:8	Joseph reiterates that it had all been the outworking of God and declares his lordship over the house of Pharaoh and the land of Egypt.	Jesus said, *"All authority has been given to me in heaven and on earth"* *(Matthew 28:18).*
45:9	Joseph commands his brothers to tell Israel the good tidings ("gospel") of their deliverance, that they must come to him to receive it.	Jesus commissioned his twelve disciples (and others) to declare the b'sorah (good news) to Israel, and to all nations (Mark 28:19).
45:10-13	Joseph tells them, "You shall be near unto me," in the place he had prepared.	Jesus said, *"Father, I will that they also whom you have given me, be with me where I am, that they may behold my glory, which you have given me ..."* *(John 17:24).*
	Joseph said, *"And you shall tell my father of all my glory in Egypt, and all that you have seen."* In Matthew 11:4-5	Jesus said, "Go and tell John that which you hear and see; the blind receive their sight, the lame walk, the lepers are cleansed, the deaf hear, the dead are raised up, and the poor have good news brought to them."
45:14-15	This is one of the most touching moments in all Bible history, as the children of Israel receive their brother and deliverer who had been hidden from their eyes, embracing each other with profound tears of joy.	Such joy will be at the revelation of the Mashiach.
45:16	The Gentiles heard of this and were pleased. In Psalm 126:1-2 it is written, *"When the Lord returned the captivity of Zion, we were like them that dreamed. Then was our mouth*	

Ref	Joseph	Jesus
	filled with laughter, and our tongue with singing: then said they among the Gentiles, the Lord has done great things for them."	
45:17-20	With the suggestion and authority of the king, Pharaoh, Joseph gathers his people together. In Matthew 24:31	Jesus said, *"and he shall send his malachim[117] with the sound of a great shofar, and they shall gather together his elect from the four winds, from one end of heaven to the other."*
	Moses promised, *"If any of yours be driven out unto the utmost parts of heaven, from there will the Lord your God gather you, and from there will he fetch you"* (Deuteronomy).	
45:21	Upon this joyous occasion Joseph gave his people gifts.	Paul stated in the letter to the Ephesians, quoting Psalm 68:18 and 68:19 in Hebrew, *"You have ascended on high and returned the captivity and took gifts for men."*
45:22	Joseph gave his brothers new clothing. Isaiah 61:10 says, *"For he has clothed me with the garments of salvation, wrapped me with a robe of righteousness."*	In Revelation 6:11 we find, *"And white robes were given unto every one of them."*
45:24	Joseph told his brothers not to become angry at each other on the way.	Jesus told his Talmidim[118], *"Whoever is angry with his brother without cause shall be in danger of judgement,"* and, *"Love one another"* (Matthew 5:22, John 13:34).
45:26	The centre of Joseph's message to Jacob here was: *"Joseph is alive,"* but he did not believe them.	

Luke 24:11 describes how when it was first reported to Jesus' eleven disciples that he was alive, *"They believed them not."* The Brit

---

[117] Messenger
[118] Disciples

Ref	Joseph	Jesus

Hadasha report that Jesus is alive, has been, for the most part, disbelieved by Israel. The prophesy of Isaiah 53 begins, *"Who has believed our report, and to whom has the arm of the Lord been revealed?"*

45:27 | When Israel finally did believe the report, before actually seeing Joseph, *"the spirit of Jacob their father revived"*, literally, *"Jacob's spirit came back to life."* | Paul states, regarding Israel's return and their relation to Jesus, that it will be *"life from the dead"* (Romans 11:15).

46 Here we see the gathering of Israel to Joseph in Mitzrayim, for the purpose of making there "a great nation."

In the prophesies of Ezekiel we see that the gathering of the Jewish people to King Mashiach will in fact be in the Land of Israel, for a similar purpose, *"For this declares the Lord God, 'Behold, I, even I, will both search for my sheep, and seek them out. As a shepherd seeks out his flock in the day he is among his sheep that are scattered, so will I seek out my sheep, and will deliver them out of all the places where they have been scattered, in the cloudy and dark day. And I will bring them out from the people, and gather them from the countries, and will bring them to their own land, and feed them upon the mountains of Israel by the rivers, and in all the inhabited places of the country ... Therefore will I save my flock, and they shall no more be prey, and I will judge between lamb and lamb. And I will set up one shepherd over them, and he shall feed them, even my servant David, he shall feed them, and he shall be their shepherd. And I the Lord will be their God, and my servant a Prince among them; I the Lord have spoken it'"* (Ezekiel 34:11-13, 22-24).

And in Ezekiel 37:24-26, *"And David my servant shall be king over them, and they shall all have one shepherd: they shall also walk in my judgements, and observe my statutes, and do them. And they shall dwell in the land I have given unto Jacob my servant, wherein your fathers have dwelt, and they shall dwell therein, even they and their children, and their children's children forever: and my servant David shall be their prince forever. Moreover I will make a covenant of peace with them; it shall be an everlasting covenant with them: and I will place them, and multiply them, and I will set my sanctuary in the midst of them forevermore."*

46:27 | Seventy souls in the house of Jacob. Seventy, in Judaism, is the traditional number of the nations, probably coming from Deuteronomy 32:8, | In Matthew 28:19 Yeshua said, *"Go therefore, and teach all nations."* The Hebrew letter ("y" ayin) is the number seventy. This is the last letter in the name Yeshua.

Ref	Joseph	Jesus

Joseph

"When the Most High divided to the nations their inheritance, when he separated the sons of Adam, he set the bounds of the people according to the number of the children of Israel." The prophesy of the prophet Isaiah 49:6 states, *"It is a light thing that you should be my servant to raise up the tribes of Jacob, and to restore the preserved of Israel, I will also give you for a light to the nations that you may be my salvation unto the end of the earth."*

Joseph was sent forth by God for the salvation from hunger of both the Gentiles and Israel.

Jesus

Amongst the Jewish people for two millennia, the last letter in his name has been traditionally dropped, making Yeshu. Ayin ("y") also the Hebrew word for "eye".

In Paul's letter to the Romans, chapter 11:25-26 we find, *"that blindness in part is happened to Israel, until the fullness of the Gentiles be come in. And so all Israel shall be saved, as it is written, There shall come out of Zion the deliverer, and shall turn away ungodliness from Jacob: for this is my covenant unto them, when I shall take away their sins."*

It is written in Isaiah 42:6-7, *"I the Lord have called you in righteousness, and will hold your hand, and will keep you, and give you for a covenant of the people, for a light to the nations, to open the blind eyes ..."* In Luke 4:20-21 it is recorded that Yeshua read these words in the beit knesset (synagogue) after which "the eyes of all of them that were in the synagogue were fastened on him. *"And he began to say unto them, this day this scripture is fulfilled in your ears."* In numerous places it is recorded that Yeshua also healed the physically blind.

46:28

Joseph

Judah was sent first to direct Israel unto Joseph in Goshen. This interplay between Judah and Joseph and the dynamic between them in the entire account, plus the prophesy given by Jacob over Judah (Genesis 49:8-12), is a remez to the Mashiach ben Joseph

Jesus

The inheritance of the tribe of Judah - the Land of Judah (Judah) - therefore actually does contain the name of the Lord. David ("beloved") ben Ishai, from whose seed was to arise the "son of David", or "Mashiach ben David", was born from the tribe of Judah, in the Land of Judah, in

Ref	Joseph	Jesus
	coming forth ultimately from the tribe of Judah. The name Judah in Hebrew actually contains the four letters of the tetragrammaton, or the name of the Lord, plus one letter "d", from which comes David. In Deuteronomy 12:11 we find, "Then there shall be a place which the Lord your God shall choose to cause his name to dwell there."	the town of Beit Lehem, all of which is true also of Yeshua (Luke 2:1-7; Matthew 2:1-6). In Micah 5:2 it is prophesied, "But you Biet Lehem Ephrata, though you be little among the thousands of Judah, yet out of you shall come forth unto me that is to be ruler in Israel, whose goings forth have been from old, from everlasting." We read in Sh'mot 23:20-21, *"Behold I send a malach before you, to keep you in the way, and to bring you into the place which I have prepared. Beware of him, and obey his voice, provoke him not, for he will not pardon your transgressions: for my name is in him."*
		In Jeremiah 23:5-6 it appears, *"Behold, the days come, declares the Lord, that I will raise unto David a righteous branch ... and this is his name by which he will be called, 'the Lord (the tetragammaton) our righteousness' "*. Is it not possible, therefore, that Mashiach ben Joseph and Mashiach ben David, are in fact one and the same person, an individual in whom the Holy One, blessed be he, has chosen to place his name?
46:29	Israel embraces his son whom he thought was dead, after a long passage of time, with tears of joy. First we saw the reunion of the brothers, now of the old father, with Joseph. The coming together of Israel with her Mashiach will be the fulfilment of the dreams, visions and hopes of our	Yeshua said, *"... when you shall see Abraham, Isaac and Jacob and all the prophets in the malchut haElohim (kingdom of God) ..." (Luke 13:28),* and in John 8:56, *"Your father Abraham rejoiced to see my day: he saw it and was glad."*

Ref	Joseph	Jesus
	fathers, indeed of all the prophets of Israel.	
46:30	*"And Israel said unto Joseph, now let me die because I have seen your face, because you are yet alive."*	In Luke 2:28-32 we see the aging Shimon hatzadik in the Temple at the time of the brit mila/circumcision of Yeshua, when he took the infant up in his arms and said, *"Now let your servant depart in peace according to your word, for my eyes have seen your salvation which you have prepared before the face of all people; a light to illuminate the Gentiles, and the glory of your people Israel."* Luke 24:5-6 reports of Yeshua at the tomb in which he had been placed, *"Why do you seek the living among the dead? He is not here but is risen."*
47	This portion deals with the situation of Israel as shepherds and their flocks. And yet through the Tenach the people of Israel are referred to as sheep, as the flock of the Lord, as in Psalm 79:13, *"So we your people, and sheep of your pasture will give you thanks forever,"* and in Jeremiah 50:6, *"My people have been lost sheep."*	

Likewise, God himself is called a shepherd, *"The Lord is my shepherd"* (Psalm 23:1) and *"Give ear, O shepherd of Israel"* (Psalm 80:1).

As a good shepherd leads his flock to grazing, God, through Joseph, has led Israel from famine to fullness and rest, as we read in 47:12, *"And Joseph nourished his father, and his brethren, and all his father's household, with bread, according to their families."*

In the Brit Hadasha, Yeshua is described, like Israel, as both lamb and shepherd, *"Behold the lamb of God, who takes away the sin of the world"* (John 1:29), and *"They overcame him by the blood of the Lamb"* (Revelation 12:11), and, *"I am the good shepherd: I lay down my life for the sheep."* (John 10:14-15).

The name Judah in Hebrew actually contains the four letters of the tetragrammaton, or the name of the Lord, plus one letter "d", from which comes David. In Deuteronomy 12:11 we find, *"Then there shall be a place which the Lord your God shall choose to cause his name to dwell there."*

Ref	Joseph	Jesus

The inheritance of the tribe of Judah - the Land of Judah - therefore actually does contain the name of the Lord. David ("beloved") ben Ishai, from whose seed was to arise the "son of David", or "Mashiach ben David" was born into the tribe of Judah, in the Land of Judah, in the town of Beit Lehem.

All this is true of Yeshua (Luke 2:1-7; Matthew 2:1-6). In Micah 5:2 it is prophesied, *"But you Biet Lehem Ephrata, though you be little among the thousands of Judah, yet out of you shall come forth unto me that is to be ruler in Israel, whose goings forth have been from old, from everlasting."*

APPENDIX G   MESSIAH AS THE BRANCH

A consideration of the kingships of David and the Messiah

It is important that we understand the meaning of the word 'root' used in Isaiah 11:1 where it relates to lineage so that we can understand the position of the Messiah in regard to the kingship of David and the lineage of David. The word 'root' refers to the underground part of a plant that enables it to draw nourishment. When the word is used figuratively for family connections it relates to the ancestor from whom a person derives their name or character. In the spiritual context, Paul tells us that if the root be holy then so are the branches, which is particularly relevant if a branch from another tree, such as a wild olive tree, is grafted into the tree with holy roots, such as the cultivated olive tree that is Israel. (Ro. 11:16 – 18; cf. Col. 2:1 – 6)

Why is this so important? In this context it is important for two reasons.

The first is that just as with our understanding of the important place Melchizedek played in establishing a superior priesthood to that of Aaron, so we cannot deny the fact that the Son of God as the Messiah, being part of the triune God, could not become a king purely because He was born on earth in a certain lineage. To put it another way, as He is God, He cannot accept a subordinate kingship originally given as a gift to a sinful human being (David).

The root of mankind is God, for He is the creator and therefore Father of all that exists, and the 'holy root', which feeds the vine of Israel with nourishment, that Paul referred to in Romans (11:16 – 18). The creation of man was God's final and supreme act in the original creation. Man was tasked with taking charge of God's world. The act of sinful rebellion then separated man from God which triggered the launch of God's plan of salvation, prepared before the creation, the revelation of which was initially confined to prophetic utterances regarding the future appearance of the Messiah and the revelation of the means, or way by which man could regain a proper, spiritual relationship with God. This led to the final act of fulfilment of God's salvation at the appearance of the Messiah.

As part of the revealed promises regarding the coming of the Messiah, God tells us that there shall come forth a rod or sapling from what remained of the tree of David which grew out of his father Jesse (Is. 11:1), a branch, symbolic of a new kingship, from out of the roots of Jesse, and the ultimate root of Jesse is God.

Therefore, any kingdom that the Messiah would rule as King could not be of this temporary world of dust (Jn. 18:36, 37). This allowed the tribe of Judah no excuse to boast in their exalted position with their own independent, God-appointed king and, although *the sceptre shall not depart from Judah* it was only, *until Shiloh comes.* (Gen. 49:10)

The fact that the Messiah was born into the tribe of Judah and particularly of the house of David meant that He was taking over the Davidic throne because of His superiority of rank above that of David; for David, under the influence of the Holy Spirit, called Him 'my Lord' (Ps. 110:1), just as His high priesthood was superior to that of Aaron.

But who is this Shiloh? The name is variously interpreted as the one God sent into the world (Jn. 17:3), the branch that would come out of the root of Jesse (Is. 11:1) and the man of peace who would bring together the two schism of man (Eph. 2:22), that of the chosen people of God, the nation of Israel, and the rest of humanity for whom God's plan of salvation was designed.

For surely the central purpose of God's plan of salvation was not confined to His chosen people, Israel. It is a nonsense for the Jews to believe that they alone should be saved to the uttermost. They were, however, to be His mouth-piece, His means of communicating to the rest of the world the truths regarding this salvation and, through their obedience to God, become a show case of what God was able to do for mankind and therefore cause mankind to realise there was a better way to live life to the full, thereby causing others to realise it was available to all mankind. (Jn. 12:32) The concluding part of Genesis 49:10 amplifies this with these words, *and unto Him shall the gathering of the people be,* confirming the teaching of Paul who had been enlightened by the Holy Spirit. (Eph. 2:11 – 18)

Gentile believers in the Jewish Messiah, and I am one of them, must realise and accept that Israel is God's first-born. From Abram, God has spoken solely through his chosen offspring. The Messiah, Himself born a Jew of the tribe of Judah as prophesied, said that salvation is of the Jews (Jn. 4:22) and it was those Jews who believed that Jesus was the Christ (Yeshua or Jehoshua – in Hebrew), led by the disciples, who first announced the way of salvation to the World.

It was an Italian army officer with his family who were the first Gentiles to be baptised with the Holy Spirit as the disciples had been. The Christian Church is not senior to the true God–fearing Israel, but has grown out of it.

As Gentile believers, we, as wild olive branches, have been grafted onto the cultivated olive tree that is Israel so that we can share the same root. (It is essential to read Ro. 11:11 – 36) The Deliverer did not come from the church for it did not exist at that time, but scripture says that the Deliverer will come from Zion, which is exactly what happened with the birth of the Messiah in Bethlehem. (Is. 59:20, 21)

Messiah as The Branch

Unless we are prepared to gain a balanced knowledge of the truth from the perspective of both the first and second testaments, then there is a danger of gaining only half-truths. This book is dedicated to putting the facts before those who are ready to listen.

Throughout scripture it has been made very clear that just because the father is a believer in God and full of faith, it does not mean that their offspring will be like-minded. We can see from the example of Jacob that his personal journey brought him so close to God that he wrestled with Him, but of his sons it was only Joseph who believed as he believed. So too the kings born to David gradually fell away from the true faith in God until evil and self-serving kings finally lost the kingship of the people of God at the time of the exile.

However, since the arrival of Shiloh, over two thousand years ago, it can truthfully be said that there has been no king in Judah, but the root of Jesse has drawn to Himself those Jews and Gentiles prepared to believe in Him. (Is. 11:10; Ro. 15:12) It is interesting that Paul makes another important point when he says that *not all Israel ... are of Israel,* for it is only people of the promise (true God-accepted, and God-accepting believers, not necessarily all those who were born an Israelite for some were unbelievers, rejecting God) who are counted as the seed of God. (Ro. 9:6 – 13)

The second reason is the importance of lineage which gave legitimacy to each element of the plan of God as it was revealed throughout the history of God's chosen people (Matt. 1). It was essential to maintain the purity of its revelation and fulfilment.

God, through Jacob, (Gen. 49:8 – 12) foretold that a lawgiver would not be absent in Judah *nor a lawgiver from between his feet, until Shiloh come* (v10). But who is this lawgiver? Was it not God who gave them the commandments and laws and instructions on how to live a life worthy of Him? Surely it was also He who supplied the Israelites with food, showing them where water could be found in the barren wilderness (Num. 21:16 – 18)?

The lawgiver is identified as being in Judah (Ps. 60:7, 108:8) because it was into that tribe that a God-focused king and prophet, who was ultimately bound by God's laws, became a human lawgiver. But then *(until Shiloh come)* into that tribe the Messiah would be born. We are reminded that *the Lord is our Lawgiver* (Is. 33:22), for it was He who, from the environmental turbulence on the mountain, spoke to His people and gave them the law through His prophet Moses. God is pure; therefore, the purity of the Messiah's lineage had to be established through the prophetic word as *spoken by holy men moved by the Holy Spirit* (2 Pet. 1:21) and clearly revealed in the history of man, particularly Israel.

In the prophetic utterance of Jacob, Judah is given prominence. Chief amongst the twelve tribes – thirteen when considering Ephraim and

Manasseh[119], which were technically half-tribes – it was chosen by God to be host to the Messiah. Growing from a lion's whelp, having little power, to a calm but formidable adult lion *as a lion, who shall rouse him*, for David and a greater than David spring from it (consider Matt. 12:42). But the prophetic utterance of Jacob goes into further detail, establishing beyond question, the true lineage of the King who was to come for it also speaks of one *binding his foal unto the vine* (the grape bearing vine was plentiful in Judah), *and his ass's colt unto the choice vine*. It was in the land of Judah that the Messiah revealed Himself as the true King of all Israel by riding into Jerusalem on the colt of an ass (Jn. 12:12 – 15).

This revelation, so despised by those who considered themselves as the religious elite (Jn. 12:19, consider Lk. 19:39, 40), was strictly according to scripture (Is. 40:9; Zech. 9:9) but sadly unseen as such by those who should have understood (Jn. 5:39). As prophesied, their studies of scripture were from man's perspective and understanding, not through seeking after a God perspective, spiritual understanding in spite of all the signs He had performed in their sight. (Jn. 12:37 – 43)

Judah was blessed with fine wine, the grapes of Eschol in the Judean hill country producing very fine grapes. (Num. 13:23) The vine is used in scripture to refer to the health of people and nations. Isaiah likens Moab to a spreading vine which is trampled down by other nations. (Is. 16:8 – 12) But as far as Israel is concerned the vine refers to the nation's temporal and spiritual blessings. (Ps. 80, Is. 5)

Joseph, so loved by his father Jacob because of his desire and love for God, is described as a, *fruitful bough by a well whose branches run over the wall* because of the work of God he performed in Egypt through his tenacious faith and trust in the God of his father Jacob. (Gen. 49:22 – 26) Jeremiah calls Israel a noble vine, planted by God as a seed of the highest quality that had turned into a degenerate plant because of the iniquity of the people. (Jer. 2:21)

The Messiah refers to Himself as the vine and the Father as the vinedresser. (Jn. 15:1 – 6) Every branch that grows out of the vine is dependent upon the vine for its nutrition and fruitfulness. Lack of belief and trust in the God whose main desire is to sustain them (Matt. 15:8, 9) will result in unfruitfulness and the danger of being pruned and taken away and cast onto the fire.

The failure of the vine that was Israel to perform the duties God required of them is clearly seen in the state of the people at the time of the coming of the Messiah. Four hundred years had passed with no prophet

---

[119] Although Ephraim took a leading role in the history of the ten tribes of Israel that broke away from Judah with Benjamin, the tribes of Ephraim (who was the younger of the two) and Manasseh took the place of what would have been the tribe of Joseph, therefore they were in fact two half tribes.

declaring, *Thus says the Lord.* The worship of the people had also reached a low point, being empty of meaning, which is not surprising given that even Nicodemus, a ruler of the Jews, had no concept of the spiritual aspect of the relationship they needed to have with their spiritual God for that relationship to have any meaning and hope of success.

Indeed, none of the leaders, apart from exceptions like Nicodemus, believed in the Lord Jesus, and even Nicodemus did so privately for fear of being ostracised and excommunicated from the synagogue and therefore unable to worship God in the official manner, the empty ceremonial to which they had become addicted. (Is. 1; Mal. 2; Matt. 23)

The praise of men is a powerful attraction to those who prefer to be at one with those around them rather than God, unlike Jeremiah who, although in an extreme way, was mocked by everyone just because he alone was prepared to be the voice of God. (Jer. 20:7)

In speaking about the Servant that was to come, Isaiah (Is. 49[120]) proclaims to the world *you peoples from afar* the prophetic arrival of the Messiah *the Lord has called me from the womb … He has made mention of My name …He has made My mouth like a sharp sword.* (Heb. 4:12) But more than that the Messiah became the True Israel because, born into the house of Israel as the Son of Man, He is the True Vine, as the Son of God, into which those who are of the true Israel (Ro. 9:6 – 13) must be secured as living branches.

The gradual decline of Israel to the still proud but awkwardly subservient and subjugated nation it became under the Roman occupation, is testimony to the truth that there was to be no true blessing of Israel until the Messiah (Shiloh) had come; not to lead them to an earthly victory over the occupying forces, but into a new and intimate relationship with their God *to bring Jacob back to Him* by way of the altar of sacrifice.

The cross, through prophecy, therefore became the altar of a sacrifice that was to include Gentiles, for His salvation was to extend to the ends of the earth (v6). This act will ultimately lead the nation of Israel to both temporal blessing on this earth and eternal blessings in the new world that is to come in the form of the New Jerusalem that God will have ready at the right time to house all those who truly believe in Him (Rev. 21:1, 2).

It was God's task to provide the means by which men must be saved, there being no alternative. He could not work through men to achieve that task because of inherent sin, which is why He had to tread that path alone (Is. 63:3 – 5). The gulf that opened up between God and man because of sin could only be bridged from God's side.

That salvation is of God and God alone means that the judgement for the unbeliever and enemy of God is also of God. Consider the subject

---

[120] It is important to read the whole of Isaiah 49

matter of Isaiah 63 (please read the whole of the chapter) for this prophecy concerns the triumphant judgement of the Messiah, who became King of kings after His glorious victory on the cross and by His resurrection, on all those who have defied Him since His sacrifice. Edom, the nation that sprang from Esau, was often opposed to Israel, so it is reasonable for the name (which means red) to be symbolically used for the enemies of Israel and of all believers. *"Who is this,"* asks the prophet, *"who comes from Edom, with dyed garments from Bozrah* (at one time part of the country of Edom was situated in an area that abounded in grapes), *glorious in His apparel and travelling in the greatness of His strength?"* In answer we are told that it is the only One who can, *speak in righteousness and is mighty to save.* (v1b)

Sin attracts the vengeance of God upon the sinner; therefore, in order for God to provide repentant sinners with the antidote for sin, the Saviour had to get personally involved by taking upon Himself the sin of the world and defeating the hold sin had upon the sinner declaring, *It is finished.* (Jn. 19:30; Heb. 9:23 – 28, cf. Ro. 7:23 – 25)

Jacob tells us, after the reference to the appearance of the king sitting on the colt of an ass to declare His Kingship that was not of this world (Jn.18:36, 37), that, *He washed His garments in wine and His clothes in the blood of grapes.* (Gen. 49:11) With the prophecy of Jacob before us, Isaiah (ch. 63) asks the question, *Why are your clothes stained red, as though from treading a wine press?* The answer is, *I have trodden the winepress alone for there was no one of the people righteous enough to help Me. For I will tread them in My anger and trample them in My wrath; and their blood shall be upon My garments ... for the day of vengeance is in My heart and the year of My redeemed has come.* Because the One who speaks is He who is mighty to save through His own work, He also has the right to enact judgement (the meaning of the winepress) on all those who are hostile to Him or ignore Him as irrelevant.

By taking the scriptures as a whole we cannot accept as past, and now irrelevant, the events in the Garden of Eden where deception brought about the separation of man from God. We have discussed at length in this book the relationship of Satan, also known as the Devil, with the creator God. We have also been enlightened over the matter of those offspring of Adam, and later Abraham and Isaac, who decided to live their lives totally ignorant of God such as Cain, Ishmael and Esau. Sin has therefore abounded on the earth though them.

The cost to the Father and the Son to provide a means of salvation whereby man can once again, if he so chooses, respond to the call of God and enter into an active relationship with God, thereby gaining a lasting spiritual union through the second birth, is incalculable.

The eternal salvation offered by God as the result of Christ's sacrifice upon the cross is freely available to all mankind, but it is necessary for those wanting to receive benefit from that salvation to make a definite decision to ask God to forgive their sin and allow their lives to be changed by the work of the Holy Spirit, allowing Him to enter into their lives to dwell with and in them. Just as Adam was born with the freedom to choose, so are we. Those who either choose to ignore the offer of salvation or reject it will find themselves in that place where God is not present, which is hell.

Unfortunately, those who reject salvation are greater in number than those who accept it for wide is the gate and wide the way that leads to destruction. (Matt. 7:13, 14)

The fulfilment of the plan of salvation by first requiring a sacrifice for sin at the altar of sacrifice, according to the illustration of the tabernacle complex built by Moses in accordance with what he saw in heaven, was essential. Without that way back to God by first tackling the sin of rebelliousness that caused separation and then through the rebirth of the spirit within man, God was unable to bring in the judgement of those who rejected His salvation. By providing that all-sufficient sacrifice for sin on the accursed tree and broadcasting the good news of full salvation to the world firstly through those Jews prepared to believe in Him and then Gentile believers, God was able to prepare the world for the enactment of His judgement on Satan and all those who have conspired against Him.

A human baby grows physically from their complete dependence upon their mother into childhood. During their childhood and further growth into youth they start gaining knowledge through schooling and life's experiences that will train them to become mature and to gradually become independent, so that by the time they reach adulthood they can go to work and earn a living.

But what happens in the spiritual context? New birth in the Spirit should lead by inquiry into spiritual childhood, youth and mature adulthood. But how is this achieved? Except we study scripture, both testaments, and gradually through prayer and by meditating on those scriptures grow in the knowledge of God, we will not be able to personally grow in the Spirit and into a real and developing relationship with God. We will in fact remain as new born babes in Christ. (Heb. 5:12 – 14)

The knowledge we gain through the Holy Spirit is of the Father, therefore as we grow in our understanding of the truth to become mature in the faith, we are spiritually drawn by the Father to Himself and, through the sacrifice of the Son, we are accepted by the Father because of the Son. There is a very grave danger in believing that we are required to do nothing, thinking God has done it all.

Our eternal responsibility is whether or not to believe in the Messiah of Israel, and then how far we need to commit ourselves to His service. It is a decision that only the individual can make, and it is that decision that will decide if we go to heaven or hell.

APPENDIX H THOUGHTS ON THE TRINITY

This was on an email from my Jewish friend Derek:

> Bit complicated sometimes.
> Holy spirit is the presence of God.
> Does the Holy Spirit move, with God? Is God. One with God but independent?
> Some say that the Holy Spirit was created by God to interact with Man. God cannot abide evil or sin. Who is without sin on Earth now?
> Every time, with an exception here and there. Holy Spirit is the spokesperson or presence of God.

My reply:

Having been challenged by what you wrote above, it suddenly came to me.

The person of God is beyond our ability to imagine for He has never been born, can never die and is pure spirit, which means that He has no form as we have visible recognizable physical form. This means that He is not in one place at any time, but everywhere at the same time.

He is not restricted in His ability, knowledge, understanding, wisdom or any other attribute, so that nothing is unknown to Him or impossible to Him.

The Father, who is the source of all love which impregnates the Son and the Spirit, is the decision maker as acknowledged by the Son, to whom He gave birth of Himself, for before the creation there was no one else but Him, and after the creation there was still no one like Him or His equal.

The Son voices the thoughts of the Father (Jn.7:15 – 18) but has no power of decision making of Himself, for He is merely obedient to the will and purposes of the Father. The Son, by that very distinction, is subservient to the Father, but the Father loves the Son as the Son loves the Father and for the moment the praise for our salvation goes to the Son, because of His physical death on the cross in place of mankind for our sin, because He alone was totally pure before His physical birth and during His physical life, and could therefore die for sinful mankind.

It is because He died for man's sins that Jesus attracts the praises of man, but all the praise truly belongs to the Father for as Jesus looked up to heaven said,

"Father, the hour has come. Glorify your Son so He can give glory back

to you. For you have given him authority over everyone. He gives eternal
life to each one you have given him (see Jn. 17:1 – 5).

Humanly speaking, Jesus died in place of man so that the Father could
be satisfied that the objective of the sentence He imposed on man could be
fulfilled, *"You shall surely die".*

As the Father can never die, the Son will always be the Son of God.

It is also possible that God, who is referred to as the Father and
therefore the central figure of the Godhead, needed someone to enact His
decision to create the physical things including man, so the Father of
Himself provided a Spirit for Himself that was of Himself, who would be
the one producing the physical as a result of the Father's spiritual decisions
as spoken by the Son.

That is why the Spirit cannot attract praises to Himself, for He is merely
being obedient to the will and purposes of the Father according to the word
spoken by the Son (Jn. 16:13). He will not speak on His own authority for
He cannot.

The Spirit, has to be an individual person, for independently He created
all that exists according to the plan and will of the Father and finally created
man in the image of God the Father. When Jesus called for the storm to be
stilled, the dead raised to life, the blind to see etc., it was the Holy Spirit
who caused it to happen. For such things also happened after Jesus had
ascended when the Spirit worked with and through the disciples.

He is also the channel through which man communicates with the
Father through the offices of the Son. He is also the barrier between the
purity of the Father who cannot look upon sin, hence Him 'turning His
back' on His Son as He hung on the cross. So the presence of God that was
with man from the beginning is through the Holy Spirit who has dealt
directly with sinful man on behalf of the Father.

Because it was the Spirit of God who created all that exists, He is able to
see into and understand the workings of men, including all that is
happening in their minds and hearts. The heart is understood to be the very
centre and hub of a person.

Because of this attribute He was able to tell the Son what the men
listening to Him were thinking. It is also He who applies the blood because
He witnessed the Son shedding His physical blood on the cross.

Also, because the Son is also a Spirit being who was housed in a human
body for a time, as soon as He left the body hanging on the cross, the body
died, which is why the soldiers did not need to break His legs.

Whilst in the human body the Son experienced what it was like being a human being, and suffered the extreme agony of the pain of hanging on the cross, as any human being would. For that reason, He not only sympathises with our weaknesses (Heb. 4:14- 16), He is also our advocate before the Father (1 Jn. 2:1).

So, although the three separate persons of the Trinity are all members of the Godhead, it is the Father who is the source and inspiration of the other two.

Thus, we have the three members of the Godhead explained. Each an individual in their own way and equal in the Godhead and bound by a depth and intensity of love that man could not possibly understand, but the Father is, and always will be, the source and head of the Trinity.

ABOUT THE AUTHOR

After an electrical engineering apprenticeship in the Royal Navy, Peter went on to serve on a number of ships in different parts of the world, finally being responsible for the weapons maintenance department of a frigate and lecturing to trainee officers on weapon systems. He also spent two years at the Royal Navy's training college in Fareham, Hampshire instructing on underwater weapons and defense systems.

Leaving the service at 30 in 1969, Peter worked as a quality engineer for the British Aircraft Corporation at Filton, Bristol on spacecraft and guided weapon systems before moving to R. A Lister (Diesels) where he became a technical author in 1984. He then worked as a contract author, mostly in the nuclear power generation industry, writing instructional and training documentation before finally retiring in 2011.

For over 20 years, Peter was a Methodist Local Preacher before leaving Methodism in the late eighties. He became an official prison visitor on January 1st 1990 and from 1994 worshipping with his wife at the prison he visited in order to focus on supporting prisoners who wanted to change their lives around. After retiring from that work in 2016 he and his wife continued to worship at the prison until January 2020. He still supports a few released prisoners.

Peter met a Jew named Derek who had become a Christian in prison. On his release to the local community, Peter was able to help him adjust to a new life of going straight.

It was Derek who first asked Peter to write on scripture in 2002, after which Derek's brother Aaron, a rabbi serving in the USA, came under the influence of Peter's writing and became a Christian. Aaron asked him to write first on the book of Revelation and then on the subject of Moses' Tent of the Meeting, which he self-published early 2011. He currently has 25 books on Amazon for downloading to an eBook reader or as a paperback.

Peter was married in December 1961 and has three sons and six grandchildren. His autobiographical book explaining how he came to write his books is called "A Tale of Three Men".